THE AVENGERS FILES

THE AVENGERS FILES

ANDREW PIXLEY

Reynolds & Hearn Ltd

London

To Julie
More wonderful than Cathy, Emma, Tara and Purdey put together

First published in 2004 by
Reynolds & Hearn Ltd
61a Priory Road
Kew Gardens
Richmond
Surrey TW9 3DH

Reissued 2007.

© Andrew Pixley 2004, 2007
The Avengers © Studio Canal
The Avengers illustrations © Canal+ Image UK Ltd
The New Avengers/The New Avengers illustrations © Mark One Productions Ltd

A CIP catalogue record for this book is available from the British Library.

ISBN 1 905287 38 0

Designed by Chris Bentley.

Printed and bound in Great Britain by Biddles Ltd, Kings Lynn, Norfolk.

CONTENTS

FOREWORD

BY BRIAN CLEMENS

I think I first met John Steed, the *real* John Steed, one wintry afternoon when, leaving the Saville Club, I collided with an unkempt and apparently blind beggar. Shortly after, I discovered my wallet was missing.

Two days later Steed himself turned up at my office in Elstree Studios to return the wallet, which he said he had found on a train. The contents were intact. Naturally I offered him coffee and we got to talking, or rather he did. He was a natural raconteur: urbane, cultured and with a mellifluous voice that could charm not only the birds, but possibly the leaves too, off a tree.

It was common knowledge that at that time I had just finished helping create *Danger Man*, a TV series concerning the adventures of a secret agent, and somehow the conversation got around to that. Steed apparently liked and admired the series, but thought it was 'only half the story' and that in actuality 'it was madder than that'. He said that he had an acquaintance actually working for 'them', and that the reality was unbelievable. I was intrigued – who wouldn't be? He promised to 'whiz some real life incidents your way', which might inspire me. He left and, my curiosity aroused, I watched from my window to see him get into a vintage Bentley alongside a spectacularly beautiful young woman and a large Boxer dog.

Soon after, Steed's 'real life incidents' started to arrive in plain brown envelopes, turning up on the seat of my car, under the cushions of my sofa, and once, in the shower – thoughtfully stuffed into a Wellington boot.

He was right, they were quite unbelievable, but I remembered another of his comments that, 'it was a world of its own'. I was especially taken by the fact that in these astounding adventures, there largely figured a young, attractive and amazingly resourceful young woman. It was the Sixties, and women were just beginning to flex their feminist muscles, but no one – so far – had the temerity to put a female on equal par with a man. I decided the Time Was Ripe.

I met Steed again, several times, in a number of strange locations: atop of a bus, below ground in a sewer, and once even in the basket of a balloon. Steed seemed to appreciate that the wild, and obviously exaggerated, adventures he was engaged in were akin to my own imaginative work – and soon I was being co-opted as one of his colleagues, while simultaneously maintaining some links with the television industry.

By 1963, I was acting as one of the Department's intelligence operatives in addition to my duties documenting Steed's cases – where my skills in screenwriting could be put to additional use. Indeed, Keller – one of our 'best enemies' – kept my photograph on the wall in his office.

I struck a deal with Steed. He would be paid for his story input into some scripts I was writing, but the methods of those payments were bizarre; some monies were sent to a home for aged horses, another to the Benevolent Society of the Horse Guards, and the rest required in yen, Swiss francs, American dollars, and even Indian rupees.

Steed had little further input to my television work, although on one occasion he called to ask that the female partner in a certain series be 'clad in leather – because I like it'. On another more curious occasion we were on location when the actor Patrick Macnee had his entire wardrobe stolen from his car. I told Steed of this, and that it would hamper production, but he replied, 'not to worry, old boy'. The next morning the full set of clothes miraculously reappeared, and the body of a known felon was found floating in the Thames. I think I am the only one who wondered if there might have been a connection between the two incidents.

Of course this was all a long time ago, and I have not seen John Steed in some years. I do, however, receive the occasional letter from him. It is always delivered by hand, and always at night. It invariably offers his good wishes, and sometime encloses a photograph of Steed in company with a series of stunning young women. He looks hale, hearty, and always tanned, so I can assume that, wherever he is, he is under the sun, happy, and very much alive.

You know, initially I doubted Steed's veracity, and yet, witness this book, it all now seems to have been true. But then, didn't someone once say, 'truth is stranger than fiction'?

Brian Clemens
Film and television writer/producer... and former Department operative
April 2004

INTRODUCTION

'The Avengers *is such a turkey that Warner Bros would have done better to hand*
over its distribution to Bernard Matthews.'
'*This film is an insult to cinema...'*
'*How does* The Avengers *fail? Let me count the ways...'*
'*A coherent plot might have helped. It is all rather sad.'*
'*"That was the worst movie I've ever seen," muttered the house manager...'*
'*It has elegance, wit and repartee but not nearly enough action and excitement.'*

These were just some of the comments to appear in the columns of disgruntled film
reviewers on 14 August 1998, the day after they had finally got see *The Avengers*, supposedly one of Warner Bros' biggest movies of the year but in fact a film which had been
plagued with difficulties in the run up to a troubled launch.

The plot of this motion picture included many elements of a typical blockbuster or an
endearingly wacky spy spoof of the sort popular in the 1960s. It concerned the exploits of
a suave, larger-than-life gentleman called John Steed, a 'secret agent' working for a crippled boss code-named 'Mother' at 'The Ministry'. In the movie's narrative, Steed was partnered with Dr Emma Peel, a government scientist, to investigate the sabotage of Dr Peel's
Prospero Program – a combined weather shield and defence umbrella for the United
Kingdom. This process (in a profusion of gibberish associated with science fiction movies)
bombarded protons and ions to create anti-matter – but the main suspect for the destruction
of the program's laboratories was Dr Peel herself, whose name Steed was assigned to clear.
The true culprit was actually a clone of Dr Peel created by a fanatical ex-Government meteorologist called Sir August de Wynter. De Wynter, and his associates from BROLLY[1],
aimed to take control of the Prospero Program and use it as a weather-controlling weapon,
demanding a ransom from the Council of Ministers who would now have to buy their
climates from him. Steed and Emma worked together to smash this blackmailing scheme,
killing Sir August and destroying his secret base – an island in the middle of the Serpentine
in Hyde Park, London – in the classic explosive finale so beloved of the cinema world.

However, while the mass audiences were offended by the apparently incoherent plot
(the result of writer Don Macpherson's script having several key sequences removed from
it at the decree of nervous studio executives), there was a smaller proportion of those

---

[1] British Royal Organisation for Lasting Liquid Years.

present who were equally offended – but for a totally different reason. These were the select band of enthusiasts who were appalled to see such a complete work of fiction woven around one of the greatest undercover agents that Great Britain has ever seen: John Steed.

John Steed was indeed a real person who – from the 1950s to at least the late 1970s – tackled a wide range of missions encompassing the mundane elements of crime and security concerns such as blackmail, extortion, drugs smuggling, arms dealing and murder, through to more bizarre and exotic assignments including killer pussy cats, giant rats roaming London's sewers and devices which could swap the psyche, memory and personalities of individuals. However, until recently, most of his work for the bureau known variously as 'the Organisation' or 'the Department' has been kept closely under wraps.

However, the film did contain many truths – indicating that Macpherson probably had an inside source at British security. Yes, there was a John Steed. Yes, he worked alongside a young widow called Emma Peel. Yes, Steed dressed in a well-tailored suit and bowler and carried a swordstick umbrella. Yes, Steed would train in a simulated village test ground. Yes, Steed drove a green 4^1/$_2$-litre vintage Bentley. Yes, Steed and Emma did once encounter a man who had the ability to create rainstorms to order. Yes, Steed had a wheelchair-bound boss called Mother whose 'number two' was a blind woman called Father. Yes, Steed and his colleagues came up against many bizarre threats to civilisation which would defy the credulity of most people. Yes, Steed and Emma enjoyed a *very* close relationship.

But equally there were many distortions of the truth and inaccuracies, and it was these that upset and annoyed those who have studied Steed's remarkable career over the years. No, Emma Peel was not a government scientist. No, the organisation Steed worked for was seldom referred to as 'the Ministry'. No, Steed and Emma did not meet because of an attack on her Prospero Project. No, Steed was not a member of Boodles club. No, the weather-controlling genius was called Dr Sturm and not Sir August de Wynter. No, Father was not a traitor to her organisation. No, Steed was not regularly reporting to Mother during the time he worked with Emma. No, Steed did not use a rosewood handled umbrella. No, Steed didn't go around kissing Emma on the lips in the middle of assignments...

It is now 27 years since Steed's last recorded mission for the Department, and all attempts to locate his current whereabouts have proved futile. It is not clear whether Steed is living or dead; certainly at the time of writing he would be in his early 80s. Being attached to national security work, so much of Steed's life has been shrouded in mystery, with many references even to his existence – or indeed those who were his associates – carefully expunged from recorded history by the meticulous work of the Department, a section which operates with a frighteningly zealous attention to detail. Many major incidents which Steed tackled were never covered in the newspapers of the day, hidden by D-notices issued by the government. Organisations and individuals have similarly vanished as the Department thoroughly covered the tracks of threats to British security. Visiting Companies House and attempting to locate organisations such as the Business Efficiency Bureau, the Briantern Health Farm or Mandrake Investments will prove fruitless – as if the companies never existed. All evidence of the visit of the Radeck State Circus to London around early 1960 has been carefully deleted; the videotapes and films of their appearance on the TV programme *Limelight* erased or incinerated. Indeed, entire communities involved in Steed's exploits have apparently vanished off the face of the planet; picturesque villages such as Tinbey, Little Bazeley-by-the-Sea and Pringby[2] have evaporated from the British gazetteer, rechristened by the almost sinister machinations of the Department which protects us and our country.

Notable amongst Steed's friends and colleagues is the world famous actor Patrick Macnee, a friend since their days together at Eton in the 1930s. Ironically, Macnee himself 'appeared' in Warner Bros' ill-fated motion picture in the unlikely cameo role of 'Colonel "Invisible" Jones'. Many of those who have studied Steed regret the fact that such a film was never made in the 1960s or 1970s when Steed was still active – for the younger Macnee would have been perfect and inspired casting to have portrayed this legendary gentleman adventurer.[3]

Nevertheless, despite all the secrecy surrounding Steed's exploits, security regulations have now allowed researchers to access material pertaining to assignments over 25 years old, and as such a total of 186 firmly documented missions are available for study. Almost all of these are supported by the most amazing visual material, surveillance films made by the Department during Steed's actual missions for use as both evidence in national security trials, and also to aid in the training of fledgling operatives. This was standard policy – apparently – between 1960 and 1969, and then again over the period 1975 to 1977.

It is at this point that we must acknowledge the outstandingly generous help of the current head of the Department, a role which – on many occasions since at least 1967 – has been traditionally code-named 'Mother'. The current Mother is an affable gentleman and – in keeping with his predecessor's security policies – his headquarters are continually on the move, appearing in all manner of incongruous locations. At the time that we were able to visit him and view the material pertaining to Steed's remarkable career in March 2004, Mother's base of operation was within a film vault at Pinewood Studios – ironically the same venue where the much maligned and misleading Warner Bros biopic of Steed's career began shooting on 2 June 1997.

To clarify the source material on which this book is based further, there were originally at least 161 surveillance films and tapes covering the exploits of Steed and his associates between 1960 and 1969, and a further 25 incidents spanning the period 1975 to 1977. With the strange sense of humour which has frequently been associated with the Department over the years, these have generally been edited together into films running to some 50 minutes for a single case (apart from one incident, mostly taking place in France in 1977, to which two films have been devoted). It is quite amazing how these films have been constructed – almost like episodes of some unbelievable television series. Department regulations apparently dictated the continual, multi-camera surveillance of the various homes of Steed and his colleagues for internal security, while the Department also had various mobile film units which could keep surveillance on known hand-over locations or 'safe houses' used by the opposition during the Cold War. Furthermore, footage and tape recorded for similar reasons by the opposition or private organisations was often seized at the end of a mission and cut into the Department's own material to tell the story of events more fully (such as the film shot by the late Dr Clement Armstrong in his United

---

2 While there is no trace of Tinbey at all, the surveillance film of Little Bazeley bears a strong resemblance to the village of Wighton near Wells-Next-The-Sea in Norfolk, while the village of Pringby appears to have been rechristened Aldenham and can be found in Hertfordshire.

3 Indeed, the Telemen production company made an abortive attempt to shoot a television film series with Macnee playing Steed – or at the very least a character inspired by Steed – in November 1964, but it was abandoned after four weeks of production.

Automation factories to study the performance of his robotic creations, the Cybernauts).

This material was then available both as evidence and also for training and review purposes; Emma Peel, one of Steed's partners, is seen reviewing film of a March 1965 assignment in her flat in a surveillance report shot in November 1967.

It seems that from late 1960 to spring 1964, surveillance was generally undertaken on monochrome videotape with a few inserts on 16mm film; these tapes have long since been destroyed, and of the 78 tapes we know were recorded, 54 of these exist in their entirety as 16mm film recordings taken from the tapes. Of the 24 wholly or partially missing films and tapes, mission transcripts exist for ten assignments (it seems that the remaining 14 have been lost over the years – either destroyed because of no further interest, misfiled or possibly even still existing, but now in the hands of an unfriendly power).

From late 1964 to summer 1966, another 26 missions of Steed's were subject to surveillance, this time on 35mm monochrome film which exists to this day. With autumn 1966, the Department switched to colour film, which became the norm for at least the next 11 years (although it seems it was not Department policy to conduct such surveillance from late spring 1969 through to autumn 1975). Transcripts exist for all missions from 1962 onwards, and it is from these that spellings and facts have been double-checked as far as possible. For all the assignments, there are also mission summaries – although these differ rather alarmingly at times from the evidence available in the films and transcripts themselves.

Also emphasising the black humour which Department operatives clearly depend on to get them through the often gruesome and depressing cases of betrayal and murder, at some time or another some film archivist with a particularly strong funny bone has been though many missions – including the ones logged against Steed – and allocated names to them, alongside their formal Department codes. These unofficial designations range from the straightforward (such as *The Frighteners*, an incident where Steed and his colleague Doctor Keel dealt with a London based gang who beat people up for money) through to the bizarre (for example *Mission... Highly Improbable*, a play on the title of the popular 1960s and 1970s American undercover television series *Mission: Impossible*, here used to recount how miniaturisation was being used to smuggle secret technological advances out of the country). The most notable of the unofficial 'titles' (for want of a better term) is the one which appears on most paperwork associated with Steed and his cohorts – a nickname which became legendary in the Department, synonymous with some of the strangest security issues on British soil, and indeed cemented itself as the title of the 1998 movie: *The Avengers*.[4]

Because these were not official nomenclature for the Department, it has been decided to relegate these to simply a means of referring to the surveillance films and reports in terms of a four-letter code. For this biographical work, it has been decided to use a coding method designed to chronicle the adventures of Sir Arthur Conan Doyle's world famous fictional consulting detective Sherlock Holmes. These codes were originally outlined in the 1947 work *An Irregular Guide to Sherlock Holmes of Baker Street* by Jay Finlay Christ,

---

[4] It is possible that Steed and his associates were known by this nickname in the espionage and crime world. One unfilmed adventure depicts one of Steed's adversaries saying 'Ah, those notorious nosey-parkers the Avengers, I believe?' as he confronted Steed and Tara. *TV Comic*, Issue 975, 22 August 1970.

who abbreviated the famous *The Hound of the Baskervilles* to the less intrusive HOUN, or *The Disappearance of Lady Frances Carfax* to the briefer LADY. Devotees of Holmes have attempted to piece together coherent histories of this literary character for almost a century, and since a similar exercise is being undertaken here – albeit with a real-life hero – it seemed strangely appropriate to borrow the same method of reference. As such, it is easier to refer to the incidents surrounding Steed's investigation of the exclusive marriage bureau Togetherness Inc by the code [MARK] as opposed to the frivolously dramatic title *The Murder Market* or the meaningless alpha-numeric code E64.10.2, or the smashing of the espionage ring run by occultist Dr Cosmo Gallion as [WARL] rather than *Warlock* or 3502. A full list of these four letter codes – along with the dates the missions were documented and issued as well as a list of the Department operatives who so brilliantly transcribed Steed's exploits – appears in Appendix A.

There are some further observations to be made regarding the often strange editing of the surveillance films. For example, in some instances there is clearly surveillance footage from other sources spliced in to cover a 'gap' in narrative from a different source. The first of the two reels concerning the sleeping attack force established by the Russian General Stanislav in 1946 [KIL1] begins by showing events dated as 25 July 1965. However, when Emma Peel is seen accepting Steed's phone call from the scene of the incident at her flat this is actually footage taken from a later surveillance film [WING]; this film shows Emma at the apartment which she moved into during 1966, around a year later than the inserted scene would have the viewer believe. Similarly, when she is seen talking to Steed on 15 August 1977, material of her from another 1966 film was again spliced in [TIGE]; as such, Emma had not aged a day and was still inhabiting her 1960s studio flat. Some of the events would also be resequenced, meaning that the attire of Steed and his colleagues would appear to have a lack of continuity (such as the clothes Steed wears when investigating the Neoteric Research Unit in November 1967, or when walking around the grounds of Castle De'Ath in 1965).

Another example is the incident of Intercrime's 'Great Great Britain Crime' where original film showing Steed and his partner Tara King in action, apparently shot around late 1967 or early 1968, has been integrated with other material filmed at the mews flat of Mother's two aunts, Harriet and Georgina, which seems to have been shot at the start of 1969 [LACE]. To confuse matters further, additional footage representing murders committed by Intercrime was taken from other surveillance films [eg BIRD, MDVL] while their attacks on Steed were similarly depicted using what in the movie industry would be referred to as 'library' material [eg FEAR, NEVE]. It should be noted that there is evidence to indicate that more surveillance footage for both this assignment and the theft of a consignment of FF70 rifles to sell to the revolutionary Colonel Nsonga [GUNS] was originally in existence, but is not currently available.

Material of Steed at the Target Range from 1976 [TARG] was inserted into a 1977 film showing him under stress [ANGE]. In fact, the Department also inserted footage from other official bodies; a film called *The Engineer in the RAF* provided material of fighter planes in action during an aerial exercise executed by RAF Squadron Leader Larry Doomer [OBSE]. A lapse of security meant that somehow, the motor manufacturer British Leyland acquired film of Steed's expert driving of their Rover 3500 SD1 around hazardous country and quarry roads in what appears to be Cornwall in pursuit of an assassin's associate. This was inserted into one of the company's 1977 advertisement films [LION]. Similarly, restricted footage of the Saracen FV 603 armoured vehicle being put through its paces in October 1967 [MISS] surfaced in *Who Plays the Dummy*, an episode of the television adventure series *Department S* (coincidentally named after the Department's private medical facility) broadcast in London on 23 March 1969.

The films also have appended a list of key figures implicated by the events which occasionally gives names which are not evident in the footage itself, such as a gentleman in a gymnasium changing room during a psychological attack being called Saunders [FEAR]. On some occasions, the spellings given in these lists of protagonists is at fault; one film refers to a 'Dr Haymes' in its appendix, whereas the true spelling as given at the man's consulting rooms is clearly 'Dr JF Haynes' (Haymes is only the pronunciation) [MDVL]. It is also worth noting that in the following work, whenever a currency has not been specified in a surveillance film, it has been taken as being that of the native country where the film was shot.

In addition to the films and official reports are a number of other relevant documents to be considered – some visual, some textual. However, the films are the core source material as these other unsubstantiated documents are often unreliable. For example, an alternate document (in report form rather than transcript) exists concerning Steed's 1977 encounter with the Cybernauts, but this contains many errors such as naming Professor Dormeuil as the creator of the robots rather than Dr Clement Armstrong and referring to the Purlington Research Establishment as opposed to the correct name, the Turner Laboratories.[5] For that matter, this record also shows Steed's protagonist, Felix Kane, being defeated in completely different circumstances to those documented on celluloid. To confuse matters further, a set of images relating to the same incidents refer to Armstrong by the name of 'Professor Aronov'.[6] Other English language material such as this has been considered whereas there has been no attempt to look at documentation in other languages.

When information from outside the films has been considered, every attempt has been made to clarify its source. There are even further sources – the exact provenance of which is unknown – which have generally been treated with extreme caution. Some of these appear to be unfilmed missions – or events which were not captured by Department surveillance film. Some of these were written up as text reports (rather than transcribed in script form as with the films) and a number of the shorter ones were filed as 'Annual' reports on Steed's activities in 1967, 1968, 1969, 1977 and 1978. Other items, of even more dubious reliability, are filed in a 'disguised' form as books and children's comics – a form by which they could be transported from office to office without arousing suspicion. Because of the unconfirmed nature of these incidents, they are dealt with only briefly in the main text and are considered in detail in Appendix B.

Most infuriatingly, most of the surveillance films and reports have little to fix them chronologically. The dates available include a 'completion' date (presumably of either shooting, recording or editing the material) and dates on which the files and celluloid were made available to the Midlands, London and New York offices of the Department. These issue dates often differ in sequence from the code numbers, which generally tally with the 'completion' dates – and it is presumably this sequence in which the events occurred,

---

[5] *The Cybernauts* (Cave), p36, 98.

[6] 'The Cybernauts' (LeGoff), *The New Avengers Annual*, 1978, p1; a translation of 'Le Cybernaute', *Chapeau Melon et Bottes de Cuir*, Collection 1, 1977.

presumably shortly before the 'completion' dates.

Unfortunately, not all these dates can be correct. For example, the film relating to Steed's investigation of the Ministry of Technology's Neoteric Research Unit was apparently completed on 14 February 1967, and issued to the UK bureau on 18 March 1967. Yet viewing the footage clearly shows that the month is November 1967 – some nine months after 'completion' – because of a diary entry shown for the October, some weeks before the events depicted. As such, there are times when the sequence of events may differ from the more accepted chronologies compiled by other scholars of Steed's affairs. These are offered as an alternative rather than a definitive solution – and in the years to come further evidence will most likely come to light to allow even greater refinement of some of the theories presented herein.

There have of course been other works on this subject in the past. One of the most useful for fleshing out Steed's early life through to the late 1940s was the first volume of an aborted series of 'authorised' biographies about Steed from the journalist and writer Tim Heald, later Chairman of the British Crime Writers' Association. Former singer Dave Rogers has also published numerous books on Steed's career since his groundbreaking *The Avengers* in 1983, leading the field at a time when such complete access to the Department surveillance films was undreamed of and a great reliance was placed on the few summary reports which had escaped into the world at large. These and other such sources such as newspapers and comics have been referenced as footnotes at the appropriate places in the study and are listed fully in the bibliography.

The scope of this work is first of all to attempt to give an overview of the life and work of John Steed (as far as autumn 1977, the date of his last recorded mission) and then to present biographical details of his colleagues and the historical structure of the Department, which the current Mother assures us is now obsolete. The result is a document which it is hoped will promote further research and investigation into the otherwise overlooked career of the gentleman who is surely Britain's most secret agent. As you will see, many contradictions and inconsistencies arise as cover stories become confused with the truth. Indeed, at times Steed's behaviour is so erratic it is tempting to compare his life to a fictional character, being tugged this way and that by different collaborative writers. For some of the questions raised, there are no answers – only theories.

As with any biographical work though, the reader should be aware that the interpretation of the information available is only one possible perspective. There are many other ways of binding together the established facts and inferences – and given the clandestine nature of the subject matter, there are countless other combinations of truth and falsehood which could be woven together from the same source material.

A study into the greatest secret agent who ever lived, so terribly misrepresented in the eyes of the public by a box office flop – or a mass of unsubstantiated trivia assembled from documents and films hitherto kept from the eyes of the nation? Hopefully, this work will lie somewhere between the two.

Andrew Pixley
March 2004

JOHN STEED

A LEGEND IN HIS OWN LIFETIME

'John Steed, 38, is a man of many faces. In the course of my inquiries I discovered that some people believe him to be a ruthless adventurer. Others know the second face of Steed – the charming man-about-town with a taste for Edwardian elegance in his clothes... jackets with cuffed sleeves and patent leather, Chelsea-style boots.'[1]

This summation of Steed was one of his rare mentions in the popular press, and appeared in late September 1963 as part of a cover story which allowed him to expose the machinations of Miles and Jasper Lakin, two barristers at law who had successfully concocted 11 'briefs for murder'. This cover story also maintained the perfect image of the true Steed who – even as an undercover agent for the Department – was every bit as charming and stylish as this piece of journalistic window dressing made him out to be.

'That increasing rarity, a real English gentleman,' is how the art and restricted information dealer Gregorio Auntie described Steed in 1965 [AUNT] while another art dealer going by the name 'Paul Beresford', later described him as an 'agent, adventurer extraordinary' [RETU]. This combination of cultured exterior alongside ruthless national security work fascinated many operating in the field; 'A dangerous man, a worthy adversary, and yet he looks like an English gentleman,' pondered the oriental-styled drugs baron Soo Choy when one of his operations was foiled by Steed's team [TRAP]. Steed's cover, as described by his opposite number Comrade Zalenko of Russia was that of a 'man about town', with the addendum that 'his other activities are rather obscure' [CONC].

'A legend in his own lifetime,' was how Steed's colleague McBain described him in the 1970s [RARE], just one of the many accolades accorded by those serving with the Department. However Steed was admired not just by his colleagues, but also by his opponents such as The Unicorn [LION]. He was described as a 'cunning old fox' by his rival Comrade Nutski [CORR], and even the misguided cosmetic surgeon Arcos rated him as 'the most respected agent in the country' in 1968 [KEEP]. In jocular mood, Steed described his true role to his ecclesiastical friend, the Reverend Teddy Shelley, saying 'You baptise and bury them, and I'll try to see that the interval in between is as long as possible' [THIN]. However, Steed also modestly claimed that his greatest contribution to mankind was the

---

[1] *TV Times*, 20 September 1963, p4.

creation of the 12-tier champagne fountain [THAT].

There was little that Steed would stop short of in the performance of his duty. 'I wouldn't put anything past you,' commented Dr David Keel during one investigation alongside him [FRIG], although Steed himself informed the GP at the outset of their association that he was 'on the side of the angels' [SNOW]. Keel was just one of those working alongside Steed who would be amazed by what the operative was prepared to do in pursuit of his work. 'Sly, devious, cunning [and] scheming,' was how Catherine Gale – whom Steed worked with on and off for over a decade – described his approach to work [CHAR], while Emma Peel, with whom Steed was associated from 1964 to 1967, found him 'Ruthless, devious [and] scheming'[MARK].

'With Steed, nothing is impossible,' commented double agent Coldstream, who worked alongside Steed in the 1970s [ANGE]. Indeed, the maxim of the Russian Captain Malachev was, 'Never underestimate Steed. The prisons and graveyards are littered with those who made that mistake' [BASE]. However, along with all his skill and training, Steed's career was also blessed with something more than a little cosmic in terms of good fortune which allows him such longevity, leading one of his closest colleagues, Purdey, to quip that her boss was 'Found under a four leaf clover' [DEAD].[2]

In his role as an undercover man Steed also saw himself as having one specific role, and when offered the code-name of the Roman God Mars – known as 'The Avenger' – he felt that the choice of this epithet, 'Hit it on the head' [ROME]. 'He's a fascinating man and there will never be another John Steed,'[3] said actress Linda Thorson, who knew Steed during the late 1960s via her working relationship with one of Steed's old school friends from Eton, Patrick Macnee.

Attempting to determine the true life story of Steed is not the easiest of tasks – not least because, as a trained undercover agent, he was supremely skilful at dispensing mistruths and misinformation in a highly plausible manner, placing him on an equal footing with other larger-than-life figures prone to embellishing their life stories such as Orson Welles or Baron von Munchhausen. Indeed, added to Steed's own sense of the dramatic, the biographer must also contend with the many security precautions and cover stories laid down over the years by the different sections of the Department, which serve to muddy the waters of research.

While the primary source of research has been the surveillance films made available by the Department, much of the detail on Steed's early life up to 1949 has been drawn from *John Steed: An Authorised Biography*. Published in October 1977, this work was assembled by journalist and thriller writer Tim Heald. Heald's family had been acquainted with Steed since at least the early 1950s.

However, there is one very important caveat to bear in mind with Heald's work. At the front of the volume it states, 'Spectacularly well-informed and observant readers may think they have spotted a number of factual errors in this book... At several points in the narrative I have changed one or two names and facts on the grounds of legality, taste or national security... to avoid causing innocent people either undue embarrassment or, in some cases, almost certain death!'[4]

---

[2] Steed allegedly once commented 'I come from a lucky family.' 'The Golden Game'. *Steed and Mrs Peel*, Book Two, p49.

[3] McGown, Alistair and Rea, Darren, 'Bizarre Inc.', *Dreamwatch*, Issue 19, March 1996, p19.

[4] *John Steed: An Authorised Biography – Volume One: Jealous in Honour.*

JOHN STEED

FROM KING NOFFIN OF THE FENS
TO ALEXANDER STEED OF RAMZAK

Before arriving at Steed himself, it is worth recounting some of his lineage. As Steed commented, he was born with a silver spoon in his mouth [CATC]. He once even plotted a family tree for the Steeds as a hobby around 1968 and completed this work in early 1969. His research confirmed his suspicion that royal blood ran in his veins. On his great-grand-father's side through a great-great-cousin twice removed through his great-uncle's cousin's aunt's sister – from his mother's side – and taking into account his father's father's father's brother who was four times removed from his uncle's sister's brother's nephew, he had an ancestor related by marriage to the brother of the father of the sister of King Noffin of the Fens. Other figures apparently included Steed-the-Ready who dominated three shires in the Dark Ages, and also Sir Steedalot who was credited with the invention of King Arthur's Round Table. Indeed, the invention of this fabled piece of furniture was apparently an acci-dent, since Sir Steedalot had a bad habit of whittling away with his sword at any piece of wood which came to hand... [REQU]

Much of the other detail about the Steeds was turned up by Heald's extensive researches from which he concluded that 'the family has always been highly individual.'[1] There was evidence of Steeds as far back as the Roman age, but the first definite records tell of a Stede the Sturdy who was the henchman to Port the Pirate in Hampshire at the start of the sixth century. Also known as Stede the Steady, Stede the Surly or Stede the Stout, he was a warrior who died in battle. Heald notes that there was also a Stedius, a minor poet from St Albans around the time of Christ.

Steeds and Stedes seemed to flourish in North Hampshire and Wiltshire, principally engaged in the crafts of piracy and looting. One of the Steed women, Ethelreda, was married to the King of Mercia while another, who changed her name to Gudrun, was the mistress of Ivar the Boneless. Another Stede, who came from near Wilton in Wiltshire was noted by Asser, the Bishop of Sherborne, in his chronicles as warning King Alfred's West Saxon army about a Danish force at the Battle of Ashdown in 871. There was a Guthrum Stede who fought alongside King Harold at both Stamford Bridge and Hastings in 1066,

---

[1] *Jealous in Honour*, p11.

and a few weeks after Hastings, there are records that one John Steed – whom Heald speculated might be Guthrum Stede – had been granted land near Binfield in Berkshire. This was the site of the manor which became Stede Regis, the family estate of the Steeds.

However, the exact location of this regal building is disputed. One stately home where the later John Steed grew up was in fact near Henley-on-Thames, since Steed recalled stealing the binoculars which had belonged to his father and setting off across the fields to watch the Regatta on the Thames. The young Steed played by the river and recalled that – by spring 1969 – there was a retired eccentric called Captain Cleghorn who lived nearby, tooting his horn at passing ducks. The River Thames was apparently a quarter of a mile away from the estate across the fields [REQU]. Another theory that has been put forward from viewing of one of the surveillance films is that it was near Fulmer [HOST] – ironically very close to Pinewood Film Studios where in 1997 Steed's 'life story' was filmed by Warner Bros.

By 1800, Stede Regis was very similar to a country house which Steed later took his junior colleague Tara King to sometime during 1968; he observed this place bore a marked resemblance to the house which he used to live in. There was a wall with Victorian urns along the top, roses around the front door of the house itself which stood in its own grounds, and large iron gates bearing two faces – one laughing, one crying – which the young Steed used to swing on. There was also a weather vane in the shape of an ecclesiastical figure which Steed always felt was a canon, but was in fact a bishop [REQU].

Regardless of Stede Regis's actual location, there were a few other scattered middleages Steeds of note, many being the lords of Stede Regis who were never slow to take up arms in a war. Godfrey Steed was part of Richard the Lionheart's forces in the Crusades and killed at Joppa in 1192.[2] The historian Holinshed mentions a William Steed at the Battle of Agincourt in 1415.

However, Stede Regis was almost lost by the Steed family in the 16th century. In 1537, Walter Steede became embroiled with Anne Boelyn, and as a result was beheaded at the Tower of London on 12 May. Because of this royal offence, Stede Regis was forfeit to the crown, with the family fleeing first to exile in Flanders, and then in northern Spain.

However, the Steeds were soon back in favour; Walter's grandson, John Steed, operated as an agent in Spain for the British government and was able to supply Queen Elizabeth's forces with the plans of the Spanish Armada some six months in advance of the attack on England in 1588. As a mark of thanks, Stede Regis was restored – with John narrowly escaping from Spain when his part in this act of espionage was revealed, much in the manner of his namesake centuries later.

One Philip Steed sailed with Sir John Hawkins to the Spanish West Indies in the 1590s, giving his name to Steedstown in Haiti – a settlement later renamed Duvalierville and now best known as Cabaret. An American arm of the family was founded when cousin Wilbraham settled in Massachusetts in 1634, and the Steeds quickly proliferated in the colonies.

One of our Steed's ancestors was his great-great-uncle Sir Everington Steed who fought at Waterloo in 1815. Sir Everington was a brilliant soldier who apparently taught the Duke of Wellington all he knew about military tactics, and therefore was instrumental in the

---

2 In jovial mood, Steed apparently claimed that Robin Hood was one of his ancestors. *The Floating Game*, p23.

defeat of Napoleon. As with his descendent, this Steed was a man who was clearly admired by both English and French forces [KIL1]. One of his most quoted observations on warfare was 'A battle cannot be lost until it has been fought' [KIL2]. Sir Everington was one of the more notable soldiers in the family, one member of which rose to the rank of general while another attained the heights of colonel.

By tradition, the eldest Steed boy of any generation would remain at home to manage the affairs of Stede Regis while his younger brothers were free to seek adventure and fulfilment around the world. Our Steed's great-grandfather was RKJ de V Steed [CHAR] apparently known in his day as 'Stallion'[3], who was immortalised in a fine portrait in oils presented by the Bagnell and Wintle Hunt in 1892 [NUTS] which later hung over our Steed's fireplace at his Westminster Mews flat and clearly displayed the family resemblance across the generations. John Steed's grandfather, also named John Steed, was born in 1832, and Steed later inherited his gold Hunter pocket watch [KEEP]. Of his siblings, it is possible that one was his grandson's Great Aunt Emily, a lady who impressed on the younger John the importance of the phrase 'waste not want not' and saved silver paper until she had five tons of it – whereupon she went off with a scrap metal dealer with a big moustache [FALS]. Steed also made reference on one occasion to a Great Aunt Florence as part of a background story to allow him entrance to the Gaslight Ghoul Club of London, and while Florence's diary giving an account of a murder in 1888 was certainly a fabrication by the Department, it is at present unclear if Florence herself existed or not [FOG].

A particularly roguish member of the Steed clan, John ran away from a formal education at Eton, that most venerated of public schools, and set sail for adventure. He travelled to Calcutta and was present at both the pacification of the Punjab and the expropriation of the Kohinoor diamond. During the Indian Mutiny of 1857 he lost a leg. Returning to Stede Regis, he bred racehorses at the family home and was a reckless gambler, two traits later shared by his grandson. Some sources claim that he was in fact the inspiration for Long John Silver in Robert Louis Stevenson's acclaimed romantic thriller *Treasure Island* in 1883.[4] It is presumably John Steed whom the elderly Miss Gladys Culpepper remembered as being 'a charming old man' in 1969 [THAT].

The year after his literary alter-ego appeared in print, John Steed travelled to America to find a wife. Although having turned 50, the adventurer became engaged in a whirlwind romance with Emerald Cabot, the youngest daughter of a well-connected Boston family. The couple were married within a fortnight of meeting. They then returned to Stede Regis, where their first son Walter was born in 1887. However, within a year of the birth of Walter's young brother Alexander in 1889, Emerald had died of consumption. Her condition had apparently been brought on by a chilly visit to Newbury races where Emerald had been present to watch her favourite colt, Boston Boy, romp home first. Family history records that John blamed himself for his wife being out in England's wet weather, and never attended a race course again. Presumably it was Emerald whom Steed referred to when he commented in 1965 that 'They do say I take after granny' [AUNT].

It was young Alexander who would be the father to possibly Britain's most respected

---

[3] The nickname appears to stem from an unconfirmed report which referred to the ancestor as 'RKJJ de V Steed'. *The Avengers* (Enefer), p63. This is also how the name is given in the transcript.

[4] An unconfirmed report suggests that Steed may have encountered a version of Long John Silver created by a 'Three Dimensional Books' machine in 1969. 'Fable Land'. *TV Comic Annual*, 1969, p53.

undercover agent. He was a typical Steed and had 'inherited his father's dark good looks.'[5] Educated at Eton like his elder brother, Alexander was fascinated by botany – accumulating one of the finest collections of butterflies indigenous to the Thames Valley – and travelled to Palermo by motorcycle in his youth. Having been introduced to Indian dialects by his father at an early age, Alexander pursued his talent in this area by reading Oriental Languages at Oxford; he then joined the Indian Civil Service so that his skills could now be employed while he would be able to visit exotic locales. When war broke out with Germany in 1914, Alexander felt it best that he served in India. This was something of a disappointment to his father who had wanted him to join the Guards.

In the meantime, Walter – a keen cricketer, a passion which later resurfaced in his nephew – had been on to study at King's College at Cambridge and read for the bar where he practised briefly. After working for the Foreign Office, he married Lady Eithne Wimborne at St Margaret's Westminster in January 1914. At the outset of hostilities, Walter was drafted to the Royal Navy and served as a lieutenant with the Hood Battalion.

Alexander joined up with the explorer Eric Bailey and travelled to India via China and Tibet. Because of the demand for officers who could speak Urdu, he was drafted to the 34th Sikh Pioneers – part of the Indian Expeditionary Force formed to fight the French – and accorded the rank of second lieutenant. Wounded by one of his own Mills Bombs during a midnight skirmish with a Prussian patrol, Alexander was awarded the Military Cross, and then transferred to the 1st-5th Gurkhas, promoted to the rank of captain.

On an expedition to the Dardanelles in 1915, Alexander was reunited with Walter – but the happy meeting of brothers ended in tragedy. Shaving the next morning, Walter was shot through the temple by a Turkish sniper. This major blow to Alexander was compounded when he received a letter from Eithne to say that the boys' father had died in his sleep three days earlier at the age of 83. Since John had pre-deceased Walter, the estate passed to Eithne as his widow. This double tragedy formed a strong bond between Eithne and Alexander.

After the end of the war in 1918, Major Alexander Steed was posted to Amritsar to act as Political Adviser to Frontier fighter Brigadier-General Rex Dyer; he arrived to take up this role in spring 1919 shortly before widespread riots broke out across the Punjab. With Dyer's forces trapped in the fort at Amritsar, Alexander bravely disguised himself as a Sikh and moved among the population to gather vital intelligence in a manner similar to the undercover work his son would later undertake. Steed was with Dyer at the defeat of the Afghan forces at Khadimakh, but the Brigadier-General was relieved of his post after collapsing. After the subsequent committee of enquiry, Alexander spent a tedious period at Government headquarters, shuttling between Delhi and Simla.

It was during summer 1919 that Alexander was invited to a soiree being given by the wife of the Adjutant-General. Although initially reluctant, it was here that he met Krystal Zamoyska, a brilliant young pianist whom – it was said – had arrived by hot air balloon from Delhi via Chandigarth to the government base in the northern hills. Alexander was captivated by Krystal, even enjoying her rendition of works by the Polish composer Frederic Chopin, compositions which he previously had little time for. As with his father, a whirlwind romance followed and the couple were married within a month, with Belvoir Pottinger, a young subaltern with the 17th Lancers, as Alexander's best man.

---

[5] *Jealous in Honour*, p17.

Born in Chicago, Krystal was the eldest daughter of a Polish father and an American mother. In her late teens she left her home city to travel in search of adventure in New York and appeared in a couple of films for DW Griffith – small roles which, regrettably, have defied being traced – before turning her hand to writing screenplays and having some short stories published in *The Anglo-American*. Outgoing and gay, she also had a serious streak which manifested itself via her work as a pianist and her passion for the work of Chopin, her father's countryman. Her skill at the keyboard was a talent which would later manifest itself in her son.

Steed's Grandfather Zamoyska[6] had been part of a once noble but now impoverished family in Poland who had set out across the world to seek his fortune. In Chicago, he had met the lady whom he would marry, the daughter of a local soda-fountain owner. Of this generation of the family from America, little is known. Steed later recalled a great-aunt on his mother's side who displayed a ruthless way with a knitting needle [WILD].

Grandfather and Grandmother Zamoyska were blessed with many, many daughters of which Krystal was the eldest; her numerous sisters formed the eclectic network of aunts to John Steed all over the world. Over the years, Steed stayed in touch with many of them and most seemed to have some form of eccentricity. His colleagues often found this amusing, with Tara King once commenting that the behaviour of his aunts was in fact quite predictable [FOG].

At least one aunt seemed to have a drink problem; she could not keep off the bottle and did a skating act in the music halls as well as dancing on marble table tops [BREA]. It is possible that this is the same aunt whom Steed was reminded of when horsewoman Miss Beryl Snow told him of her mount who 'can't keep away from the trough – just wants to keep drinking all the time' [DUST]. On one occasion, Steed joked that he was writing an academic work entitled *Advanced Research into the co-relationship of the Lesser-Crested Newt and Mrs Sybil Peabody*, explaining further that this was his Aunt Sybil who drank like a fish – and was thus possibly either one, both or a third alcoholic aunt [HIST].

Many of Steed's aunts sent him presents at regular intervals. Auntie Penelope would despatch rock cakes which had the constituency of lead weights [TREA] while Aunt Emily periodically sent hampers of cold goodies to his apartment [PAND] and had also given him a battered, ancient alarm clock which kept excellent time although it was, in fact, missing one hand [GAME]. One aunt was adept at making biscuits shaped like gingerbread men [SURF] while another apparently worried continually about who was darning his socks well into the 1960s [MIND]. His Auntie Ermyntrude had a 'Patent Cold Cure Remedy', a very heady mixture which was supposed to clear the sinuses, although the effectiveness of this potion must be questioned as Ermyntrude herself had died at an early age from a cold [CATC]. Steed also wrote to one of his elderly aunts who had settled in Eastbourne [CHAR]. Aunt Tibby used to comment on the weather being inclement for the time of year [LOBS] and apparently – as Heald recalled – Aunt Alberta made fudge.

The mention of a typewriter whose hammers included a 'blunt f, squint i [and] h above the line' reminded Steed of his Auntie Queenie [NOV5], while a photograph of a miscreant with 'a face full of avarice' found him musing about another auntie of his [TIME]. On another occasion, Steed claimed to have an aunt in Rottingdene, but it is most likely that

---

[6] An unconfirmed report notes that Steed recalled his grandfather telling him about film star Rudolph Fairbanks; this was presumably Gradfather Zamoyska. *TV Comic*, Issue 904, 12 April 1969.

this was part of a ruse to send a coded message [FROG].

The name of Steed's very favourite aunt is not known, but certainly one of her frequent sayings was, 'If Christmas came in August, chestnut stuffing would never have been invented'. Neither Steed nor the rest of his family ever understood exactly what these words of wisdom were meant to mean, but this did not deter the lady from saying it [THIN]. More lucid was his Aunt Clara who was well known for saying that 'Life is not a bowl of cherries' – a phrase so common that it was well known to Steed's colleagues [FOG].

Of his aunt's husbands. Steed had an Uncle Joe who left him a gold toothpick which he wore as a tie-pin in the 1960s [BREA], while another heirloom from this side of the family was his Hunter pocket watch bequeathed by another uncle – the timepiece in question had been dented at the Battle of the Somme in 1916 by a kick from a Canadian mule [DIAL]. Another uncle on his mother's side became a grand master at chess – a game which Steed also played on occasion, albeit not to the same level [REQU]. Although one of his uncles alone sired 19 children in addition to being a keen bicyclist [SLEE], there is only one direct reference in connection to a cousin, this being one Desmond, better known as 'Demon Desmond' the 'Demon Dice Loader' who won the World Ludo Championship some time prior to 1969 [REQU].

With Krystal now part of the Steed dynasty, it was time for Alexander to be posted again, this time to Razmak. The Afrids were revolting in Waziristan, and Krystal agreed to accompany her husband there without hesitation – providing that the Bechstein grand piano could also come with them. Although there were many hardships, the marriage between Krystal and Alexander was a strong and loving one, and within two years she was pregnant with their first child. Alexander sent a protesting Krystal to Peshawar, the nearest town with medical facilities, but as it turned out this was not where their son would enter the world. Heading off on a railway excursion one day, Krystal felt the contractions soon after Nowshera and alighted from the train at Campbellpore.

According to Heald's work, Steed's mother was pregnant with him towards the end of 1921, a fact which seems to square with his attendance at school in the same year as his good friend, the actor Patrick Macnee, who was born on 6 February 1922. Since Steed commented that his star sign was Aquarius [WARL], this means that he was born between 21 January and 18 February, presumably of 1922. This is however at odds with newspaper reports at the time of the faked murder of Catherine Gale in September 1963, which suggest that he was 38 when he should have been 41. Yet, since this is no more than a 'cover story' (and bearing in mind the notoriously unreliable nature of many periodicals), the age in this article can most probably by discounted. It is also worth noting that, during 1977, Mark Crayford – one of Steed's old friends from school days – was described as being in his 'mid-40s', which probably reflects better on Crayford's physique and appearance, since to be a contemporary of Steed's at that time would place him nearer his mid-50s [DEAD].

Thanks to a qualified nurse who was travelling in the same railway compartment as Krystal, John Steed was born in the stationmaster's office in Campbellpore, not far from the Khyber Pass. A telegram was despatched to Razmak, informing Alexander: 'John arrived safely. Eight pounds two ounces.'[7]

It is worth noting at this point that of the other famous contemporary Steeds, one was the English journalist and author Henry Wickham Steed who was born in Long Melford in

---

[7] *Jealous in Honour*, p25.

1871. Henry Steed began a long association with *The Times* at the end of the 19th century, becoming foreign editor during World War I and then editing the world famous newspaper from 1919 to 1922, prior to a career writing books and lecturing on European history and affairs into the 1930s. As Henry came from the East Anglian wing of the family, exactly how John Steed was related to this man of words is unclear, but according to Heald – who had extensive access to Steed's family papers – Steed's full name was John Wickham Henry de Trafford Steed, which seems something more than a coincidence.[8]

---

[8] Another source – of all things a stage play about John Steed's life written in 1971 by Brian Clemens and Terence Feely two of the Department operatives who had prepared transcriptions of Steed's missions – gave Steed's full name as John Wickham Gascoyne Berresford Steed. However, the script also noted that he was the youngest of a family of eight and had seven elder sisters, none of which is substantiated by other evidence.

JOHN STEED

STEDE REGIS AND LYDEARD LODGE

By all reports, the young Steed was bestowed with blue eyes (which became hazel in adulthood), wiry black hair and the knees peculiar to the Zamoyski family, while he would later develop the highly recognisable primped nape of the neck – a tough trait when inflicted on the Steed girls as Steed himself observed [FOG]. A very important figure in the early years of his life was Ruth, a young local Roman Catholic girl who acted as his 'ayah' or nanny and cared for young Steed back at Razmak when his parents were away.[1] Indeed, Steed's first words were in the Urdu and the local Waziri, picked up from either Ruth or Abdul Haq, his father's bearer. Steed's Aunt Eithne despatched Primrose, the Boston built rocking horse beloved by both Alexander and Walter as children, to Razmak, and in March 1923, Alexander wrote to her saying that his young son had very much taken to the toy and enjoyed riding. By now, Steed had also experienced his first stiff drink, having downed a bottle of Krystal's perfume which left him stoned!

According to Heald's work, Steed became a big brother when he was two as his mother gave birth to a fair and delicate child. Steed's younger sibling was christened Walter in honour of his late uncle. However, in one of the Department surveillance films, Steed stated that he did not have a brother on an occasion when he was not undercover and had no reason to lie [DWAR]. This seems to indicate that Department operatives were advised not to make mention of family members who could possibly be used by the 'other side' for the purposes of kidnap or blackmail, thus eliminating potential security risks. One press item in September 1963 erroneously referred to Steed as being 'the younger son of a younger son'.[2]

Certainly further evidence for Steed having a brother comes from the fact that he has nephews and nieces – presumably Walter's children. It seems that in the absence of any children of his own, Steed would later dote on these and particularly delight in buying gifts for the boys which he could first play with himself. One nephew's birthday in 1965 gave him an excellent excuse to invest in a gun which fired ping pong balls [GRAV] while for another nephew's tenth birthday the same year he purchased a toy aeroplane to assemble –

---

[1] There is an unconfirmed report that Steed once admitted to having 'teething trouble as a baby'. *Diana*, Issue 204, 14 January 1967.

[2] *TV Times*, 20 September 1963, p4.

not realising that it would take him three years to actually complete work on the model [LEGA]. When visiting the offices of Winged Avenger Enterprises in 1966, he also claimed that he was trying to obtain back numbers of the comic *The Winged Avenger* for his young nephew [WING]. Steed also made reference to a niece in 1963 although it is most likely that she was an invention to allow him a plausible excuse to investigate the famous fashion designer Fernand. Supposedly, the niece was 'coming out' the following season, was fair, five feet four inches tall and had vital statistics of 34-24-36 [WHAL]. However, there certainly was a niece who seemed to be a teenager – and apparently being educated in London – whom Steed would go to meet from school in 1968 [LOVE].

But the nieces and nephews were in the future, and Walter had only just been born, let alone become a father. By 1924 there was more unrest on the frontier; indeed, around the time that Steed was born there had been 22 policemen killed during a riot at Chauri Chaura on 2 February 1922 and 11 days later, the Indian National Congress had been forced to suspend the civil disobedience campaign in the face of mounting violence. Alexander had taken it upon himself to keep appraised of local feeling by visiting the local maliks and conversing with them in their native tongues. On these visits, he would now on occasion travel with an entourage which included his wife, two sons and Ruth. The village of Hazmat Khel – subsequently renamed Steedsabad – was their venue for the night of 17 April 1924 where they experienced the hospitality of Akbar Khan who enjoyed drinking whiskey with Alexander. That night, Akbar warned Alexander about his son, Basmati Khan, who was in league with the Mullah and opposed the British forces in his country.

The following morning, it was the mountain rebels in league with Khan who attacked Alexander's party as they stopped by a stream. Although putting up a valiant battle, the British party were wiped out – save for Ruth and her two orphaned charges who were captured by the natives and bundled away on horseback to their secret base in the hillside caves.

News of 'The Massacre of Zamoyska Hill' was soon a prominent feature in the British newspapers, with the infant John and his baby brother major news in the political arena. Lady Eithne's father, the Duke of Dorset, spoke on the situation surrounding his daughter's captured nephews in the House of Lords, and support for the missing children was fostered by Hannan Swaffer's headlines in *The People* (eg 'Steed Children. Government must Act!'). However, when the British Government failed to bow to newspaper pressure, it was up to Lady Eithne – the guardian of the two brothers – to step boldly in.

While many believed that the boys were in fact dead, Eithne took it upon herself to travel to Peshawar to discover the truth. Riding with the company of the Poona Horse, she met with Akbar Khan and established that his estranged son and the Mullah had the children and their ayah safe and well. Terms for the return of the brothers were agreed, and Eithne met with Basmati for the hand over. The rebels departed with their ransom payment, and Eithne was left with Ruth and her two nephews. After some months of captivity, young John's first words to his aunt were in Urdu.

Steed's parents were later avenged when the men from Akbar Khan's village rid themselves of the local rebels, including Basmati who was put to the sword. Memorial tablets to Walter, and to Alexander and Krystal, were placed in the parish church at Stede Regis; Alexander himself had been buried with full military honours at Peshawar. For the rest of his life, Steed made little or no reference to the parents he had hardly known. At one point in the mid-1960s, he commented that his father would spin in his grave at the rising price of gun cartridges [DUST].

However, while his father's premature death was a matter of public record, later in his life it seems that Steed would delight in concocting anecdotes about him. He once joked that when the Harteinsch grape went out, his father made his family vow not to drink another hock, commenting that this is what killed him [BROK]. On another occasion, Steed claimed that one of his childhood recollections was that he would creep up to his father's study every night and help himself to a glass of soda water from the liqueur cabinet. Fair enough; no doubt there was still a study at Stede Regis which would have been Alexander's. However, he then embellished the anecdote by saying that he felt rather guilty about this act, not however because of its covert nature, but rather that he would have preferred lemonade while the 'old man' said such a soft drink would ruin his palette [WILD]. Of course, it is open to debate who the 'old man' was. Possibly it was actually the Duke of Dorset and these events in fact occurred at the Duke's family estate, Vole.

On one occasion around September 1962, it was necessary for Steed to pose as a married diamond merchant to investigate a trade in illicit stones. With Cathy Gale taking on the mantle of his wife, Steed threw a party at their new home in Highgate for other members of the gem industry. One lady present – presumably a member of the Organisation – posed as Steed's mother, whom Cathy described as 'really quite a character' [ROCK].[3] The absence of Steed's mother would later mean there was a lack of confusion about whom he was referring to when he would say he needed to call his Department superior – code-named Mother [BIZA].

Eithne, John, Walter and Ruth set sail from Bombay, and Steed got the first view of what would become his beloved England when their ship docked at Southampton amidst the drizzle characteristic of the climate. It was a very different world for young Steed, whose English had improved substantially on the voyage. He and Walter were then whisked away to the first of the grand and stately homes which would litter Steed's childhood – as Tara later observed [REQU]. However, this was not the ancestral home of Stede Regis, but rather Vole, the great house which was home to the Duke of Dorset and Eithne's birthplace.

Rejecting the advances of many highly eligible suitors, Eithne devoted herself to raising her nephews as her own children. Much of the time they lived at Stede Regis, but spent periods at Vole and also Balwhinnie Castle, the Duke's highland home near Balmoral where as a teenager, Steed would learn to use a rifle when deer stalking with the ghillies. The assorted Zamoyski aunts would visit the boys, but never interfere with Eithne's upbringing of them as little English boys. She read them children's stories written by Beatrix Potter, and the new works of AA Milne as they were published. Fred Gotobed, one of the staff from the days of 'Long John' Steed, taught John and Walter all about country lore as they grew up. The elderly Duke coached the brothers in cricket and croquet when they came of age. Algy, Eithne's brother who was the Marquis of Yetminster, taught them tennis, while an elderly nanny at Vole showed them how to play cribbage.

Another talent which the young Steed acquired in his formative years was how to fight – although this was not generally known to the rest of his family. He had been shown his first moves in India by Abdul Haq, and had then studied the combat techniques of his captors at Basmati Khan's hideout. But his tuition in combat now continued in secret cour-

---

[3] In the Warner Bros. biographical movie set in 1999, the cinematic Steed told Dr Emma Peel that his mother, Mrs Steed, was still alive and living in Wiltshire.

tesy of Ruth who had been part of a secret sect which practised martial arts. Ruth herself had attained a rank in 'Pathan fighting' which Steed later told one of school friends was called 'emerald slipper'.

Young 'Johnny' – as he was called by his family – grew accustomed to the English gentry's way of living in the coming years. Steed suffered bouts of mumps, chickenpox and whooping cough, and also broke his leg in a fall one October while scrambling up a conker tree. Nevertheless, he remained a keen climber despite this mishap. As a child, Steed seemed to be a rather solitary figure when it came to mixing with his peers. Lady Eithne's diary entry for 18 September 1928 shows that the six-year-old preferred his own company to that of potential playmates Hugo and Cecil Framlingham. This could be in part due to the fact that Hugo and Cecil were two other little boys. Already Young John found such company boring, whereas he was developing a fondness for the company of the opposite sex, in front of whom he became a rather debonair little figure. He also enjoyed stealing kisses from girls in cupboards when playing sardines at parties.

There seemed to be two regular places that the young Steed used to play – both on his own and presumably with other children and young Walter. One of these was a summer house in an estate, possibly called 'Lyndon', which by summer 1968 was up for sale. Steed paid a return visit here when the property was on the market and seeing the summer house brought back memories of playing cowboys and Indians[4], and doctors and nurses; the room itself was still full of all manner of junk including a guitar, dolls (suggesting it was once the haunt of little girls as well as little boys), a ventriloquist's dummy, bird cages, an old gramophone player and numerous toys including Harry the Dragon. Steed also had fond recollections of an old tree-house, which was presumably in the same grounds [LEGA].

Similarly, there was 'Fort Steed', a room in a unidentified building which had walls excitingly painted to resemble those of a mediaeval castle. As mentioned, it is possible that this was located at Stede Regis – providing that Stede Regis was at Henley-on-Thames rather than Binfield. Certainly it was from here that Steed went to play on the river a quarter of a mile away and stole his father's binoculars to watch the Henley Regatta across the nearby fields. The existence of 'Fort Steed' was apparently only known to two of Steed's childhood friends, 'Stinks' Wilkins and 'Fatty the Gorger', both sworn to secrecy on the oath of 'last one in's a ninny'. As with the summer house, when Steed returned in spring 1969 it still housed items from his childhood, including a rocking horse (possibly Primrose), hoops, toy trains, drums and another guitar. The state of the playroom also suggested that since John and Walter, there had been no other children living at the house. The room reeked of military history with plenty of toy soldiers and model ships to re-enact great battles.

During his childhood, the young Steed fought many moments of history in 'Fort Steed' including Sir John Moore and the British defeating Marshal Soult and the French at Corunna in Spain in January 1809, Wellington's British forces and their allies triumphing over Napoleon Bonaparte's French army at Waterloo in June 1815 (thus re-enacting the tactics of Sir Everington Steed), the Russian attack on British positions at the Battle of Balaclava in October 1854 during the Crimean war, Wellington's pursuit of Napoleon and General Declare's 'ignominious retreat' from Corby. In adulthood, Steed was secretive

---

[4] In an unconfirmed report, Steed revealed how he was quick on the draw in a Western-style shootout, explaining to Tara that it was 'A childhood craze'. *TV Comic*, Issue 988, 21 November 1970.

about this venue and claimed that the only person he ever mentioned it to amongst his colleagues was Tara. In spring 1969 he was sure that nobody in the Department – not even his superior, Mother – knew about it, making it the safest place he knew. As it turned out Steed was mistaken, since surveillance film of him in hiding with Miss Miranda Loxton is in existence [REQU].

Steed's other toys included a model roundabout which played a melody that seemed to run through his life [NURS]; indeed, this was one of the tunes which he was known to play on the piano [VENU]. It is also possible that one his childhood hobbies was the collection of stamps from the reign of Napoleon III [MAUR].

Steed could be an exasperating and precocious child. Already he enjoyed disobeying the rules, reading story magazines like *The Magnet* and back issues of *The Gem Library* under the sheets by torch-light, despite his aunt's dislike for these titles. Days out included visits to Harrods, or a pantomime at Christmas, or – best of all – the local point-to-point races. Since his days in the saddle of Primrose, young Steed seemed to have had an affinity for horses, and as he grew older he relished riding out on the Dorset or Berkshire downs. Thus, by the age of seven he was already an excellent horseman.

Early education for Steed seems to have been handled at Stede Regis by Eithne herself and a variety of tutors including a French mistress who left when the young John put pepper in her marmalade pudding. However, in 1929 Aunt Eithne decided it was time that he should be educated at school. The selected establishment for John's first taste of formal education was Lydeard Lodge at Swanborne, a prep school where boys generally passed through to Eton, Harrow or Windsor.

So it was that in September 1929, John Steed was dressed in his tweed jacket, grey flannel shorts, knee length socks and black shoes, and duly despatched to Swanborne. The seven-year-old was a little upset at the parting – as was his aunt – but neither party displayed their feelings.

From the outset, the young Steed was rather cautious of Somerset Andover-Bigge, the somewhat right-wing headmaster who ran Lydeard Lodge with his wife, Susan. Although Andover-Bigge had been very friendly when initially meeting Steed and Eithne, now he had the new boy on his books his true colours were revealed. The school itself was a draughty Victorian edifice atop the Swanborne cliffs, with its oak-panelled dining room and a rostrum that squeaked whenever the headmaster stood on it [DEAD]. The headmaster was lazy and usually drunk, sadistically taking a riding crop to boys who displeased him in any way. Steed soon realised that his letters home to Aunt Eithne were being censored and so wrote with great care, saying that he liked his new school and was learning Latin. This 'dead language' was yet another tongue in which Steed would eventually become adept, although his first school reports indicated that his 'command at Latin is not good'.[5] In adult life it would surface in everything from the use of odd phrases – such as 'Quo Vadis?' ('Where are you going?') [LEGA] or 'De mortuis nil nisi bonum' ('Don't speak ill of the dead') [LOVE] – and showing off by giving the origin of words (claiming that 'exit' comes the Latin 'exodus' whereas in fact 'exit' is pure Latin and 'exodus' is Greek [LIVI]). On one strange assignment in 1963, Steed even became entangled with a sect who held by the principles of the ancient Roman empire [ROME].

Finally, Steed started to forge friendships at school, and some of these would last him

---

[5] *Jealous in Honour*, p56.

for many years. One of the first was Grantley, whose father was in the Grenadier Guards. Steed's exploits with Grantley featured at length in his biography, while his associations with two other boys – Mark Crayford [DEAD] and Mark Frederick Clifford [FACE] – were deleted, supposedly for security reasons since Crayford later defected and Clifford had been a prominent politician. It is indeed possible that some of the escapades which Steed went through with Grantley actually took place with either Clifford or Crayford.[6]

Mark Crayford was a good friend of Steed's at school and would remain part of his life through to his death. The two boys were very similar at this stage and very much competitive rivals. However, Steed always had the edge in a schoolboy situation which would unknowingly lead to tragic consequences [DEAD]. There was less rivalry with Mark Clifford, and later in his life Clifford would comment that Steed was the closest thing to a brother he had ever known [FACE].

While he did not like the headmaster, Steed's life was heavily shaped and guided by his form master Mr Edward Lorrimer, a new teacher at the school who smoked Turkish cigarettes and had a rather Bohemian air to him. Lorrimer was keen on country strolls and natural history, and his cliff top walks to study gulls eggs fired the enthusiasm of Steed and Grantley who embarked on their own illicit expedition of this nature. The idea behind this came from Steed, who explained to his protesting young cohort, 'I know it's not allowed... That only makes it more exciting.'[7]

However, during the escapade, Grantley slipped on the cliff-edge and became trapped on a ledge with an injured leg. Steed tended to his friend and kept his spirits up with rousing choruses of *Ten Green Bottles* before seeking the help of Lorrimer. Lorrimer and Steed got Grantley back to school safely, but the affair was discovered by Andover-Bigge who dismissed Lorrimer and then gave Steed six of the best with his crop.

When Steed wrote to Aunt Eithne to tell her of these events, his guardian was outraged. Checking into Andover-Bigge's affairs, she discovered that he was heavily in debt, making it easy for her to assemble a new board of governors for Lydeard Lodge – headed by herself – and buy the headmaster out. Andover-Bigge was replaced by the rehired Lorrimer. 'She really was the most remarkably satisfactory aunt,' Steed recalled in Heald's biography.[8]

Apart from his shaky grasp of Latin, Steed's reports at Lydeard indicated that he enjoyed reading poetry, but that his spelling was not good and he had problems with his French. This was one language which Steed was never to seem entirely at home with; although it would prove vital during the impending war, he seldom seemed to use it in the missions for the Department which exist on surveillance film [CART, PRIN].

However, where Steed did excel was at sports, with his report declaring that, 'His performance in the high jump was truly remarkable.'[9] The sports master was 'Pinman' Perry, a tall man and thin and as post. 'Pinman' believed in encouraging rivalry amongst his charges to bring out their sporting instincts, but doing so without showing any favouritism so that all boys would be given an equal chance to shine. A keen cricketer himself, Perry saw the talents for the game which Steed had already developed from his

---

[6] It is possible that another – later – pupil at Lydeard was 'Bumble' Corf, by 1968 a British Colonel who had a similar background to Steed and attended the same school and clubs [LACE].

[7] *Jealous in Honour*, p50.

[8] *Jealous in Honour*, p53

[9] *Jealous in Honour*, p56

coaching by the Duke and made Steed opening bat for the school team. In comparison, Mark Crayford did not make the team while Mark Clifford did. A breeder of fish later in his life, Perry retained fond memories of Steed through to his retirement in the 1970s [DEAD].

Soon Steed was a legendary figure in the sporting annals of Lydeard and the chants of his name from his school friends rang in both his ears and those of other former pupils some 40 years later. Steed was the winner of the School House Trophy – with Mark Crayford coming a close second. It was then Steed's name which was engraved on a silver shield which took pride of place in the trophy room and proclaimed 'Victor Ludorum – John Steed' meaning that the boy was the overall champion, the 'top dog' in sports. It was an award which no other pupil at the school would win until after 1977 at the very earliest[10] [DEAD].

Nevertheless, Steed's new headmaster was confused as to where the boy was destined, and even unsure if Lydeard was the right establishment for him. Apparently unruly at times, Steed later claimed that he was always breaking windows when he was at school [MIND]. Despite this, Lorrimer was very proud of Steed's accomplishments. Steed also remained extremely proud of his time at Lydeard. In 1967, he found himself unable to undo a knot in a tie of his old school colours (navy blue with thin red and white stripes) and had to resort to cutting through the item of clothing with a knife – despite the fact that it had been used to restrain one of his colleagues [CORR].

In 1931, Walter joined Steed at Lydeard Lodge. A quieter figure than his brother, Walter was already showing a religious streak and was soon bullied by some of the other boys for dutifully saying his prayers each night. It was big brother John who came to his aid, and in adulthood cited the family motto, 'God aids Steeds if Steeds themselves do aid' (a phrase which Heald was unable to confirm in any of the family papers).

The main miscreant making Walter's life a misery was a fearsome older boy called Oliver Bodger to whom Steed issued a forthright challenge for a showdown in the changing rooms. In a flurry of action, Steed emerged victorious from the scrap, nimbly avoiding Bodger's jabs and securing the bully in a full Nelson so that he might be propelled face down into a sink full of indelible ink until he apologised for his actions. This fight was a major triumph for Steed and – as with some of his later victories – he exuded a rather superior charm over those he had defeated. Word of Steed's prowess at unarmed combat spread, and soon he was teaching friends such as Grantley the martial art techniques he had learned from Ruth at the rate of a toffee a lesson. It was later commented that Steed could outwit and out-fence anyone in school [DEAD]. It was also in these prep school days that fun was made of Steed's equine surname for the last time in many years...[11][DRES].

While Lorrimer had started to make Lydeard a more progressive school, Steed's academic work did not improve, despite near photographic memory and fine eye for detail. Steed enjoyed performing in plays, and from 1932 to 1934 won the school elocution prize every year; the theatricals would aid him immensely in adulthood when working under-cover. His sporting prowess also continued. In winter 1933 he scored the winning try in the dying seconds of a rugby match with rivals Connaught House from Weymouth. Some time

---

[10] This award was actually defaced by Mark Crayford some time in spring 1977 [DEAD].

[11] When undercover in spring 1964, Steed's surname when undercover as a criminal was 'Johnny the Horse', prompting another law-breaker called Harry to ask if Steed 'worked the gee-gees' [WOND].

after his 11th birthday, Steed was also in the scouts which impressed certain values of behaviour and bravery on him, such as not deserting women [HOST]. He also experienced his first crush, on a temporary under-matron at the school, while his regular pin-up was film star Greta Garbo.

Towards the end of their time at Lydeard Lodge, the rivalry between John and Mark had become rather painful for the latter. Steed was just naturally better – if even fractionally – at everything than Mark; he was however aware of the effect this had on his chum. One of the games the pair would play was at an old Victorian folly, a bell tower – presumably near the school – where two ladders ran upwards into the gloom above. The boys would have races, each scurrying up a ladder with the victor being the first to sound the bell. On one occasion, Mark cheated – using a stone thrown upwards to sound the bell in the darkness when Steed was in fact further up his ladder. Steed was aware of the duplicity, but, knowing how desperately his friend needed to win something, remained silent. For Mark, this was a shining moment in his life – but although he had been victorious over Steed, the fact that he had cheated twisted in his soul for the rest of his life [DEAD].

In February 1934, Lorrimer wrote to Lady Eithne saying that Steed needed to cut down on the theatrical and sporting side of school life to focus on his academic studies since he was 'a naturally bright and gifted child.'[12] At the end of his final term at Lydeard that June, Steed gave a tremendous performance as Peter Quince in Shakespeare's *A Midsummer Night's Dream*, which pleased the audience so much that he had to give three encores. He also took ten wickets against the Summerfield team from Oxford and became the first Lydeard boy to score a century against the Dragon. Then, with a last chorus of *Floreat Lydeardiana*, he was leaving Lydeard for the last time, clutching Lorrimer's leaving gift, a bound volume of the works of the 19th century English poet Sir Francis Hastings Doyle.

Judging by a visit made to the school by Department operative Michael Gambit in 1977, Lydeard Lodge had become a far more welcoming place since the days of Andover-Bigge. Attitudes had changed, and Gambit was particularly taken with an attractive young mathematics teacher, Miss Penny Redfern, who helped him research Steed's childhood from all the old school records now housed in the establishment's Trophy Room – a chamber decked with tributes to one of their greatest pupils [DEAD].

---

[12] *Jealous in Honour*, p65.

JOHN STEED

A NEWBURY WIN AND AN ETON SACKING

In autumn 1934, Steed arrived at Eton College – having passed his Common Entrance Examination after a tutor had been hired by Aunt Eithne to give him extra coaching in the holidays with regards to Latin, Greek and French. Eithne was delighted that the Eton tradition was being maintained, as most Steeds had been educated at the historic public school. This was indeed something which Steed was rather proud of later in life, and would later remark upon the benefits of the public school [FRIG, LAST, GUNS] and what he described as a 'classical education' [RAT]. Certainly he would later wear his Eton tie [CHAR] and his status as an Old Etonian was known to colleagues such as Major 'B' [WHO?].

Some years later, Steed was to have fond memories of his college days, recalling tea and crumpets, the Proctor and his bullfrogs, times spent larking about on a punt, and also his moments of triumph on the rugger field [HIST]. In fact, while Steed very much enjoyed rugby, the game was not taken seriously at Eton, and instead – because of his then small, stocky stature – he was pressed into service as a coxswain in the school's famous rowing team. Another element of life at Eton that he reportedly disliked was some of the mildly sexual attentions of some of his seniors. One press article about Steed in September 1963 also claimed that while at Eton he 'spent most of his time in amateur theatricals.'[1]

Despite his later comments about being at the prestigious college, young Steed disliked most things about it, from classmates such as the sons of Lord Camrose through to the antiquated customs. Soon he was engaged in more fisticuffs with another school bully, a youth some two years or so older than himself called James Bond, who would also work with Her Majesty's Secret Service from the 1950s. One day, Bond ordered the young Steed to stir his evening mug of cocoa; this act led to Steed flinging down another challenge, this time for Bond to meet him behind the Fives Court. As with Bodger before him, Bond was quickly despatched.

Little is known about some of Steed's classmates at Eton. One of them was possibly Richard Davis who later became a research scientist at St Luke's College, and whom Steed

---

[1] *TV Times*, 20 September 1963, p4. Macnee seems to support this, commenting that Steed played the role of Portia in *The Merchant of Venice* in 1935 – although he attributes this to Steed's prep school days. *Dead Duck*, p25. In the 1999 biopic, Ralph Fiennes's version of Steed was familiar with the character of Prospero, Shakespeare's magician in *The Tempest*.

had not seen until around January 1963 [SCHO].[2] However, as with Grantley and/or Clifford at Lydeard, Steed finally made another good and life-long friend at Eton when another new boy, Daniel Patrick Macnee, arrived there in the Lent Half of 1936. The two boys literally bumped into each other by the Burning Bush that January, and Steed noted the name 'DP Macnee' inscribed in one of the books scattered by the other pupil as a result of their collision. Better known as Patrick Macnee[3], this new bug would later be famous across the world as an actor in films and television series. But for the young Steed, he was already an object of fascination since Macnee's father was 'Shrimp' Macnee, one of the best racehorse trainers in the business who stabled some of Aunt Eithne's horses. Indeed, Steed recalled seeing young Pat Macnee riding at various events, while Macnee had noticed the young Steed at Newbury races. Approaching the age of 14, Steed already had his own mare, an eight-year-old called Abigail, and rode with the Whaddon Chase.

At 14, Steed joined the Officer Training Corps, largely because he was a boarder at JJ Horton Fawkes's[4] – Horton Fawkes having been a soldier-turned-schoolmaster who made all second year boys join the OTC. In the meantime, it was arranged that after the Lent Half, Steed would ride Abigail over from Stede Regis to Rooksnest, the Macnees' stables at Lambourn, for a weekend. Passing out of the Vale of the White Horse and across Icknield Way up onto the Downs, Steed came across a saddled but riderless powerful black gelding. Having used all his horsemanship to catch the rogue, Steed quickly located its missing rider, a 14-year-old girl with a beautiful Latin face called Jeanne de Saint-Rambert.

Discovering that Jeanne's arm had been hurt in a fall, Steed gallantly made a sling from a scarf given to him by Algy and rode her back to Red House Farm near Lambourn where she was staying with her cousins, the Berringtons. It transpired that she lived in the Jura region of France; her father Pierre was a French Comte and her mother Mary was English. As they rode together back to Lambourn on Abigail, Steed was delighted to feel her arm clutched around his waist, and he thought about her long after departing to continue his journey to the Macnees. Indeed, Aunt Eithne soon noted in her diary that she believed her nephew to be in love for the first time.

While staying at Rooksnest, young Steed found himself riding in his first horse race at Pickersgill Mill when 'Shrimp' Macnee felt that his horsemanship was good enough to replace one of his own lads who had fallen ill. So well did Steed ride that 'Shrimp' suggested he rode in the Vale of Lambourn point to point the following week. At the time, the race was the most exciting thing in Steed's life, although he was also delighted when his scarf was returned to him with a note giving the de Saint-Rambert's address in France and signed 'with love, Jeanne'.

Dressed in some silks loaned by the Macnees so that there was no danger of a rider in

---

[2] Another uncorroborated report suggests another classmate was Hilary 'Four Eyes' Fox. *The Golden Game* Part Three, p56.

[3] It is interesting to note that although Macnee remained life-long friends with Steed – and indeed had a cameo role as Colonel Invisible Jones in the Warner Bros biographical picture of Steed's life in 1998 – he omitted totally his friendship with Steed in the account of his own time at Eton in his 1988 autobiography *Blind in One Ear*.

[4] It should be noted that Steed made a reference to being at 'Youngs', presumably the Eton house named after its master, in December 1962 [MAUR]; Horton Fawkes may have been an instance of Heald altering the truth.

Aunt Eithne's colours being noticed, Steed rode Abigail in the 2.30 as planned and came third in a field of eight; 'Shrimp' observed that Steed had gone too early in the race. Nevertheless, that night Steed tasted champagne for the first time in the form of Pol Roger and developed a rapid liking for it. After this, Steed visited Patrick and the Macnee family whenever he could. There he was tutored further in horsemanship by 'Shrimp' while enjoying games of ping pong and Monopoly with Pat. Meanwhile his correspondence with Jeanne, who was back in the Jura, continued.

The covert racing moved on to new proportions for Steed on 18 June 1936 when the eight stone 14-year-old deputised Geoff Bramble, one of 'Shrimp's' riders who had broken his leg. However, this time the event required Steed bunking off from Eton for the 4.00 race which was none other than the Ascot Gold Cup, the biggest all-aged race of the Flat season. Entered under the name of 'A Smith' (possibly the first of many aliases that Steed would use over the years), Steed rode Easter Parade owned by Clarence Roehampton... and in a final burst won the race by a head over Quashed, the winner of that year's Oaks.

Unfortunately, also attending the race was the Reverend Hartington Rowse, Steed's Greek master from Eton who recognised the victorious boy's features rather than the family silks. Rowse had never liked 'Steed Major' and reported the incident to the headmaster, Claude A Elliot, who summoned the teenager before him. Steed admitted that Rowse's tale was true and forthrightly said that he was not sorry for doing it; however, he did not implicate Pat Macnee in events. Taking a leaf from Charles Dickens' *A Tale of Two Cities* – which he had just read and enjoyed[5] – when Elliot informed Steed that he would be expelled (or 'sacked'), the 14-year-old calmly thanked him and shook hands in true Sydney Carton style.[6]

A family inquest into what should be done with Steed now was held. Aunt Eithne decided that his education should continue at a very new experimental establishment called St Jude's which catered mainly for the sons of aristocratic families who were unable to qualify academically for the established public schools. Far more progressive under the guidance of headmaster Arnold Moberley, activities such as creative writing were given emphasis over traditional subjects like Latin and Greek, and the curriculum for each student was designed to bring out their strengths – whether that be Serbo-Croat or landscape gardening. Chapel was voluntary, there was no OTC, but boys could instead learn to sail[7] or even fly a Tiger Moth bi-plane. The school itself was located in a grim Victorian gothic edifice on the edge of Exmoor, just south of Minehead.

---

5 Steed was able to recognise characters from the Dickens story when confronted by them in a particularly strange and unfilmed incident. 'Fable Land'. *TV Comic Annual*, 1969, p50.

6 Steed found himself cast in the role of doomed hero Sydney Carton again when he attended a Dickensian themed Christmas party at the home of publisher Brandon Storey in 1964 [XMAS]. When working undercover as a bit of a rogue in late 1964, Steed claimed to have been expelled from no less than three public schools as his many extracurricular activities left him no time for academic study [MARK]. Also, the previously quoted news item about Steed by the 'crime reporter' of the *TV Times* in September 1963 commented (erroneously) that Steed was 38 years old but left Eton just before the war. This elicited a comment from reader Phillip Turner of Swey in Hampshire who pointed out 'That puts him at 14 when he left. Expelled?' A reply from Steed was printed in which the subject proudly confirmed: 'Expelled? Of course, what else?' 'Readers Letters', *TV Times*, 11 October 1963, p21.

7 Steed's skills in a boat were used in some unfilmed missions. *TV Comic*, Issue 771, 24 September 1966; Issue 973, 8 August 1970.

Before leaving for St Jude's, Steed went to spend part of his summer holiday in France with Jeanne and her family, first in their Paris home at the end of July and then at their chateau near Pierrotville in Juba for a few days. Although both Steed and de Saint-Rambert families had been initially wary of their offsprings' new friends, a close bond was soon formed as the teenage romance between John and Jeanne blossomed in the French capital. Finally, walking back across a meadow of buttercups on the eve of his departure for England, Steed and Jeanne kissed for the first time.

Back in England, Steed started at St Jude's in September 1936 and quickly threw himself into a great variety of subjects in the less restrictive atmosphere. The Finnish language appealed to him, as did classes in karate and learning the skills of a radio ham. There were also classes in 'practical economics' which encouraged the boys to invest a small amount in shares, and when at the offices at the hub of the Litoff Organisation's financial empire in October 1962, Steed commented that his good education had not dulled his business instincts [DANE]. In the non-competitive atmosphere, Steed was again free to indulge in cricket (he was part of the Somerset Stragglers Schoolboy XI which trounced the Eton XI in Summer 1938) and rugby (playing as fly-half)[8], while the fortnightly Victorian society allowed him to render his favourite poems by the likes of Sir Francis Doyle and Sir Henry Newbolt. Furthermore, Steed's time at St Jude's encouraged him to develop his palette, acquire basic cooking skills (over and above bread and butter pudding, a recipe he had mastered one winter at Vole), master ballroom dancing and develop his attention to clothes which would later become his trademark in adult life.

Another trait which the English public school system had left in Steed was the ability to mask his emotions. This aspect of Steed's character would later prove most useful in the often depressing and dirty world of counter-espionage when it was not a good idea to have close friends, nor to grieve at length for them should any ill fate befall them. He became the master of the euphemism and some of his contemporaries at St Jude's felt he was 'a cold fish'.[9] However, one subject which soon stirred a passion in Steed was European affairs, notably the looming menace of the Nazis which he became increasingly aware of after an address at the school's sixth form from none other than his distant relative, the former journalist Henry Wickham Steed. This threat to Europe was compounded by tales from fellow pupils such as Leo Himmelbad, a Jewish refugee whose family had been taken away by the secret police leaving him to escape to England alone. Steed also continued to visit the Saint-Ramberts in France, aware that their country chateau was perilously close to the German border and that the Comte was vehemently outspoken against the 'Boche'.

As the situation with Germany deteriorated through 1939, Steed saw the Nazi threat at close quarters during a visit to the chateau in August, just after the German nation had signed a non-aggression pact with Russia. A few days later, Steed was forced to kiss his sweetheart goodbye and return to England. Her parting gift to him was a photograph of herself in a silver frame which became Steed's dearest possession. Within days of his return to Stede Regis to join Aunt Eithne and Walter, Steed heard the wireless broadcast from Prime Minister Chamberlain declaring that the country was at war with Germany.

Returning to St Jude's as captain of games, Steed continued to receive letters from Jeanne who was being schooled in Paris. In late November as 120 Czech students were shot

---

[8] Macnee observes that Steed made three tries against Harrow Colts in 1937. *Dead Duck*, p25.

[9] *Jealous in Honour*, p102.

by the Gestapo and Helsinki went up in flames, Steed saw the full menace of Adolf Hitler's idealism when he read *Mein Kampf* and was horrified when Finland – a country and people he had studied – was invaded by the communists. This was the final straw for Steed. He wrote three letters – to Jeanne, Aunt Eithne and Arnold Moberley – explaining that he now regarded himself as a man, and he now had no option other than to enlist under a false name to fight the Nazi menace. It was the end of Steed's formal schooling which, by 1963, he described as being 'a long time ago' [SCHO].

JOHN STEED
THE HORRORS OF WAR

Already a clever strategist, Steed used a very roundabout and cunning method to cover his tracks as he travelled to London by train, often switching lines and getting off before the destination on his ticket – a shrewd behaviour pattern, again useful in later life. By the end of the day he was enlisted as a trooper in the 49th Dragoon Guards, again under the alias of 'Albert Smith'. He was trained extensively at Aldershot, becoming adept with grenades (recognising a 1945 X5 pin grenade over 30 years later [KIL1]), rifles, the Bren gun and the light sub-machine gun. Because of his knowledge of ham radio, Steed was put in charge of a wireless set.

In January 1940, Steed was sent to France where he and his comrades took part in night patrols between forts along the Maginot line. One incident that March saw Steed's group taking on a German armed with a flame-thrower. It is possible that this lone German was the first man to be killed by Steed. The 18-year-old found his victim to be pathetic, while not feeling guilt over firing the potentially fatal shot from his rifle. 'I don't like having to kill and when I do it is always in self-defence,' he told Heald during the compilation of his biography, adding, 'But everybody else thinks I'm getting away with murder.'[1] Certainly, the experience of battle going on around him would never leave him anything other than relaxed and in control, as evident during a meeting with one Major Prentice during a British Army war game exercise in 1976 [DIRT].

The major German attack on 9 May 1940 shattered the Maginot line, and the 49th were left isolated when the French retreated. The objective of Steed and his fellows was now to cover the retreat back to the Channel coast, avoiding German dive-bombers and taking pot-shots at foot patrols. By June, British forces at Dunkirk had been defeated and many of the French were now surrendering as the Germans took over the ports. The Dragoons' commanding officer now gave the order for the 49th to split into small groups and escape as best they could. Steed and three companions made for a coastal village where Steed – in an early example of his later approach to tricky situations – calmly approached two French fishermen and in his Etonian-accented French asked them, 'Would you be so good as to take us to England... Be a good chap and run us across, there's a dear.'[2] When the locals

---

[1] *Jealous in Honour*, p86.
[2] *Jealous in Honour*, p111.

proved uncooperative, Steed had them bound and gagged, commandeered their boat and set off across the sea, navigating by the sun and his watch. Abandoning their uniforms, the four men avoided a close call with the Luftwaffe and reached land at Weymouth Bay where they were detained by the Navy as possible French deserters or German spies. Handed over to the 7th Battalion of the Dorset Yeomanry at Portland Bill, Steed was relieved to find that the Lieutenant-Colonel commanding officer was none other than Algy, Aunt Eithne's brother. The family were immensely relieved to know that after being out of contact for seven months, Steed was safe and sound.

However, Steed was primarily concerned for Jeanne and the Saint-Ramberts now that France was effectively under the control of Germany. Now aged 18, he could enlist under his own name. It was felt that he should go before a commission board, where he was made a second lieutenant and joined the Life Guard regiment near Dover in late summer 1940.

In spring 1941, the battalion was mobilised to North Africa to fight Field Marshal Rommel's German forces, the Afrika Korps having landed on 14 February.[3] Here Steed served under the disciplinarian Lieutenant-Colonel Piers 'Foxy' Liskeard who appointed him Intelligence Officer – apparently because he believed Steed spoke German, while in fact his fluency was not good. This position kept Steed away from the action, and he was critical of Liskeard's tactics. It was this background that Steed later used in 1964 for a military cover as 'Major Steed', claiming to have been in the Tank Corps as part of the desert campaign against Rommel prior to being 'bowler hatted' [ESPR].

After an embarrassing incident when Liskeard attacked a visiting General Montgomery, a new commanding officer was appointed in the form of a man called Millington who was far less autocratic. He welcomed Steed's suggestions for night-time sabotage raids using both new plastic explosives and the expertise of Trooper Albert Pierce, a safe blower by trade. The mission – undertaken by Steed, Pierce and a large unidentified East Ender – successfully blew up oil tanks at a German fuel depot and dealt a massive blow to the Nazis. However, Steed covered the retreat of his colleagues and was shot three times – chest, thigh and left shoulder – by German soldiers. Rescued by his two colleagues, he underwent an emergency operation to remove one bullet which had perforated his lung. Steed remained in a coma for eight weeks, and within a fortnight of the incident had been shipped back to England. He finally awoke to see the face of his Aunt Eithne, who was massively relieved when he asked for champagne and his Newbolt poetry.

The recovering Steed was not terribly happy to hear that Walter was seriously considering taking holy orders at a time when he felt his younger brother should be fighting alongside him for his country. However, it would be some time before Steed himself could be in combat again as his recovery was not rapid, least of all on a psychological basis from the shock he had suffered. Steed seemed detached from events when discharged from hospital on 20 November 1942 – five days after the victory at El Alamein. Christmas was spent at Vole where Steed met a mysterious and dashing Frenchman known as 'Maurice' who had been invited to the house by Algy Yetminster. The same age as Steed, Maurice had been operating as a saboteur behind enemy lines, but had recently received a beating from

---

[3] The battalion's morale in Africa was apparently looked after by 'Message' Morrison – although Morrison claimed he and Steed were there in 1943 and Steed apparently recalled Morrison bringing a German into the camp one Christmas as a demonstration of brotherly love. *The Laugh was on Lazarus*, p23, 25.

the Germans and narrowly escaped from a train bound for a prison camp. Although the Frenchman was at first taciturn, he was soon discussing the latest situation in his invaded country with Steed and outlining the guerrilla fighting techniques adopted by the resistance against the occupying soldiers. When Maurice departed for his London HQ on 27 December, he commented to Steed that there were Englishmen working in the French resistance, and gave him a telephone number to call if he was interested becoming one of them.

In one of his first cloak-and-dagger operations, Steed made the vital phone call and was told to come to Flat 73a of the Belvedere Mansions at 4.30 pm that day. Giving his aunt the excuse of meeting a girl for tea at the Ritz, Steed headed up to London from Stede Regis and was shocked to see the effects of the Blitz. At the appointed place and time, Steed faced a major and a colonel in a dimly lit room. His background and war service were discussed, before the men ascertained that his French was not good enough to pass in the occupied territories. Already aware of his devotion to Jeanne, the officers sternly told Steed that the only people they put into France were professionals with useful skills – not amateurs with 'a pash on some French girl.'[4] There could be no degree of sentimentality in his mission.

It was Steed's experience as a wireless operator which swung his acceptance, and he was sent for intensive training before being deployed to a unit of the maquis. According to Steed's biography, he was ordered to report to a Special Operations officer training camp at a country house some miles from Vole the following Tuesday. In the early weeks of 1943, he and others were taught to handle explosives, kill silently, encode and decipher, and how to parachute into enemy territory.[5] He was also given a cover story as a former insurance salesman from Paris – which he claims he never memorised properly. His field name was 'Heloise' and he would be dropped into the Jura region to meet a cell which needed a radio operator. It was now that he was promoted to the rank of Captain.

It seems most probable that this is another area where Heald had to hide the truth, since although he claims Steed was trained near Vole and flown out from Tangmere Aerodrome, it seems most likely that both events in fact took place at Station 472 – RAF Hamelin. Steed later claimed that he spent a lot of time at the camp during the war and that it was an 'agents launching pad'; the trained men would receive a posting and be flying out on a plane somewhere [HOUR]. Steed had very fond memories of Hamelin, and indeed seemed to enjoy being at other air bases (even if, 20 years later they were now merely ruins) such as the former HQ to 33 Squadron at Little Bazeley-by-the-Sea [TOWN].

Steed was dropped in the Jura region where he was met by members of the resistance, only to find that Guillaume, the contact he was meant to meet, had been killed the previous day outside Champagnole. A youth called Francois and a man called Albert guided Steed across the dark countryside to the maquis cell, camped deep inside a forest. Steed found them to be disorganised in the wake of Guillaume's death and so took control, declaring that they would attack the railway junction at Mouchard that night. A train was stolen at St Lothain, explosives laid, and the sabotage successfully carried out by the unit under Steed's

---

[4] *Jealous in Honour*, p135

[5] This would seem to disprove one later unconfirmed report in which Steed had never made a parachute jump in his life and did not relish the prospect. *TV Comic*, Issues 737-738, 29 January – 5 February 1966. Another report suggests that by 1969 Steed was a member of a sky-diving club declaring, 'I've become quite an addict of the sport'. *TV Comic*, Issue 921, 9 August 1969.

command.[6] The next night, Steed had his men successfully destroy a signal box near Voiteur.

However, Steed's actions were immediately disapproved of by Colonel Renard, who was in charge of all resistance in the region and who – according to Steed's memoirs – summoned 'Heloise' to meet him the day after the operation near Voiteur at the Cafe des Sports in Doucier-les-trois-eglises. Renard was unhappy that Steed had taken rash action without prior approval from himself, since the Mouchard incident had already been planned for execution by another unit. Steed was relieved of command and restricted to his primary function: radio operator. This was a bitter blow to Steed, who felt that he was achieving something in the thick of the action. However, he could not believe his good fortune when he was driven to the safe house from which he would operate – the chateau of the Saint-Rambert family.

When Renard delivered Steed to meet the young 'mistress of the house', both Steed and Jeanne were careful to act as if they had never met – since any recognition would have immediately seen them separated. After a meal, the Colonel departed and the sweethearts were free to exchange their respective stories. A tearful Jeanne explained how her father had been outspoken about the Germans. Thus just over two years ago, armed men had arrived at the chateau and taken her parents away. As Madame la Comtesse, the young woman had helped maintain the local farms, and also involved herself in the resistance, with the chateau forming part of an escape route to smuggle downed airmen into Switzerland. Finally, after an emotional evening together, Steed and his beloved went up to the principal bedroom and made love.

In the coming weeks, the couple's love flourished. Jeanne went about her normal business as Madame la Comtesse while Steed maintained radio contact with London from the attic. One Monday morning in May 1943, three weeks after his arrival, Steed and Jeanne married at the village church.

A week after the wedding, Steed was spurred into more direct action again by Emile Mallarme, a fanatical anti-Nazi friend of Jeanne's who was opposed to Renard's cautious approach. Emile suggested that the maquis could attack a component factory in St Claude where parts for Messerschmitts were manufactured. Steed and Jeanne were reluctant, but an attack was made that Wednesday night. Steed's forces moved in and – ever keen to avoid bloodshed – Steed confronted the factory manager to give him and his men a chance to flee before the establishment was destroyed. The explosives were planted and detonated as planned.

However, on returning to the chateau, Steed faced the worst experience of his life. SS officers were leaving the estate. In the hall was the dead form of Renard, lying where he had been shot. In the courtyard, tied to a heavy piece of piping, was the lifeless body of Jeanne – her white night-gown stained red from the bullet wounds.

The tragic events of the night were related to Steed by old Hortense, the family maid, who had been badly beaten up. The Colonel had arrived at the chateau, allegedly to warn Jeanne about a traitor in the resistance, but it soon became clear when the Germans had arrived that it was he himself who had led them to her. The German commander, Obersturmbannfuhrer Schmidt, had Renard shot and ordered a search of the chateau, calling Jeanne a whore. When she had slapped him for the remark, Schmidt's loss of face

---

[6] Steed had apparently always wanted to drive a train. *TV Comic*, Issue 1005, 20 March 1971.

could only be restored by immediate execution. As Schmidt offered her a blindfold, Jeanne spat in his face and died proclaiming the words of French dramatist Pierre Corneille, 'Faites votre devoir et laissez faire aux dieux' ('Do your duty and leave the rest to the gods').

These events are what shaped Steed in the eyes of Heald who noted that the tragic death of his young bride and the loss of his parents in infancy '*marked* John Steed, but [have] never *broken* him.'[7] Steed's brief marriage to Jeanne was an exceptionally secret one which none of his friends and colleagues knew about until publication of his 1977 biography. In 1976, Steed claimed that he had only married once – to his career. 'My one and only marriage,' he explained to his girlfriend Joanna, 'I married a job. I married a profession. I've been very faithful' [CARD].

After Jeanne's funeral at the village church where he had wed only days before, Steed and Emile took to the hills with the maquis. Steed was now acting like a man possessed, performing many reckless raids. It is possible that it was around now that an act of bravery on Steed's part saw him awarded the Military Cross (issued to commissioned officers or rank of Captain or below and warrant officers for distinguished and meritorious service in battle), but it was something which he did not like to talk about. The citation for this honour read like a boy's adventure story and told how Steed had taken on a machine gun post single-handed. Steed joked that the action was only described as 'single-handed' because a grenade fragment had torn his belt off and he was having to use his other hand to keep his trousers up [DEAD]. Certainly, Winston Churchill himself found time to write to Aunt Eithne to say that 'the nation has due cause to be grateful for your nephew's service. He is performing his task with the utmost valour and distinction, but such is its nature that I can tell you no more than that he is well and that he is bringing desolation to the ranks of the Nazi foe.'[8]

The Nazi target that Steed really had in his sights was more specific: the vicious and corpulent Obersturmbannfuhrer Schmidt who bore the nickname 'Le Boucher'. This is where the official story of Steed's later war days in Heald's book must have diverged from reality somewhat in terms of dates, as Steed's war service was to continue in other countries after this personal vendetta in France was resolved. For months, Steed studied the behaviour of Schmidt and discovered that he and his equally obese aide Hauptmann Flott liked to gorge themselves at the expense of Nazi sympathiser Gaston Richard, the proprietor of the Hotellerie du Moulin on the outskirts of Pierrotville.

After the allied landings in Normandy in June 1944, Steed felt that it was time to strike before Schmidt could be removed from the area. Emile and the maquis peacefully took control of the Hotellerie and waited to spring the trap when Schmidt made his next gastronomic visit. After almost a week of waiting, the resistance were rewarded when Schmidt and Flott arrogantly entered the establishment in search of food on their last visit before returning to Berlin.

Allowing the Nazis to consume their meal first, Steed then revealed his identity as a British officer and announced that both Germans were his prisoner. Like the French, Steed would have been only too pleased to extract a fatal punishment for Schmidt, but he was now the hardened professional who could see the bigger picture. Taking control of the

---

[7] *Jealous in Honour*, p164. Heald's emphasis.

[8] *Jealous in Honour*, p166.

General's Mercedes staff car and disguised in Flott's uniform, Steed had his captive driven through a German checkpoint to a small landing strip where they rendezvoused with the Lysander monoplane that would take Schmidt to England to stand trial.[9]

It is now that the most severe divergence between the official biography and the evidence of the Department surveillance films takes place.[10] The official version as told to Heald by Steed himself will be related first – although its inconsistency with other events referred to in the Department's surveillance films clearly calls into question much of the contents of *Jealous in Honour*. In this history, Steed remained in France as the Germans were repelled and returned to London after the liberation of Jura[11], arriving back at Northolt in late spring 1945. Aunt Eithne noted in her diary that by now her nephew was to receive a Distinguished Service Cross, a silver medal awarded for courage and devotion to duty on active service (although, oddly enough, this duty should be as an officer serving on a naval vessel). Steed later commented that he had won his decoration for 'dedication to duty', and he would proudly wear it on a scarlet sash to formal occasions [HOST].[12]

However, these events seem to be extremely vague in the account as related to Heald by Steed – and probably because of another traumatic event which was to leave a scar on Steed for some time. It seems far more likely that Steed may have actually captured Schmidt at an earlier juncture in the war – possibly within months of the murder of his wife. Then Steed returned to England in late 1943 to be despatched on further missions. Judging by Steed's comments about RAF Hamelin, it seems likely that he departed from the airfield on various missions in the later years of the war – although how many of these are his own tall stories is unclear. He claimed that one Christmas (possibly 1943), he and 14 of his colleagues crammed into a four seater car for an alcohol-fuelled outing and that the fire brigade had to cut them out. He said he had driven along the approach road about a 100

---

[9] Schmidt was interrogated by Military Intelligence and in 1945 faced a trial in France on 17 counts of murder, including that of the Comtesse Jeanne de Saint-Rambert. Found guilty on 24 December, he was executed by the guillotine.

[10] For that matter, a completely different cover story of Steed's time in World War II was fabricated for press coverage in September 1963. In this version, Steed was still at Eton until 'shortly before war broke out and had a fine war record. It was distinguished by the fact that, as a lieutenant in the Royal Navy, he commanded a motor torpedo boat... after 1945 he was running an ex-naval launch in and around Eastern Mediterranean ports at a time when cigarette trafficking was in full swing. Later he turned up in London and, to some extent, re-established himself with his family by taking a respectable job with the Civil Service. Shortly afterwards he appeared in the Middle East as economic adviser to Sheikh al Akbar Ben Sidi Ben Becula, ruler of the oil-rich state of Kurim. While he was there the Sheikh became involved in a quarrel with two neighbouring states. Some people say this row nearly started World War III... Steed returned to England with an award from the Sheikh, the Order of The Golden Ram (second class) and life royalties from two of the oil wells. From this income he lived the life to which he had accustomed himself – rare wines, fancy waistcoats, pretty girls and polo. About this time he is said to have done some work for the State. But no official record exists of such work.' *TV Times*, 20 September 1963, p4.

[11] One unreliable report placed Steed in Paris during its liberation when he supposedly met a rather nice girl who turned out to be a spy. *Heil Harris!*, p9.

[12] There is an unconfirmed report that Steed was due to be decorated for a 'third time' by the Queen herself at Buckingham Palace some time in 1977. 'A Funny Thing Happened On The Way To The Palace'. *The New Avengers Annual*, 1977, p15.

times, and knew the short cut and back entrance to the camp through a gap in the wire fence used by the men to get back from the pub after 'lights out' – a talent which earned him the nickname 'Cats Eyes Steed'. Indeed, in true Steed hyperbole, he claimed to know similar ways into every camp in the British Isles apart from one in Scotland which he had somehow missed [HOUR].

The antics of the agents stationed at Hamelin clearly had a near legendary status in the intelligence and armed forces. There was a jolly officer's mess of highly competitive men, and Steed recalled everything from rugby matches with the Royal Navy through to beer drinking contests between Peewee Hunt and Bussy Carr. He was also the one who tended to make the punch, while Sergeant Henderson made some truly astounding cakes – including one containing a WAF girl on the occasion of a commanding officer retiring. With the skills acquired from the controls of the Tiger Moth at St Jude's, Steed performed stunts in the two-winged training plane[13], and claimed that on one occasion they had the police of three counties after them. In terms of professional airmen, Steed also became good friends with Squadron Leader Geoffrey Ridsdale DFC, and later attended his wedding with an appropriate gift – brandy glasses [HOUR].

Apparently during his time at Hamelin, Steed now also had a batman. This was a 'fine man' by the name of Pratt who didn't smoke, didn't drink and had eight children – but who had died by 1965 [HOUR].

One thing that is certain is that Steed spent at least the later part of 1944 and much of 1945 in a Japanese prisoner of war camp at Nanking[14], a Chinese settlement where 300,000 civilians had been slaughtered within eight weeks of the Japanese occupation in December 1937. Exactly what Steed's mission was in the Far East is still not clear even now, but he and a fellow soldier, Bill Bassett, were taken prisoner. The two men quickly lost track of time, and although they made their own calendar while in confinement, when they were finally released they found that they were over a month adrift and believed that they had probably celebrated Christmas in February – a tradition which they continued to maintain for many years [OVER]. The experience left Steed traumatised somewhat – notable in his reactions to a discussion about the Nee San prison camp in North Manchuria which he was party to in spring 1965 [ROOM].

By the end of 1945, Steed had been repatriated and shipped out again to what remained of Munich – now apparently with the rank of Major. His role in occupied Germany was as an attachment to I Corp, initially keeping an eye on an adjutant who was smuggling coffee beans, and then casting an eye over other illicit trafficking by soldiers in merchandise such as penicillin. His new batman at the time was one Clarence Arthur Wrightson, a loyal man to whom Steed loaned £10 to enable him to buy some draughtsman's tools, and so start a new career after he was demobbed [BATM].

Steed recalled that Munich was a busy place just after the war, with army units in and

---

13 An unconfirmed report notes that Steed flew an old bi-plane in Norfolk on one assignment. *Diana*, Issue 210, 25 February 1967. Another suggests he flew a similar plane near Swanton Air Base. *TV Comic*, Issues 994-995, 2-9 January 1971.

14 One unlikely version of events which seems to be at odds with all other evidence apparently stems from Steed's unpublished war memoirs, compiled around 1966-67. In this he indicated that he was working as a Captain for MI5 in 1945, and entered Berlin on 30 April, meeting Adolf Hitler before his apparent death. *Heil Harris!*, p9.

out the whole time. As well as his investigations into smuggling, Steed also served on several military tribunals, with one such case in 1946 being to try Sergeant Daniel Edmund for black marketeering.[15] The other five officers serving alongside him were Captain Clive Dexter, Captain 'Cootie' Gibson[16], Major Henry J Averman, Brigadier Wishforth-Brown and Major Witney. Steed continued to meet up with Wishforth-Brown on many reunions prior to the Brigadier's death in 1968 when he was in charge of the 2nd Battalion, and they would recall escapades such as the incident with the colonel's daughter in Montagne, France. However, he lost touch with Dexter. Gibson later became prominent in the field of motor racing, Witney achieved notoriety as a professor and a man of words, while Averman evolved into a successful financier [GAME]. Indeed, Steed commented that he only kept in touch with a few 'fellas' from the war [CHAR]. He was apparently still a major when he was demobbed; 'Friends still call me Major,' he remarked once when undercover some years later, adding that he had served in 'the Guards' [MARK].[17]

---

[15] There is an unconfirmed report that Steed also sat in on the court martial of one Captain Kettle who was cashiered for cowardice; Steed was the only surviving member of the tribunal by early 1970, which suggests this could have taken place concurrent with the Edmund incident. *TV Comic*, Issue 943, 10 January 1970.

[16] Erroneously referred to as 'Williams' in the summary report.

[17] A number of highly dubious reports suggest that Major Steed was 'retired' and was still referred to regularly by this rank in 1968-69 by his colleagues. *The Floating Game*, p68; *The Afrit Affair*, p13; *The Gold Bomb*, p5; *The Magnetic Man*, p5; *Moon Express*, p3. Heald recalled Steed wearing a Guards tie in June 1962. *Jealous in Honour*, p4.

JOHN STEED
ENTER THE DEPARTMENT

Details of Steed's life from 1946 to 1961 are even more vague than what happened to him at the end of the war. It seems that with the situation in Europe now under control, Steed returned to England and was initially at something of a loss for what to do with himself. He spent much of the time bored and, according to his biography, dabbled with mescaline and hashish. Aunt Eithne had introduced him to numerous diplomats, bankers and lawyers – but none of these careers appealed to him. When working undercover in 1964, Steed claimed that he tried working once, but it didn't work out for him; he then 'footled' around at the Foreign Office for a while but found it all quite baffling [MARK].

There had been so many changes during the war – not least the death of the old Duke of Dorset and the early death of Ruth, struck down with bronchial pneumonia by one of London's killer smogs. Grantley, his school friend from Lydeard Lodge, had been killed serving as a lieutenant with the Guards in Burma and been awarded a posthumous Victoria Cross. Another change was that Walter – now a six foot tall moustached man in his early 20s – was sporting a dog collar as part of his otherwise khaki uniform when he met Steed at the Great Western Hotel in Paddington.

It was probably around now Steed spent some time at university[1] to complete his studies, most likely from autumn 1946 through to spring 1949 along with many other young servicemen who had been denied their time in higher education on leaving school. Certainly, he was reunited at this point with his old friend Mark Crayford – and in a case of history repeating itself, Steed was again in the university cricket team while Mark failed to pass selection [DEAD]. Another acquaintance whom he made in 1947 was a figure called Peter Borowski who was in fact a double agent [SHAD]. It is indeed possible that Steed was still deployed on certain military security operations during his education. An unsubstantiated report says that he encountered the Irgun movement in 1947 when there were attempts to create a Jewish state in Palestine; it is possible that this was the occasion when Steed was sentenced to death in Jerusalem alongside one Archie Newman who became a good friend in the 1960s.[2]

If his claims are to be believed, Steed was 'in Prague the night Jan Masaryk fell from

---

[1] In the 1998 Warner Bros film, Steed was shown wearing a tie from Magdalen College, Oxford.
[2] *Heil Harris!*, p91,107.

the window'[3]; this was 10 March 1948, when the Czechoslovakian diplomat was found dead in the courtyard of the Foreign Ministry.

Exactly which university Steed attended, or what he studied, is unclear – although his references to 'Varsity' mean it was one of the more established and noble seats of leaning [DEAD]. Certainly he was living in Herefordshire in 1948 and had particularly fond memories of the spring there that year [CONC]. After the tragic loss of Jeanne, Steed had shown little interest in women, many of whom he was introduced to by Aunt Eithne. He was always polite to these young ladies and the perfect escort to a restaurant or a screening of the film *Brief Encounter*, but he was bored by many of them. One of his dates at university was Dorothy, a tall red-head allegedly built like the Albert Memorial whom he described as 'well endowed'. Dorothy was Steed's date at the Varsity Ball – to the irritation of Crayford whom she was meant to be accompanying [DEAD].

It is not known if Steed emerged from higher education with a degree of any sort, but certainly he had a firm grasp on the antiquated terminology in use by the established bastions of learning (such as saying that one was 'sent down') [SCHO]. Without doubt the Steed inheritance had left the young man financially secure and he did not have to work if he did not want to. When undercover in 1967, he once quipped that he was 'following father's footsteps. He spent his life depositing money – I spend mine withdrawing it' [VENU]. There was more than likely some truth to this statement...

Another claim of Steed's later in his life was the extraordinary one that, at the age of 21, he rode point for the Lazy Tee Ranch, a genuine cattle drive from Arizona to the Black Hills. This unlikely cowboy claimed that here a man was judged on his ability to sit on a horse – which would have given the equestrian expert no problem – and also on his capacity for beans. More importantly, he learnt about a maverick, an animal that cuts out from the herd and is difficult to tie down [HOST]. Whether this story is a completely fabricated anecdote or not is unknown, but it is tempting to believe that maybe this Stateside sojourn did take place after Steed's further education when he was around 27 and increased the feeling that he did not fit in with everyday life.[4]

Even after education and overseas travel, Steed was still apparently at a loose end. Aware of the personal loss that Steed had suffered, Wally – as John called him at this stage – talked to him about God, and asked his big brother if this was possibly an avenue he should pursue. At this juncture, Steed was considering that civilian life might either consist of playing cricket on a professional basis (having made a bad debut for Somerset at Bath while suffering from the sandfly fever he had contracted in North Africa) or teaching games back at Lydeard Lodge. However, Wally persisted and Steed finally agreed to visit one Father Humphrey at the Society of the Sublime Will, the headquarters of which was a forbidding Victorian house in London's East End.

Steed's visit to Father Humphrey was dated by Heald as soon after the defeat of Japan in August 1945, but it was more likely that this occurred – if at all – in late 1949. The thin old monk listened for two hours while Steed related his life story and then told the young man that his organisation would very much like to have him join them.

---

[3] *Jealous in Honour*, p9.

[4] It is worth noting that in an unconfirmed mission report, Steed used a leap to knock an adversary from a horse and commented that this was an old cowboy trick 'I've always wanted to try'. *TV Comic*, Issue 745, 26 March 1966.

The following week, Steed informed his family that he was leaving to join the sect in Flintgarth, North Yorkshire, to take up what he felt to be his vocation as a monk. Aunt Eithne felt that her nephew was 'running away from things'[5] when she wrote in her diary, as she did not feel he had the strength to endure the monastic life. Indeed, the clerical existence suited Steed – or 'Brother Basil' as he had been renamed since the order already had a Brother John – as little as his time at Eton. The rules annoyed him, and his faith was weak. One morning, after a long walk across the deserted moorland, he went to visit Father Adam, the Father Superior who had founded the movement, and asked if there was a vacancy in an African mission. The next morning, Father Adam told the young monk that he could go to Africa but 'in the nature of a challenge and not an escape.'[6]

A week later, Steed left Flingarth and took the train to London where he was due to spend the night at a seamen's hostel run by Father Adam's friend Sister Cynthia before sailing for Cape Town. At the ticket barrier of King's Cross he was unexpectedly met by a young and attractive nun who introduced herself as Sister Catherine, sent to collect him by Sister Cynthia. Once outside the station, Sister Catherine ushered Steed towards a chauffeur driven black Humber and – when Steed hesitated – bundled him inside. As the car accelerated away into the London streets, Steed noticed that the nun was wearing black leather boots. Removing her cowl to reveal golden hair, the 'nun' offered him a Black Russian cigarette before saying 'I know you're John Steed of course, but I don't suppose you know me. How do you do. I'm Cathy Gale.'[7]

It is at this moment that the first and only volume of Steed's biography frustratingly comes to a conclusion, and the researcher is plunged into the vagaries of throwaway references for the next ten years until the first of the Department surveillance films become available. Certainly it would appear that with his Special Operations training in 1943 and his incredible army career behind him, the powers that be saw Steed as too resourceful and skilled a patriot to have his talents deployed at an African mission. So it seems that John Steed was recruited into the career at which he would excel – an undercover counter-espionage agent for a group which became known as the Department.

Steed's grounding in his new career was now even more extensive than that for either the Army or the Special Executive – and much of the basic training apparently took place at the ruined Mitrum Glass Works known as 'the Glass House'[8] [KNOT]. 'Trained in arson, burglary, forgery, explosives, codes, poisons and murder... trained to withstand *torture* and *brainwashing'*[9] were all points noted on Steed's Departmental dossier by 1963. He was already adept with a gun – reminiscing on one occasion how he was once at the wrong end of a charging rhinoceros which taught him that in some situations the only chance of survival was a shot to the brain rather than the flank [TRAP]. Steed's 'superior training' as he later called it [TOWN] allowed him to withstand pain [NUTS], move without making any

---

[5] *Jealous in Honour*, p188.

[6] *Jealous in Honour*, p190.

[7] *Jealous in Honour*, p192. This meeting is contradicted in various other unsubstantiated reports (eg *Too Many Targets*, p12), but since one surveillance film [BEHI] shows that Steed and Cathy were working together as early as 1953, it would seem to prove that they met prior to their regular partnership between 1962 and 1964.

[8] Erroneously referred to as 'the Heights' in the summary report.

[9] *The Complete Avengers*, p59. Their emphasis.

noise [TOWN] or in such a manner as to get the drop on an opponent [eg SELL]. There were also basic techniques in how to conduct private conversations in public places (such as using phone cubicles at an airport as Steed did in Bogota [DISP]) and how to palm useful items (for example, a brooch off model Jane Wentworth at a New Year's Eve party [DRES]). Operatives were taught how to bait traps and thus get on the trail of suspects; an example of this occurred in Lima in 1962 when Steed wanted an opposing force to steal a batch of dispatch papers. This he achieved by leaving the dispatch case in his hotel room, Room 30, but then angling a mirror in the corridor outside to allow him to keep watch from the door of the adjoining Room 31 which was occupied by Cathy Gale [DISP]. A variation on this technique allowed him to see an attacker creeping up behind him at his desk at home [RARE]. Another simple trick was to leave a thread placed across a door to see if anyone had entered the room in his absence [SHAD].

Agents were also taught caution and to watch for booby traps – a skill which served the observant Steed well when he noticed a strange wire coming out from a box under the stage at the Gemini night-club, and thus avoided a piece of theatre apparatus slicing down on himself and his companion, singer Venus Smith [BOX]. Bomb disposal was also covered, and was a technique which Steed found useful in a variety of non-explosive situations as well – notably when he used a stethoscope to carefully open a mysterious refrigerated case which had been recovered by Cathy [EGGS], and also when dealing with chocolates sent to Emma Peel from a possibly dubious source [DANG].

Some of the lessons taught to Steed by his instructors would reverberate in his ears over 25 years later. One in particular was about how to survive when captured by the opposition. 'In the course of your work, you will fall into the enemy's hands,' said the instructor. 'Let us accept that as inevitable. You will be subjected to physical brutality. Worse, you will be subjected to modern hypnotic drugs. There are ways of fighting such drugs. The first, most basic way, is to take advantage of your own nervous system. Pain makes the adrenaline flow. Adrenaline fights the drug. So you must inflict pain upon yourself' – advice which Steed later called upon while drugged and trapped at a health farm [ANGE]. Steed was quite an expert at resisting torture and interrogation, such as when Gerald Shelley threatened him with dental tools in December 1962 [MAUR], and could even employ techniques to counter psychic assaults on his mind [XMAS]. Those in the Department knew that he was a 'pretty tough nut' [XMAS] – although he was not immune to hypnotic suggestion [STAY].

Another useful piece of advice dispensed to the young agent was to look for 'The unexpected. Always the unexpected. They expect you to move right, you move left. The first law of survival in this jungle that you will inhabit. The unexpected move' [ANGE]. This included the notion of making often unconventional entrances; 'Basic training – old habits die hard' he would apologise on occasion [POSI]. He entered the flat of his associate Dr David Keel through a window on their first proper meeting [SNOW] and in 1967 claimed that this was his new habit when arriving at the studios of photographer Tom Savage [BIRD].

'A whizz with locks,' was how Emma described Steed's skills at gaining entry [MDVL]. He was able to easily and undetectably pick locks or get into secured premises [CART, KNOT, INVA], often with nothing more than a bit of wire [INVA] while his Gray's plastic bank card was ideal for Yale locks [STAY] and he employed a knife to open a locked chest on one occasion [OVER].[10] For some locks, he would occasionally use a special device such as the one he used on a studio belonging to artist Claire Summers; when his companion Venus Smith curiously asked what this was, he quickly assured her 'never you mind' [SCHO]. Macnee recalled that Steed had a metal toolbox like a cigarette case[11] which may be the tool kit he prepared for breaking and entering at Art Incorporated in 1965 [AUNT]. Sometimes it seemed that he used skeleton keys [SECO, BROK, MEDI, GRAV, ROOM, HOST] but he could normally enter a building easily and undetectably [DWAR]; his adversaries soon realised that even locked laboratories would not be safe from Steed for long [FROG]. He could also pick the locks of handcuffs with objects such as a brooch clasp or safety pin [DRES, WHO?, GUNS] – his record in opening such bracelets during training being 32 seconds [GUNS]. He was similarly adept at manacles [DONE].

Another tactic was to assess easy points of entry on a prior visit or even to leave a door or window open for a later return, such as when Steed needed to look around the design rooms of Fernand one night [WHAL]. Steed also knew how to use a penknife to open a window [INVA]. Agents were trained not to leave clues of their clandestine visits; while in the hotel room of a shady operative called De Groot, Steed was careful to wipe any prints off De Groot's revolver and return it to the drawer where it had been found by another uninvited guest, Mara Little [CLAY].

Steed also discovered how to crack safes which meant he could break the security of criminals and miscreants – and their associates – such as Steve Bloom [ROOT], Jack Dragna [REMO], Lady Cynthia Bellamy [BATM], Colonel Martin Nsonga [GUNS], Lord Edgefield [FALS] and even colleagues such as Tommy McKay [HOST] and Wallace [RARE]. Steed could open a safe within a minute [GAME]

Another couple of skills that Department operatives needed were to be able to tail effectively (such as when Steed had to follow Henry Barker of the Ministry of Science [DWAR]) and, conversely, to determine when they are being tailed and lose their pursuers (such as when Steed was tailed in Aluda by one Bug Siegel [REMO], when he needed to lose followers from his own side such as Walters [HOST] or McBain [RARE], or when followed by around London [SELL]). He also knew that there were two effective ways to disembark from an aeroplane without being noticed – either go out with the crowd, or lag behind to make the other side think you were not on board [MIDA].

When establishing a safe house on a mission, it was also vital that the agent should be totally familiar with the venue and all exits and approaches to it; on such a basis, Steed chose 'Fort Steed' to hide Miss Miranda Loxton when she was targeted for death in early 1969 [REQU]. Steed also learned how to tell if a phone was being tapped [COUR] and became even more adept in ciphers and codes than when trained by the army [STAT]. Drugs were being used more and more in the espionage and crime worlds, and Steed learned how to detect the use of concoctions such as hexabarbitones [PROP]. Another skill which Steed acquired was how to conduct an internal debriefing or interrogation [ZEBR, SHAD, SPLI, CARD].

Steed would often have to learn about a completely new subject for some of his undercover work at very short notice [CLAY, MAUR], and this gave him an excellent grounding for quickly and thoroughly acquainting himself with paperwork on reactivated cases (eg knowing which roads Burt Brandon drove along nine years earlier [TALE]). He often found

---

[10] See also *TV Comic*, Issue 981, 3 October 1970; Issue 1012, 8 May 1971.

[11] *...deadline*, p164.

himself tested on his new skills, and an intensive session with a work such as *The World's Rare Stamps* would equip him with enough background not to be caught out by talk of a Maltese 2d blue [MAUR]. When his swotting had paid off he would allow himself a crafty smile – although he would then make a basic mistake, such as confusing Sunderland China with Gloucester when posing as a ceramics expert [CLAY].

All in all, Steed was the 'star pupil' during training [KNOT]. Also on the training course were Hal Anderson (whom Steed claimed to have known about 12 years by 1963) [WRIN], Freddy Marshall [XMAS], Paul Ryder and George Neville [GETA]. Of his colleagues, Steed formed a particularly strong and affectionate bond with Ryder and Neville through to their deaths in 1968. Together they worked on various (undated) cases such as the EBA[12] and the GAP[13], and indeed both of them saved his life on at least one occasion [GETA]. He also felt a certain amount of responsibility for Marshall who became another close friend, and with whom he found himself in many tight spots. By the mid-1960s, Steed and Marshall would be the only two Department operatives entrusted with some particularly vital secrets [XMAS]. He also socialised with Anderson, and at one point went on what he referred to as a 'Yugoslavian hike' with him although admitted that by 1963 he had not seen his old friend in a 'long, long time' [WRIN].

Along the way, there were naturally refresher courses for Steed's basic training; one such piece of tuition in late 1963 was a course on how to extricate oneself from handcuffs. This proved advantageous the following New Year when Steed had cause to release himself from cuffs using a brooch he had pocketed [DRES].

Armed with his new skills, Steed set to work on undercover assignments concerning counter-espionage and organised crime which involved work in England but more frequently in Europe. Steed also seemed to make a habit of co-opting civilians with specialised skills to his cause – manipulating them by one means or another. One of the first was his old army colleague from North Africa, Albert Pierce, who by 1950 was three years into a ten year prison sentence for his part in raids on three Hatton Garden jewellers. Pierce's skills as a safe blower would come in handy for Steed's new line of work – and somehow during 1950, pressure from high up was brought to bear which led to Pierce being released. According to Heald's research, Pierce than associated unofficially on a number of assignments with Steed before his death in 1968.

Assigned the codename 'The New Doberman' (which was abbreviated to 'The New D') [RAT], Steed started to operate more and more in Europe as the Cold War between East and West started to set in. It was on 7 February 1952 – the day after King George died – that Steed met one of his future biographers, an eight-year-old lad called Tim Heald. Major Steed was an acquaintance of Heald's father and visited the family, who were then living at the Worther See in Carinthia, Austria. Arriving by staff car after a journey from England, Steed was muffled up in an army greatcoat, and gladly accepted the hot chocolate offered by the Healds to warm him. Steed had continued his interest in rugby, and enthusiastically told Heald senior about the match he had seen at Twickenham the previous Saturday. Young Tim was also given some fudge made by one of Steed's many aunts before the Major departed for business in the Russian zone.

---

[12] Exploding Bootlace Affair.

[13] Great Assassination Plot. The summary report suggests that this was in fact the scheme for three Russian agents Rostov, Lubin and Martin Ezdorf to eliminate Steed, Ryder and Neville.

Another colleague whom Steed continued to work alongside was the young Cathy Gale. One of their missions in August 1953 took them to Berlin where they had to apprehend Martin Goodman, a man who had tricked £3,000,000 out of refugees before handing them over to the military for an additional fee. Cathy was the bait while Steed worked with the German police to move in for the capture [BEHI].

In summer 1956, Steed was working for a John Benson of 'security' and based in Berlin. The pair got each other out of one or two scrapes, and on 8 July 1956 were able to arrest a man called Malik in Beirut [MAND]. Shortly after this, Steed was back in England and glimpsed by young Tim Heald at Hengist Hall, his prep school in Somerset. This covert visit saw Steed addressed as 'Colonel Steed' (although it is not clear if this was his true rank) and its purpose seemed to be to collect the school's history and Greek tutor Mr Basil Clerides, a native of Alexandria. Clerides never returned to the school – and was posthumously awarded the Military Cross.[14]

As well as rugby, Steed remained a keen cricketer and in 1957 his name was added to the Honour's Board of the Cricket Pavilion at his cricket club. By now he had renewed acquaintances again with his schooldays friend Mark Crayford who had also joined the Department. However Crayford's cricketing skills – as ever – were no match for Steed's, and his name was never to appear on the same board [DEAD].

By 1958 Steed had already attracted the attention of enemy agents, and a man of similar build and looks in the Eastern Bloc was already being trained to replace him at a date in the future [SHAD]. Some time prior to 1963, Steed had been captured by 'them' – an experience which he never talked about. He was the only one of his Department ever to escape after being held for four days [SHAD]. Otherwise, Steed seemed to be on amiable terms with certain figures from behind the Iron Curtain. He was good friends with one of his opposite numbers, Comrade Zalenko, and his wife Madame Zalenko [CONC]. Steed also 'crossed swords' with Ludovick Croza – 'International Agent Number One' – in Istanbul and upset his 'fiendish scheme'.[15]

While working in Vienna, Steed was able to stay in luxury at the Theodore Hotel on expenses; this allowed him to indulge in losing 800 Marks at baccarat, a champagne party, a private plane to Berlin and a blonde. It was also in Vienna that he came across Keller, a Russian agent operating in a slightly more impoverished manner for the opposition. In the coming years, Steed always felt close to Keller when their paths crossed, and was 'best of enemies' with Martin, another agent from the 'other side' who was later assigned to London [CHAR]. Also while in Vienna, Steed encountered Nutski, another member of the opposition who later occupied a similar role to Keller. When reunited in 1967, the pair would recall incidents such as exploding tuna fish, a poisoned tooth pick and a Swede with a sense of humour whom Nutski allowed to fall 13 floors down a lift shaft [CORR]. Steed had also become aware of other enemy agents, crossing swords many times with Boris Groski prior to Groski's death in London in 1967 [CORR], as well as getting to knew George Vinkel [CHAR]. It is also possible that during this period he became 'old enemies' with the villainous Henley Farrer [LEGA] and encountered unarmed combat expert Captain Tim [TAKE].

---

[14] In June 1962, Steed told Heald: 'His cover broke. He should never have been sent. Not my idea.' *Jealous in Honour*, p5.

[15] *TV Comic Holiday Special*, June 1969.

Steed spent some time in Moscow examining black market operations there which is where he earned the respect and friendship of a man called Toy [KIL1]. Some time prior to 1967, he had also run into one 'Admiral' Shaffer, a head of intelligence for the 'other side' [MISS]. Steed spent a while on the Corinthian Pipeline trafficking people and secrets via Austria (possibly during his visit to the Healds). This task was referred to as being 'on the line', and Steed became very friendly with a girl he knew as 'Lisa' [WRIN]. There was an incident in Istanbul which involved an unorthodox use of a garlic sausage [RAT] and a sojourn with a girl in Cairo where something else bizarre happened within the space of 16 minutes [CAT]. This incident in particular suggests that Steed was regaining his old reputation with women after the tragedy of his brief marriage.

In 1960[16], Steed did some work on the border of Aburain[17] which involved a 'little blood-bath', and was possibly where he had met the man who later became the Aburanian ambassador to London in a little incident before the country gained independence [OUTS]. A frequent venue for Steed's assignments were former colonies which were now seeking independence. Once such state[18] which was being presided over by two would-be presidents saw Steed sent in to oppose the ambitious, dictatorial Colonel Martin Nsonga and ensure that a President more friendly to the United Kingdom was appointed. The elected President was deeply grateful, and throughout the 1960s he and Steed never missed a Christmas card [GUNS]. Prior to 1961, Steed had come up against an enemy agent called Kolchek [SLIP]. In 1963 he was also to comment that his old friend Hal Anderson and himself had helped each other out of the fire at least twice [SHAD].

With all this training behind him – from the Department, the War Office and his school days – Steed was now a superbly equipped agent, ready to do battle for the security of his country in some of the most bizarre crimes and act of espionage to be chronicled throughout the Swinging 1960s.

---

[16] Four years before the visit of General Sharp of Aburabia to London on 17 February 1964.

[17] Referred to in the summary reports as 'Abarain'.

[18] The state was in Africa according to the summary report.

JOHN STEED
THE MAN – PROFESSIONAL AND PERSONAL

At this point in our study of Steed's life, it is probably best to pause on the chronological journey and consider his traits, knowledge and experience as an adult agent, since the main period with which it is possible to fully associate oneself with him begins with surveillance material in 1960.

As an adult operative, Steed had dark hair and hazel eyes. He stood around 6 foot 1 inch [KILL] or 6 foot 2 inches [TWOS, TIME] tall – with the metric equivalent noted as 1.855m by 1977 [COMP]. His weight in 1966 was about 170 pounds [TIME], increasing to 175 pounds in 1968 [KILL] and then to 85.729kg (ie 189 pounds) by 1977 [COMP]. Although normally very dextrous when in the field, off-duty he could occasionally be clumsy [TIGE].

In his 40s, he still had the strength to unbend a metal spear [SUP7] – in the manner of the fictional Sherlock Holmes's treatment of a poker in *The Adventure of the Speckled Band* – and was quite capable of smashing a sturdy museum door off its hinges [MDVL]. His eyesight was excellent; he could spot a dropped contact lens on the ground several feet away [VENU]. While it was felt that his eyes themselves betrayed him when he felt sceptical about some matter [WILD], others felt that he had a 'nice kind face' [NURS].[1] Despite his middle-age weight increase, even in the 1970s Steed remained extraordinarily fit, able to leap over a high wall into a multi-storey car park in Windsor with ease [TRAP]. Health-wise, a medical in 1964 found that his heart was perfectly strong, although Mr A Beardmore of Harley Street observed that Steed was probably overworked [WOND]. He had no recorded history of natural amnesia up to an incident in October 1968 where he was kidnapped and hypnotised [STAY]. Steed certainly did not suffer from vertigo, and had no qualms about shuffling along a ledge at the top of a tall building [CART, BREA]. In 1968, it seems that his doctor was Dr Winter [LEGA] while by 1977 he was well acquainted with Dr George Culver at his local hospital [DEAD].

Although Steed hated getting up early [MEDI] he did not normally get tired or sleep in the afternoons [XMAS]. A number of Steed's other habits are apparent from viewing the surveillance films. He rather meanly did not put stamps on the postcards which he mailed to his friends [UNDE], liked to snap his fingers when signalling the change of slides in a

---

[1] On one occasion in 1966, Emma invented a missing cat which she called 'Little John' and whose nose she described as 'more aristocratic' in a possible reference to her partner [TIGE].

briefing (mainly because he knew it was a trait of Viscount Montgomery's) [MAND], slept with papers over his face [ELEP], would spend up to four hours in the bath ('Some people take longer than others') [FLEE] and liked to walk through Alley Gate (better known as Shaft Alley near Leadenhall Street) when the blossom was out [CLUE].

Steed was aware that he had led a charmed, exciting and not altogether blameless existence [BIZA]; when his past life flashed before his eyes in front of a firing squad he described it as 'infinitely enjoyable' [LIVI]. Although he took his job very seriously, he was also known to comment 'Pleasure before business' [MIRR]. When it seemed as if doomsday for the human race had arrived in the form of the wandering White Dwarf Richter Alpha, Steed declared that he aimed to have as good a time as possible with what was left [DWAR]. However, as the Cold War dragged on and more of his friends died, Steed's views crystallised more on the natural wonders of the world – a world at peace. By 1976, his new motto for life was 'Make jokes, not war' [CARD], and he took a positive enjoyment in the country views and clean air which fed his soul even when his usual luck seemed to have left him [TALE].

As a well-brought up member of the gentry, Steed's breeding made him tolerant and polite as a person. A punctual man [GAME], his politeness seemed infinite – readily agreeing without argument to strange requests, such as posing for a fashion shoot when mistaken for a photographic model at the studios of Tom Savage [BIRD]. Even when levelling a high velocity rifle at crime lord Soo Choy and the syndicate who had tried to kill him, Steed was the perfect gentleman [TRAP], and his excellent manners were noted by his adversaries [GAME]. His request for the unconditional surrender of the Russian submarine Forward Base once its location had been revealed in Lake Ontario was incredibly pleasant [BASE]. And he could also be perfectly polite at his own defeat [CORR].

Emma once commented that Steed was 'always the perfect host' [MARK] and it was a mantle which he attempted to retain whenever possible, offering champagne to the dubious figure of Old Gorky who had been spying on his flat, and making no remark at all when the interloper started to break his glasses in a drinking ritual [LEGA]. Similarly he treated an injured criminal called Palmer to wine while the safe cracker was incapacitated in the bedroom at Steed's Westminster Mews flat [INTE]. He was felt to be 'too generous' by some people [LAST], but explained 'I like people to have what they like' [LAST].[2]

In his 1963 dossier, the Department noted that Steed 'displays GRACE and CHARM.'[3] 'We're few and far between,' said Steed when discussing chivalrous gentlemen in 1966 [TIGE]. This was clear in the simplest of actions; when he picked up a lady's handkerchief, he did it perfectly, with economy of movement and style [CHAR].

As fiercely loyal to Queen and country as he had been during the war, Steed was a true patriot and felt true nationalistic feelings. He agreed strongly with the board members of the Reniston Group about their desire to manufacture a ground-breaking vessel using only British technology, and felt it was a pity that two of the directors had to resort to murder to facilitate it [HAND]. However, Steed had a low opinion of politicians and their brand of truth [DOOR] and believed that most had nothing to say [TALE]. When it came to the general election in October 1964, Steed did not vote for Harold Wilson who became the new Labour

---

[2] An unconfirmed report indicates that by 1970, Steed and Tara gave a Christmas party for orphans 'every year'. 'The Spirits of Christmas'. *TV Comic Annual*, 1970, p53.

[3] *The Complete Avengers*, p59. Their emphasis.

Prime Minister [STAT]. Nevertheless, by 1967 he was secretly hoping for an OBE... although he was not keen enough to actually want to meet Wilson who was coming to thank him for saving his life after an assassination attempt [STAT].[4]

Steed's extensive life-experience and chequered education meant that he brought a wide variety of skills and knowledge to the Department – much of which was then added to during the 1950s. By the 1960s his originally poor skills in French had been refined [CART, PRIN]. He also retained his schoolboy Latin [ROME, LIVI, LEGA, LOVE] as well as a grasp of Italian [FRIG][5] with some impeccable Neapolitan [FRIG]. Unconfirmed reports suggested that he also spoke both Turkish[6] and German.[7] He spoke a little Russian (apologising for his accent as 'Steedski') [CONC, FOG][8] and could understand Greek [GAME]. He could not, however, speak Spanish [DISP].

When it came to literature, Steed could quote Alfred, Lord Tennyson's 1954 work *The Charge of the Light Brigade* [ANGE], 'A loaf of bread and thou' from *The Rubaiyat of Omar Khayyam* (18th century translations of 11th century Persian verses) [RETU], 'The flowers of the forest are aw'ede away' from Alison Rutherford Cockburn's 18th century piece *The Flowers of the Forest* [CAST] and delivered a variation of J Milton Hayes's 1911 rhyme *The Green Eye of the Little Yellow God* ('There's a little yellow idol...') [KILL]. He was also familiar with Dr Samuel Johnson's words on the angler (misquoted slightly as 'A stick and a string, with a fool at one end and a worm at the other') [SCHO]. Having enjoyed his times on the stage at school, Steed was well versed in a number of the classics. He quoted 'poor Yorick' from Act 5 Scene 1 of Shakespeare's *The Tragedy of Hamlet, Prince of Denmark* [WARL], Banquo from Act 1 Scene 6 of *Macbeth* ('the temple-haunting martlet') [DUST], 'it's only the superficial qualities that last' from Oscar Wilde's 1895 play *An Ideal Husband*[9] and was familiar with John Galsworth's first play *The Silver Box* from 1906.[10] He could recognise quotations from works such as Edgar Allen Poe's 1849 poem *For Annie* ('the lingering illness is over at last – And the fever called 'living' is conquered at last') [FOG] and on meeting a gamekeeper called Mellors asked 'not *the* gamekeeper' in reference to DH Lawrence's controversial tale *Lady Chatterley's Lover* which, although written in 1928, did not receive full publication in Britain until 1959 [DUST].

Steed's historical knowledge seemed to be focused on only one area – military strategy. He could reproduce a copybook attack of Nelson's fleet at Trafalgar [REQU] had a basic knowledge of military history such as the Battle at Spion Kop in January 1900 [DANG] and the Battle of Vimy Ridge in 1917 [CATC]... but believed that Marie Antoinette was held in

---

[4] An unconfirmed report suggests that Steed was still hoping to get an OBE in 1976 for saving the life of another Prime Minister, and that he would not vote for him 'again'. This rather oddly means that he would not vote for James Callaghan, who had become Labour Prime Minister following the resignation of Harold Wilson earlier that year, Wilson having returned to power in March 1974. 'The Sleeping Dragon'. *Daily Mirror*, 14 October 1976, p21.

[5] Which he apparently used on an unfilmed mission in Naples, adopting an accent which Cathy Gale said was 'execrable'. *The Avengers* (Enefer), p103.

[6] *...deadline*, p37.

[7] *A Question of Intelligence*, p83.

[8] It has been reported that Steed once said, 'My command of Russian's not all that good.' *The Afrit Affair*, p45.

[9] *...deadline*, p67.

[10] *The Laugh was on Lazarus*, p123.

the Bastille [PROP]. He did however know about the existence of the Hellfire Club which was so influential in London in the 1760s [BRIM], and from Greek mythology knew the legends of both King Midas whose touched turned all to gold [MIDA] and Daedalus who flew with wings of feathers and wax [RAT]. Similarly, it seems that optional chapel at St Jude's had left Steed's religious knowledge somewhat shaky; he could badly paraphrase the Bible [DANE] and did not know the difference between a canon and a bishop [REQU]. However, when lonely, he mournfully compared himself to Adam from the book of *Genesis* [ANGE].

Fred Gotobed's country lore and Mr Lorrimer's natural history lessons at Lydeard seemed to leave Steed with an interest in this subject. He was intrigued to find a nest of the lesser throated warbler (usually found in the higher branches of oak tree) [MISS] and was delighted to discover the blue periwinkle on a Surrey hillside, carefully placing his find in an envelope so it could be recorded [TALE]. Fake owl calls did not fool him [HIST], and in 1976 he had even heard of Professor Waterlow, the leading authority on bird migration [CAT]. He also knew how to brew a potent concoction which attracted rats with its distinctive smell; this was mixed in his best silver over a small flame and stirred anti-clockwise at 30 stirs a minute [GNAW]. However, he still needed to read up on whales in the *Encyclopaedia Britannica* [WHAL] and had little or no interest in Cathy Gale's wildlife photography when there was official work to be done [DANE].

Science was to play an increasingly important role in espionage in the coming years.[11] Steed knew about the developing field of cybernetics which had emerged in the late 1940s [LAST], realised that a device producing static electricity in the office of research scientist James Mankin was a development of the early 19th century Wimshurst Machine [POSI] and was familiar with the work of another physicist called Kruger at the Royal Establishment into the 'Projection of Electric Power through Space' [THIN].[12] It is also possible that Steed had had dealings with the Nuclear Fission Committee by May 1968 [MORN]. From his own schooling, he would attempt to use rudimentary mathematics and science to figure out the equations of a problem – sometimes unsuccessfully [WING]. However, he was able to solve the riddle of subliminal microdots used by Casanova Ink using a light and a magnifying glass [LOVE]. Steed was not adept in the field of chemistry at all [ZEBR]. He had a basic medical knowledge, sufficient to comment on Tara's tibia and astrogalus when studying her X-rays [CLUE].

It has to be said that – domestically speaking – Steed was not an immensely practical man. When he attempted to mend Emma's automatic toaster with the help of an eyeglass he succeeded only in blowing it through the roof [RETU]. And despite the fact that by the 1960s he had nieces and nephews courtesy of Walter, Steed seemed to have little or no experience with babies and Emma observed that he would make a dreadful daddy [NURS]. Nevertheless, he would baby-sit for his neighbours' infant at Stable Mews [WISH].

Steed's mental and emotional processes were still generally kept very much shrouded

---

[11] Steed apparently once claimed that he was lost beyond his 'fourth form science knowledge'. 'The Runaway Brain', *Look Westward/The Viewer*, 21 March 1964.

[12] An uncorroborated assignment had Steed displaying a basic knowledge of the operation of a laser. *TV Comic*, Issue 728, 27 November 1965. He also apparently knew how to rewire a bomb to make it explode using 'a trick I picked up in Rangoon'. 'Operation Harem', *Look Westward/The Viewer*, 22 February 1964.

as they had been in the wake of Eton. His doodles of a cat and his writing of his name on a wall indicated a 'repressed personality with extrovert undertones' [TIGE], while he had a nightmare of being beaten with a large bunch of black grapes in a Sultan's harem [DOOR]. When he hallucinated following a bullet wound, he apparently believed that Emma was a Red-Eye drinking Wild West doctor treating himself as a sheriff (an image which was later re-enacted, apparently for fun, and spliced into the surveillance film) [DUST]. His greatest fear was apparently a lack of champagne [FEAR].

Steed believed that 'the simplest pleasures of life are the most enjoyable' [DONE] and – as some of his enemies knew – valued the lives of his compatriots above his own [GAME, LAST, HOST]. 'We're all expendable,' he grimly observed to his colleagues in 1976 [TARG]. He also stated that he did not believe in coincidence [DOOR] – although the phenomenon would seem to stalk his career.

However, while Steed believed that he and his colleagues were as nothing compared to their united aim, he was as reluctant to waste life as he had been while repelling the Nazis in France. He stated that he only killed when had to [GETA] and no matter who the enemy, he wanted them taken alive if at all possible [LION]. He could not bring himself to kill the pleading, possessed Ministry of Top Secret Information security officer Major Peter Rooke[13] and instead knocked him out [SPLI]. However, early in his career he would coldly shoot down a traitor from his own side like Mark Harvey – particularly if he was a killer who had one of Steed's friends at gun-point [SELL]. He was less concerned about other people spilling blood, telling the Balkan Ambassador Stepan that he would be happy to allow him to kill his President, Yakob Borb, in his own country – but not in Britain [DECA].

In the early 1960s, Steed fervently held the view that the ends justified the means to any mission [TOY], echoed in his 1961 Departmental report: 'To him, the *success* of the mission is the only important thing and therefore his *means* may sometimes be questionable'.[14] Even in 1977, Mike Gambit suspected that Steed would sell his grandmother if it came to a choice between that and performing his mission [HOST]. As far as Steed was concerned, you could lose battles along the way, as long as you won the final one [KEEP] – as such he saw himself as a 'realist' [RARE].

Steed's colleagues were of the opinion that Steed was very dedicated [3HAN]. Like Tommy McKay and others of the 'old school', Steed did not start what he could not finish [HOST]. Admitting 'I'm extremely stubborn,' [MORN] Steed would overcome massive odds and considerable pain to complete an assignment. Even when shot in August 1977, he struggled on to toll some church bells which would knock a Russian sniper to his death and avert an assassination [KIL2].

Looking back on his career, whatever his other faults of behaviour, it is unquestionable that John Steed was an outstandingly brave man. He volunteered himself as a guinea pig for radiation experiments [DRAG] and when facing a firing squad refused a last cigarette (largely because he had given up smoking) but accepted a blindfold, feeling 'It's important to do these things well' [LIVI]. He would not ask his subordinates to do anything which he himself would not do first, such as the desperate attempt to obtain a vital hand-print from the roof of a burning car [EMIL]. He was also determined not to endanger others, such as fellow inmates at Department S once he had isolated himself as the target of an attack

---

13 In the summary report, Rooke was referred to erroneously as 'Colonel Rooke'.

14 *The Complete Avengers*, p15. Their emphasis.

[NOON]. Even when confronted by an armed Gambit during his bid to rescue a kidnapped Purdey, Steed informed his colleague that he would have to kill him if he wanted to stop him [HOST]. And when informed that his partner Tara King had been found dead, Steed summoned up his stoicism to refuse the leave of absence offered to him by his superior, Mother [PAND].

Fortunately Steed was blessed with very acute senses. He was soon aware if he was being watched [DUST, LEGA] and would remember bits of information as his ever-analysing gaze flitted around a room [BREA, XR40]. He had a knack for analysing both tyre tracks [MISS] and stray hairs [CLUE], and was curious about people with an odd appearance (such as sticking plasters on their throats) [OVER]. Other tiny clues came to light under his gaze, such as a cigarette burnt down to a stub yet held by a cipher secretary in a vital surveillance photograph which helped unravel a major security breach in April 1968 [CYPH], or a moment when he pressed the hand-print of a traitor onto a car roof in a struggle at Hank's Auto repair in Woodbridge, Canada [EMIL]. The fact that he remembered seeing tools in the back of this vehicle meant that this vital piece of evidence could later be saved from an inferno [EMIL].

Steed's sensitive hearing allowed him to hear assailants creeping up behind him [INVA, GETA] or the sound of Tara digging down towards him when secreted beneath a luxury cemetery [BIZA]. He could often smell drugs when added to his drink [MOUS, WRIN] as well as trichlorocetic acid [SCHO] and the odour of ambergris [WHAL]. Even when blindfolded, he could collect enough information about a journey to later retrace his steps [TIME].

These skills were powerfully coupled with what Steed saw as one of his few weaknesses; 'My most insatiable vice is curiosity,' he revealed in 1969 [THIN]. This was certainly true – on one occasion he deferred a mission in the Middle East for several days because he was intrigued by a situation which Cathy had got herself into at a computer establishment [BIGT]. This 'inquisitive nature' was very evident to Dr Keel [FRIG]. However, he had an open mind as he began an investigation. Steed believed that there were 'two sides to every story' [DUST], but his suspicious nature often made him err on the side of caution. He was even suspicious of chocolates sent to Emma by one Major Robertson [DANG]. 'Relentless and thorough as ever,' was how mercenary agent Jimmy Merlin admiringly described the professionalism of Steed [MORN] – a thoroughness which extended to checking the contents of each and every bird seed found on the body of his late colleague Percy Danvers [BIRD].

Steed's training made him extremely adept at observation and deduction [NUTS] – notably in analysing his surroundings when trapped [WRIN]. In particular, he looked for the reactions in those around him during an investigation – such as when Emma went missing at Little Storping in-the-Swuff and his mention of her name in the pub The Jolly Ploughman caused barmaid Jenny Prewitt to drop a glass [MDVL], the reaction of occultist Dr Cosmo Gallion upon reference to the late physicist Professor Waterson [WARL] or the recognition of arcade owner Mike Brown to a photograph of missing cipher clerk Victor Trevelyan [MIRR]. Similarly, from his experience of human nature he could sense that his acquaintance Sir William Burgess was off-form when playing snooker and probably on edge from involvement in a murder [CLUE], that his old friend Chuck Peters of Canadian Intelligence was 'jittery' [GLAD] and detect a flicker of recognition in the eyes of intelligence officer Charles Minnow when showing the man a vital photograph [INTR]. Another photograph – of the French General Gaspard – bothered Steed because it was too new to have been issued to a man in the 1940s [KIL2], while a shot of Mafia employee Carlo Bennetti informed him that Carlo was short-sighted and wore contact lenses [CONS]. He was curious about traces of soap being on a telephone used by a murdered girl which helped unravel aspects of one case [DECA], and he quickly spotted a fake policemen who was wearing non-regulation boots during another [MAUR]. Another excellent method of gathering clues was distraction, drawing somebody's attention elsewhere while he pocketed a vital piece of evidence [CYPH, LOVE]. Steed's observational skills were aided by his near photographic memory; as such he tended not to write addresses down when they were given to him [LACE].

However, although Steed's abilities to gather clues were powerful, another of his strengths was that he was not narrow-minded enough to be completely led by them [CLUE]. Fortunately, Steed believed very strongly in instinct [ANGE], commenting as early as 1962 that he had 'developed a sixth sense – we get it in my job' [PROP]. When suspicious about the involvement in an air crash of village simpleton Vincent O'Brien and air hostess Deirdre O'Connor, he connived to have them on board a Montreal flight to extract a confession [COUR], and could quickly identify opposition agents, such as Siebel, by their behaviour [PROP]. His 'sixth sense' even allowed him to detect a squeaky step on the descent into a cellar [LIVI]. Feeling he understood the approach of the assassin known as The Unicorn, he gambled that the killer would not try a head shot to kill a religious minister, and that a bullet proof jacket alone would protect the target [LION]. After only working with Steed for a few months, Gambit learnt that Steed's instincts were something to be trusted [SLEE].

Steed once commented that he valued 'loyalty amongst other virtues as something they impressed upon me at Eton' [GUNS]. He was privy to a great many secrets, carrying vital information in his head [XMAS], and by 1967, his position in the Department gave him access to every file and every secret document [WHO?]. He knew when and where cabinet meetings were taking place [BRIM], could stroll into a high security conference room barred to everyone except 'Top Brass' [DOOR], knew the layout of Buckingham Palace [LACE], and when and how large amounts of currency were being transported [COUR].

'I'm Caesar's Wife,' claimed Steed on one occasion to indicate that he was loyal beyond the point of suspicion [SELL], and he appeared high on the Department's list of 'incorruptibles' – behind the Queen, Prince Phillip, the Director of SIS, the Deputy Director, the Prime Minister and Coldstream, a senior figure in the Department [ANGE]. By 1968, Steed was also increasingly instrumental in new security initiatives, staking his reputation on the supposedly invulnerable security devices protecting the War Room (including a hidden entrance, a camera detector, and a magnetic field which jammed guns in the vicinity of the Field Marshal computer) [THAT] and some years later developing the 'Three Handed Game' method of using a triumvirate with photographic memories to convey secret US policies from America to Britain [3HAN].

In terms of security clearance and identification, he seldom used formal cards and passes. In 1967, he was a privileged Red Card Holder; this plastic punch card, signed by an authority figure, was kept in his bowler and read 'PRIORITY PASS. JOHN STEED. 379905 LONDON HAS BEEN PERMITTED ACCESS TO ALL MINISTRY FILES CLASS A3-C7'; it was signed by somebody whose initials appeared to be 'SR' or 'SK' [POSI].[15] Around the same time, an investigation at a Ministry of Defence testing area saw

---

[15] It is possible that another holder of such a card was Fletcher of MI5. *The Magnetic Man*, p126.

him issued with an ID card from the Treasury [MISS], while he also carried an ID pass which projected an image of his face when scanned on a special device at the Ministry of Technology's Neoteric Research Unit [NEVE]. By 1968, the Department seemed to have issued its operatives with a folded ID card marked 'Ministry Security Pass'[16] which on the left hand page carried name ('John Steed'), location ('London') and signature, while on the opposite leaf was a monochrome 'Picture of Holder' again signed by somebody in authority [KEEP]. His security clearance in May 1968 was KR5 [MORN], although Father had this reduced to 'Third Class' when – because of his amnesia – Steed was temporarily removed from the active service list the following November [STAY]. Furthermore, over and above any official standing, Steed was somebody whom everyday people, like old Josh Machen at the Marlings ceramic factory in Staffordshire, felt that they could trust [CLAY].

Trust was a vital quality for Steed, and after many years in the spy game, perception of loyalty and dependability started to distort. In 1976, Steed commented regretfully, 'I have to suspect everyone. My recurring nightmare is that one day I may have to arrest myself' [RAT]. By the 1970s, Steed's reliance on organised security was not as firm as he would have liked – particularly when working in Canada. He was actually wary of his old friend Paul Baker and trusted the word of a spy called Keith Greenwood over and above him [COMP]. The situation was compounded later when – deciding that he did not know which member of Canadian Intelligence might be the double agent known as The Fox – he felt it was safest that he, Purdey and Gambit should accompany Phillips of Canadian Intelligence back to Toronto Headquarters with vital evidence [EMIL].

In the prime of his career, Steed was very fit for a man in his 40s, although he did not like exercise [SUCC]. He could jump over a fence [DUST] or his classic Bentley [NURS] with ease, scale an estate wall [HAND], lift himself up by the arms on a bar [FROG], perform back-flips [SURR, THAT], twist around with great agility to avoid a knife blade [INTE], kick in a locked door [CATC] and would swing on bars to avoid assailants with great agility [GAME]. He could also rip manacles out of crumbling brickwork [CAST]. His resilience allowed him to bounce back from blows to the head from vases [AUNT] or horseshoes [TREA].

Even in his mid-50s, Steed could remain awake for almost 24 hours and still tackle a heist gang operating on a hot Sunday morning [SLEE]. Despite infection by a lethal dose of curare, Steed's stamina allowed him to stagger onwards in order to save Purdey's life [TARG].

Steed claimed that his reflexes were in 'top form' in 1965 [HOUR]. His driving benefited from this when a dog shot out into the road [HOUR], while he moved swiftly behind cover on seeing an impact grenade fall from his umbrella [BIRD] or when shot at [CONS, LIVI]. A gunman appearing at the door also failed to faze him [CORR, STAT] and he was able to grab a hypnotised Tara on one occasion when she was about to leap to her death from a window [LOVE]. A movement in some bushes would send his fist crashing instinctively into the foliage [CARD, LAST]. His sensitive hearing meant that he could hear a rifle being cocked and act first [HUNT, SUP7]. He could anticipate attacks [NEST] and quickly move to counter them [TOWN].

'I never promised to fight fair,' said Steed, having defeated Emma Peel in a bout of fencing by wrapping her in a curtain, a move she declared was 'very, very dirty' [TOWN]. Some 12 years later when he faced his close colleague Mike Gambit – something he had

---

[16] Tara King was seen to carry a similar card in one surveillance film [NOON].

hoped never to have to do – the armed Gambit was swiftly disabled when Steed's knee made contact with his groin; Steed had earlier warned him, 'You're too young to die Gambit – besides I never fight fair' [HOST]. By the end of his career in intelligence, Steed had some 30 years of combat and training behind him – more if one included the lessons taught to him by Ruth and observed from the captors who had killed his parents.

Steed claimed to be opposed to physical violence and would attempt to deal with any given situation without resorting to fisticuffs [TAKE]. Although he did not look muscular, Steed could even deal with a former 'contender' such as Goliath (or 'Golly'), the devoted bodyguard of Lady Cynthia Bellamy [BATM]. By and large, Steed could look after himself in a fight [eg FRIG, MOUS], being able to throw a man with one arm [CYBE], lift a man up on his shoulders [QUIC], hurl an assailant over his head [BUTL] and lift a man by his necktie [AUNT]. He could better either a squad of enemy soldiers [TOWN] or his own security guards [KEEP]. He made flying attacks [NURS, TREA, INVA], knocked the legs from beneath heavies [SURF, FEAR], delivered winding punches to the stomach [MAUR, TIME, ROTT] and indulged in traditional fist-fights [WHO?]. Certainly, it was clear why he refused a special bodyguard offered by Colonel James in 1968 [GETA].

Women tended to give him little trouble when being overpowered or disarmed [CLAY, FROG, BROK, TIME, BIRD] – often in a rather demeaning manner, such as pulling down the jacket of Elizabeth Purbright before pinioning her with a stool and putting Sara Penny across his knee and tickling her [SUCC]. And oddly while he was no match for the robotic duplicate of the male Professor Frank Stone, he was able to deal with the similar replica of Dr Betty James and lock it in a cupboard with ease [NEVE].

Rarely, Steed could be overpowered by people such as Evans the zookeeper [FEED] and was losing badly in the ring against a wrestler called Ito until helped out by another veteran of the ring, Harry Ramsden – better known as 'the Decapod' [DECA]. Generally those who got the upper hand were fellow experts; Hal Anderson [WRIN], Cathy Gale [WARL, BEAR, ZEBR, BROK], Emma Peel [TWOS, SURR, WHO?] and Tara King [INVA] all managed to better Steed at one time or another.

When forced into a fight, Steed would frequently employ any objects which came to hand against his adversaries – or would-be adversaries. Such articles included a pan lid [HIST], a vat of hot oil [CART], a cash box [MEDI], a piece of wood [ROME], a bottle [TROJ, DIAL], handfuls of wedding cake [MARK], a horse collar [TREA], a horseshoe [TRAP], an antiquated spear from a museum [MDVL], a pike [TIME], books [SCHO, MDVL, GUNS, LOVE, TALE], boxes [GETA], a tea trolley [CYPH], automated filing cabinets [CYPH], a coal shovel [GAME], milk crates [FALS], a paddle [FALS], a cart [KILL], an electric arc gun [THIN], a swivel based rocket launcher [OVER], a swinging lamp [BIZA], fruit [BIZA], a fishing line [NEST], a snooker cue [LAST], spray-on Plastic Skin ('Good for 100 and 1 Uses') [LAST], an arm splint [TRAP], a pot of tea [ROTT], brandy [WILD], shaken bottles of champagne [LION], a soda siphon [SUCC], a burning bucket [BASE], a telephone [CONC], a child's ping pong ball gun [BARG], a cricket bat [BARG], a mop [ROOM], dance shoes [QUIC], boards with comic strip fighting words (eg POW! SPLAT! BAM!) [WING], a metal waste bin [PRIN], the bonnet of his Bentley [CLUE], a rock [GUNS], and – most ironically – a placard proclaiming 'Down With Violence' [DUST]. Many of his disabling blows with such objects could be quite vicious [CONC, CART, MEDI, TROJ].

Whisking a rug away from under an attacker's feet always produced results [GRAV, WILD]. Pulling a man's hat and coat down over his face and arms was an effective disabling method [LEGA].[17] Disarming techniques included holding an assailant's weapon hand over a fire [BASE], placing it under scalding water [HOUR] or smashing it on the edge of piano [ROTT]. To subdue to an attacker, Steed would beat a man's head against metal railings [ELEP], a wall [GUNS] or a bar top [MDVL].

In 1962, Steed regularly practised his unarmed combat using exercise mats at his Westminster Mews flat [BEAR] and knew techniques such as the 'single handed death grip' which he himself could also counter [KNOT]. He had a knowledge of Judo which he then passed on to Tara in 1968 [INVA][18] and he could deliver a chop to the neck to put a man out cold [MONT, INTE, SEET, LOOK, KEEP, NEST, RARE] – no doubt developed from the karate studied at St Jude's. He was aware of body pressure points (such as below the right ear) which could render a victim unconscious [ESPR, KNOT]. On other occasions he would resort to a traditional punch [CLAY, TREA, MISS, SPLI, XR40] which could put the recipient out for hours if the blow contained 'a great deal of venom' [XR40]. Most notable of all, he could overpower an opponent almost silently and take his place [CORR].

Sometimes during confrontation, Steed could not help his sense of the dramatic coming to the fore, such as acting as a toreador when attacked by a pair of motorcyclists one night [DIAL]. Makeshift missiles included popping a cork from a bottle of Grand Marque to hit John Harvey squarely between the eyes [DIAL] and an otherwise useless empty pistol [NEST].

Steed knew that three breaths was just enough to let a man stay alive when he chose to throttle him [CLUE] and cutting off the air supply of a man wearing a respirator was easy for him [ROOM]. He seemed to relish throwing or punching his opponents through a window [PRIN, POSI], and later when instructing Tara in combat advised her to create a spectacular effect by propelling opponents through the plate glass variety [INVA].

In combat, Steed would co-ordinate well with his colleagues [eg DISP, SURF, GAME, GLAD]. However, by 1976, Steed indulged in fisticuffs far less – claiming to abhor violence [NEST]. As the film of his struggle with the double agent The Fox demonstrated, by 1977 Steed – although in excellent shape for his age – was decidedly past his peak [EMIL].

Up to around 1965, Steed would often carry a firearm of some sort [DANC], usually a revolver [SELL, DISP, WARL, REMO, MAUR, DWAR, HAND, WHAL, FLEE, UNDE, ELEP, CHAR, XMAS, BARG, DIAL, AUNT, CLUE] which he carried in his left breast pocket [DISP, BARG], his right hand pocket [WARL, REMO, AUNT], in his waistband [WHAL], a briefcase [MORN] or even in his boot [XMAS]. Steed once commented that he preferred a Smith and Wesson Magnum to a Beretta [GETA] and had 'no great admiration for the automatic carbine' believing that 'in the right hands, one shot should be enough' [DOOR]. From 1964, he initially favoured a Combat Masterpiece Model 18 K-22 .22 Smith and Wesson [CHAR], but by the following Christmas was using what appeared to be a Webley revolver [XMAS, AUNT, NURS], switching to a .357 Smith and Wesson Model 19 Combat Magnum on most occasions from late 1967 [BARG, CLUE, LOOK, MORN, TAKE, STAY, FOG, REQU]. By spring 1977, Steed owned both a Walther PPK 7.65mm automatic [HOST] and a .38 Smith and Wesson Model 15 K-38 Combat Masterpiece [HOST]. When investigating a counterfeiting operation, he used a gun

---

[17] There is an unconfirmed report that Steed used a similar technique on one Professor Merlin Jones. *TV Comic*, Issue 1014, 22 May 1971.

[18] It is possible that Steed did not practice judo until late 1966. On one unfilmed mission, he is believed to have moaned 'Why didn't I learn judo?'. *TV Comic*, Issue 749, 23 April 1966.

fitted with a silencer [MEDI].

Like any law-abiding citizen, Steed had a full licence for his revolver, keeping the piece locked in the top drawer of his apartment desk [MAUR, NURS, STAY, FOG] or the top drawer of the bureau in his country seat [HOST] when not in use. He also had a certificate for his ammunition [MAUR]. If he trusted somebody enough, such as Cathy, he would hand the revolver on to them to use [ELEP] and loaned his Smith and Wesson to Tara when she was assigned to protect Lord Dessington[19] [LOOK]. His only 'novelty' firearm appeared to be a harpoon-firing mechanism secreted in his crutch while incapacitated at Department S [NOON].

However, by 1963 Steed was already starting to make less use of his revolver, commenting on one occasion that he would not consider carrying a gun in a tight well-cut suit [CAGE]. In 1968, Tara remarked 'That's not like you,' when she saw Steed preparing his Smith and Wesson, to which Steed explained that he took no chances with an agent as slippery as Jimmy Merlin [MORN]. Similarly, a few months later the sight of Steed preparing his Magnum told Tara that the protection of Miss Miranda Loxton must be a 'very important' assignment [REQU]. By 1977, Steed stated that he now abhorred using guns, and claimed not even to have a gun except for his old Colt .45 which he kept for 'sentimental reasons' (meaning that either he had got rid of his Walther and his Smith and Wesson... or, more likely, that he was lying) [RARE]. Certainly Steed had very little to do with guns when working in the 1970s, claiming by now that loud gunshots tended to make him blink [NEST].

Sometimes, Steed would enter the fray with other weapons which were to hand, such as a rifle from the Wonderland amusement arcade's shooting range [MIRR], a gun from a Russian embassy guard [TWOS], a firearm used by a woman called Vesta [TIME], the army issue revolver of Colonel Corf [LACE], or an automatic handgun used by a Russian agent [GLAD]. He also acquired a gun from somewhere while aboard 'Archipelago' Mason's yacht [FROG]. However, by 1968 he was more likely to cast aside the handguns confiscated from his adversaries than to use them himself [GUNS] or empty them of bullets and hand the useless item to one of their associates [LACE].

With a firearm, Steed's aim was excellent. He was an expert with a revolver from his army days [SECO] and could down a model Spitfire at some distance [TWOS], fire a bullet close to somebody in what gun expert Hana Wilde knew was 'fancy shooting' [SUP7] or place four shots in the wall perfectly behind Mother's head – confirming his superior's belief that Steed was 'a superb marksman' [STAY]. By 1976, he was also the only person ever to get 100 per cent on the Department's tortuous and complex Target Range – a feat which he achieved three times in a row [TARG]. Steed was similarly skilled with a rifle [CAST], being able to hit the bullseye when firing at Rifle Ranges International Ltd [INTE]; he also carried a rifle when hunting a 'big cat' near the home of one Major Nesbitt [TIGE].

Usually, Steed employed a gun purely as a warning – such as when he left his revolver deliberately beneath his bowler hat on a visit to Gutman's Circus so that a simple raising of the brim from its resting place would warn off any would-be killer [CONS]. However, when necessary he could inflict a flesh wound in the arm [MIRR], shoulder [UNDE] or hand [GLAD] to overpower an attacker; such a shot saved Cathy from execution by Abe Benham [CAGE]. He could also shoot a gun from the enemy's hand [MEDI] or – when left with no

[19] Incorrectly referred to as 'Lord Bessington' in the summary report.

other option to protect himself or others – shoot to kill [XMAS, NOON].

Steed had a fine taste in firearms [ELEP] and collected old-fashioned firearms which could be seen at both his rooms in both Queen Anne's Court and Stable Mews. He could identify a single action flintlock as being made around 1650 – although he could not tell it was a replica [ELEP]. Some of his own flintlock pistols came from a dealer called Xavier Smith[20] who had a shop close to Stable Mews [PAND] and even in the 1970s he was still the proud owner of a silver flintlock [FACE]. In terms of other weapons, Steed knew the three-foot effective range of a gas pistol wielded by a card-sharp's girlfriend called Clarissa[21] [BIGT] and recognised the latest Belgian model of .22 rifle [INTE].

Outside the arena of firearms, Steed really seemed to relish a good sword fight or workout [CAST, TOWN, DANG, BRIM, VENU, CORR, LOOK, FOG], having been taught the sabre by Kisorky of the Russian Imperial Guard [FOG] and claiming that it was the sabre he truly preferred [CHAR]. Kisorky's training regime was unique; he fired darts faster than the eye could see to develop instinctive reflexes so that Steed would learn to deflect the darts with the blade [FOG]. Steed fought with a claymore at Castle De'Ath [CAST] and selected a curved blade to hunt with when offered a choice of weapons on another occasion [SUP7]. Three simultaneous opponents were nothing for him [DANG] and he once sliced an opponent's false hand off with a swift manoeuvre [BRIM]. Fencing from the position of an armchair [CORR] or with a walking stick [LOOK] did not dull his skill.

Even though Steed was famed from the mid-1960s for his amiable approach to the dirty business he was involved in, there were a few situations which truly caused his temper to erupt. Mother knew that it was a serious mistake to make Steed angry, as this made him even more dangerous in combat [LACE].

Rather irritable at times, Steed got stroppy when being ignored [UNDE], when he did not get his questions answered [HOUR] or when somebody refused his help [JUST]. The irrational behaviour of others in critical situations also angered him and he was prepared to admonish even people such as Lord Melford for such actions [DOOR], became annoyed by a vow of silence taken by a vital witness like Sister Isobel of the Convent of St Mary [COUR], or to viciously discuss with a woman like Angela Craig her reluctant attitude to bringing the killers of her husband to justice [ESPR]. Frustration at his own inability to solve a mystery would send a drinks glass flying into a wall [HOUR]. Betrayal of fellow operatives was – naturally – the worst trigger to unleash Steed's wrath. One moment he could be quite charming – and the next he could be throttling a man for causing the death of a colleague [MAND, INTR]. He could also be a stern interrogator of his own people [SHAD, INTR].

The late Sydney Newman, a Canadian TV executive who was a long-term friend of Macnee's, encountered Steed in the early 1960s. His verdict on the agent concluded that Steed was 'a ruthless cold killer who's got no morals – he's totally amoral'.[22] Certainly up until 1964, it seems that one of Steed's most valuable traits for the Department was that he would take whatever steps were necessary to achieve a result – often endangering the lives of those around him, sometimes without their permission. Occasionally this ruthless streak manifested itself physically. Steed held a thug called Moxon in terror by wielding the man's

---

[20] Referred to erroneously in summary reports as 'Murray'.

[21] Referred to erroneously in summary reports as 'Clarice'.

[22] Collins, Tim. *DWBulletin*, Vol 4 Nos 5/6, p13.

own razor blade at him and – according to Moxon – threatening to slice his ear off [FRIG]. When joining his superior Charles in the interrogation of his former colleague Peter Borowski, Steed seemed to go berserk at one point, viciously kicking him and barking at his protesting elder to 'shut up' [SHAD]. Betrayal of colleagues ruffled Steed's feathers. When let down by his backup, an agent called Melville who had fallen victim to a lying drug, Steed took his colleague to a remote woodland clearing to punch and threaten him harshly [FALS]. Moving to the next stage, Steed would often throttle people to get the information he needed [COUR, DISP, CLUE] and treated the horrific tools of pain used by others lightly to add to his menace – such as referring to knuckle-dusters as an 'article of bijoulry' [FRIG].

Even after his considerable change in approach in 1964, Steed would resort to drastic action to get results. Emma was doused in herbicide and fed to a lethal form of plant life to ensure its destruction [SURR] and on another occasion he threw lighter fuel over an enemy agent called Keller and threatened to set fire to him [XR40]. When enemy agent Joe Franks planted a bomb in the Central Control of *HMS Zebra*, Steed locked him inside the room with his own explosive, telling the man that the blast 'may not kill you, may just mess you up a bit' [ZEBR]. Even in 1976, Gambit still described Steed as ruthless [3HAN].

When he felt the need, Steed could be a very threatening figure – even after his character changes following the departure from his life of Cathy Gale. When a student called Eric Duboys attempted the ill-advised act of restraining Steed, the agent hurt the young man's hand and calmly threatened to break the student's arm if he had any more trouble with him [HIST]. During the same assignment, another student called John Pettit experienced the sort of pain Steed could deal out to the human hand, and was also struck on the head when unco-operative [HIST]. A blackmailing car mechanic called Stanley found himself spread-eagled under a car bonnet, which Steed said he would slam on his neck and face [CLUE]. Knowing the fine medical requirements of hotelier Max Chessman, Steed threatened to open a window of Chessman's penthouse and so disturb the critical temperature vital for his life [ROOM]. He told a butler called Fleming that he would punish him in a manner that would confine him to a wheelchair unless the factotum answered his questions [CAGE]. Steed threatened to send Carlo Bennetti back to Naples where he knew he would be killed by the Mafia [CONS], and indicated to French low-life Henri Duval that unless he helped to locate the new aide of the assassin known as The Unicorn, he would tell the Parisian underworld that Henri had supplied all the information he required anyway... and let his fellow criminals extract their own punishment [LION]. Similarly, he played on the fear of The Unicorn's underlings when dealing with them [LION].

When adopting a callous attitude towards the family of a man involved in a car crash, Steed apologised to Cathy, saying 'Sorry, runs in the family' [DANE]. The younger Steed would use the misfortune of others to ensure co-operation, such as when he bluntly informed Pamela Johnson that she was a murder target, later visiting her and cheerily saying 'Hello Miss Johnson. Not dead yet?' [INTE]. Steed could be a master of the friendly threat – telling two divers called Aristo and Helena not to get involved with his affairs, '...or I'll tan your hides' [FROG]. Even when not being physically threatening to a person, a deliberately smashed head off a figurine [FEAR] or a crisp clear 'I'll wait' [NURS] let those he was addressing know in no certain terms that the pleasantry in Steed's voice masked dire consequences if their co-operation was not forthcoming. Similarly, the tone of his voice when telling millionaire George Unwin that he would kill him if any harm came to Emma through Unwin's schemes left his companion in no doubt about Steed's feelings on the matter [JUST].

However, by and large Steed liked to expend minimal effort to maximum effect. The optimum way of entering the premises of Schnerk Studios over an electrified wire was to walk up a series of mobile steps and gracefully step over the fence before descending the other side [EPIC]. By the late 1960s, Steed was more than happy to let others do the work. Thus it was Purdey and Gambit who energetically distracted Russian master spy Ivan Perov[23] and his men so that he could quietly whisk the defecting Professor Vasil[24] to safety [CARD]. He could relax while letting Tara shake off those pursuing them by car [LEGA], left the tailing of the mercenary spy Juventor to his colleague Larry [3HAN] and felt the most leisurely way to uncover the truth behind a Russian operation in Canada was to lean on enemy agent Ivan Halfhide and see where he ran to [BASE].

One of the reasons that Steed could take such a relaxed attitude was his supreme confidence in his own skills and being able to produce a result – quite natural after his amazing wartime experiences. Indeed, ultimately it seemed that Steed could walk into almost any situation and take over with a voice of authority [eg THIN]. Some of his acquaintances found that Steed's self-confidence made him appear smug [WILD] and sometimes he could come across as condescending, which could annoy associates and make him unpopular [COUR]. Nevertheless, Steed remained mentally confident and sure of his actions even when Tara – held at gun-point – contradicted him in an attempt to shake his sanity [STAY]. The same belief also allowed him to play devil's advocate with colleagues who were over-confident [CAT]. However, Steed himself could also be over-confident and liked to show off – one such instance resulting in crushing his own bowler when claiming he knew how to operate a powerful pressing machine [SURF].

The sheer confidence added immensely to Steed's approach to his undercover work – an affable approach which fitted his foppish 'man about town' image. He liked to employ 'Subtlety at all costs,' as he told the enemy agent Olga Volowski [CORR], a sentiment he echoed to freshman operative Basil Creighton-Latimer [WISH].

Steed found that being light and breezy when meeting potential suspects was a useful way of putting people off their guard [eg HUNT]. Even after being shot at on the Benedict Estate in 1966 he was still jovial with the clearly menacing figure of Masgard the game-keeper [LIVI], was amiable and affable when probed by country gentleman Peter Omrod [DUST], walked straight into the home of former government scientist Dr Cresswell and started helping himself to the sherry [POSI] and adopted a light air of innocence when trying to purchase some Lizard Vodka at the Magnus Importing Co Ltd [GETA]. This affable, charming approach would often command respect from those in junior authority positions [GLAD] or obstructive officials [DISP]. The airy charm of the gentry came in handy when visiting a dolls hospital [WOND] or staying close to opposition agents [PROP]. When held at gun-point by a diver called Helena, Steed simply offered to buy her a drink if she was a 'good girl' [FROG].

His sense of humour was what Steed once described as the only saving grace in a terrible problem he was faced with [LION]. Much of the time, Steed gave the impression that he treated life very lightly – always ready with a smile and a joke [SURR]. This could

---

[23] An alternate transcript of the assignment gives Perov's first name as 'Nikolai'. *House of Cards*, p13.
[24] The same alternate transcript gives Vasil's full name as 'Anton Vasil'. *House of Cards*, p10.

give him the appearance of being flippant when discussing weighty matters such as the horrific effects of the Silent Dust fertiliser [SURR] or when accused of murder [SUP7]. 'Does it keep good time?' was all he could ask as a watch which would rob him of control of his own nervous system was about to be forced onto his wrist [RETU].

Even when escaping death from a deadly four poster bed, Steed would beam the next morning that he had 'that glad-to-be-alive feeling' and that somebody 'tried to press my best shirt last night while I was still wearing it!' [CAST] When exposed as a spy at the Hellfire Club, he simply grinned and confirmed, 'He's right you know,' and when subsequently challenged to a duel he asked for 'feather dusters at 400 yards' [BRIM]. 'Come here often?' he asked Cathy as they both stood surrounded by Cosmo Gallion's acolytes [WARL] and when encircled by a troupe of armed women he merely observed that he should have brought his ray gun [SUCC]. 'Tails I lose,' was his comment when double agent Spelman made short work of his attempted bluff to pass off a 10p piece as an incendiary device [HOST]. When asked for a last request before execution, he would reply with a flippant request to have his milk cancelled [LIVI] or espouse an impractical desire to ride on a Tornado Roadster [BARG]. When most would be terrified at gun-point, Steed delivered quips about mixed metaphors [FALS] and could even quickly laugh off a near fatal dose of curare [TARG]. As Tara once remarked in a confirmation of Steed's identity, 'Who else would smile at a time like this?' [KEEP].

However, some of the incredible incidents which Steed encountered were too bizarre to take seriously, such as an invasion from Venus [VENU] or encounters with ghosts [LIVI]. When undercover as a dealer in Roman antiquities, Steed cheekily gave the phone number of the British Museum to Sir Bruno Lucer as the contact details for another of his clients [ROME]. Occasionally, his humour would be directed at the demise of his adversaries. 'He died flat,' he commented after seeing an enemy courier called Shepherd impaled on a cello spike [TAKE].

Many of Steed's quips were suggestive in nature. Seeing an ivy-wrapped female mannequin at Sir Lyle Peterson's, he observed 'Come autumn, I hope to see more of you' [SURR]. He enjoyed wordplay [KNOT], such as his declaration 'I'm a herbicidal maniac' as he destroyed an alien form of plant life [SURR] or this joyful 'Pop goes the diesel' as a plan to blow up the Prime Minister's train was revealed to him [STAT].

Steed liked having fun when he was on his own, such as a quick spin on a roundabout [TOWN] or raising his hat to a skeleton while breaking into a surgery [MAND]. He would also find amusement when playing with items like a dentist's drill [HOUR] or pulling a Christmas cracker while searching for a nuclear bomb [BARG]. He also enjoyed going off on flights of fantasy [WING].

With a repertoire which included a lot of vicar jokes ('Ours was a quiet wedding – the vicar had laryngitis') [THIN], Steed's humour was also one of his charming ways of dealing with women, and he soon had the initially stony Ministerial top-hush secretary Cynthia Wentworth-Howe amused by his unlikely story about fish [POSI]. When Venus messed up introductions to a man called Jack Roberts, Steed simply said 'Call me Bert' which sent Venus into a fit of giggles [SCHO], and he was able to whisper a private something to Cathy to make her laugh [SHAD]. In the 1970s, it seems that Gambit occasionally shared Steed's sense of wit as the pair would come up with the same quips [CAT] and his 'English humour' began to rub off on those who respected him such as the French Colonel Martin [KIL2]. However, Steed did not even grin at Gambit's other jokes [LION].

By 1965 Steed's general approach to his career was now less serious than that of many of his colleagues. Even when warned about a looming reprimand from a Minister, he airily responded that he would 'probably have to hand in my umbrella' [ROOM]. Nor did he bother to keep up with all the professional publications devoured by the more officious and trivial minded [ROOM]. Another manifestation of Steed's humour was his wicked streak of sarcasm, deployed against both colleagues ('I could have coupled up my train set' he smiled when Turner accused him of wasting his time [CAT]) and criminals ('You astonish me,' he remarked to the dubious antique dealer Mervyn Sawbow when told there were 'shady people' in the industry [ROTT]).

A good judge of character, Steed would quickly assess those around him to determine who would and would not help him in a given situation [eg NOON]. He preferred a peaceful solution if at all possible, appealing to the better nature of a butler called Glover who was implicated in a series of killings [BREA]. He seemed to relish the art of detection, referring to Tara as 'Watson' while she addressed him as 'Holmes' [FOG]. And, having observed the behaviour of others, Steed capitalised on their weaknesses. Sensing the thirst for danger in Major Robertson, Steed knew he could persuade the officer to take part in a deadly game to grab a gun first rather than just allow himself to be shot [DANG]. He also took advantage of people's nervousness to calmly put the pressure on them [MAUR, ROCK].

Having studied the evidence at the scene of the crime and the reactions of those around him, it was then a matter of assembling all the clues and observations to fit the pattern that revealed the truth, and fortunately Steed's powers of reasoning were excellent [eg HOLE]. He was congratulated for being 'astute'[25] enough to deduce that the vibrations he felt in Castle De'Ath were generators for a nefarious purpose [CAST] while when a dubious fellow called Sidney Street made enquiries about Steed in 1968 he soon determined that he was dealing with a man of 'considerable perception' [LEGA].

When it came to thinking, Steed could deduce a *modus operandi* [WILD, KILL, DEAD], reason an accused killer's innocence [FOG], isolate the one guilty person linking a series of events [FACE] and determine technological tricks [eg SURR, TAKE]. When confronted with a circle of six doors, five of which contained something lethal, he knew that to open two facing doors would cause the threats to eliminate each other [GAME], and realised that if he knew his way into a maze, he did not need to determine his way out [ANGE].

Steed was also clever enough to deduce how things looked from other perspectives – inverting instructions given to him by Emma which she related from an upside-down position [SURF]. While locals believed that fish in Meadow Pond had been killed by dynamite, Steed pointed out that no debris had been thrown up and the water was clear [THIN]. From the evidence suggesting a variety of creatures from a snake to a shark lurking in the London sewers, Steed deduced it was in fact one vast rat [GNAW]. Sometimes he would discuss his findings with colleagues like Emma and they would brainstorm possible solutions [DANG], and at others he would reach his conclusions independently at precisely the same moment as his colleagues [3HAN].

Having deduced what was going on, the next step was to set a trap or execute a plan to catch the culprit or acquire vital evidence. Fortunately, as Steed himself claimed, he was a 'devious fellow' [BIRD]. Wherever possible, Steed liked to plan ahead. He had a special coffin with hinged sides prepared for Emma to escape burial after her supposed murder as

---

[25] Tarquin of SNOB also felt that Steed was an 'astute' adversary [CORR].

part of a plan he hatched in 1964 [MARK], and would wait patiently for an opponent to return to its lair like a hunted animal [SUP7]. Although he seemed reckless at times, Steed liked to play safe wherever possible. Indeed in 1965 he even purchased a place on board Jonah Barnard's Ark in case the biblical Great Flood should return [SURF].

There was one recurrent part of Steed's scheming early in his career. He would use people a great deal prior to the departure from his life of Cathy. David Keel and Cathy Gale were the two figures most usually ensnared like flies in Steed's web of intrigue, a technique he used a lot in the early 1960s on others such as Dr Martin King and Venus Smith. And it didn't end with regular associates – any other members of the public were fair game. Cathy's young friend Joey Frazer was ideal to send into Sam 'Pancho' Driver's boxing ring, with Steed dangling the offer of management as bait [WHAL]. He manipulated the Greek diver Helena into attacking the laboratory containing enemy agent Anna Lee, and got her to threaten 'Archipelago' Mason for him by letting her think that Mason had killed her friends [FROG].

Many of Steed's promises were well-meant but empty. Guaranteeing that he would look after arcade owner Mike Brown if he spilt the beans about the defection of cipher clerk Victor Trevelyan, Brown agreed to accept Steed's protection, but had been shot within seconds [MIRR]. At St Luke's College, Jack Roberts and Ted East were persuaded to play along with blackmailers until Steed could make his final move [SCHO]. After his character-changing experiences in 1964, Steed became a less ruthless person. However, in spring 1966 he was still forced to use economist Richard Carlyon as live bait in a trap [HIST]. Untruths were also part of the undercover agent's basic tool kit, but Steed would also reluctantly lie to a woman to save her distress. He kept the fact that fellow agent Mark Pearson was dead from Pearson's girlfriend Samantha Slade for as long as possible before coldly breaking the truth to her [BIRD].

'A master of the double-play,' was a phrase which Gambit associated with Steed [3HAN]. Steed's persona made him a plausible trickster, with people never quite being sure if they could trust him or not. He played upon this skill for subterfuge, handing over a joke-shop laughter box instead of secret documents in exchange for a kidnapped Purdey [TALE] and trying to pass off a 10p piece as the aforementioned incendiary device [HOST]. Twice he used dummies of himself to divert unwanted fire or attention [VENU, ANGE], although when Purdey suggested using a wax model of the dead Unicorn to fool observers in 1977, Steed dismissed this as 'Too 19th century.'[26] [LION] The use of a pill in Mark Harvey's drink was also an excellent excuse to have his colleague Dr King called in when Harvey fell ill [SELL].

Sometimes, Steed would also bluff that although he had walked alone into a dangerous situation, his allies had the building surrounded [HOST]. Even complex medical regulations which sounded authentic would trip off his tongue; one moment he would inform Dr George Culver that a wounded man may assume responsibility for his own discharge from hospital in accordance with Paragraph 5 Subsection 14a – and then seconds later admit this edict was a complete fabrication [DEAD].

Steed would cheat when he had to [GAME].[27] 'I never did believe in rules,' he observed

---

[26] Steed was no doubt referring to Sir Arthur Conan Doyle's 1903 story *The Adventure of the Empty House* in which Sherlock Holmes arranged a wax bust of himself to draw the fire of Colonel Moran.

[27] In comparison, the version of Steed depicted in the 1998 Warner Bros film commented 'Play by the rules... Or the game is nothing'.

as he grabbed a gun in a duel on the count of 'two' only moments after he and his opponent had agreed not to make their move until 'three' [DANG]. Cheating was part of Steed's undercover way of life, such as writing the answers to an exam paper on his shirt cuff as crib notes in a test... at which he still performed miserably [MIND].

Even in the 1960s, fellow agents like Fraser knew that Steed did not play by the book [SELL], but as far as Steed was concerned 'there's no rules in this game' [MORN]. Gambit felt that when it came to procedure, Steed broke the rules more often than anyone else he knew [HOST]. However, as Steed observed, rules and regulations were not always made to keep people alive and he often could not wait for clerks to give him clearance before acting [LAST]. While at the British consulate in Santiago, he ignored the house arrest he had been placed under by Sir Henry and calmly started to tear up invitations for an official reception until Travers, Sir Henry's desperate aide, let him go [DISP].

Like falsehood, bribery was a way of life for Steed when he needed information in a hurry. During his active service, Steed paid money to Vincent O'Brien [COUR], a double agent who posed as his barber [BUTL], the staff of the Oriental restaurant Yan Sing [FLEE], the elderly gunsmith Joseph Gourlay [ELEP], Kermit the Hermit who lived at the Benedict Mine [LIVI] and a soldier of the Highland Guard [ESPR]. Seldom did these bribees betray Steed. Steed also paid a man called Cooper to work for him as an inside man at the merchant bank of Teale and Van Doren before letting him escape to Johannesburg [BATM], and offered either £1,000 in cash or an Earldom to the Right Honourable Lucien ffordsham to expose goings on at Meadows Stables [TROJ]. Steed's promise to double the prize money offered by Sir George Benstead for his car rally treasure hunt would probably have persuaded Sir George to reveal the location of his treasure chest (containing vital papers), had Sir George not perished first [TREA]. Steed offered cash to the patrons of Dos Pajaros in Santiago for information about Cathy [DISP], and his bid to buy the services of a wrestler called Harry Ramsden was vital in proving the fighter's innocence in a murder when Ramsden declined the payment [DECA]. A ticket to a foreign shore was waved under the nose of a criminal called Palmer to get him to spill the beans about his employers [INTE]. After an initial £50 paid to Private Jessop to keep his presence in the kitchens of the Highland Guard secret, Steed then gave the same avaricious soldier £5,000 and 750 guineas-worth of tie-pin to arrange his salvation from a firing squad in March 1964 [ESPR]. A hotel lift operator was paid by Steed to ferry him to the restricted sixth floor and then keep the elevator out of action while he investigated the suite of his old adversary Colonel Nsonga [GUNS]. And Bill and Charlie – a lorry driver and his mate – were amenable to delivering Steed to the Grosvenor Auction Rooms in a crate for a small fee [MAUR].

However, enemy agents could seldom be bought, such as Zerson who rejected his offer of £500 in cash to release Steed from imprisonment [KEEP]. Similarly, the sweetener offered to the butler Gregory at the Litoff Organisation in an attempt to see tycoon Alex Litoff proved fruitless [DANE]. And at times the initial deal Steed offered was not enough; young Miss Sally Graham rejected an offer of 20 large lollipops in exchange for the vital key of a courier case, but acquiesced when £25 was on the table – commenting that she knew Steed would not take advantage of her just because she was a little girl [TAKE]. If bribery failed, blackmail was another weapon in the Steed arsenal of enforced co-operation, such as threatening to expose Brother Sampson's back-handers to ensure that a shipment was unloaded from the SS *Jan de Krup* [BAIT].

When corrupting monetary traffic flowed the other way, Steed was unbribeable and retained his integrity. When investor John Harvey and banker Ben Jago offered him £200,000 in a Zurich bank account to keep quite about their chain of murders, Steed refused [DIAL]. Nor did double agent Jimmy Merlin's pitch of £20,000, a yacht, a private plane, a string of Arab ponies or a Villa in St Tropez in return for his freedom cut any ice [MORN]. When undercover as a dubious character, Steed asked for £5,000 and £4,000 to return smuggled diamonds to the Litoff Organisation on two separate occasions [DANE, BREA].

Steed frequently respected many of his more worthy adversaries. He liked killer Jack Dragna [REMO] and when assigned to track down assassin Olaf Pomeroy commented that it would be a pleasure to deal with 'a real professional again' [DANE]. Similarly he admired the work of the hit-man known as The Unicorn [LION] and had respect for the embezzling but cultured butler Gregory [DANE]. He also allowed Fleming, the butler to the villainous JP Spragge, to flee the law because the gentleman's gentleman was, after all, a gentleman [CAGE]. On the other hand, he dismissed hustlers like Nicky Broster and Clarissa as 'amateurs' [BIGT] and believed that drug dealers were worms [TRAP]. Steed was tough and resolute with his enemies – informing Purdey's kidnappers that he would simply hang up unless they allowed her to speak as proof of their claims [HOST].

In association with his bravery, Steed was also able to remain calm in many strange situations – even when being shrunk to an inch or so in height [MISS], being directly accused of murdering a man called Pasco by the Peruvian authorities in Lima [DISP], or when cornered at gun-point by the French gendarmerie [PROP]. When he knew he was a target, Steed could remain in control and was far more concerned about the fate of others [GAME, NOON].

Because he stayed calm, Steed could think clearly and come up with schemes in a flash. When attempting to expose a fake training establishment, Centre 53, as being run by the enemy, Steed suggested that his fellow agents fired the gun which Colonel Mannering assured them were loaded with blanks at the Colonel himself – thus discrediting the villain [INTR]. In Paris in 1977, he managed to set up an exchange with the gang run by The Unicorn, exchanging his dead captive – The Unicorn himself – for a kidnapped prince in a scam using two lifts travelling between the fifth and ground floors [LION]. In the London sewers in 1976, Steed used the liquid lure intended for a massive rat to drench a man threatening Purdey – thus causing the rodent to attack him [GNAW]. Attacked by birds, he dived into a swimming pool to escape death [CAT], while a quick switch of distinctive headgear atop an old car was enough to fool the Canadian police who had specific orders to locate a vehicle 'wearing' a bowler [EMIL]. If a plan he had concocted in advance went awry, Steed would quickly adapt it to the new situation [DISP]. While captured, he quickly covered cameras that could track his movements [BEAR, ANGE]. To distract people he would do anything from throwing cigarette cases [BOX] to overturning tables [REMO].

Another great knack of Steed's was to think laterally. When set the Ultimate Test of the Hellfire Club, Steed's approach to the removal of a pea from beneath a vicious falling blade was to blow it clear with his breath rather then risk losing his fingers [BRIM]. When unable to enter the sealed Canadian Security building, he used the post-box as a means to get matches and lighters inside to the trapped Purdey, enabling her to trigger the internal sprinkler systems and short-circuit the controlling computer [COMP]. The purchase of a Magnetic Fish Pond game from Harper's Trading Post allowed him to locate Forward Base [BASE] and the use of one of his aviator's maps helped him to fathom out the clue left by a one-time pilot in the riddle of *The Tale of the Big Y* [TALE].

Steed's quick reactions saved his life on many occasions. When he received a phone call telling him to 'sleep well', he realised that the receiver he had just lifted up was coated with a nerve gas and blistering agent, but his lightning reactions in wrapping the flex of an electric lamp around his wrist bought him time until he could administer the antidote [BEAR]. His quick response on hearing that Venus had received face cream from an unknown source led him to vigorously wipe her features clear from any secreted acid – although Venus had thankfully not used the product [SCHO].

Ever ingenious, Steed made use of the items around him in a most resourceful manner, be it using a tyre pump to capture perfume detected in a car [SUCC], a surgeon's mirror to reflect a deadly light beam [VENU], his own tuba as a cannon to dispose of a bomb [NURS], a live cartridge knocked through a hole in a wall with a stone to 'shoot' an attacker [DOOR], a nail to force open links on handcuffs [KEEP], a giant paperknife to cut bonds [MISS], a spray gun of dry rot to dissolve the stairs beneath a fleeing killer [ROTT], a tree trunk hurled through a window as a distraction [INTE], spectacles to magnify vital photographic evidence [TALE], Fun Fireworks as a distraction when dealing with kidnappers [HOST] or lighted matches to burn through his bonds [WARL]. A hat on a stick made an effective decoy [OVER][28] while a similar arrangement with a glove and a weighed-down bag simulated his own demise in some marshland [OVER]. A metal shield snatched from a wall made a makeshift bullet-proof vest for an encounter with Perov [CARD] and he purchased cats to devour killer birds [CAT].

Towards the end of his career, Steed declared that nobody would catch him behind a desk [ANGE]. Although slightly lazy, like Sherlock Holmes he hated inactivity. He had an intense dislike of filling out forms and would rather be attending an inquest, telling one of his superiors 'Office work isn't quite my line' [MIRR]. Although he could type, he was not terribly quick at the keyboard [NOV5, KILL].

More oblique skills which Steed seemed to pick up during his adventures included a talent for quick changes (with his repertoire including a Mandarin, an Admiral, a Red Indian and a dinner jacket with an illuminated 'Eat at Joe's' sign) [LOOK] and a sleight of hand acquired from Jimmy Merlin which allowed him to produce handcuff keys from thin air [MORN]. However, it turned out that his claims to have a superior mind capable of hypnotism using a watch were unfounded [CYPH].

When he became a senior figure in the Department, Steed worked those who reported to him hard – too hard according to his medical officer Dr J Kendrick [TARG]. Nevertheless, he would not ask anyone to do anything which he had not done himself – thus earning the trust and respect of many of his colleagues. In the 1960s, he felt that many of his colleagues were impulsive and impetuous, bemoaning 'Why can't any of 'em wait?' as a string of eager young operatives were disposed of, having run directly into danger [KILL].

During 1961, Steed often worked with the police [DOWN, FRIG, DOUB, BAIT] but this relationship all but evaporated over the coming years apart from a few rare occasions [HAND]. When in Ireland, Steed worked with the Irish police, the Garda [COUR] and liased with other local law officers in Switzerland [MORT]. However, when on his home turf from 1962 he was reluctant to become involved with the police on some occasions [SELL, MAUR,

---

[28] Apparently Steed used a similar trick with his bowler to trick a villain called Chang Tu. *Diana*, Issue 224, 2 June 1967.

CLAY], but happy to call them on others [WARL, DECA, BIGT, CLAY, MIRR, CONS] while sometimes using the alias 'Carruthers' when summoning the law [BIGT, WHAL]. Likewise when dealing with French security at Marseilles Airport, he did not reveal his identity to the authorities [PROP]. He also liased with both Immigration Control [INTE] and the Home Office [INTE]. Steed had the power to get a search warrant [COUR], have phone lines tapped [COUR, MAUR] and have a helicopter ferry him from Ballyknock to Shamrock [COUR]. He could arrange for the loan of two priceless Chinese porcelain figures [CLAY] or a Goya [AUNT] from museums to be used as bait, set up appointments via the British Cultural Council [CONC], Ministry of Science [DWAR] or Imperial War Museum [FLEE], and could order the power to an entire village cut off [THIN].

On occasion, Steed was seen to use a certain amount of the latest gadgetry in his private and professional lives, and his 1963 dossier noted that he had access to 'poison capsules, time bombs [and] microscopic transmitters.'[29] Although old-fashioned, he would often take the chance to try out new technology, and Emma knew that Steed was one 'for the big toys' [TREA]. The eavesdropping tape recorder with concealed microphone was one of the most frequently employed devices [HAND, MAND, ESPR] along with the miniature camera [ESPR, MISS] and an adhesive transmitter which could be fired from a gun and tracked with a hand-held unit [JUST]. There were also tiny directional microphones which he and Emma deployed to track big game [TIGE], along with walkie talkies for bodyguard duty [DOOR]. In the days before mobile phones, Steed used a portable radio telephone to stay in touch with colleagues like Major Plessey [TWOS] and had a similar device when working in Canada [BASE]. Simpler items included the traditional use of a stethoscope to listen at a door [LION]. By 1976 Steed also recorded radio messages on his Dictaphone [CAT].

Steed was however sceptical of machines like lie-detectors which attempted to replace human instinct [FALS]. After several nasty experiences in the 1960s, by the 1970s he had healthy dislike of computerised buildings, recalling a friend in New York who wanted to have his car horn repaired at a garage where you had to sound your horn to enter [COMP]. He would use a simple torch for night time break-ins to premises such as vintners Waller and Paignton [BROK] or Taylor's print works [MEDI].

However, no matter what gadgets and skills were available, working undercover meant living in a world surrounded by death and suffering. Originally, Steed was very tough about this aspect, advising Cathy, 'It's bad to feel sorry for people in our business. Slows you up.' [CLAY], although he did express a momentary sadness at the horrific loss of life in a charter plane crash in Ireland [COUR]. From 1964, the regrets which Steed experienced seemed to be more sincere, such as that of Pettit whom he had forced into investigating for him at St Bede's [HIST]. The notion of autopsies seemed to trouble Steed from around 1968; he would not discuss the details, and even referred to the process as the doctor doing 'what they have to do' [GUNS]. By 1977, he was becoming a more stoic figure. Casting his mind back to the death of a colleague a year earlier, he observed 'You have to learn when to close the file. It's in the past. Forgotten' [LAST].

Away from work, Steed could relax and rub shoulders with the rich and famous. Having hijacked the bodies of Steed and Emma in 1967, enemy agents Basil and Lola soon realised that the couple knew all 'the right people' [WHO?]. When it came to titled personages, Steed knew Sir Andrew Ford (Head of Department at the Ministry of Defence – Special Section

---

[29] *The Complete Avengers*, p59.

(Inventions)) [SEET], the famous explorer Sir George Robertson [SUP7], top meteorologist Sir Arnold Kelly [SURF], the investigator Sir Arthur Doyle [CLUE], industrialist turned politician Sir William Burgess [CLUE], and possibly Lord Tweezle.[30] He was also allowed to borrow classic vehicles from the collection of Lord Montagu [TIME, BIRD, SEET] while Sir Andrew Boyd was an old friend [DOOR]. By 1967 his banker was Lord Maxted, the chairman of the British Banking Corporation [JUST] and he also knew millionaires such as George Unwin (another long term friend) [JUST] and Gilbert Jarvis [JUST] as well as attending a party thrown by a womanising ambassador [MDVL].

Other friends and acquaintances included Tony Linkletter who made a fortune out of fertiliser (and spent New Year 1964 in the Argentine) [DRES], Tony Mercer who designed the Mercer Twin motorcycle [MOUS], Dr Henry Padley [CATC], Bertie Bartram [THAT], a friend with a son of an age to play cowboys and Indians in 1963 [EGGS], the Reverend Teddy Shelley ('a very old friend of mine', possibly via Walter's church connections) [THIN], the Major who ran London's Gemini club [BOX], Freddy Firman (who took a live skunk into the Turkish Baths) [OVER], the 73-year-old balding Rear-Admiral Keever [XMAS], a 'long-standing friend' who was a shareholder at Anderson's Small Arms Ltd [BULL], and electrical science expert Professor Harvey Truman [THIN]. He also stayed in touch with Miss Gladys Culpepper – apparently the best lip-reader in Britain after years of watching silent films – who knew his grandfather [THAT]. Other friends ran a nurseries on the Surrey Downs [SURR] or had cottages on the coast with a string of polo ponies [BEHI]. Unconfirmed reports identified other possible friends as Sir Ronald Lindley Loring the Minister for Research[31], Darwell scientist David Herston[32], noted huntsman James Cardew[33], fellow Bentley enthusiast Nigel 'Bunny' Bennett who lived in Lytham St Annes[34], Peter Crabbe who lived near the A4[35], Professor Brand[36], Sir Jocelyn who had an estate and castle in Scotland[37], Dick North[38], television reporter Tom Partridge[39], Bertie Clivesdale who won a Ministry of Defence contract around 1964[40], and Stuart who was one of the chiefs at the Ministry of Agriculture and Fisheries.[41]

In particular, Steed always tried to visit Bill Bassett in February to celebrate Christmas as they had done in Nanking – with Steed bringing presents, a tree, party hats and crackers. Bill was married to an interior designer called Laura and had done well in the antiques business, thus living in a lavish country house some seven miles from Critchley Manor with a vintage car on display in the hallway [OVER]. At the other end of the social scale, Steed knew a fellow called 'Leftie' who once tried to shoot off a pair of handcuffs [DRES] and it also possible that he knew a stoolie called Charlie around 1962-64 whom he paid in

---

[30] *Diana*, Issue 221, 12 May 1967.

[31] *The Avengers* (Enefer), p6.

[32] 'The Runaway Brain', *Look Westward/The Viewer*, 21 March 1964.

[33] *TV Comic*, Issue 741, 26 February 1966.

[34] *The Passing of Gloria Munday*, p10,77.

[35] *Heil Harris!*, p19.

[36] *TV Comic*, Issue 767, 27 August 1966.

[37] *TV Comic Annual*, 1966, p26.

[38] *Diana*, Issue 202-203, 31 December 1966 – 7 January 1967.

[39] *Diana*, Issue 216, 7 April 1967.

[40] *Too Many Targets*, p13.

[41] *TV Comic*, Issue 990, 5 December 1970.

Scotch.[42]

In addition to the gentry and nobles of Great Britain, Steed established many friendships around the world, including three Canadians – Security Chief Charles 'Chuck' Peters [GLAD], Bailey [BASE] and Paul Baker [COMP]. He also had friends in Rhodesia [WOND] and New York [COMP].

A number of Steed's friendships were even with members of the 'other side'. By 1967 he had known Ambassador Brodny[43] for years [TWOS, SEET] and was also on friendly terms with the doorman at his embassy [SEET]. Steed was good friends with both Olga Volowski [CARD], and the diplomatic attaché Illyanovitch Pushkin Tarnokoff[44] ('Boris') [GLAD] a decade later. He knew George Vinkel 'well' [CHAR], was 'best of enemies' with Martin [CHAR], felt he was 'always close' to Keller [CHAR] and clearly knew Joseph Ivanoff[45] who was operating in London in 1965 [AUNT]. His friendship with Toy bloomed from work in the black market of Moscow [KIL1]. He knew of and admired master spy Comrade Ivan Perov [CARD] and was also quite fond of Hong Kong Harry, a hapless Oriental courier [MIDA]. Steed also had an on-off relationship with double agent Jimmy Merlin. Steed treated Jimmy as being very dangerous, but the two would also work together, and Steed would let him go free if he promised to stay out of trouble [MORN].

Close work colleagues included Freddy (surname unknown) [MIDA], Craig [FACE], Frank Hardy (who had a photograph of himself with Steed on his desk) [SLEE], Peter 'Mandy' Manderson (Steed said he was 'one of the best friends I ever had' and knew his wife Sally) [ANGE], Colonel Tomson [ANGE], Freddy Mason[46] [RARE], Tom Fitzroy of the ministry [CYBE], General Canvey [OBSE], Major Prentice [DIRT] and – apparently – Purdey's uncle, Colonel Elroyd Foster [DIRT].

Of his old family friends, Steed seemed particularly close to Dr Spender. He and Spender shared the same club and although Spender was rather old-fashioned (commenting that Cathy was 'competent enough for a woman'), Steed respectfully called him 'sir' [SECO]. Steed also apparently remained in contact with Bailey-Gibson, the family solicitor.[47]

Steed was usually addressed – even by close friends – as 'Steed' (which is why this work has adopted it in his adulthood as opposed to 'John'), which is how he instructed Lady Diana Forbes-Blakeney to refer to him in preference to 'Mr Steed' [KILL]. Only a handful of people addressed him by his Christian name. These included old colleagues like Tommy McKay (and oddly enough the junior agent Walters) [HOST] and some of his friends in Canada like Chuck Peters and Bailey [GLAD, BASE]. Gambit would call him 'John' when socialising off duty [SLEE] – the rest of the time it was 'Steed'.

It was believed by many in the Department that Steed's Achilles Heel was the 'opposite sex' [KNOT] – an astute deduction of a man who arranged to take his calls in a French lingerie department whenever possible [PROP]. Cathy was very used to Steed's wandering

[42] *Too Many Targets*, p82.
[43] Brodny referred to himself as Vladimir Yurislav Brodny [SEET] but recalls his mother calling him 'Sergei' [TWOS].
[44] Erroneously referred to as 'Elisnevitch Tolstoy Tschaikovsky Pushkin Tarnakov' in the transcript.
[45] Erroneously referred to as 'Colonel Ivanov' in the summary report.
[46] Erroneously referred to as 'Jimmy Mason' in the transcript.
[47] *Jealous in Honour*, p138.

gaze when she started working with him again in 1962 [DISP, FLEE] and was not surprised to discover that his contact at the Reniston Group was a woman [HAND]. In the 1970s, his old colleague Freddy remembered that Steed could 'always pick 'em' [MIDA], echoing the comment made by Paul Ryder when Steed introduced him to Tara [GETA]. When Purdey told Steed that he was 'A roué', he corrected her by replying, 'An optimist' [MIDA]. However, in his younger days he would boastfully quip that unlike Cathy's ornithological photographs, he usually got the birds to pose for him... [DANE].

It was said that what Steed needed in an ideal woman was a cross between Lucretia Borgia and Joan of Arc [MARK]. On one occasion he claimed to prefer a 'switched-on' Swedish *au pair* [THIN] and on another said that he wanted a woman who had a good seat on a horse, played a good game of bridge, mixed a good dry martini and whipped up a fair soufflé [MARK].

While he joked that he had a weakness for 'big brown eyes' [SURF], it seemed that 'beautiful grey eyes' had a greater effect on Steed [LIVI]. Blondes such as Pamela Johnson [INTE] and Miss Mara Little [CLAY] seemed to be particularly attractive to him, and he was similarly captivated with Samantha Jones [TIGE] and Inge Tilson – although he put business before asking her for her life story [THIN].

Steed's beliefs regarding the fairer sex were that 'Women should never be kept waiting' [DANG], that with ladies one should 'Always leave 'em laughing' on good terms [DEAD], and always obeyed the rule 'Ladies first' – even when in a hurry [ZEBR]. He also told Purdey that 'A beautiful woman belongs to the world' [OBSE]... while on the subject of rivalry in dating decreed 'All's fair in love and war' [DEAD]. And despite all his mottoes and rules, there were still times when he claimed that he did not understand the 'fairer sex' [MAUR].

Steed would not swear when there were ladies present [ANGE], always attempted to be charming and thoughtful [eg BRIE], and made sure he paid plenty of compliments [SELL] or at least flattery [WILD]. Even in the middle of a fight, he would take the time to stop and reposition an entranced female clerk who had being knocked round in her chair [CYPH]. He was sensitive to women who were truly upset and would dispense genuine comfort [ROCK]. However, he could be tough with women when the situation demanded, becoming angry with the spoiled actress Nicole Cauvin when she did not take his story of being sent to kill her seriously [REMO].

Scantily clad women proved distracting to Steed [DISP, WING] as did women in short skirts [TREA] or women with garters [POSI]; the idea of shrinking mini-skirts appealed to him greatly [MISS]. He and Gambit were both keen to visit the Moulin Rouge while in Paris [LION] and enjoyed watching the dancing girls [KIL2].

Steed would often dreamily eye up or flirt with secretaries, maids and assistants at organisations that he visited [eg BOX, WHAL, CART, MAND, TROJ, MARK, DIAL, SURF, SEET, LOVE] – occasionally in a way which would disarm and distract while he searched for clues and information. Barmaids [WARL], airline stewardesses [DISP] and sales girls [PROP, MIRR, BARG] were other targets for the Steed charm, along with girls at clubs such as Henriette at the Gemini (of whom he wondered what her vices were and gazed at while dancing with Venus) [BOX], Miss Dicey Hunt (a 'brunette with a touch of gold' who does 'interesting things with stuffed snakes' at the Green Cockatoo) [BRIE], or the odd cigarette girl (whose bottom he slapped) [DECA]. Sometimes though, the girl at the club would find that Steed's eyes were focused on his work rather than her [BOX].

In December 1964, Steed received Christmas cards from various lady friends including Amy ('Come Fly With Me'), Carlotta ('Yes... Carlotta'), Urma (whom he had met in Monte Carlo and was not fond of) and 'Boofums' (a post mistress at Ongar) [XMAS]. He was also admired by Sara Bradley (the ignored girlfriend of John Cartney) [BRIM], model Jane Wentworth thought he was 'fabby' [DRES], and the strange Circe Bishop thought he had nice ears and hair [OVER], while on another occasion he apparently had great difficulty in shaking off the attentions of a beautiful Bolshoi ballerina [GLAD]. At Brandon Storey's party, Steed made sure at least one lady guest had his phone number in her diary by midnight [XMAS] and – as a gentleman – would never refuse an address given to him by a lady [KNOT].

However, Steed would not take advantage of a drunken woman who draped herself over him [BRIM]. He also became increasingly responsible for women who got dragged along in his work, notably Miss Kim Lawrence, an actress hired in 1964 by his adversary Keller to pass herself off as a top enemy agent. Steed found the lady charming, and was concerned when her life was later imperilled [CHAR]. He felt similarly for enemy agent Olga Volowski, despite the fact that she was fully trained [CORR]. Steed found himself becoming attracted to Olga, and almost a decade later charmingly told another 'cultural attaché' also called Olga[48] that she was 'an exceptionally beautiful spy' [CARD]. He was also known to flirt with the Oriental 'diplomat' Sing [MIDA].

The women that he was seriously devoted to and cared for were somewhat fewer. Certainly one of these was Wendy, the wife of his dearest friend Mark Clifford [FACE]. He seemed to have been very close to a girl called Ann Lisa Pravicz (whom he knew as 'Lisa') [WRIN] – and was 'once close' to Janice Flanders, the sister of the wealthy Robert Flanders. When meeting her again in December 1967, Janice seemed rather intolerant of Steed, knowing at once that he had not come to see her [CLUE]. In 1976, Steed also became particularly involved with a woman called Joanna[49] – and it upset him deeply when she was revealed to be an enemy sleeper [CARD].

Steed could turn on the charm when he needed co-operation on an assignment [WARL]. He made a beeline for Miss Beryl Snow when infiltrating the hunting set at the Stirrup Cup Inn [DUST], and was usually excellent at exploiting a situation with romantic overtones, without dropping his guard [MOUS, SUCC]. Steed would sometimes date in the course of duty, his evening guests including a girl at a cracker factory called Judy [MAND], Katie Miles [LOBS] and Lady Cynthia Bellamy [BATM]. Other dates – like the blonde in the swimming costume at the Ocean Hotel pool in Jamaica – were purely for pleasure to kill time during an assignment [DISP]. Steed went out riding with Ann Meadows whose company he enjoyed [TROJ] and got on very well with a girl called Fay who called him 'John' and stayed at his Westminster Mews flat with her little dog, Sampson, before leaving to model in Paris [MEDI].

The standard 'Steed Date' for the lucky girl circa 1964 appeared to be a glass of champagne, then dinner at a club, a diversion to Richmond Hill to look at the river (with fog obscuring the gasometer at Kew), then up to Steed's Westminster Mews flat for coffee – although as he explained to Cathy this 'depends on the lass' [LOBS]. Sometimes his gifts often betrayed very little thought – such as daffodils grabbed from the grounds of a zoo

---

[48] Possibly Olga Perinkov. *House of Cards*, p18.

[49] An alternate transcript gives her name as 'Joanna Harrington'. *House of Cards*, p69.

[FEED] – while on other occasions he would be outstandingly generous towards a lady who had helped him on what seemed like a minor matter [STAY]. In Steed's murky globe-trotting past there was also a liaison with a blonde in Berlin ('on expenses') [CHAR], the incident with a Colonel's daughter at Montagne [CYPH], and a young belly dancer called Yvette in Tangiers [LION].

As Steed matured, a number of women now wanted to flirt with him, including the scientist Doctor Marlow [LAST] and architectural agent Miss Cummings [COMP] – in addition to the various women who were seen with him at his country house. In a dangerous situation, Steed was generally very gallant in protecting women [LAST]. 'We're emancipated now,' Purdey had to explain to Steed in 1977, to which the senior agent smiled and replied, 'I'll remember that' [LAST]. Indeed, Steed had already been praised for his increasingly positive attitude towards women since 1963 in an anonymous letter which arrived addressed to him around autumn 1975 – on the eve of the Sex Discrimination Act becoming law. Signed simply 'Yours sincerely, an Educated Feminist and Nice Girl', Steed was commended for having 'done so much to further our emancipation. You treated Mrs Gale, Mrs Peel and Miss King with an unusual degree of intelligence and civilisation that is rarely found in men... I congratulate you for your vision'.[50]

With older women, Steed was chivalrous, offering to carry pruning baskets [ROTT], being charming to those who seemed slightly senile [EMIL] and displaying his usual patience and politeness when being delayed by an old lady doting on a dog with an absurd name like 'Posy Puff' [NEST].

Steed 'visits the best clubs'[51] noted his 1963 Department dossier, and indeed he belonged to one of those bastions of tradition, a London gentleman's club [SELL, MEDI, LOBS] whose members also included Dr Spender [SECO], Lord Darcy [BRIM] and Colonel 'Bumble' Corf [LACE]. This was not Whites or the Athenian, and he was blackballed at Boodles [CHAR]. After he moved out to the country in the 1970s, he would sometimes stay at hotels in London and was well acquainted with a hotel porter called George who had got him hundreds of cabs by August 1976 – although Steed had never realised that George wore red socks [SLEE].

As with so many other things in his life, Steed's tastes were often expensive. He was well known for his liking of caviar [TROJ, XMAS, BIRD, GLAD] which he would eat while on surveillance [TROJ, BIRD] and liked to have chilled, but not frozen [GLAD].[52] Also among his other gastronomic treats were quails' eggs [XMAS], asparagus [XMAS], soufflés [MARK], moussaka [GLAD], pheasant [ESPR], lobster [LOBS] (possibly hoping that Emma might cook one for him [AUNT]), roast chicken with mushrooms [NUTS], something with an apple in its mouth at the Savoy Grill [HOST], a grouse basted in red wine [BIRD] and *escallop a la crème* with parmesan, a touch of garlic and crepes [MARK]. One ideal meal that he outlined comprised Whitstable oysters, *la tortue claire au xeres* (turtle soup), *la saumon d'Ecosse belle vue, la supreme de volaille a la Kiev* and peeled walnuts [WING].[53] He also commented that his favourite dessert of all was brandy balls [WOND].

---

[50] *Blind in One Ear*, p269.

[51] *The Complete Avengers*, p59.

[52] It has been suggested that Steed was particularly fond of Belugan Malossal caviar. *The Magnetic Man*, p29; *House of Cards*, p89.

[53] Steed reportedly liked lasagne al forno Piemontese. *Heil Harris!*, p19.

Steed was always prepared to try new and exotic foods such as the left eye of a mountain rat, which was considered a rare Barabian delicacy at Prince Ali's dinner party [PRIN]. He deplored both the notion of a Blue Chip special combining prawns, scrambled egg and mayonnaise on lightly toasted rye bread [DIAL], and the idea of putting mustard on lamb [LOBS]. Nor did he like porridge [CAST], sugared mangoes (a jar of which he tried to get rid of for a year)[54] [UNDE] or jellied bumble bees from Japan [UNDE] – and felt that a great big juicy rare fillet steak was somewhat mundane, even though he would keep one warm on his Rolls-Royce engine for Tara [DONE].

There were certain cheeses Steed was partial to [ESPR, XMAS] – such as ripe Stilton [BARG] – and he preferred his butter unsalted [ROOM] keeping his own supply at home at the front of his fridge [EGGS]. In terms of sandwiches, he liked cucumber [HUNT]. For tea at his flat he liked to have biscuits (often chocolate ones) [NUTS, SPLI] or – best of all – Cornish cream with Swiss cherry jam, thin brown bread and Indian tea at the stroke of 4.15 pm [MAND].

Between meals, Steed would accept mints when offered [FRIG], liked the wrapped chocolates in a selection box [DANG], seemed partial to marzipan delight [TOWN] and admitted to always having a taste for French cake [PROP]. He was known to eat peanuts by tossing them in the air and catching them in his mouth [MOUS] and had the occasional ice cream [CATC]. Steed also liked grapes [DONE] – which featured in one of his strange dreams [DOOR].

The Department noted in 1963 that Steed ate at the 'best restaurants'.[55] His favourite venues included The Cock Pit[56] [MIDA], a floating venue where diners sat on board a canoe over water (with waiter service) [BIRD], the Savoy Grill [HOST], a Greek taverna on Dundas Street in Toronto [GLAD], the Yan Sing restaurant (which in 1963 did the best Peking Duck outside Singapore) [FLEE], a place in Montmartre [WHO?], the Ritz[57] and another unspecified restaurant which he and Tara frequented in 1968 [CYPH] which might or might not be a stone's throw from a library [MARK].[58] Steed also used any excuse to 'console' Emma with a meal out in 1967 [MISS].

Whenever possible Steed preferred to eat with cutlery instead of his fingers [HIST, BIRD]. When travelling, rather than miss afternoon tea he would often take cutlery and serviettes with him [BIRD] and he even had a carpet bag which housed a portable table, cups, saucers, tea spoons, a milk jug, a cake rack, a tea pot, sugar lumps and tongs and a kettle [TOWN].

For breakfast, Steed liked eggs [COUR], 'Wild West Cornflakes' [EGGS] and toast [MEDI].[59] Although Cathy claimed that Steed himself could not cook [OUTS][60], it seems that he could rustle up a rather tasty spaghetti [DWAR], *Boeuf Bourguignon* [CART] and poached

---

[54] Another report indicates that Steed was keen to offload kangaroo soup and pickled red ants in cranberry sauce onto Cathy Gale. 'The Runaway Brain', *Look Westward/The Viewer*, 7 March 1964.

[55] *The Complete Avengers*, p59.

[56] Which appears to be the establishment on Windsor Road in Eton.

[57] *The Golden Game*, Book Three, p91.

[58] There are also unconfirmed reports that Steed and Emma would grab a late bite in an all-night London coffee bar. *Diana*, Issue 204, 14 January 1967. With Tara, Steed would apparently eat at a restaurant just off the Strand – *The Gold Bomb*, p127 – or at the Mirabelle on Curzon Street. *The Magnetic Man*, p26.

[59] It is possible that he also ate kippers. *The Afrit Affair*, p9-10.

[60] It has been suggested that Emma would prepare supper for herself and Steed at his flat while he took a nap. *Diana*, Issue 219, 28 April 1967.

eggs [CART] – but not pheasant [CART] and he was seen to burn an omelette [BIGT].[61] There were also several recipes which he seemed very proud of. His best preparation for steak made use of tomato, two egg whites, half an onion and a pint and a half of burgundy [BARG]. There was also his crusted omelette of mushroom which demanded four dozen eggs laid by pedigree hens in the last three hours, llama's milk, wild cane sugar, flour hand-milled on stone, ground salt from the coast of Brittany and pimentos – all mixed for ten minutes and then cooked for ten minutes [ROTT]. When he went away, he liked to clear the kitchen cupboards of food he didn't want and dump it on his friends [UNDE].

'Always on time when there is a drink to be had,' was one of Steed's memorable traits from his time at RAF Hamelin as recalled by Geoffrey Ridsdale [HOUR], and his code-name chosen for the Danger Makers organisation was, appropriately, Bacchus – a name used by the Romans for Dionysus, god of wine [DANG]. Steed had a great capacity for alcohol, and even the two pint goblet which members of the Hellfire Club were expected to drain in one gulp apparently failed to slake his thirst [BRIM]. He was aware of how to drink milk before a wine tasting to prevent intoxication [DANE]. Able to remain sober while his friends such as Major Prentice got drunk [DIRT], Steed never drank when driving [SLEE]. More than happy to accept the role of barman at Centre 53 [INTR], even when undercover as a ship's steward, Steed could not resist consuming the drinks of passengers such as Dr King [MONT] – and seldom turned down the offer of an alcoholic beverage, unless, when undercover as Major White, it was 'too early in the day' [BUTL].

According to his Department assessment in 1963, Steed apparently used the 'best wine merchant'.[62] He certainly claimed to have 'everything' in the way of drink at Stable Mews [SPLI] and his cellar was the envy of many – particularly his boss, Mother [NOON, REQU]. In particular, Steed very much enjoyed a good brandy [WARL, CLAY, BOX, DWAR, CONC, BRIE, NUTS, FLEE, UNDE, LOBS, DIAL, GRAV, ROOM, SURR, DUST, TOWN, CAST, AUNT, DANG, BRIM, SUP7, NURS, RETU, JUST, POSI, KNOT, SPLI, WILD, ROTT, INTR, LOVE, STAY, FOG, OVER, LION], particularly an older distillation such as a Five Star Napoleon [UNDE, RAT, LION] or Napoleon Special Reserve [KILL].[63] He found it was a drink which eased his tension [SUP7] and an excellent restorative after a shocking experience [POSI, SPLI, STAY]. Such was his love of this drink that he even knew how to warm a brandy glass like a professional butler [BUTL] and even Daniel Edmund was able to safely gamble on Steed selecting the brandy from an array of drinks [GAME]. He also took soda with it at times [FRIG, SELL, HUNT, DEAD], and accompanied by an aspirin found that this was another excellent pick-me-up after being wounded [DEAD]. For high quality brandy, he relished a fine cognac [REMO, DEAD, KIL1] and even offered the drink by name in word association sessions [STAY]. Steed tended to look down on people who took liqueurs [BROK] as he himself preferred a cognac.

Increasingly from 1962, one of Steed's favourite treats became champagne[64] [DISP,

---

[61] An unconfirmed report noted that Steed enjoyed cooking a recipe from a 1597 edition of *Good Huswives Handmaid*. *The Floating Game*, p31. He could also rustle up bangers and mash. *TV Comic*, Issue 1027, 21 August 1971. He also claimed to cook a Philadelphian Fricassee *a la* John Steed (a fancy name for stew). *TV Comic Holiday Special*, June 1969.

[62] *The Complete Avengers*, p59.

[63] Steed apparently has a '48 Napoleon Brandy at his flat. *The Laugh was on Lazarus*, p62.

[64] Emma referred to her mythical missing cat 'Little John' as being bad tempered first thing in the morning until his first glass of champagne – presumably inspired by Steed's behaviour [TIGE].

DECA, UNDE, DRES, TROJ, LOBS, MARK, TWOS, HOLE, TIME, BIRD, TIGE, NEVE, SUP7, NURS, JOKE, TREA, JUST, MDVL, SPLI, GETA, XR40, LEGA, KILL, THAT, DONE, NOON, LEGA, THAT, PAND, REQU, BIZA, CARD, LAST, TALE, OBSE, LION, KIL1, KIL2, COMP]. Having first tasted Pol Roger at the Macnees' in 1936, the strictly defined sparkling wine from France's Champagne region became his most 'trusted pick-me-up' of all [BIRD]. So much did he like this expensive libation that he admitted it was a craving of sorts by 1969 [WILD] and a lack of the drink was his greatest fear [FEAR].

At his flat he kept bottles of the '45 which was a splendid year [DRES] and had the traditional silver bucket to chill it in [NURS]; by 1968 there were generally a couple of bottles hidden in the desk drawer at his apartment [SPLI] and he even kept a stock in his self-assembly rocket [BIZA].[65]

Steed was disappointed by non-vintage material [LOBS] or anything over-chilled [TWOS] while he relished finding 'a rarity from Reim' at the home of Sir George Benstead [TREA]. There was also one occasion when his vintner mistakenly sent a '27 instead of a '26 [MDVL]. Purdey commented that Steed got his 'strong supple wrists' from pulling champagne corks [NEST], an action which Steed had performed increasingly since 1968. He would even take it with him while on surveillance in a cooler flask [TROJ, BIRD, TIGE] and when going into hiding [REQU].

Steed found it a very useful drink when trying to get the co-operation of a lady [DISP, DECA] or as a treat when one of the fairer sex had been particularly brave [DIRT]. It was also one of the few drinks he would never consider poisoning as it would destroy the bouquet [LEGA] and by 1976 was seeing even the smallest celebration as an excuse to crack the bubbly [TALE, LION, KIL2]. When Steed held his infamous 13 June parties it was the only drink available [OBSE]. Eventually, Steed would find his favourite champers hidden in the strangest places – including a teddy bear [SUP7] – and Tara soon knew it was a gift guaranteed to delight the partner she admired so dearly, cheering him up with an extra special vintage ('every grape hand trod') when he was at Department S [NOON]. Steed modestly claimed that his 12-tier champagne fountain was his greatest contribution to civilisation [THAT].

Sometimes Steed would enjoy a whisky [ROOT, BOOK, MONT, SELL, SCHO, MOUS, MARK, DANG, GAME, FALSE, CATC, ROTT, PAND], and often took ice with it [GAME]; on one occasion in 1969, all of Steed's own whisky was consumed by a former agent called Hubert Pettigrew [PAND]. One special brew – including weed bark and a little touch of snakehead – Steed downed out of politeness as it meant a lot to Professor Lopez [TARG]. Occasionally, Steed also took soda with his whisky [SELL, DISP, WARL, KNOT, KIL2].

In 1968, Steed claimed that he was a 'connoisseur of wine and people' [KEEP] and he would not be fobbed off with anything other than the 'proper stuff' [DISP]. His love of the grape was even known to the 'other side' [KEEP]. Steed took his wine very seriously and it was a common treat for him prior to his specific burning passion for champagne [DANE, ROCK, MAUR, DWAR, NUTS, ROME, MOUS, BROK, CAGE, ELEP, ESPR, CHAR, DIAL, ROOM, DUST, TOWN, HIST, VENU, CORR, RETU, TREA, LEGA, KEEP, INTR, TALE, 3HAN, HOST]. A wine lover for years, Steed's favourites included a '49 Carbonnieux (a terrible year because of the lime-

---

[65] An unconfirmed report suggests Steed took an 1879 Bollinger on a picnic with him. 'The Golden Game'. *Steed and Mrs Peel*, Book One, p38. Another incident says he liked a 1947 Barolo. *Heil Harris!*, p19.

stone layer) [MAUR], the '52 Gevrey-Chambertin [BROK][66], the Lafite Rothschild [BROK], a '52 Burgundy [BROK], Pouilly Fume [LOBS], a Chateau Rothschild '28 or '29 [WING] and a '47 (which he was appalled to find that Basil and Lola drank the last of without chilling) [WHO?]. Liking 'a wine that fights back' [DUST], Steed did not take the St Emilion seriously in 1962, knowing that the Chateau petit village would be superb in a couple of years [DANE] and felt that the Chalons '58 served to him at the Officer's Mess Kitchen of the Highland Regiment was a 'lousy year' [ESPR]. Steed took a rosé out with him for a day's punting, keeping it at river temperature by dangling it into the estuary [DUST].

Sir James Arnell[67] observed that Steed had 'a palette in a million' [DANE] and at a tasting the agent could identify a Pontet Carnet '52 [DANE], a Corque-Michotte '49[68] [DANE], a stimulating Chambertin pinot noir [BROK], a hock from the Rhine [BROK], a poor '34 [DIAL], a '65 Algerian Red [DIAL], and a Premier Croup Chateau Lafite Rothschild 1909 from the North End of the vineyard [DIAL]. He was more than happy to pitch his taste buds against a palette in a tasting duel [DIAL] and only too happy to criticise other people's tastes when looking through their fridge ('Plucky, but from the wrong side of the hill') [FALS]. Like champagne, Steed saw wine as a fine gift for his female friends, bringing Tara a 1957 bottle when she was ill [CLUE]. He also enjoyed helping to drink the world's most expensive red wine – its value enhanced by the precious Black Pearl dissolved in it [LEGA]. Steed also had fond memories of a Chablis which he and Emma shared on a trip to France [WHO?], while rating a 1959 Chablis very highly [WING].

Claret – or red Bordeaux – also attracted Steed's attention; at St Jude's, he was a genuine connoisseur of claret – but never sound on Burgundy.[69] One variety which did not travel well he declared to be his favourite wine [VENU], while he treasured a '61 at his country home and was most worried at the thought of his unscrupulous double consuming it while imprisoned in his cellar [FACE]. He was delighted by clarets at the homes of Brandon Storey [XMAS], the Duke of Benedict [LIVI] and 'Paul Beresford' who served him a notable '29 [RETU]. He also knew that such wines were an excellent solvent for pearls [LEGA].

'Beer is for thirst, wine is for the senses,' said Steed [KIL1], and would sample the hops on certain occasions [MOUS, QUIC, VENU, MDVL, SLEE, ANGE]; FB Mild Beer was also his choice for a liquid lunch [QUIC] while he would take beer with him on surveillance [VENU]. Ice cold, Steed found it particularly refreshing [SLEE, ANGE], although he was appalled when Gambit quaffed his straight from the bottle [SLEE].

From the environs of the Douro Valley in Portugal, Steed also kept port [NOON] and would sample this at parties [XMAS]; he particularly savoured tawny or crusty varieties [WING]. Occasionally Steed drank the wine-brandy fusion of sherry [WHAL, BATM, DIAL, JUST, POSI, KEEP], notably a rare brand offered by Lord Maxted at the British Banking Corporation [JUST]. Seldom would he drink vodka [CHAR, DIAL, CORR], although when he did he knew how to smash the glass and shout 'Zamir' in true Russian style [CORR]; the Russian Tarnokoff also knew that Steed would appreciate vodka from the Crimea with a

---

[66] Steed also apparently liked the Chambertin '53 – *The Drowned Queen*, p70 – and a Dom Perignon – *House of Cards*, p89.

[67] Erroneously referred to as 'Sir James Mann' in the summary report.

[68] Erroneously referred to as ''47' in the transcript.

[69] *Jealous in Honour*, p102.

second fermentation [GLAD].[70] Steed would drink the odd dry martini [MARK][71] or straight gin [ZEBR].[72] He quite enjoyed the sparkling Buttercup Brew distilled by Grannie Gregson's [SURF] and quaffed the 'Super' in 'Standard' quantities from the petrol pumps of Sir George Benstead [TREA].

Having made some famous punches at RAF Hamelin (usually with too much brandy) [HOUR], Steed was partial to this at Christmas [XMAS] and was delighted to find that his recipe was still in use at RAF Hamelin around two decades later; 'Wherever I linger I leave my mark' he observed, recalling the days when his standard order was 'one dash and half a splash' [HOUR]. Similarly, he reminisced with George Neville and Paul Ryder about their home-made Granny Tiddyfeather's Rum (or GTR) which fortified the drinker against the dawn rituals [GETA].

Sometimes Steed would indulge in cocktails [REMO], occasionally mixing them at home [TIME, XR40]. He had an aperitif called 'Romantica' [BUTL] while another involved diced melon and ice which one should then 'agitate vigorously' [UNDE]. When given access to the computing facilities of George/XR40, he asked for the recipe to the most deliciously potent cocktail in the world, something it would take 500 bartenders four years to come up with; the resultant explosive concoction included a thimbleful of Scotch and an olive [XR40]. However, Steed was quite appalled by Tara's disagreeable request for a tall crystal glass of crushed ice permeated with grenadine laced with a mixture of Cantonese saki and crème du violette topped with a measure of calvados, a tablespoon of Devonshire Cream and a fresh, unripe strawberry [SPLI].

The young Steed's preference for lemonade [WILD] had been fairly well stamped out of the adult who occasionally would have a soft drink such as pop [WOND][73], Worcester Sauce in tomato juice [BREA] or a tomato juice 'with everything' [KILL].

Believing that a drink at home helped him mull over a problem [TALE], Steed would also have a tipple at his club [SELL, BRIM], a pub in Covent Garden where he would meet his superior One-Ten [WARL], at night-clubs [DECA, BOX], in the bar at the Department HQ (especially if Gambit was paying) [RARE], in officers' messes [ZEBR] and various other bars which he would gravitate towards [CLAY, ZEBR, SCHO, MOUS, DUST]. He would happily meet people in a pub cellar for a drink [COUR] and was not above being found in an attempt to 'unravel the intricacies of the drinks cabinet' at Cathy's flat [WHAL]. Indeed, Steed was also happy to help himself to a drink when at a pub [BOX, DUST], Emma's apartment [VENU], Tara's rooms [GUNS, OVER], Mother's HQ [INTR] or when breezing into the home of Dr Cresswell [POSI]. Even having broken into the flat of Lord Darcy, Steed could not resist a quick tot while Darcy's manservant was hoovering in the next room [BRIM].

Steed sometimes carried a hip flask [MIND, DUST, KILL, TAKE] containing one of his favourite treats like a Napoleon Special Reserve [KILL] or any other drink which he could collect at a pub [DUST]. He had a patent hang-over cure called the National Anthem since it soon got one on one's feet [BRIM]. Usually, Steed could detect a drug in his favourite

---

[70] An unsubstantiated report suggests that Steed felt that vodka and slivovitz were 'ghastly'. *The Afrit Affair*, p43. He also apparently drank vodka with Olga Perinkov, *House of Cards*, p80.

[71] Steed was apparently quick to point out to a girl that she 'can't mix a martini. That one tasted terrible.' 'Epidemic of Terror', *Look Westward/The Viewer*, 19 October 1963.

[72] One unfilmed incident noted Steed ordering a gin and tonic. *The Magnetic Man*, p11.

[73] Apparently, Steed did not like Pepsi-Cola. *The Afrit Affair*, p43.

drinks by smell [MOUS, WRIN] although sometimes this skill failed him [GAME].

Steed was partial to tea [SELL, DANE, ZEBR, EGGS, SCHO, BEHI, MEDI, WRIN, ROOM, AUNT, PRIN, DOOR, BREA, SPLI, NOON, ROTT, DEAD] and while he did not take sugar at first [SELL] he soon picked up this habit [DANE] and took two sugars [BRIE, NOON].[74] At his flat, he had Hyderabad Green-Tipped tea [NUTS], and liked both Indian [MAND, BRIE] and China tea [NOON] with milk or lemon [TOWN] (preferring Indian over China [BRIE]) and Formosan Tea [ROOM]. At his Stable Mews apartment, Steed would serve tea to his guests in an ornate silver tea service [DOOR, BREA]. As the departing Emma informed the arriving Tara, Steed liked his tea stirred anti-clockwise [KNOT].

Steed also drank coffee [FEED, COUR, REMO, EGGS, DWAR, MIRR, FLEE, BEHI, NOV5, WRIN, LOBS, MIND, ROOM, XMAS, DIAL, CAST, TOWN, ROOM, JACK, HIST, KNOT, CLUE, GETA, GAME, FALS, 3HAN, SLEE, KIL2] which he usually took black [MIRR, FALS] and with anything from no sugars [FEAR], through one sugar [3HAN] up to three sugars [KNOT], although during 1966 he commented he preferred it with milk if it was available [HIST] and was taking his coffee white again by 1976 [3HAN]. He was partial to blends kept by both Cathy [BEHI, NOV5] and Emma [TOWN] and developed a taste for a continental brand used by Richard Carlyon [HIST]. Steed drank coffee when he needed to stay awake [MIND] and without sugar or milk when dealing with a headache [XMAS]. A lover of an early morning brew [CAST, SLEE], with breakfast Steed liked an Irish coffee laced with spirits [COUR] and was fond of Kenyan Coffee with 'a dash' [DIAL]. When offered milk to drink at the headquarters of PURRR[75], Steed declined [TIGE], although he drank it before wine tastings [DANE].

In the early 1960s, Steed smoked cigarettes [FEED, DOWN, COUR, MONT, DISP, BEAR, DANE, BOX], sometimes using a cigarette holder [DECA, REMO, SCHO]. He carried a cigarette lighter [FRIG, BEAR, DECA, ROCK, BOX] and a cigarette case [DISP, PROP, DECA, MAUR, BOX]. He would smoke cigarettes which he bought for other people [MONT] and their purchase would give him a chance to fraternise with cigarette girls at night-clubs [DECA]. They were similarly useful objects to offer to ladies he encountered [BOX] although Steed himself believed that women were 'always safe with a pipe smoker' [ZEBR]. When being frisked on one occasion, he asked to have his cigarettes left on him [PROP], possibly because one of his techniques to obtain release was a bluff involving an explosive cigarette [TUNN].

By December 1962, Steed claimed that he was trying to give up smoking [MAUR] and although he was still having the odd puff over the next few months, it seems that by late 1963 Steed had given up cigarettes [NUTS, SHAD]. When in front a firing squad in 1966, he refused a last cigarette [LIVI] and at other times turned down both cigarettes [WILD] and cheroots [FEAR] when offered. Nevertheless, a cigarette lighter was still a useful item for Steed to carry [LIVI, GUNS, XR40][76] while he also pocketed other people's matches [OUTS].

Steed was also smoking cheroots in 1961 [FRIG] and would take snuff on occasion [BRIM]. A regular enough customer of cigar merchants Herrick Brothers to know Jerezina [BREA], Steed enjoyed the odd cigar [DISP, BULL, BRIE, FLEE, MOUS, WOND, TROJ, OUTS, BREA, NOON], particularly a good Cuban [DISP] and was able to spot such a hand-rolled product with ease [ROOM].[77] Cigars were a particular passion of his when relaxing [FLEE]. Even so,

---

[74] In the 1998 film about Steed, he was shown taking his tea with a twist of lemon.

[75] Philanthropic Union for the Rescue, Relief and Recuperation of Cats.

[76] See also *TV Comic*, Issue 1010, 24 April 1971.

[77] An unconfirmed report suggests he still smoked the odd panatella around 1967. *Heil Harris!*, p9.

Steed was not always in a hurry to savour the precious leaves [WRIN, DIAL, HOUR]. He was aghast at the appalling treatment forced on his favourite brand by an enemy agent called Basil, ruminating 'What sort of a fiend are we dealing with?... A man who could bite the end off a cigar is capable of anything' [WHO?]. By 1977, Steed seemed positively anti-smoking, commenting that although he no longer smoked himself, he still carried a silver case of cigarettes for those of his friends who 'foolishly' did, in his left breast pocket. It was this case that protected him against a bullet fired by a Russian gunman [KIL2].[78]

Not earning in the seven figure bracket himself, Steed generally found talk about money to be dull [JUST]. In 1962 he banked at Peterson's bank [DANE] whose Sir John apparently thought very highly of him [ROCK] – certainly he was able to buy a 12 room exclusive 1930s modern maison in Highgate for £30,000 cash [ROCK]. However, by 1967 his banker was Lord Maxted, the chairman of the British Banking Corporation [JUST] and in 1968 had a credit card for Gray's[79] [STAY]. He still kept a piggy bank in 1966 (which Emma smashed) [PRIN] and also saved a little in half-pennies each week until in 1967 he was just one short of 1,000,000 [JUST].[80] By 1977, his account was with the London Bank Ltd [RARE].

Steed was rather old-fashioned in his monetary outlook, preferring to deal in guineas rather than pounds [MORN, LEGA]. He always liked to leave a tip as it 'makes better service' [SLEE] and was careful to leave money in exchange for any materials he might have to appropriate from the innocent during the course of an assignment [EMIL]. That said, he expected Mother and the Department to settle expenses occurred in his work – such as paying his old family friend Miss Gladys Culpepper £200 in cash for her help with lip-reading [THAT].

When posing as Cathy's broker in 1962, the wealthy Henry Cade[81] had observed that Steed was a shrewd business man [BULL]. Steed dabbled a little in shares [CLUE] and made a killing from some in Anderson's Small Arms Ltd which he purchased to get Cathy a place on the board and hence investigate the firm [BULL]. In comparison, when he later applied for 230 shares elsewhere, he got none of them [BATM], and some other stocks went down three days running around the same time [MEDI].

So – where did all Steed's money go? A fair amount of it – at least from 1966 onwards – must have ended up at some of the finest outfitters in London. Those inside British security such as DISCO knew that vanity was one of Steed's weaknesses [NUTS] – a fact which even the enemy were conversant with in 1963 [SHAD]. The age old cliché of the man waiting for the woman to dress herself for an evening out was reversed when Emma found herself waiting for Steed as they kept an appointment at the Hellfire Club [BRIM]. At the outfitters H Cleeves, Steed was unable to resist the lure of a new bowler hat and gloves, swiftly donning them to admire himself in the mirror [CHAR].

According to his 1963 Department Dossier, Steed had the 'best tailor'[82] and in a letter to the *Daily Telegraph* from Macnee about his friend's attire (with reference to the Warner

---

[78] Steed voiced near identical sentiments during an unfilmed 1976 mission. 'The Sleeping Dragon'. *Daily Mirror*, 13 October 1976, p21.

[79] The same bank was also used in 1969 by enemy agent Gregor Zaroff [THAT].

[80] Rather bizarrely, one report suggests that Mother reduced Steed's salary in late 1969. 'The Spirits of Christmas'. *TV Comic Annual*, 1970, p53.

[81] Erroneously referred as 'Calder' in the summary report.

[82] *The Complete Avengers*, p59.

Bros biopic), the actor gave a full run-down on where his old school chum had obtained his wardrobe. Steed's 'suits were tailored by Bailey and Weatherall of Regent Street, where they were cut and fitted by Mr James, their senior cutter. The jackets were shaped to the body, as on an 18th century man, full-chested and low-waisted, sporting collars of matching lady's velvet. The trousers were pencil-thin and settled neatly on a pair of elastic-sided 'Chelsea' boots, and [Steed's] shirts were ready-made from Turnbull and Asser.'[83] Another of Steed's tailors was actually an agent called Lovell whom he consulted in late 1963 [WRIN], while various sources confirm that he purchased his suits in the famed Saville Row.[84] In 1966 he was using the same tailor as his colleague Frank Elrick [BIRD], and their very touch made them uniquely identifiable to Steed's blind superior, Father [STAY].

Steed admitted to always having a hankering for the 18th century [TIME] which came across in the cut of some of his suits in the late 1960s; in 1963 his tailor was persuading him towards an Italian style which Steed seemed rather unsure about [BEHI]. At this time, some felt that Steed's look was a little old-fashioned – and in February 1965 Emma voiced the opinion that he would not be out of place in the Department of Discontinued Lines at Pinters in New Oxford Street [BARG]. However, Steed had a sense of style – realising that his bowler and brolly were just what was needed to add contrast to a photoshoot in which a girl was advertising a watch [MARK] and others – such as fence Charlie Binaggio – declared that Steed was a 'snazzy dresser' [REMO]. Certainly he was amused by the styles which he saw in the fashion magazine *Svelte* [WHAL].[85] His outfits were sharp, simple and striking, seldom overcomplicated; he did not require a 'JS' monogram on his clothes [BRIE].

When studying the fashions of others, he would remark on well-cut suits [LACE] and was keen to know the name of the tailor who serviced an elegant enemy agent called Dangerfield [THAT]. Steed was able to provide duplicates of his clothes for Bobby Cleaver to wear as a decoy [REQU] – although his opponents could also obtain duplicates when they needed to frame him with their own double [HOST].

Steed was most famous of all for his finely crafted suits – most of which were three-piece affairs with a distinctive waistcoat. One of his most notable suits which he was wearing as early as 1961 was a three-piece affair in a grey Worsted. This had a flap on the

---

[83] 'Steed's bowlers', *Daily Telegraph*, 24 July 1997.

[84] *The Avengers* (Enefer), p5.

[85] Two items exist in the archives of Pathé newsreel which have for years been believed to show Steed taking part in a fashion show, despite the fact that one unconfirmed report suggests that he was not keen to attend such events. *Diana*, Issue 205, 21 January 1967. One item, dated 26 September 1965 (when Steed was most probably investigating a threat posed by Silent Dust), shows 'Steed' wearing suits designed by Jean Varon, while another on 5 January 1967 had him posing with Twiggy (a famously slim model of the period), Olympic swimmer Linda Ludgrove and others to show further designs by Alun Hughes and Pierre Cardin. One explanation had been that this was further undercover work in the guise of, or one akin to his persona of, male model Gordon Webster. However, further research has revealed that the 'Steed' figure was in fact Steed's old actor friend Patrick Macnee. Dabbling in the world of male modelling at the time, Macnee also appeared in a photostory called *Strange Case of the Green Girl* which appeared in the April 1966 edition of *Man's Journal*, a supplement of *Woman's Journal*. In this he again wore outfits very similar to those sported by his old Etonian friend. Furthermore, from late 1967 to 1969, Macnee helped to design some of the principal items in Steed's wardrobe. The confusion over the Pathé footage seems to have arisen because some of the outfits on display were the same as, or of the same style as, apparel worn by Emma Peel and Steed.

breast pocket and lapels on the waistcoat [eg BOOK, KING, SELL, HAND, BROK, LOBS], a look which became part of the established Steed image. This was cut for Steed by Frith Brothers of Saville Row and cost around 70 guineas [CAGE]. Rarely, Steed wore it without the waistcoat [INTE], or occasionally with a glittering lapelled waistcoat to contrast rather than match [INTE, WHAL]. The right shoulder of this was ruined in one fight [PROP] and the quality of this item was impressive, with a butler called Gregory commenting on it [DANE]. There was also a darker three-piece suit [eg DOUB, WINT, MAUR, HAND] which came with a double-breasted waistcoat [BOX].

Between 1961 and 1965, one of Steed's favourite items of apparel was a grey sports jacket with blue, brown and black Prince of Wales check and a flap pocket [eg MORT, BAIT, BULL, WHAL, UNDE, ESPR, MARK, QUIC]; this was damaged in 1962 during an encounter with a guard dog which mauled the right sleeve [WARL]. Usually Steed wore this with a dark green waistcoat with metal buttons[86] [eg SLIP, BAIT, BIGT, WHAL, CAGE, ESPR] and some light tan trousers. It seems that this was effectively replaced in 1966 by a brown checked twill sports jacket with buttoned breast pocket [eg WING, NEVE, MISS, DONE].

Although the pinstripe suit had gone out of fashion in the late 1950s, Steed felt that by 1963 it was on its way back in and availed himself of a sharp black edition which went superbly with his now ever-present bowler and brolly [eg CONC, BATM, OUTS, LOBS]. He also started to veer towards an Edwardian look in his clothes. From 1964, his wardrobe of suits increased considerably, now including a dark navy chalk pinstripe three-button suit [eg MARK, BUTL, HIST], a similar version with a pocket flap, double hip pocket and lapel on waistcoat [eg DIAL, BARG], a grey with lapelled waistcoat and pocket flaps [eg MARK, HIST], a pale grey with a felt collar [eg CYBE, PRIN], a dark grey with a silk collar [eg GRAV, HIST], a navy three-button pinstripe [eg FEAR], numerous variations on a grey three-piece three-button with a lapelled waistcoat [eg FEAR, SEET, NURS], a distinctive light grey double-breasted Edwardian cut with a dark silk collar [eg BIRD, STAT], a grey three-piece with a dark stripe [eg NEVE, RETU] plus a charcoal grey [eg WHO?]. From 1968, Steed had some two-piece suits [eg LOOK, XR40, CATC] and moved more towards single button jackets with 'Chesterfield' fur collars and sometimes a lack of breast pocket. This new look included a grey with a flap pocket and silk collar [eg SPLI], a black three-piece [eg GETA, WILD], a brown three-piece with felt collar and gold backed waistcoat [eg LOOK, CATC, OVER], and a charcoal grey one-button with silk collar [eg GAME, BIZA].[87]

The waistcoats also made Steed stand out, with one person referring to him as someone's 'friend in the fancy waistcoat' [MAND]. He wore a dark silk waistcoat at times during 1965 [eg MARK, PRIN]. In addition to all his suits, he also had a black, high-collared hessian 'Chinese Admiral' blazer without lapels which he wore from 1963 to 1964 [eg SCHO, BATM, MARK] and a similar white 'Pandit Nehru' cotton suit which he wore while convalescing after an accident in 1968 [NOON].

Steed was known to steal white [UNDE] and red [MOUS, MARK, GRAV, ROOM] carnations for his buttonhole, although he also grew his own 'Morning Sunrise' [SURR]. His style was simple – even Ambassador Brodny knew that Steed would never have greenery or silver paper wrapped around his bloom [TWOS]. He accepted a carnation from Miss Daly in

---

[86] In the 1998 film, Steed had a 'bullet-proof waistcoat' from Trubshaws, a firm based on Anderson Sheppard's in Saville Row who also supplied Ralph Fiennes' suits in the picture.

[87] Macnee also makes reference to a 'lavant-green suit' with velvet collar. *Dead Duck*, p23.

Canada [EMIL] and purchased a white one from a London flower seller as cover to speak to an informant [FRIG]; sometimes Emma also arranged them for him [TWOS]. By 1968, he had red carnations in his flat [STAY] and favoured these in the 1970s [ANGE, OBSE]. He also wore a small flower like a daisy in his buttonhole [HUNT] and a distinctive black rose for a visit to join the Danger Makers at Manton House [DANG].

By and large, Steed wore plain shirts, often white or at least light in colour [eg REMO, MAUR, ROCK, BIGT, MIRR, VENU, JOKE, MISS, GUNS, LACE]. These were made to measure from South Sea silk and cost ten guineas in 1963 [CAGE] and – according to Macnee – ordered in Duke Street[88] as well as Turnbull and Asser. Sometimes Steed's shirts were striped [eg BOOK, FRIG, MEDI, DIAL] and in an attempt to keep up with new trends, during 1962 he was often seen sporting a very striking example with horizontal stripes [eg COUR, BEAR, MAUR, DANE]. In 1968, his collar size was 15 [KILL] and since 1965 he had been more daring with their colours; these included beige [eg CYBE], khaki [eg GRAV], gin [eg AUNT], pale blue [eg MISS], tan [eg POSI], grey [eg TREA], gold [eg INVA], pale green [eg CLUE], cream [eg SPLI], yellow [eg WILD], lilac [eg GAME] or gold with fine brown stripes [eg LOVE] as well as old favourites like the pinstripe with a white collar [SUCC]. Steed liked to wear ornate silver cufflinks [eg SELL, CLAY, FLEE, SECO, MIND, TIME, DONE] including some of Cabochon Crystal [CAGE].

Steed generally wore a tie except when relaxing [eg FLEE, MEDI]. According to Macnee, Steed purchased his ties from Mason's Yard[89] – in addition to his old school tie from Eton [CHAR] which was apparently from 'Youngs' [MAUR]. From 1961, Steed tended to wear a silk tie [FEED, FRIG, WINT, etc] including ones in dark blue silk [EGGS], a blue Paisley [UNDE] or one with a fine check [SPRI] or a dark pattern [DOUB]. In 1962-63 he often wore dark ties [eg COUR, DECA, WHAL] with the occasional lighter silk variant [eg DISP, WHAL] or a pattern [eg BEAR, HAND]; Heald also recalled Steed wearing a Guards tie during an encounter in 1962.[90] Rarely, Steed wore a woollen tie [eg DECA, BARG]. Again, as the decade rolled on, Steed's increasingly brave approach to colour and patterns increased the range of his collection. His favourite ties included a metallic grey [eg DIAL, PRIN], a navy with white polka dot [eg TIME, MISS], a gold (sometimes with matching hankie) [eg RETU, WISH], a silver [eg CYPH], a green [eg POSI], a brown [eg LOOK], a maroon [eg CATC] and a yellow and black check which came with a matching hankie [STAT]. Steed's range of favourite silks included navy blue [eg DIAL, ROOM, TIME, POSI, CLUE, LOVE], black [eg FEAR], brown [eg FEAR], light blue [eg KILL], gold [eg BIRD], red [eg TIGE, LACE], silver [eg WHO?, POSI], and purple [eg LOOK]. A Paisley design was popular (particularly from 1968), with Steed sporting examples in red [eg MARK], green [eg XR40], pink [eg FALS], blue [eg KILL] and brown [eg CYPH]. Bright floral designs were another way in which Steed kept pace with the current vogue [CYPH, GAME, PAND], but he drew the line at having dogs on his tie [BREA]. When undercover, he sometimes wore a spotted bow tie [ROME, UNDE].

Until 1965, Steed frequently accentuated his ties with a diamond pin [eg FEED, BAIT, PROP, CONS, UNDE, LOBS, MARK, SUCC, FEAR, LOOK]; the best of these was worth 750 guineas which Steed traded with a soldier called Private Jessop as a bribe in order to survive a firing squad [ESPR] while another which he often wore was a gift from Emma and contained a

---

[88] ...deadline, p11.

[89] ...deadline, p11.

[90] Jealous in Honour, p4.

miniature camera [TWOS].

The cravat was another form of neckwear which Steed wore on occasion [eg SECO, MEDI]. One particular polka dot item served him well around 1963-64 [eg BROK, TROJ, OUTS, CHAR] and was incredibly useful for concealing the microphone of a surveillance tape recorder [MAND]; he also tended to wear a cravat when riding [eg MARK, SURF, SURR, DUST]. Around late 1966, Steed occasionally favoured a cravat over a tie, although he wore these less often by 1969 [PAND, FOG]. His range included items in black and a white polka dot [TIGE], brown [eg TIGE, EPIC], blue silk [CORR, NEVE] and light grey with white polka dot [EPIC]. Again, these items were often highlighted by his tie-pin [eg CORR, BREA, FOG] or an ornate bar pin [TIGE].

Outdoors, Steed wore a number of different high quality coats including a dark overcoat with fur collar [FEED, FRIG], a light double-breasted trench-coat [eg DOWN], a heavyweight light coloured single-breasted overcoat [eg COUR], a short, light single-breasted overcoat with tartan lining [eg ZEBR], a longer light single-breasted overcoat with a double-hip pocket [eg BIGT], a heavy oatmeal broadcloth overcoat with a velvet collar (like an old coach-driver's coat) [CONC], a dark double-breasted overcoat with Astrakhan collar [eg BROK], a light tan overcoat with a wide collar [eg MARK], a light grey overcoat with a black collar [eg XMAS], a black single-breasted overcoat with a felt collar [eg MARK], a short slate grey double-breasted overcoat with a dark fur collar [eg HOLE], a brown single-breasted overcoat with a velvet collar [eg FEAR], a pinstripe double-breasted overcoat [eg SEET, GUNS] and a dark grey double-breasted overcoat [eg WING]. He also had a light brown zipped suede windcheater [HOLE]. Some of his finer coats were made for him by Baldwin's of Jermyn Street [FLEE] and these quality items attracted the attention of M Roland [SELL].

When it was cold, Steed sported a scarf [eg FRIG, MONT, CONS, XMAS, BUTL], while his gloves had other uses apart from keeping his hands warm [CONS]; primarily, they were effective for keeping telltale fingerprints away during a break-in [WHAL, UNDE, DIAL, AUNT, DANG, GUNS, CATC] or even as an excuse to linger [MEDI, ELEP]. He favoured black leather for a while [eg MAND] as well as string-backed [SURF] and later had well-cut items in grey [eg CORR, LACE] and brown [eg EPIC].

For formal occasions, Steed had a sharp-looking dark dinner jacket [eg FRIG, ROCK, ESPR, DIAL, PRIN, RETU, GETA, OVER] with white silk scarf [eg FRIG], a satin waistcoat [ESPR] and a bow tie [eg FRIG, BRIM, PRIN, VENU, DOOR]. As the decade wore on, Steed's tuxedos started to come in various colours such as a dark blue [eg VENU] and a rich red [eg VENU, FALS, BIZA], augmented by pleated shirts [eg OVER]. When going out to dance he had an opera cape with white tie and cane [QUIC], and he also had formal wear appropriate for a Scottish castle, including a kilt which appeared to be of the Macgregor dress tartan [CAST].

Steed was equally well provided for with clothing for relaxing at home or braving foreign lands. He had a light jacket with a dark stripe [DIAM] and out in Jamaica sported a striped blazer [DISP]. Similarly for warmer climes, Steed slipped into a light two-piece linen suit with a striped cummerbund which matched his Panama hat [DISP, REMO]. Again when in Mediterranean mood, he had a short-sleeved smock with a toggle neck [REMO, FROG], a V-neck smock [REMO], a striped top [FROG] or a short-sleeved shirt [FROG]. From climates that were tropical even when not actually in the tropics, Steed had a white linen safari suit [HUNT]. At the other end of the atmospheric spectrum, he braved the cold winds of Scotland aided by a chunky sweater, thick shirt, boots and kagoul [WRIN].

Steed had a loose dark casual jacket [REMO, FROG], a dark sports jacket [ZEBR], a zipped leather suede jacket [ZEBR, INTE], a light two-button jacket [DECA, CLAY], a dark check jacket [MOUS], and a navy blazer with gold stripes which was perfect for punting [DUST]. When at home or relaxing, Steed would sometimes wear a green V-necked tank top with a waist pocket [eg MAUR] and light [eg SCHO, DUST] or dark [eg MIND, PRIN] polo neck sweaters. A dark cardigan protected him from paint when decorating [ROCK] while he also relaxed in a similar V-neck [eg MOUS]. The cardigan became one of his favoured 'lounging' items, including some outrageous examples like one with suede leather panels [eg CYBE] and a silk lined model with patterned fur panels [eg MARK]. From 1963, he also started to wear casual polo shirts with a button collar [eg SECO, CAGE, MIND, PRIN] which later came in green [BREA]. He also had a blue silk smoking jacket [TREA].

After the Summer of Love, the fashion explosion came in 1968 – and Steed attempted to remain 'trendy' in his 40s. He was now wearing striking floral [INVA, GAME] and other casual pattern shirts [CLUE, SPLI, GETA, SPLI, XR40, LEGA], sometimes with neckerchiefs [CYPH, ROTT]. He had more cardigans, now in beige [LOOK, XR40], black with blue stripes [CATC], green [CATC] and brown stripes [CYPH]. He had a short, brown suede jacket [PAND, REQU, OVER] which he usually wore with a beige polo neck [PAND, REQU]. There were also his polo shirts in black [WILD, CATC, LOOK, XR40], a white knitted pullover with a button collar [PAND] and a green pullover [CATC] as well as a black polo neck [CYPH]. With these he would sometimes wear striped trousers [CATC, CYPH].

In 1963, Steed was wearing charcoal grey silk hose [CAGE][91] and took size 9¾ socks [AUNT]. Once, he also resorted to using a stocking as a mask when posing as a criminal [LACE]. Steed's preferred type of footwear was invariably a slightly-antiquated elastic-sided suede Chelsea boot [eg WINT, REMO, MAUR, AUNT, MARK, FEAR, EPIC, MISS, CATC, STAY, FACE, KIL2] which he took in various colours such as grey [KILL] and brown [LOVE] in size 9 [DUST].[92] These were handmade for him [WILD] by Teale of St James and polished like mahogany [CAGE][93], and he joked that his Achilles Heel was rubber-soled shoes [KNOT]. When things got wet, Steed wore Wellington boots [SURF] while danger of electrocution brought out his rubber galoshes [POSI].

From the surveillance films it seems that Steed wore silk pyjamas [DWAR, XMAS], although Macnee's writings suggest that he also sported a Cossack-style night-shirt[94]; Steed also joked about owning some lemon spot pyjamas in 1967 [VENU]. He wore a variety of dressing gowns [DISP, DWAR, BATM, CAGE, XMAS] – some in silk [BATM, CAGE] – which were ideal camouflage for visiting Cathy's hotel bedroom [DISP]. He cringed at the Chinoiserie dragon dressing gown sported by his associate Dr Martin King [MONT].

When in golfing mood, Steed wore a chunky knit cardigan [MEDI] while he had a suede fronted model for riding [MARK] along with a brown hunting jacket [SURF, SURR, DUST, PRIN]. Golf called for plus-fours [HOLE], while rowing brought out a naval greatcoat and sailor's cap [HUNT]. His hunting togs included a trilby, a study coat and leather gloves [OVER].

By the 1970s, Steed favoured a dark grey three-piece suit [eg NEST, RAT, 3HAN, HOST, KIL2,

---

[91] Macnee confirmed that Steed wore silk socks. ...*deadline*, p37.

[92] An unconfirmed report suggests that Steed may have kept a spring-loaded knife in the toe of his shoe. *Diana*, Issue 207, 4 February 1967.

[93] Steed apparently liked to shine his shoes himself. *Diana*, Issue 205, 21 January 1967.

[94] ...*deadline*, p57.

BASE], a light grey three-piece suit with a felt collar and a patterned back to the waistcoat [eg NEST, TARG, TALE, HOST, LION, EMIL], a black three-piece suit [MIDA, KIL2], and a light brown three-piece suit with a felt collar (from which sometimes he just wore the jacket with slacks) [CARD, LAST, TRAP, LION, KIL1, GLAD]. There was also a yellow waistcoat [eg CARD, RARE, ANGE] which he tended to wear around the estate when working with the horses, and a similar green version which he wore less often [RAT, ANGE]. By now, Steed's build meant he needed to wear braces [LION]. The temperature did not seem to bother Steed any more; he failed to remove his jacket and tie when in the tropical domain of Professor Lopez saying that he could take whatever the plants could ('I just think cool') [TARG], nor when having treatment under a sun lamp at a health farm, which he did not find hot enough [ANGE].

At this time, Steed's shirts were generally blue [eg NEST, CAT, GNAW, HOST, KIL2, EMIL] or white [eg LAST, FACE, DIRT, ANGE, LION, EMIL]. His favourite ties included white polka dots on navy blue [eg CARD, EMIL], brown [eg CARD, EMIL] and maroon [LAST]; others came in brown [eg NEST, ANGE], green [DIRT], purple [eg LAST, EMIL] and various patterns [eg MIDA, ANGE, GLAD] while those in silk were silver [NEST], brown [eg MIDA, GLAD], gold [LAST, TARG] and green [CAT, ANGE].

For outdoor wear, Steed now had a brown single-breasted overcoat [NEST], a black overcoat [MIDA] and brown gloves [NEST]. While pursuing his passion for riding, Steed had a checked brown jacket [eg CARD, DIRT] with a dark waistcoat and beige slacks [CARD], On formal occasions, he retained the reliable tuxedo [eg MIDA, DEAD, LION, COMP] and in 1977 also sported a green velvet dinner jacket [HOST, TRAP]. Sometimes he would now wear his medals at formal functions [HOST].[95]

Steed was used to having his laundry taken care of by somebody else [WOND], and hence did not know how to use an automatic washing machine or an electric mangle [ESPR]. Because of this, he accidentally cleaned Cathy's leathers in a washing machine on one occasion [ESPR]. However, when it came to ironing he had a nice 'easy style' which won him commendation from Hubert Hemming of the Butlers and Gentlemen's Gentlemen Association [BUTL].

Choosing fancy dress apparel, Steed fancied himself as a well-dressed gambler from the Wild West for a party on New Year's Eve 1963 [DRES] and attended a similar event in 1967 in an old-fashioned military uniform described as 'Kitchener's Valet' [SUP7].[96] However, his Sidney Carton outfit from *A Tale of Two Cities* was selected for him with a sinister assault on his sanity in mind at Christmas 1964 [XMAS]. He enjoyed dressing as an 18th century dandy to attend the Hellfire Club [BRIM][97], and became the Sheriff of Nottingham to attend a Robin Hood themed rag ball in 1966 [HIST]. While working undercover, Steed felt that a Naval Commander's uniform suited him [ZEBR].

---

95 Such as the retirement party for one Sir James. 'Hypno-Twist'. *The New Avengers Annual*, 1977.

96 Other reports suggest Steed attended similar functions in costume: a Hogmanay party with Sir Jocelyn as a knight in armour. *TV Comic Annual*, 1966; a do at the country estate of Lord Tweezle as 'Sir Lancelot Steed'. *Diana*, Issue 221, 12 May 1967; a party at the 'Lazy J' Western Style Dude Ranch and Holiday Camp as a cowboy. *TV Comic*, Issue 987, 14 November 1970.

97 It is possible that Steed also disguised himself as an Edwardian dandy to attend a party given by Sir Hubert Corringham. 'What's A Ghoul Like You Doing in a Place Like This?', *The Avengers Annual*, 1969, p59.

Steed tended to wear a wristwatch on his left wrist [eg TUNN, COUR, GRAV, BIRD, ANGE, EMIL] and occasionally on his right wrist [DEAD]. Generally, Steed kept his wristwatch in his desk drawer [RETU], and found that it was an excellent object to focus on when resisting brainwashing [WRIN]. For a time in 1965 he wore a Hunter pocket watch left to him by an uncle which played a tune (a little out of key) [DIAL]. He had a chiming pocket watch in 1968 [CYPH] as well as his grandfather's gold Hunter [KEEP] and in 1976 he wore a similar model bequeathed to him by his close friend Mark Clifford [FACE]. In one rare 'trendy' move, Steed once sported a medallion on a chain with his formal wear in 1969 [OVER]. Steed sometimes wore spectacles when undercover [MAUR, INTE, ROME] or dark glasses when in sunny climes [DISP, FROG]. Another accessory – the pocket handkerchief [CATC] – proved useful for wiping away telltale fingerprints during room searches [CLAY].

One of Steed's regular barbers appeared to be a double agent – killed in early 1966 – whom he would drop in to visit for a 'Quick scrape and a hot towel or two' [BUTL]. According to Macnee, Steed also had his hair trimmed at Jeffrey ('Styling for the Hair from 1792') in Jermyn Street.[98] Steed used both electric and cut-throat razors [XMAS], but by late 1964 favoured an electric [XMAS, DOOR]. In 1967, he purchased the latest and most powerful electric motor available. Economical but noisy, it did 5,000 shaves to the gallon, required a 1,000,000 whisker service once a year and had four forward speeds and a reverse [TREA].

In particular, Steed loved hats. He could not resist trying on a naval hat and a top hat at a gentleman's outfitters [QUIC] and took to the peaked brim of a Royal Navy Commander [ZEBR]. But the hat most associated with Steed was a bowler[99], which was seen as suggesting some form of 'off-duty' uniform as with the Brigade of Guards. Steed was often seen wearing such an item as early as 1961 [FRIG, SLIP, BAIT], and from late 1963 it became his headgear of choice [eg MONT, CONC]. By 1964, he found the lure of trying on a bowler hat difficult to resist (witness his visit to H Cleeves [CHAR]), and the item of apparel soon became inextricably linked with him, suiting his manner perfectly. Steed's doffing of his bowler – with such superb economy of movement and elegance of style – vastly impressed Tarquin Ponsonby Fry of SNOB Inc[100] [CORR]. It was this gesture that, for some of his adversaries, summed Steed up [LAST].

In 1962, Steed got his bowlers from Batesons, which was run by Young Master Jack Bateson (who was in his late 40s with seven little trilbys) [DANE]. By 1963, he was shopping at Hemmings and Ford, St James, whose beautifully blocked headgear cost him not a penny under ten guineas [CAGE]. By 1967, it was a well known fact to security personnel that Steed still got his bowlers from St James [STAT], although he was now wearing bowlers that came from Bensons (run by Young Master Arthur Benson, also in his late 40s with seven little trilbys!) [BREA]. By 1977, Steed was getting his bowlers from Herbert Johnson of New Bond Street, London, W1S 1LA[101], a firm established in 1889 which maintains its

---

[98] ...deadline, p11.

[99] The first bowler hat was made for William Coke II – latterly the Earl of Leicester – by James and George Lock of Lock & Co. St James Street London in 1850.

[100] Sociability Nobility Omnipotence Breeding Inc.

[101] In a letter to the Daily Telegraph, Steed's friend Patrick Macnee recalled that the bowlers 'were flat-ironed, curled and fashioned by Herbert Johnson of Old Bond Street.' 'Steed's bowlers', Daily Telegraph, 24 July 1997.

high reputation in the field of millinery to this day [HOST]. In terms of design of his bowler, Steed favoured a curly brim [BARG].

From 1964 onwards, Steed's bowler was usually firmly lined with a light steel crown or a steel brim, making it a potent hidden weapon to have hidden about him; he referred to this as his 'armoured hat' [AUNT].[102] This headgear was highly effectively at knocking out adversaries (and occasionally friends) on many occasions [TOWN, BARG, KNOT, CATC, LEGA, LOVE, TAKE, NEST, BASE] or at least to disarm somebody with a blow to the hand [GLAD]. After use, an occasional quick tap might be needed from Steed to bring his headgear back into perfect shape, removing any tell-tale dents [TOWN].

The bowlers were also effective against firearms, spectacularly so when a man called Poole discharged a pump-action shotgun into the crown of one and was blown back through Steed's French windows [TALE], or when an assailant called Jacobs fired a handgun under similar circumstances, causing a backfire which killed him [XR40]. Against bayonets, the reinforced headgear would simply bend the blade [INTR]. At longer range, it was an effective missile against assailants [GRAV, CLUE, SPLI, HOST, GLAD], or to loosen a larger object to perform the same concussive job [HOST].

One of Steed's metal-lined bowlers contained an extendible aerial and radio set [NEST][103], while another had a secret flap in the crown where Steed could secrete a handgun such as a Walther PPK 7.65mm automatic [HOST]. Steed would also hide other items in the hat band, such as firecrackers [HOST] and could attach accessories such as a miner's lamp when venturing down the Benedict Mine [LIVI]. Steed would also keep his Ministry Priority Pass red card inside the bowler's crown [POSI].

Furthermore, as a hat alone, Steed found his bowler useful when he needed to cover a vicious falcon placed inside his Range Rover by Zarcardi [CAT], to protect the vital hand-print which could identify the double agent The Fox on the roof of a car [EMIL] and to trap an enemy agent and his cohort who had become miniaturised [MISS].[104] According to an unconfirmed report, Steed would also use the adjustment of his bowler as a signal to the watching Emma that he was in trouble.[105] At home, Steed used his bowlers to chip golf balls into when practising [MEDI, ANGE]. While he was often very reluctant to let somebody else take such a vital weapon from him [GAME], he would occasionally let others wear them, such as Katie Miles [LOBS]. Nevertheless, it was a piece of attire which Steed would happily cast aside when enjoying a walk on a summer's day through the Surrey country-side [TALE].

Several of the bowlers were casualties in action over the years. One was peppered with gunshot [ANGE], one was sliced in two by a sharp blade [GAME], a light grey model had its crown ripped by an impact grenade [BIRD], one was crushed during Steed's over-confident

---

102 In the 1998 film *The Avengers*, Steed was shown using a metal bowler hat – and being most angry when one was damaged by poison darts thrown by Sir August de Wynter ('You'll pay for that'). These bowlers were supplied by Patey Ltd of Gowlett Road, Dulwich, London.

103 Also possibly used on other occasions. 'Fangs for the Memory!'. *The New Avengers Annual*, 1977, p11.

104 An unconfirmed report suggests Steed also used his bowler to ward off a toxic red gas. *Diana*, Issue 220, 5 May 1967. Another shows him throwing it like a Frisbee to cut the burning wick on a keg of gunpowder. *TV Comic*, Issue 962, 23 May 1970.

105 Both 'The K Stands for Killers', *The Avengers* (Anglo) and *TV Comic Holiday Special*, June 1966.

demonstration of a pulping press [SURF], another was swapped for a Stetson in a Canadian junkyard [EMIL], a black model had two holes shot in it by Eastern Bloc 'observer' Albert Becker [DOOR], one was punctured by a burning arrow [HIST], one was bleached by a laser beam [VENU] and another was rendered invisible by a strange liquid [GETA]. Steed stepped on one by accident when descending the fireman's pole in Tara's flat, requiring her to perform the world's first ever brim graft to get it back into shape [CLUE]. One which survived through the years was auctioned for £550 at Christies on 18 December 1988, by which time a growing cult had sprung up of admirers who studied Steed's formidable career and wanted to own his personal artefacts.

Aside from the iconic bowler, Steed also wore a Homburg [DOWN] and a dark trilby [FRIG, WINT, COUR, WHAL, FLEE, etc] which, alongside his bowler, was his favoured regular headgear through to late 1963. When in warmer climes such as South America or Aluda, Steed wore a light straw Panama with a striped band [DISP, REMO, SHAD]. Another piece of headgear he sported from 1962 to 1964 was a checked flat cap, which he generally wore when undercover or travelling [INTE, CLAY, DWAR, DEAD] or when in golfing mood [MEDI]. He also had a fur hat which he used when undercover as a native of Iceland [MEDI] and when braving the cold of Scotland [WRIN]. Hats with a Soviet flavour came to him from friendly enemy agents [CONC, CORR]. There were also top hats for hunting [eg SURF, SURR, HOLE, PRIN] with one brown model being sliced open with a sickle [DUST]. Somewhat sturdier was Steed's golfing trilby which was lined with chain mail and thus protected his cranium from a high-velocity golf ball [HOLE].

'Maybe it's the way I hold my umbrella,' replied Steed when asked what sets him apart from the rest [SUP7]. Even the earliest existing surveillance film of Steed from 1961 shows that he was already carrying another trademark item – his knobbly bamboo (or 'whangee') handled umbrella[106], which he took great care to hang up safely before rushing into fisticuffs [FRIG]. During his career, Steed was seldom separated from his umbrella, taking it with him on a break-in to Dr Macombie's surgery [MAND] or when responding to a Red Alert call indicating global crisis [TRAP] – although, like the bowler, he might cast it aside to enjoy a gorgeous day in the country [TALE]. In his 'man about town' persona, he had a jaunty swing in his handling of it, and when explaining the use of this accoutrement to others, he described the brolly motion as being 'sprightly but not eager; eagerness [is] untrustworthy... almost the next worst thing to enthusiasm' [AUNT].

The umbrellas were very finely balanced pieces of craftsmanship, of which J Nathan Winters (expert purveyor of gentlemen's quality goods) commented, 'I don't think you're going to better this model' [CORR]. In the surveillance films, the only manufacturer which Steed was known to use was Bolton and Son, who provided him with their 1963 model with a slightly weighted handle to give perfect balance [CAGE]. From 1963, Steed's umbrella often concealed a swordstick [CORR], although he seldom drew the blade [ROME, HUNT, FOG]. A number of other special devices were fitted into some of Steed's umbrellas, including a miniature camera at the base of the handle (useful for photographing papers on a desk) [CYBE], a knockout gas ejector in the tip [TIME], and an audio recording device

---

[106] The 1998 movie of his life incorrectly had Ralph Fiennes' Steed wielding a swordstick umbrella with a rosewood handle. This was supplied by James Smith & Sons of New Oxford Street. An unfilmed report suggests that Steed would on occasion refer to his brolly as his 'gamp'. *TV Comic*, Issue 725, 6 November 1965.

operated by a switch in the bamboo handle [STAT]. Steed even suggested that one model could possibly be a 'loaded' gun to one of his colleagues [CAT] and brandished it in such a manner when surrounded by a group of nannies [NURS]. These improvements seemed to be something secret which Steed did not necessarily share with his colleagues [STAT]. Occasionally, Steed would even use it for protection against the rain (usually indoors) [SURF, COMP] and prove, as Gambit suspected, that it would always come in handy [COMP].

The brolly was an ideal item for the cautious agent to use when pointing or probing. It was good for ringing doorbells [TOWN, GAME], knocking on doors [DECA], smashing windows [UNDE], attracting the attention of an enemy with a prod [LAST], pushing open a door behind which might lie danger [SPLI] and probing rock or earth which might prove to be a façade [LIVI, BIZA]. When the tip was placed in the back of an assailant, it could also masquerade effectively as a firearm [BIGT], while in desperate combat it could function as a foil to fend off an attacker [CORR] or throttle a man to within an inch of his life [MAND].[107] It was also an effective pinion in a fight [CHAR, SURF][108] and Steed even used it to carry certain items with him [MEDI].[109] 'Accidentally' dropping it, the brolly also allowed Steed to have a crafty look beneath a vehicle when necessary as he moved to pick it up [NURS].

The bamboo handle was an ideal item to use in a scuffle to trip people up [NEST, DEAD, GLAD] or unbalance them [AUNT] while it was also superb to grab an enemy by the neck [CHAR, TOWN, CYPH, SLEE, DIRT] or hand [HUNT, FEAR, VENU]. A swift strike from the handle was another effective disarming manoeuvre [ROME, BIRD, TIGE, CORR]. In a full-blown fight situation, the umbrella as a whole made an effective club which was capable of rendering a man unconscious or winded [CONC, UNDE, BRIM, HIST, PRIN, BIRD, LIVI, LACE, XR40, THIN, GLAD]. The brolly was also an excellent missile which enabled Steed to douse the lights at the Business Efficiency Bureau [FEAR] and to knock Soo Choy's man from the parapet of a multi-storey car park in Windsor before the villain could shoot Gambit [TRAP]. Seldom were Steed's brollies damaged – although the accessory was used against him by a man called Verret who secreted an impact grenade inside its folds so that it would be detonated when the umbrella was opened [BIRD].

Although not seen in the surveillance films, there have been references to other specialised brollies used by Steed. One supposedly contained a mountaineer's scaling ladder made from a light alloy with nylon rope[110] while another apparently concealed a hacksaw blade and collapsible frame.[111] In addition to his usual brolly, Steed was also known to use a walking stick with a carved handle [COUR], a swordstick which resembled

---

[107] Steed apparently also used the metal tip of the umbrella to short-circuit robots. *TV Comic*, Issue 734, 8 January 1966. Another brolly had a knife blade which extended from the tip. *TV Comic Annual*, 1966, p69. Another variant simply had a stiletto point on the end. *The Magnetic Man*, p15, 50.

[108] Further unconfirmed reports suggest that Steed also used it to keep vicious animals at bay. *Diana*, Issue 216, 7 April 1967. When soaked in water, it was a shield to enter a burning building. *Diana*, Issue 204, 14 January 1967. Another saved Steed from losing an arm to an exploding model boat. *Diana*, Issue 212, 11 March 1967. On another occasion, a brolly was used to deal with a tarantula. *The Magnetic Man*, p31. Steed also used his umbrella to burst a plastic sabre-toothed tiger. *TV Comic*, Issue 1013, 15 May 1971.

[109] Another unfilmed incident had Steed secreting the plans of a nuclear reactor in his 'gamp'. *TV Comic*, Issue 725, 6 November 1965.

[110] 'The Hidden Helps', *The Avengers Annual*, Atlas, 1968, p29.

[111] *TV Comic*, Issue 729, 4 December 1965; Issues 753-4, 21-28 May 1966.

a walking stick [JOKE], a cane (for occasions such as hunting or hobbling around his flat with an injured ankle) [JOKE, DUST] and a shooting stick [SURF].

Steed carried items such as a monocular [TOWN], a pen-knife [CHAR], a knife blade [MAUR, MIRR, MDVL], a candle (when testing for heroin) [LOBS], a pocket radio (for the cricket scores) [NEVE], a black notebook of phone numbers [CATC, MORN], a 'park pinger' to remind him to feed 6d into the parking meter [MAUR] and a hip flask [MIND, DUST, KILL, TAKE].[112] It has also been suggested that Steed may have carried a two-way transistor radio on him.[113] He kept his wallet [MORN] and a cigarette case [DISP, PROP, DECA, MAUR, BOX] usually in his right-hand breast pocket and generally had his cigarette lighter [FRIG, BEAR, DECA, ROCK, BOX] in his right hand hip pocket. Sometimes Steed would carry handcuffs [TAKE] – once quite a few pairs [BIZA] – and skeleton keys [SECO, BROK, MEDI, GRAV, ROOM, HOST]. For writing, he had a large red fountain pen [CYPH] and a golden propelling pencil with a crown on top which Tara gave him one Christmas [REQU].

Part of Steed's cover was various cards with his contact details [BEAR, UNDE, BROK, ELEP, MAND, LACE, ROTT, FOG][114], some of which he gave to his friends to use [LOOK] and others of which – such as those for 'Wayne Pennyfeather ffitch' [AUNT], the 'Steed Foundation' [CATC] or a fictitious stockbroker [DWAR] – were fakes. The genuine article was useful for giving out to prospective dates [MAND]. He also carried business cards for others such as Dr Martin King [SELL] and the night-club where Venus Smith might be singing [DECA].

Steed's favourite places to visit in the world were Paris, staying at his suite with roof garden at the George V Hotel [ANGE, KIL1, KIL2], and Scotland [RARE]. He preferred Provence to St Tropez [MORN] and was less than keen on the idea of being in the middle of the Channel in February [OVER]. It seems that Steed had also done his fair share of cycling over the years [BRIE, BARG], rode on a two-seater tandem with Emma [JACK][115] and even had a folding cycle which he took with him to Scotland in April 1976 [NEST]. In 1966, he commented that he used to cycle around the Pendlesham area of Hampshire and knew the B31 [JACK].[116] On one occasion in 1963 he travelled on the back of a motorcycle driven by a biker called Dave, of the Salts gang [MOUS]. In addition to these conventional forms of transport, Steed could also handle a go-kart [DANG] and knew how to fly a balloon [DUST].[117]

---

[112] One unconfirmed report suggested that Steed carried a magnifying glass in his top pocket. *TV Comic*, Issue 730, 11 December 1965.

[113] 'No Jury... No Justice!'. *The Avengers* (Anglo). Another unfilmed case had Emma commenting that Steed always carried a 'radio gadget' on him. *TV Comic*, Issue 726, 13 November 1965. This may be the device which Tara contacted him on in another report. *TV Comic*, Issue 991, 12 December 1970.

[114] The one Steed was using in early 1968 read: 'JOHN STEED, 3 STABLE MEWS, CITY OF LONDON 460-9618' [LACE].

[115] Steed apparently also used a three-seater tandem with Emma and Tara. 'The Golden Game', *Steed and Mrs Peel*, Book Three, p91-92.

[116] Steed apparently borrowed a vicar's bicycle without permission while on one mission in Scotland. *TV Comic*, Issue 879, 19 October 1968. He also cycled around Buckinghamshire on another unfilmed case. *The Gold Bomb*, p87. Another borrowed cycle was one belonging to an ice cream salesman. *TV Comic*, Issue 1024, 31 July 1971. Another report suggests he could ride a unicycle. *TV Comic*, Issue 962, 23 May 1970.

[117] Other reports suggest that Steed could drive a scooter. *TV Comic*, Issue 721, 9 October 1965. He soon mastered how to control a tank on *two* occasions. *TV Comic*, Issue 766, 20 August 1966; *TV*

As Father knew, Steed did not like dimly lit rooms [STAY], and while he felt that Gambit's flat in Central London had style, he had to admit that its modern functionality was not his style [SLEE]. Steed liked things traditional, steeped in 'old English customs' such as calling one's wine the 'cellar' [LIVI], although he simultaneously dismissed some of his traditionalist elders, such as the academic Dr Ashe at St Luke's, as being like a 'late Victorian tea cosy' [EGGS].

Steed described himself as a 'sportsman' [LIVI], and indeed the surveillance films show that he was happy to turn his hand to many pastimes... at least until they bored him and he moved on, often having acquired all the paraphernalia which would reside unused in his rooms. From his various comments, it seems that Steed maintained his interest in cricket alongside his dangerous assignments, making good use of the Duke's coaching and his time on the pitch at Lydeard, St Jude's and university. Never taking the sport up professionally after his dalliance with the Somerset team in his post-war doldrums, he was not the Steed who used to play for Worcestershire [DISP]. He continued to enjoy the intelligent flow of cricket over and above other sports like baseball and basketball [DEAD]. Proficient at batting and bowling, Steed was an all-rounder [PRIN]. He bowled to middle and leg [DANG, PRIN] while as a batsman, he felt technique was all in the grip [BARG] and could deliver a straight drive to mid-on [BARG]. When wicket keeping, he could get as low as a forced leg-before-wicket [TRAP]. He had played in Rawpindi in Pakistan [PRIN] and at Lords (with Major 'B' who did not seem to up to Steed's standards) [WHO?]. The sight of a cricket bat would often cause him to wield it for a bit of practice out of season [FOG].

By 1977, Steed was still part of a cricket club and knew the captain [DEAD] as well as playing with Mark Clifford at the 'Old School' match (presumably Lydeard) up to Mark's death in 1976 [FACE]. Although he often just watched cricket, he still enjoyed the odd workout at the stumps with Gambit, whom he felt had a weird delivery [DEAD]. And, whether home or abroad, Steed would always attempt to check on the cricket scores in the paper [REMO, SLEE] or on his pocket radio [NEVE].[118]

When out in the country, Steed liked to indulge in a little fishing [ROME, DRES, CAST, AUNT, POSI, OVER] and favoured a dry fly [DRES]. Although he would sometimes claim that this was not one of his pursuits [DIAL], even Steed's Canadian colleagues knew it was a sport he indulged in [GLAD]. Leasing a stretch of water on the famed River Test in Hampshire [POSI] for his own fishing, Steed cast for trout [DRES] and used a flaming kestrel fly [POSI] while also commenting that he usually needed luck with his bent pin and string fishing [CAST]. When on the coast, he also knew the best time to catch deep sea bass [NEST].[119]

Comic, Issue 903, 5 April 1969. He quickly determined how to drive a hovercraft. *TV Comic*, Issue 1042, 4 December 1971. Under an unlikely set of circumstances, he also drove a model fire engine. *TV Comic*, Issue 889, 28 December 1968.

[118] An unconfirmed report suggests that on one occasion Purdey believed that Steed was once 'either worried or very, VERY ill. Do you know he missed the Test match at Lords?' 'The Sleeping Dragon'. *Daily Mirror*, 13 October 1976, p21.

[119] Apparently Steed fished in Scotland and cast for Pike in Ireland several times. 'Steed's 'Holiday'', *The Avengers Annual*, 1967, p70. He also angled in the Norfolk Broads. *Diana*, Issue 209, 18 February 1967. Steed did some fishing with a friend's rod. *TV Comic*, Issue 991, 12 December 1970. He allegedly commented to Emma once 'I should have chosen the sea as a career, Mrs Peel'. *Diana*, Issue 209, 18 February 1967.

Alongside fishing, Steed's associates also knew that he dabbled in hunting [TIGE, GLAD], a pastime stretching back to his days stalking deer at Balwhinnie Castle. In 1965, Steed owned a Weatherby's shotgun with a walnut stock [DUST] and very much admired a double-barrelled shotgun belonging to Tara's uncle [OVER]. He seldom used shotguns in the course of his assignments – a rare example being when he looked for the apparently indestructible man who was roaming the woodlands near the Neoteric Research Unit [NEVE]. As with a handgun or rifle, he was yet again a first class shot [VENU] who indulged in such sport periodically [DRES, SUP7, OVER] including his trips to visit Bill Bassett [OVER], possibly some grouse shoots [BIRD, KILL], and presumably the occasion when he was at the wrong end of a charging rhino [TRAP]. In 1967 he recalled how exciting the hunt for 'big game' could be [TIGE]. He was very confident about his abilities in this area, and happy to bet 100 guineas with a ruthless fellow called Fenton Grenville that he would get the first kill of the day [OVER]. To keep his hand in between shoots, Steed would practice firing at beer cans propelled into the air [QUIC] or competing with friends like Gambit or Colonel Tomson at clay pigeon shooting [FACE, ANGE]. Steed condemned Gambit's use of a pump-action shotgun on these occasions, observing that it was 'not a gentleman's gun' [FACE].

Apparently the owner of a yacht in 1968 [MORN], Steed swam [REMO, BASE], was an experienced aqualung diver [CAST, AUNT, STAY][120], and by 1963 was certainly aware of the dangers of Caisson Disease (or decompression illness) [FROG]. It is also possible that he canoed [AUNT] and claimed to be a 'a rowing man' [FOG].

After his training on the St Jude's Tiger Moth and stunts in the Hamelin training plane, Steed had acquired a pilot's licence. Although by 1962 he was doing little flying [COUR], he was still familiar with the use of auto-pilot and fuel consumption [SUP7]. He was expert enough for discussions with Mr Hughes of the Aeronautical Research College, knowing about the danger of fuel bursting on hot engines, the melting point of key aluminium parts, and identifying a rudder control coupling [COUR]. Steed flew a lightweight plane with Tara around 1968 [KEEP].[121] However, he had never handled anything as big as the craft used to trap himself and his friends by Soo Choy in 1977 [TRAP] which was presumably bigger than the Canada Jet-Ways flight he piloted in 1962 [COUR]. It also appears that Steed could possibly pilot a helicopter [DIRT] and in 1976 he still kept aviators maps at his home [TALE].

Of course, Steed's first love had always been the equestrian world and he pursued this with vigour in adulthood [DRES, MOUS, TROJ, MARK, TWOS, DUST][122] – even if he was a little tall in the saddle [DUST]. Horsemanship led to a passion for polo in late 1963.[123] Steed purchased a pair of polo ponies which 'a very important person' was also trying to acquire; he then bought a mallet and received a polo helmet from Lady Cynthia Bellamy [BATM]. However, things seemed to go wrong over the next few months. The two ponies took a fancy to each other and lost all interest in the competition they were trained for [MEDI]. It seems that Steed persevered with the sport for a while, or at least kept track of the 1963-

---

[120] It is possible that Steed also went scuba diving on other assignments. *TV Comic*, Issue 747, 9 April 1966; Issue 952, 14 March 1970; 'Come on In – The Water's Deadly', *The Avengers Annual*, 1969, p48.

[121] Steed may also previously have flown a glider with Emma. *TV Comic*, Issue 738, 5 February 1966.

[122] See also other reports. eg *TV Comic*, Issue 982, 10 October 1970; Issue 1036, 23 October 1971.

[123] One unconfirmed report suggests that Steed had already become adept at polo, and that at his Westminster Mews flat was the Hyderabad All-India Polo Cup. *The Avengers* (Enefer), p63.

64 season [WOND]. A saddle was one of the items to be found at his Westminster Mews flat [DRES] and in 1964 he was a member of a riding club where – so he claimed while under-cover – he hired his polo ponies [MARK]. Even in 1965 he commented that he played polo 'when I can' [HUNT]. In early 1964, Steed received a race horse named Sebastian II from a grateful Sultan. He was initially delighted by the acquisition of the four-year-old until Cathy pointed out that Sebastian II's teeth told a different story about his age... [TROJ]. By 1968, Steed commented that he preferred Palominos to Arab ponies [MORN].

After moving out to the country in the 1970s, Steed indulged his passion for breeding horses in the stables at the large estate. Three fillies in particular were rosette winners, whose pictures he proudly displayed in his lounge. One of these was beautiful, faithful and reliable and went through some tricky situations with Steed. The second was a fantastic, very spirited creature which – unfortunately – he had to take the whip to sometimes. The third[124] liked her oats too much and Steed heard that the Arab prince he sold her to even-tually had to shoot her [CARD]. According to comments made by Purdey, Steed was prob-ably also taking part in steeple-chasing by now [NEST]. Out in the countryside, the grounds were large enough for Steed to enjoy a canter with colleagues like Gambit (who seemed equally skilled in the saddle) [TARG] or any of his numerous new lady friends [CARD, TRAP]. He was now attending hunt balls, along with friends like Joanna [CARD] and saw a horse as the perfect gift for a special lady like Laura who shared his passions [LAST]. Other female visitors like Helga would help him with the grooming [RAT]. Steed's skill with horses extended to taking the reins of a horse and trap [XMAS] or guiding a Hansom cab through the streets of London [FOG].

'I'm a gambler from way back,' claimed Steed in 1963 [WHAL]. In the 1950s and early 1960s, Steed often liked to indulge in betting and his internal 1963 report noted he used the 'best bookmaker'.[125] His playing the odds included losing his shirt on Revenue Girl in the St Michael Stakes in 1951 [TROJ], gambling on the greyhounds at White City [ROOT], asking a parrot for a tip for the Derby in 1961 [FRIG], talking about racing tips at Kempton [FLEE], losing £5 on Transfer Supervisor at Crediton when it failed to even start [TROJ], not wanting to miss 'the 3.30' [LOBS] and taking an interest in hearing the racing results on the car radio [RAT]. This behaviour was useful for undercover work; a comment that he had to phone his bookie gave him an excuse to contact his colleagues [ROOT, FLEE]. However, it seemed to be the gambling which excited Steed – sometimes he actually took little interest in seeing the animals perform [TROJ]. He enjoyed playing at the casino on a visit to Deauville [NUTS], and gambled on boxing bouts at the ring run by Sam 'Pancho' Driver [WHAL].

Another hobby which Steed seemed to take up after his disappointing dabble in polo was golf [MEDI, MARK, HOLE, NEST, ANGE], starting off by chipping practice balls around his flat with a handicap of 24 [MEDI]. When the mood took him, he would stand on a footstool to drive off the table [MARK] or chip balls into his bowler hat if he was on form [MEDI, ANGE] or Cathy's cup of tea if he wasn't [MEDI]. By 1965, he commented that his grasp of the sport had been 'good at Glen Eagles, fair to middling at Pebble Beach' [HOLE]. At times his attention to detail was a little too scientific, employing gadgets to check the wind and the position of the sun before playing his shot [HOLE]. Normally playing a Number 3 ball (which he kept under his hat) he was actually very skilled at putting, while his drive was

---

[124] Apparently called Connemara Princess. *House of Cards*, p123.

[125] *The Complete Avengers*, p59.

accurate enough to down a fleeing man [HOLE]. Steed also appeared to be the pioneer of the rather bizarre game of 'invisible golf' which was much harder to master than normal golf and demanded enormous concentration [OVER]. Steed's 1963 dossier made reference to him playing croquet, a fact which seemed to be supported in the surveillance film about his internment at Department S [NOON].[126] He also knew how to play boules [LION]. As a spectator, he would occasionally go to watch stock car racing (even in a thunderstorm) [SECO] and probably first became aware of Zoltan the Terrible when seeing him losing at another wrestling match [LEGA].

On one occasion when he floored a lady called Davinia Todd, Steed was reusing skills from the game he had loved in his schooldays and explained to her that he had been a Wing Three-Quarter [MIND]. Although he still took a rugby ball on holiday [AUNT] there was little evidence of him actually playing. Coached in childhood by Algy, Steed played the occasional game of tennis [BEHI] and was known to take his rackets on vacation [AUNT, STAY]. When distracted, he was a poor shot with a bow and arrow [MIND] although when concentrating his aim was true [HIST]. The fact that boxing gloves were amidst his holidaying equipment in 1965 suggest that this was another noble art which he still practised [AUNT]. Steed owned a set of skis which were stacked in the back room at Stable Mews [WHO?] and went on holiday with him [STAY]; he also owned snowshoes [NEST].

When it came to indoor sports, Steed played dominoes [ZEBR], darts [ZEBR, MIND][127], 'pick a stick' [HOLE], tiddly-winks [HOLE], draughts [MISS] (sometimes with himself when killing time [BIRD]), ping pong (having a table at Stable Mews) [LOOK] and was a demon at Ludo [REQU].[128] In 1968, Steed even devised his own very complex game Steedopoly [GAME].[129] Apparently taught by his grand master uncle [REQU], Steed played chess [CONC, ELEP, LOBS, ROOM, CYPH, KEEP] to a decent level; he could recognise situations such as a 'Scotch Gambit' [LOBS] and work out strategies well ahead, while relying too much on his knight [KEEP]. He was able to beat Zalenko [CONC] and Arcos [KEEP] but usually lost when playing Cathy [CONC, ELEP] and was also defeated by Miss Miranda Loxton [REQU].[130] He was unfortunately a 'bad loser' [OVER].

'A proficiency at snooker is another sign of a mis-spent youth,' Steed explained in 1977 [LAST]. While claiming that he was 'extremely rusty' at the game in 1962 [ZEBR] it was a pastime which Steed enjoyed turning his hand to [ZEBR, CLUE, BIZA, LAST, 3HAN], later having a billiards room at his country home [LAST, 3HAN]. It was also a technique which he used on a cannon shot with golf balls to avoid an explosive fate at Craigleigh Golf Club

---

[126] An unfilmed report suggests Steed played croquet at Mother's. *TV Comic*, Issue 1070, 17 June 1972.

[127] Steed also possibly played this at home at Stable Mews. 'The Golden Game'. *Steed and Mrs Peel*, Book Two, p51.

[128] Steed was probably also familiar with the pub game crown and anchor and was reasonably good at jackstraws. 'The Golden Game'. *Steed and Mrs Peel*, Book One, p40; Book Two, p67-68.

[129] Amongst the many diverse rules of the game... a player landing on a black square is paid a pound by their opponent on the first round, and again when landing on a red square on the second round; when a '5' is thrown the player moves back to the start unless they threw a '4' the previous time; there was a forfeit to pay which involved missing six shakes; and if a '6' was shaken the player had to pay their opponent a pound.

[130] Steed was seen playing chess against Dr Emma Peel in *The Avengers* in 1998 – and was shown losing to her.

[HOLE]. Steed was also known to raise a cue for bar billiards [SCHO].

Gambit, quite rightly, did not trust Steed at cards [TALE]. Steed had an understated talent in this area [SNOW, LACE, KEEP] and played bridge (which he did not understand the mathematics of and claimed he 'sprained a tendon' playing it) [MARK, JOKE, POSI, OVER], cherme [WOND], bezique [WOND] and baccarat (which he once lost 800 marks on – on expenses) [WOND, CHAR]. When alone, Steed enjoyed a game of solitaire [JOKE], was still skilful at cribbage after his tuition back at Vole [FALS] and played a rather bizarre version of snap [HUNT]. Although he claimed to be a novice at solo, he shuffled the cards like an expert [TALE]. He could build an amazing card tower [THAT], did a bit of basic conjuring [DANE] and performed card tricks [JOKE, LOOK].

In addition to playing the piano [VENU], Steed could make a scratchy attempt at playing a violin while thinking in a tribute to fictional sleuth Sherlock Holmes [CLUE, NEST] and on another occasion was walking around with a guitar which he had acquired [FRIG]. He could not play the tuba [TAKE] but could pick out JS Bach's famous *Toccata and Fugue in D minor* on the 1970s gadget fad, the stylophone, with the aid of a device which told him the numbers to slide the metal probe onto [LAST]. When examining a violin, he betrayed his ignorance when decreeing it was unmistakably made by a pupil of 'Stradivarius' (ie Antonio Stradivari) when the instrument's label revealed it as the product of the East Indian Plywood and Timber Box Company [TAKE].

Steed was far happier listening to music than playing it. He was very fond of the clarinet [ROTT] and preferred the popular American concert pianist Van Cliburn in his younger vein for his renditions of 19th century French composer Frédéric Chopin [CONC]. Steed's knowledge of classical music recordings was astounding. He knew that Scorofino's *Concerto for Percussion and Woodwind* was conducted by Hemmplehoffer who has a baton like a sabre and that it was recorded at the Deutsche Records Studio in Hamburg where there is a distinctive resonance to anything recorded before 1959. He also knew that Hans Rhiner used ivory drumsticks whereas his brother Fritz Rhiner used whale drumsticks [OVER]. Steed enjoyed putting this knowledge to use at trivial games such as identifying music recordings [OVER].[131]

'You've got a voice like a saw,' Cathy once remarked to Steed [HAND], who was not known for his singing, but could bellow out renditions of 'Green Grow the Rushes-O' and 'Oranges and Lemons' amongst others [XMAS].[132] He would whistle 'Colonel Bogey' (a composition by military bandmaster Lt FJ Ricketts, published under his pseudonym 'Kenneth Alford') which had become a tune popularised in the 1957 film *The Bridge on the River Kwai* [NEST].

Despite his ballroom dance classes at St Jude's, Steed seemed to be an increasingly reluctant dancer in the 1960s [MONT, ROCK, BOX, SCHO, MOUS, XMAS] although he could possibly do the fox-trot [CORR].[133] Generally, a quick jig was simply a means for Steed to

---

[131] Other reports suggest that Steed enjoyed listening to a recording of JS Bach's 1721 *Brandenberg Concerto – The Floating Game*, p44 – and to the work of Claude Debussy – *House of Cards*, p122.

[132] When feeling 'chirpy' at the coast, Steed would sing 'Oh I Do Like To Be Beside The Seaside'. *TV Comic*, Issue 1023, 24 July 1971.

[133] An unconfirmed report noted Steed commenting that he pulled a thigh muscle executing a sedate waltz on VJ night in 1945. *The Laugh was on Lazarus*, p125. He could also do a gavotte. *TV Comic*, Issue 934, 8 November 1969.

get close to a woman whom he either fancied or needed to keep close to [MONT, ROCK]; he did however take to the floor at a Student Rag Week [SCHO] and at Christmas [XMAS]. He also performed a Scottish crossed-sword dance, commenting that he was once the 'junior all-England amateur hopscotch champion' [CAST].

Steed seemed to enjoy celebrations and parties [MAUR, DRES, PRIN, OBSE] some of which were apparently quite riotous [MAUR, DRES]. Other hobbies for Steed included tracing his family tree in the late 1960s [REQU] plus a bit of ventriloquism [SUCC]. He seemed to do little gardening due to the restriction of his London flats, but did keep an orchid in 1961 [BAIT] and a cactus in 1965 [SURR]. He also briefly dabbled with yoga to improve his concentration by watching daffodils and balancing two wine glasses on his forehead [ELEP].

Although he may have collected stamps in his childhood, he could not believe that true philatelists would pay £1,000 for such tiny items at auctions. In December 1962, he ended up with the stamp collection of the late Major Wilde which Cathy accidentally bid £50 for [MAUR].[134] Mother knew that Steed was a keen 'student of crime' and so knew all about the Gaslight Ghoul killings of 1888 [FOG]. Similarly, Steed was familiar with terms like 'Omerta', part of the Mafia conspiracy of silence [CONS].

Steed's childhood war games were also something which he still practised from time to time [REQU, DIRT] and he maintained his collection of model soldiers at both Stable Mews and his country house[135]; one of his prize pieces was the only 95th rifleman in existence, while he was also proud of a French lancer complete down to his leather brandy pouch, and he still used the pieces to re-enact battles[136] [DIRT].

The fondness of models of all scales probably stemmed from Steed's childhood. He made a model ship with Major Carson at his flat [TWOS] and apparently had a train set [CAT]. A model Spitfire intended for his nephew's tenth birthday gave him some problems following the instructions for three years [LEGA], but his crowning achievement was a full-scale rocket which he assembled himself in his 'own back yard'. This item was very expensive, but it was something Steed had always wanted and even came with its own launch gantry – along with a very detailed booklet. Judging by Steed's comments, this was some sort of 'part work' since he did not have the circuitry to bring the rocket down at the time when Tara inadvertently launched it skywards in 1969 [BIZA].

Watching television was not one of Steed's major pastimes. In 1962, he would watch discussion shows such as *The Man and the Place* [BEAR]. From September 1968, Steed enjoyed watching the American sketch show *Rowan and Martin's Laugh-In* on BBC2 – notably the 'Sock it to me' catch-phrase of British actress Judy Carne [MORN]. When he wanted something intellectually stimulating, morally uplifting and with humour, he sought out a party political broadcast [NEVE].

Steed claimed to be a 'true patron' of the National Gallery, and the revered establishment was happy enough to loan him the 1805 oil painting *Dona Isabel de Porcel* by Francisco de Goya as part of a scheme to rescue Emma in 1965 [AUNT]. He could recog-

---

[134] Another unfilmed report suggests that Steed may have known about rare coins, being able to recognise an octadrachm from Egypt, 3rd century. *The Afrit Affair*, p29.

[135] Steed was well known as a collector of model soldiers around late 1969. *TV Comic*, Issue 942, 3 January 1970.

[136] An alternate report suggests the battles included Edge Hill and Waterloo. *Fighting Men*, p47.

nise a miniature by the American painter John Singer Sargent [CAGE], the work of 'Gibson' (presumably Richard Gibson) who never used down-strokes on a Thursday [AUNT], and used his skill to test the knowledge of Fenton Grenville by asking him about the 1877 painting *La Premiere Sortie* (*At the Theatre*) and attributing it to French impressionist Claude Monet rather than Pierre August Renoir from the same school [OVER]. When it came to his own creative talents, Steed could at least produce rough sketches of anything from a fine meal [WING] to an oriental face [STAY], and one unconfirmed report suggests that he painted while staying with friends in Cornwall.[137] When it came to sculpture, he thought that the bronze 'A portrait of the artist as a young man' was a monstrosity [RETU].

Steed's continued love of the theatre seemed to have continued from his school days and he attempted to see live entertainment on a regular basis, recalling actor Stewart Kirby's stirring performance of *Hamlet* [EPIC].[138] Sometimes he was frustrated in that the shows he wanted to see were sold out for up to three months [BAIT]. Steed would go out to see French musicals [DOOR] and the opera [LOOK, NOON] but rarely the ballet [WILD, RARE] which he generally went to see to gaze at the ballerinas [RARE] – although he did once make reference to Vaslaw Nijinsky [TAKE].

Steed dabbled in photography himself but had little interest in the pictures taken by others unless they were work related [DANE]. He developed his own photographs [ROME, JACK, VENU, HOST] and had a patent do-it-yourself portable darkroom (which consisted of a black bag that he stuck his head inside) [JACK]. He claimed to have shot a bull elephant using f8 at five 100ths of a second [HUNT] while he also talked of another snapshot which he took at a distance of 80 yards [NOON].

While on an assignment, the volumes which Steed would consult for research included *The World's Rare Stamps* [MAUR], the *Boys' Book of Astronomy* [DWAR][139], the *Encyclopaedia Britannica* [WHAL], *Visual Optics* [SECO], the *Handbook of Ophthalmic Surgery* [SECO], *Venus – Our Sister Planet* by Venus Browne [VENU], *Common Disorders in Timber* [ROTT] and he was able to read the paperback Western *The Tale of the Big Y* twice in one day [TALE]. He tended to have books sent on subjects he needed to learn in a hurry, and when requesting books on astronomy was accidentally sent *Instant Astrology And What The Stars Foretell* by mistake (which he still believed he would read) [DWAR]. *Brush Up Your Judo* proved an effective refresher in unarmed combat for him in 1968 [INVA]. In 1963, Steed had a bad habit of not putting books back when he had finished with them, but just dropping them on the floor [SECO]. The periodicals he consulted included *Form* [CLAY] and *Battalion News* [ESPR], plus the House of Commons records collated in *Weekly Hansard* – notably No 601, 27 July – 2nd August 1963 [SECO].

For leisure, Steed's reading included *Great Disappearing Acts* [TOWN], *The Ventriloquist* [SUCC] and *Hypnosis – It's* [sic] *Theory and Practice* [CYPH] and the work of French novelist Marcel Proust (which was so overdue from the library that he owed £2.14.6) [WRIN]. One particular form of reading material which Steed was very fond of was the stories of Tintin, the intrepid young Belgian reporter who featured in comic strips

---

[137] 'A Brush With Disaster', *The Avengers Annual*, 1967, p89.

[138] Steed was apparently in the third row of the stalls for Margaret Allington's first night around 1963. *The Avengers* (Enefer), p8.

[139] Steed did apparently actually learn some basics of some subjects. In 1966 he was still aware of galaxies such as Alpha Centauri. *TV Comic*, Issue 736, 22 January 1966.

written and drawn by 'Hergé' (the pen-name for Georges Remi); he referred to Tintin as a 'very bright little fellow' [SHAD] and enjoyed the oaths uttered by Tintin's colleague Captain Haddock such as 'blistering barnacles' [OUTS]. Amongst the Tintin adventures in Steed's collection were English editions of *Tintin in Tibet* (1958's *Tintin Au Tibet*) [SHAD] and *The Secret of the Unicorn* (1942's *Le Secret De La Licorne*) [OUTS], while he devoured 1934's *Le Lotus Bleu* (*The Blue Lotus*) [LOOK] and 1939's *Le Pays de l'Or Noir* (*Land of Black Gold*) [FLEE] in their original French (since at the time neither title was available as an English translation). He also read Emma's article in the June 1967 issue of *Bridge Player's International Guide* – but didn't understand it [JOKE]. He did not seem to keep up with publications related to his profession [ROOM].

Steed usually had a newspaper delivered [STAY] and enjoyed doing the crossword when he got the chance [CYBE]. The newspapers he read included the *Financial Times*[140] [MEDI], the *Daily Mail* (at his flat) [PRIN, WING], *The Times*[141] (both at his home [BIRD, BREA, MIDA] and while in a waiting room [CORR]), the *Daily Clarion* [STAT], the *Daily Express* [OBSE], possibly the *Sunday Times* [MIDA] and the *Guardian* [KIL1].

Shortly after meeting Steed, Baron Von Curt quickly voiced his feeling that Steed was a man who could look after himself [KEEP] and junior agent Lady Diana Forbes-Blakeney soon reckoned there was little that she could teach Steed when partnered with him on a temporary basis [KILL]. People like Joshua Rudge found Steed's approach to be 'over-dramatising' or 'hysterical' [SUCC] and Steed himself admitted to Tara that he had an 'overdeveloped sense of the dramatic' [LEGA]. This sense of the dramatic would at times display itself when Steed – aware of the surveillance camera from the Department covering his every move – would deliver asides to the 'audience', such as his observation that Purdey and Gambit were 'irreplaceable' [FACE]. It is odd moments of direct intimacy like this which give the viewer of the films the most direct bond to the true psyche of John Steed[142] – the man who took such incredible pride in his work [LEGA] and who was called 'a professional' by friends and colleagues [CLAY].

This was the man who would now face some of the strangest British security cases in the 1960s and 1970s.

---

[140] The cinematic Steed also read this in the 1998 movie *The Avengers*.

[141] Steed's 1963 profile notes that he 'reads the Royal Edition of *The Times*'. *The Complete Avengers*, p59; *The Avengers* (Enefer), p83. It has been suggested that Steed believed *The Times* was 'sacred to an Englishman'. *The Eagle's Nest*, p128.

[142] One theory which has been put forward concerns the often comical sequences appended to many of the surveillance films from late 1964 to early 1969. These may have been specially staged little events between the theatrical Steed and the surveillance teams, and then spliced into the full surveillance films by the Department editors as some form of light relief at the conclusion of a dangerous assignment.

JOHN STEED
PAGING DR KEEL

Late 1960 is the point at which the biographer can really get to grips with Steed, aided by the surviving surveillance tapes, the files of paperwork and transcripts, and numerous internal records about him. By now, Steed was starting to divide his time between international assignments and undercover work fighting crime back in England – particularly in London. On home turf, he had easily created a distinctive persona which made him highly recognisable in society and in the City. Cathy Gale was to describe this version of Steed as 'a man about town', noting that he 'seems to have lots of money and does precious little for it' [CAGE]; this was a textbook description from Steed's 1963 Department dossier which outlined him as a '"man about town" with a private income.'[1]

Steed himself outlined his daytime occupation as a 'gentleman of leisure... Ride, shoot a little, cast a creditable dry fly' [DRES]. According to the Department, this persona was 'suave, witty, debonair; foppish even'[2], the perfect front to disarm opponents in the manner of Baroness Orczy's fictional hero Sir Percy Blakeney, better known as the daring philanthropic agent the Scarlet Pimpernel. Steed's true status as an 'undercover man' was confirmed by the rival security chief DISCO[3] [NUTS] and Steed himself agreed that he was a 'sort of agent' [ROME]. Obliquely, family friends knew that Steed had become a 'Whitehall Man' [SECO]. 'Thoroughly professional and efficient undercover man'[4] was the Department's 1963 appraisal of him, emphasising that he was *dedicated, ruthless* [and] *unscrupulous.*'[5]

One Departmental document on Steed assembled in February 1961 included the note 'He has owned a Great Dane (now dead).'[6] However, within a few weeks of this memo being compiled, Steed had a new pet, a Great Dane bitch of around 18 months called Puppy [ROSE], whom he would ask his new associate Dr David Keel to walk on occasion when he was busy [ROSE]. In October 1962, Steed made comments about a previous Great Dane of

---

[1] *The Complete Avengers*, p59.

[2] *The Complete Avengers*, p59.

[3] Director Intelligence Service and Combined Operations.

[4] *The Complete Avengers*, p59.

[5] *The Complete Avengers*, p59. Their emphasis.

[6] *The Complete Avengers*, p15.

his who was 'a racer', and that his association with her had made him fond of the breed [DANE].

Apparently by now Steed had acquired a distinguished form of transport. 'He has a Rolls-Royce'[7] noted Steed's Department dossier in February 1961, although there is little further information on this vehicle – and whether it was the one he was using in 1962 [BEAR], in an unfilmed incident in 1963[8], or any of those he drove in 1968 and 1969, is unclear. On one occasion in early 1961, Dr David Keel was amused to find Steed using a beaten up old banger which he referred to as his 'runabout' when following a cipher clerk called Felgate [FEED]. Steed's passion for cars meant that he knew all manner of trivia, from the technical specification of an eight cylinder Rolls-Royce [FEAR] to how eggs could be used to plug holes in a radiator [EMIL].

As he admitted himself [POSI], Steed was quite a driver – and as Emma Peel would later comment he was the most able person she knew behind a wheel, after herself [DOOR]; his driving was also admired by Penny Playne who navigated for him on a car rally treasure hunt in August 1967 [TREA]. When made to believe that he had killed a 25-year-old woman with drunken driving in 1961, he was sure this could not be the case [DIAM]; Steed always avoided an extra drink when he was driving [SLEE]. While he did not always wear his seat belt, he did take care to apply it when accelerating rapidly [HOST].

Over the years, Steed's skill in handling a vehicle was often tested as he sped along narrow coastal roads above a quarry[9] [LION] or through winding French country lanes [KIL2]. In desperate situations, he was not above using a car as a weapon to drive at his adversaries [KEEP]. When necessary, Steed could negotiate spiked blocks thrown into the roadway [TREA], swerve a car smoothly off a road into cover [INVA], lose a trained tail [HOST], block another vehicle to stop it passing [TREA], swerve to avoid a dog [HUNT] and knew how to evade a roadblock [EMIL] or an ambush [KIL1, KIL2]. Steed was even able to keep control of a car when being attacked by a window cleaner's ladder [CYPH], by a falcon (performing the slick manoeuvre of driving into the darkness of a removal van) [CAT], or when infected by curare [TARG]. Nor was taking control of a car from a dying man while in motion a problem for him [ANGE]. However, by the 1970s, Steed was prone to being distracted by his passengers [RAT], driving on the wrong side of the road when abroad [KIL1] and sometimes his handling of a vehicle was not been what it was a decade earlier [EMIL].

Based in London, one of Steed's first regular associations after his periodic assignments with Cathy Gale ended – because she had moved to Africa with her husband during the 1950s – was with a general practitioner called Dr David Keel. Their working relationship – chronicled in the earliest surviving surveillance films – appeared to begin shortly before Christmas 1960, weeks after John Kennedy had scraped in as the new President of the USA. The partnership was the result of one of Steed's home turf assignments to catch a supplier of heroin operating in London. With his undercover skills, Steed was soon well in with Charlie, Spicer and the other gang members. A struck-off medic called Dr Treading was also implicated, but when Steed visited his flat he found the man dead. On this occasion he also encountered Keel, who was investigating Treading himself in an attempt to

---

[7] *The Complete Avengers*, p15.

[8] 'Epidemic of Terror', *Look Westward/The Viewer*, 14 September 1963.

[9] Apparently Delabole Quarry in Cornwall.

find out who had shot his fiancée, Peggy Stevens, three days earlier [SNOW].

Steed quickly got the background on Keel and knew he had been working with the police.[10] Entering Keel's living room via a window, he waited for the doctor to return home and – in his cautious and mysterious way – played upon Keel's desire for justice for Peggy to ensure his co-operation in further surveillance. What Steed wanted Keel to do was pretend that he was tired of his everyday medical practice, and now quickly wanted to make a lot of money pushing drugs so that he could retire to the Continent [SNOW].

Soon realising that he could play on the doctor's incredible compassion, Steed kept in touch with Keel by phone, instructing the GP to tell the gang that he wanted to pull out of the operation after he had received his first delivery. Now Keel would be a target for Spicer, Peggy's killer. Steed carefully primed Charlie and the gang to whisk Keel away in a car and have him killed at the docks. Superintendent Wilson of the police was then tipped off and was on the scene when Keel confronted the gang – only to see them escape after one of them was shot by an unknown gunman [SNOW].

While investigating two gangs of protection racketeers run by rivals Ronnie Vance and Nick Mason, Steed went undercover at a racecourse, supposedly working for Mason. Learning that Mason was to hire Spicer to deal with Vance, Steed realised that he again needed Keel's help. Having his associate Lila lure Keel to a pub called The House of the Rising Sun, Steed finally introduced himself properly to the GP as a 'kind of civil servant'. This time Steed was more trusting, explaining how Spicer was back in London and how he had infiltrated Mason's gang. To control the situation fully and bring all to justice, he needed Keel in Vance's gang – and saw just such an opportunity by having Keel administer to 'Pretty Boy', Vance's younger brother, whose face had been razored by Mason. Again tipping off Wilson, Steed had the pub raided to make it seem as if Keel was a heroin dealer and thus attract Vance's attention [BOOK].

Soon, both Mason and Vance realised that Steed was manipulating them and hired Spicer to kill him. Steed and Keel set a trap at The House of the Rising Sun where they extracted a confession from the hit-man on behalf of Wilson. With all the gang members named, Steed commented to Keel that his unspecified 'colleagues' could use the doctor again: 'Crime is a disease. Work with us and you can probe and examine it – perhaps understand it... We'll only call on you when you're needed – really needed.' With a hollow promise from Steed that his practice would not suffer, Keel agreed – unaware of how he was to be used in the coming months [BOOK]. Steed would call upon Keel when he needed backup [SNOW, FRIG] or the use of his surgery to keep matters away from the police [FRIG]. He addressed the doctor at times as 'old boy' [FRIG].

Now with his work regularly documented or preserved on videotape, Steed was next assigned a case by his superior – a man known as '5' – which had previously been handled by an undercover colleague called Tobert prior to his death. Extremely good forged bank notes were to be distributed across Europe by a gang run by Chris Hooper, and '5' gave Steed three weeks to learn all about Timothy James Riordan, an Irish master forger who had been in jail for eight years for counterfeiting. Infiltrating the gang as Riordan, Steed took a particular interest in a gangster-style killer called Jimmy Bishop who called himself 'the Cardinal'. While hiding at the secret print works, Steed's hand received an injury from

---

[10] It is possible that Steed was able to get some background information about Keel from a surveillance tape made of Keel's investigations at the Radeck State Circus earlier in 1960 [GIRL].

a trolley cart running over his knuckles, which he had tended by Keel, telling the GP 'just enough to put him in the picture.' With Keel's help, Steed captured Bishop and Hooper's gang, and planned to put undercover men in their place to nail the head man of the outfit [ROOT].

An espionage assignment with scientific overtones came next when the eminent scientist Professor Braintree disappeared. Since Braintree was a patient of Keel's, Steed asked the doctor to pose as Braintree to expose the enemy agents, and then saved Keel's life when an operation on Keel was infiltrated by one of the opposition posing as an anaesthetist [NIGH].

The Caribbean island of Pascala was the venue for Steed's next mission. Carmelite Mendoza, the daughter of the late General Mendoza – a Western ally – had been kidnapped; the General himself had been killed in an accident a week earlier. Believing a concurrent jewel theft was a cover for something political, Steed intercepted police reports and discovered that the kidnapper was a man called Paul – whom it turned out had been taking Carmelite to her father who was not really dead at all. Mendoza was being threatened by his wife who was in league with their retainer, Vasco, to bring their own political party to power [MOON].

Although a 1961 dossier on Steed indicated that 'He has NO ORGANISATIONAL ties whatsoever'[11], this was not entirely true. After reporting to figures of authority such as '5' [ROOT], from spring 1961 he would sometimes receive assignments from a man known as 'One-Ten'.[12] Steed's interaction with One-Ten over the coming couple of years was interesting. At first, the pair tended to meet at One-Ten's London office, although later they would arrange to keep each other informed of developments in the field. Their relationship was uneven. Steed, ever the maverick, would not be above arguing with his superior [BEAR] – yet would also apply oil to One-Ten's back when the latter was sun-bathing [REMO].

Operating for One-Ten, Steed posed as John Ryan, an airline steward who had been arrested on smuggling charges in Australia, to infiltrate a diamond trafficking operation from London to New York. Living at a bungalow near Heathrow once owned by one of the smugglers, Steed started working for Globe Airlines and soon found himself framed for killing a woman in a hit-and-run accident – over which he was then blackmailed by the airline's Dr Collard into taking a package with him on one of his New York trips. The arrival of Keel, whom Steed had been working with, rescued Steed from becoming another 'suicide' victim at the hands of Collard [DIAM].

While Steed was getting a tan with an overseas mission, he still found time to telephone Keel with a vital lead in tracing Marko Ogrin, an immigrant worker from a secret government Medical Research Laboratory who had gone missing with some deadly radioactive isotopes [RADI]. On his return to London, Steed was plunged into an arson investigation where the only lead was the telephone number of the Jacques Beronne hairdressing salon. With the help of Keel's receptionist Carol Wilson, Steed was able to stop another fire started by criminal Johnny Mendelssohn, whom Steed was able to knock out while preparing an incendiary device. Carol's life had been endangered in the blaze – a fact which

---

[11] *The Complete Avengers*, p15.

[12] Documents are inconsistent over the hyphenation of One-Ten and his colleagues; it appears on films both with [REMO, SCHO, FROG] and without [DISP, WARL, BEAR, MIRR, FROG]. The hyphen has been retained as standard in this work.

Steed felt somewhat guilty about and made reparation for by taking her to dinner [ROSE].

Steed's next case was to follow Frank Preston who had just served a long sentence in jail for a £100,000 robbery, the spoils of which were never recovered. Preston was attacked by two other criminals in league with his wife, and required treatment from Keel. When Carol was then kidnapped, Steed promised to use his people's resources to find her, and brought the police to the London sewers to rescue both Keel and Carol from the thugs [DOWN].

The next case for Steed was to check on the behaviour of Felgate, a cipher clerk, whom it was believed was connected with one of his colleagues being found dead at Brinkley House Zoo. Going undercover as Felgate's new office colleague, Steed claimed to be married and had a cover story in which he had a wealthy wife whom he stayed with because of her money. Having got to know Felgate, Steed then asked Keel to help him follow the subject – who visited the zoo. When Steed investigated the establishment after hours, he was apprehended by a zoo-keeper called Evans and informed Major Renton-Stephens, the zoo owner, that he was one 'Mr Archibald' who worked in ciphers and codes. Felgate was being blackmailed into handing over secrets at the zoo, dropping packages into the crocodile pit to be collected by a trained monkey called Jimmy which belonged to the Major's daughter, Christine. Steed allowed himself to be similarly blackmailed by Yvonne, a stripper at the Bromango Strip Club... and received a black eye in a scuffle there from a heavy called Harrigan who was employed by the club's blackmailing owner, Kollakis. Eventually, Steed was able to prove the blackmail link between the zoo and the strip joint [FEED].

Keel's involvement with the murder of a woman called Elaine Bateman at her dance school led Steed to joining the classes there. Steed soon identified the pianist, Philip Anthony, as a man who had escaped a charge of murdering his wife but was wanted by the police for electrocuting women in the bath. He and Keel then managed to save another young woman, Valerie Marne, from the same fate at Anthony's hands [DANC].

Needing to get a vital new medical formula for a dangerous drug to a conference in Geneva, Steed used Keel to unwittingly carry a microdot containing the information on a document belonging to one of his partners. When Keel give the microdot away by accident, Steed followed him to Geneva where he was able to get Keel released into his custody from being held on a murder charge. It transpired that the doctor to whom Steed was meant to deliver the microdot had arranged for some thugs to steal it so that he could sell it to the highest bidder, but Steed, again working with the local police, recovered the formula and apprehended the greedy medico [MORT].

Back in England, Steed asked Keel to pose as a criminal in prison so that he could execute an assignment from One-Ten, identifying an escape route being used to spring inmates from jail. Posing as a parent with young agent Caroline Evans as his daughter, Steed also investigated a girl's finishing school which he believed was implicated and was able to reveal a man called Neame operating the escape route under cover of the college [SPRI].

While Sir Wilberforce Lungi was in London for negotiations relating to the independence of his African state, Tenebra, Steed left the diabetic VIP in the care of Keel who was an old friend of Lungi's. In the meantime, Steed himself travelled to Tenebra in the guise of a journalist and uncovered a plot to kill Lungi by Chief Bai Shebro, a tribal nationalist rival. Captured and released, Steed was able to escape Tenebra and return to London in time to stop Shebro's killer, none other than Lungi's secretary Jacquetta Brown, administering a dose of yellow fever to Sir Wilberforce in the guise of insulin [NEED].

Around now, Steed tangled with an organisation called Murder International which was headed by a man called Gerard Kafka. On 19 June 1961, Steed finally tracked Kafka down and saw that he was sentenced to life imprisonment [NOON]. Steed's next cover was that of a metallurgist at a dockyard where a nuclear submarine was under construction. A secret service man had been killed there, and Steed soon found that he was up against his old enemy Kolchek who was using blackmail to gain plans of a new nuclear reactor. Steed managed to foil Kolchek's scheme to detonate a bomb on the submarine, hurling a brief-case of explosives harmlessly into the water [SLIP].

A daring diamond robbery commanded Steed's attention next, and his first strong lead came from a cryptic prescription delivered to Carol from Keel, who was being held by the thieves. Working with the police, Steed used a vital clue given to Keel to locate the stolen diamonds at a cottage owned by a man called Bartholomew, and so arrested a gang led by Bruton. On this occasion, Steed was actually to personally profit from his actions, receiving the insurance company reward for the returned gems which he spent on a celebratory dinner for Keel and Carol [DOUB].

Having used Keel so much, it was now Steed's turn to respond to the doctor's call for help when a girl called May Murton went missing. Steed's investigations at a department store where May worked eventually led to him uncovering a call girl racket run by the girl's hostel housekeeper Mrs McCabe. His subsequent plan to have the police arrest Mrs McCabe meant endangering the life of young Bunty Seton, a girl in the care of David Keel [TOY].

Steed's next brush with danger was assigned to him by One-Ten, and he went under-cover as an Oriental-style magician – accompanied to his delight by some very pretty showgirls – at a funfair in Southend where top secret information was being passed on. He managed to resist being interrogated by hypnotism when captured by Jack Wickram, the man in charge of a telephone line tapping scam. Wickram had Steed and a girl called Claire chained up in a disused Ghost Train tunnel, but Steed used a bluff with an explosive ciga-rette to overpower Wickram and his gang with the help of Keel [TUNN].

In August 1961[13], Steed and his various associates kept tabs on a young cad called Jeremy de Willoughby, a man heavily in debt but planning to marry young Marilyn Weller[14], the daughter of the wealthy Sir Thomas Weller. Learning that de Willoughby was to be the latest victim of a gang operating a 'massage contract' (a beating delivered for a fee), Steed co-opted Keel to help him with the injured Jeremy and apprehend Moxon, one of the gang, whom he wanted to interrogate at Keel's surgery. During this operation, Steed seemed to be operating from a telephone box – which Keel could call him at – and had obtained the services of a cabby called Fred who seemed to be continually and reluctantly at his disposal; other associates acting as informants appeared to be a flower lady, a street sweeper who kept surveillance, and a black agent who posed as a bus conductor. With evidence from Keel about the operation run by 'the Deacon', Steed worked with Inspector Charlie Foster to make the necessary arrests. He then posed as a man sent by an escort

---

[13] The surveillance film recording makes reference to the date being 'Tuesday 15th', suggesting August 1961 – despite the fact that Steed asks a parrot for tips for the Derby which was run on 31 May.
[14] The family was erroneously referred to as 'Waller' in the summary report.

agency to take Marilyn Weller to a party at Lady Faraday's – part of a plan of Keel's to show Marilyn the true nature of her beloved who only wanted her money [FRIG].

Another foreign dignitary visiting London required Steed's protection – this time the Oriental King Tenuphon who was due to sign an oil treaty, in spite of assassination attempts from dissidents in his own country which so far had injured his adviser, Prince Serrakit. Steed was able to effectively protect Tenuphon from a sniper's bullet fired by Major Harrington, a hit-man hired by the King's enemy U Meng; Harrington was in a hotel across the road from Tenuphon's suite which Steed had earlier checked. Serrakit was killed, although General Tuke, the King's bodyguard, then shot Harrington [KING].

An attack on a scientist called Heneager at a top secret laboratory threatened work on a vaccine to cure a deadly disease, with Steed involving Keel for his medical knowledge. After another scientist was murdered and sabotage committed, Heneager was exposed as the killer. However, further investigation led Steed to learn that Dr Owen Craxton – who, along with Dr Hugh Chalk, was in charge of the work – was trying to discredit his own vaccine and then market it elsewhere. Craxton planned to kill Steed with a lethal concentration of the vaccine in a hygiene test room, but was foiled when his superior, Herbert Truscott, switched the phials – although Steed believed he had received a fatal dose. Project security then apprehended Craxton [AIR].[15]

Steed discovered a scam being worked by Mr Barker of the Finance Loan Corporation over insurance claims on investments. Part of this involved Barker's strike rigger, Lemuel Potts, having Peter Sampson at the London docks blacking certain boats containing a perishable cargo. Posing as 'Brother Steed' from 'The Congress', Steed visited Sampson and his men and blackmailed Sampson into disobeying Potts. Steed also impersonated a representative of the firm Fletcher and Calpes in a rigged phone conversation with Potts, forcing through a rotten banana consignment which Potts had previously ordered to be 'blacked'. Steed then followed up on a similar scam worked by Potts and Barker at a failing antique business run by a man called André which was due to suffer a fire. Obtaining photographic evidence of the two arsonists, Herb Thompson and Charlie, at work, Steed left Keel to summon the police. Steed then tricked Potts into making a phone call to Barker, implicating them both [BAIT].

Steed worked alone when investigating sabotage at a scientific research centre, this time for another of his superiors, One-Fifteen. Here Dr Reddington's team were attempting to find a radiation resistant material for space travel, although one of them had been exposed to radiation and others were having security-threatening affairs. Steed bravely volunteered to act as a guinea pig for one experiment – stripped to the waist and strapped into a chair in a test chamber covered with electrodes, and nearly dying when somebody sabotaged the equipment. Working with Saunders, a security officer, Steed was able to expose the strangling space-suited saboteur as Susan Summer, the assistant to Dr Alford, and apprehend her and her accomplices before she could strangle Lisa Strauss, one of the other members of

---

[15] Strangely enough, these events mirror the narrative of a BBC Light Programme radio serial called *Test Room Eight* which ran from 22 December 1958 to 26 January 1959. This concerned a research establishment where work on a flu vaccine was sabotaged and a murder committed. The serial starred Robert Beatty as private detective Philip Odell and featured characters called Herbert Trustcott, Win Craxton and Hugh Chalk. By an amazing coincidence it was written by Lester Powell, who later joined the Department and documented the same events for Steed and Keel.

Reddington's team [DRAG].

Steed's next case came about when the frozen body of missing Nazi war criminal Gerhardt Schneider was found amidst a consignment of meat at the London docks. Schneider was connected with a new fascist party called Phoenix which included a Dr Kreuzer and a thug called Willi. Steed was lured into a trap at the docks – only to be rescued by some dockers he had primed. He managed to rescue Keel, who had gone into Phoenix undercover, from some deadly freezing experiments in the nick of time [WINT]. This seems to have been the last time that Keel worked with Steed – possibly due to the fact that Steed had caused Archie Duncan, Carol's landlord, to suffer a minor heart attack because of the ill-considered actions which he took to achieve a result [BAIT]. However, another unsubstantiated report suggests that Keel was lured away from his London practice by an excellent post in the World Health Organisation.[16]

---

[16] *Too Many Targets*, p12.

JOHN STEED
THE COLD WAR SETS IN

Despite all the home-grown crime in London, Steed also spent some time in Paris in 1961, which is where he met Jean Pierre Avalon[1], a Slav double agent [NUTS]. It is also possible that it was on this occasion that Steed's contact man was Jonathan Winters [LOBS]. A major event for the Department was when the Berlin Wall was erected by the Eastern Bloc in August 1961. Over the next few years, Steed was to make various trips back and forth across the wall. On the first occasion, he picked up three bullets and fractured a thigh. The event was highly traumatic and it turned the hardened agent to jelly for some time – presumably late 1961 or early 1962 when there seems to be a gap in the surveillance films. As soon as Steed was well, the Department made him go over again at the earliest opportunity. 'The best way to destroy a fear is to face it,' he later sagely commented of the experience [OBSE].

Certainly it seems that Steed made various skirmishes across the wall between 1962 and 1964, along with other agents for both sides such as Willi Fehr. Indeed, by 1966 Steed looked back quite fondly on the old days when operatives like himself and Fehr were 'back and forth across the wall' [QUIC]. He made the acquaintance of Canadian agent Charles 'Chuck' Peters, and on one occasion Chuck stood on his shoulders while shinning over 'the wall' [GLAD]. Using his 1950s code-name 'The New Doberman' saved his life on one occasion when he was coming back across the wall. The abbreviation 'The New D' was misinterpreted phonetically by the opposition security forces, who instead arrested a coach full of innocent nudists – including an eccentric dancer, a bishop and a taxidermist from Fife [RAT].

During 1962, Steed made three visits to NUTSHELL[2], a security area deep beneath the War Office and Embankment in London which was the most secure place in Britain and housed the National Security Archives [NUTS]. Also early in 1962, Peter Borowski – whom Steed had first met in 1947 – went missing, having not been in the west since 1959 [SHAD]. By early 1962, Steed had been helped on some assignments by another general practitioner, Dr Martin King [COUR]. The relationship between Steed and King was similar to that which the undercover agent had experienced with Keel – slightly less friendly and with King less

---

[1] Erroneously referred to as 'Pierre Jean Avalon' in the transcript.
[2] thermo Nuclear Underground Target zone SHELter.

argumentative but also less committed in general. How the two met is not clear. One version of this event as related by Steed was possibly just a cover story which he dreamt up for the benefit of Lillian Harvey, the wife of his colleague Mark Harvey, possibly merely to get her to accept King's business card and so have him gain her confidence. In this instance, Steed claimed that two years earlier – presumably 1960 – he had been feeling ill, and that it was King who brought an end to his headaches, dizziness and spots before the eyes [SELL].

Charm and flattery were useful weapons in the Steed armoury to ensure King's co-operation [COUR], and if these failed, then Steed would play on his sense of humanity – for example, persuading him to carry on investigating to find the gunman who made an innocent lady called Mrs Alan Price into a widow [SELL]. Addressing King as 'old boy' [COUR], Steed always seemed to act as if King would help him anyway, regardless of any protest [SELL]. Steed would guide King in his investigations by advising him who to talk to [COUR] – but would also taunt him about his dress sense and embarrass him by asking about his tastes in women [MONT]. In return for all King's help, Steed did not even tell him where he lived or could be contacted [SELL].

Some time around spring 1962, Steed was made responsible for monitoring the smuggling of some microfilm with details of the new DEW Line[3] stations across Canada to Alaska, acting on information from an opposition agent picked up in Montreal. When film actress Carla Berotti was clearly implicated, Steed arranged for King to have a free trip to Montreal on board the luxury liner *MV Calpurnia*, acting as Carla's doctor. Steed himself joined the ship at Le Havre under the guise of a steward called 'Jim' – and was surprisingly effective in this role. The voyage took four days[4], and during the trip Steed was able to expose his old associate double agent Sheila Dowson and an enemy agent called Brand as those forcing Carla into acting as a reluctant courier [MONT].

Having returned to London, Steed found himself flying overnight to the coast of Ireland to investigate a possible case of sabotage which caused a Canada Jet-Ways aircraft to crash. This disaster had similarities to another crash three months earlier. Arriving at 3.00 am, just over three hours after the crash, Steed summoned King and worked alongside the Gardai, the Irish police, in the area of the Convent of St Mary for several days until a wrecking plan devised to target planes carrying currency was exposed. This was being run by a local called Vincent O'Brien from the village of Ballyknock and some fake nuns at the Convent; Steed extracted a confession from O'Brien by manipulating him into boarding the next doomed flight, for which Steed himself was one of the pilots [COUR].

Returning to London again, Steed now found himself somewhat reluctantly reporting to One-Twelve when One-Ten was not available. Having not met One-Twelve before he was rather cautious over his new assignment in which he was ordered to work alongside Mark Harvey, arranging for the visiting United Nations official M Etienne Roland to conduct vital negotiations with a minister over a dangerous situation in East Africa. As Roland was the only man whom it was felt could bring a peaceful settlement, there were certain groups who were keen to remove him before he could get all the necessary parties together for talks [SELL].

There were various attempts on Roland during his stay in London, and again Steed

---

[3] Distant Early Warning Line.

[4] Although no firm date was given, it was a 'good time of year' to cross the Atlantic.

found it necessary to involve Dr King. On this assignment, Steed drove a white AC Greyhound sports car with spoked wheels.[5] In a technique which he would use again over a decade later when protecting Professor Vasil [CARD], Steed donned Roland's Homburg and borrowed the distinctive cane given to the dignitary by his father when he was commissioned in 1915. He also learnt to imitate the walk caused by Roland's lame right leg. The security leak in the meeting arrangements was identified as Harvey, whom Steed shot when Harvey captured King and killed a fellow agent called Fraser. King and Steed ensured that Roland boarded his New York flight at London Airport safely, despite threats from another gunman [SELL].

King had appeared exasperated and reluctant on this assignment. Although Steed had always claimed that he really needed King's help [SELL], it seems that the incident with M Roland was the final time the two worked together; certainly there is no further reference to him on the subsequent surveillance films from the summer onwards. Steed would later comment that 1962 was a terrible summer [MAUR].

By June 1962, Tim Heald was now completing his final year at Oxford and had been encouraged to apply for a post at the Foreign Office by his parents. At his interview, it was intimated to him that he might like to consider working for 'another branch' and was lured to a clandestine rendezvous at the Weeping Beech in Kew Gardens the next morning... where he was amazed to find Steed sitting, reading *The Times*. Steed chatted in a round-about way about his work, but seemed reluctant to allow his friend's son to become enmeshed in his business – instead sending him a copy of *The Collected Works of Sir Henry Newbolt* to encourage him along a path of literary merit rather than espionage.[6]

It is possible that the reason for One-Ten's earlier unavailability in London was that he had been in the Caribbean. When their colleague, Washington courier Allan Baxter, was murdered at the Ocean Hotel in Jamaica en route to Santiago, it was Steed whom One-Ten summoned at short notice to ensure the safe delivery of the papers that Baxter was carrying. It seems that it was this occasion which saw Steed renew his acquaintance with Cathy Gale, the woman who had originally inducted him into the undercover world. With Cathy as his cover, Steed flew to Bogota in Columbia and then onto Lima in Peru the next day before arriving in Santiago the following day. It was here that Steed confronted and defeated Senor Miguel Rosas, the would-be political leader who had attempted to intercept the papers; when arriving at Rosas's home, Steed initially posed as a newspaper reporter [DISP].

'Steed likes working with women,' said his old opponent Keller [CHAR], and Steed generally relished his 1960s partnership with Cathy Gale, his first regular female colleague of the decade. Although Steed had worked with Cathy before, it is their working relationship from the surveillance tapes recorded after the Santiago incident between 1962 and 1964 which is the most fascinating. When dealing with Cathy, he would generally address her as 'Mrs Gale' [WARL, CLAY, HAND, WHAL] although he referred to her as 'Cathy' on occasions [DISP]. He also addressed her as 'luv' when in a playful mood [BIGT, CONS] or 'my dear' when trying to charm [INTE, EGGS, CONC], but when concerned for her safety would still call out 'Cathy!' [BIGT].

Although there was a great closeness between Steed and Cathy, there was little true intimacy. Steed invited her up to his flat (which she refused) [WARL], would take her for lunch

---

[5] Registration 680 DFA.

[6] *Jealous in Honour*, p4-6.

[BULL] and would at times unnervingly stare at her classic good looks [PROP]. He seemed to relish the idea of pretending that they were a married couple living in Highgate on one assignment and took this opportunity to indulge in some unappreciated horseplay [ROCK]. Another time, Steed offered to scratch Cathy's back when she took her next bath [CONS]. Any closeness between them was generally an act, such as a kiss on Cathy's cheek for the benefit of a hotel maid in Lima [DISP] or on her lips to keep his cover amongst criminals – an experience he clearly enjoyed more than she did [WOND]. 'Am I the same Steed you knew a year ago?' he asked Cathy after an assignment which involved his double – and then whispered something in her ear that made her laugh [SHAD].

When working together, Steed very much took Cathy's co-operation for granted, which she disliked [PROP] and on some occasions he could not even be bothered to be very subtle about it [MAUR]. He would even manipulate her domestic arrangements to force her to join him undercover [ROCK] or just climb into her private room [HAND]. Even her drinks cabinet was not sacred to him [WHAL]. On their assignments, Steed would use Cathy as a decoy [PROP, OUTS], bait [ROCK, CLAY], an impostor [INTE], to go undercover [EGGS, DWAR, HAND], to collect things [HAND] or simply to do research for him [DANE]. He would also make arrangements for her without waiting for her assent [EGGS, DWAR] and generally he knew that he could trust her instincts [WHAL]. At times he saw himself very much in command and would sternly tell her to follow his instructions [BEAR]. However, when Cathy asked to be extricated from some undercover work, fearing for her life, Steed would not always comply [DISP, BULL, ROCK, INTE, BATM].

Yet Steed clearly cared deeply about Cathy's wellbeing and safety [ROCK] and wanted to comfort her or cheer her up when she was upset [HAND]. When he discovered that Cathy was missing one night in 1964, he bustled his date for the evening off home so that he could investigate and was deeply shaken when it seemed that she had been killed in a fire. 'Mrs Gale was my responsibility,' he grimly declared [LOBS].

Steed would deliberately irritate the highly qualified and intelligent Cathy by teasing her about scientific work for women [ZEBR] and joke about her prowess in the undercover field by referring to her as 'Mata Hari' [BIGT]. He even delayed a trip to the Middle East for three days to observe the 'mess' she got herself in with one assignment [BIGT]. He also felt that he knew her tastes in men [BIGT].

However, Steed and Cathy often found themselves at odds about the execution of their assignments. While Steed saw the best way of getting co-operation from Carlo Bennetti as threatening to send him back to certain death in Naples, Cathy felt that he should offer a carrot rather than a stick. 'You're an idealist,' said a bemused Steed. 'And you're a cynic,' retorted Cathy [CONS]. Cathy also felt that Steed could be rather lazy in his assignments, commenting: 'He's a good agent – even if he is inclined to take the easy way out sometimes' [WRIN]. On another occasion, Cathy angrily rounded on him and accused him of 'using my expertise to cover your indolence.' [ELEP] These angry outbursts against him apparently had little effect on the smiling undercover man [CONS], but he in turn respected some of her more moral actions – such as destroying the GF Fund[7] records to protect innocents [FLEE].

By 1964, Steed referred to Cathy as 'a very old friend' [LOBS]. Occasional gifts to her included £500 so that she could buy herself a fur coat after she was nearly frozen to death

---

[7] Golden Fleece Fund.

[BIGT], some Fernand perfume which he had pilfered from the Treasury as a 'mark of our appreciation' [WHAL], £10 to cover her expenses at the Regency Turkish Bath [MEDI] or a Christmas present which she tried in her living room but felt worked better in her bedroom [DRES]. He would pick flowers for her on a day out as he drove her towards danger [BEHI], but a paid-for holiday to Switzerland came with the usual strings attached [SECO].

By now, Steed was living at 5 Westminster Mews, London, SW1 [PROP, MAUR, INTE, UNDE], a flat in a tower block [WARL] which was serviced by a lift [INTE]. The flat was near Phoenix Square, meaning that when Steed needed to visit NUTSHELL he only had to cut through Buckingham Gate [NUTS]; the nearest place to get a taxi was on the corner of Horseguards Parade [NUTS]. Parking was awkward at this venue with the newly appointed traffic wardens very hot on overdue meters – even fining a fire engine on one occasion [MAUR]. The apartment was within five minutes of a delicatessen [EGGS], and Cathy was able to get over in 30 minutes at a push from her new flat at Primrose Hill [DWAR]. The foot of the M1 was also nearby, allowing Steed quick access to northern cities such as Birmingham [OUTS]. The flat's location apparently made Steed a constituent of Major Gavin Swinburne[8] [NOV5]. Steed later made reference to two concierges, Parkin [MEDI] and Harry (who could make sandwiches) [LOBS] who could possibly have been the same person.

Beside the front door was a bear-shaped hat and brolly stand to the right as one entered [BEAR, INTE, EGGS], although Steed periodically replaced this with a rubber plant [MAUR]. The front door itself could be secured by a chain and a lock [EGGS]. On the walls of the hallway were small frames containing Victorian theatre bills [BEAR] such as *Gulliver's Travels* [BEAR, DWAR], *True Core* [DWAR], *Hughes Macready* [MAUR], *Marco* [MAUR] and *Magic Mirror* [MAUR]; this collection presumably harked back to the schooldays when Steed had taken such an interest in all things theatrical and the bills were regularly rotated around the picture hooks in the apartment, with small paintings sometimes gracing the hallway instead [DWAR]. There was also a mirror to the left of the front door [EGGS]. A door led off the hallway from the right to the small kitchen, which had a serving hatch through to the lounge area [INTE, DWAR].

Judging from the surveillance films, Westminster Mews was originally a compact apartment on two levels. The lounge was an open plan affair with some pine walls and others painted grey with navy blue décor. A staircase led up past a brick wall – lined with what appeared to be female nudes [INTE, EGGS] – to a landing. Thus the landing overlooked the living area [BEAR], and initially had a bear's head mounted on a shield attached to it [BEAR], although the bruin was later replaced by two decorative plates bearing pictures of women [INTE, EGGS], and then later still by prints, again showing women [DWAR].

The main seating in the apartment was a few modern-looking chairs [BEAR]. There was a desk with a black telephone [BEAR, INTE, DWAR] and an ornate lamp [BEAR]. Steed kept the top drawer of the desk locked as this is where he kept his revolver [MAUR]. Similarly, his wine cupboard beneath the stairs was under lock and key [MAUR, DWAR]. There was also an abstract sculpture [BEAR]. Steed owned a reel-to-reel tape recorder [BEAR, MAUR] which he did not feel like carrying over to Cathy's apartment [MAUR]. He exercised on mats which he laid on the lounge floor [BEAR]. Presumably Steed also had a TV in his flat somewhere as he was watching the discussion programme *The Man and the Place* when Colonel Vernon Wayne-Gilley was killed on air [BEAR].

---

[8] Erroneously referred to as 'Swinburn' in the summary report.

The door off the living room seemed to lead to a small bedroom where Steed kept some of his clothes [BEAR] and which he used for guests such as the wounded Intercrime operative Palmer [INTE]; this had a bed, bedside table and a few pictures on the walls [INTE]. Above this door and the bookshelves – which did not house any volumes earlier than 1600 [MAUR] but included a book borrowed some time ago from a Mrs Pringle [EGGS] – were stuffed fish in glass cases [BEAR]. More theatre bills, similar to those in the hallway, were on the wall beside the one doorway [BEAR]. At the end of the landing was a doorway which led to the bathroom [EGGS] where Steed kept his medication [BEAR]. This apartment was kept clean by an unmarried char lady called Elsie who came in to vacuum, and who was not in the least surprised to find Steed spark out on the floor – which she assumed was due to a good party rather than an attack by an adversary [MAUR].

Although Steed had been delighted to renew acquaintances with an old friend as beautiful and professional as Cathy, she was not necessarily as pleased to start working regularly alongside a man who was every bit as manipulative as he had been a decade earlier. Back in London, One-Ten arranged to meet Steed at a pub in Covent Garden where Steed had 'not been in in some time' and now assigned him to protect Mr Peter Neville, the creator of a new propellant fuel who seemed to have fallen ill. The illness appeared to be connected to the occult, and knowing Cathy's experience of this, Steed sought her out at the Natural History Museum where she was working. By now, Steed was also driving a different car – a Triumph Herald[9] [WARL], although around this time he also had access to a Rolls-Royce which he used to visit the offices of Sorenso Imports Ltd [BEAR].

Accompanied by Cathy who infiltrated the occult society run by Dr Cosmo Gallion, Steed attended one of Gallion's lecture; claiming it was 'elementary', he posed as a physicist working at Bancroft and claimed to have been interested in the occult for years, borrowing books from Professor Waterman who – like Neville – seemed to have fallen foul of Gallion's powers. Gallion was using occult ceremonies to supposedly place scientists under his power and hence obtain their secrets to pass onto an enemy agent called Mogom.[10] Steed had to pose as Pasco, a member of Gallion's coven, hurriedly donning the robes of the man he had overpowered. Gallion then collapsed, apparently of heart failure, during one of his ceremonies [WARL].

Steed's next assignment was on the continent again and seemed to be quite a simple one. He was briefed one morning to collect a package from the Austrian Jules Meyer when he arrived in Marseilles from Tripoli that evening and bring it back to London. 'Head Office', whom Steed was reporting to by phone, did not tell Steed what the package was. Steed's subterfuge of sending Meyer a wireless message saying that he would instead meet Meyer in Paris caused Meyer to panic and complicated the assignment, for which Steed had co-opted the help of Cathy who happened to be in Paris on business of her own. Within 24 hours, Steed and Cathy had located Meyer's package – a sample of a powerful oriental propellant – and out-manoeuvred enemy agents Siebel and Paul Manning, although Meyer had been killed [PROP].

By now, Steed had acquired a new canine to keep him company at Westminster Mews, with Puppy not having been seen since the previous year. This was Freckles, a young Dalmatian bitch of about two years. When Cathy was introduced to Freckles for the first

---

[9] Registration 7061 MK.

[10] Erroneously referred to as 'Mogam' in the summary report on the incident.

time, the dog was in the process of moulting [BEAR]. Seldom seen, Freckles would be around in Steed's life for the next few months through to the end of the year [MAUR].

The next assignment from One-Ten for Steed was to track down Olaf Pomeroy, an extremely professional hit-man known as 'Mr Teddy Bear' who had just executed Colonel Vernon Wayne-Gilley live on television. Again, Steed requested the help of Cathy, intending that she should employ Pomeroy to execute Steed and so bring the killer out into the open. Pomeroy was most intrigued by this offer but requested £200,000 to take on the contract. This was more than his usual amount because he was curious about Steed; Steed was the first victim he had been asked to kill twice, by both Cathy and a small time criminal called Henry Farrow. Cathy and Steed worked well together, and the result was Pomeroy's suicide upon capture [BEAR].

With Cathy heading off to a conference in Paris, Steed needed a different accomplice for his next assignment – to head up British Security for the visit of the influential Balkan figure Yakob Borb. When Steed's job was complicated by the death of a woman at the Balkan Embassy in Kensington, Steed arranged to place somebody close to Borb. This was a young night-club singer called Venus Smith whom Steed seemed to know well, and who was gullible enough to visit Borb believing that she was arranging a singing tour when in fact the dignitary was hiring a secretary [DECA].

It is not clear how Steed came to know Venus. According to actress and agent Julie Stevens who worked with Venus during the 1960s, the singer 'wasn't involved with anything [to do with Government work] and just met up with Steed who, at some point in Venus's career, saw her in a night-club and said 'I can get you work' – and used her as a lure for his enemies.'[11]

The Department's assessment of Venus was that 'She is involved in Steed's 'escapades' for several reasons. She does it for the *excitement*.'[12] This was certainly true in part as when Steed later placed her at the Gemini club in London, the story of a murder excited her and she eagerly decided to look for the bullet holes made in the magic cabinet [BOX]. Steed also knew how to exploit this trait to have her snoop around the bar of Les Centaurs in Aluda [REMO]. Although he did not seem to flirt with her or attempt to start a relationship, he was not above pushing a business card into her cleavage [DECA]. Venus's friendship with Steed was strong enough for her to quickly forget the terrible risks which he seemed to casually take with her life. When fuming over the fact that Steed had placed her in peril, baited by a non-existent singing tour, Venus found that Steed's attitude was glib. After she demanded that he never did this again, Steed's reply was a highly unconvincing, 'As if I would' [DECA]. Whether Steed genuinely believed that it was in Venus's best interests to keep her in the dark or not is unclear, but he would make comments such as 'She doesn't know much about this, you know' [FROG] in an attempt to keep her out of any direct threat from his opponents – even though he would probably just have used her as a dupe to send a coded message to his colleagues anyway [FROG].

Nevertheless, the pair had a good friendship – if a little one-sided. Steed would often call her 'luv' [MIRR] or 'my love' [SCHO] in a casual manner, the former presumably chiding her on her own use of this term in her increasingly Northern dialect [SCHO]. Venus was happy to do little favours for him such as walking one of his dogs [MIRR], and he indicated

---

[11] Stocker, Andrew and Tipton, Paul, 'From Venus, With Love', *DWB*, Issue 89, May 1991, p19.
[12] *The Complete Avengers*, p36. Their emphasis.

that he might take her to the Richmond Horse Show in Surrey [MIRR], an event which would presumably otherwise be denied to her. Venus's 1962 dossier notes that Steed referred to her as 'Smith'[13], although there is no evidence in any of the six existing surveillance films to confirm this.

Initially Steed believed that Yakob Borb was being threatened by his own people and wanted to avert an execution on British soil; he even replaced Borb's bodyguards when they were killed. However, it soon transpired that Borb was an embezzler who had killed his own aides Georgi and Sarko in the guise of a masked wrestler called the Decapod, and now planned to flee the country taking Venus with him. Ultimately, Borb was shot by his own ambassador, Stepan [DECA].

A few weeks later, One-Ten and Steed travelled to the Riviera where Steed had to infiltrate the hit mob operated by one Jack Dragna from the province of Aluda; Dragna worked across Europe arranging hits for characters like Godard, a Parisian who paid 100,000 Francs for an Italian political killing pulled off by Bug Siegel.[14] Part of Dragna's operation was the night-club Les Centaur, 12 miles from Minoma where Steed was staying. Apparently by coincidence, Venus Smith and her trio were halfway through a month-long cabaret booking at the club. Steed claimed to Venus that he was on holiday – but could not resist tempting her into investigating the running of Las Centaur under the pretext that he was thinking of retiring and buying the bar from Siegel [REMO].

Steed studied his quarry thoroughly in advance and decided to pose as a thief and con-man, mirroring the career stage where Dragna had been ten years earlier. Claiming responsibility for an emerald job in Nice, Steed's first move was to break into Dragna's home and steal some jewels which he then deliberately tried to fence to Charlie Binaggio, one of Dragna's men, before returning the cleaned and restrung gems to the hit-man and asking to join his firm. Working with the authorities, Steed had Binaggio arrested – whereupon the ruthless Siegel killed him in his cell while posing as Binaggio's visiting lawyer [REMO].

Dragna's latest job – which Cecile, his wife of 12 years wanted to be his last – concerned a group which wanted independence for Aluda. Steed was able to undertake small jobs for Dragna like collecting Godard. Godard's next target was to be box office star Nicola Cauvin, the uncrowned Queen of France, who was filming in her native Aluda and had donated a million Francs to a local university as well as writing an article in an international magazine backing independence. The Frenchman paid a quarter of a million to have Cauvin killed and it was decided that Steed would carry this out. Steed got access to the rather spoilt Cauvin by claiming to be one Mr McGrath of Homeric Studios who wanted to discuss a script. He then seemed to carry out the hit, faking a fatal car crash for her and returning to Dragna with proof of the killing – a bracelet taken from her 'body'. Steed claimed that Cauvin's body could not be recovered, 42 fathoms down in the Corniche. In fact, Steed had hidden the star with her mother to the north at Aix-en-Provence. Unfortunately, Venus's presence at Las Cadenas complicated matters, and a jealous Siegel exposed him. In a shoot-out at the bar, Steed rescued Venus and disposed of both Dragna and Siegel with a revolver from Siegel's till [REMO].

When Cathy returned from France, she soon found herself involved – against One-Ten's best instincts – in a murder at Marlings, a small pottery in Staffordshire where director

---

[13] *The Complete Avengers*, p36.
[14] Erroneously referred to as 'Bud Siegal' in the summary report.

Allen Marling claimed to have developed a strengthened clay that could cut steel. During a meeting in a Turkish Bath[15], One-Ten assigned Steed to investigate possible espionage at the factory by setting him up with a cover as an expert from the Ceramics Research Council; this involved giving Steed a copy of the trade journal *Form* and telling him that he was expected him to acquire a decade of ceramics knowledge in 24 hours. Not all went well for Steed on this case as Marling's unbreakable experimental tile was stolen by a rival agent called DeGroot, and One-Ten told Steed it was up to him to recover it. DeGroot was eventually subdued and the tile recovered – largely because one of Marlings's staff, Josh Machen, happened to trust Steed[16] [CLAY].

The murder of a girl called Valerie during a magic act at a club called the Gemini was somehow connected with Steed's next assignment, the leakage of information regarding NATO troop movements which seemed to come from the home of General Sutherland where discussions took place in a specially screened office. Acting on behalf of NATO HQ, Steed took a dual approach to the mission. While he posed as a masseur sent to look after the invalid General, he arranged for Venus to be employed – as if by pure coincidence – by the Major, an associate of his who ran the Gemini. Two weeks after Valerie's murder, Steed's investigations began to bear fruit, and it was clear that somehow a faith healer called Dr Gallam[17] was involved with both Sutherland and the Gemini. Steed had Venus set him up as a new client for Gallam. In thick glasses, bowler, paisley scarf, heavy overcoat and carrying a silver-topped cane, Steed visited Gallam posing as a man called 'Thackeray' who claimed he was a chronic invalid with internal disorders, dizziness, a crushing sensation and coughs. Tired of other medics' prescriptions of diet or exercise, 'Thackeray' claimed to have just returned to England and was seeking a quiet hotel to reside in. While Gallam quickly saw through this disguise, Steed was able to identify the connection to the Gemini where the NATO secrets were being passed on by a radio operated by magician Gerry Weston, and thus stop the leakage [BOX].

Cathy was away from mid-October.[18] When she returned on the morning of Friday 26 October she was instantly involved by Steed in a rather strange case which occupied them while the rest of the world held its breath to see if Premier Kruschev would withdraw the Soviet missiles stationed in Cuba. A man called George Miller had been caught in a car crash and found to have £50,000 of diamonds in his stomach. Since Miller was regularly travelling to Switzerland, it was felt that he was smuggling part of a £3,500,000 fund which had gone into a Swiss account from England over the last week and a half. It transpired that Miller had been connected with the Litoff Organisation, a major corporation which Steed visited posing as a dubious 'management consultant' who blackmailed the company for the return of their clearly illicit diamonds. The smuggling was part of a plan hatched by Getz, a senior figure in the Organisation, to make it appear that Alexander Litoff, the company

---

[15] The notion of a meeting in a Turkish Bath was later used in the movie *The Avengers* to show the 'first' meeting between John Steed and Emma Peel.

[16] These events seem to have taken place during one week in September 1962; a calendar at Marlings appears to show a 30 day month starting on a Saturday.

[17] Erroneously referred to as 'Dr Gilman' in the summary report.

[18] The telex sent by Cathy Gale to the Litoff offices was dated '29th October 1962'. The surveillance tape therefore seemed to have spanned from 26 to 29 October, and Cathy had been away for a fortnight beforehand.

founder, was still alive – whereas he had in fact died several weeks earlier. Getz and his accomplices planned to embezzle the remaining assets and flee the country, but the scheme was thwarted by Steed and Cathy [DANE].

The following week[19], Steed was on another case which required Cathy to work undercover for him – this time at Anderson's Small Arms Ltd. Purchasing 20 per cent of the company's shares for Cathy, Steed explained that this munitions company was somehow involved in smuggling weapons into Africa where they had been recovered by his colleagues. The apparent suicide of Anderson himself was just the excuse needed to get Cathy in. During the course of this investigation to find who was aiming to get control of Anderson's and who was in control of the gun-running, Steed posed as both a window cleaner to keep an eye on Cathy's flat for her, and also as Cathy's broker – having arranged with one of his long-standing friends who was a shareholder in Anderson's to have Cathy voted onto the board. Cathy was able to flush out the company secretary Miss Doreen Ellis as being in charge of supplying a smuggler called Karl with the weapons to take out of London on a boat which was intercepted by the river police [BULL].

Steed's next mission was to determine the source of a security leak which had been going on for six months at *HMS Zebra*, a naval base in Wales where a new defence system using ruby crystals to track enemy satellites and missiles was being developed. Cathy was infiltrated first as part of Professor Richard Thorne's team, and was joined almost a week later by Steed. Working with the co-operation of the Navy, Steed's cover was that of Commander Steed, a service psychiatrist on a temporary short term commission, acting unpaid and at present attached to the Admiralty; Steed's cover was complete right down to his security pass which he presented on arrival in his latest car, a racy open sports Lagonda dating from the 1930s.[20] This was the first firm indication of Steed's fascination with classic cars. At *HMS Zebra*, Steed was able to clear Sub-Lieutenant Michael Crane, who had been accused of the acts of espionage, and identify Joe Franks, the enemy agent out to destroy the project – extracting a confession in a ruthless manner by sealing Franks in a room with his own sabotage bomb [ZEBR].

An organisation known as Intercrime which co-ordinated crime and murder across Europe was Steed's next target after he nurse-maided a safecracker called Palmer, shot by his own organisation for doing an unauthorised job in Hampstead. Palmer gave Steed – and One-Ten – a lead on Hilda Stern, a German executioner, who was due to visit London. With the help of immigration and the prison authorities, Steed arranged to have Stern apprehended and imprisoned at Holloway with Cathy as a cell mate. Arriving as a bespectacled solicitor to see Cathy at the prison, Steed then advanced his plan and asked her to pose as Stern to penetrate the organisation. Intercrime was fronted in London by Rifle Ranges International Ltd which Steed investigated undercover, posing as a flat-capped gentleman making a trade enquiry about setting up his own shooting gallery. The front for the organisation was soon exposed, and further hits averted, with Steed actually working alongside Intercrime boss Jack Manning to deal with Manning's eager upstart and London manager, W Felder, who was planning a coup [INTE].

---

[19] The year is confirmed in the surveillance tape as 1962, while a letter to be typed from a taped dictation was dated Monday 5 – suggesting 5 November 1962. This means the surveillance tape probably covers the period 6 to 13 November.

[20] Registration CPT 75.

As premiers de Gaulle and Macmillan remained in deadlock about Britain's entry to the EEC in the run up to Christmas 1962[21], Steed was given a lead on the killing of a colleague in Rome back in September. The dead man had an envelope addressed to a Mr Peckham[22] at a stamp dealers in London, and a phone tap finally confirmed that the shop was somehow involved. Investigating the outlet, Steed posed as a stamp collector specialising in Empires and claiming to know Lord Matterley – who had been mentioned on the phone surveillance; it is possible that Steed's childhood philatelic knowledge of collecting Napoleon III issues was genuine. Later, Steed took on the identity of the late Paul Goodchild to keep the dead man's appointment at 3.00 pm with Miss Sheila Gray, a dentist working at 33 Wimpole Street. This was another step in the uncovering of a right-wing organisation led by Matterley which was planning to take over the country in a coup one weekend [MAUR].

Cathy's redecoration of her flat in the New Year gave Steed an excellent excuse to use her on his next assignment – to trace the origin of £1,000,000 in illicit stones found in Hatton Gardens and learn if these were connected to the sudden death of Mrs Ross, the wife of diamond merchant Samuel Ross. The implications if the smuggling was not stopped were widespread; if those responsible moved into industrial diamonds it was feared that they could get a grip on the manufacturing and munitions trades. By having one of his colleagues assigned to work on Cathy's flat at a leisurely pace, Steed was able to suggest that she could move into the Ross's former home in Highgate with him for a short while – and pose as husband and wife. Having gone to the London Diamond House, Steed had also set himself up as a diamond merchant with Samuel Ross to make him the next target for the smugglers. Diamond merchant Max Daniels, beautician Liza Denham and a man called Fenton were identified as behind the smuggling, blackmail and murders. 'Mrs Steed' was then able to return to her redecorated apartment [ROCK].

By early 1963, Steed had a new dog in his life – a mongrel whippet called Sheba[23] [BIGT, DWAR, MIRR, CONS] whom he took around with him far more often than Freckles, even feeding her while visiting other people [BIGT]. While Steed was out of the country, he asked Cathy to look after Sheba – saying that each day she needed half a pound of raw meat, some seaweed powder, a special teaspoon of cod liver oil and a long walk [BIGT]. Both Venus [MIRR] and Steed [CONS] would take Sheba for a walk, with the bitch given a little coat to keep her warm when taken to the park to play with her ball [CONS].

Steed was due to go off to the Middle East on an assignment, but remained behind for three days when a situation evolved at the Plato computer project outside London where Cathy happened to be doing some of her own research. One scientist was killed inside the sub-zero machine and another, Dr Jimmy Kearns, seemed to be the victim of blackmail. Arranging to meet Cathy at the gaming arcade 'Doctor Death's Parlour', Steed became fascinated by the 'mess' that Cathy seemed to be making of things. He remained in England long enough to see the attempted sabotage on the project by Dr Farrow exposed, before departing for the Hotel Miramar in Tel Aviv in the persona of 'J Carruthers' – the name by

---

[21] According to the brochure for the meeting, the 'International Philatelic Convention' which was the cover for the organisation was due to be held on '18th December 1962'. Thus the events of the surveillance tape seem to span around 16 to 18 December 1962.

[22] Referred to as 'Percy Peckham' in the summary report.

[23] Steed apparently acquired Sheba from actress Katherine Woodville, who married his old friend Patrick Macnee in March 1965.

which he also called the police to have blackmailer Nicky Broster and his accomplice Clarissa arrested [BIGT].

During January[24], it seems that Steed was still busy overseas – this time in Cairo – concurrent with another assignment, this time from One-Seven. One-Seven was concerned with Richard Davis, a university research scientist at St Luke's College who was being blackmailed. Since Davis was an old friend of Steed's from school days who had long drifted out of touch, Steed and One-Seven set about feeding him fake research to pass on and keep the trail warm. Steed subsequently arranged that Venus should provide the musical entertainment at St Luke's rag week – as well as keeping an eye on Davis in his absence. Unfortunately, by the time Steed returned to the country, Davis had been killed in a faked suicide. Meeting with One-Seven, Steed was informed that he would now enter the scene under the guise of a literary researcher. His subject would be Mrs Hesther Lynch Piozzi, the close friend and biographer of English lexicographer Dr Samuel Johnson. In the following days, Steed managed to uncover the blackmail ring – run by Dr Shanklin of St Luke's along with artist Claire Summers and publican called Higby – which aimed to get control of the young undergraduates who would be tomorrow's top men [SCHO].

That winter[25], when Cathy sold her flat and was looking for a new apartment, Steed gallantly allowed her to use his Westminster Mews flat while he moved into a nearby – and ice cold – hotel; in return, she had to provide him with slap-up bumper meals. While Cathy was replacing Steed's shelves of books with her current work restoring old pottery, the newspapers headlined a break-in at the laboratory of Dr Ashe, a researcher into bacteriology whom Steed and his colleagues were suspicious of. Although supposedly nothing was stolen, Steed arranged for Cathy to probe further – and it transpired that two golden eggs containing a deadly strain of verity prime had been procured for a mercenary criminal called Julius Redfern. Steed and Cathy managed to recover the deadly bacillus which was then destroyed by Ashe [EGGS].

When Cathy found her new abode, Steed was able to return to his flat and then spent the best part of the next month working for the Treasury, trying to find out how ambergris was being smuggled into the country and turned into illicit scent. The chain seemed to be connected to a boxing gym run by Sam 'Pancho' Driver, an establishment which Steed started to frequent to bet on fights before entering his own pugilist – Joey Frazer, a young friend of Cathy's. This gave Steed a lead to the design house of Fernand which he then visited in the guise of an uncle requesting an entire new wardrobe for his niece. With the smuggling ring uncovered, Steed again used his 'Carruthers' alias to summon the police to arrest Pancho, Fernand and their accomplices [WHAL].

With this case completed, Steed departed for a break back in the Caribbean [WHAL]. On his return[26], it seems that one of his first cases was a matter of averting world panic. Six months earlier, Professor Richter of Tor Point Observatory in Cornwall had alerted the Ministry of Science to his observations which suggested that a white dwarf was to re-enter the solar system and wipe out all life on Earth. The government did not want to tell the

---

[24] The calendar on Dr Shanklin's desk was for January 1963.

[25] There is snow visible on the surveillance tape, suggesting a winter setting.

[26] No specific date is given in the surveillance tape, but it is cold weather and Henry Barker has not yet booked his summer vacation. Astrologically, Mars is in opposition to Libra and Neptune is in ascendance.

other countries of the world until they had proof of the impending doomsday, but it seemed that there had been a leak of information. Any nation which could prove that the white dwarf's appearance was just a scare would have the upper hand and could walk into other territories. Steed's people were concerned when stock markets started to fall in all areas except armaments, suggesting that somebody had inside information. Having Cathy assigned undercover to Tor Point itself, Steed tackled the Ministry of Science direct, going to the Division of Astronomy with a fake business card and a posh accent to pose as a stockbroker for a successful financiers and investors organisation; in this guise, Steed was able to probe Henry Barker, the Head of the Division, about the security leak. This gave vital leads which enabled Steed and Cathy to confirm that the wandering star posed no threat to Earth, while also apprehending Barker's crooked brother, Maxwell, who had been planning a stock market coup [DWAR].

Spring was a rocky time for British security. Kim Philby had vanished in January, and John Profumo, the Secretary of State for War, was involved in a scandal with call girl Christine Keeler. Around March 1963[27], Steed was acting as a 'civil servant' on behalf of the Research Council and preparing for a four to five day voyage to New York on the *Queen Mary* accompanying Professor David Frederick Renter[28], a scientist who had just solved a problem in developing an industrial high speed film and was to receive development finance from the British and American governments. Although Steed referred to his 'boss' being angry if he failed on this mission, he did not specify which of his superiors he was working for. When Renter suddenly went into meditation at Adelphi Park[29] a few days before the journey, Steed became suspicious. The investigation into Adelphi Park with Cathy revealed a connection with Green's Funeral Parlour. Visiting the undertakers, Steed adopted one of his increasingly daring and outlandish aliases: 'Mr Small' of Small, Blake and Zomba, the finest funeral suppliers who offered a grave extraction unit, fragrant plastic flowers and tape recorded organ music for a more economical funeral service. Eventually, a scheme at Adelphi to keep dead millionaires 'alive' so that their widows could inherit was exposed as being run by Lomax and Mason[30] – Renter having died and been secretly disposed of [UNDE].

By now, Steed's interference in organised crime – and particularly the dope peddling rings in London, Montreal and New York – was starting to annoy the Mafia. A Mafioso drug peddler called Sica arrived in England and forced another former member, Carlo Bennetti, out of retirement to shoot Steed. Carlo attempted to kill Steed while he was walking Sheba, but failed. Tracking back on various clues, Steed assigned Cathy to go undercover at Gutman's Circus where Carlo had been working as a clown. Having taken over the premises of Billboard Office while Cathy was at work, Steed was lured to the Circus that Saturday where Sica aimed to have him murdered. Steed himself intended to contact Carlo and scare him by threatening to deport him back to Naples where he would be killed – a plan which again brought him into conflict with Cathy over their different

---

[27] Renter was born on 5 May 1902, and was due to be 61 on his next birthday – meaning the surveillance tape was recorded before May 1963. Daphne comes home from finishing school 'a month early', suggesting that maybe she had left in March rather than April at the end of the Spring Term.

[28] Referred to erroneously as 'Sayer' in the summary report.

[29] Also apparently known as York House on Richmond Road in Twickenham.

[30] Referred to erroneously as 'Marshall' in the summary report.

ways of working. Carlo, who wanted to be free from his Mafia thrall, ended up shooting Sica's aide Terry, and with Sica apprehended, Steed summoned the police to the big top [CONS].

Steed's next case took him to the North East to look into the situation regarding a massive new ship to be built by the Reniston Group and Collier's Yard, despite various disagreements over French involvement. He also persuaded Cathy to re-establish contact with Rosalind Waldner, one of her school friends 'by chance', since her father, Oliver, was a Reniston group director. While Cathy kept watch on Oliver – and formed a romantic bond with him – Steed focused on Collier's Yard, supposedly as an official from the Ministry of Works visiting with a party from the Board of Trade; in this capacity, Steed claimed that he was dealing with material requirements for the project in liaison with his opposite number in Le Havre. The Reniston Group's manipulation and murder – apparently with the motive of boosting British business – was exposed, directors Oliver Waldner and George Stanley were arrested, the strike action at Collier's was lifted, and the build went ahead [HAND].

By mid-May[31], Steed was in Norway, enjoying a solo camping holiday as he travelled from Narvik to Alta; during this time, fellow agent George Meyer was unfortunately drowned on the Austrian border while working the Corinthian Pipeline [WRIN]. By the end of the month[32], Steed was back at work and assigned to report to yet another new superior, One-Six, whom he arrived late for a briefing session with. Steed had not worked for One-Six before, and found that this rather stern and demanding figure had a very different attitude and approach to his own. Amidst One-Six's heavy workload, he issued Steed with a 'routine job', checking on a civil servant cipher clerk called Victor Trevelyan who had apparently committed suicide on a railway line when his wife walked out on him. Steed followed a lead from a ticket stub in the dead man's pocket which pointed towards the Wonderland amusement arcade. Venus Smith was happy to swallow another unlikely story which meant she took surveillance shots of the establishment for Steed, while Steed visited the widowed Mrs Jean Trevelyan claiming to be a colleague of her late husband who had come to recover any of his papers. As it transpired, Trevelyan was not dead but had defected, a plan conceived by a man called Strong which Steed was soon able to counter with the help of the police [MIRR].

Within a few weeks of the Trevelyan affair, Steed had acquired another new dog – another Great Dane bitch called Junia [CONC, FLEE] who was apparently related to Puppy. Steed's next assignment concerned the visit of Russian pianist Stefan Veliko to London, shortly after Profumo quit. Veliko was the nephew of a senior Soviet figure and there were trade talks going on between British and Russian governments. Steed arranged with the British Cultural Council that Cathy Gale should be appointed to look after the pianist on his tour – which was also a safeguard if something happened. On 11 June[33], Polly White – a girl with a criminal record – was killed in Veliko's suite. Under the alias of 'John Smith' of the Wodis Hotel, Steed visited The Stud Club to uncover background on Polly, and exposed a blackmail and murder plot concocted by Mr Peterson of the Cultural Council to

---

[31] Around 15 May [WRIN].

[32] Steed commented to Venus that he would take her to the Richmond Horse Show, which takes place at the start of June. The calendar for what appears to be July 1962 in a run-down office at Wonderland was presumably an old one.

[33] The date appears on a calendar at the British Cultural Council offices.

Right:
Autumn 1961: Dr David Keel's
medical knowledge aids Steed's
investigation into an attack at a
top secret vaccine laboratory
[AIR]

Previous page:
Early 1963: John Steed leaves
his mongrel whippet Sheba at
Cathy Gale's flat prior to an
assignment in Tel Aviv [BIGT]

Below left:
Spring 1962: Steed relaxes
in Dr Martin King's cabin
aboard the *MV Calpurnia*
en route for Montreal [MONT]

Below right:
Autumn 1962: Steed arranges
a singing spot for Venus Smith
at the Gemini club [BOX]

Left:
Late 1962: At Steed's apartment – 5 Westminster Mews, SW1 – Cathy Gale informs Steed that she has been ordered to murder Pamela Johnson by Felder of Intercrime [INTE]

Below:
Spring 1963: Claiming that she knows all about tattoos, Cathy reports to Steed about her undercover work at Gutman's Circus [CONS]

Above:
Late spring 1965:
Emma, botanist Dr Sheldon
and Steed come under fire
from Lennox the chauffeur
as they make for the estate of
Sir Lyle Peterson [SURR]

Left:
Autumn 1966: Steed gets the
better of Vesta at the home of
Waldo Thyssen [TIME]

Above:
Spring 1968: At Stable Mews,
Tara King connects the jigsaw
pieces found on the body of
Henry J Averman while Steed
thinks about his dead comrades
[GAME]

Right:
Summer 1968: Steed gets the
drop on Tara when they
investigate the home of the
supposedly late Henley Farrar
[LEGA]

Above:
Spring 1977: Steed and Purdey spray plastic skin to defeat the cybernetic traitor Felix Kane in Purdey's basement apartment [LAST]

Right:
Having risen to a senior position in the Department, Steed worked closely with operatives Purdey and Mike Gambit from spring 1976 until late 1977.

ruin the trade talks with Russia. Steed also found himself reunited with Comrade Zalenko who was handling Soviet security for Veliko; the two men swapped hats – Zalenko's trilby for one of Steed's trademark bowlers – once Peterson had been exposed and the talks were safe [CONC].

Steed was out of the country on 3 July when, coincidentally, another agent, Frederick Sempel, was shot on the Corinthian Pipeline [WRIN]. It is possible that this was concurrent with some work – or possibly a holiday – on the coast of Greece. Steed may have been working indirectly with Andreas Stephanopoulus, a shady diver and smuggler who was found dead – dumped from a luxury yacht[34] owned by 'Archipelago' Mason[35], a dubious figure whom Steed's people had been trying to monitor since 1961. One-Six arrived on the scene and assigned Steed to investigate what was going on aboard the yacht. It is unclear if Venus Smith's presence as the entertainer for the following cruise was by luck or by design, but Steed initially used her cabin to stow away, and then – when discovered – claimed to be her agent. Also on board was Anna Lee, an enemy agent of whom Steed was aware from his own people's files. With his fame in the undercover world spreading, Lee also knew Steed, and it transpired that Andreas had been killed in an accident surrounding a new bathyscaph being tested on the yacht – a piece of equipment which Lee wanted to use for espionage purposes at any cost. Steed was able to frustrate her plans, and narrowly saved Venus from being the next test subject in the submersible. Lee was defeated [FROG].

This seafaring incident was the last time that Venus and Steed appeared to work together [FROG]. During 1963, a revised dossier on Steed noted that 'Other than CATHERINE GALE there is no one working *for* STEED or *with* him, except such as may be persuaded (by any means from bribery to blackmail).'[36]

---

[34] The summary report gives the name of the yacht as *The Archipelago*.

[35] Erroneously referred to as 'Palago' Mason at points of the transcript.

[36] *The Complete Avengers*, p59. Their emphasis.

JOHN STEED
WESTMINSTER REBORN

Back in London, 5 Westminster Mews had by now undergone some serious internal redevelopment, and while Steed was at the same address as he had used since 1962 [LOBS], the interior of his apartment had been dramatically transformed [eg CHAR, FLEE, CAGE, OUTS, LOBS]. In comparison to the old apartment, the new flat was very light and airy. The main living area had two large windows looking out across London. This also meant that Big Ben could clearly be heard striking nearby, day and night [eg FLEE, CAGE, LOBS]. Opposite these large bullet-proof windows installed by Ponsonby's of Jermyn Street [CAGE] was another tall building topped with an illuminated sign [CAGE]. This offered an ideal site from which to open fire on the flat – hence the precaution with the strengthened glass [CAGE]. At night or for privacy, venetian blinds could be drawn across [SECO, OUTS].

On entering the flat from the corridor outside, the visitor stepped into a hall area where there was a mirror and small silhouette pictures on the wall [FLEE]. Although he obviously had a key to his own front door, Steed was lazy enough simply to ring his own buzzer if he knew there was somebody in [BATM]. Letters were slid under the front door [OUTS], and the buzzer was later replaced by a bell [SECO, LOBS]. Wired to the front door in 1964 was Steed's patent alarm system which caused a bulb to flash in the serving hatch from the kitchen [CHAR].

The hallway allowed access to the kitchen directly ahead [FLEE], and to the right a few steps went down as the space opened out into the main living room with its arched ceiling [FLEE]. This main room was nice and warm [LOBS], and a tiger skin rug covered the raised section of the wood-panelled floor with another rug in the main seating area [FLEE]. A set of steps led down into the main seating area by the window, with leather seating set into the sunken section [OUTS]. The furniture included some antique chairs [SECO], a rocking chair [OUTS] and a comfy sofa [LOBS], clustered around an antique table [NUTS]. There was a grandfather clock, apparently stuck at 7.15, which was moved around the flat according to Steed's whims [NUTS, FLEE]. Over the fireplace was a painting of Steed's great grandfather [CHAR], RKJ de V Steed presented by the Bagnell and Wintle Hunt in 1892 [NUTS] – although Steed later gave pride of place to a modern art item with a chess motif given to him by Cathy in 1964 [LOBS]. A hat stand stood close to the hallway and a framed naval crest was mounted on the wall near the fireplace [FLEE].

'Most of STEED's possessions have a history – or at least an anecdotal background to them'[1] noted Steed's internal dossier in 1963. Ornaments included a microscope [NUTS], a sextant [NUTS], a barometer [NUTS], an ornate chess set (possibly ivory) [ELEP], a model boat in a glass case [BATM], a globe [eg FLEE], a small brass cannon which sometimes stood on the floor by the window [eg BATM] along with a telescope [eg NUTS] and a small metal statuette of a knight in armour [eg NUTS], an hourglass and a dual-faced clock in a dome on the mantelpiece [eg FLEE], and a tuba [DRES]. There was also a low set of filing drawers sometimes set in front of the window [OUTS]. Additional decor after a party came in the form of a horse saddle and teddy bears [DRES].[2]

As with the previous configuration, there were a lot of books present [NUTS], with the bookcase hiding a radio set [NUTS]. One of the bookcases in fact masked a door from the rear of the room to Steed's bedroom. This was later redecorated so that the bookcase was replaced by an enlarged section of a historical map [eg FLEE, OUTS]. Some of the theatre bills remained on display [eg FLEE], now joined by prints of a more nautical flavour [eg NUTS]. Also in the flat, Steed still had his reel-to-reel tape machine [CAGE] and apparently had two telephones, one white [SECO] and one black [FLEE, LOBS]. Although he asked Mr Warmsley to phone him at Westminster 0011 regarding anthropologist Thaddeus Lawrence's disappearance in Burma [ELEP], this may not have been his own number. On another occasion, Steed's phone number began 124 [FLEE] and the phone line itself was prone to bugging by adversaries such as Fleming [CAGE].

Separating the kitchen from the main area was a set of open bookshelves which formed a serving hatch [MEDI] akin to that of the old flat. Sometimes, the area around this hatch was mirrored in some way [eg SECO, LOBS]. Steed kept his revolver in the kitchen hatch [ELEP] which later had a curtain placed across it [LOBS]. In his new, modern kitchen, Steed had an electric grinder (which went on the blink) [FLEE] and a portable coffee percolator [SECO]. The oven was positioned beneath the hatch to the lounge [OUTS]. To keep the flat clean and tidy, Steed had people in to help him spring clean [WOND].

By now, Steed was concerned about the security at NUTSHELL, having been alerted by double agent Jean Pierre Avalon about a file called BIGBEN[3] which listed all double agents on both sides in the Cold War. Steed set up a deliberate security leak by having a Swedish diver and escapologist called Elin Strindberg break in and photograph the files on BIGBEN. When the break-in took place one Sunday, Steed was called to investigate and took Cathy with him. Soon Elin was found dead. Mike Venner, who was in charge of security and operation at NUTSHELL, had Steed apprehended and interrogated; even Cathy was unsure about Steed's loyalty since she was unaware of his plan. Trained to withstand pain, Steed managed to go through with his plan, exposing Venner as the traitor in the organisation [NUTS].

Another VIP visit to England engaged Steed's attention again when the sheikh Emir Abdulla Akaba visited London for a health check-up while also negotiating a new contract for a vital oil supply with the British Government. Installed in a penthouse suite at London's finest hotel, the Emir wanted to sample the finest cuisine on offer. Steed became one of the three chefs on call at the hotel, under the name 'Sebastian Stonemartin' (a name

---

[1] *The Complete Avengers*, p59. Their emphasis.

[2] Another unconfirmed report indicated that the apartment contained the Hyderabad All-India Polo Cup. *The Avengers* (Enefer), p63.

[3] Bi-lateral Infiltration of Great Britain Europe and North America.

inspired by the bird) and with a pedigree which apparently included the Maria Christina Hotel in Mexico City. Cathy was also on hand as the hotel's social director. When the Emir died – despite Steed's precautions – it was necessary for Steed to determine if the cause was natural, or part of a plot to spark a revolution in the Emir's homeland. Fortunately, Abdulla had died of a coronary before troops led by Brigadier Mellor[4] were in place to stage a coup at Ibra – and Mellor was tricked into confessing his plans [CART].

In the midst of a summer heatwave, Steed's old friend Peter Borowski now turned up, found by American sector patrols and turned over to another of Steed's superiors – a portly man referred to in documentation as Charles – for questioning. Borowski seemed to be insane, housing numerous different personalities in his mind. During a chilling questioning, the deeply distressed Steed resorted to kicking his old friend and took over Borowski's interrogation, even rounding on Charles; the traumas of his four days held prisoner by the other side came flooding back to Steed. It seemed that doubles of key people were being infiltrated and Steed investigated William Gordon of the Atomic Energy Commission claiming to be part of the medical security team at Deepdale where Gordon worked. 'Gordon' had already been replaced by his double at Baxter's Holiday Camp and the same fate was in store for Steed – who was now being investigated by Cathy on Charles's orders. However, Steed was quickly able to kill his *doppelgänger*, suffering only a cut to his left temple. He then pretended to be his own double, revealing the foreign agents at work at Baxter's and exposing the main duplicate, Frank Cummings MP [SHAD].

Steed was out of the UK again at the start of July – concurrent with the death of another agent in Austria [WRIN]. By now, Steed had bought himself what he described as a 'spanking new' car, but was in fact another classic 1930s Lagonda[5], this time a 2-litre Speed model with low chassis in which he was delighted to take Cathy for a drive at the first opportunity when – one Friday – she had been invited to Resagne Hall[6], the home of Sir Cavalier Resagne in Devon. Unfortunately, this trip was one which Steed believed was taking Cathy directly into a trap. He had read that three days earlier Martin Goodman – the ruthless profiteer whom they had apprehended a decade earlier – had been allowed to escape by the authorities in the hope that he would lead them to his hidden money. Goodman had instead set up a trap at a lonely house for Cathy, which Steed allowed her to walk into – claiming that he was going on to visit friends on the coast. After Goodman had been drawn into the open and killed, it was an aghast Cathy who learnt that Steed had been on hand all the time throughout her terrifying ordeal [BEHI].

Steed's next assignment came from the Ministry of Agriculture, whom he would represent on an investigation as to how areas such as Dumfries, Yorkshire and East Anglia were all experiencing crop failures from ergotism. The common link appeared to be the fertilisers and insecticides from United Foods and Dressings (UFD), and while Steed had his 'Ministry of Ag' cover he arranged for Cathy to work with him on behalf of Universal Health and Famine Relief. This eventually led Steed to tangle with one of the increasing breed of eccentrics whom he would meet in the coming years, in this case Sir Bruno Lucer, the chairman of UFD who was obsessed by the culture of ancient Rome and who had

---

[4] Referred to erroneously as 'Pentner' in the summary report.

[5] Registration GK 3295.

[6] Resgane Hall had a very similar architecture to St Mary's Training College in Richmond Upon Thames.

founded the World Empire Party to bring peace and unity to the globe. Steed posed as a dealer selling objects d'art including Roman antiquities when he first visited Sir Bruno, and later disguised himself in a Roman toga as a member of the World Empire Party. Unfortunately the Party was also being used by Gordon Dobbs who aimed to wrest power, and a scheme to unleash Type 'A' Botulinus to recreate a plague of the Roman era via UFD produce was thwarted [ROME].[7]

The village of Vernon had been suffering strange mechanical jamming – which oddly enough did not affect the nearby Winterwell Atomic Research Station. After two months of these incidents, Steed was assigned to investigate posing as a man from the Ministry of... (Steed coughed mysteriously), an inspector for the National Distrust, a new organisation allied to the National Trust for people they didn't trust to look after buildings of national importance like Verne Mill. Cathy meanwhile put her love for the motorcycle to good use joining a biker gang called the Salts. The jamming device had been developed years earlier by the late Professor Peck and left to his daughter Cynthia, but was now a target for Soviet agents operating in the area. Steed managed to quickly identify a woman called 'Caroline' as one such member of the opposition, and she was soon apprehended [MOUS].

Around mid-September[8], Steed picked up the wrong coat while visiting one of his regular haunts – the Yan Sing Restaurant – with Cathy; in the pocket was a cheque made out for £5,000 to George Jason. This was part of a payoff being made by Mr Lo for a smuggled shipment of gold which was being taken out of Europe to the Orient. The smuggling was being undertaken by Captain Jason of Blore Camp at Aldershot who, along with other officers and soldiers, was trafficking the gold under the cover of military supplies and putting the money earned into the Golden Fleece Fund to support ex-colleagues living in poverty as the result of an army purge. Steed arranged with the Committee of the Imperial War Museum to send Cathy to Blore Camp. Although the smuggling was exposed and the officers apprehended, Steed did not stop Cathy destroying the Golden Fleece Fund records to prevent the beneficiaries being identified [FLEE].

Steed's next assignment required press coverage and a cover story at the end of September 1963. His aim was to expose Miles and Jasper Lakin, two barristers at law who specialised in helping those committing murder or selling state secrets to be acquitted in court by telling them how to plan their crime and lay false evidence to play on loopholes in the legal system. Posing as a figure called 'Jonno', Steed arranged to buy secrets from Ronald Henry Westcott who was acquitted as the Lakin's 11th case. Steed had arranged that Cathy should then 'expose' him as 'Jonno', whereupon he approached the Lakins for advice on how to kill Mrs Gale. Steed and Cathy faked her murder – which made the press with their prepared cover stories[9] – and after Steed was arrested by Inspector Marsh, he was acquitted when tried in the Number 1 Court at the Old Bailey one Tuesday. Cathy and Steed were then able to spring one of the Lakins' traps on the brothers themselves [BRIE].

By now, yet another dog had become occupant alongside Steed at Westminster Mews, an immature Great Dane called Katie [BATM, CAGE], whom Steed apparently owned well

---

[7] This surveillance tape began somewhere prior to the 'tenth' of a month and concludes on the '15th', probably in August 1963.

[8] The last meeting of those involved in the Golden Fleece Fund was noted as being 14 September 1963. The surveillance tape most likely spans 19 to 23 September 1963.

[9] *TV Times*, 20 September 1963, p4.

into 1964 when he was still asking for shin bones for her [OUTS]. Something – although it is not clear what – after this time must have changed Steed's traditionally favourable attitude towards canines since, after several years as a dog owner, he had no further pets from late 1964. Indeed, in 1967 he was heard to comment that although he claimed to be a dog lover, he preferred to have the animals neither in his domain nor on his tie [BREA] and in 1968 was only too happy to evict Fang the Wonder Dog from his apartment [TAKE]. Around this time, Steed also started taking an interest in polo, purchasing a mallet and a brace of polo ponies [BATM].

Steed's next investigation did not come from his colleagues at the Department, but began when he attended the reading of the will left by Clarence Wrightson, his batman in Munich in 1945. Wrightson had left the army shortly afterwards[10] and had remembered the £10 Steed had loaned him. Steed was however astonished when Wrightson's widow, Edith, was left his estate worth £180,000 in property – despite the fact that Wrightson had earned £20 a week as a draughtsman. Wrightson's wealth had come about through another officer whom he had served back in 1918, Lord Basil Teale, who was now a major merchant banker with his company Teale and Van Doren. Steed was able to pull some strings with emigration to enable Jenny, the secretary at Teale and Van Doren, to suddenly be allowed passage to Sydney. Thus, at short notice, he placed Cathy as her undercover replacement at the firm's offices and aimed to 'produce action'. Meanwhile, Steed flirted with one of Teale and Van Doren's best clients, Lady Cynthia Bellamy, claiming they had been drunk together at Jeremy Barnes's party in Mayfair; he also claimed to run 'Steed's Dog Kennels'. Lady Cynthia gave Steed a polo helmet, while Cathy helped to reveal how Wrightson had tipped Teale off about new share certificates and notes, giving the company an advantage when making investments. The profits from the illegal advantage had been poured back into supporting Britain's electronics and science industry – in a patriotic, well-meaning but misguided vision akin to that held by the Reniston Group [BATM].

Steed became suspicious about an operation to restore the sight of the blind millionaire Marten Halvarssen which involved the then unusual surgery of a corneal graft – the donor being interned at the Mondblick Clinic in Switzerland. Although this was a private affair, Steed claimed to represent HM Government because there were 'odd people involved' and wanted two allies present in Europe during the operation – Cathy Gale and his old family friend, Dr Spender. Cathy was presented as a medical friend to Halvarssen while being asked to look after Spender in Switzerland. Tragically, Spender stumbled upon evidence that the operation was a fake and was killed when pushed 800 feet off a balcony. Steed took charge of the plane scheduled to make the return flight with a heat-insulated sterile case to convey the live grafts through customs; in fact the whole operation had been staged in order to smuggle diamonds worth a quarter of a million. The diamonds were stolen by Dr Neil Anstice, the medic who had hatched the plot with Halvarssen; Anstice was shot by the blind millionaire who was now fighting alongside Steed [SECO].

During October 1963, Steed spent some time briefly in Berlin where he was 'involved in quite a little fracas,' the exact details of which are not clear but the conclusion of which was certainly that he was involved in a shoot-out with an enemy agent called Boris Kartovski, apparently triumphing with a well-aimed bullet straight through his adversary's

---

[10] Referred to as 18 years earlier, suggesting a demob of late 1945 and the surveillance tape being late 1963.

heart [SPLI].

One Sunday around now, Steed's colleague David Marshall was killed and left in an alley close to Bridlington's Research Centre; the one lead on Marshall's death was the wine dealer Waller and Paignton. With Bridlington's developing an underwater tracking device which was then in testing, Steed took an interest on behalf of his 'elders and betters in Whitehall' and became known at the establishment as the 'man from the ministry' or 'ministry spy' (a title which Steed disliked). Becoming a customer with Waller and Paignton, Steed was soon able to uncover a link to the electronic work while arranging for Cathy to carry out inspections at Bridlington's on behalf of Whitehall. Within days, a scheme of blackmail and espionage using microdots had been exposed, involving a fake spiritualist called Millie Wilson, her daughter Julia and the adjoining wine merchants run by Jack Waller [BROK].

Cathy played a major part in the next assignment with Steed, the entrapment of John P Spagge, a wheelchair-bound and apparently retired criminal who could not resist the bait of £3,000,000 in gold bullion offered to him by Steed. Spagge and Cathy's cohorts – who pulled off the vault robbery with her – were soon in custody [CAGE].[11]

While Beatlemania gripped Britain's youth in late October, Steed's colleagues were more concerned about a five Megaton nuclear warhead which went missing when travelling to an East Anglian RAF station in thick fog. When Michael Osborne Dyter was then apparently shot and killed 1.5 seconds after being declared the winner of the elections for the Parliamentary Division of South East Anglia, Steed took an interest. He approached his Member of Parliament, Major Gavin Swinburne, claiming that he was an old friend of Dyter's. Learning that Dyter had been about to expose a scandal, Steed had Cathy stand for the constituency re-election while he offered to pay her deposit, become her agent and write her speeches (which he filled with clichés). Steed's investigations into the world of politics was aided by the first lady of the Brentwood Ladies' Guild, an elderly woman who snooped around the Houses of Parliament for him and passed him notes. Eventually, it was revealed that Dyter was not dead, but had a scheme to explode the missing warhead on midnight of 5 November – a plan which Steed was able to foil by shooting Dyter [NOV5].

The suffocation of Tu Hsiu Yung, a female agent from Hong Kong, at the Regency Turkish Bath was as a result of her investigation into imitation medicines being sold in the Middle East with fake British trademarks. The main victim was Willis Sopwith Pharmaceuticals Ltd whose packaging was being almost perfectly duplicated. Steed initially investigated the firm as an agent for the Overseas Export Board (a new Government Department whom, he quickly added, was not in the phone book) who had experience of the Middle East markets and the task of analysing the complaints of companies who had fallen victim to the imitators. With Cathy's help, Steed found that the trail led to an action painter called Leeson whom Steed visited, posing as an art mogul from Reykjavik – complete with long fur coat, fur hat and cigar – on a buying trip in the UK. The imitation scam was revealed to be part of a plot to disrupt oil negotiations between Britain and Karim by shipping poison in packages of stomach powders. Behind this was none other than Geoffrey Willis, but his plans were cleverly averted by Cathy. Steed now acquired a temporary visitor at Westminster Mews; this was Fay, a model and former *Lilt*

---

[11] The surveillance tape included references to the Great Train Robbery, a theft of £2,600,000 on 8 August 1963.

girl, who stayed with him along with Sampson, her pet dog, en route to an assignment in Paris [MEDI].

Steed was next prompted into action by a report from UNESCO[12] on Wildlife Preservation which highlighted the increase in the slaughter of male elephants for their ivory in the African states and the political implications of the smuggling of this valued commodity. When an albino elephant went missing at a private zoo called Noah's Ark, Steed arranged for Cathy to become the group's new resident zoological director. Cathy was soon able to determine that the zoo was being used unwittingly to smuggle ivory by secreting it in the bars of animal cages made by the firm of Jordan and Moss – the operation being run by Professor Thaddeus Lawrence and his wife Brenda Paterson [ELEP]. It seems that shortly after this, Steed travelled to America, since he later claimed that he 'was in Dallas the day Kennedy was shot'[13], although exactly how Steed fitted in with the tragic events of the Presidential assassination on Friday 22 November 1963 is unclear.

Steed's next operation turned into a nightmarish experience for him as – for the second time that year – he fell foul of his own people's security. Once again he was working for Charles who asked him to find his old friend Hal Anderson. Anderson had gone missing six weeks beforehand while on an assignment to find out why six agents had been killed on the Corinthian Pipeline. After four days searching and with the use of their mutual contact Lovell, who worked as a tailor, Steed found Anderson in Scotland. However, his old friend accused Steed of being the traitor in the organisation and arrested him. It transpired that Steed had been out of the country on the six occasions when agents had died on the Austrian border, including Ann Lisa Pravicz – Steed's close friend 'Lisa'. Steed was sent up to the Unit for interrogation by the Wringer, a beatnik-styled man who deprived people of any means of measuring time so as to disorientate them in confinement. Steed managed to resist the techniques by using his training until he was rescued by Cathy. With the help of Anderson, they were then able to prove that Steed had been framed by the Wringer, who had planted false memories of Steed's treachery in Anderson's mind as the first stage of a plan to destroy the Department with mistrust from within [WRIN].

While Steed was recovering from his ordeal at the Unit, it seems that the Department had to intervene to stop his cover being blown. Even an operative as good and as active as Steed could only maintain his cover to a certain extent before somebody would spot a recurring pattern. In this case, Steed – and indeed Cathy – somehow came to the notice of an American film producer called Louis de Rochemont who set in motion plans to bring the undercover man and his anthropologist accomplice onto the silver screen. An outline prepared by Howard Thomas, an executive at ABC Television, suggested that the movie's plot would concern Steed and Cathy joining forces with Washington agent Drew Vernon and his female colleague in avenging the deaths of numerous young diplomats, slaughtered by gunfire at the School of Asiatic Languages in Beirut. This cinematic Steed was assigned by the 'head of the Secret Service' and lived in a 'splendid Belgravia flat.'[14]

The Department quickly and effectively averted a security breach, and although their methods are not clear, the film never went into production. Nor did an even stranger idea – a musical proposed by American producer Cheryl Crawford about Steed and Cathy which

---

[12] United Nations Educational, Scientific and Cultural Organisation.

[13] *Jealous in Honour,* p9.

[14] *The Complete Avengers*, p84.

would open on Broadway and then transfer to London. Again, the Department moved swiftly and killed the project at birth.

In late December, having recently undertaken a handcuff course, Steed next embarked upon a plan to draw into the open those who were buying up all the land close to early warning installations via a Swiss bank; on this case he reported to an unidentified male boss on the phone. This was somehow connected with a false alarm for World War III that was called by Westwell radar station a couple of days after Christmas 1963; signals for a missile attack appeared and then faded away which, in the event of a true attack, might have caused a vital delay. Acting quickly, Steed took an option on a bungalow plot on the Millhouse Estate in Smallcroft overlooking the Smallwood installation [DRES]. Steed's festivities at Westminster Mews [DRES] were marred somewhat by news that his old boss in Beirut and Berlin, John Benson, had died of a coronary on 29 December and was being buried in Cornwall, as was apparently his request, in the New Year [MAND]. Steed was then invited to a fancy dress party on board a train travelling from Paddington to Chester on New Year's Eve. Knowing the invitation, supposedly from his friend Tony Linkletter, was a fake, Steed donned the garb of a Wild West gambler and soon found that he – and others who had optioned plots on the Millhouse Estate – had been segregated into a carriage which was abandoned at the deserted station of Badger's Mount in order to prevent them completing their land deals on New Year's Day. Cathy had infiltrated the party in London and helped Steed expose Frederick Preston, who was working on behalf of an enemy power, as the figure behind the land purchase scheme. In a Western-style draw on the Badger's Mount platform, Steed's reactions were faster than Preston's [DRES].

No sooner had 1964 begun than Steed was in Cornwall attending Benson's funeral which was being held at St Alban's, the parish church of Tinbey. Although the village near Bodmin was almost empty, Steed was intrigued to learn that Benson was the latest in a series of burials of wealthy people from London who seemed to have no connection to the place. Within a week, Steed and Cathy had determined that those interred at Tinbey had been murdered by doses of arsenic, a condition which would soon be undetectable after their internment in the arsenic-rich soil of the St Alban's churchyard. The scheme was being operated by Roy Hopkins of Mandrake Investments in association with Doctor Macombie[15], who had duped the vicar, the Rev Adrian Whyper MA.[16] Steed was deeply upset and angry to discover that his old boss had been poisoned by Benson's own son, who had even claimed to have nursed his father in his last 'illness' [MAND].

When a sultan involved in delicate oil negotiations allowed his horse to be stabled in Britain, Whitehall asked Steed to look after the animal – Sebastian II – on behalf of the Foreign Office. As it transpired, there was no threat at all to the horse, who was ultimately given to Steed as a gift by a grateful sultan. However, during the security operation at Meadows's Stables, Steed stumbled upon evidence of a blackmail scheme being operated by bookmaker Tony Heuston and with some investigation from Cathy was able to clear up 12 unsolved murders of businessmen and politicians over the last year [TROJ].

In mid-February, Steed was co-opted to work for Mr Quilpie of PANSAC[17] where he was placed in charge of security for the visit to London of General Andrew Brian Sharp of

[15] Erroneously referred to as 'Dr Macrombie' in the summary report.

[16] Erroneously referred to as 'Wyper' in the summary report.

[17] Permanent Agency for National Security And Counter-intelligence.

Aburain for arms talks with the Prime Minister. With British troops being flown into hot spots like Cyprus, it was a sensitive time for the country and its international relations; as such, Steed was to liase with Special Branch and the airport police. Steed had experience of the Aburanians from 1960, and was aware that Sharp was a former British subject who had defected, and whom in 1959 they had attempted to kill. Cathy was asked to look after accommodation for Sharp, and was then used as a decoy by Steed when it became clear that the Aburanians aimed to kill Sharp themselves now that he had outlived his usefulness. The Aburanians had released one of Steed's former colleagues, Mark Charter, after five years imprisonment for attempting to kill Sharp in 1959, so that he could now complete his mission in London, disrupt the talks and discredit Britain. Steed and Charter hatched a plan to expose the Aburanians involved – without killing Sharp when he arrived on 17 February[18] – and so engaged in a successful stand-off with Major Zulficar who, along with the London Ambassador, was behind the scheme [OUTS].

Steed's high profile in the Department now meant that he ranked third on an Enemy Identification Chart used by a third party which aimed to set Steed's people of the West and the 'other side' at each other's throats by attacking both parties, starting with the death of Steed's colleague Matthews. Returning from a weekend break in Morocco with his moustachioed friend Otto, Steed discovered that George Vinkel, a Soviet agent whom he knew well, had been found murdered, and that the Russian operation in London, run by his old rival Keller, believed Steed to be responsible for Vinkel's death. Calling a truce with Keller, Steed offered his and Cathy's services to work together to expose the third party which was operating primarily via the Academy of Charm for Aspiring Young Gentlemen. This murderous organisation was in fact run by Keller, bitter at being passed over for promotion and aiming to sell secrets to the highest bidder. During this assignment, Steed commented that he received information from 'undisclosed sources'. He also found himself responsible for Miss Kim Lawrence, an actress hired by Keller to pose as one of Keller's top agents. Coming from a large theatrical company which included a great grandmother who was still doing her knife-throwing act at the age of 89 (which was how Kim got started when she was five), Kim was out of her depth in the espionage world – having only found three 'dead bodies' before while on stage in Cardiff. As such, Steed felt very protective of her – although it was Kim who deftly put Keller out of action with a foil in his back, thanks to the skills of her great grandmother [CHAR].

At the start of March 1964[19], Steed took on an assignment from Army Intelligence to investigate the Highland Guard over the death of one Corporal Craig who had been shot. This was a sensitive matter with 'wider implications' which Army Intelligence could not handle themselves, so Steed was assigned to work for CIGs (Current Intelligence Groups), regaining his former rank of Major Steed and claiming to have been in the Tank Corps repelling Rommel's desert campaign (which his manner seemed to clearly indicate was a lie) before being 'bowler hatted'. In this capacity, he claimed to be writing a history of the Highland Regiments. Much of the investigation was undertaken by Cathy, who concocted a background which allowed Brigadier General Sir Ian Stuart-Bollinger[20], the regiment's retired commander, to believe that she was the rightful heir to the throne and so put into

---

[18] The events of the surveillance tape seem to span from 15 to 17 February 1964.

[19] The events on this surveillance tape seem to span 3 to 5 March 1964.

[20] Referred to erroneously as 'Stewart-Bollinger' in the summary report.

operation his plan 'Operation Claymore' whereby the Highland Guard and their cohorts aimed to take control of London. With sufficient recorded evidence about the plans, Steed could then take steps to avert the coup [ESPR].

Around mid-May 1964[21], Steed set about infiltrating an organisation known as Bibliotek, a bizarre Commonwealth Mafia set-up which operated under the guise of ecclesiastic figures. The way in for Steed came in the form of the Reverend Harbuttle, the Vicar of Ndola (better known as a criminal called Sachs), who was arrested when arriving at an airport for a 'full assembly' in Lambeth. Posing as the Reverend 'Johnny the Horse' Steed of Mabote and claiming to have had a criminal record since he was nine, Steed joined the other 'men of the cloth' to clarify operations and territories, while confirming that members of Bibliotek were also smuggling microfilm of top secret information, a fact unknown to the Right Reverend Bishop of Winnipeg who ran the crooked organisation. When internal factions attempted to take control of the group, Steed received a flesh wound in the left shin from Sister Johnson's machine gun, but soon the Bishop was defrocked and the strange organisation put out of action [WOND].

After a couple of weeks walking with a stick [WOND], Steed was suitably recovered to return to active service. It was the death of Jonathan Williams, a contact man Steed had known in Paris, which triggered an investigation into a heroin smuggling operation. The drug was being secreted in chess pieces hidden inside lobsters being caught on the coast, a scheme set up by Quentin Slim who had been presumed dead just before the authorities could arrest him in 1963 but whom Steed's people believed had been continuing to operate from Le Havre in France. Steed's investigation in Stannage saw him claiming to be from the Ministry of Agriculture and Fisheries, and operating for an unseen boss who clearly irritated him by stating the obvious over the phone. During this assignment, Steed dated singer Katie Miles who was Quentin's 'widow'. Cathy again found herself in peril, only narrowly escaping from a burning beach hut set alight by Quentin. On hearing that a body had been found in the charred remains, Steed was badly shaken and feared for Cathy's safety – but the corpse was that of Quentin [LOBS].

However, it seems that the heroin smuggling incident was the final straw for Cathy who now decided to sever her working relationship with Steed. Again, she had been placed in danger and he was now simply asking too much of her now. When Steed attempted to involve her in an assignment to the Bahamas where there was a 'little bit of trouble', she firmly told him 'Goodbye Steed' and departed. Apparently unconcerned, Steed picked up the phone and contacted a female friend of his with some troublesome pet salukis to offer them a 'job on the beach' [LOBS].

Although he did not seem to show it outwardly, the loss of Cathy Gale as a colleague must have been a major blow to Steed and affected him very deeply. Certainly, during 1964 there was a marked change in his character. His attitude to his work was now far more light-hearted and less intense, and he no longer as frequently imperilled others outside the Department in his missions without their agreement. It is possible that this was a result of the stinging words left ringing in his ears by Cathy.

---

[21] In the surveillance tape, Steed commented that the polo season was over, suggesting this was some time after April. The Bibliotek organisation used St Timothy's Primary School for their meetings when it was closed for a week, suggesting the half-term in May.

JOHN STEED

TITIAN TRESSES

Within months of Cathy's sudden departure, Steed began working regularly with a new partner, Mrs Emma Peel, whom he almost invariably addressed as 'Mrs Peel'.[1] Every bit as emancipated as Cathy, Emma was also a widow; her husband had been test pilot Peter Peel who went missing in the Amazon during 1964 [KNOT] and since January 1960 had been in control of Knight Industries, the business built up by her father Sir John Knight [JACK]. According to the surveillance films, Steed commented that they met when he ran into the back of her car, with Steed recalling that he was distracted by her 'Titanian tresses' [DOOR].[2] However, another theory put forward was that this 'accident' was a deliberate move by the Department to look after Emma since either Sir John's military contracts or Peter's aviation assignments may have involved work of national security. This is in part supported by the otherwise unreliable 1998 cinema film supposedly concerning Steed's first mission with Emma in which Father, one of Steed's real-life superiors, observes that Emma's missing husband was 'one of ours'.

The relationship which Steed and Emma were to enjoy over the next three years was a very close one. Cathy had been a professional who enjoyed the excitement and intellectual stimulation of her work with Steed... but only to a certain point. In contrast, Emma showed no such reservations. When Steed involved her in another undercover investigation there would be only a token rebuke, if any – and then generally because of some role he had accorded her which she felt was beneath her. One such incident was when Steed persuaded Emma to take the post of receptionist at the Chessman Hotel; Emma initially refused, saying that she had had her fill of 'new fascinating experiences' [ROOM]. As with Cathy, Steed blithely assumed that he would have Emma's full co-operation in advance, having already booked a train ticket to Little Bazeley where Emma would pose as a school mistress before informing her of his strategy [TOWN]. At other times Emma was simply

---

[1] Steed directly addressed her as 'Emma' only once, at the end of their working partnership in 1967 [KNOT]. He also jokingly addressed her as 'Lady Emma' [DUST], referred to her as 'Dame Emma' [STAT] and introduced her to Prince Ali as 'Emma, Star of the East' [PRIN].

[2] An erroneous version of this meeting is described as being at a party given by Steed's friend Berty Clivesdale where a glass of Chivas Regal was knocked from Steed's hand over Emma's crepe and leather evening suit. *Too Many Targets*, p13.

around to help fetch and carry for Steed, such as when she collected meteorological equipment from a station [SURF], to perform routine tasks like breaking into a Rolls-Royce [BREA], doing research at the library [MARK] or going through Dr Palmer's files at an Early Warning Station [GRAV]. However, Steed was confident enough in Emma's abilities to leave her to carry out her own enquiries by mid-1965, leaving her to discover on her own why a birdwatcher called Quince had been watching them [DUST], or later to look round the former laboratories of Risley Dale on her own while he went for a drink with the scientist Dr Creswell [POSI]. On occasions though, Emma was not obedient to his schemes. When Steed worked out a way for her to covertly enter the offices of Winged Avenger Enterprises, she calmly informed him that she was going home to put her feet up [WING]. In most respects though, the pair saw each other as equals – tossing a coin to see who should stand guard inside and outside Lord Melford's hotel [DOOR]. Emma once commented that although she knew Steed could handle a situation on his own, she didn't want him to know it [RETU].

While Cathy had had to fight to show that she was as good as a man in a male-dominated arena, this was an attitude which Emma had accepted from an early age. Initially, Emma was clearly an outsider to Steed's work with the Department, and Steed accepted full responsibility for her at this stage [ROOM], commenting to Lord Maxted that Emma was 'extremely trustworthy' [JUST], and that he was happy to use her on matters of 'national importance' [BUTL]. When describing Emma, Steed referred to her as an 'old friend' rather than 'an associate' [TIME], and his 'thank you' gift of chocolates after her experience at the Business Efficiency Bureau in 1966 was a superficial sign of their deep friendship [FEAR].

However, unlike his working relationship with Cathy, Steed's friendship with the young widow extended far more into their private lives. As early as Christmas 1964 there was a possibility that the pair would exchange a seasonal kiss beneath the mistletoe [XMAS]. The duo would engage in a great deal of lively banter, and Steed would sometimes tease her, or indeed pass on friendly advice while they were fencing [TOWN]. They socialised together far more, experiencing the finer things in life. Once they drove from Montbert to Dijon[3], enjoying a Chablis at a gourmet's paradise which they found when she took a wrong turning [WHO?]. He would take her out to formal functions [HOUR], all-night parties [PRIN], offer to drive her to the coast for dinner in the evenings [EPIC] and take her to the theatre for shows such as a Parisian Musical – Seats 11 and 12 in Row D [DOOR]. On Emma's birthday in 1967, he arranged a lavish trip to France for them [WHO?]. When a grateful Prince Ali wanted to thank Steed for saving his life by giving him anything he owned, Steed chose Emma – who had become one of Ali's harem [PRIN]. Steed could also recognise Emma purely by her eyes [POSI] and when they socialised together at the home of 'Paul Beresford,' Steed was clearly jealous of his potential rival's attentions towards her [RETU].

Discovering that Emma was adept at sewing, Steed was reminded by her that, 'Our relationship hasn't been exactly domestic has it?' [TIME] while enemy agents Lola and Basil – who temporarily hijacked Steed and Emma's bodies for a day in 1967 – came to the conclusion that the couple were 'just good friends' [WHO?]. Nevertheless, while redecorating Emma's apartment in late 1966, Steed at one point painted a heart symbol on her wall,

---

[3] This may or may not be connected with an assignment which Macnee recalled Steed and Emma being involved in at Rouffach in Alsace. ...*deadline*, p47.

added the initials 'JS' and then hurriedly painted over his handiwork as she looked round at him [TIGE]. Twice Steed was seen to kiss Emma lightly on the cheek; once when she had rescued him from a firing squad [LIVI] and once as a 'consolation prize' after she had located missing papers at the end of a rally [TREA].

Certainly, there were many private moments for Steed and Emma – and it seems that Emma became the person closest to him since Jeanne. On one occasion she whispered something private to him to prove his identity which mildly embarrassed his gentlemanly nature [WHO?], while on another occasion after an amnesia attack she whispered, 'Are you the man who...?' to which he responded 'I'm afraid so' [KNOT]. Although there is no firm evidence on the surveillance films apart from the obviously magical chemistry between them, according to many of those who knew Emma and Steed at the time, the pair were sexually involved. By the mid-1960s, 'the Pill was part of life,' recalled Macnee. 'We took it for granted that Emma and Steed slept together, but simply didn't dwell on it.'[4]

Since spring 1964, Steed had moved to a new apartment in London: Flat 4, Queen Anne's Court, Tothill Street in Westminster [MARK]. This was a quiet suburban road of tall, old-fashioned buildings with a few shops at street level [JACK], about half an hour from the Russian embassy [TWOS]. The phone number is unknown, but seemed to comprise of seven digits beginning 3833 [TWOS]; Steed's line could be connected to a reel-to-reel tape recorder for Emma and others to leave messages on [PRIN].

Entering the apartment by the main door, there was a raised hallway space from which some steps led down to an open lounge-dining area, with an ornate old-fashioned street lamp-style light sticking out at a jaunty angle from the banisters [MARK]. Steed sometimes hung his umbrella on a picture to the right of the door as he entered [XMAS], although beneath this was a stand at the top of the stairs which was the correct home for his collection of umbrellas and walking sticks [XMAS]. This was unfortunately an ideal position for Steed's old rival, Russian Ambassador Brodny, to leave a bugged umbrella during a 'social visit' on one occasion [TWOS]. There were also some small cupboards immediately to the left of the door [PRIN]. Visitors could indicate their presence using the doorbell [TWOS]. As well as Steed, Emma had a key so that she could get into the flat when its owner was out [CYBE].

Amongst the decor was Steed's Regency sofa from his original Westminster Mews flat placed by a pillar at the foot of the stairs, a model of a sailing ship and some porcelain figures on a sideboard near the main windows [XMAS], lots of toy soldiers [MARK], and Steed's tuba [MARK]. Near to the recliner was a pendulum clock on a table [XMAS] while Steed tended to keep his drinks and a table light on the table behind the sofa [XMAS]. Steed's telescope had made the journey from Westminster Mews and took pride of place in the large bay window adjacent to the door [MARK].

To the left of the main room – by the kitchen door – was a shelving unit which contained various cups, trophies and horse photographs [eg XMAS], while on the other side of the doorway was a bureau with numerous drawers, in which Steed kept both his cut-throat and electric razors [eg BRIM]. Steed's black phone moved around the flat according to his whims, sometimes being on the bureau [eg JACK] and at other times on a low table by the settee [SUCC].

At the rear of the flat were two smaller arched windows – which apparently looked down on the street below. On the wall to the left of these were a collection of antique

---

[4] *Featuring The New Avengers*, p60.

firearms, a sword and a few more trophies along with some cacti, another clock and some more military photographs [eg SURR]. The area over the hearth in the furthest corner from the front door was dominated by a painting of a soldier, while a photograph of another army officer stood on the mantelpiece along with some detailed model soldiers [eg MARK]. When it came to Christmas, Steed placed cards sent by his friends and relatives on a special screen which he set up in this corner of the room [XMAS].

To the left as one entered was the kitchen, a brick lined and partially tiled room [eg JACK]. There was a window opposite the door with a sink beneath, some drawers and cupboards on the left hand wall with hooks for cooking implements, while the crockery was kept on shelves above the fridge behind the door. There was also a kitchen table which dominated the room [DIAL]. The cooker was in the corner by the window, along with the bread bin [JACK] in which Steed kept the London phone book [SUCC]. Steed had storage jars for items such as currants, pearl barley and – naturally – tea [DIAL], although he kept his sugar in the one marked 'Wild Thyme' [XMAS].

Opposite the kitchen door – between a large wall-mounted mirror on one side and a chair and a large glass-fronted cabinet on the other – was the door to Steed's bedroom [DIAL]; this was a partially wood-panelled room with a sumptuous, old-fashioned four-poster bed in it [XMAS].[5]

The news that Steed was now working with the famous Emma Peel of Knight Industries proved a tantalisingly romantic notion for ABC Television, a company that had earlier used Dr David Keel as the blueprint for their short-lived *Police Surgeon* series in autumn 1960. A company called Telemen decided to make a filmed TV adventure series based at Associated British Elstree Studios in Borehamwood, which they hoped to sell into America. Steed would be portrayed as a super secret agent (akin to Napoleon Solo in the popular series *The Man from UNCLE*, itself adapted from the real-life work of the United Network Command for Law and Enforcement which had debuted on NBC that September) undertaking offbeat and light-weight adventures alongside Emma. Steed's old friend, Patrick Macnee, was the perfect casting as Steed himself – indeed comparing the few production pictures which exist of the filming it is almost impossible to distinguish Macnee from period surveillance shots of Steed. 'The only difference between Macnee and Steed was one between a silk topper and a bowler,'[6] quipped the actor in his autobiography.

Shooting on the series, which had the working title of *The Avengers*, began in Norfolk on Monday 2 November[7] with actress Elizabeth Shepherd playing a blonde Emma Peel in a red leather flying suit. However, within four weeks the Department and – presumably – the legal wing of Knight Industries had made their move. With two partially-completed episodes, Telemen were forced to shut down production. A cover story about casting problems with Elizabeth Shepherd (who went on to star in another offbeat thriller, *The Corridor People*) was cited.[8] The footage which was shot mysteriously vanished.

---

5 Macnee seems to refer to this apartment in ...*deadline* p38-40, although giving the address as '5 Westminster Mews' (p11) but notes that the flat had a 'back stairs... [a] wrought-iron spiral which dropped straight from [the] kitchen to the garage beneath' (p40). The garage was apparently sealed off from 'the Mews' by electric gates.

6 *Blind in One Ear*, p227.

7 *Daily Cinema*, 6 November 1964.

8 *Daily Cinema*, 4 December 1964.

In real life, one of the first joint ventures for Steed and Emma appears to be the investigation into a series of 11 clueless murders over a six month period where the coincidence – if the killings were *not* connected and organised – was 27,000,000 to one [MARK]. This was typical of the assignments now being given to Steed who seemed to have less and less direct contact with his superiors, and now operated generally autonomously and investigated strange killings with possible connections which were not necessarily linked to security or smuggling operations. Similarly, it was now increasingly rare for Steed to operate on the Continent; his missions were generally home grown counter-espionage or threats to industry.

When the latest victim was prominent businessman Jonathan Stone, Steed sent Emma undercover to interview Stone's widow, Jessica. The lethal linking factor turned out to be the marriage bureau Togetherness Inc, which Steed infiltrated posing as an ex-Major of 'the Guards' who had been expelled from three public schools and was the 'black sheep' of the family; his income came from a trust while his cousin had the real money. However, Steed was then forced to 'kill' Emma to maintain his cover. The fake death allowed him to identify that it was Jessica Stone running the operation, and so apprehend those involved such as Togetherness boss Mr Lovejoy and his Counsellor of True Love, Mr Walter Dinsford [MARK].

By late 1964, Steed's passion for vintage vehicles was in full swing and he took great pleasure in driving his green 1926 4^1/$_2$-litre Bentley. When Emma suggested that he should get a newer car, Steed refused, commenting that he was 'Loyal to my Old Lance' and adding in a gentlemanly fashion, 'The quality of a lady's performance is not measured by her years' [XMAS]. One of the most notable things about Steed's vehicles was that, presumably due to some arrangement with the vehicle licensing wing of officialdom arranged via the Department, he was able to swap number plates between his favourite cars. Thus the Bentley which he drove to Brandon Storey's house in Christmas 1964 [XMAS] and to the Dorrington Dean College for Young Ladies bearing the number UW 4887 [MIND], was not the same vehicle which inherited the same number plate some months later.

Shortly before Christmas 1964[9], Steed and Freddy Marshall became aware that certain secrets were getting into the wrong hands. Steed also started to experience nightmares in which Freddy died. Freddy's subsequent death from a brainstorm on 22 December was quite a blow to Steed; the two had been good friends and Steed felt responsible for him. Aware that he would be the next to be attacked in the same way, Steed arranged a plan with Dr Felix Teasel, a psychoanalyst from the War Office's Security Intelligence Psychiatric Division who would monitor Steed for forms of telepathic attack. Emma – to whom Steed gave a Christmas gift of a tear gas pen – invited Steed to a Dickensian-themed Christmas party given by the publisher Brandon Storey, unaware that she too had been mentally manipulated. Through will-power, Steed and Emma resisted the telepathic forces at work and exposed Storey as the man behind the mind-reading security leak in the early hours of Christmas Day [XMAS].

Recovered from the psychic traumas and the death of Freddy, Steed's first mission of 1965 appears to have been an investigation into Pinters Stores Ltd on New Oxford Street,

---

[9] It seems that this was Christmas 1964 since the film and transcript were logged in early 1965. Thus the surveillance film begins – interestingly enough – with a dramatised recreation of the nightmare suffered by Steed on the night of 22 December 1964 and concludes on Christmas Day.

since a receipt dated Sunday 7 February 1965[10] was found on the corpse of Steed's colleague Moran which had been dumped in an alley. While suggesting that Emma should become an assistant at the store, Steed himself used two false stories to elicit information on the business. When meeting Horatio Kane, the store's owner, he claimed to be an efficiency expert who stepped in and 'gingered up' failing businesses. Later, sensing the disgruntled nature of Mr Glynn the chief window dresser, he posed as a shareholder of Pinters who was concerned about the way the business was being run [BARG]. In addition to this, he also flirted with Julie Thompson on the Food Market counter. While at Pinters, Steed was caught off-guard and struck by Major Wentworth, making a tremendous fuss over the black eye which he sustained. It transpired that Pinters Store itself was a bomb which could destroy London in a blackmail attempt launched by Horatio Kane and his cohorts (such as the mercenary Major Robert Wentworth), a plot averted by Steed at the last moment when he halted the lift which was the device's detonation mechanism [BARG].

In late February 1965[11], a spate of thrombosis amongst prominent businessmen was the next assignment to confront Steed, with the bereavements affecting share prices in key companies. Used to responding rapidly, Steed was at the scene of death of the sixth victim, Norman Todhunter, within two hours. The connecting factor between Todhunter and the earlier victims was that they all dealt with Boardman's Bank, a firm which Steed approached on the pretext of investing £2,000,000 representing the Trust Fund of the Armed Forces. Steed was in turn referred to the offices of broker Frederick Yuill[12], where he flirted with a lady called Suzanne who discussed the investment portfolio with him. Moving through the banking and investment world, Steed and Emma discovered that investor Ben Jago and banker John Harvey were behind the deaths – caused by a paging device which, upon receiving a phone call, administered a fatal injection to the carrier [DIAL].

It seems that in mid-March[13], Steed began an investigation into a three violent deaths of businessmen who were involved in bidding for new circuit elements from the Horachi Corporation. Again, Steed adopted two covers during the investigation. Firstly he posed as the replacement for the deceased Bob Lambert of Industrial Deployments[14] so that he could attend the meeting with Horachi. Then when visiting United Automation, another company in the franchise bid, he claimed to be a journalist writing about automation in a modern society. It was at United Automation that Steed soon came face to face with one of the increasing range of technological menaces he would encounter – the Cybernauts. These man-like machines had been created by Dr Armstrong as part of a step towards government

---

[10] This surveillance film seems to cover the period from 7 February to 16 February 1965.

[11] When consulting his diary to make a note of a wine tasting the following Tuesday, Steed read the annotation 'Ladysmith relieved 1900'. The British garrison was relieved in the Anglo-Boer War on 28 February and – given that the year is presumably 1965 it suggests that this surveillance film begins with the death of Norman Todhunter on 23 February and concludes on 4 March. The 28 February was actually a Sunday in 1965, but presumably Steed was consulting a diary which showed a week per page.

[12] Also referred to as 'Brian Yuill' in the surveillance film.

[13] The surveillance film seems to be logged after the Todhunter incident [DIAL] and spans from the 11th to 13th of a given month; Tusamo's meetings in London all took place on the 12th.

[14] A firm also referred to in the surveillance film as 'Industrial Developments'.

by automation, and to develop them he needed the new circuits. Emma and Steed watched as Armstrong was killed by his own creations [CYBE].

Some time shortly after this assignment, it seemed that Steed had purchased or borrowed another old car – this time veteran rather than vintage. Emma found Steed doing the newspaper crossword at the wheel of a 1909 16-horsepower Talbot [CYBE]. By the time spring arrived, Steed was more interested in post-War vintage vehicles and had acquired a 1927 Vauxhall 30-98[15] which he drove to villages such as Pringby [GRAV] and later used to visit the Craigleigh Golf Club [HOLE]. It is possible that this was the car which was nick-named 'Fido' – a fact known by both close friends like Emma and acquaintances like Brodny – and which was in need of an oil change to be ready for Steed attending an Owner's Club meeting one Sunday [TWOS].

Defence work occupied Steed next as one sector of the country's early warning system was blacked out, apparently by a jamming device akin to that being devised by the late Dr Hubert Marlow. Discovering that Marlow had been buried at the village of Pringby in the blackout area, Steed investigated further. While following a lead at the Sir Horace Winslip Hospital for Ailing Railwaymen, Steed posed as a representative of the Footplateman's Friendly Association when found snooping by a thug called Sager; this was also his cover story when he subsequently visited the eccentric, steam engine loving Sir Horace Winslip himself to ask for a donation to the fictitious fund. Needing further investigation of the hospital, Steed pulled some strings at the Ministry to have the medical authorities assign Emma to the Sir Horace Winslip Hospital as a qualified nurse. This exposed a scheme conducted by Dr Johnson to bury Marlow's jamming devices in coffins to knock out the Early Warning System [GRAV].

While mods and rockers clashed at Brighton at Easter, it seems to have been around now[16] that the presence of an injured Sir Clive Todd during a break-in at a Government strong room became a State Security matter requiring Steed's attention. On this investigation, Steed worked with Sir Jeremy, one of Sir Clive's colleagues who reported directly to the Prime Minister, and again Steed wasted no time in assigning Emma as a nurse to keep an eye on Sir Clive. The linking factor between Sir Clive and Dr Fergus Campbell – a 'security' psychiatrist who attempted to kill Sir Clive under hypnosis – was RANSACK, a club for people boasting a high IQ. Although Steed's own intellect was not sufficiently exalted to enable him to join, he successfully completed the entry exam with some help from Emma, and so uncovered the fact that a sports teacher called Holly Trent was using hypnotised geniuses to help her execute espionage missions such as gaining access to a naval base and stealing a plane from an airfield [MIND].

The sudden reappearance of John Wadkin, a cryogenics expert who had gone missing two years earlier, led to the search for a security leak which seemed to be centred at the grand and expensive establishment of the Chessman Hotel in London. While checking out the luxury business, Steed adopted two cover stories. Initially he claimed to be a rival of one Leonard M Pasold[17] from the New York office who wanted to hire Wadkin's colleague Dr George Cullen. Later on Steed passed himself off as the renowned but anonymous food

---

[15] Registration XT 2273, XT 2275 or XT 2276 – the surveillance film is unclear which.

[16] The time of year appears to be spring, and Holly Trent commented that she had been left in charge of Dorrington Dean College for Young Ladies during the school holidays.

[17] Erroneously referred to as 'Pascold' in the summary report.

critic 'M Gourmet'. Having persuaded Emma to take on a receptionist job at the Chessman, Steed was soon able to uncover a Manchurian-style prison camp secreted adjacent to Room 621 where kidnapped scientists had been interrogated – part of a service which Max Chessman hoped to offer the enemy agent Pushkin in each of the hotelier's establishments around the world [ROOM].

A particularly important assignment given to Steed by the Department was being in charge of security at a Ministry briefing of the Western Defence Chiefs – such as Admiral Le Frere, who was ultimately delayed in Paris with plane trouble – in a third floor Conference Room at Westminster. The purpose of this meeting was to ensure an ongoing armed peace by planning the basis of supply routes of Polaris submarines. Knowing that the meeting was to be a target for a Russian spy known only as 'Colonel Pzev', Steed set a trap with the help of his Departmental colleagues Major Carson and Major Plessey who appeared to act as Steed's bodyguard, while actually helping Steed to maintain the illusion that he had a double. In the meantime, Steed asked Emma to sell model kits, knowing that this was one of Pzev's passions [TWOS].

Steed's plan revolved around him convincing the Russian operatives that a model called Gordon Webster was Steed's double, and to this end ensured that he was present at a men's fashion show modelling items such as a champagne resistant suit from 'The Dandy Collection' along with a trendy tropical holiday outfit (including summer shirt and Panama) and a sporting man's wardrobe. The background for 'Webster' had been very firmly established by the Department, and when Ambassador Brodny checked into it he discovered that Steed's alter-ego was a cashiered pilot-turned-criminal-turned-actor – an opportunist who drank, gambled and womanised. As 'Webster', Steed wore loud clothes very unlike his own taste, and referred to people as 'Duckie' in a very theatrical manner. The performance was sufficient to fool even Emma and convince the Russians to employ him to 'kill' Steed and break the security of the Conference Room. As 'Webster' posing as himself, Steed drove a Humber Imperial[18] which was presumably an official vehicle from a car pool. Returning successfully from his mission, he was able to learn that 'Pzev' did not exist and was a combination of four Soviet agents[19] who were then overpowered when their embassy was attacked by one of their own deadly model planes [TWOS].

When Laura Burford, an old friend of Emma's, became the fourth horticulturist to go missing, Steed unearthed some clues as to the disappearances. When he went to see Sir Lyle Peterson, the President of the Horticultural Circle, Steed adopted the guise of a representative of the Trees Preservation Society, a body which was supposedly against tree felling and wanted the government to encourage compulsory tree planting in cities and towns.[20] In a horrific turn of events, it turned out that Peterson and the missing scientists had fallen under the mental control of a plant of extra-terrestrial origin. This had arrived on Earth in a manned space-shot which had been presumed lost when a technical fault occurred after

[18] Registration AWK 948B.

[19] Josef Pudeshkin (third assistant – cipher expert), Boris Schvedloff (second assistant – sabotage and elimination), Alicia Elena (fourth assistant – finance and administration) and André Vogel (first assistant – planning and operations); the correct acronym was thus 'Psev', which the Department had erroneously documented as 'Pzev'.

[20] Comments from those involved indicate that the season is neither summer nor autumn, suggesting this is spring.

take-off a year earlier. The carnivorous vegetation was shortly to seed itself and spread across the planet, but Steed's ruthless use of herbicide again saved the world [SURR].

By now, Steed had a second Bentley[21] which he had used when visiting Sir Lyle [SURR].[22] A few weeks later, this vehicle was badly damaged on a Saturday when Steed had to swerve off the road to avoid a dog as he approached his destination – his old stomping ground RAF Hamelin. Despite the impact with a sturdy tree, Steed was sure that the 'old girl' could be straightened out [HOUR], although this particular vehicle was not seen again. It is possible that Steed also used the car to travel to the Stirrup Cup Inn, since the barman there knew that he ran a 'vintage job' [DUST]. This may also have been the vehicle which Steed earlier used to visit the home of John Wadkin [ROOM], while over the summer of 1965, Steed was also seen to be driving another 1926 3-litre Bentley in racing green[23] [POSI, MISS, KNOT, CLUE, SPLI, GUNS, KIL1]. This vehicle, which was fitted with a black telephone by the driver's seat [SPLI] could be started by a crank handle [CLUE] and was used by Steed periodically for around three years. During this time it came under attack from broadcast electrical power which burnt out its wiring [POSI] and was also sabotaged by two criminals called Earle and Gardiner to frame Steed for murder [CLUE].

Steed's visit to Hamelin was not a formal assignment, but a day out with Emma to say goodbye to the camp which – after its long service – the Air Ministry was now closing. Rather than the thousands of men Steed recalled being at RAF Station 472 in the war, there were now just 30, destined for various overseas postings. However, on arrival at the camp, Steed found it deserted. After being knocked out with a blow to the right temple from the main gate bar, Steed found himself strangely reliving the last hour of his life at the camp, but without Emma and with his former colleagues such as Geoffrey Ridsdale now present and in party mood. The men had been conditioned by Philip Leas, the base dentist, using ultrasonics; Leas now planned to auction the 30 conditioned men to the highest bidder, but had not reckoned on the presence of Steed and Emma [HOUR].[24] RAF Hamelin actually remained active for a few more months and Steed returned there to visit Wing Commander Watson towards the end of the year [DANG].

Around the time that Sir Alec Douglas Home resigned as the Tory leader, Steed was involved in a solo case on 25 July 1965 which would not be fully solved for another 12 years. A Salvation Army group was killed in the village of Wentwick in Berkshire[25] by a Russian soldier wielding a machine gun, who moments later fell off a wall and died of old age. Only Steed apparently visited the scene, but it was a case which both he and Emma would remember [KIL1].

---

[21] Registration XR 6056.

[22] In ...*deadline* (p40), Macnee makes reference to a 4½-litre 1930 Bentley driven by Steed which was restored in 1947 by HM Mackenzie. It is possible this is the vehicle Macnee was referring to, which had a top speed of 104 mph (p146). Other uncorroborated reports also refer to a 1929 Bentley which may be the same vehicle, suggesting that it was later fitted with a 1966 Rolls-Royce engine. *The Floating Game*, p91. The vehicle was also referred to as Speed Six in which Steed apparently took part in Bentley rallies up to Blackpool in 1966. *The Passing of Gloria Munday*, p9. Another unfilmed report suggests that one of Steed's Bentleys from 1965 had a distinctive 'old hooter' with which Emma could signal to him. *TV Comic*, Issue 721, 9 October 1965.

[23] Registration YT 3942.

[24] Comments from a tramp called Hickey seem to confirm that this was in the early stages of summer.

[25] The village has distinct similarities with Sarratt in Hertfordshire.

It was a lack of fish being caught by the home fleets which prompted an undercover mission up to Castle De'Ath in Scotland, and for this Steed donned a kilt to pose as Jock McSteed, a Scottish Historian writing a book on the 13th Laird of De'Ath, one 'Black Jamie'. Steed's claim to be of Scots blood was backed up by his story of how he was carried south by the 'Sassenachs' when he was only 'a bairn'. For this journey north, Steed acquired the use of an Amphicar[26] in which he could simply drive out into a loch for a spot of fishing. Emma soon joined him, posing as a publicity consultant for a stately homes organisation to discuss opening the castle to the public. Detecting a secret area of the dungeon with an underwater dock off the moat, the presence of a mini-sub was discovered, with a team led by Angus De'Ath using ultrasonics to drive the fish into deep waters away from the British fleets [CAST].

The corpse of a man called Arthur Peever pitched from a runaway pram allowed Steed to renew acquaintances with his old rival, one-time top agent Willi Fehr, in mid-August.[27] The evening suit worn by Peever had been hired from men's outfitters Lichens and Co which Steed visited, claiming to be undertaking top secret work for Baggy Pants Ltd (Diplomatic Corps), ensuring that visiting Russian diplomats were given terrible clothes to wear. The trail eventually led to Terpsichorean Training Techniques Inc, a dance school where lonely young men were targeted by principal Lucille Banks and band leader Chester Read and killed, to be replaced by foreign agents who could then infiltrate British society. Steed joined the classes as 'Jonathan Steed' whose family 'came over with the Vikings' between raids and discovered America. Claiming to be British 'by birth, nature and inclination,' Steed's background included a girlfriend who had been eaten by a crocodile on an Amazonian trek and how he had returned from abroad a week ago with no friends and family – thus feeling that a dancing brush-up would kick-start his social life [QUIC].

In the later summer[28], the drowning of a poacher called Ted Barker in a field at Lower Storpington during a freak rain storm was rapidly linked by Steed with ten letters to *The Times* from Jonah Barnard, a local eccentric of the same village, who insisted that the Great Flood of Biblical times was returning. When visiting Grannie Gregson's Glorious Grogs Incorporated, a factory which seemed to be at the centre of the strange events, Steed introduced himself to secretary Joyce Jason as representing 'Steed, Steed, Steed, Steed and Jacques Ltd – Wine Merchants Extraordinary.' Steed quipped that in fact he was the only director of the company and that the other Steeds were made up as they simply looked good on the card, while the non-existent Jacques had been added because 'in the wine trade you must have that French touch.' This cover was certainly a strong one; Dr Sturm of Grannie Gregson's was able to check on Steed and was left certain that he was indeed a bona fide wine merchant. Eventually Steed's mission revealed that Sturm had developed a method of creating rain to order which he planned to sell as a weapon to the highest bidder. After a

---

[26] Registration ELF 981C.

[27] When Steed visited Mulberry's Bank Ltd the first time, the calendar read 19 August, and it showed 23 August when he returned some time later. Thus, this surveillance film seems to span events from 19 to 24 August 1965.

[28] This is an instance of the documented dates not matching the evidence of the surveillance films. Although the assignment was completed and filed with a date of around 11 May 1965, the sales chart at Grannie Gregson's Glorious Grogs clearly chronicled sales up to the end of August, suggesting that this was late August 1965.

fight between Steed, Emma and Sturm's men in a rain-filled room at the factory, the rain machine exploded on burning out and killed Sturm [SURF].

The death of security agent Ted Murphy, found with a series of golf cards on his body, took Steed and Emma to Craigleigh Golf Club (CGC) in Surrey. Joining as members, within the space of a weekend they had revealed a control room secreted beneath the 13th hole which allowed treacherous scientists such as missile guidance expert Dr Peter Adams to relay their secrets by television signals beamed via the Vostick 2 satellite to scientists in Eastern Europe. Steed drove a fine golf ball which stopped the fleeing mastermind behind the scheme, Colonel Watson, in his tracks [HOLE].

In late September[29], Steed reported directly to a minister, a poor soul plagued both by hayfever during the summer months and also having to organise the Ministry hockey team because nobody else wanted the job. The reduction in wildlife in one area of the British countryside – allied with a fertiliser called 'Silent Dust' which had turned a hamlet called Manderley into a barren, infertile wasteland in 1955 – meant that Steed had to track down the family of Prendergast, the man in charge of the destructive project. As Steed's mission proceeded, his excuse for being present at the village where Prendergast's daughter now lived was that he intended to buy farmland near Peter Omrod, and there cultivate stock, sugar beet and grain. This mission was a particularly hazardous one for Steed who sustained two injuries. He was shot in the right breast by Mellors, a gamekeeper wielding a double-barrelled 12-bore shotgun, and also caught his left foot in a man trap – although he managed to stay silent and not give his presence away to Mellors. Ultimately though, Omrod and his compatriots – including Miss Beryl Snow, Oliver Mellors, Juggins and Croft – were put out of action before their £40,000,000 blackmail threat to release 'Silent Dust' across Dorset and other counties could be put into operation [DUST].

With these events behind him, Steed allowed himself the luxury of an autumn holiday in some warmer overseas climes. On his return he was surprised to discover a woman who was clearly not Emma living in Emma's flat and passing herself off as his friend and colleague. To observe the impostor, Steed first posed as a mutual friend of both himself and 'Emma' in an attempt to confuse her, and then made a telephone call from a nearby phone box when he adopted an upper-class accent announcing himself as 'old lover boy himself – back from Karachi.' This had the desired effect in making the fake Emma panic, allowing him to follow her. It turned out that the real Emma had been kidnapped by a firm called Art Incorporated and put up for auction. Visiting Art Incorporated, Steed posed as an art expert named Wayne Pennyfeather ffitch, a man who liked to establish a 'rapport' with his surroundings... and an identity backed up by one of many business cards which he happened to be carrying. With help from Georgie Price-Jones – the fake Emma – he was able to rescue Emma from being sold to a foreign power and defeat Gregorio Auntie of Art Incorporated [AUNT].

Around mid-October 1965[30], Steed was asked to investigate the small coastal hamlet of Little Bazeley-by-the-Sea because of vague reports of something strange which had

---

[29] Miss Clare Prendergast told Steed that her father died during the cold snap at the end of March six months ago. Since the surveillance film seems to climax with a hunt on a Sunday, it is most likely that it spans 23 to 26 September 1965.

[30] The reason given to Emma for the school being empty was that it was 'mid-term' and the weather conditions seemed to indicate autumn.

reached the Department. Again, the power of the Department was such that Steed could arrange for the education authorities to have Emma sent to Little Bazeley as a qualified teacher. Steed himself posed as a property developer with a roving commission to look for likely sites in the Little Bazeley area. The entire community had been replaced by foreign agents commanded by a fake school inspector called 'Mark Brandon' who were amassing a military force in a bunker beneath the abandoned air base of 33 Squadron. Overpowering the key agents, Steed and Emma were able to seal the infiltrators in their own underground shelter [TOWN].

Sometime around late October – during the 'rainy season' – the appearance of a local farmhand called Jack Kendrick in Hertfordshire prompted Steed's investigation, since Kendrick seemed to be a victim of Shirenzai, a form of voodoo peculiar to the tropical country of Kalaya. One of Steed's lines of enquiry was the nearby Kalayan Settlers and Ex-Servicemen's Association where, on meeting the eccentric Colonel Rawlings (who believed he was still living in Kalaya), Steed passed himself off as a former member in No 2 Company who had been at Colonel Rawlings's farewell party in Selunda; Steed further claimed to have subsequently bought a rubber plantation in Kalaya with his army gratuity, but had it taken from him by the new Kalayan government. At the Association, Steed soon discovered that a group of expatriates forced out of Kalaya – including entomologist Professor Swain, hunter Simon Trent and a man called Fleming – were planning to release a new strain of tsetse fly in Kalaya to paralyse the country and punish the government. He and Emma quickly disposed of the lethal insects in the British rain [HUNT].

Steed had a new recipient for the UW 4887 registration plate by now, a fourth Bentley. This green 3-litre model, again from around 1926, first appeared in surveillance films when he visited Professor Swain in Hertfordshire [HUNT]. This vehicle became one of Steed's favourites and he used to visit the Faversham Military Hospital [DANG] in the coming weeks. In the New Year, Steed drove the vehicle when dashing to the Hall of Friendship [BRIM], going to check up on Emma when she was lured down to a house in Pendlesham [JACK] and to deliberately collide with Emma's Lotus to give him a pretext to talk to her [SUCC]. This vehicle was actually fitted with a small television set on the passenger side, allowing Emma to watch live television coverage of the dedication of the Hall of Friendship while Steed drove towards it [BRIM]. Steed also had no hesitation in using the Bentley to smash through a fake 'Road Closed' barrier which stood in his path, although moments later the vehicle's tyres were shredded by automatic metal spikes which were hidden in the country lane [JACK]. After Steed's investigation of a Keep Fit Class for Young Ladies [SUCC] in spring 1966, it seems that this Bentley was garaged for over a year until Steed selected it to follow a lead at the estate of George Benstead, where it subsequently had its windscreen shot out – despite the fact that Steed had been assured that the glass was bullet proof [TREA].

By November 1965, Patrick Macnee had taken a break from his successful acting career and had pursued the notion of fictional adventures about his friend Steed, akin to the glorified biographies concerning their school bully James Bond which Ian Fleming had been issuing since *Casino Royale* in 1953. Macnee collaborated with Peter Leslie, a professional writer who had written tie-in publications for the *Danger Man* television series and concocted a work entitled *...deadline*. Steed's taste and style such as his Chelsea boots and even his former address of 5 Westminster Mews were all perfect details which Macnee brought to the manuscript. This fictional tale of Steed saw him reporting to a food-loving boss referred to as 'His Nibs' in a tale of how fake newspaper headlines were being printed to inflame public reaction to key political speeches. Emma also appeared, her age given as 27 and described as 'a woman of independent means.'[31] Macnee and Leslie then completed a sequel manuscript entitled *Dead Duck*, this time pitting their fictional Steed and Emma against Sir Albert Warbeck-Simner, a mad ornithologist who was planning to have Helimanthine, a synthetic version of curare, spread across the world by migrating birds. Although completed by May 1966 for Hodder and Stoughton, neither book were to appear in the book shops and only a few trade sample copies are known to be in existence. As with the television series, the Department moved quickly and the manuscripts only appeared in print much later from Titan Books in August and September 1994 when they no longer had any relevance to Steed's confidential career.

Meanwhile, the real Steed operated on behalf of the War Office when investigating the strange behaviour of the 60-year-old General 'Woody' Groves who was involved in a 'chicken run' incident with a motorbike, despite being in line to be the next Chief of Staff. Groves was the eighth in a string of military men undertaking unnecessarily hazardous tasks. The senior soldiers involved were all members of a secret organisation known as the Danger Makers which aimed to put the spice back into life during peacetime for those who thrived on peril. However, this organisation was being manipulated by Dr Harold Long, a consultant with the Psychological Warfare Department, who had found how to control these trained men and aimed to use them on the 'Crime of the Century', the theft of the crown jewels. Posing as a member from the society's Northern Chapter, Steed infiltrated the group at Manton House Military Museum[32] with the code-name Bacchus and put an end to their activities with help from Emma [DANG].

From late 1965, a series of vicious, childish and damaging practical jokes were played on visiting dignitaries and members of gentry. Steed got involved in earnest on 11 January 1966[33] when he and Emma attended a gala at the Queen's Theatre where a Middle Eastern VIP was the latest victim to a prank. The main suspect was the Honourable John Cleverley Cartney who had re-established the Hellfire Club, an 18th century clique which had aimed to topple the government. After the practical jokes, Cartney was now moving on to destroy the British cabinet by detonating explosives beneath Calverstone House. Steed joined the society where Emma became the 'Queen of Sin', and together they thwarted the club's plans – with Emma manoeuvring Cartney to fall into one of his own subterranean traps [BRIM].

A leak of secrets from the War Office was narrowed down to the three officers comprising the CFEE[34] when Steed was tipped off by a double agent working as a barber. Steed approached each in turn under a different guise. When visiting Vice Admiral Willows he donned a false beard and arrived with a WREN in a motor launch as 'Commander Red' on Admiralty Business. To learn about Brigadier Percy Ponsonby Goddard, he posed as 'Major White' of the War Office and arrived in a tank to ask questions for a regimental

---

[31] ...*deadline*, p44.

[32] This later apparently became the British Rail Centre at Watford.

[33] In the surveillance film, Emma visited the Hon John Cleverley Cartney the following day, which – according to Cartney's diary – was Wednesday 12 January 1966. Thus the film spans Steed's experiences from 11 to 14 January 1966.

[34] Commission For Eastern Europe.

magazine. With a handle-bar moustache, he dropped in by helicopter as 'Squadron Leader Blue', a PRO from BHQ seconded from RHB, to research the career of Group Captain Miles. Having asked Emma to investigate Miles further, Steed established a connection between the three officers at the Butlers & Gentlemen's Gentlemen Association which he then applied to join to train as a butler. Steed's fake references from the Duke of Duffup, Earl of Isley and the Honourable Flegghorn (all names of pubs) made Benson believe that Steed was a thief and so allowed him to become part of the espionage ring, which hid tape recorders in the dress uniforms of the officers. Exposing Benson and his boss, Sergeant Moran, Steed and Emma closed down the operation [BUTL].

It seems that around now, Steed may have taken a European holiday. On his return, his suspicions were aroused when a property called Seven Pines at Pendlesham in Hampshire was bequeathed to Emma by an Uncle Jack of whom she had no recollection. As well as having his friend Frederick 'Pongo' Withers keep an eye on her, Steed departed in pursuit in his Bentley – arriving at the remote house to discover that Emma had survived a horrific automated trap left for her by the late Professor Keller, a man she had once fired from Knight Industries [JACK].

In late March[35], Steed became involved after the murder of James Broom CBE, an economist with plans to banish poverty from Europe forever. Broom had been en route to see a rival economist at St Bedes[36] college, where Steed volunteered Emma's services as a lecturer while he guarded the nervous Richard Carlyon, Broom's right hand man, before himself posing as a former student of St Bedes. Once again, Steed found himself in fancy dress and attending another college rag week, this time as the Sheriff of Nottingham in which guise he unmasked university archivist Dr DB Grindley MA as the economist who aimed to change the face of Europe with ideas which opposed those of Broom and Carlyon [HIST].

On the next case, Steed reported by phone to 'the Colonel' [SUCC], who was possibly the short-tempered Colonel Robertson with whom Steed would argue [PRIN][37] and whom he had called to have Emma tailed to Pendlesham [JACK]. This investigation concerned the deaths of numerous businessmen including Sir George Morton. Speculating that there might be embezzlement going on, the Minister himself made an appointment for Steed with Joshua Rudge, a chartered accountant. Knocked out by a blow from what turned out to be a stiletto heel, Steed set himself up as a target by establishing his own four million pound business in stocks and shares at his flat, and asking Rudge's office for part-time help in the evenings. The assistant sent to him, Miss Sara Penny, was one of a number of ambitious secretaries attending keep fit classes run by Henry and Henrietta Throgbottom – although when Steed tailed Henry in an Austin he found that Henrietta was in fact dead. The mentally ill Henry was using secretaries to attack business men like those who had driven his wife, a successful ballerina, to a premature grave. Throgbottom was subsequently

---

[35] The students of St Bedes were in high spirits because it was the 'end of term'. Although this film seems to have been completed and documented in February 1966, it seems more likely that this is late March 1966 at the end of the Spring term.

[36] Pronounced 'St Bodes'.

[37] It is possible that Steed and Emma also reported to Robertson as 'the Colonel' on a number of other assignments around 1965-66. *TV Comic*, Issues 731, 18 December 1965; 736, 22 January 1966; 751, 7 May 1966; 761, 16 July 1966.

killed in a shoot-out with Steed [SUCC].

Steed's discovery of fellow undercover man Ronny Westcott fatally wounded at his flat on his return from an all-night party with Emma led him to take over the investigation handled by Westcott and his similarly deceased partner, George Reed. Posing as Reed, Steed kept an appointment at the outlandish Quite Quite Fantastic Inc organisation where it was possible for people to live out their wildest dreams. At the QQF offices, one of the fantasies being prepared was the assassination of the cricket-loving Crown Prince Ali of Barabia[38], who was visiting London to offer oil concessions in exchange for Britain's full military protection. Steed approached Ali claiming to represent the Ministry of Eastern Affairs and the British Government, and offered the 'poorly educated' Emma as a gift to Ali for his harem. Arkadi, a foreign rival for the oil concession, was soon identified as the man behind the planned assassination which was averted [PRIN].

It seems that Prince Ali was so grateful for having his life saved that, in addition to giving Emma back to Steed, he allowed the Department to shoot a short humorous training film as an experimental item using colour stock in the main chamber of his London embassy. Entitled *The Strange Case of the Missing Corpse*, this ran to three minutes and featured Steed and Emma along with a girl who seemed to be one of Ali's cricketing harem. The piece, conveyed with the pair's unique humour, emphasised the importance of locating a corpse at the start of an assignment, otherwise an agent would be 'defunct – obsolete – out of business.' Emma displayed her 'feminine wiles' and fighting skills while Steed admired a vintage champagne when dining with a 'diabolical mastermind'. At the end of the demonstration, the secret of the 'double-barrelled atomic sock knitter' was declared safe and Steed discovered the harem girl whom he decided to 'handle personally'.

On a more serious note, it was possibly in summer 1966[39] that Steed found himself effectively repeating a strategy he had used in 1953 on a rare overseas mission. An Eastern European called Max Prendergast was operating a racket similar to that of Martin Goodman – betrayal and causing suffering to refugees. Adopting the same approach as he had with Cathy, Steed allowed the same dangerous romantic situation to be played out in Berlin by Emma. Prendergast was apprehended by the police the day he was due to leave for Rio. Unfortunately, it was not the last that the happy couple of Emma and Steed would hear of the matter [JOKE].

---

[38] In the summary report, Prince Ali was described as being a 'Bahranian'.

[39] In late 1967, this was referred to as being 'not long ago'.

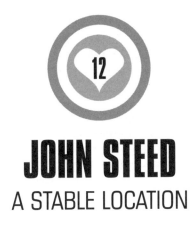

JOHN STEED

A STABLE LOCATION

Around mid-1966, Steed moved from Queen Anne's Court to the 'clubman' flat which would be his home for the next three years. This was Apartment 3 [KNOT] at 3 Stable Mews, City/County of London[1] [KNOT, CATC, LEGA, LACE, FOG], situated in a quiet cobbled mews near the middle of the city [eg WHO?] with a call box round the corner [WHO?]. The address was known to Steed's fellow agents like Penman [FALS], Trouncer [KILL], and courier Bobby Danvers [TREA] and also to more dubious characters such as Jimmy Merlin [MORN], foreign agents like Ivan Peppitoperoff [CORR], Merridon and Brinstead [KILL] and assorted criminals [LEGA, ROTT].

Overlooking the end of the Mews was a fine brace of stone sphinxes [KNOT, CATC]. The far side of the building, angled away from the Mews, was covered in ivy [NURS]. The flat was 35 miles along country roads from an airfield used by Bobby Danvers [TREA], 15 miles from High Pines at Edgington[2] [TREA], 30 minutes drive from Risley Dale [POSI] and 15 minutes drive out into the country to the office used by Steed's superior, Father [STAY]. It was also handy for the opera [LOOK], round the corner from Xavier Smith's antique shop in Sturmer Street [PAND] and close to Gunthorpe Street in London's East End as well as both a hotel and a railway station [FOG]. Local trades-folk in the area seemed to include a knife grinder, a lady selling lucky white heather, an organ grinder, a rag and bone man, and a blind beggar [FOG].

The yellow door from the Mews [KNOT] led into the building. The main entrance to Steed's was then up some stairs inside the main building [KNOT] to a landing with a curtained alcove [LEGA]. Visitors rang a doorbell mounted beside the dark green front door [eg TIME]. The door could be secured by a bolt and chain in addition to its Yale lock [JOKE]. Again, Emma had a key to the apartment [STAT] and later on Steed's new colleague, Tara King, could also gain access in his absence [eg GETA]; Steed and his friends also used a secret door release to open the lock, with the catch being located in the top right corner of

---

[1] There seems to be some confusion over this address. One work notes that '5 Westminster Mews, near London's Houses of Parliament, had now been given a face lift. Having been able to buy the freehold of the property...' *The Complete Avengers*, p127. It seems that since Steed's days, the street has been re-named Duchess Mews and is in London W1 near Regent's Park.

[2] Which strongly resembled Shenley Hall at Shenley, Hertfordshire.

the front door [WHO?]. The flat was not impregnable to the enemy. Prendergast or one of his agents was able to plant a trip wire and poisoned razor blade on a joker card in the apartment [JOKE] while a man called Benson broke in to stage a burglary and exchange Steed's watch for a duplicate [RETU]. Neither was the door any defence against a deter-mined Cybernaut [RETU] and on some occasions Steed left the door open anyway when he was at home [FOG].

By the front door was a glass panel [STAT] which Emma smashed with a vase from the landing outside on one occasion so that she could gain entry [JOKE]. To the left as one entered the vestibule area was an 18th century red leather hotel porter's alcove chair [eg TIME] beside which Steed kept his boots [CORR] while he sometimes placed his bowler and brolly in the alcove itself [eg FALS, FOG]. The light switch for the living area was by the alcove [KNOT].

The main living room – as with the vestibule – was finished with pine-panelled walls. Principal items of furniture were Steed's rich red leather sofa and armchair [TIME] which were augmented by a rotating chair [LEGA]. On the floor was a white sheepskin rug [eg DOOR]. Silver cups and model soldiers stood on a chest of drawers to the right of the front door, with rifles mounted on the wall above them [eg CORR]. Close to this was a lacquered cabinet where Steed kept his drinks including his port [NOON, REQU] in addition to his other wine cellar [PAND].

In the hearth was a gas fire [NURS]. Marble surrounded the fireplace [TIME] on which there were model cannons ('Model of 1672') [eg CORR] while above it hung *The Charge of the Light Brigade* painted by 19th century British painter Robert Alexander Hillingford [eg TIME]. From around Autumn 1967, this was later replaced by a pastoral scene [eg KNOT, etc], which in turn Steed on one occasion removed since he was expecting to receive a gold clock from the President of an African nation whom he knew well in thanks for putting paid to the schemes of Colonel Martin Nsonga [GUNS]. To the right of the fireplace was an arched alcove painted red which housed two flintlocks from Steed's antique handgun collection [eg TIME].

The tuba from the previous two flats remained on display, housing daffodils [TIME] or other bright flowers [WING], although the original instrument was unwound when Steed had to place a bomb inside it for his own protection in 1967 [NURS]. He soon acquired a replacement [JOKE] and it sprang a leak [GETA]; he later explained that he now kept the instrument solely to put flowers in since he could not play it himself [TAKE]. Later on, it appeared to be used to house pokers [THAT].

Also in this corner were paintings of soldiers in old-fashioned uniforms on either side of the main window [eg TIME] along with a tall mirror [NURS]. Other items seen around Steed's flat included a rocking horse (possibly Primrose from his childhood) [TIME] and ornamental military porcelain figures on the corner bookshelf [eg DOOR], some of which had their heads shot off when Steed traded gunfire with the enemy agent Martin Ezdorf in early 1968 [GETA].

The main window looked down into Stable Mews itself [eg KNOT] and was lockable [STAY]; it was smashed by Tara using her shoe from the street outside [WILD], a heavy called Zoltan shooting a fortune hunter called Gorky [LEGA] and also by an errant model Spitfire made by Steed [LEGA]. It was generally covered by yellow drape curtains [DOOR] in velvet which were dangerous to hay fever sufferers [CATC]. In the window itself was usually a table with a table lamp [LEGA] while other ornaments included a model vintage car on a tabletop [TAKE], a globe [eg LEGA] akin to the one at Westminster Mews, a vase of red carnations [STAY] and a silver box on a round table [JOKE].

There was an impressive desk with a leather jotter and letter knives [LEGA] and a glass ashtray [THAT]; Steed kept champagne in one of the drawers [SPLI] and a revolver in one of the other drawers [FOG]. He usually kept a black telephone on his desk [eg BIRD, KNOT, STAY, REQU] although he also used white [eg DOOR, JOKE, KILL], grey [TREA] and green [CYPH, JOKE] receivers which he moved about the flat. Attached to his phone line was a reel-to-reel recording machine which could take messages [FEAR, JUST].

At Stable Mews, Steed's telephone number was Whitehall 9819 [STAY] and while he was away he arranged to have calls transferred to 'the usual number' by the operator [STAY]. However, one version of Steed's calling card gave his phone number as 460-9618 [LACE] while – rather oddly for an undercover man – Emma remarked that Steed was 'in the book' [VENU]. In both cases it is possible that these were security lines of some sort and did not go directly to Steed's flat.

The rear wall of the apartment – opposite the fireplace – was where Steed erected a projector to view films [BREA, CYPH]. Steed also had a record player [WHO?, CYPH], an electric fan [DOOR] and a television [MORN, PAND]. In fact by early 1969 he had a colour television to receive BBC 2 in its full glory – the only problem being that the best aerial position for reception was being dangled outside the window [PAND]. He also used a Dictaphone with cassette tapes to record informal reports for Tara or Father [STAY].

From the corner by the porter's seat, bookcases snaked around to the kitchen and the back door [TIME]. It was here that Steed kept his reference books [LOOK]. At the rear of the flat was the back door [TIME] which – although on an upper floor – sometimes gave the appearance of being on the ground level with a hedge outside [NURS]. This back door was in fact a half-door like that found in a stable [WHO?]. This was presumably accessed by the fire escape [WILD].

To the left of the back door was the kitchen and some shelves [NURS], while on the right was a spiral staircase which led upstairs. Behind the staircase were some curved windows [JOKE]. It is most likely that Steed's bedroom was up these stairs [SUP7] and it seems that he had an electric blanket [STAT] on a bed which was missing one of the knobs on the bedstead – Steed later located a perfect match when dredging the Meadow Pond [THIN]. Steed's bedroom did not appear in the surveillance films, but other material suggests it was a large room with a standard lamp, tall windows with long curtains and a phone on the table.[3]

On the wall opposite the kitchen doors were more pictures, military cap badges, a bugle and firearms [WING, NURS, WILD]. The kitchen had black-tiled surfaces [WING] and a brass hood above the cooking hob [CORR]. The room was decorated by red checked curtains and a green lamp [SUP7]. Steed was appalled when enemy agents Basil and Lola left a dirty tea towel in his kitchen [WHO?].

The flat also had a dark room where Steed could develop photographs [CYPH]. Although the main living room originally had a doorway in the corner to the right as one entered (where Steed kept his sporting equipment) [WHO?], this was panelled over in late 1967 and another table of drinks was housed in this space [CATC]. A further door exited the room in the far corner between the window and Steed's desk [SPLI]; this led to a room where Steed

---

[3] 'Steed's 'Holiday'', *The Avengers Annual*, 1967, p68.

would leave the neighbours' baby – a 'lively lad' – when he was on baby-sitting duties in 1968 [WISH].

Steed was happy to let Tara use his flat when he was away on holiday in October 1968, saying that she could help herself to his drinks and play his records [STAY]; he also let the timber expert Forsythe stay in the flat and help himself to a drink while he was out [ROTT]. The flat was also occupied by Steed's boss Mother for use as a temporary HQ when Steed was injured and confined to Department S [NOON]. Steed found the apartment was just the right size for him on his own – and certainly not large enough for Fang the Wonder Dog to live with him too [TAKE]. To quote the opposition agent Olga Volowski, the apartment was 'Opulent, luxurious, expensive and *thoroughly* decadent' [CORR].

Three unconfirmed stories hint that around 1966 Steed also owned a cottage in Wiltshire that was built in 1573.[4] This was apparently two miles from the village of Berniston, not far from Swindon.[5]

By now, Steed apparently had a new source of classic period vehicles which he could use – the collection of Lord Montagu housed at his public motor museum at Beaulieu House near Brockenhurst in Hampshire. Ralph Montagu, the son of Lord Montagu, recalls some of Steed's visits there around 1966.

'Growing up at Beaulieu in the 1960s involved meeting a lot of different people – mostly distinguished guests of my father. Many of them came to see his rapidly expanding car collection in the Montagu Motor Museum, and this included a number of motoring enthusiasts. My father believes in running the museum as a working collection, and was always pleased to have an excuse to take his cars out.

'One of those who helped to keep the cars in regular use was a dapper man called John Steed, who was introduced to my father by an old army friend. My father evidently had great faith in Mr Steed as he was allowed to borrow almost any car from the museum and drive it on the public roads completely unsupervised. These valuable old cars usually only come out for organised rallies, but Mr Steed was allowed free reign. Quite what he got up to in these veterans I never understood; at first I thought he might have been a motoring journalist, but I never saw an article written by him, so that can't be the reason. Even my father was rather vague when I asked him why Mr Steed was allowed such unfettered access to his priceless collection.

'Our bower-hatted guest was usually accompanied by a very nice lady who I assumed to be his wife (I was only eight years old at the time) but I later discovered that she was called Mrs Peel and not married to Steed at all! I remember that she was always keen to get out and help, although on one occasion Mr Steed got her to stay at the controls whilst he swung the starting handle of the Unic — a former London taxi.[6] The engine sounded very sickly, so he went round the back to listen to the exhaust, at which point the car, or Mrs Peel, did something and the engine backfired, producing a violent cloud

---

[4] *The Floating Game*, p32; *The Laugh Was on Lazarus*, p39; *Heil Harris!*, p10.
[5] *Heil Harris!*, p52.
[6] A 1907 burgundy and black model, registration MD 1480 [TIME].

of smoke. His face was absolutely blackened! On another occasion they both got out to push the 1909 Rolls-Royce Silver Ghost[7], but just as they got behind the car, she seemed to fire up on her own, and started away without anyone at the wheel. I have an abiding memory of them running after the car as it went through the stone arch of our gate house – I suppose they must have caught up with it eventually, as it was safely returned to the museum and is still one of our prize exhibits.[8]

'I haven't seen either Mr Steed or Mrs Peel for many years. However my sister, who was only four or five when they first visited, treasures a photograph of them together, her in a small yellow Edwardian pedal car, and Mr Steed looking his usual gallant self.'[9]

One of Steed's latest habits was to inform Emma that he was in need of her services by an array of strange methods – each more convoluted and fantastic than the last. The phrase he selected was 'Mrs Peel – We're Needed'[10] and the methods in which Steed delivered this call to arms included a card inside a box of chocolates left in Emma's flat [FEAR], the reverse of a Grand Hunt Ball invitation [TIME], an arrow fired into her apartment [BIRD], a tiny card placed under her microscope [SEET], an inscription added to one of her paintings [WING], the colours on a set of traffic lights [LIVI], in writing under the wallpaper at Emma's flat [TIGE], a card on the end of Steed's umbrella [VENU], the headline on a newspaper [CORR], a card carried by a clockwork train [STAT] or model carousel in her flat [NURS], and finally appearing on Emma's colour television set [NEVE]. On one occasion, Emma was ready for him and when he asked 'Mrs Peel...' she responded 'Sorry Steed – I'm needed elsewhere' [EPIC] while another time she took control, having him shoot down a yellow plastic duck marked 'Steed' and then emerge from behind a bush to add 'You're needed' [SUP7].

Steed's high profile in the counter-espionage [BIRD, CORR, TREA] world now meant that there seemed little point in him acting as an 'undercover' agent with a back story[11]; Comrade Nutski, who had now taken over counter-counter-espionage for the opposition in London rated Steed as 'DANGEROUS. HANDLE WITH CARE' [CORR]. Thus Steed continued his autonomous existence, apparently seldom reporting to superiors and occasionally liaising with other members of the Department when necessary – often taking over cases from agents who were killed in action [TIME, BIRD, NURS]. Many of his assignments were to investigate strange serial killings – with fewer operations directly stemming from the schemes of the 'other side'. The threats which he started to encounter now became increasingly outlandish, and the attitude with which he faced these perils was an almost surreal unflappability and an extremely light-hearted nature, rather unlike the manipulative and merciless figure who had angered Cathy and Dr Keel so much in recent years.

---

[7] A Rolls-Royce 40/50 model, registration 'R 1909' [SEET].

[8] Steed also had use of a 1905 Vauxhall, registration MV 9942, a car which drove off backwards on one occasion [BIRD].

[9] Correspondence with Ralph Montagu, 25 January 2004.

[10] This phrase was even worked into the dialogue for Steed in Don Macpherson's movie screenplay.

[11] Unconfirmed reports suggest that Steed was actually prominent enough to be recognised by members of the public, such as a boy called Slim Dexter. *TV Comic*, Issue 721, 9 October 1965.

By autumn 1966, Steed had access to a fifth Bentley, a 1928 Green Label model in British Racing Green[12] with – on occasion – a Union Jack flag attached to its radiator [FEAR].[13] He was driving this at the time of an investigation into why a number of prominent manufacturers in the ceramics industry were all found in a traumatised state, having been exposed to their innermost fears. Visiting another ceramics firm, Fox, White and Crawley, Steed claimed to be from the Central Productivity Council dispensing the Prime Minister's views on the industry, while later he approached British Porcelain as a 'minor official' of the Monopolies Commission. Establishing that the common link between the incidents was the Business Efficiency Bureau (BEB), Steed offered himself as a customer with the unlikely cover story that he ran a group of travel agencies which offered luxury igloos in Iceland and had a gross turnover around the £100,000 mark. Steed confirmed his suspicions that the Bureau were literally eliminating competition for their clients by working on their fears – a tactic he exploited in the defeat of Pemberton, their President [FEAR].

Before the next assignment, Steed acquired a sixth vintage Bentley, a 1926 Speed Six, again in British Racing Green[14] which would become his favoured vehicle for the next year or so [TIME, BIRD, VENU, SEET, WING, LIVI, TIGE, EPIC, NURS, JOKE, WHO?, DOOR, RETU, BREA, JUST]. Steed seemed to relish this car, jauntily leaping into her driving seat without opening the door [eg SEET]. It was a rather temperamental vehicle which Emma believed only Steed could start properly [WHO?], and it apparently suffered from 'ghosts' in the engine, which Emma was able to remedy [LIVI]. It was equipped with items such as a green telephone receiver between the front seats [DOOR], a walkie-talkie in the glove box [JUST], a reel-to-reel tape recorder for bugging operations [SEET] and Steed also kept a torch on board [JOKE]. The Bentley was ultimately sabotaged when its linkage was tampered with causing the brakes to fail on Spout Hill as Steed drove to Sir Andrew Boyd's residence in October 1967; Steed fought to keep control, crashing through a fence and into some woodland [DOOR].[15]

Steed next inherited a case being undertaken by fellow agents Clive Paxton and Tubby Vincent who had stumbled upon an escape route being used by embezzlers and criminals who were fleeing to England. The escape chain began at Mackidockie Court[16] and Steed followed this, supposedly offering illicit diamonds. The service offered by Waldo Thyssen was apparently an escape into the past using a time machine, but this was a con trick to get the clients' ill-gotten gains before killing them. Steed and Emma easily overpowered Thyssen and his cohorts in the faked-up period chambers [TIME].

The death of undercover man Percy Danvers meant another case for Steed to inherit, although two more colleagues – Frank Elrick[17] and Mark Pearson – were then killed when

---

[12] Registration YK 6871.

[13] There is an unconfirmed report that one of Steed's Bentleys was rigged with an explosive around 1967 by a group of killers known as the Secret Six; this may be the vehicle. *Diana*, Issue 221, 12 May 1967.

[14] Registration RX 6180.

[15] There is an unconfirmed report that Steed acquired yet another Bentley, a 1933 model, around 1969/1970. *Too Many Targets*, p11.

[16] Erroneously referred to as 'Mackidockie Mews' in the summary report.

[17] Erroneously referred to as 'George Elrick' in the summary report.

engaged in similar ornithological activities. Furthermore, Steed's notoriety made him a target when he entered the affair since he was now well known to elements of the espionage fraternity. Emma was sent undercover as a model to a photographic studio run by Tom Savage which was somehow involved. The mystery surrounded Captain Crusoe, a missing parrot who had been trained to memorise details of the Muswells Back missile installation – obtained by flying pigeons carrying cameras over the site – and was then to be taken abroad to relay the data to the enemy. The man behind the plan was George Cunliffe, a public relations officer to Edgar J Twitter, the organiser of a bird show which was about to leave Heathcliff Hall to tour Europe [BIRD].

Steed and Emma were then summoned to investigate a possible security breach by an 'invisible man' at a Records Office of the Ministry of Defence; on this assignment Steed reported direct to the government. Once again, Steed found himself outwitting his old rival Brodny, the Russian Ambassador, and by now, Steed was a well known visitor to the Soviet Embassy. The luckless Brodny was again being duped by his own people, in this instance Major Alexandre Vazin and his wife Elena who had concocted a fake 'invisible man' scare to force British scientific research to study a useless formula and so upset the country's economy. Steed and Emma penetrated the specially-rigged control room at the Embassy used by Vazin and his wife, overpowering the Major and discovering the truth [SEET].[18]

In late November[19], Steed and Emma were assigned to investigate the murder and mutilation of Simon Roberts, a ruthless publisher killed in his locked office at the top of a tower block – the fourth such murder of a heartless businessman in a high place. The killer turned out to be Arnie Packer, a deranged comic strip artist and co-creator of *The Winged Avenger* who was now acting out his masked vigilante's form of justice while dressed as his creation – and aided by boots which allowed him to walk up walls and across the ceiling. Taking a page from Packer's work, Steed defeated the madman with over-sized comic strip panels [WING].

Steed and Emma next found themselves investigating sightings of a ghost at a church near the Benedict Estate; it was said that these spirits were either the ancestors of the current Duke of Benedict, or those lost in a mine disaster five years earlier. Steed investigated the Benedict Estate himself by claiming that he was in the shooting business, and had heard how good the game was. Later on, having entered the estate cellars for a look around, he donned the gas mask, white helmet and lab coat of a strange workman whom he had overpowered. What Steed had stumbled upon was another underground invasion force, similar to the one at Little Bazeley but on a far grander scale. An entire town with 20,000 fighting men had been established in the old mines – and once again Steed and Emma managed to seal in the foreign foes [LIVI].

The next strange death for Steed to look into was that of Sir David Harper's butler who was found mauled at Harper's home, as if by a big cat. On this assignment, Steed had

---

[18] Ambassador Brodny mentioned having tickets for the next Beatles' concert – but the Fab Four's final live concert in Britain was at the Empire Pool, Wembley on Sunday 1 May 1966. Presumably Brodny, a gullible individual at the best of times, had been conned over the tickets.

[19] The film shows Steed reading about the death of Edward J Dumayn (erroneously referred to as 'Damayn' in the summary report) in the *Daily Mail* dated Wednesday 23 November 1966. As such, this surveillance film appears to span 21 to 25 November 1966, and fits in with the completion date of December 1966.

access to an olive green Land Rover SWB with a canvas cover.[20] Similar attacks around Harper's Experimental Husbandry Farm led back to an establishment called PURRR – the Philanthropic Union for the Rescue, Relief and Recuperation of cats – which Steed joined by claiming that he had a pedigree cat called 'Emma'. Unknown to the eccentric Edwin Cheshire who ran PURRR, one of his aides, Dr Manx, had hatched a plan to decimate the population using a transistorised circuit which turned the domestic pussy into a savage killer. Ultimately, Manx was defeated by the fear of one of his own creations [TIGE].

As 1967 arrived[21], the death of Ernest Cosgrove of the War Ministry was the first in a series of strange killings where astronomers were discovered with their hair and clothes bleached white. Steed's involvement appeared to be at the behest of the Ministry; according to Crawford of the BVS[22], Steed was 'from the authorities' when he tried to join their numbers as a keen astronomer to watch Venus and donate to an ambitious space programme. Liaising with Ministry experts, Steed soon confirmed that the attacks were not extra-terrestrial, but the result of a laser – light amplification of stimulated emission of radiation – being employed by Dr Henry Primble, a bitter ophthalmic surgeon who was taking revenge on those whom he considered to have stolen his research funds [VENU].

For the first time in Steed's career, history seemed to repeat itself in a case which involved him again in counter-espionage. The deaths of two enemy agents in London made Steed a target for the opposition and he was attacked by Ivan Peppitoperoff, the second-in-command to Steed's old friend Comrade Nutski who had assumed charge of counter-counter-espionage operations in the city. Steed was innocent of the eliminations and – as he had done with Keller in 1964 – suggested a truce so that both sides could work together against the third party. On this occasion, Steed was partnered with a bona fide Soviet agent – Comrade Olga Savonovitch Negretiskinka Volowoski whom he clearly found attractive at their first meeting. Although Olga was highly trained in comparison to the duped Kim Lawrence, Steed still felt responsible for her, and Olga's communist attitude towards him thawed during their partnership. The killings were being performed by third party agents trained at charm school called SNOB Inc[23], which Steed successfully infiltrated as one of its well-turned out members. Again Steed found that it was the top Soviet man, Nutski, who was trying to build up his own new super-power by trading on secrets; Nutski was finally killed by Olga [CORR].

Finding Olga quite charming, Steed dated her after the events at SNOB Inc and was 'Embraced to the bosom of glorious motherland' [CORR]. However, he was soon dining out with Emma again. On one such occasion when they had arranged an evening out, Steed became concerned when he found Emma missing from her flat. By identifying a voice on her answerphone as the once prominent actor Stewart Kirby, Steed was able to trace Emma to the largely derelict Schnerk Studios where she had been imprisoned and forced to take part in a surreal film which would culminate in her death. By impersonating a dead actor

---

[20] Registration OPC 109D.

[21] The next meeting of the British Venusian Society members is given as Friday 13; this suggests that it is January 1967. However, this does not agree with what must be an erroneous completion date of November 1966. Emma comments 'We've got to the moon', referring to the soft landings of Lunar 9 on 3 February 1966 and Surveyor 1 on 2 June 1966.

[22] British Venusian Society.

[23] Sociability Nobility Omnipotence Breeding Inc.

who had been hired to play the corpse of 'John Steed', Steed arrived on the set in the nick of time to save his friend from a rotating saw mill blade operated by insane art movie genius ZZ von Schnerk [EPIC].

Steed's next dangerous encounter was again provoked by a personal scheme rather than an official investigation. Attired in period military uniform and described as 'Kitchener's Valet', he attended a fancy dress party on an aircraft – similar to the one he was lured into on New Year's Eve 1963. Once again, Steed knew in advance that his invitation from the famous explorer Sir George Robertson was a fake and had arranged for Emma to follow the plane. Steed and his six colleagues – all fellow experts in armed and unarmed combat – were flown to a desolate island. Here they were informed by a man called Jessel that one of them was a highly trained killer with super-human reflexes who would kill the others in a demonstration for a foreign power. Steed killed the test subject – a hunter called Jason Wade – and, with Emma's help, exposed Jessel's training regime as a fake [SUP7].

Back in England, Steed was assigned to meet his colleague Lucas who had intercepted radio messages plotting the assassination of a VIP. Lucas went missing on the Liverpool to London train, leaving clues which propelled Steed and Emma into a plot which was connected with the British Rail network. Steed's investigations led to him being captured by a ticket collector who was planning to kill the Prime Minister by detonating an explosive on a special train, but Steed managed to disconnect the equipment sending the destructive signal. Although he hoped this action would win him an OBE, Steed's personal dislike of the current Prime Minister – Harold Wilson of the Labour party – meant that he did not wait to receive the premiere's official thanks [STAT].

Another security leak – this time concerning a recent defence meeting – was investigated by Steed when he took over the work of one of the Department's best agents, Dobson, who had been killed. The link between the three possible suspects was that they had all had the same nanny in childhood, Nanny Roberts. By now, Nanny Roberts was old and frail and resident at GONN[24] which she had established; posing as another of her former charges, Steed paid a visit to the training centre which turned out to have been taken over by Mr Goat and his cohorts. Disguised as Roberts, Goat was using drugs to extract secrets from top men, and was planning to sell on the locations of missile bases in the North West of England when he was stopped by Steed and Emma – and then shot by General Wilmot [NURS].

The 'other side' went on the offensive again, luring Steed and Emma into a trap by attacking the flower-coded agents from the Floral Network run by Major 'B', apparently another section of the Department. Two enemy agents – Basil and Lola – had studied the behaviour of the pair and, using a machine developed by Dr V Krelmar, took control of Steed and Emma's bodies, leaving Steed and Emma's minds trapped in the bodies of Basil and Lola. Suspected and hunted by the team of Major 'B', the pair only narrowly managed to trap the impostors and reverse the effects of the machine in time [WHO?].

It was around now that Steed encountered an enemy agent who would become a deadly rival for the next decade; this was 'The Unicorn', another legendary figure in the crime world, a brilliant killer and one of the top spies in the world. The two crossed paths for the first time in 1967 [LION]. A more personal assignment saw Steed receiving a minor physical wound and also a deep personal injury. Mark Crayford's progress through the

---

[24] The Guild Of Noble Nannies.

Department had not been as spectacular as Steed's, and he still remained in his school rival's shadow. Although the men had both been through school and university, trained to be ruthless Class A1 agents and drunk warm bitter beer at a riverside pub together, the anger inside Crayford could no longer be contained. Driving a black Mercedes[25], Steed had agreed to see Mark off across the border to the 'Eastern Sektor' on a mission, but as they evaded the guards Crayford revealed that he had made a deal with the 'other side'. Now he could be his own man – and turning traitor gave him an opportunity to kill Steed. Crayford's shot caught Steed in the shoulder, while Steed's bullet hit his old friend in the chest. Mark's new allies took him across the border and on to Moscow – while Steed managed to struggle back to safety [DEAD].

Steed was mildly jealous when Emma attracted the attentions of art dealer 'Paul Beresford' – not knowing that Beresford was in fact the brother of Dr Clement Armstrong and was seeking revenge on the duo for the events at United Automation two years earlier. Beresford's aim was to make both Steed and Emma suffer intensely, and aimed to trap them using his brother's Cybernauts before turning them into beings who would no longer be in control of their own bodies. While Emma fell victim to the nerve control device which Beresford had had constructed, Steed managed to fight back at the last moment. Like his brother, Beresford perished at the metallic hands of a Cybernaut [RETU].

Steed's next mission was an extremely odd one, and there is a train of thought to believe that the entire spool of surveillance footage was nothing more than a more extensive training film in which Steed re-enacted one of his textbook cases – the 1962 investigation into the Litoff Organisation [DANE] – only this time accompanied by Emma rather than Cathy. Assuming that this incident is genuine material and not staged, the similarities are remarkable. A ventriloquist called Dusty Rhodes was caught in a road accident and found to be smuggling a fortune in diamonds to Switzerland, at the same time as the Treasury called in Steed, anxious about the valuables and currency leaving the country. It seems that somehow the financier Alex Litoff had died *again*, and once more his personal assistant – this time a woman called Miss Pegram – was creating the illusion that he was still alive until she and her cohorts could flee overseas with the conglomerate's funds. Whereas the plans concocted by Comrade Nutski [CORR] and – later – Max Prendergast [JOKE] bore a coincidental resemblance to the machinations of Keller [CHAR] and Martin Goodman [BEHI], it is not at all clear how the same world famous financier with the same organisation could die both in September 1962 and again during summer 1967 [BREA].

In late August, Steed found that he and Emma had a hectic week. First of all, Steed was expecting some hot papers to be delivered to him by courier Bobby Danvers. Danvers arrived at Steed's flat and died in the early hours of 21 August[26], having already posted an invitation to Steed which would lead him into a car rally treasure hunt run by motoring fanatic George Benstead. Danvers had apparently been fatally wounded by two members of the opposition, Carl and Alex, who were well aware of who Steed was, although he did not know them. Furthermore, a third party was at work in the form of an opportunist who passed himself off as one 'Major Mike Coborne' and who had also recognised Steed. After a deadly race around the countryside near Edgington, Steed and Emma recovered the vital

---

25 Registration B-NP 374.

26 The invitation to George Benstead's Annual Car Rally gives the date as 'August 21st', suggesting the mission effectively took place that day, despite the fact that the file date is 5 July 1967.

papers, having defeated the opposition [TREA].[27]

Later that week[28], Steed was involved with threats on the lives of millionaires. His investigation began when he was coerced by Lord Maxted, the Chairman of the British Banking Corporation, into going to a party hosted by millionaire George Unwin. Unwin and a number of other rich men were acting strangely, the reason being that a hit-man called Skelton[29] had demonstrated to them all how easy it was to murder them at any time – unless they paid one million pounds in cash to his employer, Nathaniel Needle. Steed and Emma laid a trap to lead to Needle – who was hidden in a haystack – and put him out of business within days [JUST].

Around now, Steed started to regularly use his 1926 3-litre Bentley again through into early 1968. His next investigation was again on behalf of one of the Ministries and involved another strange death – this time Dr Charles Grey, an electronics expert engaged on secret work, had been electrocuted with such force that he had been embedded in a concrete wall. Steed was introduced as being 'from the Ministry' when meeting James Mankin, and was now issued with a red punched computer security card from the Ministry. Steed and Emma uncovered the history of Project 90, a research scheme into the broadcast of electrical energy via radio waves which had been abandoned some months earlier. Now its chief researcher, Dr Creswell, had developed the notion to an extent where he had created a prototype invincible soldier charged to be a lethal walking dynamo with a deadly touch – but still able to be earthed by Steed and Emma [POSI].

Shortly afterwards in the last days of the legendary Summer of Love, Steed found himself summoned to the village of Little Storping in-the-Swuff[30] by a cryptic phone call from his 'wife' Emma who had been helping her old friend Major Paul Croft move into a house there. Steed arrived to find that Little Storping was a 'boom town' that Emma had inadvertently wandered into, and managed to rescue her while overpowering the murderously greedy villages led by Dr JF Haynes[31] [MDVL].

One Friday, most probably in late September[32], Steed was injured in his own apartment – falling down the stairs to his lounge by what he later realised was a deliberate trip wire. With his left leg hurt, he had intended to rest and recuperate while Emma went to visit Sir Cavalier Rousicana, the greatest bridge player in Europe, at his remote home on Exmoor. It was not until Steed received the news that Max Prendergast had broken out of jail in Germany two weeks earlier that he realised the trap had been meant for him, and that Prendergast was playing out the same revenge on Emma that Goodman had subjected Cathy to four years earlier. Steed managed to arrive at the remote hall just in time to overpower Prendergast for an unnerved Emma – a contrast to the way in which he had allowed

---

[27] In honour of Steed and his associates, this rally has been re-enacted by enthusiasts each June since 1987.

[28] The invitation to George Unwin's cocktail party is given as Saturday 24 August (despite the fact that 24 August was a Thursday in 1967, which is when the film must have been shot; presumably a printer's error was to blame). This suggests that the surveillance material covers events from 23 to 26 August 1967.

[29] Erroneously referred to as 'Shelton' on the summary report.

[30] The village later seemed to be given a new lease of life, rechristened Aldbury in Hertfordshire.

[31] Also erroneously referred to as 'Dr Haymes' at the end of the surveillance film.

[32] The surveillance film shows that it is starting to get dark at 5.20 pm.

Cathy to walk unknowingly into the same peril in 1963 [JOKE].

In mid-October[33], Steed and Emma were called in by Steed's acquaintance Lord Melford to investigate the strange behaviour of Sir Andrew Boyd at a conference relating to his aspirations for a United Europe organisation. At night, Boyd and later Melford were falling victim to drug-induced dreams which predicted death for them should they go ahead with their work at the conference the next morning. The precognitive warnings were being created by a press attaché called Stapley and Eastern Bloc observer Albert Becker in order to wreck the European discussions [DOOR].

A few days later[34], Steed was called in to investigate the disappearance of a chauffeur-driven Rolls-Royce Silver Cloud carrying Treasury supremo Sir Gerald Bancroft to a Ministry of Defence Testing area. Although Steed would probably have attended a demonstration of the Saracen FV603 armoured vehicle at the establishment anyway, on this occasion he was present carrying an ID from the Treasury since he had been working with Sir Gerald. Sir Gerald's planned audit of the Metal Fatigue Division had threatened to expose some unconventional research by Professor LT Rushton who had developed a shrinking ray, which his aide, Dr Chivers, was planning to sell to an enemy agent, Comrade Shaffer. Both Steed and Emma were temporarily miniaturised by the device before using it to cut Shaffer and Chivers down to size [MISS].

Steed was concerned when his colleague Sean Mortimer arrived at his mews apartment suffering from amnesia, and went to contact Mother – the portly, crippled senior member of the Department who seemed to be in charge of personnel and disappearances. At Mother's country estate, he was attacked by a new trainee agent, Agent 69, better known as Miss Tara King. When Emma was captured by the enemy agents and one of Steed's Bentleys was stolen, Steed battled his own bout of memory loss to find the traitor in Mother's establishment, and was helped immensely by Tara, who clearly hero-worshipped him. By now, Steed was a very prominent figure with legendary status; Tara and other new recruits were taught many 'Steed Methods' every day in training. Eventually, Steed was able to rescue Emma and Sean and also expose George Burton, one of the trainers, as the traitor testing the memory drug on his colleagues [KNOT].

Towards the end of November 1967[35], Steed and Emma were called to investigate a supposed death where the corpse – a man knocked down in a car accident – had got up and walked out of hospital. To find the walking dead man, Steed had the use of an olive green open Land Rover SWB.[36] The gaunt figure was also tracked down by a team from the Neoteric Research Unit (known as MOT-NRU), a scientific establishment so secret that the Ministry of Technology would not even discuss it with Steed. By getting 'official consent',

---

[33] Lord Melford's first day in charge of the conference was Friday 13, as shown on the calendar and in his dream. This suggests possibly January or October 1967, with October better fitting both the sequence of the surveillance films and the weather – although disagreeing with the completion date of 7 June 1967.

[34] The calendar in the office of Comrade Shaffer covered Thursday 12 and Friday 13, suggesting that these events occurred on a day the following week and that the calendar sheets had not been removed over Shaffer's long and drunken weekend.

[35] The diary at Professor Stone's cottage had an entry for Sunday 22 October 1967, and since the real professor had been a captive at the Neoteric Research Unit for a month or so, these events must have taken place around four weeks later.

[36] Registration VX 897.

Steed was able to visit the base's Experimental Section, looking after 'security' surrounding an imminent VIP visit. Steed and Emma soon discovered that the senior scientist, Dr Frank N Stone, had been replaced by his own robotic double which was susceptible to radio waves – a weapon used by the pair to immobilise the amazing creations[NEVE].[37]

It was now that Emma and Steed stopped working together because of the sudden reappearance of Peter Peel who had miraculously survived the crash in the Amazon. Steed was deeply upset to say goodbye to Emma as she left to rejoin Peter – even allowing himself to address her by her Christian name. However, he was somewhat flattered to discover that the dear friend whom he promised to remember in his will [LIVI] was in fact married to a gentleman whose cultured tastes perfectly mirrored his own [KNOT].

Moments after Emma had departed his apartment to continue married life, Steed contacted Mother and requested to have somebody new assigned to him. Indeed, Mother had clearly anticipated this since before Emma could leave Stable Mews, Tara King had arrived. As the women passed on the stairs, words of advice were passed from the old hand to the novice who would partner Steed for at least the next two years.[38]

---

[37] Oddly enough, ten years later when it was suggested that a robot double of a killer called 'The Unicorn' should be used to confuse the enemy, Steed dismissed such a notion as 'science fiction' – despite his earlier encounter with these near-perfect human replicas [LION].

[38] One unconfirmed and unlikely report suggests that 'Major' Steed and Tara King had adjoining offices at 'the Ministry'. *Moon Express*, p5.

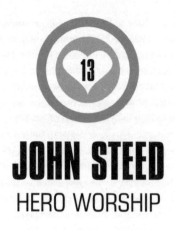

JOHN STEED
HERO WORSHIP

While Steed was still a gentleman, his relationship with Tara was very different to his previous partnerships with Cathy or Emma. Cathy and Emma had been women; Tara was little more than a girl. Indeed, it was more akin to how Steed dealt with Venus at times, largely because Tara was so very young while he himself was now in his mid-40s and an increasingly senior member of the Department. Added to this, Tara's wide-eyed devotion to the legend that she was working alongside was only too obvious – although after a year or so, this puppy dog loyalty started to blossom into a more equal friendship.

Initially, Steed called Tara 'Miss King' [GUNS, LACE], but – as the decade loosened up – Steed became less formal himself and addressed her as 'Tara'. Even more so than with Emma, Steed would frequently take Tara out for a picnic [WISH] or a romantic dinner [DONE, FALS] such as a candlelit table for two with champagne and red roses in the middle of a field [DONE]. He also enjoyed buying her presents, such as champagne, a floppy hat, a parasol and a luminous sundial all crammed into a redundant plaster cast [NOON]. For her birthday he gave her pearls [KEEP], and after a holiday on the continent he brought back a gift for her from Breton et Fils, 17 Rue de Balzac, Bordeaux [STAY]. He was also able to recognise intimate items of hers, such as her wristwatch [PAND].

The close relationship Steed enjoyed with Tara made him the envy of her other suitors, such as the Honourable Teddy Chilcott[1] [WILD] although the closest Steed seemed to get on the surveillance films was a kiss on the cheek [KILL]. Ultimately, in 1969, there was ample opportunity for the pair to get better acquainted when they spent some time together unchaperoned in Steed's home-made rocket which accidentally blasted off with only them on board [BIZA].

Soon after they started to work together, Steed learnt that he could trust Tara with many intimate details about his life, talking to her about his childhood [WILD, REQU] more than he had with former colleagues. The thought that she could have 'gone over' to the other side was inconceivable to him [THAT] and he grimly told Mother that he would handle an investigation into her behaviour himself – officially or unofficially [THAT]. Department archivist Henry Lasindall commented that Steed would certainly not stop looking for Tara until he was absolutely sure that she was dead [PAND].

---

[1] Erroneously referred to as 'Lord Teddy Chilcott' in the summary report.

On a professional basis, as Tara became more experienced in the counter-espionage world, Steed knew that he could leave tasks to her to perform without worries, such as losing a string of cars that might be following them [LEGA]. He was determined to protect Tara – the younger more inexperienced agent – and indeed would use a gun on her to lock her away somewhere safely until a danger had passed [NOON]. Daniel Edmund knew that Steed valued Tara's life more than his own [GAME]. Steed was furious with Tara when she placed herself in any danger – and on one occasion had to knock her out with his bowler when she attacked him [LOVE]. When she fell asleep because of gas bombs deployed by Jimmy Merlin, Steed carefully left her to slumber on a sofa and ensured she was covered up [MORN]. Yet in other respects Steed could be very remote, failing to understand Tara's frustration at being forced to lie when under the influence of drugs and not being capable of understanding why she was acting so oddly [FALS]. He could also be thoughtless and show a lack of respect, slapping her bottom [GAME], tricking her into doing his baby-sitting for him so that he could go to the pub [WISH] or assigning her the less pleasant jobs such as taking the night watch at Happy Meadows [BIZA].

One of Tara's first assignments with Steed was an investigation into the daring theft of a consignment of FF 70/9 rifles from a State Ordnance Depot. The weapons had been obtained by Lady Adriana Beardsley who was planning to sell them to Steed's old adversary Colonel Martin Nsonga, still an ambitious would-be dictator of a newly independent African country. Since Steed was still a good friend of Nsonga's president, he bid against the Colonel for the rifles in an auction – and eventually managed to destroy the firearms. As a mark of gratitude for Nsonga's defeat, the President sent Steed a rather big cat as a 'thank you' gift – which Steed swiftly disposed of [GUNS].[2]

During December[3] while Tara was on leave with a skiing injury, Steed was invited to help in the investigation of one of his friends, the cabinet minister Sir William Burgess, who was the chief suspect in the murder of Reginald Hubert Dawson[4], a former employee at one of his companies. This was one of a string of meticulous framing and blackmail operations being carried out by three men called Earle, Stanley and Gardiner, whereby unless the victim handed over art treasures, a murder of an innocent person connected to them was committed and personal items stolen from the mark were left at the scene of the crime. Steed himself was to be set up for the murder of the invalid Tara – but Tara proved herself more then adequate at the art of defence, even when injured; Stanley fell foul of Steed while Earle and Gardiner's assault on Tara's flat saw them firmly trounced [CLUE].

A recovered Tara found herself helping Steed to track down Grant[5], one of Steed's colleagues who had been missing for three weeks. The trail from Grant's last hotel room led to the Alpha Academy, a strict military-style school run by Brigadier Brett which was preparing young people to be the astronaut soldiers for the approaching space age. Visiting the school as Civil Service employee 'Colonel John Steed, late of the 9th Lancers', and accompanied by Tara as his wife, Steed gave a cover story about wanting his son, 18-year-old Aubrey Neville (from his first marriage) to be enrolled while he and 'Mrs Steed' travelled

---

[2] In the surveillance film Lady Adriana Beardsley says that it is autumn.

[3] The surveillance film spans the 12th to 15th of a month and – since a tax disc for January 1968 is visible on Robert Flanders' car, this was most probably 12 to 15 December 1967.

[4] Erroneously referred to as 'Herbert Dawson' in the summary report.

[5] Referred to in the summary report as 'Bernard Grant'.

around the Commonwealth. During this operation, Steed drove Tara's AC 428 which he handled superbly, skidding off a road smoothly into the cover of bushes when followed. Grant had uncovered Brett's bizarre plans for the domination of space with ruthless, highly trained, cryogenically frozen youngsters, and it was up to Steed and Tara to incarcerate the pupils underground and overpower Brett [INVA].[6]

Around now, Steed received strawberry shortcake from Tara for his birthday [KEEP]. With assignments again taking on more of a security aspect from the Department, Steed and Tara were called in when agent Frank Compton was found shot dead at the Ministry of Top Secret Information – TSI. This case brought Steed up against Boris Kartovski, whom he had shot through the heart just over four years earlier[7]. Although Kartovski was immobile on a life-support system at Nullington Private Hospital and tended to by Dr Constantine, his mind was fused with a number of Steed's colleagues to make them extensions of himself. It had been another agent, Harry Mercer, who had unknowingly shot Compton while possessed by Kartovski. Although in a lot of pain from fisticuffs with Constantine and the enemy agent Hinnell[8], Steed finally triumphed over Kartovski one last time as the equipment keeping his adversary alive expired [SPLI].

There was then tragedy for Steed when – in the space of a few hours – his good friends and colleagues Paul Ryder and George Neville were both killed by escapees from the Monastery, one of the Department's top security detention centres for enemy agents.[9] The escapees had used a strange liquid, which conferred chameleon-like properties, to pass unseen out of the establishment and had each been assigned targets to kill in the Department. The third escapee, Martin Ezdorf, had been allocated Steed as his victim, and Steed only narrowly defeated him by using the bizarre camouflage technique in a shoot-out at Stable Mews [GETA].

Although Steed had referred to owning a Rolls-Royce since the start of the decade, there was infuriatingly no visual evidence of what sort of vehicle it actually was. However from spring 1968, Steed eschewed his faithful Bentleys of the last three years in favour of these more grandiose vehicles. The first was a yellow Rolls-Royce Silver Ghost dating from 1923[10] [GETA, LOOK, WILD, XR40, CATC, DONE, CYPH, GAME, FALS, LEGA, WISH, KILL, ROTT, INTR, MORN, LOVE, TAKE, STAY, FOG, BIZA]. This four-seat open-tourer was to become Steed's regular transport for the next year or so.[11] There was a rather quaint old-fashioned telephone fitted under the dashboard on the passenger side [CYPH, KILL] which could also be located behind Steed's driving seat [INTR]. It was in this car that Steed planned to drive across three countries from France to Italy while on holiday in October 1968, although in the event it spent some of its time in London and was in collision with an Italian car driven

---

[6] The incident took place some time after 8 August 1967 which is when one of the Alpha Academy pupils, Penelope Kenwood, had been frozen.

[7] Harry Mercer's memo of his assignments refers to incidents dated '18.11.67' and '29.11.67', suggesting this could be early 1968.

[8] Erroneously referred to as 'Himel' in the summary report.

[9] The agents were specified as being Russian in the summary report.

[10] Registration KK 4976.

[11] Steed may still have been using this vehicle as late as 1971. eg 'Fable Land'. *TV Comic Annual*, 1969, p49; *TV Comic*, Issue 942, 3 January 1970; Issue 982, 10 October 1970; Issue 997, 23 January 1971; Issue 1033, 27 February 1971.

by a girl called Sally[12] in Fitzherbert Street [STAY]. Other damage sustained by the classic vehicle was a windscreen smashed by a ladder wielded by a van from Classy Glass Cleaners in an attempt to make Steed crash [CYPH]. Steed was also known to use the heat of the engine to keep a fillet steak warm on a silver salver when dining out [DONE]. He was already happy to let Tara drive this vehicle on a couple of occasions [WILD, FOG]; she herself could identify its unique sound as it ferried her beloved Steed towards her [WISH].

In late March[13], the murder of a board member of the Caritol Land and Development Corporation[14] involved Steed and Tara on a security basis, since Caritol were contracted to construct the government shelter for Project CUPID.[15] The Caritol board members were being wiped out in a darkly humorous manner by Merry Maxie Martin and Jennings, two unemployed clowns from Vauda Villa.[16] The inmates of the retirement home for music hall artistes were being manipulated to destroy CUPID by Seagrove, a Caritol board member who wanted to clean up with a foreign power. Steed infiltrated Vauda Villa posing as retired artiste Gentleman Jack ('A Smile, A Song and An Umbrella') and later joined Tara in a pantomime horse costume to attend a meeting of the inmates whom they then overpowered [LOOK].

A few days later[17], Steed was selected as the perfect witness for a series of dream-induced killings planned by Frank Tobias. Tobias was manipulating the work of Dr A Jaeger, an aggresso-therapist who was using drugs to treat patients for aggressive urges, to kill his fellow board members at the Acme Precision Combine Ltd. Supposedly, Jaeger's clients were harmlessly working out their anger against partners and colleagues – but at a critical point Tobias's cohorts would direct them to live out their dream and kill their antagonist. Steed was lured to the murder of one Acme director, Aloysius Peregrine, by another, Paul Gibbons who had been treated by Jaeger. When visiting Jaeger, Steed posed as a man who believed he was a horse because of his surname. When Steed's investigations got too warm, Tobias took advantage of the Right Honourable Teddy Chilcott's jealousy of Steed – because of his working relationship with Tara – and programmed Chilcott to kill Steed. Together, Steed and Tara were more than a match for Tobias's group – and Tobias had the rug pulled out from beneath him at Stable Mews [WILD].

Steed and Tara were called in on the matter of another security breach, this time when a crude attack was made on George/XR40, a computer at the Ministry of Technology's Cybernetic and Computor [sic] Division Administration building. Representing the Ministry, Steed discovered that the machine was being targeted because of the equations developed by its creator, Sir Wilfred Pelley, who was being held captive by enemy agents at his country house. Steed and Tara dealt with the operatives of the 'other side' such as

12 Although not confirmed in the film or transcript, the summary report names this lady as Sally Unstrutter.

13 According to the calendar in Bradley Marler's office, it was the 24th – meaning the security film spans the 21st to 24th. Since Tara commented that there were 230 shopping days to Christmas, this would place it around late March.

14 Erroneously referred to as the 'Capital Land and Development Company' in the summary report.

15 Cabinet Underground Premises – In Depth.

16 Erroneously referred to as 'Greasepaint Grange' in the summary report.

17 According to Paul Gibbons's diary, he had an appointment with Dr Jaeger scheduled for Monday 1 April 1968. Since Tara's hair had not yet been cut short – as with her work at Cypher HQ – this suggests it was a future appointment and that the events took place from Wednesday to Friday in late March.

Keller and Jason and released the hostages [XR40].

From spring 1968, it seems that the Department underwent some reorganisation, with Mother effectively taking charge of the whole organisation. From now on, it was usual for Steed and Tara to report direct to Mother for their mission briefings at whichever venue he had selected for his HQ. Steed was now a 'top executive' in the Department [REQU] and his role firmly established again as a 'secret agent' [NOON]. No agent on either side could fail to recognise John Steed – an impeccably dressed fellow with a bowler [INTR]. Generally he held security clearance KR5 [MORN], although when he had to be taken off the active service list temporarily, Father – Mother's subordinate – reduced his security rating to third class [STAY].

Whereas Mother had once referred to Steed as 'John' [KNOT], now that they were in direct superior-subordinate positions he usually called him 'Steed'. The two men clearly had a great experience of each other's working methods. Mother would comment how he had received many reports of Steed being missing (in his former capacity) [DONE] but observed that Steed 'usually knows what he's up to' [FALS]. Often Steed was used on important cases, to keep an eye on less able agents [FALS] or to solve complex problems of internal security in matters which Mother could not entrust elsewhere [WISH].

At the very start of April[18], one of the first assignments under Mother's aegis was at Cypher HQ at Lessington[19], a division of MOTC[20], which Mother described as their 'biggest job in months' as assigned to them by the Minister. Photographs of the most top secret codes were being smuggled out, and it seemed as if a window cleaning company, Classy Glass Cleaners (CGC), were somehow involved. Steed visited the company's offices, claiming to have a house where his family had to board up their windows because of death duties. Having established that CGC was placing the HQ staff in a trance while conducting a raid on the codes, Steed posed as 'Fred', a white-overalled CGC man, to help defeat the espionage organisation on the same day that Dr Martin Luther King was shot dead in Memphis [CYPH].

Around now, Steed spent two weeks investigating security leaks at the Carmadoc Research Establishment. When he failed to prevent these, Steed had to be placed under house arrest by Mother following the death of a man called Roger. He was soon cleared by Tara who unveiled the true form of the surveillance at the coastal station – although by this time he had released himself from his luxurious confinement at Mother's swimming pool [DONE].

Also at around this time, Tara helped Steed to battle one of his old enemies, the organisation Intercrime, as they aimed to pull off 'The Great Great Britain Crime'. Mother had heard that 'something big' was about to happen and after a number of agents were killed, informant Freddie Cartwright managed to get to Steed with information about a planned diamond heist from a Bond Street jewellers worth £750,000. Steed was unimpressed, feeling that this was really the province of Scotland Yard, but Cartwright persuaded him that this was connected to the 'Crime of the Century'. By robbing the robbers at the appointed time, Steed left his calling card and attracted the attentions of Dunbar, Elected

---

[18] Since the day that agent Roger Jarret goes missing is established by a calendar as Monday 1 April 1968, this suggests the surveillance film runs from 1 to 4 April 1968.

[19] Apparently now acting as Brookman's Park Transmitting Station in Hertfordshire.

[20] Presumably Ministry of Top Secret Codes.

President of Intercrime. Although Intercrime was efficient, they seemed to have no details of Steed's previous encounter with them, allowing Steed and Tara to infiltrate their ranks as criminals. Because of Steed's background, it was decided that he should trick one Colonel Corf into announcing Operation Rule Britannia, a security drill which would allow Intercrime to seize all the major works of art in the country in one go. Steed and Tara were ultimately able to overpower the international Intercrime delegates led by Dunbar and save the country's treasures [LACE].

It is possibly around now that Steed was engaged on two of his increasingly rare assignments outside Great Britain. The first of these, accompanied by Tara, was to rescue a little Lama, a friend of the Dalai, in Tibet. For this the pair used a lightweight plane with two passenger seats fore and aft. Tara and Steed shared the open pilot's cockpit to keep warm, and delivered the young Lama safe and sound [KEEP].

Steed then encountered Tim Heald again during May 1968. Heald was now working for the *Daily Express* and based in Prague, Czechoslovakia when he saw Steed, adorned with an East European felt hat complete with feather, reading a copy of *Rude Pravo* in Wenceslas Square. Maintaining his cover, Steed met Heald at the Charles Bridge, leading the journalist to a small attic flat in an 18th century block. In private, Steed was able to comment that the Russians were about to arrive and that he was trying to delay their approach aided by a colleague called Jitka; the Warsaw Pact army eventually arrived in Prague on 20 August 1968. Most significantly, it also seems that Steed's attitude to his career was changing somewhat and that he now saw the end in sight. It was during this brief discussion that he first mooted the notion of Heald collaborating with him on his biography. 'You're on,' replied Heald without hesitation.[21]

On 20 May[22], Steed was back in England and able to move in on Jimmy Merlin, a former colleague gone rogue who had stolen capsules of a newly developed sleep gas from the Ministry of TSI. When Steed and Tara sprang their trap, Jimmy used some of his newly acquired bombs, putting the trio to sleep until the next day. On waking, Steed found that an evacuation had been called and martial law declared, supposedly because an atom bomb had been found at the vacated Eastern Hemisphere Trade Commission building. This turned out to be the cover for a nuclear blackmail plan hatched by Brigadier Hansing, a disillusioned senior officer. The plan was defeated by Steed with Jimmy's help and at the end of escapade, Steed let Jimmy go free, urging his wayward associate to keep out of trouble [MORN].

Steed's past again returned to haunt him when he received a game of snakes and ladders on the same day that Clive Dexter, with whom he had served on court martials in Germany just after the war, was killed by venom from a snakebite. As his other military colleagues were killed off in macabre games, Steed was fed clues in the form of jigsaw pieces left on

---

21 *Jealous in Honour*, p10. There is an unconfirmed – and probably inaccurate – report that around 1966/7 Steed had attempted to write up his war memoirs covering his time supposedly entering Berlin for MI5 in April 1945. *Heil Harris!*, p9-11.

22 The calendar in the bank reads Tuesday 21, suggesting 21 May 1968. The closing scene of this film was shot sometime later; Steed was watching the comedy sketch show *Rowan and Martin's Laugh-In* on television. Although the show appeared on NBC from 22 January 1968, the series did not debut on BBC 2 in the UK until 8 September 1968. Thus Merlin's present was presumably delivered months later.

their corpses, leading him to the home of Monty Bristow, the games king. When Steed visited Bristow, he found himself meeting Sergeant Daniel Edmund who was now seeking revenge – and who forced Steed to play a game called Super Secret Agent to rescue Tara. Steed's training and reflexes won out, and he finally deflected the flight of a lethal razor-sharp playing card back at Edmund [GAME].

In June[23], Mother briefed Steed and Tara about a report from New York where three 'ear, nose and throat' specialists had died at a top American clinic. Although Steed attempted to dismiss this as 'not our territory', there seemed to be a connection with the demise of Dr H Ralph Camrose in London. Camrose choked to death on a concentrated powder of the common cold virus, and the clues led to the Anastasia Nursing Academy which Steed visited posing as a man planning to offer the establishment an endowment from the 'Steed Foundation'. Steed and Tara exposed Dr Frank Glover who planned to sell the lethal dust to the highest bidder [CATC].

Steed was called in by Mother to keep an eye on less able agents when a series of disasters occurred during the compilation of a dossier against Lord Edgefield, who had been accused of extortion and blackmail against security personnel. Mother's main concern was Melville, a young agent who seemed to have let his partner, Penman, die while on assignment. Key people who could testify against Edgefield – and members of the Department – were being fed a drug in their daily milk delivery which made them lie. Tara was affected, but Steed eventually deduced that Dreemykreem Dairies (DKD)[24] was behind the outbreak of untruths and dealt with their operatives [FALS].

However, by mid-June Steed had been removed from active service with a broken leg. This he had sustained while pursuing a saboteur over five garden walls and then stepping into a cucumber frame just when he had the miscreant trapped behind a bed of Queen Mary Roses. Now being such a prominent figure in the Department, Steed was whisked away to Department S, the remote farm which was used as a security hospital by the authorities. Tara went to visit him on 19 June – the very day that another of Steed's old enemies, Gerard Kafka[25], the head of Murder International, decided to celebrate the seventh anniversary of his capture with Steed's death. With one leg in plaster, Steed had few allies ranked alongside him as Department S came under attack, but with the help of Tara and the bedridden Edward Sunley, he managed to kill Kafka and his hired hit-men [NOON].

Shortly after Steed's plaster cast was removed and he returned home to Stable Mews, he found himself pitched into a strange but brief incident reminiscent of the Humphrey Bogart film *The Maltese Falcon*, based on the novel by Dashiell Hammett. One night he was visited by an unsuccessful ex-wrestler called Zoltan the Terrible and bequeathed the Dagger of a Thousand Deaths – an heirloom which was being sought by a number of undesirables, all of whom were being flushed out into the open by one of his old enemies, Henley Farrer. Over the next few hours, a series of fatal incidents dogged Steed's steps until he shot Farrer dead in a gun battle and saw Farrer's much-sought riches, a black pearl, destroyed [LEGA].

By now, Steed had been placed in charge of being an 'official observer' at a peace

---

[23] The Anastasia Nursing Academy purchased stationery on 13 April which was two months ago, suggesting the surveillance film covers three days in the first half of June 1968.

[24] Erroneously referred to as 'Peter Pan Dairies' in the summary report.

[25] Erroneously referred to as 'Gerald Kafta' in the summary report.

conference held in England – a liaison assignment which he treated as being a bit of a holiday. However, the role made Steed a target for enemy agents who again planned to infiltrate British security using a double – this time one created using a new technique developed by a scientist called Arcos. Steed was kidnapped and a mould taken of his face so that an operative could use the mould to adopt his features. However, Steed sent their plan awry by having five duplicates created: Georgio, Mintoff, Nadine, Bowler and Perova. In the chaos at the Conference, Steed was able to convince Tara of his true identity and a shoot-out at Arcos's hideout put paid to both the plan and Arcos, who had himself taken on the face of Steed in an attempt to escape [KEEP].

1968 was a notoriously bad year for leaks within British security. A traitor in the section meant that Mother needed the help of the trusted Steed to carefully go through the agents closest to the leak one by one. However, after a couple of days' work, he became concerned about his inability to contact Tara at the Elizabethan Hotel where she had gone to visit her uncle. On arriving at the hotel that Saturday evening, Steed found that Tara had indeed been imprisoned there by the staff – but now had the situation quite under control [WISH].

With Tara off on a week's holiday, Steed was engaged in finding who had killed one of his colleagues, Trouncer. To stand in for Tara, Mother assigned Lady Diana Forbes-Blakeney of Special Services whom Steed addressed as 'Forbes'. Lady Diana proved herself most able on the assignment to discover how trained agents were being killed by a variety of methods and then deposited, gift-wrapped, in a graveyard. The ruthlessly efficient murderer was REMAK[26] – a machine programmed to devastate the Department. Steed managed to set REMAK to self-destruct, wrapping up the case before Tara's return from vacation [KILL].

Autumn arrived, and when Sir James Pendred of the Department of Forestry Research was found shot dead after trying to telephone the Prime Minister with information of national importance, Steed and Tara were assigned to find out what menace Pendred had uncovered. This propelled the pair into the woody world of forestry and timber, with Steed claiming to represent 'the Ministry', and going undercover to dubious antiques dealer Mervyn Sawbow as Steed of 'Steed and Heppelwhite' – antique experts with offices in New York, Los Angeles, San Francisco, Montreal, Toronto, Seattle, Winnipeg and all points west – who was looking for select quality pieces. Steed and Tara eventually uncovered a bizarre plan concocted by a man called Wainwright who had a super-strength strain of woodworm which he was planning to release from fake letter boxes unless the authorities paid him £100 million [ROTT].

The lapses in internal security continued when informants used by the Department began to be killed off – the contact man for the informants, Lt Roy Casper[27], had gone missing two days before. Mother assigned this investigation to Steed and Tara, who discovered that Casper was only one of several agents being lured to Centre 53 by a faked telephone message from Mother himself. Once there, operatives believed they were undergoing mock interrogations on a TOHE[28]; during the 'rest periods', they were passing on vital information to fake officers like Colonel Mannering and Captain Soo. Steed and Tara were able to shut down the scheme within days [INTR].

---

[26] Remote Electro-Matic Agent Killer.

[27] Erroneously referred to as 'Roy Caspar' in the summary report.

[28] Test Of Human Endurance.

Two months' surveillance of one of the Ministries also came to fruition around this time, plugging a leak of information about missile deployment to the 'other side'. Again Mother sent in Steed and Tara who discovered that high level security personnel with top QR security ratings were being made to fall in love by the subliminal use of microdots, and then divulging their confidential data to a woman called Martha working at the Ministry as a cleaner. The operation was being run from the romantic publishing company Casanova Ink, which Steed visited posing as the greatest fan of the publisher's most prolific author, the fictitious Rosemary Z Glade, and claiming to own all 437 of her books. Saving the life of a suicidal Tara, who had become lovelorn under the microdot influence, Steed then employed the devices against their creator, Nigel Bromfield, and his staff [LOVE].

A more serious conduit for secret information was also shut down at this time. For 18 months, a talking courier case had been taking codes, secrets and plans to the 'other side', and Mother was determined to intercept and track the case as it passed from hand to hand. This time, it was containing the final payoff for the 'man at the top'. Steed took on the identity of one 'Richard Strauss' early on in the chain, taking the case to the Cremorne Hotel[29] where it was collected; later, when apprehending a contact called Cavell, he introduced himself as 'Steed – Security'. At last, the case was delivered and the traitor – Colonel Stonehouse – was exposed [TAKE].

Steed was now planning another holiday and booked himself three weeks in Naples where he could travel by ferry and relax on the beach. However, when he was about to leave on 14 October, he was kidnapped and taken away to a house in London. Here, he was hypnotised intensively by a man named Kreer for enemy agents led by Proctor. Steed's programming was to kill Mother upon hearing the trigger word 'Bacchus', Proctor's team having sent a postcard on behalf of Steed to Mother showing this rotund deity. With no memory of the processing, Steed was returned to his apartment three weeks later believing it was still 14 October – and being forced to relive the day again and again, as well as attempting to kill himself and Tara when she mentioned the postcard of Bacchus. Steed was soon suspended from active service by Father, Mother's second in command, and was made to believe that he had killed Collins, a fellow agent. Steed was finally able to break through his hypnotic conditioning and see Proctor, who had been following him around but had previously been edited from Steed's consciousness. With Mother safe, an unsuspecting Proctor was soon overpowered by Steed [STAY].

Having very quickly tackled a case in Bermuda with Tara at around the time that Richard Nixon was elected as the new US President [STAY], within days[30] Steed found himself representing the British Government in welcoming Haller, Vailarti, Stretlsov and Gruner, members of the World Disarmament Committee who had arrived in London for talks. This night was to be a dramatic one for Steed as it appeared that the Victorian menace known as the Gaslight Ghoul was again stalking the streets close to Stable Mews and attacking the delegates. With a fake diary revealing another 1888 murder, Steed joined the Gaslight Ghoul Club and was able to expose Mark Travers, the club secretary and a professional armaments trader, as the true killer [FOG].

At Christmas, Steed received a golden propelling pencil with a crown on top from Tara

---

[29] Erroneously referred to as the 'Cremone Hotel' in the summary report.

[30] A hire document for a horse-drawn hansom cab from Bartholomew Sanders was dated '7th November 1968', and Tara commented that they were just entering the month of November.

[REQU]. During late 1968, Steed had designed a whole array of new security measures for the British War Room, and from the start of 1969, Tara was assigned to test these out with practical assaults. After two weeks, Tara found that she was being set up as a traitor and was eventually framed for the murder of her colleague, Jimmy Fairfax. Mother was forced to place Tara under house arrest while Steed took a personal interest in proving the innocence of his partner, who had now become a deep and trusted friend. The fake evidence planted around Tara by a man called Dangerfield was revealed and Tara was cleared as those involved were apprehended [THAT].

From the start of 1969, Steed switched briefly to the use of another Rolls – a yellow New Phantom Tourer Mark I made in 1927[31] [THAT, THIN, REQU, LACE, OVER]. Again, he was happy to leave this prized vehicle for Tara to drive when he was busy elsewhere [REQU]. Steed's next case came not from the Department but from his old friend, the Reverend Teddy Shelley. At an archaeological excavation beneath a church there had been a strange death by electrocution. Working alongside archaeologist Inge Tilson, Steed discovered the presence of some strange metal boxes which devoured and emitted electrical power – the creation of a man called Kruger who had worked for the Royal Establishment but was now selling his inventions to a foreign representative called Stenson. Steed was able to prevent this deal reaching fruition and destroyed one of the boxes after it had killed Kruger [THIN].

Even though Steed had killed Kafka, Murder International were still a very active organisation. When Miss Miranda Loxton became a key witness against these killers, Steed was assigned to protect her after an attempt on her life sent her into hiding.[32] For this, Steed secreted Miranda at his boyhood haunt of Fort Steed, whiling away the hours by recreating famous military battles... and learning the hard way that his grasp of tactics had become a little rusty over the years [REQU].

Steed was deeply concerned when Tara went missing after a visit to an antique shop near his flat. By careful research from the available clues, Steed deduced that she was being held against her will at the home of Henry Lasindall, a controller in charge of records at the Ministry. Steed arrived in time to rescue her from being used as a pawn in a plan which required a vital day in 1914 being recreated, allowing Henry and his brother Rupert access to great riches [PAND].

In February 1969, Steed set off to keep his usual Christmas celebration date with Bill Bassett, who was by now living in a large and remote country house with his wife, Laura. On arrival, Steed discovered that the Bassetts had other house guests, comprising the forceful Fenton Grenville, his strange lady friend Circe Bishop and his aides Ernest Lomax and Gilbert Sexton. The Bassetts were actually being held hostage by Grenville, who had allowed Circe to insert radio-detonated phosphor bombs in their throats; Grenville needed their home as a vantage point from which to launch a long-range weapon at a meeting of foreign ministers being held at Critchley Manor seven miles away. Presumed dead after a morning's hunting with Grenville – but in fact only shot in the right leg – Steed returned to the Bassetts' home and was able to rescue his friends with a little help from Tara [OVER].

Steed, Tara and Mother were called in during spring 1969 to investigate a lady called Helen Pritchard who had been found wandering in the snowy wastes of the British coun-

---

[31] Registration UU 3864.

[32] Collecting Miss Loxton, Steed made use of a grey Morris Oxford, registration LGF 942D, and then switched to a red Triumph 2000, registration MBH 545C.

tryside. Helen's tale involved a man who was destined to be buried at Happy Meadows, a luxury cemetery. What the proprietor of Happy Meadows did not realise was that the rich corpses buried in his Paradise Plot were not really dead, but entering a secret base beneath his graveyard where they shared their embezzled funds with The Master, a man who had arranged an escape route for them. Steed managed to infiltrate this bizarre scheme fronted by Mystic Tours[33] by claiming to be a city financier who had met one of the absconders, Jonathan Jupp. With Tara's help, Steed was soon able to overpower The Master's gang and bring the thieves to justice [BIZA].

Shortly after this, it seems likely that Steed and Tara spent some time together unchaperoned on board a space rocket which Steed had assembled [BIZA]. It is at this point that the Department changed its policy on surveillance filming, and no more of Steed's missions were held on celluloid until early 1976. Presumably Steed and Tara continued to work together with Mother for some time – some reports suggest as late as August 1972.[34]

---

[33] Erroneously referred to as 'Paradise Holiday' in the summary report.
[34] *TV Comic*, Issue 1078, 12 August 1972.

JOHN STEED
AVOIDING THE DESK JOB

Obviously without full Department reports and films, the years from 1970 to 1975 are somewhat sketchy – which is a shame as there were clearly some great changes in Steed's career and outlook on life. Certainly, the encounters with The Unicorn seemed to continue during this period as Steed and the top assassin stalked each other from country to country, neither having the edge to dispose of the other and both showing an increasing admiration for their opponent. Steed got to know more about The Unicorn's contacts on the continent – notably Paris. On one occasion in Tangiers, Steed got an excellent shot in at The Unicorn; the bullet was not fatal, but put The Unicorn on a strict diet for life. Connected with this case was a belly dancer called Yvette whom The Unicorn trusted, unaware that she found Steed more attractive [LION]. It seems likely that Steed had also been over to Toronto to spend time with Chuck Peters [GLAD] and may well have been in California one summer [ANGE].

After having spiked movies, musicals and a television series, the Department next managed to suppress a stage play about Steed's career which was set to open in July 1971. A storyline had been written which dwelt upon the more fantastic and 'kinky' elements of Steed's career – with details apparently leaked from the department by Brian Clemens and Terence Feely, two of those responsible for documenting many of Steed's assignments. Actor Simon Oates, who had played suave but ruthless espionage agent Anthony Kelly in the 1965 BBC adventure series *The Mask of Janus* – and its 1966 spin-off *The Spies* – was chosen to play a younger Steed, who was apparently to be given a contemporary image. Furthermore, the script would partner him with a lady called 'Hannah Wild' – no doubt inspired by the world-famous shot Hana Wilde whom Steed had encountered when lured to the island training course in 1967 [SUP7], a mission chronicled by Clemens. Some of the details about Steed were authentic (he still drove a vintage Bentley) while others were not (he lived in a penthouse apartment and had a female butler called James). A superior called 'Mother' appeared – but this was an Irish gentleman who was not confined to a wheelchair. The far-fetched plot concerned one Madame Gerda who planned to make herself and her shapely female gang invisible using a Giant Computer Brain. After a few performances to small audiences in Birmingham, the show vanished into the backwaters of theatre legend as it opened in the West End. Poor ticket sales were to blame publicly – but it seems that the Department had again worked its official brand of prohibitive magic.

The Department were rather less successful with their next attempts to obscure Steed's work to the public. During 1971, Sonovision Ltd decided to make a radio series about Steed's 1960s career for the South African Broadcasting Company station Spingbok Radio – a company well beyond the jurisdiction of British security in the same way that Peter Wright's 1987 book *Spycatcher* would initially be published and sold outside the United Kingdom. Sonovision's owner, David Gooden, produced around 20 serialised adventures based loosely on many of Steed's exploits between 1965 and 1969 – all of which were restructured to feature Emma rather than Tara and had Steed always reporting to Mother. London born actor Donald Monat, who had been working frequently in Johannesberg, played a rather plummy but highly acceptable Steed and the series – like the aborted 1964 television films – was called *The Avengers*. Clearly the Department were immediately unable to stop these broadcasts which ran from 6 December 1971 to 28 December 1973.[1]

It seems that by early 1976 – which is when the surveillance films and reports begin again – Steed had attained a senior position in the Department similar to that occupied by Mother from spring 1968.[1] High on the Department's list of 'incorruptibles' [ANGE], Steed was seen to report direct to government ministers on different cases [RAT, CAT, TALE] and had the authority to ask to have radio channels cleared [RAT]. However, he did report to Craig, the Executive in Charge of Home Security, along with colleagues such as Torrance [FACE]. Steed did not occupy a specific office at the established HQ – and seemed determined not to end up trapped behind a desk [ANGE]. Indeed, it seems that during 1976 it was usual for other members of the Department or any of the Ministries to report direct to him at his home either in person or by radio [MIDA, CAT, 3HAN, LAST].

Steed's fame now meant that he was one of a handful of agents whose features were identifiable at the Department's new Target Range – the espionage equivalent of Madame Tussaud's [TARG]. Steed was the only person that a double agent such as Karavitch was prepared to deal with over vital information, over and above Canadian intelligence [COMP], and Marco, one of The Unicorn's men, could not believe one occasion when Steed himself answered his phone call [LION].

By 1976, Steed had left the well-furnished but confined apartments which he had occupied in the heart of London for one of the more stately dwellings which had apparently littered his formative years. His new home – which according to some unconfirmed sources was known affectionately as 'Steed's Stud'[3], a name which appeared on an area of the Target Range [TARG]; to the north west was the village with a windmill where Steed hid Professor Vasil[4] [CARD]. The signpost would seem to indicate that it is in the region of Fulmer, not far from Eton and north west of Stede Regis, while the architecture is reminiscent of the private property Fulmer Hall.

'I just adore his house,' said Purdey.[5] The large white mansion with its impressive frontage stood at the end of a long drive [FACE] in its own grounds which included expansive

---

[1] Some of the shows were subsequently aired in the mid-1980s on WBAI in New York.

[2] An unsubstantiated report suggests that Mother was still Steed's superior during 1976. *The Eagle's Nest*, p5-7, 107.

[3] *The Eagle's Nest*, p168; 'Room at the Top'. *The New Avengers Annual*, 1978, p48; *The Avengers* (Rogers), p173. Also the transcript of the Perov incident [CARD].

[4] This appears to have been the village of Turville in Buckinghamshire.

[5] 'Room at the Top'. *The New Avengers Annual*, 1978, p49.

lawns, a lake [MIDA] and lots of well maintained bushes creating secluded areas [LAST]. The grounds were expansive enough to allow many pastimes which Steed had been forced to forego on his confined London premises; he could ride horses [MIDA, TARG] and indulge in clay pigeon shoots [FACE]. The countryside setting allowed Steed to enjoy more natural pleasures, such as a dawn chorus in the summer months [SLEE].

Considering Steed's position and the remoteness of the building, there was very little security installed and people could stroll in easily through an unlocked side door – something which Steed now seemed unconcerned about [3HAN]. From the front porch [HOST], a hallway with statues and vases [FACE] led to both the lounge and the dining room; the door to the lounge had a Nash handle dating from around 1800 [TALE].

Behind this door, Steed had a green walled lounge with shuttered shelves full of leather-bound books and maps [TALE], a large fireplace and a bas relief along one wall [NEST]; Steed kept his drinks beneath this frieze [FACE]. There were leather chairs and a settee [eg NEST, TALE], a piano [eg NEST, DEAD], a military drum (useful for playing cards on) [LAST, TALE], small statuettes (useful for holding maps in place) [TALE], a wooden kidney shaped table by the hearth [TALE], a wooden globe [DIRT], a golden clock on the mantelpiece beneath some armour [MIDA, CAT], a breastplate and helmet on a stand [CARD], a grandfather clock [CAT], a sphinx (which Steed put his bowler on top of and his brolly beside) [CAT], and framed colour photographs of Cathy, Emma and Tara in the lounge area [CARD], along with another three photos depicting a trio of Steed's most successful fillies, each accompanied proudly by its rosette [CARD].

Adjoining the lounge area was the dining room with a large and lavish wooden dining table and chairs [CAT]; the table was smashed by a flying motorcycle in 1976 [3HAN]. There were French windows leading to the bushes outside [CARD]; these were broken by gunshots [FACE], flying bodies of assailants [TALE] or Steed's colleagues crashing through them on a motorcycle [3HAN]. There was a green telephone [LAST, TALE] (which could take calls from car radio phones) [TALE] and sometimes Steed had a radio telephone unit in his lounge [CAT]; another extension led to a white receiver which could be taken out into the garden [TARG]. Steed's number was known to the Department agents [TARG].

Leading up from the hallway was a flight of stairs with banisters (which got smashed in a fight) [TALE]. Upstairs, there was a guest bedroom where things would occur that might offend people of 'high moral standards' after parties [LAST]. Beneath the house, Steed was delighted to maintain a proper wine cellar [FACE]. Steed could often be found indulging the pleasures of his mis-spent youth in his billiards room [LAST, 3HAN]. As with his Westminster Mews flat, Steed employed a housekeeper, Mrs Weir, who could play the overture to Gioachino Rossini's 1829 opera *Guillaume Tell* (*William Tell*) on the Stylophone [LAST]. Sometimes weeks would go by without Steed seeing her [TALE].

The stables were Steed's major passion in his life, and he kept a number of horses there [MIDA, RAT]. Some of the stables area was now reserved for parking Steed's cars such as his Range Rover [CAT].

By early 1976, Steed was driving a yellow Rover 3500 SD1 Automatic[6] [NEST, MIDA, HOST, RARE, LION]; this vehicle had an arm rest in the rear [HOST] and by spring 1977 had clocked up 11,725 miles [HOST]. On one occasion, its tyres were let down by a man called Richards as part of a plan to discredit Steed [RARE]. Steed also drove an olive green 5.3-litre

---

[6] Registration MOC 229P.

Jaguar XJ 12 Coupé Automatic[7] [CARD, LAST, RAT, 3HAN, SLEE, HOST, TRAP, DEAD, ANGE]. This car was fitted with a radio [RAT] and a sun roof [SLEE] and in spring 1976 was tracked by Steed's old adversary Perov, who had arranged to have a large cross painted on the roof which was only visible through special glasses [CARD]. 'A docile monster,' was how Steed apparently described the wide-wheeled 'Big Cat', adding 'It's capable of 200 mph... It's hand-made – of course – *and* tailored; and a worthy stable mate for the Bentley.'[8] These two vehicles were parked side by side in Steed's large garage at his estate [HOST].[9]

For off-road work and other rough terrain, Steed used a green Range Rover[10] [CAT, TARG, TALE, OBSE]. This vehicle, which was garaged in the stables [CAT], also had a sun roof [CAT] and had its tyres shot out by both Miss Irene Brandon [TALE] and agent Purdey [OBSE], prior to its destruction by a stolen rocket when Steed used the vehicle to avert a disastrous launch [OBSE].

By early 1976, Steed was operating closely with two agents in particular – Michael Gambit and Purdey, apparently the two people he could really trust [ANGE], even if at times he found them a little impetuous [LION]. The pair of young agents had already been working together for some time [GNAW], he as her superior [BASE], and they now fulfilled the same role on vital cases which Steed and Tara had for Mother as far back as 1968. By the following year, Steed was immensely proud of his working relationship with Gambit and Purdey, commenting that he taught them both all they know [KIL2]. Steed referred to the former as 'Gambit' when at work and as 'Mike' when off duty or late at night [SLEE, HOST]. Knowing that Gambit trusted his judgement, Steed would send Gambit into the attack without hesitation [TALE] and would also allocate him undercover assignments in preference to Purdey [FACE]. He encouraged Gambit to cultivate instinct [ANGE] and worried about the junior operative on occasion [TRAP]. However, as an elder and superior, Steed was happy to let Gambit tackle more manual or strenuous tasks such as digging for Burt Brandon's box in Surrey [TALE] or releasing their car from a mudbank [EMIL].

It seems that by spring 1976, Steed and Purdey had not been working together for very long; in April, he still did not know that she was in the Royal Ballet [NEST]. Ever the old-fashioned gentleman, Steed worried about Purdey and on occasion would ask Gambit to keep an eye on her [LAST] or simply not assign her a role in the investigation [CAT]. When she was kidnapped in spring 1977, Steed was deeply troubled and was prepared to hand over the real Allied Attack plans for her release, explaining to her that the documents were, 'Only paper – you're Purdey' [HOST].

It was Steed's fondness for Purdey – already developing in spring 1976 – that Felix Kane played upon a year later, deciding that the best way of making Steed suffer was to let him see the results of his attack on her [LAST]. When fearing that Purdey was dying of curare, Steed declared that he would join Gambit to hunt down her killers – even though he knew they were all expendable [TARG]. At work, Steed liked to give Purdey perks, such as arranging for her to be part of the security team for an Arab bigwig [OBSE]; at play, after

---

[7] Registration NWK 60P

[8] 'Room at the Top'. *The New Avengers Annual*, 1978, p49. Steed's emphasis.

[9] Erroneous transcripts also suggest that Steed was also driving a Lancia – *House of Cards*, p86 – and a Bentley – *To Catch a Rat*, p93; *Hostage*, p110 – despite the use of other vehicles in the surveillance films.

[10] Registration TXC 922J.

an evening meal, he would give her a rose [SLEE]. Steed was protective of her with regards to her former fiancé Larry Doomer [OBSE], and also informed Commander East that her irrational behaviour was not an act of treason, but that she was obeying his direct orders and that he would deal with anyone who disagreed with him [OBSE]. He would also forgive Purdey her tactless moments in circumstances which she was not aware of [FACE].

Despite his affection for Purdey, Steed could still be tough; he locked her out of his hotel bedroom and left her in the cold April night of a Scots island, quipping that he would not let her into a gentleman's bedroom. 'You're no gentleman,' said Purdey. 'That's where the danger lies,' he smiled back [NEST]. Similarly, Steed would send her off on work rather than let her celebrate with champagne [TALE]. He trusted Purdey well enough to let her check his own files [DEAD], but nevertheless had moments of uncertainty with her, such as when she told him that Joanna – the latest love of his life – was going to kill him [CARD].

By 1976, Steed was dating a succession of beautiful ladies who were generally a fair few years younger than himself; he was now in his early 50s. At the time of his birthday in early 1976, Steed was seeing Trisha, who was helping him celebrate at his home with Purdey and Gambit when Terry, one of the Department operatives, staggered in fatally wounded to reveal that Felix Kane was the traitor in their organisation. The following morning, Steed's team pounced on Kane as he prepared to meet a contact. Kane crashed his car into a fuel tanker, and was presumed dead [LAST].

At the start of the year, Steed was helping a General in British security with a method of transferring American war policy documents to London; his solution to avoid interception, line tapping or kidnapping was the 'Three Handed Game', the use of three people with photographic memories each to memorise a third of the 4,000 page document in America and return to England where the information could be re-assembled [3HAN].

Shortly before Harold Wilson's shock resignation as Prime Minister in mid-March[11], Steed was dating a lady called Sara who shared his passion for horses. One night, Steed encountered his old colleague Freddy who had fallen on hard times since being forced to leave the Department because of his drinking. However, Freddy witnessed a strange hunt being conducted by one Professor Turner – which was connected with the arrival in London of 'Hong Kong' Harry, a courier well known to Steed who was carrying £750,000 in gold dust so that his countrymen could make a purchase. The object for sale was Midas, a man created by Turner as an asymptomatic carrier for a host of deadly diseases – an assassin whose very touch was deadly. Steed managed to save a visiting princess[12] from Midas's fatal greeting at an exhibition of antiquities [MIDA].[13]

Steed's next assignment was to help with the defection of Professor Vasil[14], and successfully kept him out of the clutches of rival master spy Comrade Ivan Perov.[15] To save

[11] The invitation to a costume party where Midas's powers were demonstrated was dated 'Saturday 14 March 1976' – although 14 March 1976 was actually a Sunday.

[12] A visual record of this incident refers to the Princess as being the Princess of Boltania. 'Midas Secret'. *The New Avengers Annual*, 1978, p6.

[13] Two alternate versions of this assignment are held; a transcript as part of *The Eagle's Nest* compiled by John Carter and a set of sketches by Pierre Le Goff entitled 'Midas Secret'. *The New Avengers Annual*, 1978 – a translation of 'Le Secret de Midas', *Chapeau Melon et Bottes de Cuir*, Collection 1, 1977.

[14] An alternate transcript of the assignment gives Vasil's full name as 'Anton Vasil'. *House of Cards*, p10.

[15] An alternate transcript of the assignment gives Perov's first name as 'Nikolai'. *House of Cards*, p13.

face, Perov faked his own death and unleashed a Cold War operation known as the House of Cards in which sleepers would be activated to eliminate key British agents -- and hence force Steed to lead him to the hidden Vasil. Implicated in this plan was none other than Joanna[16], Steed's latest lady friend whom he rode with and attended hunt balls. When Purdey revealed that Joanna was planning to poison him over a romantic drink, Steed adopted a stoic face to mask his upset. Joanna asked 'John' to let her run claiming, 'We meant something to each other.' However, this was the occasion when Steed stated that his only marriage was to his profession – moments before Purdey led Joanna away. By employing the same decoy technique as he used with M Roland in 1962, Steed was able to protect Vasil and apprehend Perov [CARD].

On 19 April, Steed visited George Stannard to give him an informal briefing about the security for a lecture by Dr Maybach von Claus later that day. Stannard was missing, his room was being searched and then von Claus was kidnapped, apparently by a group of monks from the Brothers of St Dorca, a remote island to the west of the Outer Hebrides. Steed followed the trail and discovered that the brethren were what was left of Nazis who had fled from Germany in April 1945 – and who were keeping the inert form of Adolf Hitler alive in suspended animation at their monastery. Disguising himself as Jud, one of the Brothers, Steed infiltrated the Order, helped to rescue von Claus and had rounded up the remains of the Third Reich by the following morning [NEST].

As the burning hot summer of 1976 got underway, Steed received a report from Merton, one of his agents, that Hugh Rydercroft, a controller for the Ministry of Ecology, was going to be killed. Rydercroft perished in a co-ordinated bird strike, which led Steed's team to the Sanctuary of Wings, a bird sanctuary run by the strange Zarcardi who opposed official plans to control the bird population. Using a strange pipe which allowed him to communicate with birds, Zacardi planned to mass his feathered friends across the world as a vast army – similar to some of the horrors seen in Alfred Hitchcock's 1963 cinema thriller *The Birds*. Fortunately, his plans were foiled and Zarcardi fell to his death [CAT].

Around now, Steed gave a party at his home on 13 June [OBSE]. Over the period of a month, four agents in the Department – McKay, Potterton, Talmadge and Palmer – had suddenly died, apparently of natural causes. In Palmer's case he knew he was going to die and phoned Steed just before he expired. The common factor was that all the dead agents had just undertaken a session on the Target Range, not realising that the air pellet markers fired at them had in fact been infected with a lethal dose of curare – part of a scheme hatched by a man called Draker to decimate British security. After George Myers also died, Purdey was next on the range, giving Steed and Gambit a race to find the antidote for her in the midst of the lethal firing range, with Steed already having been injected in the left leg with the poison by Draker's tiny colleague, Klokoe[17] [TARG].

Steed was horrified when his old friend Mark Clifford, who was now being tipped to be the next Prime Minister, collapsed and died in front of him from a heart attack moments after they made arrangements to attend that Saturday's 'old school' cricket match. *The Times* covered Mark's death as their major story, but for Steed this was like losing a brother; Mark had always said that Steed was the closest thing to a brother he ever had. Steed did his best to comfort Mark's widow, Wendy, whom he deeply cared for.

---

[16] Again, the unconfirmed report names her as 'Joanna Harrington'. *House of Cards*, p69.

[17] Erroneously referred to as 'Kloekoe' in the summary report.

Unfortunately, the autopsy on Mark revealed that he still had his appendix which had been removed in July 1969. Aware of the trauma for Wendy, Steed arranged for an exhumation, and it soon became clear that the dead man was not actually Mark. Steed's investigations were to reveal that a number of doubles had been infiltrated into key security positions [FACE].

However, Mark was still to save Steed's life. Wendy gave Steed a watch which had belonged to Mark's great grandfather and had been in the family for over a century. While Wendy had in fact handed over the wrong watch – actually one presented to Mark by his party – it was this bequest which stopped a .38 bullet fired by Steed's own *doppelgänger* from killing him. By impersonating his own double as he had back in 1963, Steed in due course exposed his own superior, Craig, who also turned out to have been an impostor called Terrison since 1971 [FACE].

The next ministerial security job for Steed's team was to trail Burt Brandon when he emerged from jail after nine years, still claiming that he had evidence which would shake the government to its foundation. When Brandon's much sought-after treasure was finally located, it revealed to Steed that George Harmer, an under-secretary at the Ministry[18], was in the pay of Kommissar Voslavski, and a security scandal was averted [TALE].

Steed had close tabs kept on Juventor, an independent mercenary agent, when he entered the country and approached a number of foreign embassies. Juventor's target was to breach Steed's Three Handed Game scheme, using a stolen mind-draining machine (similar to the one which Steed had been subjected to in 1967) to acquire the memories of the three civilians with photographic memories who had conveyed the American attack plans back to the General in London. Although Juventor acquired all the information, he was overpowered by Purdey before he could put the data to use [3HAN].

After witnessing a test of S-95[19] – a sleep gas which could be deployed in a terrorist situation – one Saturday in mid-August[20], Steed waited for news from his old friend and colleague Frank Hardy about a lead he was following. When Sunday dawned, Steed, Gambit and Purdey were the only people to wake up because of their prior inoculation against S-95; a stolen consignment of the gas had been deployed over an area of London by a bank raid gang assembled by Brady, whom Hardy had been investigating. Steed and Gambit posed as gang members to infiltrate Brady's ranks and foil the thieves' getaway [SLEE].

Seismograph activity alerted Steed's Department to something large moving about in the London sewers beneath an area from Hyde Park to Buckingham Palace – and hence below a number of embassies. This led Purdey and Gambit back to a case which they had begun 12 months earlier when looking into the death of fellow agent Edward Harlow at a Ministry.[21] Down in the sewers was roaming a giant rat, an unwanted by-product of a serum developed by a greedy former Ministry scientist called Charles Thornton which made plants and animals swell to massive proportions. Thornton perished at the jaws of his

---

[18] The Home Office, according to the summary report.

[19] Erroneously referred to as 'Z 95' in the transcript.

[20] This surveillance film would appear to cover 14 and 15 August 1976. Dawn is at 4.45 am, and Steed checks the England cricket score – suggesting this was concurrent with England playing the West Indies at the Kennington Oval from 12 to 17 August.

[21] This was the Ministry of Agriculture according to the summary report.

creation which Gambit finally managed to kill with some substantial fire power [GNAW].

Steed was next called in by Major Prentice to an Army Training Centre from which General Stevens had gone missing on one of his routine spot inspections of 19th Division Special Commandos, a ruthless band of men moulded into a lethal fighting force by Colonel 'Mad Jack' Miller. Stevens had discovered that the unit was AWOL, taking part in mercenary action overseas. Gambit and Purdey infiltrated the Commandos by different means, with Steed and Prentice arriving with reinforcements to rescue them in the nick of time – plucking Purdey from a minefield by helicopter [DIRT].

Around now, it seems that Steed had decided to take up the notion he had floated to writer Tim Heald in May 1968. Since 1973, Heald had been writing whodunits such as *Unbecoming Habits* and *Blue Blood Will Out* which featured his character Simon Bognor of the Board of Trade. The biography of Steed was a new career move for Heald, who would later write some notable biographies of Prince Philip, Barbara Cartland and Denis Compton amongst others. Like Steed, Heald was keen devotee of cricket. Although still an active man, Steed managed to fit in tape-recorded question and answer sessions about his life, and also give Heald 'the run of the library at Stede Regis'[22]... with the exception of one bundle of letters tied with a green ribbon. Steed also put Heald in touch with his many aunts around the world for further background on his noble family.

The next woman to share Steed's life – and his beloved equestrian pursuits – was a lady called Helga, whom Steed falsely claimed to Gambit did not speak a word of English. Early in 1977[23], monitoring stations for the Department picked up regular nightly transmissions in Morse which seemed to be from Irwin Gunner, an agent who had gone missing while undercover in Leipzig in July 1960. Following obsolete code-names and signals, Steed's group raced to locate Gunner before the opposition, and it became evident that Gunner – who had been suffering from amnesia in the 17 intervening years – was still determined to identify the 'White Rat', a traitor in his Eastern cell who had betrayed his friends. The Minister[24], Quaintance, was a chief suspect for a while before the true double agent was revealed in the form of Cromwell, the head of D16[25], whom Gunner finally shot [RAT].

A year after the death of Terry and the apparent demise of Kane, Steed celebrated his birthday once again with Purdey and Gambit. This time the trio were joined by Laura who also shared Steed's love of horses – to the extent that he presented her with a fine brown filly which she had taken a liking to – and was understanding enough to be ushered out of the way when ministry business demanded Steed's attention. Around this time, a man called Frank Goff who had worked for Dr Clement Armstrong[26] was released after serving ten years in prison. Despite the existing footage of the event, Department surveillance was apparently frustrated by Goff being let out a day early – and then turning up dead next day. When a government scientist called Professor Mason was kidnapped while employed by the government, Steed looked into his project – a 'seducer' – which was being developed

---

[22] *Jealous in Honour*, p10.

[23] Irwin Gunner went missing around mid-July 1960 and was missing for '17 years' according to the surveillance film. Since the original décor of Purdey's apartment was still intact prior to Kane's attack, this must have been around January 1977.

[24] An alternate transcript referred to Quaintance as being the Foreign Minister. *To Catch a Rat*, p128.

[25] Erroneously referred to as 'DIC' in the summary report.

[26] Erroneously referred to as 'Professor Armstrong' in the summary report.

at the Turner Laboratories. It was here that Steed encountered a Cybernaut again, apparently after nearly a decade. Further evidence came to light to show that the Cybernauts were being controlled by the crippled remains of Felix Kane, who aimed to use Armstrong's technology to rebuild himself and take a vicious revenge on Steed, Purdey and Gambit. Steed's use of spray-on plastic skin defeated Kane during his deadly attack on Purdey a couple of weeks later [LAST].

It seems that in spring 1977, Steed took some sort of sideways move in the Department. Certainly he seemed to have been ill at ease at times when his young colleagues were assigned into the thick of the action, and he had been left little to do other than co-ordinate. While Steed was a cornerstone of the organisation, other senior figures in the Department such as Tommy McKay knew that Steed preferred to play his own games [HOST] rather than being forced to work by the book. Judging by the surveillance films, it appears that Steed was now free to pick and choose his cases, popping into HQ when he wanted, or agreeing to take on assignments for other senior figures such as Graham Wallace [RARE]. The fact that in the coming months, Steed was able to select one mission which involved him working on a topless beach [OBSE] indicated that he had a very free hand in what he did and didn't do. Nevertheless, he continued to work with Purdey and Gambit, now that the close-knit team had been established. As McKay commented 'John Steed is the hub of this organisation' [HOST] and as such Steed was a key figure for the oppostition to attack in order to render the entire Department ineffectual by shattering its internal confidence [HOST].

Steed himself seemed less and less enamoured of the killing trade he was caught up in as he reached his 50s. He did not like germ warfare as it 'never seemed quite sporting' [MIDA]. Similarly, he was dismissive of the work at the Turner Laboratory, feeling they were merely 'devising new ways of destroying people' [LAST]. By 1977, the career was really getting to him and he ruminated on his lonely job: 'Hideous the work we do... not the cause, the side effects... friends, cut dead' [ANGE].

During spring 1977, Steed relocated to a similar large country house, even more impressive than the last. Judging by the signpost close to the main gate, this abode was apparently two miles from Stoke Poges, two and a half miles from Farnham Common, and three and a half miles from Burnham [HOST] as well as 20 minutes drive from both the north side of Pembury Park [HOST] and an airport which Gambit and Purdey could reach (presumably Heathrow) [TRAP]. The signpost would seem to indicate that it is in the region of Fulmer, not far from Eton and north west of Stede Regis, while the architecture is reminiscent of the private property Fulmer Hall. The large white mansion with its impressive frontal columns [DEAD] was located in its own extensive grounds which included a sundial [DEAD]. White gates led to the garage and stables area to the left of the main porch [DEAD, RARE]. The stables allowed room for at least three cars [HOST] such as Steed's beloved Bentley [DEAD] plus his Jaguar [HOST] and Rover [HOST].

The tiled hallway led directly into a large open area [DEAD]; there were two tall oriental pots by the door, one holding Steed's walking sticks and canes [RARE]. The stairs opened onto the large dual-roomed area, and had an elaborate window at the top of them [HOST]. The décor for this was now generally a deep red in comparison to the green of Steed's last home [DEAD]. A rug covered the wooden floor [RARE] and what were effectively two linked rooms could be closed off from one another by wooden doors [RARE].

Steed's familiar furniture – such as his bureau – was relocated in the new living area.

Although Steed had given up smoking in the 1960s, there were ashtrays in the lounge [HOST] and flowers were now kept in the fire place [HOST]. There were impressionist pictures [DEAD], Dresden and Le Moge porcelain (including a Buddha and a horse and rider) [DEAD], Waterford glass containing a fine cognac [DEAD] and lots of mementoes of Steed's school days [DEAD]. However, by now Steed seemed to place far less value in these mere objects, commenting thoughtfully, 'The only thing that can't be replaced is the love and life of an old friend' [DEAD].

There was a grey telephone in the lounge [DEAD], while a black phone [RARE, OBSE] or white phone [KIL1] was on Steed's desk; it is even possible that he was in the telephone book since would-be psychic Miss Victoria Stanton was able to trace 'John Steed' with ease and simply arrive on his doorstep [RARE]. This desk was situated by the French windows, along with some bookcases [RARE]. Unfortunately, Steed's home was soon the target for a break-in one evening, with Steed's revolver being stolen from his bureau [HOST].

By now, Steed was seeing a lady called Suzy.[27] Suzy did not usually pursue men, but saw something special in Steed, although she was a little put out by her gentleman friend's sudden preoccupation with Purdey. The reason for this was that Purdey had been kidnapped and Steed was ordered to undertake a series of tasks to ensure her safe return. After he was tested by making a ransom delivery of £5,000, Steed was then ordered by the kidnappers to obtain the Full Allied Attack Plan from the HQ office of his old friend Tommy McKay. Steed carefully copied the plans as required, but in the meantime was framed for killing Walters, an agent sent to tail him. Working against his friends, Steed managed to rescue Purdey without handing the plans over to Spelman[28], a double agent in the Department whose true objective was to create doubt about Steed and render the section ineffectual for years. Once rescued, Purdey agreed to square things between Steed and Suzy [HOST].

Suzy was soon replaced in Steed's affections by a lady called Miranda whom he went riding with. It was now that Steed's team worked alongside Marty Brine of the CIA upon a report from the fatally wounded agent Williams[29], indicating that a major drug delivery was to take place in Windsor. Steed, Purdey and Gambit intercepted the drop successfully [TRAP].

A short while afterwards, Steed, Purdey and Gambit were informed of a 'Red Alert' situation by operative Henry Murford[30], and boarded a plane which they believed was taking them to a rendezvous in the midst of a global crisis. This was in fact a trap to bring the trio to an estate in East Anglia where the drug baron Soo Choy wanted to take revenge against them for the Windsor incident which had made him lose face with the gang syndicates. Steed broke his left arm when the plane crashed in Soo Choy's territory, and in the following battle of wits with the Oriental's soldiers he posed as an officer called Tansing, giving a less than convincing version of an Eastern accent. At Soo Choy's house, the injured Steed and his friends were able to apprehend the drug baron [TRAP].

After his arm had set, another figure from Steed's past came back to haunt him with a series of vicious and thoughtless incidents which destroyed items precious to him. Steed's home was again broken into and vandalised – notably his school trophies – and one of his

---

[27] An unconfirmed alternate document gives her full name as 'Suzy Pilkington'. *Hostage*, p39.

[28] The same document refers to 'Paul Spelman'. *Hostage*, p79.

[29] Erroneously referred to as 'Marvin' in the transcript.

[30] Referred to in the summary report as a 'Ministry official'.

remaining Bentleys which he cared about was destroyed by explosives planted in his garage. Over the next nightmarish day, Purdey and Gambit looked into Steed's past and soon realised the connection was Mark Crayford, who had been declared dead over a month ago under his Eastern Bloc name, Comrade Commissar Bukovski. An apparent attempt was made on Steed's life when he was shot at his home, although he sustained only a graze, supplemented by a secondary superficial wound when the gunman tried again at a hospital. Purdey was then kidnapped by Crayford, who wanted to triumph over Steed just once before he died. As Steed confronted Crayford back at the Victorian folly where Crayford had cheated in his only win over his school friend, the bullet fired into Crayford by Steed a decade earlier finally entered Mark's heart and killed him. Mark's death deeply saddened Steed [DEAD].

The death of Department paymaster Freddy Mason, thrown from a bridge close to HQ, was another terrible blow for Steed; the two had been good friends over the years and Steed was determined to find out who was responsible. A couple of days later, Steed was visited by Miss Victoria Stanton, a young woman who claimed to be a medium and who had received a message through the ether saying that Steed was to be murdered. At HQ, Graham Wallace asked Steed to attend a Russian ballet to get information from double agent Ivan Petrovich, but this was a lure to ultimately frame Steed for the murder of colleagues George Cowley[31] and Derek Wigmore. Placed under house arrest by security officer McBain, Steed counted upon the help of Purdey and Gambit to prove his innocence and reveal that it was Wallace who had killed Mason to cover up his embezzling activities, and had now hired a hit-man to eliminate a discredited Steed [RARE].

Steed was able to stay at one of his favourite haunts, the George V Hotel in Paris, when he joined Purdey to collect information about the return of an agent called Martin from behind the Iron Curtain; on this assignment, Steed had to disguise himself as a Monsignor. Although he evaded the Russians, Martin only got chance to say that he had information on the 'Angels of Death' before being shot. Back in England, several of Steed's friends and colleagues – including Peter Manderson – became the latest in a string of sudden but apparently natural deaths since 1975. Curious about Manderson's attendance at the Briantern Health Farm, Steed took the place of agent Simon Carter for an intensive detox session. Trapped in a maze as part of a programme to destroy agents by remote control using their stress levels, Steed managed to keep control until he could be rescued by Gambit and Purdey. Coldstream – an 'incorruptible' sleeper agent who had been working inside the Department for many years – was revealed to be behind the plan and apprehended [ANGE].

Concurrent with all the celebrations for Queen Elizabeth's silver jubilee, on 12 June[32] Steed was curious as to why Purdey should turn down a plum security job in London, but soon the team were involved in a potential security incident at an RAF base where Purdey renewed the acquaintance of her former fiancé, Squadron Leader Larry Doomer. Steed invited Doomer to his party the next day – the reason for the party being the anniversary of the one held the previous year – after which he became involved in the hunt for General Canvey, who had been kidnapped on leaving the festivities. It transpired that Canvey was

[31] The late George Cowley later had a lead character in the television series *The Professionals* named after him by Brian Clemens, once a top Department agent [CHAR] who left security work around 1977 to return to his career as a highly successful script writer and producer.

[32] Steed's desk calendar reads '12 June – Tuesday' although 12 June 1977 was actually a Sunday.

being held by Doomer, who had stolen a strike rocket and hidden it near Milton Keynes. The weapon was readied for an attack on the Houses of Parliament during a visit by a foreign VIP whom Doomer believed was responsible for his father's death seven years earlier. Still emotionally attached to Doomer, Purdey's irrational actions were defended by Steed who used his own Range Rover to block the launch of the warhead [OBSE].

Steed managed to get advance warning that his old enemy The Unicorn was planning another killing – this time the intended victim being a Minister of the cloth rather than the government. The target was saved by the use of a flak jacket and Steed's team quickly got on The Unicorn's trail with the RAF hurtling them back over to Paris. After ten years, Steed was finally able to capture The Unicorn alive, but his enjoyable chat with the assassin he admired was cut short when his captive was accidentally shot by one of his own men. Working with the French authorities, Steed had to maintain the illusion that The Unicorn was still alive so he could negotiate for the safe release of a royal prince whom the late hitman's subordinates had kidnapped [LION].

On 15 August 1977[33], Steed was intrigued by a report in the *Guardian* about a 'Mystery attack in a French town' by Russian soldiers which sounded strangely similar to the incident he had failed to solve at the Berkshire village just over 12 years earlier. Indeed, Steed took the steps of contacting Emma – who by this time had changed her name from 'Mrs Peel' – before heading over to France to investigate the situation himself. In the French countryside, Steed's team soon found themselves fighting a Russian force with obsolete equipment attacking out of date targets – and who looked impossibly young for their age. While in Paris, Steed was approached by one of his old acquaintances, Toy, who was now the Russian Ambassador and who claimed that these events could be the start of World War III [KIL1]. The soldiers had been in an artificial sleep and awakened by accident, and while most were dealt with quickly by French forces, Toy warned Steed that there were still two 'K' agents at large, briefed by the rogue Russian agent Colonel Stanislav.[34] Toy was killed delivering this information, shot on the roof garden of Steed's suite at the Hotel George V; Steed was deeply saddened, covering Toy with his jacket as a mark of respect [KIL2].

General Gaspard, a national figure, was killed in order to draw the President, Valery Giscard d'Estaing, out into the open for a funeral at which one of the 'K' agents was to strike. Steed attempted to alert the French Council to the 'K' agent situation, but a senior minister failed to believe him. The assassination was averted, although Steed was shot in the left arm during the funeral. He was subsequently decorated by the Russian Comrade Kerov who awarded him the Siberian Star – an honour which Steed felt he should keep secret from MI5 [KIL2].[35]

As autumn began[36], a photograph taken in Toronto which purported to identify the ruthless enemy agent Scapina arrived at an airfield in Kent. Steed wanted Scapina put out of

---

[33] The surveillance film dates the attack in France as taking place on 'August 14th 1977' at 9.43 am, while Steed's newspaper – presumably the following day – is rather strangely dated 'Tuesday May 3'.
[34] Also referred to as General Stanislav [KIL1].
[35] A heavily modified and abridged account of these events with Oriental rather than Russian agents also exists on file. See Appendix B.
[36] The incident with Karl Sminsky, which happens during Steed's holiday after the SCAPINA case, appears to have taken place in late September 1977; posters can be seen advertising Markham Fair from 29 September to 1 October.

business and travelled to Toronto to make a deal with a double agent called Karavitch, liaising with his old friend Paul Baker of Canadian Intelligence. Within a day, the investigations of Steed's party had revealed that SCAPINA[37] was none other than the computerised building in Toronto which was the HQ for Canadian Security, and that agents had been killed from the inside by automated systems [COMP] in a manner similar to the automated traps of REMAK [KILL] and Professor Keller's house [JACK].

While in France, Steed had driven a golden left-hand drive Rover SD1[38] [KIL1, KIL2] and also taken the wheel of a jeep [KIL1]. Now in Canada, Steed drove an automatic yellow Jaguar XJ-S[39] [COMP, GLAD, EMIL]; this was equipped with a radio telephone [GLAD, EMIL]. For rougher terrain, he made use of a green Toyota Landcruiser jeep[40] [BASE].

After exposing SCAPINA, Steed remained in Canada for a holiday along with Purdey and Gambit, but made this a 'working holiday'. Relaxation was soon forgotten when Chuck Peters, Steed's old friend from Berlin and now the Security Chief in Toronto, informed the vacationing agent that the enigmatic Red Army Colonel Karl Sminsky had arrived in the area and vanished – and that he would welcome Steed's advice. Vicious attacks by unarmed men confirmed that Sminsky had established a training school for local low-lifes – but Sminsky's true target was to break into the relocated Canadian Security Building with his bare hands. Steed's team were able to overpower Sminsky and his men, with Steed's quick thinking allowing Purdey to shoot the Soviet Colonel [GLAD].

While Steed remained in Toronto, it seems that Purdey and Gambit returned to England. However, when Steed was informed by Bailey of Canadian Intelligence that an enemy courier was arriving, the young agents crossed the Atlantic again to help spring a trap. Having followed various operatives of the 'other side', Steed investigated strange events on the shores of Lake Ontario. Such was his instinct that, with no authority whatsoever, he called upon an Admiral of the Canadian fleet and persuaded him to move in on a Russian submarine code-named 'Forward Base' which had been hidden in the lake since April 1969 [BASE].

It was now that Purdey went undercover as part of an operation to expose The Fox, a long-term double agent in Canadian Intelligence who was about to receive a payoff from the 'other side'. During a struggle with the wet-suited Fox in a small garage at Woodbridge, Steed managed to get a palm print on the roof of an old brown Plymouth called Emily. Unsure of which members of Canadian Intelligence he could trust, Steed took it upon himself to bring the vehicle back to HQ where the traitor could be revealed. After a hazardous journey, Douglas Collins[41] was unmasked and apprehended [EMIL]. This apparently brought the Canadian sojourn for Steed and his friends to an end ... as well as the surveillance films logged for Britain's greatest secret agent.

---

[37] Special Computerised Automated Project In North America.
[38] Registration 4253BX95.
[39] Registration MHF 291.
[40] Registration MMZ 300.
[41] Erroneously referred to as 'Gordon Collings' in the summary report.

JOHN STEED
BIOGRAPHY AND BEYOND

In October 1977, the Yorkshire Ripper preyed on women in Northern England, politician Jeremy Thorpe denied a highly embarrassing affair, legendary crooner Bing Crosby died while playing golf... and it seems that John Steed undertook his final filmed assignment for the Department. The incident with The Fox was the last of Steed's missions to be preserved by surveillance film and it seems that from around now the practice was discontinued. It is possible that it was at this time that Steed retired, having taken more of a back seat in Department affairs. There were also the terrible losses of old friends such as Mark Crayford, Mark Clifford and Freddy Mason – coupled with his changing moral approach to the work he did. Furthermore, Steed would have now been 55 years of age.

Concurrent with the last of the surveillance films came the publication of what was planned to be the first volume of his authorised biography. *John Steed: An Authorised Biography* appeared in hardback from Weidenfeld and Nicolson in October 1977. Only one instalment of what was planned as a multi-part work ever appeared. Subtitled *Volume One: Jealous in Honour*, this covered Steed's life from birth to his first post-war meeting with Catherine Gale. While poor sales of the hardback edition were blamed for the non-appearance of further volumes, it has also been suggested that the Department effectively had the title suppressed since some of the information contained within the covers was still sensitive while Steed retained a high position in the organisation. As a result, the print run was very limited and copies are scarce, known to change hands between collectors for up to £100.

Steed himself seemed to vanish – an easy skill given the three decades of loyal undercover work for Queen and Country. A couple of unconfirmed reports suggested that he might still have been working with Gambit and Purdey in early 1978.[1] In late 1978, there was a tale that a British Intelligence officer known as 'S' had helped a young American investigator called Joe Hardy to locate his father, Fenton, and his brother, Frank, who had gone missing while they were working on a case in London. Another report from 1985 suggested that Steed was working under the name 'Sir Godfrey Tibbett' alongside the latest Secret Service operative to adopt the title of his former bully James Bond – although Tibbett was allegedly killed in action.

---

[1] *The New Avengers Annual*, 1978.

In 1979, the notion of a film about Steed's exploits was again being suggested – this time by the American television network CBS. The concept of two-hour films 'made for television' had taken off massively during the past decade, and now studios were clamouring for new and fresh ideas. On 9 February 1980, the *Daily Mail* indicated that Steed's old friend, Patrick Macnee, would be given a second attempt at creating a fictional version of his Eton classmate after the abortive 1964 television series. By now, former top agent Brian Clemens had left the Department and with another ex-Department colleague, Dennis Spooner, drafted a script in which Steed and Mike Gambit would be seen joined by two new, young, fictitious female agents – Carruthers (one of Steed's frequent aliases around 1962) and American operative Suzy Stride. Again being careful not to adhere too closely to the truth, 'Steed' said that his father was 'Joshua Steed' and that his mother was 'Araminta'. The plot itself concerned the death of an American agent working in Britain, and a man who planned to take over the world using trained ants – presumably a nod to the real Steed's encounters with adversaries like Dr Manx and his plan to use the ordinary domestic cat as an instrument of death [TIGE]. Even with Steed apparently no longer active for the Department, the television film was never made.

In the meantime, the legends surrounding Steed persisted. In Australia, a devotee of Steed's career called Geoff Barlow attempted to publish his own tribute to possibly the world's greatest intelligence agent. This was a story called *The Saga of Happy Valley*, a beautifully whimsical tale about a hidden community in the heart of England. To avoid any legal issues which might embarrass the real Steed or the Department, Barlow cleverly referred to his lead character as 'John Steade', while his colleague was an athletic and highly capable lady known as 'Mrs Emma Peale'. In 1980, Barlow had a small print-run of the books published by Albion Press of Brisbane. Unfortunately for the author, the Department's intelligence reporting in Australia was extremely good at this time – and, unlike the two years taken to spike the South African radio broadcasts – pressure was brought to bear for the book to be withdrawn for security reasons in a far more effective exercise than the *Spycatcher* debacle seven years later. As with *Jealous in Honour,* copies are now scarce and true collector's items.

Many of the subsequent sightings of figures who may – or may not – be Steed have been based in America. An early unconfirmed report of Steed's whereabouts was a rumour that he was posing as a travel agent while living at a Malibu beach house with an ex-CIA agent called Robert Gavilan around 1982-83. A strong sighting was reported during 1983, suggesting that Steed was apparently working in New York with the United Network Command for Law and Enforcement; certainly there is a resemblance between Steed and the Sir John Raleigh who had succeeded Alexander Waverley as the head of the world intelligence agency. By 1984, somebody very like Steed was on the board of Empire Industries, and another common story concerns another similar figure who was somehow tied up with a cop and con-artist couple who worked as undercover detectives in Palm Springs in 1991-92. In late 1993, a retired secret agent called 'Steadman' aided a police detective called Peter Caine and his father Kwai Chang Caine to rescue a woman kidnapped by survivalists. The following year, the same 'Steadman' helped rescue Caine himself when he was kidnapped alongside the Dalai Lama. Also, somebody strongly resembling Steed was involved with the outrageous exploits of one Randolph J 'Hurricane' Spencer at the Paradise Beach Hotel from around 1994. In early 1997, a retired security agent referred to as 'Mr Black' was found on a golf course, pursuing one of Steed's favourite pastimes. His partner was one 'Mr White', believed to be an alias for Willy Armitage, a one-time opera-tive of the American IMF organisation.

The notion of a film about Steed's life was an increasingly attractive proposition to movie makers during the 1980s – especially now that the real Steed was clearly living in secluded retirement somewhere. Clemens – now a prolific and successful television scriptwriter and producer – was invited to write a pilot script for another attempted TV series with Steed as the central character. Macnee was again lined up for the lead in the story which was entitled *Reincarnation*. Working with American agent Christopher Cambridge and Mrs Samantha Peel (the wife of Peter Peel, supposedly the son of Peter and 'Dame Emma Peel'), the plot bore some resemblance to the ploy attempted by Boris Kartovski in 1968 – a reincarnation of psyche by double agent Bobby Lomax via the bodies of three other people, all of whom wanted revenge on Steed. As with the 1980 CBS script, it never entered production.

Mel Gibson, the star of box-office action spectaculars such as *Mad Max* and *Lethal Weapon* became quite a devotee of Steed's career in the 1980s and attempted to interest the major studios in a motion picture to celebrate Britain's greatest unsung hero. By 1987, mogul Jerry Weintraub was coming close to allowing Gibson to give the world his portrayal of Steed. Rather than use Brian Clemens – not only an established industry writer but somebody who had intimate knowledge of Steed's life during the 1960s and 1970s – a script was developed by another prolific writer with movie experience called Sam Hamm. Finally by summer 1993, another script was underway, this time by Don Macpherson.

It seems that Macpherson had access to material about several of Steed's assignments from the 1960s and 1970s in his research for the biographical picture. However, rather than recreate a single incident, it was decided to amalgamate many different ingredients in a new tale which supposedly told how Steed first met Emma Peel, who was reinvented as a Government scientist.

The central character of the Warner Bros 'biopic' was thus John Steed, played by Ralph Fiennes (the star of acclaimed films such as *Schindler's List* and *The English Patient*) – described as a 'Secret Agent' working for 'The Ministry'. This was a champagne-loving, Magdalen College graduate Steed who – around St Swithin's Day, 15 July 1999 – had not been blackballed at Boodles Gentleman's Club[2] which was the venue for his first meeting with Dr Emma Peel in no less a place than the members' saunas. This Steed wore a pocket watch with a chain attached to his suit lapel and drove around in a green 4½-litre Bentley[3] which dispensed tea from its dashboard. He lived in a colourful spacious London apartment with a large mirror over a fireplace, plants perched on pedestals and a piano; this flat was based on the museum of British architect Sir John Soane at Lincoln's Inn. According to the final shots of the movie, the residence had an ornate roof garden and was located near York Road, close to Waterloo Station – the frontage was actually on York Terrace East by Regent's Park while the interior was a Georgian house in Fitzroy Square. This Steed read not only the *Financial Times* but also the *City Bulletin*. While Fiennes' characterisation, as written by Don Macpherson, retained the basics of Steed's behaviour and attitudes, in so many other respects this presentation of the Department's most famous operative was rather a distortion. Perhaps particularly painful to the real Steed was his cinematic alter-

---

[2] Actually the Reform Club in Pall Mall, London.

[3] Registration RT 4700.

ego's claim that his mother – slaughtered on Zamoyska Hill in 1924 – was still alive and living in Wiltshire.

While the fundamental character of Steed was effectively captured by Macpherson's dialogue[4], overall the film won few fans from either the professional critics or the ever-growing group of enthusiasts whose passion for the career of John Steed was now reaching out to engulf the new electronic information highway of the internet. Unfortunately, this is how some of the British public remembers Steed – in the form of Ralph Fiennes trapped in one of the biggest box-office disasters of the decade, a movie quickly consigned to the remainder bins of VHS and DVD.

All in all, Steed's life – from his birth in the dying days of the Empire through to his mysterious disappearance sometime after his controversial biography appeared in the shops – was an incredible story which never fails to impress. Bigger in scale than the grandest motion picture, one could be forgiven for believing that the myriad incidents of danger and excitement packed into such a career could only possibly be the product of the most talented of creative minds such as an army of experienced television scriptwriters, or lauded figures from the prose world such as Sir Arthur Conan Doyle, 'Sapper', Len Deighton or John Le Carré.

Steed was the ultimate gentleman spy – and will always remain so.

---

[4] Macpherson's notes for Steed read: 'Devoted, remote, respectful, noble, loyal.' *The Avengers Original Movie Screenplay*, p xii.

16

DR DAVID KEEL

'Keels rush in where Steeds and angels fear to tread,' commented Steed [FRIG] of one of his short-term partners whom he worked with during 1961 – a bereaved, impulsive, caring general practitioner in London whose hatred of crime and suffering made him an often reckless and usually ideal tool for Steed's undercover work.

Little is known about David H Keel's background [SNOW]. Judging by the little available Department evidence – much of which has sadly been lost or destroyed over the years – he was born around 1931. Keel's medical training was very solid and he regularly kept up to date with advances in *Medical Journal* (old copies of which were then placed in the waiting room) [GIRL] and attended World Health Organisation conferences [MORT]. He could deliver a quick medical analysis [GIRL], knew about vaccines [AIR], was aware of the power of hypnosis [TUNN], could spot the behaviour of a heroin addict [SNOW], administer artificial respiration [GIRL], treat a black eye [FEED], relocate a joint [FRIG], test blood and urine to determine the presence of barbiturates [DIAM], give injections and identify recent needle marks [GIRL] and tend to wounds such as knife cuts [BOOK]. He was also knowledgeable as to how long an autopsy took to perform [GIRL].

In the 1950s, Keel presumably spent some time in the African country Tenebra where he became friends with the prominent leader Sir Wilberforce Lungi, who was a diabetic. Keel also got to know Judith, the wife of Lungi's rival Chief Bai Shebro, and a servant called Ali [NEED]. In England, he was also friends with Dr Seton, a country GP [TOY], and Dr Brennan who performed autopsies in the London area [WINT]. Keel would attend 'reunion dos' with old colleagues south of the Thames [GIRL] and also knew Miss Doris Courtney, an old 'forces sweetheart' trouper of both World Wars who still dabbled in acting [FRIG]. There was also photographic evidence to suggest that he had learned to read Italian on his travels.

In terms of his dress, Keel tended to wear simple two-piece suits in dark [eg NIGH, GIRL, SLIP] or medium [eg FRIG, SPRI, WINT] tone along with a dark [eg SNOW, FRIG] or striped [eg NIGH, FEED, GIRL, MORT] tie, while he also had a lighter suit which he wore in warmer climes [DIST]. When venturing outside, he wore either a dark overcoat with a rich lining [SNOW, GIRL] or, more usually, a light belted mackintosh [BOOK, DOWN, DANC, WINT]. Keel wore a signet ring on the small finger of his left hand [eg GIRL, FRIG, SPRI], and carried items such as an address card [GIRL] and – apparently – a set of skeleton keys [GIRL]. A cigarette smoker [eg GIRL, FRIG], he usually carried some of his favourite brand in a case in his right breast pocket along with a lighter [GIRL].

Keel owned a dark saloon car [GIRL, DOWN, DANC, ROSE, TUNN]. He liked to drink tea [GIRL, WINT] and coffee [SNOW] but preferred something alcoholic when celebrating [NIGH] and was particularly partial to Scotch [BOOK, FEED]. The doctor was a very fit man, stronger than men with far larger builds [FRIG], agile enough to scale walls [DANC] or iron railings quickly [GIRL] and even leap over obstacles such as ladders which might appear in his path [GIRL]. He was very useful in a fight [BOOK, ROOT, FRIG, FEED], able to knock a man out with a single punch [GIRL].

Keel's hobbies also possibly included fishing; he commented at one point that he might be going up to Scotland for a fortnight for this purpose – although this could have been a bluff [FRIG]. He had some knowledge of flowers, telling Steed that orchids thrive in the Amazon jungle at 120 degrees Fahrenheit [BAIT]. He was also known to enjoy cooking at home [TOY] and seemed to be fond of animals, playing with a cat he found in an alleyway on one occasion [FRIG].

By 1960, Keel shared a medical practice with Dr Richard J Tredding [GIRL, SNOW, BOOK, FRIG], an older partner. Known affectionately as 'Dick', Tredding was an amiable balding man with a penchant for his pipe [SNOW]. The practice was situated in a white fronted building on the corner of a street [SNOW] apparently in the 'Chelsea-Victoria district'[1] of London – certainly on the north side of Westminster Bridge [GIRL]. The 'relatively small surgery' as Keel described it [FRIG] also appeared to be the same building in which the doctor lived [GIRL]. Entering on the ground floor, the stairs leading upwards were to the right, while on the left was a modest waiting room with the receptionist's desk and phone; the phone number for the surgery was Sloane 0181 [SNOW, FEED]. An adjoining door led to the next room down the corridor which was the main consulting room. This had an examination couch and the doctors' framed certificates as well as a glass cabinet full of drugs [SNOW, FRIG]; it was also equipped with a fridge [BAIT]. The door leading off from the right of the corridor was the lounge with a television, a radiogram, various bookcases and a clock kept beneath a glass dome [GIRL, SNOW]. A door at the far end of the corridor led out to the back yard behind the surgery [SNOW].

Dr Keel's patients included the demanding Mrs Simpson whom he had seen every other Wednesday for quite some time, while other clients included Mrs Harper and Mrs Brewer [SNOW]. Keel would sometimes take on Tredding's evening surgery for him [GIRL] (the day hours ending at 5.00pm [ROOT]); indeed, one of the lady patients who was suffering from a temperature in August 1961 had a soft spot for 'nice Dr Tredding' [FRIG]. In fact, it was generally believed that David Keel was the inspiration behind Dr Geoffrey Brent, the compassionate lead character in the short-lived television crime series *Police Surgeon* made by ABC in 1960.[2]

Prior to his first encounter with Steed, Keel had been observed by the Department on one of their earliest surveillance recordings which seems to date from the early months of

---

[1] *The Complete Avengers*, p15.

[2] Dr Geoffrey Brent, played by Ian Hendry – whose resemblance to the real-life Keel was as close as that of Patrick Macnee to John Steed – was a doctor operating in the Bayswater district of London. Brent got involved with delinquents, drunken drivers, accident victims, abandoned children, refugees, cases of assault and unscrupulous landlords. The character generally worked alongside policemen such as Inspector Landon. The series ran on ITV from 10 September to 3 December 1960 – a total of 12 episodes.

1960.[3] At this time, Keel's nurse and receptionist was Carol Wilson, who was already aware of his capacity for getting overly involved; 'Here we go again,' she was heard to sigh [GIRL]. Born around 1938, dark-haired Carol Wilson had been working with Keel for some time before their adventure.

Keel became embroiled in a mystery concerning a girl who apparently tried to commit suicide by jumping into the River Thames, and soon connected the victim with the visiting Radeck State Circus. While attempting to keep Superintendent Lewis informed about his discoveries in connection with the death, Keel bravely visited the stadium where the circus was making its last performance and became involved with an espionage plot to kidnap a girl called Anna Danilov and take her back to her native land; Anna was the daughter of the metallurgist Dr Igor Danilov who had sought asylum in England in 1958. Keel's tactics were vital in delaying the operatives working at the circus from forcibly repatriating the Danilovs until the police could arrive. Carol bravely agreed to swap places with the bandaged Anna Danilov, and was happy to attack adversaries such as Zippo the Clown and a girl called Vera, using her medical training to inject the latter with a sedative after having thrown a blanket over her [GIRL].

'Women find him attractive,'[4] noted Keel's February 1961 dossier, and by late 1960, he was engaged to Miss Peggy Stevens, who worked as the receptionist at his surgery. The pair were starting to plan a new home together, with Peggy choosing orange trimmings for a white bedroom – which didn't entirely meet with Keel's tastes – a couple of weeks before their big day. The engagement was a rapid and secret affair, with even Tredding unaware of the impending nuptials until a couple of weeks beforehand when he was asked to be Keel's best man; the reason for the haste was partly that Peggy's parents would not be back from America for over a year. Tredding felt it was an 'odd time of year', presumably as it was approaching Christmas. However, within hours of these plans being made, tragedy struck Keel's life when, at 5.15 pm, the young doctor was waiting for Peggy to meet him at Vinson's the jewellers to choose their wedding ring. As Peggy embraced David while looking through the selection in Vinson's window, she was fatally shot in the back, the rifle bullet fired from a nearby car. She died in Keel's arms [SNOW].

Three days later, Keel learnt from Detective Superintendent Wilson that it was believed Peggy's death was a rare example of a professional murder – but the motive for the hit seemed unclear. In fact, a package containing £4000 worth of heroin had been delivered to Tredding at the surgery in mistake for a 'Dr Treading' and Peggy had been in a position to identify Johnson, the gang member involved. Determined to track down his fiancée's killer, Keel visited Treading and found him dead in his flat – clearly having been involved in the heroin ring [SNOW].

Returning home, Keel discovered an intruder in his living room whom he had earlier seen leaving Treading's home. Keel was suspicious of the dapper interloper, but it seemed that the stranger had some knowledge which could lead the doctor closer to the killer. The man, who claimed to be 'on the side of the angels', asked Keel to risk his practice and reputation for justice by infiltrating the heroin gang and pretending he wanted to become a

---

[3] The recording takes place 18 months after the defection of Professor Igor Danilov in 1958. At the time of the recording, it was apparently winter as it was dark by 7.00 pm and many people were suffering from flu.

[4] *The Complete Avengers*, p15.

pusher so that he could retire to the Continent. The intruder said he would arrange for a package to be delivered to Keel's surgery at 4.30 pm the next day – the first step towards capturing the killer who was their joint quarry. Keel still had many questions which the well-dressed stranger refused to answer, saying, 'You'll just have to trust me – or not' [SNOW].

When the package arrived, Johnson expected Keel to administer a dose to an addict called Stella. Keel's mysterious cohort then telephoned him and told him to pull out of the operation – meaning that Peggy's killer would then be sent to eliminate him. Sending Johnson away empty-handed from his surgery the following afternoon, Keel agreed with his nameless ally to re-enact the afternoon of his fiancée's death outside Vinson's where he would be collected by a car driven by Spicer – the hit-man. As Keel got into the car, the gang was preparing to pounce when Wilson appeared with his men. The gang fled. When Wilson told Keel to leave police work to the police, Keel replied, 'That's very good advice, Superintendent, but the work isn't finished yet – is it?' [SNOW].

Existing evidence shows no further serious liaisons between Keel and other women after Peggy's murder; indeed, her picture remained on the coffee table in his flat [SNOW]. Peggy's position at the practice was soon filled again by Carol Wilson, who continued to work for Keel in 1961 [BOOK, ROOT, NIGH, DIAM, RADI, ROSE, DOWN, FEED, DANC, MORT, FRIG, YELL, DOUB, TUNN, KING, WINT, AIR, BAIT]. She too would find herself propelled into the dangerous undercover games played by Keel's new colleague. Keel was worried about this and had already been concerned for her safety during their experiences at the Radeck State Circus [GIRL]. He soon found that she would sometimes be used for additional investigation by the undercover man which would land her in further peril – despite the fact that Keel allowed her time away from the practice on what he knew to be hazardous work [ROSE].

In terms of dress, Carol was conservative yet fashionable, her jewellery including earrings and a pendant on a chain [GIRL, FRIG]. When out and about in London, she wore a dark, double-breasted overcoat [GIRL, DOUB]. She would smoke, although did not do so regularly; she coughed a great deal when accepting one of Keel's cigarettes [GIRL]. She did however enjoy celebratory drinks [NIGH] and her taste in television included programmes like the film report *The Circus Comes To Town* [GIRL]. With regards to her boss, Carol cared deeply for David Keel and often went above and beyond the call of duty, either during his investigations [GIRL] or with a simple matter of helping him prepare dinner for some guests [FRIG]. She very much felt that Keel should relax more often [GIRL].

A short time after the encounter with Spicer, Keel was again drawn into the crime world when a phone call from an oriental girl called Lila invited him to a pub called The House of the Rising Sun, and again he met the strange undercover man. The figure now introduced himself as John Steed, 'a kind of civil servant', and announced a plan whereby Spicer could be brought to justice in a swoop on two rival protection gangs. Set up by a police raid as a heroin pusher, Keel was hired by gang leader Ronnie Vance to tend to his young brother whose face had been slashed. Eventually, Keel was able to help Steed apprehend Spicer and threatened to give him a lethal injection – really a harmless barbiturate – in revenge for Peggy's death; this ruse extracted a confession from Spicer witnessed by Wilson. With Spicer in custody, Steed asked Keel if he would consider working with them again when he was *really* needed. 'You know where to find me,' replied Keel [BOOK].

A Department dossier drawn up on Keel in February 1961 noted that he had 'a sense of public service, kindled by his humanitarian instincts,'[5] and it is possible that by now Steed had viewed the film of events at the Radeck Circus, seeing in Keel a useful, reliable and malleable accomplice. While accepting the offer to help clean up crime, Keel was very determined to keep separate his professional life as a GP and his assistance to the undercover agent. He was often appalled by Steed's behaviour on the premises of his surgery, and whenever possible would avoid taking those injured in the course of these escapades to his premises unless absolutely necessary [FRIG].

Steed's *modus operandi* often gave Keel cause for concern, as – unlike his undercover friend – he did not believe that the end justified the means. He was angry to hear that Steed had stood back and let criminal Jimmy Bishop lay into his wife Lisa rather then blow his cover [ROOT]. He was furious when Steed used a young girl called Bunty Seton as bait to expose a call girl racket. On this occasion he actually struck Steed warning: 'If you ever do anything like that again, I'll beat the living daylights out of you.' When Steed remonstrated, Keel continued: 'I'm doing something I should have done a long time ago... knocking some sense into that bigoted head of yours' [TOY].

Nevertheless, on other occasions Keel would help Steed extract the information he needed from a miscreant by restraining them [SPRI]. In a tight corner, there was a great sense of camaraderie between the men. At times, Keel found Steed's foppish behaviour amusing or would tease him, and described him as a 'gay old thing' [FRIG].

Like Steed, Keel could think quickly. By telling Superintendent Lewis to take an aspirin for his flu and 'Don't take a powder,' he was subtly able to signal that he was being held against his will at the Radeck State Circus [GIRL]. Similarly when held by a criminal gang, he was able to send a message to Steed by having a prescription for 'Fonus Equus' delivered to Carol [DOUB]. He quickly decided to act drunk to protect a cipher clerk called Felgate at the Bromango Strip Club – although it meant being hauled in for disorderly conduct [FEED]. He used his standing as a doctor to get access to a phone claiming he needed to check on a patient [GIRL] and could enter a situation claiming that he had been sent from an establishment such as Barrington Hospital [GIRL].

In desperate situations he would take chances to trick his adversaries, even when held at gun-point [GIRL]. His straight-faced ability to lie and his sheer nerve stood him in good stead. When threatened by a thug called Moxon who was wielding a scalpel, Keel disarmed him by telling the man that he had a fractured vertebrae and would die if he moved his head [FRIG]. When it came to hypodermics, he made Spicer – the man who killed his fiancée – believe that he was going to administer a fatal injection [BOOK][6] and later threatened a villain known as 'the Deacon' with a quantity of hydrochloric acid ('vintage stuff') which was really witch hazel [FRIG]. This appealed to Keel's sense of the melodramatic [FRIG]. He was sickened by many aspects of crime, such as the organised beatings dished out by the Deacon [FRIG] and the various drugs rackets [SNOW]. He calmly provoked the eminent Sir Thomas Weller in his own office, knowing of his role in an illegal 'massage operation' [FRIG].

Highly observant and with a good memory, Keel could take in and retain detail such as the horseshoe scar on the left shoulder of Jeremy de Willoughby [FRIG] or recognising the face of a drowned girl [GIRL]. Although he seldom seemed to relax [GIRL], when in his

---

[5] *The Complete Avengers*, p15.

[6] A technique which he apparently repeated with a syringe of water on a workman who was part of a drug ring. 'The Drug Peddler'. *TV Crimebusters*, p92.

office during a quiet moment Keel liked to put his feet up on the desk [NIGH]. He could sometimes be irritable with those around him when they did not seem to be able to help him as quickly as he would have liked [GIRL].

Several weeks after the capture of Spicer, Keel tended Steed's knuckles which had been injured on an undercover assignment with some forgers, and Keel agreed to help Steed – who was working as a forger called Riordan – at an illicit printworks where the two men apprehended Chris Hooper's gang [ROOT]. After that, Keel was called to help one of his patients, Faith Braintree, whose husband had gone missing. Keel was mistaken for Professor Braintree by some enemy agents who attempted to kidnap him. Injured, Keel was admitted to hospital where Steed asked him to act as a decoy. During a second kidnap attempt, Keel was shot in the chest. It was Carol who discovered that the hospital anaesthetist who was going to operate on Keel was an enemy agent, which resulted in her being captured and tied up. Meanwhile, Keel almost perished during the subsequent operation when his oxygen supply was tampered with [NIGH].

Keel found himself tending the supposedly dead General Mendoza from the Caribbean when he was taken ill in London [MOON]. A while later, he was able to perform tests on Steed to prove that his shady acquaintance has been incapable of driving a car the night a woman had been knocked down and killed; he also arrived in time to help Steed deal with Dr Collard who was operating a smuggling racket at Globe Airlines [DIAM].

With Steed out of the country, Keel was asked by Steed's superior, One-Ten, to help the police track down Marko Orgin, a man who had stolen a deadly isotope capsule from the Medical Research Laboratory [RADI].[7] Following this, Carol was eager to help with some detective work alongside Keel and Steed, and was only too happy to pay a visit to the hairdressing salon run by Olive and Jacques Beronne. There she was rescued from an exploding hairdryer by Steed. The agent also saved her from an arson attempt on the premises for which she was treated for minor burns by Keel [ROSE].

Keel treated robber Frank Preston when he was brought to his surgery by Steed following an attack on Preston by rivals. This led to Preston's wife and two crooks called Paul Stacey and Rocky believing that Keel knew where Preston had stashed £100,000. Keel was forced to give Preston further treatment at gun-point. Carol was then kidnapped by Stacey and Rocky, who believed that Keel knew the location of the stolen money, and held hostage to ensure Keel's co-operation. Keel was obliged to help Preston recover his haul from the London sewers until he was rescued by Steed and the police [DOWN]. Keel then agreed to help Steed follow a man called Felgate, a cipher clerk who was being blackmailed at the Bromango Strip Club and delivering packages to the Brinkley House private zoo [FEED].

Keel tended to a woman called Elaine Bateman when she was gassed, and believed her story that somebody was trying to kill her — which the police had no further evidence to investigate. Visiting her dancing school, he left behind a scarf which was then used to

---

[7] This incident for Keel was a most strange one since – as far as one can deduce from the existing records – it was almost identical to a play made for CBC Television in Canada entitled *The Radioactive Man*. This play concerned a janitor called Marko who worked at medical research establishment and who unknowingly took a radioactive lead pellet home for his landlady's son to play with. Cec Linder starred as Shore who attempted to track down Marko. The play, broadcast in the UK by BBC Television at 9.10 pm on 28 January 1959, was credited to Fred Edge – coincidentally the same name as the Department operative who documented this incident.

strangle Elaine. Steed looked into the dance school further and found that a known murderer, Philip Anthony, had been working there and was planning to kill pupil Valerie Marne for her diamonds. Together, Steed and Keel prevented a further murder [DANC].

Attending a World Health Organisation conference in Geneva, Keel befriended a girl called Yvette Declair who was taken ill on the plane. In Geneva, Keel was arrested for murdering a man and – after he was released into Steed's custody – realised that he had been duped into carrying a microdot of lethal medical information on one of his documents. Keel had given the document to Yvette and the two men tracked her down to recover the deadly formula [MORT]. A short while after, Steed asked Keel to pose as a criminal in prison so that he could be sprung with the help of a crooked warder and thereby identify the head of the escape route from the jail [SPRI].

When Keel's old friend Sir Wilberforce Lungi visited London for negotiations, Steed asked the GP to investigate his companion Jacquetta Brown. It transpired that Jacquetta was part of a conspiracy to kill Lungi with a dose of yellow fever disguised as insulin. Assigned to protect Lungi by Steed, Keel was drugged by Jacquetta, but Steed managed to arrive and save both Keel and Lungi [NEED]. Some time later, Keel was called to tend to an accident victim called Mace, only to find that Mace's injuries were clearly connected to a recent diamond robbery being investigated by Steed. Held at gunpoint by Mace's colleagues, Al Brady and Bert Mills, Keel managed to get a message to Carol disguised as a prescription. As Mace died, Keel unwittingly became the only person to know where the stolen diamonds had been hidden, information he was forced to reveal to Bruton, the gang leader, when Carol was kidnapped. She was again rescued by Steed [DOUB].

Bunty Seton, the daughter of Keel's country friend, came to him for help when her friend May Murton went missing, apparently in connection with a call girl racket. Calling on Steed for help, Keel found that the disappearance was connected with the department store where Bunty, May and a dead girl called Chrissie had been working. The girls at the store boarded at a hostel where Mrs McCabe was organising call girls, and May had gone into hiding with a store employee called Lennie Taylor [TOY].

One of the next patients at Keel's surgery was Harry Black, an escaped convict who had suffered wounds from broken glass. Steed said this was connected with leaks of top secret information via a funfair at Southend, and persuaded Keel to help him investigate. Keel soon realised that Black had been the victim of hypnosis which had helped frame him for his crime, and helped capture the real traitor, Jack Wickram [TUNN].

At this point, Keel travelled to Chile. When the return flight stopped over at Mexico City, Keel heard that a cyclone had hit a small Mexican coastal village and lost no time in volunteering his medical help alongside Dr Ampara Alverez Sandoval. After patients at the disaster site died from food poisoning, Keel discovered that the 'cooking oil' which had been flown in was actually hydraulic fluid. Keel and Dr Sandoval followed the trail of the oil back via Vera Cruz – where the first victim had died two years before – to Marseilles. The consignment had come from a financier called Hercule Zeebrugge who was arrested by the police acting on Keel's information, but only after Keel managed to stop Ampara from killing Zeebrugge in revenge for the deaths of her fellow Mexicans [DIST].

Keel helped Steed out in a scrap with a 'massage contract' gang attacking one Jeremy de Willoughby, and used his knowledge of medicine to trick Moxon, a captured thug, into leading him to the office of his boss, a man known as 'the Deacon'. Steed then had the necessary information to make arrests, while Keel attempted some subterfuge of his own.

With the help of Doris Courtney posing as Jeremy's mother 'Mrs Briggs', Keel exposed the ruthless money-grabbing nature of de Willoughby to his intended fiancée [FRIG]. After minimal assistance to Steed during the visit of King Tenuphon [KING], Keel's knowledge of vaccines was put to the test as sabotage struck in a hygienic test room – and the doctor saved Steed from an apparently lethal compound [AIR].

Carol's landlord was Archibald ('Archie') Duncan and her digs were close enough to the surgery for her to walk home for lunch if things were quiet. In 1961, Duncan made an unwise investment: he had bought a consignment of bananas worth £12,000 for only £7,000, using £5,000 loaned by Mr Barker of the Finance Loan Corporation. When the bananas started to go rotten on board the *SS Jan de Krup*, Duncan arranged for Lemuel Potts to become his agent for a seven per cent take and Potts then arranged to have the ship blacked with the dock loading officer, Peter Sampson. When Duncan heard – in an anonymous call from Steed – that the cargo would go bad, he suffered a mild stroke and was treated by Keel. Steed arranged for the bananas to be delivered, despite the machinations of Potts, which meant that Duncan got paid. The landlord then promptly retired from the investment game and went to rest with his sister while he recovered. Keel then helped Steed investigate a similar insurance scam being worked at an antique shop run by a man called André. It was here that Steed and Keel almost became trapped in a Victorian wardrobe in the midst of an inferno [BAIT].

The final recorded instance of Keel and Steed working together involved Steed arousing Keel's medical curiosity over the frozen corpse of Gerhardt Schneider, a Nazi war criminal. When his friend Dr Brennan was killed before he could perform the autopsy on Schneider and the corpse was stolen, Keel went undercover to infiltrate a fascist party called Phoenix. Dr Kreuzer, a Phoenix scientist, revealed that he had perfected a technique of suspending life by freezing as he had done with the now-revived Schneider. Keel was the next guinea pig for Kreuzer's temperature tests, but was rescued by Steed and suffered no after effects other than a cold [WINT].

It is tempting to believe that incidents such as Archie Duncan's mild heart attack as a result of a thoughtless phone call from Steed may have heralded the death knell for Keel's relationship with Steed, since after the Kreuzer incident there are no further films, reports or surveillance photographs of them working alongside each other.[8]

What exactly became of Dr David Keel after autumn 1961 – and whether he ever fully recovered from the tragic death of his intended – is not known. One report which cannot be verified by film or visual records indicates that Keel had stopped working with Steed because he had taken up a post with the World Health Organisation, where he got some press coverage for his works and kept in touch with Steed via odd cards during the 1960s.[9] By 1969, Keel had been assigned to combat both famine and plague in the small African state of Katawa alongside genetic scientist Dr Bennett Cowles.[10] It was apparently concurrent with this work that he was again involved briefly in Department affairs concerning the once mysterious stranger, John Steed.

---

[8] One fanciful and popular theory was that Keel subsequently went undercover for the Department in Leipzig as 'Irwin Gunner', but apart from a passing facial resemblance between the men, there is no evidence to support this – and since Gunner went missing in July 1960 before Keel started operating with Steed, the notion is clearly preposterous.

[9] *Too Many Targets*, p12.

[10] *Too Many Targets*, p28.

DR MARTIN KING

An 'ordinary GP' was how Dr Martin King described himself in 1962 [MONT] – despite the fact that on several occasions he found himself ensnared in the assignments given to Steed by the powers that be. Born around 1932, King was about 30 years of age in the three surveillance films which show him co-opted to the Department. He was well-spoken, square-jawed and dark-haired, and in good physical condition. An educated and sensitive man, his style and manner was not extravagant or out of the ordinary, but even so he had a look about him which told Canadian film star Carla Berotti that King was not 'square' [MONT].

There was so much that was similar about Dr King and Dr Keel that it is tempting to think that they were in fact colleagues at one time, and this is possibly how Steed came to know Dr King. There is certainly a feeling that Steed preferred to work with Keel, and that he only involved King in his undercover operations from spring 1962 when Keel was no longer available.

Like David Keel, King was very much a humanitarian who often resented Steed's methods. Unlike David Keel, King had no particular burning desire to rid the world of wrong-doers. In a given situation, he would be brave and do what was expected of him, but he lacked the passion which had been instilled in Keel by the death of his fiancée. King had a sardonic line in humour which amused Steed, such as his quips about the National Health Service issuing a 'bullet-proof waistcoat' for his associate [SELL].

King's surgery was located at 12 Marchbank Terrace, SW3 [SELL], and the telephone number was Gerrard 1071 [SELL]. The practice was shared with one Dr Michael [MONT] and was also staffed by his receptionist and nurse, a young lady called Judy [MONT, SELL] whom he said was a 'nice girl' [SELL]. King would apparently often work late at his surgery to catch up on paperwork [SELL], and dispensed a business card to friends and colleagues [SELL].

In the medical world, King was acquainted with Dr G Walton of Millbank Hospital [SELL] and vaguely knew the ship's doctor of the *MV Calpurnia* [MONT]. As with Keel, King was very adept at his vocation. He carried the traditional little black bag associated with the profession [MONT] (as well as a briefcase with his initials 'MK' on it [SELL]) and did his own chemical preparations [SELL]. He could quickly assess a patient's needs, and depending on their condition wasted no time in arranging for appropriate transport to move them to a location which had the facilities they required [COUR].

Exactly how Steed and King came to work together is unclear. It is possible that they met around 1960 as on one occasion Steed spun a yarn as to how he had consulted King – a 'wonderful doctor' – two years earlier when he was beset by headaches, dizziness, and spots before the eyes [SELL]. Certainly, having another doctor to work alongside gave Steed an ally who could walk into many situations to help with his undercover work – with Steed sometimes recommending King on a professional basis to his suspects [SELL]. Certainly, Steed and King had worked together prior to the surveillance film showing them working on board a Montreal-bound ship in 1962 [MONT]. King was already familiar with Steed's *modus operandi*, and before long remarked that Steed was 'always' saying that he needed his help [SELL]. Steed used charm and flattery on King, calling him 'old boy' and nudging him in the right direction during his investigations [COUR]. Steed's superiors, such as One-Twelve, were aware that Steed used King to help him on some of his cases [SELL]. In return, King never asked Steed for help – and indeed did not even know where he lived [SELL]. In general, he very much disliked being used by Steed who always seemed to assume that he could take the doctor's co-operation for granted [MONT].

'I deal with people,' King told Steed, at first refusing to help on the investigation of a crashed plane [COUR]. King cared a great deal about everyday people, and believed that tolerance was one of his virtues [MONT]. It was this care that Steed would ruthlessly exploit – persuading King that if he did not continue to help him, a gunman would escape justice and an innocent man called Alan Price would have died for nothing in a shooting at the Astor Towers Hotel, leaving a grieving widow behind him [SELL]. Wherever possible, King would use honesty to obtain the results he needed from people, charming information out of Carla Berotti [MONT], or appealing to a nun called Sister Isobel to break her vow of silence in order to save lives [COUR]. He could tell when people were frightened rather than ill, and would not hold back in slapping a hysterical woman... and let her slap him back to relieve the tension [MONT].

Of the limited information available about King, it seems that he cared for the actress Carla Berotti – but attempted not to show his affections too strongly in his position as her medical adviser. Carla certainly liked him, and was reluctant to involve him in the espionage nightmare which she herself was ensnared in. When Carla won a cigarette lighter as a prize at a fancy dress party, she gave it to King as a mark of friendship [MONT].

By and large, King's dress sense was a conservative style befitting a professional man; a plain dark suit [COUR, MONT, SELL] enlivened by a striped or patterned tie [MONT] at times, plus a tuxedo with bow tie for formal occasions [MONT]. Outdoors, he had a light mackintosh [COUR, SELL] and a fine, dark-checked overcoat [MONT] plus a white silk scarf [MONT]. Privately, King allowed himself some greater sartorial extravagances – notably a Chinoiserie dressing gown with a dragon on the back which quite appalled the sensibilities of Steed [MONT]. This particular item of clothing was ruined by a knife when a man called AG Brand was killed wearing it while asleep in King's cabin on board a ship [MONT].

King wore glasses when reading [COUR] and studying X-rays [SELL]. He carried a knife in his pocket [COUR], a cigarette case and matches [MONT]. Sometimes he smoked cigarettes [MONT]. He did not drink greatly [MONT] but would take some soda water [COUR]. Although King refused champagne when he was on duty, he would indulge when in a more social atmosphere [MONT]. One of the reasons that King was useful in a tight spot was that he played three-quarter position at rugby – and hence was able to make a flying tackle on a gunman who had Steed in his sights [SELL]. King also enjoyed listening to football commentary on the radio [SELL].

In the late spring of 1962, Steed arranged King to be berthed in Room M51 aboard the *MV Calpurnia* on a voyage from England to Montreal via Le Havre. King's free holiday cruise on the luxury liner required him to act as the personal doctor to the neurotic and difficult film star Carla Berotti, replacing one Dr Bronson who was apparently 'ill'. A relationship between Carla and King was soon established, and after a stormy start with the spoilt starlet, the two developed a respect for each other. Realising Carla's fear at being implicated in blackmail and espionage, King did his best to help her on the hazardous voyage, which concluded with the reluctant Carla and various cohorts being apprehended [MONT].

Shortly after this, King found himself summoned over to Ireland to help Steed investigate a horrific air crash; a Canada Jet-Ways charter plane approaching Shamrock Airport on the Irish Coast had come down near Ballyknock and, suspecting sabotage, Steed had King check out the survivors, taking over from the local medic Dr O'Leary. While King was left very much to his own devices, he uncovered vital evidence at the village and the nearby Convent of St Mary, confirming that a wrecking party involving some of the locals and some fake nuns was using the retreat as a base, luring planes ferrying British bank notes back into the country to their doom with fake radio signals. King discovered that the surviving co-pilot from the flight was being held in the bell tower, and deployed a fire bomb to deal with the 'Mother Superior' who was running operations at the Convent [COUR].

Some weeks later, Steed's assignment was to protect a visiting United Nations figure called Etienne Roland whose presence in talks with a British Minister was vital to solving a dangerous situation developing in East Asia. Generally, Steed required King to act as cover for him as he attempted to identify a breach in his people's own internal security. Having identified his opposite number Mark Harvey as the weak link, Steed arranged for King to be in a position to treat Harvey, whose sudden illness had been artificially contrived by Steed's use of drugs. Called in by Mrs Lillian Harvey, King's attempts to find further evidence were cut short and he was held at gun-point by Harvey himself – only to be saved by a gunshot from Steed. He then raced with Steed to London Airport to prevent one of Harvey's cohorts, who was posing as a journalist, from shooting Roland while he bid Britain farewell in the Press Room [SELL].

The bond of determination that had existed between Keel and Steed was not evident in the working relationship between King and Steed, and King would point out that he was not a 'professional' like his colleague in the security game [SELL]. Deaths around him upset and angered him deeply [MONT] and he bitterly told Steed that it might be more appropriate for him to engage a pathologist as a partner rather than a doctor [SELL]. Finally after a few months of working with Steed in 1962, King's patience with the covert operations of the Department finally snapped. 'From now on I'm just going to be a doctor,' he forthrightly told Steed when his associate asked him to shadow him on another case. 'I'm not going to be anything else. I'm not going to be an agent, a counterspy, a gunman or a cover for you.' [SELL]. Nevertheless, even as King refused Steed's offer of a farewell drink, he knew that his conscience would make him see this final assignment through to the end (and he also he had patients to see) [SELL]. However, after a direct threat to his life from a traitor in British security, the amateur King apparently removed himself from the dangerous arena in which Steed had proved himself to be a deadly professional.

MRS CATHERINE GALE

Catherine Gale was a blue-eyed blonde [DISP] with two beauty spots on her left cheek. And her intellect was every bit as dazzling as her beauty. She was one of Steed's first contacts with the Department, worked with him periodically in the early 1950s, and then frequently between 1962 and 1964. In the 1960s, Steed himself described her as an 'attractive widow' [DISP] and as a 'snow queen... [an] elegant young lady, sartorially a little avant-garde' [MEDI]. The prominent medical specialist Sir James Arnell found her to be very 'elegant' [DANE], the young computer scientist Dr Jimmy Kearns [BIGT] and Department operative Mark Charter [OUTS] both felt she was 'charming' [BIGT] while a strange man posing as a film mogul called 'Zanuck' recognised her as having 'class' [BEHI]. Newspaper editor Joe Franks told her that she was a 'very attractive woman' [ZEBR], and certainly Mrs Anne Marling was jealous of Cathy's friendship with her husband Richard [CLAY]. However, many also acknowledged the skills which made Cathy such a superb associate of the Department. Even criminals such as Abe Benham could recognised that she was a 'smooth operator' [CAGE] and that, as bookmaker Tony Heuston commented, 'She's got brains' [TROJ]. Steed's old school friend Patrick Macnee once described Cathy as 'a mixture of the famous anthropologist Margaret Mead[1] and the late Margaret Bourke-White[2].'[3]

Catherine Gale was born at midnight [WARL] on 5 October 1930 [WARL, DWAR][4] and thus had the star sign Libra [DWAR]. This precise time and date of her birth later made her a perfect subject for the strange Dr Cosmo Gallion to perform the occult Ritual of Asmades – a dangerous ceremony not enacted in a century [WARL].

In common with most of Steed's associates, very little is known about Cathy's family.

[1] Margaret Mead was born in Philadelphia in December 1901, a psychologist and anthropologist who worked in Samoa, New Guinea and Bali, and who wrote landmark works such as *Coming of Age in Samoa*, *Growing Up in New Guinea* and *New Lives For Old*. Based at the American Museum of Natural History in New York, she wrote many more books and was president of several major scientific associations. She died in 1978.

[2] Margaret Bourke-White was born in New York in June 1904 and developed a notable photographic career in the 1920s, contributing to publications such as *Fortune*, *The New York Times*, *Life*, and travelling around the world to places such as Russia, Pakistan, India and the battlefields of World War II. Suffering from Parkinson's disease, she died in August 1971.

[3] *Featuring The New Avengers*, p60.

[4] A Department dossier on Cathy issued in spring 1962 is strangely vague about its former operative, noting that her age was then '28/30'. *The Complete Avengers*, p35.

She had an Uncle Joseph who, by the early 1960s, lived in Rye and who owned a bull terrier called Sam whom Steed would walk on occasions [ESPR]. There was also a great aunt, from whom Cathy inherited a fine twin-barrelled derringer with an ivory inlay handle; this aunt's husband was a gambler who had shot one of his opponents at the end of a card game [ELEP]. On one occasion in March 1964, Cathy fabricated a family background which allowed Brigadier General Sir Ian Stuart-Bollinger to believe that she could be the rightful heir to the throne of England. How much of this was created with the help of the Bruce Museum in Kinross and how much is real is unclear, but certainly a family lineage was concocted to show that Cathy had descended from the Clan Ronald, which later became the Macdonalds who helped Charles Edward Stuart to escape the English. Charles Stuart supposedly had a bastard son by Agnes Macdonald, Cathy's 18th grandmother, which would have theoretically made her second in line to the Scottish throne as Queen Anne II. During this assignment, Cathy herself claimed that she had once tried to trace her family tree but had given up when getting as far back as her great-grandfather. To add more colour to the tale, she claimed that she was taught to fight by an uncle in Edinburgh who trained her in the sword, back-sword and claymore – the latter supposedly being a family heirloom with which one of her ancestors had fought alongside Charles Stuart at Preston Pans in 1745 [ESPR].

Similarly, there is little concrete which can be deduced about Cathy's schooling. One of her fellow pupils was Rosalind Waldner, whose father Oliver Waldner was a successful businessman. However, Cathy had very little in common with Rosalind, and did not stay in touch with her for many years [HAND]. It is possible that Cathy went to a quite progressive school which gave her an emancipated outlook on life. On one occasion, she quipped that she took 'tattoos' as a subject at school over and above 'needlework' [CONS]. It is also possible that she was in the Girl Guides; she certainly later acted as a 'Brown Owl' for the organisation in later years [WARL].

One bizarre document which has surfaced helps to clarify some of the background to Cathy's life in the 1950s. There are – for some strange reason – two different transcripts of the 1962 mission where Steed and Cathy were involved with Dr Cosmo Gallion [WARL]. The second of the transcripts, dating from around December 1962, matches the surveillance film. The first, dated 7 July 1962, has a different transcription of certain exchanges between Steed, Cathy and One-Ten. When exactly (indeed, if ever) these words were spoken is unclear, but it suggests that Cathy was married at the age of 19, presumably in 1949 and therefore shortly before she met Steed – thus making her 'Mrs Gale'. According to her Departmental dossier, Cathy met and fell in love with her husband[5], a young farmer, when he was on holiday in London from his home in Africa.[6] This is slightly at odds with the recollection of Sydney Newman, a Canadian TV mogul who knew Cathy: 'She had been an archaeologist in Kenya and had married a settler there.'[7]

---

[5] Although the surveillance films do not give any hint of Mr Gale's name, it is possible that he was called Robert Stephen Gale. The evidence for this comes from another 'alternative transcript' for the incident where Steed flushed out a traitor from the NUTSHELL. In this documentation, dated 19 April 1963, when Cathy handed over an ID card on arriving at the establishment, this apparently read 'Catherine Gale. Widow. Four three two. Juba. West Africa. Jane Marianna Declame. Robert Stephen Gale. James Scott. Nineteen fifty one. Three Seventy... Blood. Five-oh'.

[6] *The Complete Avengers*, p35.

It is most likely that Cathy joined the Department in some junior capacity soon after leaving school at the age of 18, and escorting new recruits into a life of espionage and crime-fighting was probably one of her first roles. Certainly, she seemed to be very well known to One-Ten by the early 1960s, a fact even more evident in the 'alternate transcript'. However, it was presumably around 1950 to 1953 that Cathy took her honours degree in anthropology, referred to in this strange alternate 1962 transcript. According to the 1962 Departmental dossier on Cathy, this was a BA and Cathy had intended to continue her research, had it not been for her marriage; the idea of sharing a life abroad with Mr Gale very much appealed to her lively spirit of adventure.[8] An unconfirmed report suggests that during her time as a student in London, Cathy got to knew M'Begwe who later became the first Prime Minister of the African country, Katawa.[9]

Although Cathy was apparently the first person Steed encountered in his 'cloak and dagger' career, she would later tell people that she had not known him as long as – for example – Hal Anderson, who had apparently worked with Steed since around 1951 [WRIN]. This suggests that, after Steed's collection, Cathy was not directly involved with him until he had been trained. In August 1953, Cathy was still working with the Department, collaborating with Steed while in Berlin to trap one Martin Goodman – a suave criminal who had been running a supposed escape route by charging refugees vast amounts of money and then turning them over to the military for an extra fee. It was decided that the best way to ensnare Goodman was for Cathy to fuel a romance with him. This deception was designed to climax on a specific day, the day that Goodman was due to depart for South America with the three million he had accumulated. Goodman wanted to take Cathy with him, but Steed had already connived to keep their target waiting until the German police could move in. Cathy made sure that the day had been especially romantic[10], with a meal at a little restaurant on Schillingstrasse (where Cathy said the barman had a red face like a man in a Rembrandt portrait) and then a ride along the Reisenstrasse to West Tor. By the time Goodman had finally determined that he would have to leave their hotel and fly to South America alone, he emerged into the rain to be arrested. Cathy was pleased that she had helped bring justice to a man who had bought and sold people, and profited from their suffering. Goodman was imprisoned – but was now obsessed by Cathy [BEHI].

It was presumably after this that Cathy and her husband went to live on a farm in Kenya [FLEE, ELEP] in East Africa [ROCK]; the 1962 dossier describes their home as an 'isolated homestead'.[11] While Mr Gale pursued his career as a farmer, Cathy put to use her anthropological skills as a hunter [ELEP]. The alternate Gallion transcript notes that she was soon

---

[7] Payne, Stephen and Vincent-Rudzki, Jan, 'The Creator', *Fantasy Zone*, Issue 1, Autumn 1984, p4. Newman's recollections seem a little vague on some of Cathy's background. On another occasion, he mentioned that 'when her husband and kids were killed she came back to London and was working at the London Museum.' This seems to be the only reference to Cathy ever having had children, assuming that Newman's memory was correct on this point. Collins, Tim, *DWBulletin*, Vol 4 No 5/6, December 1986, p14.

[8] *The Complete Avengers*, p35.

[9] *Too Many Targets*, p46.

[10] The song the couple listened to that day was 'Ein Schiff Kommt Uber Mir' by Neumann, BIEM, Polydor 23057 .

[11] *The Complete Avengers*, p35.

a first class shot. She got to know Africa very well [BULL] and became adept at stalking big game, a career which she found developed her powers of concentration [ELEP]. Handling firearms became second nature to her and in her later spell in security work, she recognised weapons such as an EY rifle from her Kenyan days [FLEE].

However, Cathy was widowed at a tragically young age when her husband was killed on their African farm [BIGT]. Although not stated in the surveillance films, correspondence in the press regarding Cathy in December 1963 revealed that 'Mr Gale was a farmer in Kenya where he was shot by the Mau Mau'.[12] The Mau Mau uprising began in earnest when the government declared a state of emergency in October 1952; this was not rescinded until December 1960. According to the strange unconfirmed transcript of the Gallion affair, Cathy's husband was killed four years earlier – presumably in 1958 – after which she returned to England. However, Cathy herself commented that in the immediate aftermath of her beloved's death, she supported herself by running conducted safaris [ELEP]. Even as late as 1964, she still occasionally missed her hunting days [ELEP].

Yet there may be some truth about what happened to Cathy next in a cover story concocted at the time of her apparent murder at Steed's hands in September 1963. One crime reporter's biography of her noted that 'When Fidel Castro, of Cuba, was leading a democratic rebellion against dictatorship she fought in the hills with him. But as soon as Dr Castro achieved power, he deported her because of her opposition to certain aspects of his regime.'[13] Castro had been leading a rebel force in the mountains of Cuba since December 1956, and finally came to power on New Year's Day 1959. Thus it is not beyond the bounds of possibility that Cathy did indeed spend time with the Cuban rebels after her husband's death during 1958, and did not return to the UK until 1959.

According to her 1962 dossier, when Cathy returned to England she decided to pick up the threads of her former career by researching for her PhD in anthropology, a goal which she had successfully completed by early 1963 [CONC]. By 1962, the profession inscribed in has passport was again 'Anthropologist' [DISP] – a subject which she viewed very much as an art rather than a science [BIGT].

Cathy did not remarry, and although there were a number of romantic liaisons, including a man who later became the city editor on *Finance* magazine [DANE] and also widower businessman Oliver Waldner [HAND], her work was the primary element in her life.

In addition to her core subject, Cathy pursued tangential subjects with increasing vigour. The alternate Gallion transcript notes indicate that she was rapidly becoming an expert photographer, a fact backed up by her 1962 dossier.[14] Some time prior to spring 1962, her dossier also indicates that she had undertaken a photographic expedition to the Amazon. Although this was hazardous territory, Cathy proved more than capable of looking after herself. When she was separated from her party on one occasion, she was attacked by natives – and escaped having shot three of them. Cathy subsequently presented a paper to the Royal Geographical Society about the expedition.[15] Furthermore, by 1963 Steed was introducing her as a 'geologist extraordinaire' [BRIE], suggesting that this was another field she had branched out into. As well as her Amazonian trip, in 1961 Cathy spent some time

---

[12] 'Viewerpoint'. *TV Times*, 13 December 1963, p21.

[13] *TV Times*, 20 September 1963, p4

[14] *The Complete Avengers*, p35.

[15] *The Complete Avengers*, p35.

in the Kuanajar province of Borneo [PROP] where she apparently took some very striking photographs of the starving children [BEAR].

Photography became one of Cathy's main passions and she usually had a darkroom at her flat [DANE, ROME]. Cathy's photographic skills were sometimes used as part of the cover for her assignments [CONS, MAND] – but also for leisure, such as the shots she took of Oliver Waldner while staying at his estate [MAND]. This talent was also employed in her different hobbies and studies, such as four days spent in the cold getting shots of the green wood-pecker, the Greater Spotted Woodpecker and the Lesser Spotted Woodpecker (using f50 with 5.6 and gambling on employing a 500 mm lens) [DANE]. Cathy was familiar with using a miniature camera [BATM, SECO] and was also adept at developing and creating microfilm [WOND]. All in all, even those who had only briefly seen her at work declared that she was very good [CONS].

A fast typist [CONS], it seems that Cathy regularly published from her researches. By 1962, she had also written a monograph on Ohi or Voodoo, which was regarded as excel-lent by the prominent occultist Dr Cosmo Gallion [WARL]. There were also photographs of her appearing in other magazines, images which only went to feed the tortured mind of Martin Goodman as he resided in his prison cell [BEHI].

At the age of 30, Cathy had a considerable knowledge of many different subjects. In terms of languages, she was fluent in Spanish to the extent that she could pass for a native [DISP, BATM], she felt her German was 'pretty good' [INTE], spoke Russian [CONC], and also had an excellent grasp of Latin (eg 'Quis Custodiet Ipsos Custodes' – 'Who will guard the guards themselves?') [SHAD, ROME] – presumably from her academic studies. It was also possible that she spoke Welsh [WHAL].

Cathy seemed to keep abreast of developments in the world of chemistry, and was aware of the existence of Propellant 23, a Chinese rocket fuel being tested in Gobi desert in 1962 [PROP]. When it came to physics, she understood the basics of both computers and cryo-genics [BIGT] and had no problem in performing well when undercover with Professor Thorne and team as they synthesised rubies at *HMS Zebra* [ZEBR]. Astronomy was another strong subject; she was well aware of the creation of a white dwarf from the core of a supernova, how the Crab Nebula came into being in 1504, and also the work in this field of people such as Professor Richter, Professor Cartright[16], Professor James Larson of the University of New Jersey and also Dr Elizabeth Fuller, author of a paper on the asteroid belt [DWAR]. In terms of botany, she was familiar with monskeriose [MAND] and could also analyse grain for the fungus causing Ergotism under the microscope with help from *Abnormalities in Plants and Animals* [ROME]. When it came to wildlife, despite her interest in woodpeckers [DANE] she was less familiar with the subject of whales [WHAL]. Although commenting that she was closer to the medical field than Steed, she admitted that she knew little about corneal surgery [SECO].

Cathy also had a basic knowledge of history – good enough to correct Steed's miscon-ception that Marie Antoinette was held in the Bastille [PROP]. From her time in Africa, she was also very experienced with the occult and black magic which she took very seriously – aware of the power that a figure like a warlock could have. Cathy commented on previous incidents of the occult involving werewolves in northern France in 1925 and of a case of a man who was under a spell in England for five years in 1947. She was already aware of the

---

[16] Erroneously referred to as 'Cartwright' in the summary report.

standing of Dr Cosmo Gallion in this field, and of his Occult Bookshop in Elm Street [WARL].

In other fields, Cathy had an interest in ceramics, and was able to identify specific items such as Marling creamware [CLAY]. When it came to diamonds, she knew that the main source of illicit stones was Manchuria, since it was not controlled by the Diamond Federation [ROCK]. She was also a shrewd business analyst, who quickly identified the issue of rising labour and material costs when looking at the accounts for Anderson's Small Arms Ltd [BULL].

Another of Cathy passions seemed to be philately. She knew which stamps were rare along with miscellaneous information about how there were only two examples of the 1847 Mauritius Penny Red in the world – one in the Carnegie Collection, the other in the British Museum – in 1962. She was not caught out by people who tried to trick her in this field with talk of a Maltese 2d Blue [MAUR]. However, her knowledge of criminology was not as good as Steed's and she naively believed that three bodies in a burnt-out ambulance could be easily identified from their teeth [EGGS]. Nor was she aware that a clown's make-up was their trademark prior to her visit to Gutman's Circus [CONS].

Cathy tended to wear some very striking outfits which were the height of fashion. Many of these were jacket and skirt ensembles [eg WARL] such as one light outfit with ticking and a tight waist [eg PROP, BEAR], a distinctive Mary Quant suit of scarlet wool with the jacket fastened by gold chains [eg MAUR, INTE], a green Scottish wool tweed jacket and skirt [eg DWAR, ESPR], a dark two-piece Spanish cut suit [eg NUTS, BEHI], a high-collared dark jacket with a sash [eg NOV5, CHAR] and a collarless two-piece suit [eg TROJ, LOBS]. Some of these outfits were accentuated by waistcoats of leather [FLEE], leopard print [DWAR] and a dazzling gold lamé [CONC, SHAD, UNDE]. With these she would wear a number of blouses, generally white [eg CLAY, WHAL] in colour in 1962 but then becoming more daring, notably a high-collared striped blouse with a bow at the neck [eg HAND, CONC, BATM], various other striped designs [eg ROME] as well as abstract two-tone patterns [eg DANE] and a white polkadot which she wore a lot in 1963-64, sometimes with a matching cravat [eg NOV5, LOBS]. Cathy also had a range of dark polo necks [eg BULL, LOBS] and turtleneck pullovers [eg MAUR, ELEP].

When a more feminine look was required, Cathy had quite a range of dresses, many of them sleeveless [eg, DISP, DANE]. Some were in satin [eg BIGT], others trimmed with black lace [ZEBR], others glittering [eg DANE, ROCK, CART], and some woollen [eg CHAR, ESPR]. One distinctive outfit was a V-neck pinafore dress in carbon blue [eg SECO, LOBS].

The Gale wardrobe also had some notable coats including a fashionable collarless white item [DISP], a general coat which Cathy used for diving [eg PROP, ROCK], a fawn double-breasted mackintosh [eg BIGT, WHAL, ROME, CHAR], and a fur-lined coat in black leather with black and white civet cat fur [eg NOV5, OUTS]. She often favoured the use of a tartan-lined cape [eg DANE, CONS], a tartan cape trimmed with black fur [eg BULLS, WHAL] and a wool and leather cloak [eg WRIN, ESPR].

As well as keeping warm with a black fur wrap [BIGT, INTE, EGGS], Cathy normally wore black gloves [eg WARL, WHAL, UNDE, LOBS], with string-backed gloves for driving [WARL] and elegant long gloves in white [DISP, BIGT] and black [HAND] for special occasions. She also had a number of scarves [eg BEAR, CHAR] and neckerchiefs [eg BIGT, SECO] in her wardrobe, and a headscarf when driving in an open car [BEHI].

Cathy was particularly well remembered for her high black leather boots[17] [eg PROP,

WHAL, NOV5, MAND] which she periodically needed to have re-heeled [CAGE]; some sources suggest that these were made by Anello and Davide. These were excellent for hiding things in [ZEBR] and Steed apparently recalled to Heald that she was wearing such footwear beneath her nun's habit when he first met her.[18] Apart from these, Cathy tended to wear high-heeled shoes [eg BULL, BIGT].

A striking item of Cathy's wardrobe was her range of leather 'fighting suits', many of which were in black. An early example of this was a dark green V-neck jacket and trousers combination [eg BEAR, WHAL, NUTS, UNDE] which she would sometimes wear when riding [HAND]. By 1963, Cathy also had a black sleeveless leather top [eg SHAD, BATM] which was perfect for biking with the Salts after the addition of black helmet with the 'S' emblem of the Salts biking gang [MOUS]. There was a distinctive shoulder-fastening two-piece tunic in black leather [eg NOV5, OUTS] and a 'Tabbard Set' which resembled an old-fashioned butcher's apron [eg MEDI, CHAR].

Cathy also had a passion for hats which she shared with her friend actress Honor Blackman who recalled their shopping trips together. 'I remember we used to go to Bond Street for her hats, because I used to wear some wonderful hats – I love hats.'[19] Cathy's favourite item of headgear was a wide-brimmed dark Spanish hat [eg BULL, WHAL, ROME] although she was also seen to sport items such as a scarlet trilby [MAUR], a Tyrolean hat with dark band [CLAY], trendy, coloured plastic caps [eg CONS, MAND], a top hat [eg CONC, FLEE], a turban affair [NOV5, SECO], a floppy knitted hat [NOV5, BROK], a canvas item [SECO] and a white hat with a black brim [MEDI, WRIN].

Not that it was seen much by Steed or on the surveillance films, but Cathy favoured a black lacy bra and undergarments in 1962 [DISP] and also had a navy blue bikini which she wore when it was hot [SHAD]. At home, she could be found wearing an Oriental silk house gown [BEAR], a patterned housecoat [EGGS], a satin gown [HAND] or a comfy striped bathrobe [BIGT].

Cathy generally wore her blonde hair down, aside from rare occasions when she styled up upwards [DANE, BIGT, HAND, BATM], often when she was working undercover. Seldom did she tie her hair back [INTE] or use hairpins [DRES].

Cathy often carried a dark handbag of some sort [eg WARL, ZEBR, BROK, LOBS], although she used a white one when in the Caribbean [DISP] and had a slim black version for dress occasions [HAND]. This accessory was also a useful defence against knife attacks [PROP] and for secreting a tape recorder [MAUR]. On other occasions she used a dark shoulder bag [eg DWAR, MAND, LOBS] or a dark briefcase [DWAR]. There were a few items she carried with her, such as a calling card ('Mrs Catherine Gale') [WARL] which she would keep in her purse [CAGE] or handbag [OUTS]. She was also known to have about her a compass [WRIN] and possibly a cigarette lighter [WHAL].

---

[17] It has been suggested that the novelty song 'Kinky Boots' recorded by Cathy's friend Honor Blackman and Steed's associate Patrick Macnee was a tribute to Cathy's stylish footwear. This was released by Decca in February 1964 (F11843) and indeed reached the charts when it became a 'kitsch' classic in December 1990. However, the song had actually been written by Herbert Kretzmer and Dave Lee for Millicent Martin to sing live on the 5 November 1963 edition of *That Was The Week That Was*, and was only subsequently covered by Cathy's colleagues for record executive Marcel Stellman.
[18] *Jealous in Honour*, p192.
[19] Richardson, David, 'Leather and Lace', *TV Zone*, Issue 75, February 1996, p75.

Cathy wore a watch on her left wrist [eg DISP, CONS], one of these was a diamond watch which she bought legitimately in a customs auction [ROCK]. Sometimes when working undercover she would wear spectacles [BEAR, EGGS, ZEBR]; occasionally she sported dark glasses [MAND]. Cathy rarely needed to adorn herself with jewellery, aside from her wedding ring [eg PROP, WHAL]. When visiting Olaf Pomeroy, she had a diamond pendant at her neck which the hit-man asked for as a deposit against her contract – although Steed later recovered it [BEAR]. When going out for a romantic dinner with Oliver Waldner, she donned some dazzling earrings [HAND]. She filed and varnished her nails [HAND, BATM] and would use her lipstick to leave messages on the mirror in Steed's flat [WRIN].

In 1962 and 1963, Cathy smoked cigarettes [DISP, WARL, BEAR, BULL, MAUR, DANE, ROCK, INTE], often using an elegant cigarette holder [WARL, PROP, ZEBR, BIGT, CLAY]. This habit was useful for allowing her to make enquiries or assess a situation while making a purchase at venues such as Marseilles airport [PROP] or a café at Barton [BEAR]. Judging by her coughs from the smoke emanating from the Professor, she was not used to smoking cigars [CONS], although later in the year she smoked these at her Primrose Hill flat and offered them to visitors [NOV5]. Also by late 1963, Cathy had switched to smoking cheroots [BEHI, UNDE, DRES, ESPR].

One of the things that Charles – one of Steed's superiors – found particularly enchanting about Cathy was her impressive knowledge of food and wine [WRIN]. One of Cathy's favourite drinks when out and about was a gin and tonic [WARL, BIGT]. She also drank champagne in moderation [CART, UNDE, CAGE], and Steed remembered that this prized drink was effective as 'a livener' for her even as early as their meeting at the Ocean Hotel in Jamaica in 1962 [DISP]. Cathy would also periodically enjoy sampling Steed's own cellar at his flat, particularly a 'splendid year' like the '45 [DRES] or his Pouilly Fume [LOBS]. Steed was also aware that Cathy liked whiskey, ordering her a whiskey and soda at their hotel in Lima [DISP]. Cathy would drink this on a few other occasions [WOND], in one instance sampling a fine 25-year-old blend from Aberdeen [ESPR]. She was also fond of sherry which she kept in her drinks cabinet [WHAL] and also drank brandy [FLEE, NOV5]. Cathy was also astute enough with drinks to know when one had been spiked [BIGT]. When Steed presented her with an apricot liqueur (rather than a peach one), she turned her nose up at it and made a comment about 'depraved taste' [BROK].

Cathy was quite a connoisseur of wine, able to identify a Chateau Grillet '53 (which she felt was 'discrete') [BROK] and having a particular fondness for the Chateau Margot '53 [SHAD]. She kept wine at her flat [BIGT], ordered it while visiting Dos Pajaros in Santiago [DISP] and enjoyed drinking it with Steed while they posed as a married couple in Highgate [ROCK] as well as on numerous other occasions [eg BEHI, LOBS]. However, despite her familiarity with wine, Cathy had not attended a formal tasting before she went to the City Wine Cellars with Steed in late October 1962; until this time she believed that one drained the entire glass. At this function she made a point of turning down the burgundies [DANE].

Aside from alcohol, Cathy also enjoyed an innocuous soda pop with the Salts [MOUS] while she normally kept orange juice in her fridge [WHAL] which she liked to drink at breakfast for its vitamin C [MOUS].

When it came to hot beverages, Cathy was partial to coffee [eg PROP, BEHI] which she took with molasses in the absence of sugar at the Tor Point Guest House [DWAR] and at home drank a brand which Steed rather liked [BEHI]. She also drank tea [BIGT, CLAY], which she would even make at her flat for uninvited guests [BIGT]. Originally she took her tea with two sugars [UNDE, BATM, MOUS], but later cut down to one only [MEDI].

As for food, Cathy's notion of a good meal in 1963 was to eat in Lombardy, Italy, ideally a repast comprising avocado, a rump steak and a green salad, washed down with the afore-mentioned Chateau Margot '53 [SHAD]. In addition to the steaks, she also ate fish [BEHI]. She seemed to have quite a sweet tooth, being fond of chocolate biscuits [NUTS], fruit and nut [FLEE], sherbet [WOND] and jellied bumble bees from Japan [UNDE], while Cornish cream was one of her rare breakfast treats [MAND]. In other respects, Cathy was a rather careful eater, refusing cake when proffered, but not because she was worried about what this would do to her waistline [CLAY].

At her flat, Cathy enjoyed cooking simple meals for herself, and when Steed visited he would be offered a quick dish such as an omelette with a choice of herbs, cheese, tomato or ham [BIGT]. When moving between flats, one of the conditions on which Steed moved into a hotel so that she could use his apartment was an agreement that she would provide him with 'slap-up bumper meals' [EGGS]. It is unclear if the choice of Wild West Cornflakes she consumed for breakfast there was hers or Steed's, but he was aghast to find that all she seemed to have stocked his kitchen with was cream crackers and yoghurt [EGGS]. By spring 1964, Cathy had decided to become a vegetarian [OUTS], but still enjoyed meals such as smoked salmon which she helped herself to from Steed's fridge when working at his redec-orated flat [LOBS].

Cathy's reading material included various social history books such as *The Great Hunger March* by the Right Honourable Arthur Dove (which she read twice) [NOV5] and Bental's *History of World War I* (which she found fascinating) [ESPR] as well as business works like *The Craft of Salesmanship* by Willis [MEDI]. As for her knowledge of literature, she was also familiar with Herman Melville's 1851 nautical novel *Moby Dick* [WHAL] and could quote St Augustine of Hippo [MAND].

In terms of leisure activities, Cathy had quite an interest in music [CONC]. Her own taste in listening material included everything from an 1868 lullaby by Johannes Brahms from his *Five Songs, Opus 49* [SHAD] through to LPs of modern jazz at her flat [DANE].[20] While at Gutman's Circus, she seemed genuinely amused by the antics of the clowns such as Arturo [CONS]. She also used to collect dolls made by the company Simon and Holby in Germany around 1890 [WOND], and once took Steed to a lecture about Cro-Magnon Art [SECO]. Cathy also savoured a nice hot bath and did not like being dragged out of one [WOND]. In terms of finances, she dabbled in buying shares [BATM].[21]

Cathy rode horses [HAND, BEHI], presumably a skill she acquired when she was younger, since by 1963 she feared that she might have been a bit rusty when she joined a drive with the Waldner family – only to be pleasantly surprised when she took the fences well [HAND]. When spending some time at Bognor Regis, she was also known to go for donkey rides [NUTS]. Cathy was a strong swimmer [BRIE] and had a handicap of only 12 on the golf course, enjoying chipping practice balls into a hat at Steed's flat [MEDI].

When it came to games, Cathy would engage with Steed in a quick game of darts or dominoes [ZEBR] and was even able to rack 970 on a pinball machine during a visit to the amusement arcade Doctor Death's Parlour [BIGT]. Her talent at cards was something which

---

[20] Apparently *Pouffe Belle* by Dutch composer Frans Mijtz, De Wolfe, DW 2731.

[21] An unconfirmed report suggests that Cathy also had premium bonds which ERNIE had never picked the numbers of by 1964. 'The Runaway Brain', *Look Westward/The Viewer*, 9 May 1964.

she kept hidden, telling Dr Jimmy Kearns that she would rather watch him play poker than play herself – although she could see how Kearns was being cheated by Nicky Broster, the club owner. Cathy was well aware of the techniques of marked cards and used this to her advantage to make equal draws with Broster when she later played 'Win or Lose' for £500 on behalf of Kearns [BIGT].

Although a magnetic chess set was part of the décor in her Primrose Hill flat and despite the fact that she was able to beat Steed at the game [CONC], Cathy claimed that she did not play that well [LOBS]. She did however know something about the chess world, such as there being only a few places in the country which dealt with truly valuable chess pieces – one of these being the Chess Shop [LOBS].

Cathy was also a highly social lady who attended all-night parties [WRIN], whether it was 'Living it up in Paris' [WRIN] or having a more modern dance with the motorcycle gang the Salts [MOUS]. She liked jasmine and surprises [BEHI], and clearly one of her ideas of a good holiday was getting a tan in Jamaica [DISP]. She also liked to partake of a massage after a Turkish bath [MEDI].

It seems that by the early 1960s, Cathy was again taking on a few background assignments for the Department, possibly connected with her travel around the world. As such, she was used on a freelance basis largely, it would seem, by One-Ten [DISP]. The more mature Cathy was ideal for missions. Her amazing intellect proved essential on many occasions, added to which she had a fantastic memory. She could recall the details of gold finances and resources from tape almost word perfect, augmented with information from *Gold Reserves and the American Market* [CAGE]. Her powers of mental arithmetic were astounding [TROJ, BATM]. While she could apply her practical skills to matters such as cracking a chess code [LOBS], she also found the concepts involved in some of her missions – such as the creation of a *doppelgänger* – to be intellectually fascinating [SHAD].

Cathy was both confident and yet cautious – a winning combination. When working alongside Steed, she would volunteer her services in investigation if it was a subject where she had a greater knowledge such as the occult or medicine [WARL, SECO]. She would not be cowed by anyone such as Harley Street consultant Mr A Beardmore [WOND] or bookmaker Tony Heuston, who offered to pay her £70 a week to work for him although she demanded – and received – £100 [TROJ]. Harking back to her days in Kenya, she liked to see a job through to the end, reminding her colleague, 'When I find a hunt worth joining Steed, I like to be in at the kill' [WARL].

However, Cathy was also aware when the level of risk was too high. Although she would take basic precautions such as removing the bullets from a gun used by Martin, a member of the 'other side' [CHAR], there were limits beyond which she was reluctant to proceed [WARL, ROCK, INTE].

'Cathy is essentially humanitarian' noted a second Department dossier on Cathy in 1963, which then continued 'She *cares* about people and cannot *use* them like *Steed*.'[22] From her time around the world, Cathy had immense admiration for people like business tycoon Alexander Litoff, who made donations to famine relief, refugee homes, cancer research, flood disaster and mental health [DANE]. One thing that was for certain was that Cathy was a far more moral persona than her shady colleague. She ensured that the Golden Fleece Fund records were destroyed to avoid implicating former soldiers who were

---

[22] *The Complete Avengers*, p59. Their emphasis.

dependent on the illicit money [FLEE] and was extremely concerned about innocent young Julie Clitheroe marrying an enemy agent who was impersonating scientist William Gordon [SHAD]. She became confrontational with business wizard Julian Seabrook over her relationship with Oliver Waldner and his daughter [HAND], allowed small-fry criminals Hasek and Gerda to go free from the dolls' hospital [WOND], felt sorry for Allen Marling over the events at his Midlands pottery [CLAY] and was very concerned about her young friend, Joey Frazer, when he became a pawn in Steed's latest game [WHAL]. However, as Cathy's 1962 report noted, 'she is fired by the desire to fight against evil and essentially to help those who are victims of crime' and she *'cares deeply for the people involved'*[23] – making it difficult for her to have turned down even dangerous work when it might benefit others.

Cathy had a strong sense of justice. She very much wanted to help Sub-Lt Michael Crane when he was wrongly accused of espionage [ZEBR] while conversely branding the former British operative Sharp as a traitor [OUTS] and went as far as threatening to kill Sica, a Mafia dope peddler, rather than just see him in the dock [CONS]. She was not altogether happy with big business practices, observing that if British drug manufacturers did not charge such a high price for their product in the Middle East, then the counterfeiters of their medicine would not be able to operate [MEDI]. Firmly opposed to the notion of germ warfare, Cathy's attitudes convinced Dr Ashe to destroy his research into the lethal strain verity prime. When the criminal Julius Redfern tried to trade in this culture, Cathy was happy to let him believe he was exposed to the bacteria, asking 'Are you in the market for a handful of death?' [EGGS].

However, Cathy was happy to indulge in some bribery when necessary, offering money to Rant, a tattooist, to identify a specific customer [CONS] and offering Scott, the sexton at St Alban's in Tinbey, £100 to turn Queen's Evidence on his colleagues [MAND]. When the stakes were high, she could also exert verbal force to get her way with the newly-widowed Mrs Diana DeLeon (although she adopted a softer approach when it became clear that Diana knew little about the operation of Julius Redfern [EGGS]) and threatened Dr Ashe with the police to get him to confess about his bacteriological work [EGGS].

'Cathy led a very active life,'[24] recalled Honor Blackman of her very fit friend who prided herself on her athleticism... as well as having excellent teeth [CHAR]. Cathy practised yoga and would sometimes be found standing on her head against a wall [ELEP]. She also attended classes in yoga and meditation run by Miss Elizabeth Prinn with whom she went boating on the Thames [BRIE]. Certainly when she arrived at the Slimorama Keep Fit School Winter Sports Centre, she already knew how to use a rowing machine [NOV5].

However, Cathy's sporting speciality was judo. In 1963, she travelled to Tokyo for the International Judo Convention [WHAL]. It was presumably judo which she taught at the local youth club on Wednesdays around this time, where one of her pupils was promising pugilist Joey Frazer [WHAL]. Cathy's expertise became increasingly necessary in many of her escapades with Steed, where her unarmed combat skills were employed successfully against a wide range of adversaries. Most of her opponents were men, and – by and large – she gained a legendary reputation for being able to better them all. 'Some men felt very threatened by Cathy Gale,'[25] observed Honor Blackman many years later. Indeed,

[23] *The Complete Avengers*, p25. Their emphasis.
[24] *The Complete Avengers*, p37.
[25] Rogers, Dave, 'Honor Blackman', *Look Who's Talking The Avengers*, OTTA, April 1986, p6 .

Blackman herself took up judo, apparently because of the skills of her friend Cathy, reaching the level of brown belt and even writing a book on the subject.[26]

On an early mission together after their reunion, Steed learnt for the first time that Cathy could easily better him with a throw [WARL], a move which was repeated when they later sparred together [BEAR] and during missions [ZEBR, BROK]. Steed rapidly realised how lethal a whirlwind his partner could become and later referred to her as 'Mrs Whizz Bang Wallop' [SHAD].

'Do you really need a gun to deal with a woman?' was one of Cathy's taunts to fellow anthropologist Thadeus Lawrence who then made the mistake of attacking her with a rope [ELEP]. Her strength was sufficient to defeat any man, grabbing a knife from Dr Gallion [WARL], preventing one of Alexander Litoff's assistants from throttling her [DANE], taking on a trained boxer like Harry [WHAL], bettering soldiers such as WO1 Wright [FLEE] and Brigadier Mellor [CART] as well as a trained Russian agent [MOUS], a fitness instructor called Max[27] [NOV5], an Aburanian soldier [OUTS], and even taking on the 17 stone of a heavy called Blomberg, albeit with assistance from Allen Marling [CLAY]. Cathy was able to get would-be assailants in an arm lock [BULL] or throw them into submission [eg ROCK, HAND, UNDE, WOND] or even – as at New Year 1963 – through a wall at Badger's Mount station [DRES]. Her opponents would later observe that she 'fought like a professional' [EGGS] and many of her movements were reminiscent of those by the French Resistance during World War II.[28]

Cathy was adept at exhausting an attacker before moving in for the kill [BIGT] and her attack could be so swift that her victim would later be unable to identify her [INTE]. When attacked herself, she would know how to roll and regain posture to retaliate [BATM]. Her reactions were generally very sharp – and one of the few occasions when they failed her was when hunter Lew Conniston crept up behind her without her knowing, an incident she was quick to reprimand herself over [ELEP].

Cathy did not suffer fools gladly [BEHI] and, when provoked, was extremely dangerous. She twisted Siebel's arm after he slapped her in the face [PROP] and threw a man who started talking about her legs before threatening to break his arm [BEHI]. She could render a person unconscious with a single blow to the neck [PROP, MAUR, TROJ, BROK, WRIN] while a similar blow to the wrist would cause the victim to open their hand [BIGT]. Her use of hand blows developed more and more [BRIE, ROME, SECO]. On rarer occasions, she would kick out, such as when she removed a gun from the hand of Oliver Waldner with a flash of footwork [HAND] or kicked Scott, the sexton, into an open grave [MAND].

Even when tied up and gagged, Cathy was still able to pinion a woman with her booted feet [MEDI]. Confident with her skills, Cathy was truly a force to be reckoned with, and gave warnings to potential opponents that she could offer them 'any amount of bruising' [MAND].

In a combat situation, Cathy was able to think quickly. She used objects like bottles as distractions [ROCK], whisked the chair from beneath a Mafia killer [CONS] and used her handbag to stop a knife attack [PROP]. When Sergeant Marsh attacked her with a knife she dealt with him comparatively easily [ESPR], and on one occasion demonstrated a rare

---

[26] *Honor Blackman's Book of Self-Defence*, André Deutsch, 1965.

[27] Erroneously referred to as 'Joe' in the summary report.

[28] *Manchester Evening News*, 6 October 1962, p5

expertise with a fencing foil [CHAR]. Her general agility also helped her loosen her bonds when trussed up in a beach hut [LOBS].

There was little that scared Cathy at all. She rarely expressed fear, such as when she was nearly hit by a block and tackle at Collier's Yard [HAND], and even opponents such as Olaf Pomeroy admired her courage [BEAR]. Indeed, she was prepared to have a go at most things, from climbing out of a window on knotted sheets some 14 floors up [DANE] through to taking part as a moving target in a knife throwing act [CONS].

From her training with the Department, Cathy was adept at gaining access [WARL], sometimes using a special device to pick locks [BIGT] and was able to cut alarm systems where necessary [ROCK]. Once inside, she knew how to make a thorough search of a room [ZEBR, CONS], including checking ink, toothpaste, the soles of shoes [PROP], desk drawers and waste bins [ZEBR]. She was also quick to hide anything that she found during her searches on her person – such as a slip of paper at the offices of the *Echo and Chronicle* which slipped neatly into one of her boots [ZEBR]. While good at locating a hidden safe in a room, she was not so quick at cracking them as Steed [HAND].

Cathy's expertise at sleight of hand was also useful in various situations, such as when she slipped a box of cigarettes into the jacket pocket of Pierre, an airport security officer, thus giving her an excuse to enter his office on the pretext of recovering them [PROP]. She was also adept at pocketing items, such as the ticket to the supposed International Philatelic Convention which she stole from the stamp shop where she was working [MAUR]. Steed referred to her as 'Mata Hari' [BIGT], the legendary Dutch dancer-cum-spy born Margaretha Zelle who was accused of spying for Germany in World War I.

Cathy was an excellent strategist, whether it was demolishing a prosecution story in a trial [INTE], preparing a vital telex to save Steed's life [DANE] or devising bait for a trap [EGGS]. She had excellent deductive reasoning which allowed her to identify company secretary Doreen Ellis as the murderer at Anderson's [BULL], or making sound assumptions from surveillance tapes on a phone line [MAUR]. Her observant nature allowed her to recall scribblings on a telephone pad [DISP] while her senses led her to detect the scent of smuggled ambergris [WHAL].

Even in a tight spot, Cathy swiftly reasoned solutions. Her bluff of having called the police brought about the desired reactions at the homes of Miguel Rosas [DISP] and Oliver Waldner [HAND]. When trapped in a chemical lab, she quickly used a broken bottle to cut her bonds and then triggered a sprinkler system to effect her escape [WHAL], and when imprisoned on another occasion she turned off the mains power, leading to a possible germination of the deadly verity prime [EGGS]. She was also not above helping Steed use a bystander as a shield [DISP]. Ever resourceful, Cathy made good use of the tools available to her. Her high-heeled shoes became a make-shift hammer [MAUR], a torn neckerchief was used to treat frostbite [BIGT] and a nail allowed her to loosen the bars of a cell window [ROME].

Highly experienced with guns after her time in Kenya – notably the EY rifle [FLEE] – Cathy was frequently armed when working with Steed. She could make a rapid assessment of most firearms [PROP], and recognise those which she had never used such as a gas pistol [BIGT]. Her prowess with firearms was phenomenal, and one press report noted that she had been 'three times runner up at Bisley'[29], presumably 1960 to 1962. With rifles, Cathy

---

[29] *TV Times*, 20 September 1963, p4.

disliked using telescopic sights and her marksmanship with this weapon was so fine that in four shots on a target range she scored three bulls and one inner – with two of the bulls on top of each other [BULL]. Nevertheless, when undercover and impersonating Intercrime operative Hilda Stern, she asked for a .22 rifle with telescopic sights to supposedly complete the execution of Pamela Johnson [INTE]. At home in her first flat, she kept a revolver in the desk drawer [DANE], while after the move to Primrose Hill she kept her guns in the kitchen and had more powerful firearms around the flat [UNDE].

On one of her earliest missions with Steed in 1962, Cathy was equipped with an automatic handgun and ammunition which she secreted in a false top to her suitcase [DISP]. Sometimes she would carry a gun in her handbag [DISP] and at other times in her waistband [WARL, DANE, WHAL] although she experimented briefly with lodging her firearm in her right garter [PROP, OUTS] Steed advised her not to conceal a six-shooter in her stocking tops when dealing with Olaf Pomeroy [BEAR] and made references to her carrying a 'gun in your garter' [CONC]. Often she would carry a small handgun [BEAR, BULL, ROCK, BIGT, INTE, FLEE, BEHI, SHAD, CHAR] – such as a Browning Baby Automatic 6.35mm [CHAR] – in a pocket low on her leather jacket [BEAR, BIGT]. She did not always keep her handgun loaded [SHAD]. While working in France, Steed gave her a small, circular gun which fitted into the palm of the hand; firing .22 bullets it was an item once used by the ladies of Paris to defend themselves [PROP].

Despite all her skill, Cathy sometimes had a moral problem in using the weapons that she was so adept with. She was too much of a lady to disable Olaf Pomeroy by shooting him in the kneecaps [BEAR]. However, she did shoot one of Litoff's assistants during a stand-off at the offices of the Litoff Organisation [DANE], as well as disarming both the real Hilda Stern [INTE] and a funeral director called Green with a shot to the hand [UNDE], shooting both Max [NOV5] and later 'Sister' Johnson in the arm [WOND] and also firing on Sergeant Marsh [ESPR]. In a shoot-out, she would count the bullets fired by an assailant and could tell the difference between six-round and eight-round .38 revolvers [ROCK].

Although Cathy liked to visit many other places around the world, by 1963 the only place that she wanted to live was London [CART]. The London flat [BEAR] which she was occupying by 1962 was a modest and simple affair, which she had personalised with many items from her travels. Entering from the upper floor hallway landing, the visitor found themselves in a kitchen area which was separated from a light sitting room area by a dividing shelf unit which housed numerous African mementos such as carvings. Either side of the front door, Cathy originally had large photographic blow-ups of a Japanese figure and some foreign children [BEAR]; the latter were very similar to the photographs of children from Borneo which she studied while in France [PROP] and her 1962 Departmental dossier notes that – in addition to her specialised firearms and African trophies – she had on display examples of her photography.[30] The shelving unit which acted as a separator was also a breakfast bar, while in the kitchen area itself – on the right as one entered – was the sink and the gas cooker, with crockery stacked on shelves on the wall above [BEAR]. To the left of the front door opposite the kitchen was a large support pillar [BIGT].

In the sitting room area were two large windows giving a view to the London street below, with small pictures mounted between them. Close to the window, Cathy originally had a baby grand piano, on top of which she kept some of the many African carvings which

---

[30] *The Complete Avengers*, p35.

were dotted around the living area [BEAR]. There was a single chair and a lounger, angled around a low table in front of the fireplace, which housed more ornaments including a small stuffed animal under a glass dome – all of which Steed felt were rather Edwardian [MAUR]. Nearby, adjacent to the dividing bookcase, stood a standard lamp and a small African stool. To the right of the windows was the door leading to the bedrooms, and either side of this were flintlocks mounted on the wall [BEAR]. The floor was covered by a rug, and for Cathy's entertainment she often had a portable radio [BEAR, DANE] or a record player [DANE], while she used a reel-to-reel tape recorder to listen to the noises of the exotic animals which she studied [ROCK]. Later in 1962, the piano had been removed and Cathy had moved her lounger nearer the window [DANE]. Of the ornaments, at least one was verified by Dr Howell as being a Benin (one of the tribes of Nigeria) and possibly worth several thousand pounds [BEAR]. There was also a desk in which she kept her revolver [DANE].

Off the lounge down a short corridor were the other rooms, one of which had been tiled and kept darkened to act as Cathy's photographic dark room, where she was also able to look at her shots on a slide projector [DANE]. The bedroom was not large, and Cathy had positioned her bed against a bamboo screen opposite the window [WARL]. Cathy apparently kept a stuffed crocodile in the bathroom [ROCK]. She also tended to leave the bathroom window open – something which Steed chided her over [BEAR]. Cathy's flat was not terribly secure. A smuggler called Karl was able to gain entry in her absence on one occasion when Steed was thankfully keeping an eye on the apartment in the guise of a window cleaner [BULL]. Fortunately, on other occasions she instinctively seemed to know that there were intruders in her home [BIGT].

Of the various cars which she drove in the early 1960s, Cathy's usual vehicle seemed to be a modern two-seater 1961 MGA 4-cylinder sports car, a sleek and elegant model which fitted her adventurous lifestyle [WARL, PROP, BEAR]. 'I always go fast,' she proclaimed of her driving, and had a habit of stopping very suddenly [WARL]. Although she also drove a car at the time of the search for the eggs stolen from Dr Ashe, it is unknown if this was still the MGA [EGGS]. Certainly, by the time of the investigation into the activities of the Reniston Group, she was driving a different model of car – another two seater, the make of which has yet to be determined [HAND]. 'She drives a car fast and well,' noted a dossier compiled about Cathy in 1963.[31]

Cathy's other favoured form of transport was the motorcycle – notably a 500cc Triumph Speed Twin[32] model from 1961 on which she was more than happy to do 'a ton plus ten' (ie drive at 110mph) and so join the Salts biking gang [MOUS]. There are also additional surveillance photographs in existence showing her astride a Royal Enfield motorcycle[33] which is possibly a modified 500cc Meteor Minor model, but this does not feature in any of the existing surveillance film. Cathy's knowledge of motorcycles allowed her to quickly and easily disable a bike with a swift tug of a cable to prevent a man called Henry Farrow from tailing her on one occasion [BEAR].

It seems that by 1962, Cathy was not necessarily an official member of the Department, but was still used on some missions because of her previous association with them. Although One-Ten had been happy enough to employ her to act as Steed's cover on a

---

[31] *The Complete Avengers*, p59.
[32] Registration 987 CAA.
[33] Registration XH 054.

mission in South America in the summer of 1962 [DISP], a few months later during an investigation at Marlings, a pottery in Staffordshire, One-Ten told Steed that he took a very dim view of his subordinate using Cathy, whom he referred to as an 'amateur', to go under-cover at the company [CLAY]. Cathy herself reiterated her status firmly to Steed, indicating that working for the Department was not her profession; 'I'm not in your business. Might as well remember that,' she declared waspishly [CLAY]. By 1963, she was referred to as a member of the public [NUTS] and in 1964 was still described as an 'outsider' [OUTS]. Her position with the Department was also expressed as a 'lady helpmate of Steed's' [WRIN].

As a wealthy widow with connections in various different fields, Cathy enjoyed a wide range of acquaintances. Some were from her work as an anthropologist, most notably Dr James Howell, an expert on the Upper Nile, who was known all over the world. Howell tended not to remain anywhere for too long, and when in London usually stayed at the Voyager's Club. On one occasion when he was coming to Cathy's flat to view her African tribal heads in 1962, Howell was unwittingly used by one 'Teddy Bruin', whom he played bridge with at the Club, to deliver a message connected with Cathy's dealings with the executioner Olaf Pomeroy [BEAR]. She was also friends with an expert reader of Arabic [MEDI] and from the world of science was Dr Farrow, an astronomer associated with the Plato computer project. Farrow was clearly taken with Cathy's many charms, commenting that he did not know her 'nearly well enough' [BIGT].

From her writing, Cathy had numerous contacts in the publishing world. It is unclear if her friend in Fleet Street [NOV5] and a veteran court reporter called Wilson [BRIE] were one and the same or not, but she remained on good terms with her 'old flame' who by October 1962 was the city editor of *Finance* magazine [DANE]. Apart from them, she knew the bullion merchant John Thorpe [FLEE] and Richard Marling, one of the directors of Marlings pottery in the Midlands [CLAY]. She also had a female friend who, in 1964, was selling a blue Vogel Prentice convertible [OUTS]. Many of her friends were listed in her small, black address book [MEDI] and she was often making new acquaintances – such as Joey Frazer – from her work at the local Youth Club in 1963 [WHAL].

But the most fascinating aspect of studying Cathy in these surveillance films has to be her relationship with Steed over this two year period. It went through highs and lows and crackled with a dangerous energy as two highly accomplished professionals tackled deadly assignments in their own different ways. Steed tended to address Cathy as 'Mrs Gale' [WARL, CLAY, HAND] or – when he wanted be particularly charming or patronising – as 'My dear' [EGGS]; on occasion she would respond by calling him 'Mr Steed' [WARL].[34]

Although a serious academic who had seen a lot of tragedy in the world, Cathy's intel-lect allowed her to be sparklingly witty and also to have some fun – often at the expense of Steed. She would tease him by claiming that he had just purchased an outstandingly rare stamp (the fictitious British Guyana 1856 four cent black with four perfect margins) [MAUR] and would deliberately make play of similar sounding words in conversation with him [WHAL]. Cathy was also amused by his clumsy attempts at conjuring [DANE].

Patronising Cathy was a method which Steed found often made her perform at her best [BIGT]. By 1962, she already knew that when he offered her a treat such as champagne, the gift would come with strings attached [DISP]; being wined and dined by Steed was usually

---

[34] One dubious report suggests that Cathy would refer to Steed as 'John' on occasion. 'Quest for a Queen', *Look Westward/The Viewer*, 9 November 1963.

the 'prelude to a perilous adventure' [FLEE]. When Steed offered an apparently benevolent and philanthropic deal to help aspiring boxer Joey Frazer, although the young man was keen to accept Cathy astutely commented, 'I'd say there was a catch' [WHAL]. An offer of a holiday in the Bahamas came with the footnote that there was a 'little bit of trouble there' which he clearly needed her skills in sorting out [LOBS].

Their approaches to Steed's assignments differed considerably – such as how to win the co-operation of Mafia hit-man Carlo Bennetti [CONS]. There were some fiery exchanges between the pair when Steed attempted to use Cathy without her consent. Angrily she reminded him that she was 'not yours to swap and barter' on one occasion [CHAR], while on another occasion when he had set her up, her fury soon dissolved into laughter [FLEE]. Nevertheless, there were increasing outbursts where she would reprimand him for setting her up as a 'clay pigeon' [ROCK] and she was appalled when he left Joe Franks in the Central Control area of *HMS Zebra* to die with his own bomb [ZEBR]. 'You always manage to win something don't you Steed?' she berated him at the end of one mission. 'Whatever anybody else has lost, you pick up your purse and off you go. Well, I'm an anthropologist not one of your gang, and if you want my help again you'd better have a very good reason... You're using my expertise to cover your indolence.' [ELEP] However, when Cathy was cross with Steed's behaviour towards her or others, her wrath could move beyond the verbal and into the physical, such as a blow to his ribs [BULL].

One thing which particularly annoyed Cathy was when Steed took her for granted. When Steed commented that it was lucky he was able to contact her in France, Cathy retorted, 'That's a matter of opinion.' [PROP] He would make arrangements before he had an agreement from her [DWAR, EGGS] and deliberately direct her into peril to keep a trail warm [ROCK]. After a while, Steed started to drop any subtlety in getting Cathy involved and simply gave her instructions [MAUR]. For her part, Cathy was unfortunately too reliable and faithful, even coming out when called by him in the middle of the night [PROP]. She obligingly asked Steed what information he needed for 'his files' [EGGS], did the 'running around' for him [WOND] and undertook various menial tasks [HAND]. When it came to this undercover work, Steed trusted her instincts implicitly, telling her, 'If it interests you, it interests me.' [WHAL] However, she disliked it when she found Steed was letting her tell him information which he already knew [DWARF] or doing work which he had already done [ESPR].

On several occasions, Cathy would ask Steed to extricate her from the assignment when it seemed to be getting too dangerous – and Steed seldom made any moves to do this, confident in her abilities [DISP, BULL]. Similarly when Cathy was concerned about their placing of Joey Frazer at 'Pancho' Driver's gym, Steed persuaded her that the youth could not be in danger – but had unfortunately not realised that Joey was independent and inquisitive [WHAL]. When endangered by Steed because she was posing as his wife, she attempted to reason with Max Daniels and Lisa Denham that since she was not his spouse, killing her would be no threat to make him comply with their request to handle hot gems [ROCK]. Despite her often poor treatment at Steed's hands, Cathy was reluctant to make any direct move against Steed when asked to [WRIN] – although she clearly harboured potential suspicions about his motives [NUTS].

Cathy found Steed's continual attempts to make a play for women amusing, be it the air stewardess on the plane from Jamaica to Bogota [DISP] or a Covent Garden barmaid [WARL]. She and Steed would go out for trips to Bognor Regis [NUTS] and it seemed that of all Steed's associates, she was the one best placed to tell him apart from his double [SHAD].[35] She would also buy him gifts, such as a doll from Santiago which she called Juanita and suggested he could hang in the rear window of his car [DISP]. Cathy cared about Steed a great deal, but attempted not to let him see this. After one life-or-death confrontation for Steed, the undercover man airily noted that Cathy was shaking, believing that he had been killed. 'Well I never. You really thought you'd lost me?' he asked. 'Disappointing, isn't it?' retorted a furious Cathy who walked off, leaving Steed smirking behind her [CONS].

An unconfirmed report suggests that early in 1962, Cathy spent some months in Rome and Naples and met Denise Minton, the daughter of a government official.[36] Judging by the surveillance films and reports, it seems that Steed and Cathy started to work together again regularly in mid-1962 when One-Ten arranged for her to be Steed's cover on an assignment in which he had to take an attaché case to Santiago, taking over from courier Allan Baxter who had been murdered in Jamaica. Within hours of Baxter's death, Cathy had flown out to the West Indies from London, ready for her mission. Like Steed, Cathy seemed to be quite adept at donning an undercover persona as required. She passed herself off convincingly as a hotel chambermaid to get access to a hotel room occupied by a man called Monroe[37] in Lima, claiming in her fluent Spanish that she did not understand English [DISP].

At this point, Cathy's everyday work was a study into a series of rather interesting skulls in a section of the Fossil Room at the Natural History Museum which had been closed off to the public [WARL]. It seems that she was also lecturing at 'the Institute' some afternoons [BEAR]. It was her knowledge of the occult which caused Steed to seek her out to explain the strange, supernatural hold being exerted over inventor Peter Neville. With her monograph behind her, Cathy was able to investigate the work of Dr Cosmo Gallion, saying that she wanted to publish a similar work about black magic in England and hence gaining access to Gallion's rites. However, on this occasion she was reluctant to pursue her undercover work beyond a certain point – and she unwittingly became a subject in an ancient ritual from which she was thankfully able to save herself [WARL].

By mid-1962, Cathy was also very involved in doing what she could with missionary work, and was staying at the Hotel de Sanpere to discuss joining a medical expedition back to the Kuanajar province of Borneo with some friends in Toulon. It was while in France that she found her life interrupted by Steed who needed her help in acting as a courier for a mysterious package arriving from Tripoli at Marseilles airport [PROP].

When Steed required her to take out a contract on him to flush out Olaf Pomeroy, a killer known as 'Mr Teddy Bear', Cathy was given an elaborate cover story: although using her own name and background until 1960, since then she had supposedly traded in watches, operating from Berne, Stutgard and Turin, and was known as a contact called 'Silverfish' for a European syndicate; over the next 18 months, she had handled cash transactions

---

[35] Cathy was apparently concerned about what her neighbours thought regarding Steed's visits to her flat. 'I wish you would not drop in so early for breakfast,' she said in one report in 1963, 'The neighbours never see you arrive, but they see you leave. They'll start thinking...' 'That you're a very lucky girl!' finished Steed. 'Epidemic of Terror', *Look Westward/The Viewer*, 28 September 1963.

[36] *The Avengers* (Enefer), p12.

[37] Erroneously referred to as 'Muller' in the summary report.

totalling £2,500,000, ending with an arms deal financed by 'Sliverman' in Brussels; and with a visa and entry permit, she had been in the UK for four months to negotiate a hit on Steed on behalf of her superior, 'Jeffrey Bridges'. While travelling to Mantel's Hote for her first meeting with Pomeroy, Cathy claimed that she was from a preservation society when asking for directions at the village of Barton. After a powerful stand-off with Pomeroy, Cathy was free to depart for a conference in Paris the following week [BEAR].

In September, Cathy's next subject for publication was ceramics – comprising china and porcelain, such as Dresden – which involved research at both a ceramics museum and at Marlings, a Staffordshire pottery partly owned by her old friend Richard Marling. While visiting there, Cathy found herself caught up in a murder investigation which involved Steed's industrial security work [CLAY]. With this work completed, Cathy departed for a fortnight of wildlife photography of woodpeckers, and returned home in late October to be pitched immediately into Steed's investigation of the Litoff Organisation. Having checked into the stocks for the conglomerate, Cathy was further involved in the assignment, culminating in her posing as a lady from a dog kennels who returned the supposedly dead Great Dane Bellhound to the Litoff Offices [DANE].

At the start of November, Steed arranged for Cathy to become a major voting shareholder with the weapons manufacturer Anderson's Small Arms, and within a few days she owned a fifth of the voting stock. When Anderson himself appeared to commit suicide, one of Steed's long-standing friends carefully voted her onto the board to help her investigation. While applying her business skills to studying the company's affairs, Cathy looked for signs of gun-running to Africa; she was only too well aware what horrific events a supply of weapons could mean in that part of the world. Her beauty and intellect attracted the attentions of works manager Dougie Young who invited her for drinks on his houseboat. However, Cathy was far more interested in the power and charms of self-made success Henry Cade of Henry Cade Holdings, who was attempting to buy Anderson's. Cathy set up a deliberately flawed cover story to intrigue Cade; she claimed that she was Miss Catherine Gray from *Woman About London* who wanted to interview Cade as their 'Personality of the Month', knowing full well that Cade owned the title and would know she was a fake. This was another assignment where Cathy became increasingly concerned by the deaths around her at Anderson's. Either a potential murder victim or a key suspect ripe for arrest, she wanted to leave the company, despite Steed's reassurances that he would make sure she was safe as he watched her flat. Eventually Cathy identified the real killer – and agreed to a dinner date with Cade whom she respected [BULL].

To assist in understanding the security leaks from *HMS Zebra*, Steed arranged for Cathy to spend a week in her capacity as 'Dr Gale' working as an assistant to Professor Thorne who was making synthetic rubies. Although realising that this was vital work to clear an innocent Naval officer of an espionage charge, Cathy also commented that she would rather have been in Tahrain doing relief work. On this assignment, she attracted the attentions of Joe Franks, the editor of the local paper *Echo and Chronicle*, who ultimately turned out to be part of the espionage and sabotage ring [ZEBR].

Cathy was sent to jail as part of her next undercover role, posing as a thief convicted of handling £10,000 of stolen jewellery in association with a man called Palmer. This allowed her to occupy a cell with Miss Hilda Stern, a German executioner working for Intercrime, the organised criminal organisation Steed wanted to nail. While she did not mind the spell in HM Prison Holloway, Cathy was less than pleased when Steed – posing as her solicitor

– now asked her to swap places with Stern in a planned breakout. Cathy and Hilda had similar build and colouring and – having escaped posing as a warder – Cathy was able to pass as the hit-woman for some time, until the real Stern arrived on the scene just prior to Steed's final moves in the game [INTE].

Approaching Christmas 1962, Steed was not even being remotely subtle when he asked Cathy to undertake more work for him. Her next assignment saw her taking a job as an assistant at a stamp collector's shop which had been run by the late Mr Peckham – an establishment somehow connected with the death of one of Steed's colleagues in Rome. Cathy soon penetrated the philatelic façade for a right-wing organisation advocating 'new rule' and infiltrated one of their meetings to help Steed expose the sect [MAUR].

At the start of 1963, Cathy decided to have her lounge and bathroom re-decorated – possibly with a view to selling the apartment. However, when Steed arranged to have a painter come and undertake this work for her he had an ulterior motive, and wanted this process to take as long as possible. Thus Cathy would be kept away from her flat and be more amenable to moving into a house in Highgate to pose as his wife in an undercover investigation into a trade in illicit diamonds. Cathy took various possessions with her to Highgate, including a number of stuffed animal heads which she liked to keep an eye on and which Steed referred to as 'my wife's trophies' – suggesting that the lion, blue wildebeest and antelope may have been just some of Cathy's mementos from her hunting days in Africa. As 'Mrs Steed', Cathy became a target for the smugglers who wanted to force Steed to fence their stones. Although concerned about being used as bait – and at one point abandoning the Highgate home for her own flat – Cathy saw the assignment through, exposing those involved [ROCK].

Cathy was pleased to be able to return to her flat once work had been completed by Steed's cohort. Steed assisted her in attempting to mount the lion's head – which he disliked – over the door off the lounge, but did not fix it very securely [ROCK]. In the redecorated flat, the large photographic images either side of the front door had been removed, along with the cupboards and shelving which had been over the sink; this area had now been tiled. There was a busy, more decorative wallpaper in the lounge area, but the range of exotic firearms were still on the walls [BIGT].

By the start of 1963, Cathy had been conducting research which required her to undertake the translation of some dead languages – apparently in conjunction with some painting and restoration work on some urns at her flat. Thinking laterally, she arranged to perform some of this work using the powerful analytical skills of the Plato computer with the help of her associate, the astronomer Dr Farrow. While working at Plato, one scientist died and Cathy realised that one of the younger members of the team, Dr Jimmy Kearns, was being blackmailed. Kearns – a brash and loud young genius – invited her out for dinner and then a party on the first day they met, and while she initially declined she went out with him anyway as she found him amusing. Steed observed that Jimmy was 'not her type' and Cathy herself described Kearns as an 'objectionable young man'. However, she looked after him when he became incapable through drink on their night out, and later paid off his gambling debt to the unscrupulous club owner Nicky Broster. The saboteur at Plato was revealed to be Dr Farrow, who was electrocuted. With the Plato incident resolved, Cathy now acted as baby-sitter to Sheba, Steed's new pet whippet, while Steed himself was in the Middle East [BIGT].

Cathy put her flat on the market and it rapidly sold before she could find a new apartment to live in. Ever the gentleman, Steed offered to move out of his Westminster Mews flat and decamp to a nearby hotel so that she could live and work there – on the condition that she would provide him with 'slap-up bumper meals' [EGGS].

A few weeks later, Cathy was still working on the restoration of ancient pottery while temporarily living at Steed's flat; this appeared to be private research since she indicated that she was not currently working for anyone at the time. Cathy's scientific knowledge meant that she could pose as a journalist for *Galileo*, a fictitious magazine which looked at the 'personal side' of science and new ideas, and so interview Dr Ashe, a bacteriologist who had been the victim of a burglary; this piece of legwork was set up by Steed prior to Cathy's agreement. It transpired that the theft from Ashe had been of samples of the lethal culture verity prime and Cathy took a strong line on this potential germ warfare research, showing little mercy to Julius Redfern, who wished to trade the virus, and persuading Ashe to destroy his work [EGGS].

Cathy soon moved into her new rented [FLEE] flat at 14 Primrose Hill[38] [CAGE] with the help of Joey Frazer, a young man she had met at the Youth Club [WHAL]; the location of this new flat meant that – at a push – she could get to Steed's at Westminster Mews in 30 minutes [DWAR]. The apartment block had a concierge whom Steed could call when he was concerned about Cathy's whereabouts [LOBS].

In comparison to her previous abode, this new home was ultra-modern in design. The entrance to the Primrose Hill flat of the future was a sliding door [WHAL, CONC, SHAD, BROK] which Steed would get his umbrella stuck in and which caused him to use phrases like 'Open Sesame' [BROK], although he was clearly able to gain access to the flat in Cathy's absence [BROK]. Visitors would sound a buzzer [WHAL] which Cathy later replaced with chimes [UNDE] – activating an intercom so that Cathy, at the table by her couch, could determine who wanted to see her before pressing another button on the table to open the catch on the door [WHAL, SHAD]. A few months after she moved in, Cathy went a step further and had a television monitor set up to the right of the front door with a closed-circuit television camera to show her who her visitor was [NOV5, BROK]; Steed would chide her about this saying that he would 'Not be on your telly screen again, not till you've got colour' [BROK] and he generally found all the flat's 'buttons and buzzers' quite amusing [SHAD].

The walls of the flat seemed to be formed from metallic shutters, and the large central living area was sparsely populated with geometric furniture, most notably a backless L-shaped couch comprising one buttoned leather surface and a deep orange light upholstered seat with a linking pine table section [WHAL]. This was ideal for Cathy to recline on while reading. The low metallic table with the intercom and door controls could revolve in its frame and had a dual function; one side was a magnetic chess board while several telephone lines were adhered to the game board's reverse [CONC].[39] The sofa faced a modern-looking circular free-standing fireplace [ESPR].

There was also a wall phone with a message pad beneath it [SHAD]. In addition to this,

[38] An unconfirmed report gives the address as '14 Primrose Hill, NW1'. *The Avengers* (Enefer), p20.
[39] It has been suggested that the 'chessboard with magnetic pieces.... automatically revolved and offered a telephone fixed to its underside every time the bell rang,' although in the surveillance film Cathy seemed to activate this manually [CONC]. Timms, Bill. 'The Avengers Props', *The Avengers Annual*, 1965, p20.

Cathy had a black telephone [MAND] which she later replaced with a white set [ESPR]; her phone number was Primrose 0042 [WRIN].

To the left of the seating area as one entered were bookcases lined with Cathy's leather bound volumes (including, apparently, the *Encyclopaedia Britannica*), and close to this was a drinks cabinet which opened up to reveal sherry glasses lodged in its lid [WHAL], although she later kept her drinks on tables in another corner of the room [WOND]. Once again, Cathy's many ornaments were in evidence including her African carvings [WHAL]. Other items to have travelled with her included her reel-to-reel tape recorder [CONC] along with a microscope for analysis work [ROME]. Also in the living area were a hanging wicker chair, ceramic jars standing on shelves, three different balalaikas and an abstract print, all of which were close to the fireplace [ESPR]. Cathy also had a juicer and kept a box of cigarettes on the table [UNDE].

To view slides, Cathy had a white table with an overhead projector casting the images downwards onto it from above [NOV5]; she would use the screen projector, which had an automatic slide changer [MAND], to prepare her slides for her lectures [BROK]. Working in the flat on her anthropological studies, she would often have strange items such as animal skeletons in the living area [MAND]. While the living area originally had a smooth lino floor, this was later replaced by a red carpet [eg ESPR]; Cathy had this shampooed periodically, which meant – much to her annoyance – that she could not work on it for five hours [BATM].

Once inside the apartment, there were doors off to the right and left immediately before the main living room area [WHAL]. The door to the right led into the kitchen which had a wall intercom [UNDE] and all the usual facilities including the cooker and the fridge [WHAL]. It was in the kitchen that Cathy kept her gun [UNDE].

It was while Cathy was moving in that Steed met Joey and quickly realised that he could use the youth to infiltrate Pancho Driver's gym where he was on the trail of smuggled ambergris. Cathy was unhappy at this use of her young friend and did her best to protect him in the events that followed – and from which both she and Joey emerged unscathed [WHAL].

To establish if doomsday was approaching Earth in the form of a white dwarf, Steed again played upon Cathy's scientific experience and arranged for her to take the train down to Tor Point Observatory in Cornwall where he had established a cover story for her with the Ministry of Science. Cathy was to be assigned to observe Mars and study it at opposition. Under this cover, she claimed to have worked at Mandasor in India for two years. Cathy was able to set up a trap to expose those who had killed staff at Tor Point in order to gain from the potential worldwide panic [DWAR].

Cathy was glad to have had some time to herself in the spring, but around March, things went wrong for Steed. Somebody was needed to investigate the meditative retreat at Adelphi Park for signs of Professor Renter; on this assignment, Cathy initially posed as a lady collecting donations for the Architect's Friendly Society of Great Britain, and then later went undercover at Adelphi Park as an assistant matron whose history included a criminal record and a spell in jail [UNDE].

When the Mafia used a clown called Carlo Bennett to carry out an attempt on Steed's life, Cathy posed as a journalist to dig into Bennett's background at Gutman's Circus. Claiming to be researching a series of articles looking at how small businesses like the circus stood up to the moguls, Cathy lived at the circus for several days with Bennett's wife, and was instrumental in the apprehension of the Mafia drugs pusher Sica [CONS].

By the now, Cathy was back working at the British Museum, but took a trip up to the North East when Steed asked her to renew her friendship with Rosalind Waldner as a means of investigating Rosalind's father Oliver, a member of the board of the Reniston Group which seemed to be indulging in murder and sabotage. Cathy had not seen Rosalind in years, but arranged a 'chance meeting' with her and her father at a theatre in London. Cathy was initially convinced that Oliver could not be involved with the accidents which blighted Collier's Yard. Oliver, a widower, soon found her very attractive and after Cathy visited the Waldner's estate for a weekend he asked her to stay on. Rather worryingly, Oliver clearly felt that Cathy reminded him of his daughter and at one romantic moment addressed her as 'Ros'. Cathy agreed to stay – albeit on her terms – and realised that she too was strongly attracted to him. Brain Collier, Rosalind's boyfriend, warned her to beware of Oliver, which left her very unsure of herself. When Oliver's role in the murder of Brian's father was proven and he was taken away by the police, Cathy was very deeply upset and Steed did his very best to comfort her [HAND].

Cathy was particularly delighted when in June 1963 she was asked to take on the job of escorting the Russian concert pianist Veilko during a tour of the United Kingdom in association with Mr Peterson of the British Cultural Council. It was the first job of such potential that she had had since returning from Africa some years earlier, and was very annoyed to discover that she had been selected for the role simply because Steed had his own interests in Veilko rather than on her own intellectual merits [CONC].

By now, Cathy had sufficient clearance – even as an outsider – to be admitted to NUTSHELL, and helped to clear Steed's name in a security breach which her colleague had arranged [NUTS]. She was then undercover again at a luxurious London hotel, acting as the social director for the visit of the Emir Abdulla Akaba [CART]. Shortly after, Steed came under scrutiny from his own people yet again when a man Cathy did not know – Charles, one of Steed's superiors – appeared and informed Cathy that Steed had probably been replaced by an enemy double whom she had to kill [SHAD].

By now, Cathy's article *Mediaeval Influences on Fashion and Adornment* had been published in *Hers: For the Fashion Woman* and had apparently attracted the attention of Sir Cavalier Resagne, the greatest mediaeval historian in Europe, who invited Cathy to join him for a weekend at Resagne Hall in Devon. Steed drove her down to the remote house where she found that Sir Cavalier was away at a conference for SOHAA[40] and that she would be looked after by his ward, a bizarre girl called Ola Monsey-Chamberlain. The night that Cathy spent at Resagne Hall was a most unnerving one as she was confronted first by a bizarre man claiming to be a film producer... and then by elements of the day she had spent ensnaring Martin Goodman in Berlin just over ten years earlier. Having been released from prison by the authorities – who believed they could follow him to his hidden fortune – Goodman was now obsessed with Cathy and needed to extract a vicious revenge. This time, Cathy shot Goodman dead – and discovered that Steed had been aware of Goodman's presence, allowing her to walk into the trap while he lurked in the shadows [BEHI].

When outbreaks of Ergotism were detected, Steed had Cathy work for Universal Health and Famine Relief to investigate United Food and Dressings who were somehow

---

[40] Society Of Historians And Academics.

connected with the virus – which led to her being captured by the World Empire Party [ROME]. Cathy was happier to practice her motorcycling skills with the Salts in the vicinity of Verne Mill one weekend when she helped Steed investigate a strange jamming signal in the area [MOUS]. By mid-September, Steed was on the trail of smuggled gold passing through Blore Army Camp near Aldershot and arranged for the Committee of the Imperial War Museum to send Cathy there to spend two or three weeks cataloguing their Peninsular War artefacts. Cathy was glad of this different strand of work, and commented that her rent did not pay itself; Steed had offered an alternative means of income for her which she had turned down [FLEE].

At the end of September, Cathy took part in an elaborate entrapment scheme hatched by Steed in which he would apparently kill her and then expose the Lakin Brothers who were arranging 'briefs for murder' in which a murderer could walk out of court a free man. Cathy seemed to be about to expose Steed as an agent for the 'other side' called 'Jonno' when Steed apparently shot her as she stood on the deck of a motor launch on the Thames. After her faked demise, Cathy then donned a black wig and dark glasses in the guise of 'Mrs Pratchett' in the final moves of the game to trap the Lakins [BRIE].

Curious about the wealth bequeathed by his old batman Wrightson, Steed needed to investigate the company of Teale and Van Doren on Throgmorton Street at short notice – and Cathy was again persuaded into the role of undercover secretary to 'produce action'. By now Cathy had started to develop a more suspicious mind than she had before, suspecting Wrightson of being a forger, in response to which Steed quipped that she had now been 'dealing with the criminal fraternity too long' [BATM].

A three day holiday in Switzerland from Steed came with the usual strings attached, and Cathy's medical knowledge meant that she was volunteered as a researcher to Steed's old family friend Dr Spender during supervision of a corneal graft operation at the Mondblick Clinic. While at the clinic, Cathy claimed to have been in biochemistry research for five years, adding that she gave her last diagnosis 'a long time ago' [SECO].

In between the security work, Cathy still found time for some lecturing at the London Institute of Anthropology, such as a slide-show which she gave about African tribes – many of which, as she pointed out to Steed, were naked. This was concurrent with Steed's investigation into the security of Bridlington's Research Centre, and again Cathy found herself undercover – this time posing as an official from Whitehall, the sponsors for the confidential work at Bridlington's [BROK].

As 1963 wore on, Cathy seemed to become involved more and more in the affairs of the Department and being co-opted by Steed into taking on covert investigations. It seems that some time around the middle of the year, she was – at least temporarily – formally employed again by the Department on a regular basis, while maintaining her everyday profession in anthropology. 'She is now a *professional* undercover agent,' emphasised the Department's 1963 report on her.[41] Her standing in the espionage community was extremely high. As far as the opposition were concerned, she was second from the top on their wanted list behind one 'JB' (possibly Steed's former Eton bully) in 1964, although the enemy agent Martin had her removed as he had admired her for 'some time' [CHAR]. Also in February 1964, she was allowed to read the PANSAC file compiled on former operative General Andrew Sharp [OUTS].

---

[41] *The Complete Avengers*, p59.

Cathy was pivotal to a scheme hatched by herself and Steed to entrap John P Spagge in the theft of £4,000,000 in gold bullion. Having learnt about the gold market and obtained access to the security vaults, Cathy set up a heist – but was then arrested. Although it seemed that Cathy had been drugged and imprisoned in Holloway by Inspector Grant for the murder of Spagge, this was in fact a test by the gang, led by Abe Benham, who aimed to pull off the raid. Steed remained in control of the situation and rescued Cathy from the rest of the criminals, having exposed Spagge [CAGE].

After the death of newly-elected South East Anglia MP Michael Dyter at the end of October, Steed's suspicions led him to having Cathy stand for election in Dyter's place – offering to pay the deposit himself and becoming her election agent. The scheme had the desired effect in locating a stolen nuclear missile, planned to destroy Westminster on Guy Fawkes' Night [NOV5].

Trying to establish the origin of counterfeit medical supplies bearing the hallmarks of Willis Sopwith Pharmaceuticals Ltd, Cathy posed as a new customer for the pharmaceutical company, claiming that she was opening a new branch in Cork. However, she then revealed that this was merely a ruse to get to see Geoffrey Willis; she now claimed to be a business efficiency consultant for the 1960s who could save him money (for example, 23 per cent on typing an invoice), providing that her firm could be given the run of the company. Her fee would be a thousand guineas. Cathy's other cover involved investigating action painter Frank Leeson by claiming to have previous modelling experience. During a fight at a print works, Cathy received a black eye, resulting in her wearing a patch over her right eye for a few days [MEDI].

Concerned about ivory smuggling, Steed asked Cathy to become the new resident zoological director at Noah's Ark, a private zoo run by 'Noah' Marshall. This assignment reminded Cathy of much of the wildlife she had seen when hunting in Kenya [ELEP]. Cathy then spent some time in Paris and, on returning, discovered that Steed was attempting to locate Hal Anderson, a missing colleague. When Steed was subsequently apprehended as a double agent by the evidence of Anderson himself, Cathy again found herself working with Charles and was informed of the grave situation. It was Cathy who penetrated the Unit where Steed was undergoing brainwashing by the Wringer – the true double agent – and managed to rescue him, receiving a minor gunshot wound to the right arm from an agent called Bethune as the pair escaped [WRIN].

As usual, Cathy went away for Christmas, this time spending the festive period quietly in Marrakech. When she returned, she found herself trailing Steed when he knew he was walking into a trap on New Year's Eve. A fancy dress party on a train was left stranded at a disused station, and Cathy – disguised first as a monk and then in the highwayman costume worn by fashion editor Dorothy Wilson – was on hand to help Steed expose those attacking Britain's defence systems [DRES].

In the New Year, Steed interrupted Cathy's skeletal studies to ask her to investigate the church of St Alban's at Tinbey in Cornwall where a former colleague of his had been buried under strange circumstances. Her cover here was as a writer compiling an article on English country churchyards for an American magazine [MAND]. When Steed was appointed to look after the race horse Sebastian II for a visiting oil Sultan, Cathy became involved in the strange goings-on at Meadows Stables. In turn Cathy used her mathematical skills to secure employment with unscrupulous bookmaker Tony Heuston – and named her wage of £100 a week [TROJ].

When Steed went undercover to crack the ecclesiastically masked crimes of Bibliotek, Cathy used her expertise with rare dolls to have one such item repaired at a dolls' hospital [WOND]. When General Sharp of Aburain visited London for talks with the British Government, Cathy was placed in charge of looking after him and arranging a penthouse suite for him. Unaware that she was also being used as a decoy in a scheme hatched by Steed and a fellow agent called Mark Charter, Cathy was also none too pleased about dealing with Mr Quilpie, the head of PANSAC. It seems that Cathy was still dabbling with ceramics at this time – baking a pot in Steed's oven at Westminster Mews [OUTS].

Deaths of opposition agents in London which were not caused by the Department led Steed into a truce with his old rival Keller and, in the spirit of co-operation, the two sides worked together to root out the common enemy. Cathy was therefore partnered with an agent called Martin – until he vanished [CHAR]. She was next involved in an investigation into 'accidental' deaths at the Highland Guard regiment at Maroon Barracks in South Kensington, where she received the unwelcome attentions of Captain Trench whom she found a 'crushing bore'. At a formal function, Steed introduced Cathy to Brigadier General Sir Ian Stuart-Bollinger, who had a plan to restore the rightful heir of the Scots throne to power. Sir Ian fell for a faked family background which Cathy had concocted with the curator of the Bruce Museum in Kinross, and proclaimed her as Queen Anne II as part of his proposed military coup which Steed was able to avert [ESPR].

Cathy's final firmly-recorded assignment was apparently her last regular liaison with Steed, and concerned an investigation into drug smuggling via lobsters and chess pieces. Captured by Quentin Slim, the head of the smuggling operation, Cathy became engaged in a fight in a coastal boat hut when a fire broke out. For a while, Steed feared that Cathy had perished in the blaze – but the charred remains were in fact those of Slim and Cathy had suffered only minor burns [LOBS].

Nevertheless, the experience had shown Cathy that she no longer needed to have her life threatened for Steed's games. When Steed then presented her with a swimsuit for a holiday in the Bahamas the next day, adding that there was a 'little bit' of trouble there, Cathy finally rounded on Steed and informed him that he had asked too much. Ultimately, when Cathy finally said, 'Goodbye Steed,' it was clear that she did not have to put up with the risks any more [LOBS].

One report suggests that when she left Steed, Cathy had gone back to Africa to study mountain gorillas[42] and had worked towards saving the endangered species, establishing the first gorilla sanctuary at the invitation of her old student friend M'Begwe, now Prime Minister of Katawa. However, by December 1964, Cathy was at the Fort Knox bullion depository in Kentucky, for reasons which Steed could not fathom when he received her Christmas card [XMAS].[43] Files were still being maintained on Cathy by the Department amongst their top secret papers in 1969 [PAND] and there were also three 22423 MA files about her in the archives in 1977 (including 246 and DM) [DEAD]. Cathy apparently lived in Surrey by 1969, having purchased an old mansion house there. According to an unconfirmed report, six months after moving in, she was again involved briefly in Department affairs.[44]

---

[42] *Too Many Targets*, p45.

[43] It has been suggested that this was somehow connected with an operation involving Steed's old Etonian bully, James Bond, but there is no clear evidence to connect Cathy with these events.

[44] *Too Many Targets*, p44.

In 1976, Steed still had a colour photograph of Cathy on display in the lounge at his country house [CARD].

'Cathy Gale was a child of her times,'[45] commented her friend Honor Blackman while Patrick Macnee's memories of the time were that 'Mrs Gale was a spy, a crusader, and a friend.'[46] 'I know she's indestructible,' observed Steed of his first regular female partner in crime [PAND]. In many respects, Cathy Gale had been a far more well-rounded and expert operative than the supposed professional whom she had inducted into the service so many years earlier. For the Steed of the early 1960s, she was fundamentally far too good a partner – and her departure from his life brought about some significant changes in his approach to life as he finally began to understand that he could not use people indefinitely for his own ends.

---

[45] *Blind in One Ear*, p234.
[46] *Blind in One Ear*, p231.

MISS VENUS SMITH

One of Steed's less frequent helpers, Miss Venus Smith was an aspiring singer around 1962-63 whom the undercover man used – or more accurately exploited – on at least six assignments. Possibly more. 'Blonde, medium height, about 20,' was how Steed once summed her up [MIRR] while on another occasion he claimed to recognise her by her legs [DECA]. What he did not mention so often was that he played upon her keenness to take part in something exciting, nor did he dwell on her horrified reactions to the events which she became ensnared by.

It seems that Venus was born around 1942 in the north west of England; certainly she seemed to have a permanent home back in Manchester [MIRR] in spring 1963 while working in London and on the continent in her professional capacity. She was in fact born on board a barge owned by her father [FROG], possibly a gentleman involved in the transport business along the Manchester ship canal. This left her with a fondness for the water, since she always found being on her father's boats was 'great fun' [FROG]. On her 18th birthday, her mother gave her a very ornate and distinctive brooch which became one of her most treasured possessions [MIRR].

According to a 1962 dossier[1] prepared by the Department about Venus because of her frequent associations with Steed, Venus's father was indeed a barge owner, and her childhood was spent travelling England's canals. She had two big brothers who were both quite a bit older than her and who emigrated when she was 12. After a sporadic education, she decided to leave home at the age of 17. Settling in London, she worked with amateur and semi-pro jazz groups, before graduating to club work. Strangely, this dossier referred to one of Venus's most notable attributes being her '*alert commonsense*'[2] – a trait which is not altogether evident in the six existing surveillance films that show her with Steed. It further noted, '*She likes Steed*, and the aura of mystery surrounding him is an intriguing attraction for her. There is NO suggestion of any 'affair' between them. If anything she probably regards Steed as a 'special' elder brother.'[3]

It seems that Venus started singing on a professional basis around 1961, commenting in early 1963 that she had been 'a couple of years in show business' [BOX]. At this time she roomed at the YWCA in Victoria where she knew Kathleen Sutherland... a friendship later

---

[1] *The Complete Avengers*, p35-36.

[2] *The Complete Avengers*, p35. Their emphasis.

[3] *The Complete Avengers*, p36. Their emphasis.

known to – and exploited by – Steed since Kathleen's father was a retired Army General [BOX]. By 1962, Venus had an agent whom she liked all her business affairs to be arranged by, with proper contracts [DECA, FROG, SCHO] and whom Steed would sometimes use as an excuse to get rid of her [SCHO]. She had digs with a landlady in London, just a bus ride away from the Balkan Embassy in Kensington [DECA].

In terms of her professional approach, Venus never had a drink before an audition as she was aware that it affected her breathing [DECA], and also sprayed her throat periodically [SCHO]. She would generally rehearse at her venue during the day prior to her evening performances [DECA], but also practised her scales in the odd half-hour between numbers [FROG]. Although she smoked cigarettes on occasion [DECA, REMO], she would sometimes refuse, saying that she was thinking of her voice [SCHO]. In addition to singing, Venus could also turn her hands to performing numbers on the piano [REMO, FROG].

By the time Venus was old enough to be manipulated by Steed for his own ends, she was a young, blonde and petite lady whom Ted East, one of the students at St Luke's, found 'delectable' [SCHO]. It is clear that she had already known Steed for some time prior to the first surveillance film of her unwittingly helping him on a case [DECA] but, unlike most of Steed's cohorts, the exact circumstances of their initial encounter are unknown. She was clearly aware that he was involved in security and undercover work of some sort – but not entirely sure about the organisation that he worked for. Unfortunately, judging by the gullible way in which she fell for many of the supposedly innocent offers of work he arranged for her, it has to be said that she was not one of Steed's shrewdest compatriots.

One thing that is notable about Venus in particular is her accent, which changed from situation to situation. In the earlier surveillance footage – which seems to date from the second half of 1962 – Venus performed and spoke in a clear and well enunciated form of the Queen's English, no doubt cultivated to appeal to the clientele of the more refined night-clubs in London where she made her living [DECA]. However, as time wore on this accent started to slip – particularly when she was 'off stage'.

Although somewhat gullible, Venus had a fiery spirit when roused [DECA] and was indignant when people started to question her [FROG]. Like any girl, she did not like being stood up on a date [DECA] and Steed once remarked that it was most unlike Venus to be late [MIRR].

Venus could be very brave in confrontation, openly accusing a woman of stealing her precious brooch from her, and later confidently telling the thief's cohort that she would not be afraid to go to the police [MIRR]. In rare situations, she was also prepared to have a go at mild physical violence, and Steed once had to stop her hitting a publican over the head [SCHO]. Otherwise, Venus was generally a nervous woman, whether it was the childish horrors of the Ghost Tunnel at Wonderland [MIRR] or simply Steed creeping around back-stage at the Gemini night-club [BOX]. Steed would often help her find the courage she needed, such as when she was asked to take part in a disappearing trick which had previously proved fatal [BOX].

Venus was rather compassionate, once helping a stricken wife to get a job as a cloak-room girl at the night-club where she was performing [DECA]. Likewise, she did not want Green, a luckless student from St Luke's College, to get in trouble with the police when she found him searching her room at an inn called The Volunteer [SCHO].

One of Venus's most notable habits – especially after she reinvented herself early in 1963 – was to gabble away when she was slightly nervous. When Steed was carefully and quietly breaking into a studio using his professional lock-picking techniques, the eager – and ignored – Venus issued forth a torrent of impractical advice on how he could have gained entry via the window using brown paper (doubtless learnt from a second-rate television series or movie). She then offered to whistle to him if the police came while he was inside – an option which he declined in the gentlemanly manner [SCHO]. Similarly, when confined with a missing cipher clerk, she vented her frustration about Steed tricking her yet again in a torrential monologue, and later continued to chatter away while she and Steed were tied up and he worked on the bonds to free them [MIRR].

Venus was easily pleased, be it winning a large teddy bear or watching the 'Parisian Can Can' on a What-The-Butler-Saw machine, for which an amused Steed loaned her a coin [MIRR]. When going abroad for the first time to the Riviera, she was also delighted to spend as much time as possible on the beach [REMO].

Her interests did not seem to include knitting [MIRR] or photography; when Venus was loaned Steed's camera, many of her shots were overexposed and she commented that talk like 'f8 at 50' was all double Dutch to her [MIRR]. When she started to travel outside the UK, it seems she made an attempt at mastering other languages, using the *Learn Cantonese* book which came with taped instructions [FROG].

When performing, Venus tended to wear dark sleeveless dresses, often of a spangly material which were the general vogue on the night-club circuit [DECA, REMO]; these tight garments left no room for 'hidden weapons' as someone commented [DECA] and one had a daring bare midriff [REMO]. When out and about, meetings with prospective employers would see her in a fur coat [DECA], while she also wore a dark leather coat and a neck scarf [DECA]. She also liked to wear high-heeled shoes [DECA, REMO, BOX] and dark slacks [REMO, FROG].

As she started to reinvent herself for the happening new decade and the spread of the Mersey beat, Venus began to dress far more casually off stage. A towelling smock kept her warm between acts [BOX] while she liked to wear a distinctive striped top [BOX, SCHO] with either a dark skirt [BOX] or tight jeans [SCHO, MIRR].

One of Venus's favourite outfits was a tartan V-neck jacket with a chain fastening which she wore with a dark polo neck and skirt [BOX, MIRR]. Many of her outfits were now quite loose and bohemian, including a large duffel coat-type affair [SCHO] or a baggy cardigan with large buttons [SCHO]. In the Mediterranean she wore sandals [FROG]. A jaunty fire-fighter-style cap was one of her frequent accessories [SCHO, MIRR], along with a top which had a striped V-neck section [MIRR, FROG]. By 1963, Venus's clothes 'were all Beatles-type gear'[4] recalled her friend and show-biz colleague, actress-agent Julie Stevens.

At the clubs, Venus's performance outfits remained glittery and show-biz [BOX] while for the carefree atmosphere of Rag Week at St Luke's she would perform in pyjamas and mortarboard [SCHO]; at night she wore striped pyjamas [FROG].

Sometimes Venus wore a ring on her right hand and was also partial to brooches [DECA, REMO]. She occasionally wore sparkling earrings [REMO], painted her toe nails [FROG] and did not like to use face cream if it smelt so strongly of chlorine that it reminded her of a swimming pool [SCHO]. Other accessories for her included a dark handbag [DECA, REMO] and dark glasses when in the Riviera [REMO].

Although she sometimes refused a drink when working [BOX], Venus was partial to

---

[4] Stocker, Andrew and Tipton, Paul, 'From Venus, With Love', *DWB*, Issue 89, May 1991, p19.

champagne when Steed was buying [DECA, REMO, BOX] while, left to her own devices and finances, would rather order pineapple juice [REMO, SCHO] or a citron pressé [REMO]. When held captive she was happy to drink Coke [MIRR]. She took tea without milk or sugar [SCHO, MIRR] and while at the Wonderland amusement arcade bought a toffee apple and one of the little cakes which she enjoyed eating [MIRR].

Venus's lateral thinking was not good and she was highly confused by Steed's ploy to leave a blank, fake letter supposedly sent to her by Richard Davies before his 'suicide' at St Luke's College in an attempt to bring their opponents out into the open [SCHO]. However, in many cases, she was eventually able to reason out a situation for herself [BOX]. Venus was not terribly observant; only after being incarcerated with Victor Trevelyan for several hours did she recognise him as the missing man she had just photographed [MIRR]. She was thankfully better at recognising voices, no doubt due to her acute skills with sound [BOX].

Early on in her career, around summer 1962, Venus's night-club routines were accompanied by the Art Morgan trio. This group comprised a double bass, percussion and a piano – the latter played by a bespectacled musician called Dave [DECA, REMO, BOX] who did not like to drink too early in the evening [REMO]. Dave's playing was said to be very introspective and inventive, like when the jazz pianist and composer Bill Evans played the work of the legendary Illinois trumpet player Miles Davis [REMO]. Dave, who was partial to the odd cigarette, also played the jazz of Dave Brubeck [REMO], along with other dance music numbers [BOX], tunes which were used concurrently as songs by Millicent Martin on the satirical programme *That Was The Week That Was* [REMO] and even an arrangement based on Peter Sellers and Sophia Loren's 1960 novelty single 'Goodness Gracious Me', composed by Herbert Kretzmer and Dave Lee [REMO]. Venus's Department dossier indicated that her night-club associates knew her as 'Vee'[5] although there is no evidence of this in the surveillance films; Dave would occasionally address Venus as 'Julie' which was presumably a nickname [REMO].

For the night-clubs, Venus's set pieces included romantic jazz-based pieces such as Al Dubin and Harry Warren's 'You're Getting To Be A Habit With Me' [DECA] which had been sung by the likes of Frank Sinatra and Guy Lombardo, Duke Ellington's 'I Got It Bad (And That Ain't Good)' [DECA] which was associated with Ella Fitzgerald (who shared many songs with Venus's repertoire), 'I May Be Wrong (But I Think You're Wonderful)' [REMO] by Henry Sullivan, Harry Ruskin, Milton Ager and Jack Yellen from the 1929 musical comedy 'John Murray Anderson's Almanac', Ralph Blane and Hugh Martin's 'An Occasional Man' [REMO] sung by Rosemary Clooney in the 1955 film *The Girl Rush*, 'Sing for Your Supper' (on which Venus also played the piano) [REMO] by the legendary combination of Richard Rodgers and Lorenz Hart which appeared in *The Boys from Syracuse* in 1938, Billy Reid's 1946 composition 'It's a Pity to Say Good Night' [BOX] which had been another popular number for Ella Fitzgerald, as had been Cole Porter's 'It's De-Lovely' [BOX] which had originally been written for the 1936 show *Red Hot and Blue*. Her style with all these numbers was a very personal one, frequently angling herself to sing directly to certain members of the audience.

In summer 1962, Venus was working at a night-club in London where she went on at 11.00 pm and sang through to the cabaret at 1.00 am. It was on this occasion that Steed

---

5 *The Complete Avengers*, p36. This is how Venus is referred to in some of the transcripts [eg REMO].

tempted her with her first overseas tour (at this stage, Venus did not even have a passport), saying that if she visited the international figure Yakob Borb, he could organise her a series of performances in the Balkans. This was – as proved usual with Steed – nothing more than a flimsy cover and, on arriving at the Balkan Embassy, Venus found that she was in fact being interviewed as Borb's private secretary and effectively became imprisoned in his office. When she finally asked about the suggested tour of his country, Borb laughed at her. Now she understood why Steed had asked her not to refer to her knowing him – since Steed was dealing with security arrangements for the visiting Borb – and was less than happy [DECA].

Borb himself took quite a shine to Venus, taking her out to a quiet restaurant before her show and having flowers flown in from his nurseries for her before asking her to live in a flat upstairs at his Kensington Embassy. Claiming to hate being alone, Borb wanted her to go with him to resorts in Switzerland, Monte Carlo, Venice and Palm Springs, and had even arranged passports for them both under the names 'Mr and Mrs Jacob Smith'. However, Venus was by now a very unwilling participant – and Borb's true colours as a killer and embezzler were revealed shortly before he was executed by one of his own countrymen. Nevertheless, Steed treated the whole incident – which saw Venus being taking captive and threatened – very lightly, despite her protests [DECA].

By the autumn, Venus (who by now must have had a passport) and her trio had landed a good contract playing overseas at Les Centaurs in the Riviera venue of Aluda where she was booked to appear twice nightly. Two weeks into the booking, a film producer in the audience one night took an interest in her and invited her to come to the Homeric Studios for a screen test. It seems that nothing came of this flirtation with the silver screen – and worse was to come when Steed turned up again and found himself locked in a battle of wits with the organised killers behind Les Centaurs. Venus was not pleased to see Steed again, and initially suspected that he was responsible for her screen test, a notion which Steed appeared to dismiss. However, Venus soon forgot her distrust of this man who had nearly got her killed at their last meeting, and he made an empty promise to leave her alone. When Steed trotted out an unlikely cover story about looking to buy a night-club similar to Les Centaurs and wondering how much such an establishment cost to run, Venus immediately swallowed the bait and offered to snoop around and look at the business's books for Steed – with Steed's explicit request that she should not do this ensuring that she would disobey him and so help with his investigation [REMO].

Nevertheless, when Venus was later endangered by the hit mob run by the club's owner Bug Siegel, Steed became very angry and concerned for her, and did his best to hasten her safe return to London. Siegel forced his unwelcome attentions on Venus, but the spirited singer grabbed his face and repelled his advances most effectively. Because Steed was eventually forced to shoot Siegel, there was no hope of Venus getting paid. With no money, she was thrown out of her hotel room and lost her ticket back to London [REMO].

Soon after the New Year, Venus was working at the Gemini Club in the Piccadilly area of London where the owner, a retired Major, referred to her as 'The Evening Star' [BOX]. This job had come somewhat out of the blue when she had been out of work, but her booking had in fact been stage-managed again by Steed who wanted to investigate further a strange death at the Gemini less than a fortnight beforehand. Venus, again, never connected the killing and her sudden job until considerably later on, and was surprised when Steed arrived one night for one of her performances – although as far as the Major was concerned, she was Steed's client. The Major was delighted with Venus's work and was considering extending her booking since her performances had brought the customers back to his establishment in the wake of the earlier tragedy [BOX].

Once more, Steed used Venus as a pawn in his investigation about the leak of confidential information, handing her the address of her old friend Kathleen Sullivan and suggesting that they should get together again – while himself posing as a masseur to the crippled General Sutherland. When magician Gerry Weston asked Venus to take part in the disappearing cabinet routine which had already proved fatal, Venus was reluctant but agreed at a nod from Steed. Furthermore, Steed also used her to have himself recommended to the suspicious faith-healer Dr Gallam under the guise of a man called Thackeray [BOX].

And now, by early 1963 the music scene started to change. When 'Please Please Me' by the Beatles hit the charts in January of that year, the 1960s had truly arrived – all of a sudden the more casual approach to rock and pop music was in, and even Northern accents suddenly sounded cool. By the end of 1962 and her gig at the Gemini Club, Venus had anticipated the approaching trends and already changed her image. Her little blonde pageboy bob had been trimmed back severely to her scalp to give her a far more modern look.[6] Her Mancunian roots now started to show more and more as she dropped her old facade. Phrases like 'I'll get me coat' [BOX] and 'Buzz off' [SCHO] were now dripping from her lips, and frequently she fell back on her Northern dialect when she needed to sound tough and determined [MIRR] or when she was putting up resistance to questioning [FROG].

As Venus changed her image, she also changed her backing group [SCHO, MIRR, FROG]. The new trio again consisted of bass, drums and piano and worked on Venus's new engagements as she placed her feet on the lowest rungs of the pop chart ladder with some recordings. The new group offered a wider range, with anything from their own compositions 'Boogie Twist' [SCHO] and 'Pots Blues' [FROG], through Vincent Youman's 1950 number 'Tea for Two Cha Cha' from *No, No Nanette* at an open-air festival [SCHO] to a burst on the bongos in a recording studio [MIRR].

The romantic jazz theme of Venus's performances decreased and she started to cover a wider variety of styles to suit different occasions – from period through to folk. At St Luke's rag week she performed the appropriate Charleston 'The Varsity Drag' (composed by BG DeSylva, Ray Henderson and Lew Brown for the 1927 revue *Good News*) as a bit of fun, along with Charles Strouse and Lee Adams's 'Put on a Happy Face' from the 1960 Broadway musical *Bye Bye Birdie* [SCHO]. Working her passage on board the yacht of 'Archipelago' Mason, she performed numbers which were rooted in traditional American melodies such as a jazzed-up version of the folk song 'Hush Little Baby' and 'The Lips That Touch Kippers Shall Never Touch Mine' – a reworking by Burnaby Long of 'The Lips That Touch Liquor Shall Never Touch Mine', an American temperance song composed by Geo T Evans in 1874 [FROG].

It seems that Venus's booking at the Gemini Club was not extended that long, or else she was able to drop out of it for another week's work which had been arranged by Steed – although this time quite openly. In late January there was a vacancy for entertainment

---

[6] Actress Julie Stevens – who worked with Venus in her professional capacity during this period – commented – that 'her hair was cut short by Vidal Sassoon.' Stocker, Andrew and Tipton, Paul, 'From Venus, With Love', *DWB*, Issue 89, May 1991, p19.

during the Rag Week Festivities of St Luke's College. Steed was assigned on a mission to Cairo and he asked Venus to take the booking while also keeping an eye on one Richard Davies for him. Venus was delighted by the job as singing in the open of the college quad made a change from night-clubs [SCHO].

Venus could also not resist a quick impromptu performance when the moment was right, such as singing and dancing to the traditional Jamaican calypso 'Yellow Bird'[7] when it was plucked out by student Ted East on his Spanish guitar at St Luke's quad [SCHO]. Indeed, Venus was quite keen on the odd display of terpsichory now and again, whether it was dancing to jazz at a night-club with Steed [DECA, BOX] or a cha-cha-cha with the students at St Luke's Rag Week ball [SCHO]. Even then, Steed cut in on Ted East so that he could dance with young Venus [SCHO].

By May[8], Venus had set about recording some of her performances professionally for release on record, and with the trio had booked several days in studio with a producer called Peter; these sessions were generally early in the morning (when Venus was not used to singing) or at 4.30 pm in the afternoon. The numbers which Venus and the group recorded were 'There's Nothing Like Love', a piece by Jule Styne and Leo Robin from the 1955 film *My Sister Eileen* which Jackie Wilson had recorded in 1962, and also Herbert Hughes' arrangement of 'I Know Where I'm Going', a melody from the 1945 musical of the same name which stemmed from the traditional folk song 'Handsome Winsome Johnny'. It was during one of these sessions that the birthday brooch given to her by her mother was stolen from her dressing room by a woman called Betty. Shortly afterwards, Steed got her a replacement – this time an astrological sign for Venus which she thought was 'gorgeous' [MIRR].

Concurrent with the fledgling record career, Steed again used Venus as a dupe to investigate a missing cipher clerk at the Wonderland amusement arcade. Giving Venus his camera and his pet whippet Sheba, Steed asked her to walk his dog and also get some photographs of the arcade for a clearly fictitious friend who was supposedly opening up his own arcade near Manchester. Venus was less than convinced by this, but did the dirty deed anyway – thus implicating herself in more espionage activity which she later resented. Captured by Strong and his cohorts, Venus was delighted to see Steed when he was brought in as a fellow prisoner, and he in turn was deeply concerned about her [MIRR].

The next surveillance film showing Venus involved in one of Steed's missions does not make it clear whether they are thrown together by luck or Steed's continual manipulation. The latter seems more likely as Venus was amazed to be flown out to perform on the luxury yacht of 'Archipelago' Mason in Bali as it headed for the Mediterranean. Mason was extremely impressed by her renditions for his guests, and – on hearing of her love of barges – offered her one of the 300 he owned for singing so splendidly. It was also on this voyage that a Greek diver called Ariston (or 'Risto') attempted to chat her up, finding her new bubbly down-to-Earth persona attractive because she was not at all 'stuck up' [FROG].

Steed became a stowaway on the yacht, hiding in Venus's cabin. When the chanteuse discovered her undercover friend, her immediate reaction from bitter experience was that

---

[7] Arranged by Marilyn Keith, Alan Bergman and Norman Luboff in 1957, this had been recorded by the Mills Brothers in 1959 and Lawrence Welk in 1961.

[8] Steed makes reference to taking Venus to the Richmond Horse Show which takes place at the start of June.

he had set her up on the job. When he teased her, Venus became cross, complaining, 'I'm the one who's always getting lumbered mate!' Nevertheless, she supplied Steed with a cover story for Mason, claiming that he was her agent. Determined not to share her cabin with him, Venus made Steed turn around while she got changed. In return, Steed deliberately used her to send a clearly coded cable to a supposed aunt in Rottingdene – a ploy which Venus once again went along with and which ended up with her almost being killed as a guinea pig in an experiment [FROG].

It is not entirely clear why Venus stopped working with Steed. Viewing the films, it would be hoped that she finally had the common sense to stop being manipulated any longer and was able to resist any more of his avuncular charms. It seems that Venus's record career never took off for although her namesakes such as Keeley, Jimmy and even 'Whistling' Jack all attained a small share of 1960s chart success, the most thorough searches of record catalogues for the decade fail to indicate that Venus's recordings of 'There's Nothing Like Love' and 'I Know Where I'm Going' ever made it to the record stores, let alone the hit parade. There are unconfirmed reports that from the mid-1960s to mid-1970s, she was using her vocal talents as a presenter on children's television, and then that she had moved into the field of theatrical management. Certainly, it would be reasonable to believe that her life would be just as interesting and most definitely less dangerous away from the influence of John Steed.

20

MRS EMMA PEEL

'She's well and truly emancipated is that one,' commented Carl, an enemy agent, after coming off worst in a close encounter with Mrs Emma Peel [TREA]. The lady most readily associated with Steed and described as his 'close friend' [TWOS] was a particularly famous person in her own right. 'British through and through' [CORR], she was 'tall, slim [and] very attractive' [SURF] with a remarkable depth to her eyes [BRIM]. However, beneath her beauty and looks there was a vast intelligence and strength of character. Actress Dame Diana Rigg, who knew Emma from her association with Steed and Patrick Macnee, knew that she was 'intelligent, independent and capable of looking after herself'[1], a true inspiration to other women.[2] The code-names for Emma suggested by Major Robertson were most appropriate: Diana (Roman goddess of the moon and hunt) or Athene (a Greek goddess personifying reason and wisdom) [DANG]. And when offered to the highest bidder as Lot 17 by Art Incorporated, Emma was described as carrying 'most of the disposition of Western defence bases in her head, is a cipher expert of no mean ability, and would be a splendid addition for any intelligence system anywhere in the world... an outstanding example of British paltritude and learning.' Indeed, Emma would have fetched £117,000 from a foreign power [AUNT]. 'Emma Peel was extremely important in my life and I will always be grateful to her,'[3] commented Diana Rigg of the lady who had become a role model to a generation.

It seems that Emma was born around 1938.[4] Emma's father was Sir John Knight, who

---

[1] *The Avengers Companion*, p16.

[2] Indeed, as well as inspiring a generation of women as the head of Knight Industries, Emma also inspired at least two pop songs in tribute to her; *Emma Peel* written by Carl Funk and Dave Kincaid, performed by the Seattle club band The Allies (*Allies*, Light LS 5864, March 1982) and *Miss Emma Peel* [sic] by Santa Barbara pop-rock artists Dishwalla (*Pet Your Friends*, A&M Records 31454 0319 2, 1995).

[3] *The Avengers Companion*, p16.

[4] According to a press article about Emma in the *Daily Mirror* on 5 April 1965 which said she was 'Age: 26'. In ...*deadline* in late 1965, Macnee gave her age as '27' (p44) and again in *Dead Duck* (p14) in May 1966. Anthony Hussey (alias 'John Garforth') later gave her age as '28' in his unconfirmed reports. *The Floating Game*, p30; *Heil Harris!*, p23. The newspaper headline about Emma being 21 at the time of her father's death which she saw in Professor Keller's display was a fake – dated Tuesday 18 January 1966 [JACK]. In the 1998 film, the big-screen depiction of Emma agreed that she was a Gemini and thus born between 22 May and 21 June. Also in the film, Uma Thurman's fictional Emma attributes her 'over-achievements' to the fact that her father wanted a boy.

by 1950 was building up the formidable business empire of Knight Industries[5] of which he was chairman; Patrick Macnee described him in 1965 as a 'shipping magnate'.[6] At the time of Emma's birth, Sir John was a dark-haired, clean-shaven gentleman. Emma's mother – from whom she seems to have inherited her good looks – was also dark-haired and had an exotic European air to her in the existing photographs. The Knights were a very smart, well-dressed couple [JACK] and apparently had a large house in St John's Wood.[7] Of the rest of her family, it is possible that she had an uncle who wrote to her from Birmingham[8] although Emma herself seemed unsure of the full extent of her family [JACK].

'A leggy little horror with pig-tails' was how the six-year-old Emma was remembered by Paul Croft who – as a child – had lived next door to her and eagerly climbed over the wall to see her; it was a close childhood friendship which was to last through to Paul's sudden death some years later [MDVL]. It seems that dolls and dolls' houses were a major element in the life of the young Emma – particularly one little figure which said 'Mummy' [JACK] from which she soon learnt to quieten infants with a swift 'sssssssshhhhhhh!' [NURS]. Having graduated from her nursery with its many pictures on the wall, Emma started to attend a school which required the girls to wear a uniform [JACK]. Macnee suggested that one of her school friends was possibly Flavia Lyall, the biologist.[9]

One vague story about Emma's childhood days indicates that she may have spent two years in Jamaica when she was a girl. Here her childhood hero was Marcus Moziah Garvey, the Jamaican political thinker and activist who founded the United Negro Improvement Association in 1914.[10] However, the early part of Emma's life was partially documented in – of all things – a girls' comic in 1966. Between Issues 52 and 63, Fleetway Publications' *June and School Friend* ran a 12-part strip serial about a major incident in Emma Knight's childhood which, it was hoped, would be an inspiring story to show other girls that, even although she had lost her mother at the age of ten[11], Emma's tenacity and bravery had brought her many skills which she would use later in life.

This event took place around 1952 when the 14-year-old Emma was touring around the world with her father on his yacht, the *Ocean Queen*.[12] By now, Emma Knight was already learning about judo from Mao, the yacht's Chinese chef, who displayed great patience with the teenage girl as she mastered the most important throw in the martial art. Simultaneously, Emma had been taught to wrestle by Paddy, the slight but wiry chief deck hand.[13] The rest of the crew included Horace, the engineer, and a valet called Joe.[14]

However, Emma's burning passion at the time was fashion. She had even designed her own sparkling trouser suit – a daring creation a decade ahead of its time – which her father

---

[5] An unconfirmed report suggests that Knight Industries may have been formed around 1938. *Too Many Targets*, p59.

[6] *...deadline*, p44. *Dead Duck*, p13.

[7] *Heil Harris!*, p53.

[8] *Dead Duck*, p24.

[9] *...deadline*, p46.

[10] *The Laugh Was On Lazarus*, p78.

[11] 'The Growing-Up of Emma Peel', *June and School Friend*, Issue 52, 29 January 1966, p24.

[12] Strangely enough, although Emma was clearly experienced on boats, she apparently suffered from seasickness in one mission in 1967. 'Sunset in the East'. *The Avengers Annual*, 1967, p60.

[13] 'The Growing-Up of Emma Peel', *June and School Friend*, Issue 56, 26 February 1966, p25.

[14] 'The Growing-Up of Emma Peel', *June and School Friend*, Issue 56, 26 February 1966, p25.

felt looked like pyjamas. 'I've got strong feelings about clothes,'[15] declared the young Emma. Indeed, she would later continue to design many of her own clothes; as an adult, she wore a version of this design crafted in blue lamé when visiting Castle De'Ath [CAST] and attending a gala event at the Queen's Theatre [BRIM].[16]

Now a slim, bespectacled and moustached fellow, Sir John was visiting the eastern country of Fezra where he had business with King Abdullah at the Arab City of Marash. Emma was keen to talk to Abdullah's daughter, Princess Asha, about fashion. However, on arriving at Marash, Emma found that her judo skills were more in demand than her sense of style as she threw General Guptah of the Royal Guard to the ground to save a young potter called Hassan from being bullied. Very soon she was propelled into a plot with international implications. Asha had been engaged to Sheikh Abul Babul, who – unknown to Abdullah – was a ruthless man. It was clear to Emma that Asha's true love was in fact Hassan, and she worked to bring the two young romantics together in the safety of the neighbouring state of Dervain.

In the ensuing adventure, Emma also got her first taste of disguise when, grabbing a turban, she posed as a waiter boy to gain access to the tent of Princess Asha, and later became a royal coach driver to rescue the Princess. Once in the Princess's quarters, the style-conscious teenager could not resist trying one of Asha's dresses.

Emma's training in unarmed combat continued to be useful; she knew where to put pressure on the wrist of the Sheikh's bodyguard so that he would release her, bettered Hassan in a friendly struggle at the ruins of Jezbah, used Mao's judo throws on Admiral Kazan of the Fezran Navy, and combined judo with wrestling on Abul's palace guards. The young Emma could also think and plan quickly, ingeniously getting Hassan away from danger in a large vase. She was also confident enough to take charge when needed. When Admiral Kazan boarded the *Ocean Queen* to recover Asha, Emma declared that in the absence of Sir John, she was the captain of the vessel.

Eventually, Emma found herself in Sheikh Abul's palace and learnt that his marriage to Asha was simply part of a plan called Operation Happiness – a scheme for Abul's forces to invade Fezra while Abdullah's people were distracted during the royal wedding. With the scheme uncovered, Sir John was able to put through an SOS to the United Nations, the betrothal was annulled and Asha and Hassan were free to marry. So pleased was he with Emma's selfless actions on his daughter's behalf, Abdullah placed a major order with Knight Industries to re-equip the entire Fezran Navy. Sir John himself had invested a great deal of faith in Emma's judgement during the incident.

In Emma's Departmental dossier, her schooling was described as 'internationally educated'[17]; she did not attend either Rodean or Sommerville [BREA]. According to Macnee, her education was 'on the Continent and in South America'[18] and she also spent some time living in Japan with her father.[19] Similarly, the actor noted that Emma took her degree at the Universidade Federal de Bahia in mathematics[20], and had friends in the

---

[15] 'The Growing-Up of Emma Peel', *June and School Friend*, Issue 52, 29 January 1966, p25.

[16] This outfit was apparently known as 'Flash'.

[17] *Featuring The New Avengers*, p17.

[18] *...deadline*, p44. *Dead Duck*, p14.

[19] *...deadline*, p85.

[20] An alternate and unconfirmed report suggested that Emma's degree from Bahia was in zoology,

biology department there.[21]

As Emma matured into a young lady, she followed her father into both the business and social worlds. 'Sir John Knight and daughter Emma' was a familiar caption to photographs in newspapers, showing the smiling young debutante and with her proud, bowler-hatted, moustached father [JACK]. Then, in December 1959[22], came the *Evening News* headline 'Sir John Knight Dies' [JACK].[23] However, as with the situation on board the *Ocean Queen* seven years earlier, Emma was in no doubt as to what she should do. With her father indisposed, she was in control. By 18 January 1960, the headlines now read 'Emma Knight Takes The Helm of Father's Industries – 21-Year-Old Girl To Head Board.' One such article about the incredibly young woman taking over the conglomerate in what was still very much a male preserve read: 'Emma Knight, 21-year-old daughter of Sir John Knight who died tragically last month, is to take his place on the Board of the Company. It was announced today that from next month she will take control as Chairman and Managing Director. Miss Knight said today at a press conference held at Knight House that she would carry through the policy of her father, who in the last 10 years had built his empire up into one of the largest industries in the country' [JACK].

Although there was scepticism that a 'mere girl' could carry on her father's work, Emma's critics were soon proved sadly wrong. Tickertape machines disgorged bulletins such as 'KNIGHT INDUSTRIES SOAR – THE AMAZING EMMA KNIGHT RUNS COMPANY MORE EFFICIENTLY THAN EVER' into the news agencies of the world. As a woman, Emma had to prove herself even tougher than her father if she was to succeed in this arena, and was not afraid to make unpleasant decisions. She was particularly concerned by the ideals of Professor Keller, Knight Industries' automation expert, who advocated using machines to subjugate man on the basis that technology was superior to humanity. Strongly disagreeing with this notion, Emma laughed at and ridiculed his theories before sacking him from the Board one morning. This created such waves that she was interviewed by the radio news that day outside the John Knight Building [JACK].

One tragic aspect of Sir John's death was that he had not lived long enough to see his daughter happily married. It seems likely that by now Emma had already met and fallen in love with Peter Peel[24], an 'air ace'[25] who was known for dramatic reappearances [KNOT]. It seems that they married some time in 1960, and unconfirmed reports suggest that they honeymooned in Pringle on Sea before a round-the-world helicopter race.[26] There is also a story that around 1962-63 – presumably while on vacation – Emma spent some time in

which seems unlikely. *The Floating Game*, p51. While there, she apparently climbed 300 feet to the top of the Speech Room. *Heil Harris!*, p36.

21 *Dead Duck*, p40.

22 Assuming that Keller's newspaper cutting of 18 January 1966 had the correct date but wrong year – the year should have been 1960 when Emma was 21 [JACK].

23 The transcript refers to other headlines such as 'TYCOON DIES IN HUNTING ACCIDENT!', 'THOUSANDS MOURN SIR JOHN' and 'DAUGHTER EMMA ATTENDS FUNERAL.'

24 The 1998 Warner Bros biopic of Steed and Emma's first meeting had Father commenting that Peter 'was one of ours.'

25 Macnee referred to Peter Peel as a 'supersonic test pilot.' *Dead Duck*, p13.

26 *Steed and Mrs Peel*, Book Two, p10-11. This rather unbelievable series of incidentals also suggests that Emma and Peter had married in 1960, 'seven years' before Peter's return. Book Three, June 1992, p25.

Arabia where she learned to ride a camel.[27]

Unfortunately the Peels' happiness together was to be short lived. While flying over the Amazonian jungle in 1964, Peter's plane developed an engine defect and he crashed.[28] When there was no immediate trace of him, he was presumed dead [KNOT]. Emma Knight had become a widowed Mrs Emma Peel.

By 1964, Emma was already becoming quite known for writing articles in many fields as well as her position in Knight Industries. She had written items on psychoanalysis which were considered very good for the lay public [XMAS], prepared a piece on thermodynamics in February 1965 [BARG], submitted a piece for *Science Weekly* the following October [TOWN], and had her article *Better Bridge With Applied Mathematics* published in the June 1967 issue of *Bridge Player's International Guide* alongside a photo of herself [JOKE]. Her by-line for writing was firmly established as 'Mrs Emma Peel' [JOKE] and it is possible that she also wrote a paper on mediaeval history.[29]

Steed's first meeting with Emma was apparently foretold by her horoscope which predicted that she would collide with a tall dark stranger. Later that day, she ran into the back of Steed [DOOR]. Whether this meeting was coincidental is – as has been discussed – a matter for conjecture, especially if Peter Peel *had* undertaken work for the Department. Given Emma's unofficial status in her earlier Department records, it seems that Steed and Emma began as friends, and that slowly she became involved in his investigations.

Steed and Emma's friendship became a very close one – and most likely had a sexual element over the three years they worked together. It is notable that Steed bore a marked resemblance in some respects to Peter [KNOT]. There was such chemistry between them, especially with regards their stylish, unhurried manner in investigating their increasingly strange cases. 'They would casually discuss some mastermind's plan to rule the world at the same time as serving the soup,'[30] was how Macnee described the sparking dialogue he observed between the couple.

Emma got to know a great deal about Steed and his tastes – how he liked caviar, quails' eggs, asparagus and cheese [XMAS] and that he liked to drink her brand of coffee [TOWN]. One of the gifts she once gave him in the early days of their association was a tiepin with a hidden camera [TWOS]. Well aware of the demands made on her by Steed, she joked that she was an insomniac [HUNT], and could sense his bribes when a look in his eye indicated a 'nasty situation' [SURR]. Soon experienced with his flirtatious nature, Emma knew that Steed would 'pick up something' at the Stirrup Cup Inn [DUST]. However, she did not know him well enough to believe that he was actually his dubious alter-ego Webster [TWOS].

Emma described her ideal partner as being a mature man of culture and intelligence, with stamina and independent means [MARK]; she also believed that a gentleman would bow to a lady in certain situations [HIST] and that a man did not have to be handsome to be attractive [RETU]. Once commenting on how 'small' men were in Elizabeth times [TIME], Emma clearly had lingering thoughts about a male model filling out a Winged Avenger outfit [WING] and found the prospect of working late with PURRR director George Erskine

---

[27] *The Laugh Was On Lazarus*, p11.

[28] A variant description of this event was 'killed when the jet he was testing had disintegrated.' *The Floating Game*, p30.

[29] *...deadline*, p44.

[30] *Featuring The New Avengers*, p60.

at Chippenham Manor's Experimental Husbandry Farm an attractive one [TIGE]. She also fell for the pleasantries of 'Paul Beresford', finding him charming, witty and intelligent... and capable of making Steed jealous [RETU]. John Harvey of Boardman's Bank also received her attentions on another mission while she thought that Henry Boardman himself was 'square' [DIAL].

Emma's manner and looks attracted numerous admirers during her covert work including Tony Marco at Pinters [BARG] and Bertie Waversham at the Craigleigh Golf Club [HOLE]. Waldo Thyssen certainly 'appreciated' her [TIME] and George Unwin was delighted to meet her at his cocktail party [JUST]. John Cartney asked her for a date almost immediately, even though he was seeing Miss Sara Bradley at the same time [BRIM]. Always able to look after herself, Emma shut one of the hands of senior dance tutor Ivor Bracewell in a locker room door when he made advances on her [QUIC] and struck drunken Hellfire Club suitors with her purse [BRIM]. However, Emma was also able to use her looks to her professional advantage, flirting with young Peter Haworth to get a sample of make-up from his collar [POSI], launching 'Operation Fascination' to run security clearances of 'national importance' on Group Captain Miles [BUTL] and bewitching Major Robertson, who later sent her chocolates [DANG]. At the other end of the spectrum, Emma found herself catalogued as Wife No 321 in the harem of Prince Ali of Barabia, and allocated Saturday on his Duty Roster [PRIN].

Emma already moved in notable society circles even before associating with Steed. For her literary collection she was known to Jeremy Wade [XMAS] and had another friend in Victoria Grove [EPIC]. In the scientific world she was friends with botanist Miss Laura Burford and her fiancé Alan Carter [SURR], Professor Minley at Greenwich Observatory [HOLE] and the entomologist Professor Swain [HUNT]. From her childhood, she was used to attending official functions, although by 1967 embassy junkets were boring her [TREA] and she had to attend one party with an ambassador who had a reputation as a womaniser [MDVL]. People like Ambassador Brodny [TWOS] and Sir Andrew Boyd [DOOR] she presumably knew via Steed.

Towards the end of 1964, Emma had started working with Steed, at first in an unofficial capacity. Certainly she seemed to relish the danger and excitement, and unlike Cathy Gale seldom asked to be removed from a hazardous assignment. Since Emma was always keen to launch into the fray, Steed rarely resorted to trickery to involve her. Finding her 'extremely trustworthy', it seems that he had little hesitation in involving her in more and more confidential work [JUST].

Emma was well equipped to deal with the events ahead of her for the next three years. Her range of knowledge and expertise was even more staggering than that of Cathy. She had a remarkable IQ [AUNT], attaining a score of 152 on the RANSACK test papers which she completed on Steed's behalf [MIND]. Physically, Emma had excellent poise [BIRD] and expressive feet [QUIC]. Her legs caught the eye of many men [WHO?] who found themselves attracted to her. Her perfectly symmetrical face added to her magnetic beauty [JOKE].

A terribly independent woman, Emma delighted in displaying her skills and abilities. She would refuse unnecessary help such as a steadying hand when climbing down from a tree [DUST] and declared proudly, 'I'm thoroughly emancipated.' [TIME] When co-operating with Russian agents in London, she forthrightly declared, 'I am *my* choice,' when explaining to Ivan Peppitoperoff that she was not partnering him simply on Steed's say so [CORR].

According to Business Efficiency Bureau analysis, Emma had a high fear index beyond their capacity to calculate [FEAR]. Emma commented that she had learnt to live with her fears [FEAR]; certainly she was not afraid of the dark [JOKE], nor intimidated by threats [JUST]. However, she was unnerved by voices when trapped in a remote house and only just managed to retain her cool and reason – showing great relief at Steed's arrival [JOKE]. Likewise she put on a brave face when Steed found her in an automated death trap [JACK]. Indeed, one of her few fears was that on some occasion her knight in shining armour might not arrive in the nick of time [FEAR]. She did not like having a spider on her nose [MARK].[31] In terms of physical stamina, she could hold her breathe when ducked in a village pond [MDVL], was able to get up and run after being knocked down by a motorcycle [TIME], would not hesitate to dash through a burning window [VENU] and withstood pressure in Dr Sturm's automated press [SURF].

Emma's staggering intellect allowed her to deduce the schemes hatched to brainwash RAF officers [HUNT] or create an enemy bridgehead [TOWN]. Her ingenuity allowed her to carry out surveillance with a compact mirror [DIAL] and make escapes using the materials to hand [DANG]. She was a very practical lady, showing Steed that the best way to get money from his piggy bank was to smash it [PRIN]. Mary Merryweather admired Emma's initiative and skill, suggesting that Emma should get her own business – apparently oblivious to the fact that she was addressing none other than the head of Knight Industries [SUCC]. Even when trapped in Professor Keller's bizarre house, Emma's panic was only momentary and she soon started to reason out a logical means of escape, manufacturing a rudimentary bomb from the items around her [JACK].

Of her own persona, Emma claimed that she had to learn to be patient, although it was not in her nature [KNOT], while Steed would comment upon her having a prominent 'stubborn streak' [WHO?, MDVL]. Generally, she could be very chatty and unfazed by any given situation – making her ideal for walking straight into a new assignment and uncovering the facts.

Like Steed, Emma had a low opinion of politicians [NEVE, JOKE] and wasn't amongst those voting Harold Wilson to power in October 1964 [STAT].[32] Unlike Cathy, she was happy to go along with those increasingly rare plans of Steed's which involved using somebody as bait [HIST]. Although she kept an open mind and would not be trapped into a hasty opinion about the unexplained [VENU], Emma felt that it was important to only believe something fully after seeing it proved [SURF, LIVI]. She remained uncertain about premonitions and sixth sense, but possibly believed horoscopes [DOOR].

Emma could be rather theatrical with her obvious whispering to Steed [DUST]. One of her most endearing qualities was her perky wit in almost any situation – even a Manchurian prison camp cell [ROOM]. She enjoyed making fun of her enemies even when they had the upper hand [KNOT] – telling the electrifying Haworth, 'Don't blow a fuse,' when he threatened her [POSI] – and generally relished word play [JUST]. She speculated that a 'rabbit punch' had rendered a rabbit unconscious [HOUR] and quipped, 'One way to bag a man,' as

---

[31] One uncharacteristic fear apparently logged in an unfilmed mission report was Steed's comment, 'Mice give [Mrs Peel] the creeps.' *Diana*, Issue 203, 7 January 1967.

[32] An unconfirmed report suggests that Emma had never cared for either Harold Macmillan – the Conservative Prime Minister from January 1957 to October 1963 – nor Harold Wilson very much. *Heil Harris!*, p36.

she carefully placed the miniaturised Steed in a small fabric bag [MISS]. Even in direct danger, Emma would comment that death by bleaching laser would be 'Quicker than a peroxide rinse' [VENU] and that her demise from a buzz saw would make her a 'split personality' [EPIC]. She was also well aware of the clichés of her own job; when Steed asked if the drowned Lord Daviot had perished of natural causes, she responded, 'Are they ever?' [SEET].

Despite all her experiences and glib comments, Emma could still be shocked by the death of an adversary whereas the veteran Steed would have a merry quip [VENU]. Early on in her crime fighting career, she was still expressing frustration at being unable to stop the murder of JG Henshaw [MARK]. It is also possible that Emma had an affinity for animals. After the incident at the Litoff Organisation, she was concerned about the Borzoi dogs Bellhound and Dancer being abandoned [BREA], and was also happy to handle a three-foot ball python when necessary [BRIM].

From her travels, Emma could speak Russian [TWOS, CORR], had an impeccable grasp of French [DIAL, POSI] and could make comments like, 'That's the way the cookie crumbles,' in Latin [HOUR]. When it came to literature, she could recognise quotes about roses from the English poet Francis Thompson, and could reply with the words of Robert Herrick [DUST] as well as identifying Banquo's words from *Macbeth* Act One, Scene Six, [DUST] and commenting, 'And the devil claims his soul,' with reference to the legend of Faust [BREA]. In terms of architecture, she could date the house of Sir Cavalier Rousicana to being built around 1620 [JOKE] and knew that Colonel Jolyon Adams died at the Battle of Saratoga in September 1777 [DANG].

As a mathematician, Emma's grasp of statistics was strong [MARK]. However, she was more interested in applying her numeric talents in other fields, notably that of physics. She crafted an exploded molecular construction for a paper on thermodynamics [BARG], knew about cryogenics [ROOM], was 'well oiled' in industrial science [DUST], scoffed at the notion of an invisible man [SEET] and could quickly calculate velocities and weights of impact [POSI]. Emma was familiar with various electronic components [GRAV], deduced that transistorised components could function as a barrier to mind control [SURR], was an expert in cybernetics [AUNT], knew the voltage created by a generator [POSI] and rapidly deduced the function of circuit diagrams [POSI]. Dabbling in the field of chemistry [SEET] she knew the effects of nitrous oxide [HOUR] and the C11 truth drug [HOUR], was an expert in centred fuels [AUNT], and was able to perform chemical analysis on substances to deduce their make-up and use [POSI]. Her grasp of meteorology was sufficient to take and analyse humidity readings [SURF][33] and she shared Cathy's passion for anthropology [KNOT].

In the field of horticulture, Emma could identify a cactus with poisonous barbs [SURR], and had a particular interest in roses – having seen 'Whimsical Folly' grown at several shows [DUST] and recognising the 'Crimson Glory' which won first prize at the Chelsea Flower Show [WHO?]. Emma was generally aware of birds and their habits [WING], and knew that the Black Capped Petrel had not been seen in England since 1850 [DUST].

Equipped with a basic medical knowledge, Emma was able to act as a nurse to the satisfaction of a doctor [MIND], having taken a refresher course in applied medicine in February 1965 and thus able to estimate times of death [DIAL] or reset a pulled neck [HIST]. With

---

[33] In the 1998 movie, Emma's skills in meteorology were expanded to be her profession as a Government scientist.

some knowledge of phrenology [DANG], Emma believed that doodles revealed the psychic character of the subject [TIGE]. She was also well aware of the electrical activity of the brain and the effect of fundamental frequencies in inducing a breakdown [HOUR]. As for her own mind and thoughts, when asked about her fantasies Emma replied, 'I haven't exhausted reality yet.' [PRIN]

Always keen to learn and with the ability to study quickly, Emma's reading matter included *Primary Education* [TOWN], *Tribal Customs of Kalaya* [HUNT], *Tropical Diseases* [HUNT], the 1962 *Basic Nuclear Physics* by IR Williams [AUNT], *Self Defence No Holds Barred* by television fight arranger and stuntman Ray Austin [AUNT], *Advanced Ventriloquism* [SUCC], *Alchemist* magazine [SEET], *Humour in Milk* [TIGE], *Milk and Its Derivatives* [TIGE] and a thriller called *Trump Hand* [JOKE]. Emma's newspaper of choice was the *Daily Mail* [XMAS][34] and one surveillance photograph shows her calmly reading the 1966 biographical work *Privileged Persons – Four Seventeenth Century Portraits* by Hester W Chapman while being held captive by Dr Henry Primble.

Thankfully for her new undercover role, Emma was blessed with tremendous reactions, able to catch a plate which she knocked from a shelf before it hit the ground [FEAR]. She did not flinch when a spear hit the wall near her head [NURS], when an assailant produced a knife behind her [JOKE] or when a visitor pulled a gun at the door [PRIN]. Emma's senses were also very fine, detecting the scent of lavender [NURS] or spotting make-up on a man's collar [POSI]. At times, Emma could sense people creeping up behind her [CAST] and determine fear in others [JUST]. Her empathy with Steed also dictated when she needed to withdraw discretely [LIVI].

Emma was an incredibly fit lady, able to roll out of a jump [DUST], scale tall walls [BIRD], leap over hedges [WING], flip out of a chair [XMAS] and back-flip over Steed while handcuffed to him – albeit in somebody else's body at the time [WHO?]. While imprisoned, she would do handstands against a wall [LIVI]. In terms of co-ordination, she was able to pass the Danger Makers' Initiative Test of walking along a plank with electrical wires [DANG]. She swam well and could execute a perfect somersault dive [BIRD] as well as energetically jumping onto a see-saw to propel a villain into an electric wire [DANG]. She could move quietly and swiftly, even getting the drop on Steed [DOOR].[35]

One of the key pastimes which Emma poured her athleticism into was martial arts, and according to her Department dossier had adapted both karate and the judo taught to her as a teenager with her own balletic abilities.[36] Now well-versed in karate, Emma could recognise a blow such as Jinchu and could beat another lady karate expert called Oyuka (a third Dan at Judo and a first Dan at karate) because she had 'the skill of a man' which Oyuka failed to take into account [CYBE]. Macnee commented that Emma was in fact a Black Belt in karate, a skill she had learnt while living in Japan with her father[37], and by 1967 Emma was also starting to use kung fu disciplines too [WHO?].[38]

---

[34] In an unconfirmed report, Emma also said that she read the *Times Sunday Supplement*. *The Afrit Affair*, p61.

[35] An unconfirmed report also suggests that Emma used a technique to expand her muscles when being bound so as to allow her to work her bonds loose. *TV Comic*, Issue 722, 16 October 1965.

[36] *Featuring The New Avengers*, p17.

[37] *...deadline*, p85.

[38] Some surveillance photographs from around 1965-66 show Emma in the company of Chee Soo

Emma would calmly take on any opponents even if they were armed [eg XMAS, STAT, JUST]. She would throw them [eg XMAS, CAST, CORR, BREA] (at times clean through a wall [HOUR]), punch them [MIND, WHO?], kick them [EPIC], deliver vicious blows to the body [eg DIAL, BRIM, NEVE, MDVL], smash their head against any available surface [XMAS, TOWN, NURS], throttle [SUCC], apply a knee to the vital areas [BIRD] and even trample over downed victims [HOUR]. She would literally leap into combat at times [DIAL, TREA] and knew how to tumble when thrown [VENU]. A single blow from her hand could poleaxe a man [CAST] often with a concussing blow to the neck [SEET, WHO?, RETU]. She was also still aware of where to apply her fingers on pressure points in the same area to induce unconsciousness [TWOS, LIVI]. Most female opponents gave her little trouble and could be quickly overpowered [CORR, STAT].

Emma also had a powerful kick which could open doors [MIND, SURF, BIRD] or break posts [WHO?] while her strong ankles could pinion a man by his neck [GRAV, BIRD]. Her arms were powerful enough to bend metal bars [AUNT] or lift a man above her head [LIVI]; once she pinned a potential attacker to the floor by standing on his hands [TWOS]. She also had some special moves such as the 'Emma Peel Patent Push-Off' for less threatening figures [SEET].

Emma's confidence against her opponents would lead her to advance on them slowly, snapping her fingers as she closed in [BARG] or taking a rest in the middle of fisticuffs [TIME]. Indeed, she could out-perform some of the trained Department agents like Varnals [ROOM] and could better Steed quite easily [TWOS, SURR, WHO?]. Often she had a touch of humour in her victories, such as dropping flowers on the prone form of Peter Omrod [DUST]. She would employ any objects to hand (such as a staff [JUST], a pitchfork [MDVL] or large books [HIST]) against assailants, and was disappointed to find that one fire bucket which she grabbed was only plastic [HOUR]. Miscreants would be shut in car boots [BREA] or have van doors slammed in their face [TIGE].

When it came to armed combat, Emma enjoyed a spot of fencing practice at her flat [TOWN, VENU] which Steed would join in with if he dropped by; he would dispense 'friendly advice' like telling her that she was not flexible enough in the wrist and that her weight was on the wrong foot [TOWN].[39] Emma fought well with a rapier [CORR], a sword [DANG] and a sabre [PRIN], and was also capable with a crossbow [CAST] or bow and arrow [MIND, HIST].

Emma seldom resorted to firearms[40], although she was known to carry a Webley and Scott Mark IV .38 revolver with wood stocks [MARK, DUST], a silver-plated Webley and Scott Mark IV .38 revolver [JACK], an Italian Beretta 6.35mm [CYBE, GRAV], a .38 Smith and Wesson revolver [BIRD] and a silver-plated pearl-handled .38 Smith and Wesson which she took with her on weekends away, hidden in a handbag in her suitcase [JOKE]. She could also handle a double-barrelled shotgun [SURR, SUP7], a rifle [TIGE], a machine gun [LIVI], a Western-style six-shooter [EPIC] and could recognise shot from a medium calibre 16th

---

(also known as Clifford Gibbs) who was accomplished in kung fu, li style taijiquan and shuai chiao, and was also a founder member of the British Kung Fu Council.

[39] In the 1998 film, screenwriter Don Macpherson wrote a scene where the pair enjoyed some fencing practice together at a gentleman's outfitters called Trubshaws.

[40] One unfilmed report suggests that Emma once stated 'I don't like guns!' *TV Comic*, Issue 771, 24 September 1966.

century firearm [TIME].

Other talents displayed by Emma included an ability to decipher Morse [QUIC] and an astounding knowledge of the distances between British landmarks [FEAR]. However, she was told on one occasion that she could improve on her shorthand and study accountancy – although her deficiency in these areas was most likely part of her cover [SUCC].

According to her Departmental dossier, Emma lived on 'private means'[41] and seldom discussed her finances, although she was knowledgeable enough of the money world to recognise financiers like Samuel Morgan and Frederick Williams [MDVL]. After her bereavement, in late 1964 Emma was living in a very modern and functional flat in London, just round the corner from Spurley Court SW1 [MARK] and seven minutes from New Oxford Street [BARG]. Although described by some sources as 'a top-floor Hampstead flat'[42] and 'in London's Primrose Hill'[43], the building housing the top (sixth) floor flat was one of the Highpoint buildings [AUNT] akin to the pair known as Highpoint and Highpoint 2 built in Highgate. These notable structures were designed by Tecton, a famed firm of architects founded by Bernhold Lubetkin. Her phone number seems to have changed in early 1965, originally starting 274 [BARG] and then beginning 359 [CYBE].

Visitors to Emma's apartment would find a large 'cyclops' eye on the front door which allowed her to see who her callers were before answering the doorbell [BARG]; this eye formed part of a stylised face sculpture on the door along with a nose, ear and mouth [AUNT]. Emma's name appeared beneath the doorbell, and there was also a loudspeaker via which she could address her visitors [TOWN].

In the main living area, the walls were painted a warm orange; the centrepiece was a conical metal fireplace, around which were two light sofas – one straight and one curved. There was a low table to the side of the second sofa, and behind this a bureau and another low table, both of which had ornaments on them. Behind the second sofa on the wall between the windows and the door to the kitchen were a number of prints from both classic and abstract schools [eg BARG]. Beneath the windows was a low cabinet adjacent to a leather swivel chair [eg AUNT] with a pair of French windows to the left [eg TOWN]. By the door was a print and a piece of ceramic sculpture. A radio set was mounted in the right-hand wall [BARG] and other items of decor included a carriage clock [eg CYBE], china ornaments [eg TOWN] and an Inca-style mask which was mounted on the wall [eg TOWN]. There was also a white telephone [eg CYBE] and other ornaments lined along the back of the sofas, interspersed with lights.

To the left of the front door were a number of sliding doors, fitted flush with the three fascias which crept around to the window. One of the first two of these led to Emma's photographic darkroom [CYBE] while the third doorway, just to the left of the windows, led to Emma's bedroom [AUNT, DANG]. 'Few people ever saw Emma Peel's bed,'[44] observed Macnee who gave one description of the bedroom which failed to appear on any surveillance footage. It was apparently highly automated and controlled from a central console. A telephone apparently swung out when it rang, and her wardrobe was similarly

---

[41] *Featuring The New Avengers*, p17.

[42] *...deadline*, p45. This was probably a fictitious address. Note that Macnee's description of the apartment is at odds with the surveillance films.

[43] *The Complete Avengers*, p127.

[44] *...deadline*, p44.

automatically revealed as sliding doors withdrew across one wall to reveal a 'wardrobe computer' which allowed her to select from categories including 'Season' (eg Summer), 'Time of Day' (eg Night), 'Occasion' (eg Formal), 'Temperature' (eg Hot) and 'Humidity' (eg High). Macnee also made reference to a luxurious bathroom suite.

It seems that there was a balcony just outside the French windows [TOWN, CYBE] which may have led to a roof garden.[45] To the right as one entered was the sliding door which led to Emma's small kitchen.[46] This had modern storage units and sink, a kitchen table, a built-in electric oven in the wall opposite the door and an electric light in the style of an old-fashioned gas lamp [AUNT]. Emma kept the flat clean by a regular quick flick over with a feather duster [CYBE].

Emma was a keen motorist and indeed considered herself to be the best driver she knew [DOOR]; certainly one piece of surveillance film shows that she was able to hold a country road superbly when rammed by another car [SEET] while she performed admirably at a speed of 140 mph in reverse when trapped in a racing simulator [TREA]. Emma had a very good knowledge of cars, being able to check the brakes on Steed's Bentley [DOOR] and perform repairs on the car [LIVI], knowing the technical specifications of a Rolls-Royce [FEAR] and recognising certain types of tyre track [MISS]. Emma never drank when driving [RETU]. Although she was described as looking like a 'keen navigating type' [TREA] she once took a wrong turning when driving with Steed in France [WHO?].

When she started working with Steed, Emma was driving one of the latest cars, a white convertible Lotus Elan S2[47] [CYBE, TWOS, SURR, CAST, HUNT, AUNT, BUTL, JACK, HIST, SUCC]. This sporty and stylish 1600cc vehicle – which had a stopping distance of 147 feet [JACK] – was a top of the range model[48]; the S2 variant was launched in November 1964, the original Elan having made its debut at the 1962 Motor Show. There was a radio on the dashboard and also a magnetic compass [JACK], while a radio telephone had also been installed beneath the dashboard on the passenger side [BUTL]. Emma allowed Steed to drive her Lotus on certain occasions [TWOS]. Apparently by 1966, Emma was ready to replace the vehicle, and was therefore happy for Steed to deliberately drive his car into the back of it on the pretext of allowing the pair to engage in a covert discussion [SUCC].

Aside from cars, Emma was also happy to take control of a moped [TOWN][49], a go-kart [DANG], a horse drawn Chippenham Coach [BRIM][50], a helicopter [BUTL][51], a bicycle [BARG], a two-seater tandem [JACK][52], or a motorcycle with sidecar [HIST].[53]

---

[45] ...deadline, p44.

[46] 'Designed by an expert in ergonomics,' noted Macnee. ...deadline, p44.

[47] Registration HNK 999C.

[48] The vehicle could go from 0 to 50mph in 6.5 seconds, had a top speed of 120 mph and consumption of 30 mpg.

[49] Emma could also apparently drive a motor scooter which she borrowed on an unconfirmed occasion. TV Comic, Issue 760, 9 July 1966.

[50] One unfilmed report indicates that Emma could also handle a chariot drawn by two horses. TV Comic, Issue 760, 9 July 1966.

[51] An unconfirmed report suggests that Emma liked flying. TV Comic, Issue 736, 22 January 1966. She also looked forward to being able to make a parachute jump during one unfilmed mission. TV Comic, Issue 738, 5 February 1966. Another possible mission also saw Emma piloting a 'copter again. The Afrit Affair, p120.

[52] Another unconfirmed report noted that Emma rode a three-seater tandem. 'The Golden Game',

As with Cathy before her, Emma set fashions rather than followed them and was generally considered to wear 'the right clothes' during this richly-designed period of the 1960s [WHO?].[54] Other women were envious of her wardrobe [JOKE, WHO?] which comprised a lot of 'op-art' inspired items of the day. According to Eli Barker, Emma wore 'fine city clothes' [SURF]. In her wardrobe there were various jacket, blouse and skirt combinations [eg XMAS, CYBE, TOWN] as well as a pink and black trouser suit [HOUR], a wool jacket with fur collar [DIAL, ROOM], a lilac jacket and trousers with purple trim [VENU, STAT], a light mustard dress and jacket [VENU, BIRD], a light green belted jacket and skirt [TIGE, WHO?], an emerald green 'A-line' coat with matching trousers [LIVI, JOKE], a brown and beige checked tweed jacket [TIGE, CORR, SUP7], a yellow double-breasted jacket and trousers [TIGE, STAT, NURS], a lilac trouser suit [CORR, EPIC, NURS], a forest green jacket and skirt (her 'rifling Rushton's desk kit') [RETU, MISS], a twill double-breasted jacket and trousers in cream with a fine brown check [JACK, HIST, SUCC], and a yellow high-collared jacket and skirt [SUP7, NURS, KNOT]. Dark pullovers [eg MIND, WING] and white polo necks [eg DANG, JACK, WHO?] were staple ingredients of her look. Emma also wore durable dark leather trousers [MARK, MIND] and a leather waistcoat fastened by ties [MARK, MIND].

For formal wear, Emma still wore the blue lamé pantsuit she had designed as a teenager [CAST, BRIM] and a Victorian-style ruffled blouse and bonnet outfit [BARG, DUST]. Her other favourite items included a pink sleeveless dress [eg SEET, TIGE, BREA], an orange and pink print dress with psychedelic swirls [SEET, TREA] and a white silk dress with concentric circle pattern which she wore to embassy junkets and ambassador's parties [RETU, TREA, MDVL]. There were plenty of other flowing dresses in white [eg TOWN, QUIC] and cocktail dresses in black [MARK, PRIN].

For a more casual look, Emma often sported a striped lilac and white casual top [eg TIME, POSI]. Other distinctive items included a navy blue tee-shirt with a white 'E' on it [DUST], a snakeskin jacket [DUST, DANG], a white jacket with black trim [DANG, BUTL, SUCC], a collarless Chinese jacket [CYBE], and a red silken Chinese-style trouser suit [VENU, NEVE, JOKE].

For outdoor wear, Emma had a deep red woollen jacket with black fur collar [CYBE][55], various fur coats [MARK, MIND], a double-breasted leopard skin print coat [SURF], a patterned black and white coat [MIND, TWOS], a hooded mink coat [XMAS], a white PVC raincoat [HUNT, DANG, SUCC], a black plastic raincoat [SURF], and a red and orange checked tweed jacket [LIVI, TIGE]. One favourite, which Macnee felt gave her 'the look of a jaunty young zebra'[56] was apparently made of rabbit fur and had distinctive black and white chevrons [eg HOLE, QUIC].[57] There was also a striking deep blue cape worn from 1966 [TIME, VENU, NURS].

There were certain items which Emma seemed to wear when she knew she was going into combat. These included a glittering catsuit [MIND], a rear-fastening black leather

---

Steed and Mrs Peel, Book Three, p91-92.

[53] In a further unfilmed incident, Emma apparently drove a steam traction engine – with difficulty. 'Deadly Rainbow', *Steed and Mrs Peel*, Book Three, p30-31.

[54] It has been suggested that Emma attended fashion shows. *Diana*, Issue 205, 21 January 1966.

[55] An item of clothing which was also purchased by a woman called Angorra [TIGE].

[56] *...deadline*, p122.

[57] This coat was apparently an item called 'Chemin'.

catsuit with silver zips [DIAL, SURF] which was perfect for her role as a 'Space Age Woman' [BARG], a black PVC catsuit [SURF], a sleeveless rear-zipped black leather jump-suit with a low neck (and a matching jacket) [CYBE, GRAV, SURR], a 'Black Watch' catsuit in black stretch cotton with vinyl facings and buttons [TOWN, CAST, DANG] and a V-necked leather catsuit styled like a waistcoat [HOLE, BUTL]. Many of these seemed to be distinctive mono-chrome designs often in leather, but from 1966 Emma started to experiment with more daring colours in jersey and crimpolene; her wardrobe now included a sleeveless mid-blue catsuit with pale blue trim, fob watch and matching zipped jacket [FEAR], a dark green suede affair with holes at the hips [FEAR], a dark blue crimpolene one-piece with gold sleeve stripes (often worn for break-ins and night-time surveillance) [BIRD, VENU, LIVI, NEVE], a red-brown jump-suit with tan trim (again for night work) [WING], an orange jump-suit with navy blue stripes and trim [CORR, SUP7, POSI], a peach and white chamois leather buckle-neck jump-suit [VENU], a purple 'trouser dress' zipped jump-suit with suspenders (and white driving mask) [BIRD], a deep blue jump-suit with pink trim plus matching cap and boots [WING, TIGE, JUST], a blue lace-up catsuit with white boots [NURS, MISS] and a green variant [DOOR], a purple catsuit with blue trim and buttons [SEET, MDVL], a black zipped and buckled jump-suit trimmed with silver [TIGE, STAT, BREA], a blue catsuit with a white stripe [NEVE, JUST], a pale green and white jump-suit [RETU] and a black leather jump-suit with two silver chains [JUST]

For sporting occasions, Emma had hunting duds with fawn trousers, a white cravat and a dark bowler [DIST] and when exercising, she sported a black cotton leotard [MIND, SUCC]. At night, she wore a translucent white silk nightie [CAST]. Attending a fancy dress Rag Week party with a Robin Hood theme, she donned the outfit of the chief Merrie Man himself [HIST], and chose a revealing bird-like outfit for the MFU Charity Ball at Pendley [AUNT].[58]

When it came to headgear, Emma often wore a distinctive black and white target motif beret [eg TOWN, DANG] which was also borrowed by the actress Georgie Price-Jones who tried to imitate her [AUNT]. Other headgear included a black tam-o-shanter [DUST], a leather peaked cap [MIND], a black broad-brimmed Spanish hat [TWOS], a dark head scarf [CYBE], a target skull cap [SURF], a boater [DUST] a patterned head scarf (which she employed as a sling for Steed) [eg DUST, HIST], and caps in white [TIME, STAT] and yellow [CORR]. Rarely, she wore a headband [XMAS].

Many of Emma's shoes were designed to match specific outfits. Some of her most distinctive footwear included a pair of zipped white boots [eg HOUR, SUCC]. She wore rubber-soled shoes [POSI] and sported wellingtons for wet terrain [SURF]. Emma sometimes wore gloves [eg MARK, TOWN], notably for break-ins [DIAL]. From mid-1965 she favoured a pair of black and white gloves [eg TOWN, SUCC], while black gloves were the vogue from 1966 [eg FEAR, CORR]. Other accessories included fur hand-warmers [MARK, MIND], various scarves [eg ROOM, TREA], a neckerchief [SURR] and a white boa [JUST]. She often wore a bracelet on her right wrist [eg CYBE, DUST] and occasionally a medallion [MIND]. In 1965-66, Emma sported a distinctive target watch on a tartan strap [eg HOUR, JACK] and then a large metal-rimmed rectangular affair in 1967 [eg WHO?, TREA]; she was also given a silver watch as a trap by 'Paul Beresford', which she wore on her left wrist [RETU]. When under-cover, Emma would sometimes wear spectacles [TWOS, TOWN] or dark glasses when she

---

[58] Another report which was not filmed noted that Emma attended a similar party given by Lord Throgmorton as highwayman Dick Turpin. *Heil Harris!*, p20.

didn't want to be recognised [BUTL].

Emma carried a handbag [eg MARK, SURF] during 1965, although she soon dropped the accessory and was occasionally seen with a purse [RETU] or a black and white shoulder bag [HUNT, QUIC]. Items which she would carry on her included a miniature camera [HOLE], lipstick [JACK], matches [DUST], a torch for break-ins [DIAL], a diary with a map [GRAV] and a pen torch [GRAV].[59] For travelling away for several days, she had luggage bearing her initials [eg XMAS, WHO?]. Seldom did she carry gadgets – a rare example being the listening devices which relayed directional sound to an earpiece [TIGE].[60]

The brown-eyed Emma was very proud of her auburn hair, and would sometimes check its styling if a mirror was to hand [VENU]. She also wore nail varnish [MIND]. Although a couple of surveillance photographs show her with a cigarette, in the films she was never seen smoking apart from the use of a hookah [PRIN].

Like Steed, Emma appreciated fine food and drink. Of all her favourite tipples, Emma could most easily be mollified by champagne [MARK] which made her a little tipsy at times [MARK]. She always seemed to have a supply at her flat [eg FEAR, NEVE], even while redecorating [TIGE]. Emma also enjoyed drinking it at Steed's flat [JOKE, MDVL] – even if forced to use a straw! [MDVL] – and on one occasion arrived with a bottle at 3.30 am [TREA]. It was a drink she liked to sample when at receptions [TWOS], parties [JUST] and on the move [HOLE], even if it was over-chilled [TWOS]. She also drank Scotch [DANG], would sometimes ask for a brandy [JACK, JOKE, MDVL] with ice [JUST], enjoyed sampling punch [XMAS] or a pint at a local pub [SURR], and partook of the odd cocktail [VENU].[61] Her other passion was wine which she had at home [VENU] and enjoyed drinking with Steed [eg LIVI, TREA]; indeed, he would buy her wine from Pinters [BARG] and she liked heavy clarets in particular [TOWN]. However, she could only identify a 1931 Claret from the De Vere Vineyard near the Bordeaux village of St Perignon (Amerio St Claire) by reading the label on the bottle [DIAL]. Emma also had fond memories of a Chablis which she and Steed had shared in France [WHO?], and on her 29th birthday, she hoped that Steed would arrange for them to be flown to Paris, have an aperitif at Lafayette, and liqueurs in the moonlight at St Tropez [WHO?]. In the mornings, Emma began the day with an orange juice [DOOR].

For hot beverages, Emma liked to drink coffee [eg ROOM, DOOR] with milk [CORR] and no sugar [FEAR]. Also a tea lover [eg DOOR], Emma took milk [SURF, BREA] and – this time – two sugars [TOWN].[62] She also drank Formosan Tea [ROOM] and chose Indian tea over China, saying that she would prefer lemon in it rather than milk [TOWN] and also asking for lemon tea at Steed's [CORR]

When it came to food, Emma liked thick steak [TOWN], cucumber sandwiches [HUNT], dinner at Montmartre [WHO?], a sauce hollandaise worth crossing four counties for [BREA]

---

[59] An unfilmed incident had Steed claiming that Emma carried a radio micro-set in her handbag. *The Passing of Gloria Munday*, p78.

[60] An unconfirmed report suggests that Emma would on occasion carry a small listening device. *TV Comic*, Issue 722, 16 October 1965.

[61] One reports suggested that Emma liked a Campari, ideally with ice and a segment of peeled lemon. *The Laugh Was On Lazarus*, p19; *Heil Harris!*, p37. Or a Remy Martin. *The Passing of Gloria Munday*, p38.

[62] In the 1998 Warner Bros film of Steed's supposed first meeting with her, Emma (played by Uma Thurman) took only one sugar in her tea.

Right:
Spring 1962: Steed becomes suspicious about Vincent O'Brien when talking to him at Joyce's Public House in Ballyknock [COUR]

Previous page:
John Steed, the country's greatest undercover operative, here seen at the height of his powers in the 1960s

Below:
Spring 1962: Steed and Freedman pilot a Canada Jet-Ways aircraft in order to expose the brains behind a wrecking gang [COUR]

Above:
Summer 1963: Steed and
Cathy Gale go through Peter
Borowski's effects in Cathy's
apartment at 14 Primrose Hill
[SHAD]

Left:
5 November 1963: Steed and
Cathy at the Houses of
Parliament, having averted
a nuclear threat to London
[NOV5]

Right:
Spring 1966: Trapped inside a vast machine designed to destroy her, Emma Peel encounters a deranged man (named Burton according to Department records) [JACK]

Below:
Early 1967: Emma and Steed discover the corpse of chiropodist Hubert Merryweather in his consulting rooms – another victim of SNOB Inc. [CORR]

Above:
Early 1967: Ivan Peppitoperoff
introduces Steed and Emma to
Olga Volowski at Steed's
London flat, 3 Stable Mews
[CORR]

Overleaf:
22 November 1966: Emma
was painting in her apartment
when she was 'needed' by
Steed to investigate the death
of publisher Simon Roberts
[WING]

Left:
Late 1967: Emma meets
rival spiritual investigators
Mandy McKay (of FOG) and
George Spencer (of SMOG)
in the crypt of the Benedict
Estate chapel [LIVI]

Left:
Late 1967: No, it's not
John Steed. While undercover
at Henlow Grange Beauty
Farm on an undocumented
assignment, a blonde-wigged
Tara King encounters
Steed's old school friend
Patrick Macnee

Overleaf:
Summer 1976: Steed checks
on the safety of racing driver
Tony Field, a member of the
Three Handed Game,
apparently at Silverstone
racing circuit [3HAN]

Below left:
The former ballerina Purdey,
who reported directly to Steed
during 1976 and 1977

Below right:
Ex-SAS man Mike Gambit,
who reported directly to Steed
during 1976 and 1977

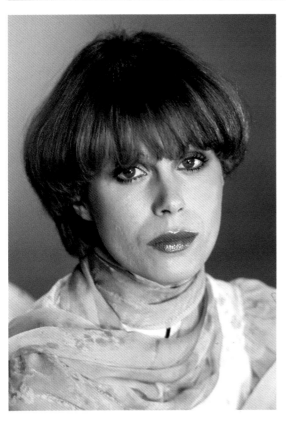

and lobster, which Steed brought her back from his holidays [AUNT]; she did however decline Marzipan Delight [TOWN]. It has also been suggested that around 1967 she experimented with 'infra-red cooking'.[63]

As well as attending auctions looking for antiques [RETU], Emma had quite a passion for art. She could do excellent sketches from memory [CAST], while when it came to painting her style was particularly cubist [WING], including her portrait of Steed [SUCC]. On a grander scale, she enjoyed sculpting from large blocks of concrete using an electric drill, or a hammer and chisel [FEAR, BIRD], and was captivated by a bronze entitled 'A portrait of the artist as a young man' in which she saw a sense of humour [RETU]. She could also sew [QUIC, TIME].

As London swung in 1967, Emma lived in the right place, knew the right people and went to the right places [WHO?]. Still in the midst of the social world she grew up in, Emma enjoyed attending all-night parties such as the MFU Charity Ball [AUNT] or going out for the night with Steed [PRIN]. Although rather tall at about five foot eight, Emma became a good dancer because of her father who entertained a good deal; this meant she became very good at making elderly gentlemen feel that they could dance [QUIC]. She seemed to be 'expert in Latin American' as well as doing the fox-trot, rumba and black bottom [QUIC], reversing [XMAS] and performing the exotic Dance of the Six Veils [PRIN]. Emma sang Top Line [TOWN] and knew melodies such as the traditional 'Green Grow the Rushes-O' [XMAS], could pick out Richard Wagner's 'Die Walküre' ('Ride of the Valkyrie') on Steed's Tuba [MARK] and discovered 'an unexpected talent' for playing the miniature bagpipes [CAST].

Emma was being modest when she claimed that she could ride and hunt 'a little' [DUST]. She was a fine horsewoman[64] [TWOS, DUST, WHO?] and was invited to equestrian events such as the Grand Hunt Ball [TIME].[65] Other outdoor pursuits for Emma included punting [DUST] and golf [HOLE].[66] She enjoyed exercise on the trampoline [MIND] and indoor games with Steed which included 'pick a stick' [HOLE], tiddlywinks [HOLE] and draughts [MISS], while she agreed to play Group Captain Miles at Ludo [BUTL].[67] Her mathematical skills made her a proficient bridge player [JOKE] and she also enjoyed attempting to do card tricks [JOKE].

At the cinema, Emma walked out of *Lasagne 6¹/₂* three-eighths of the way through [EPIC]. Attending the theatre, she enjoyed a Parisian musical with Steed [DOOR]. On television she possibly watched pop programmes [NEVE] or reviewed surveillance film of earlier cases [NEVE]. Her other hobbies included collecting for a Christmas charity [XMAS], doing newspaper crosswords [CYBE, KNOT], throwing her voice [SUCC] and a little amateur fortune telling [NURS]. She also enjoyed opening other people's Christmas cards [XMAS].

Initially, Emma's standing in Department missions was as a 'talented amateur'[68] and Steed would vouch for her as his responsibility [ROOM]. By late 1965 she was still an

---

[63] *The Laugh Was On Lazarus*, p40.

[64] One of the places Emma would go riding would appear to be St Mary's Bay in Kent [WHO?]. It has also been suggested that she could ride an elephant. *TV Comic*, Issue 755, 4 June 1966.

[65] It has also been suggested that Emma liked going to the races. 'Odds against Steed'. *The Avengers Annual*, 1967, p10.

[66] Two unconfirmed reports suggest that Emma also indulged in fishing. *Diana*, Issue 209, 18 February 1967. 'Steed's 'Holiday'', *The Avengers Annual*, 1967, p80.

[67] In the 1998 film, Emma was shown to be a superior chess player to Steed.

[68] A phrase used to describe her on American copies of the surveillance films between 1964 and 1966.

outsider, but clearly trusted [TOWN] and had acquired expertise in ciphers [AUNT] as well as being privy to the disposition of the Eastern Defence Bases [AUNT].

Emma's earliest recorded work with Steed appeared to require her to go undercover – no mean feat for a woman who was a major industrial leader and whose face had appeared in newspapers. Her first guise was as a reporter for *Industrial Times Magazine*, claiming she was writing a biography of the late businessman Jonathan Stone to investigate his death [MARK]. When Steed got her a job as a sales assistant at Pinters Stores Ltd close to her flat, Emma turned this rather demeaning post to her advantage, telling Jarvis the store detective that she was undercover from the Ministry of Labour [BARG]. In February 1965, she was undertaking her refresher course in applied medicine. A short time later when investigating Warner's Answering Service, Emma passed herself off as a relative of another dead businessman, Norman Todhunter [DIAL] and later claimed to have arrived from Barbados the previous week [DIAL].

By March 1965 when she and Steed started to investigate a series of deaths in the automation industry, it was Emma who was given the briefing notes rather than her partner; this assignment saw her pose as a buyer of toys for 'Winnel and Fentle Stores'[69] when visiting Jephcott Products Ltd. [CYBE]. Next, Steed arranged for her to be sent to the Sir Horace Winslip Hospital for Ailing Railwaymen as a qualified nurse [GRAV] and around Easter she landed a job as secretary to Professor Spencer at RANSACK where she briefly fell under a form of hypnotic control [MIND]. She was less than pleased to find herself obliged to work at the reception of the Chessman Hotel in London (which led to her being placed in what seemed to be a Manchurian prison) [ROOM] and her subsequent role selling model aircraft at Aero Models was similarly undemanding [TWOS].

Naturally, Emma felt personally involved by the disappearance of Laura Burford, and during her subsequent investigations at the village of Surrey Green[70] claimed to have bought a small-holding there [SURR]. Very good friends with Steed, Emma now often accompanied him socially to various events [HOUR]. While she did not join him to investigate the strange execution of a Salvation Army member in a small village in July [KIL1], her next mission saw her travelling up to Castle De'Ath in Scotland where she posed as a publicity consultant for ABORCASHATA[71] called in by Angus De'Ath who was thinking of opening the estate to the public. This assignment was one of the few to see Emma injured, sustaining a blow to the right temple during a fracas in the dungeons [CAST].

Emma's dancing skills were put to use when investigating Terpsichorean Training Techniques Inc [QUIC] and she was able to display her meteorological skills a short time after, as well as passing herself off as a freelance journalist at the Grannie Gregson's distillery. While at Lower Storpington, Emma drove a dark Mini Moke[72], and this investigation culminated with her catching an autumn cold [SURF]. Fully recovered, Emma joined the Craigleigh Golf Club for some more work alongside Steed [HOLE]. Then while investigating a threat to destroy the English countryside, Emma claimed to Peter Omrod that she was from

---

[69] This appears to be a Spoonerism which Emma came up with from the names of Julian Wintle and Albert Fennell, two senior surveillance personnel. The transcript erroneously refers to this as 'Gorringes' Stores.'

[70] This village bears a strong resemblance to Letchmore Heath in Hertfordshire.

[71] Advisory Bureau On Refurbishing Castles And Stately Homes As a Tourist Attraction.

[72] Registration BOX 656C.

the British Trust for Ornithology, and later joined a hunt in place of Miss Beryl Snow [DUST].

By autumn 1965, Emma's involvement in Department affairs – even in an unofficial capacity – had made her privy to much secret information, and she was kidnapped (or 'acquired') by Gregorio Auntie of Art Incorporated for sale at $140,000 to the enemy agent Joseph Ivanoff. When Ivanoff was detained by the authorities, the imprisoned Emma was put to auction with an opening price of £50,000. Steed eventually outbid all his rivals at £200,000 and rescued her from her cage. Around now, for some reason, Emma was driving a Messerschmitt KR201 Cabriolet Microcar – or 'bubble car' – rather than her Lotus [AUNT].

Having completed an article for *Science Weekly* around October, Emma had no objection to going along with Steed's pre-arranged plan that she should become a school teacher at the mysterious village of Little Bazeley-by-the-Sea [TOWN]. An investigation into sleeping sickness in Hertfordshire culminated with Emma posing as Lala, a native girl at the Kalayan Settlers and Ex-Servicemen's Association [HUNT], while her investigation into the affairs of the late General Groves saw her representing Willis and Ferguson (Auctioneers, Valuers, Specialists in Probate), allowing her access to his collection – and eventually infiltrating the ranks of the Danger Makers society [DANG].

At the start of 1966, Emma approached the charming John Cartney, the suspect behind a number of embarrassing incidents, collecting donations for a Home for Wayward Girls. Cartney was taken with her and donated generously – inviting her to join the bawdy celebrations at his revived Hellfire Club as the snake-wielding Queen of Sin [BRIM]. This kinky temptress image was one which was a million miles away from the brave and plucky teenage version of Emma which was appearing in *The Growing-Up of Emma Peel*, the serialisation of her adventures in Fezra in the British girl's comic *June and School Friend* from the end of January.

The security checking for the members of the Commission of Eastern Europe meant that Emma had to check on any potential risk surrounding Group Captain Miles, who had quite a reputation as a woman chaser. Launching 'Operation Fascination', Emma declared confidently, 'He will come to me.' Her plan began by placing photographs of herself (including a surveillance shot from her time investigating Grannie Gregson's) around Miles's office and even on the mats in his usual bar. Emma proved to be ingenious at fending off Miles's many advances, and eventually cleared him of treachery... although she would not reveal to Steed what she had offered 'Georgie Porgy' to deduce this [BUTL].

When Emma heard that she had inherited a house from her Uncle Jack, she was amazed to discover that she even had such a relative. As it turned out, she did not – a fact confirmed by Mr HW Pennington of Pennington and Co Solicitors, the long-term family lawyers for the Knights. The bequest was Seven Pines at Pendlesham in Hampshire, but the building was actually a gigantic automated trap left to ensnare her by the dead Professor Keller. The computerised house was Keller's final proof that Emma had been wrong to dismiss his automation theories a couple of years earlier. The experience of being trapped in the sense-warping mechanism of the building came close to breaking Emma's spirit. Having seen an exhibition dedicated to her 'late' self, she was able to reason out a means of destroying the house's systems and escaping – just as a concerned Steed arrived on her trail [JACK].[73]

---

[73] Don Macpherson incorporated elements of Emma's experienced in Keller's dimensionally impossible building into his screenplay for his 1998 movie, relocating this to 'Hallucinogen Hall', the home of Sir August de Wynter.

Towards the end the spring term, Steed had Emma stationed at St Bedes college as a lecturer [HIST], after which she then went undercover as a secretary to work for Miss Mary Merryweather, a secretary herself who had recently taken over the running of Sir George Morton's business in the wake of his death. As such, Emma was able to befriend Mary and so infiltrate Henry and Henrietta Throgbottom's strange keep fit classes which promoted 'ruination to all men' [SUCC]. During the investigation into a planned assassination of Prince Ali of Barabia, Emma again fell back on the cover story of a journalist to interview Ponsonby Hopkirk at QQF Inc and later became a gift from Steed to Prince Ali's harem as a rather indignant, 'poorly-educated', shy and 'retarded' (as Steed puts it) Lustrous, Luminous Star of the East... who could not even count [PRIN]. With this assignment concluded, Emma joined Steed to shoot a short training film entitled *The Strange Case of the Missing Corpse*.

Around now, Emma apparently embarked upon a rare European adventure, acting as a lure to trap a man called Max Prendergast who had preyed upon refugees and betrayed many people. In Berlin, Prendergast believed that he was in love with Emma, buying roses for her and listening again and again to Carl Schmidt's recording of 'Mein Leibling, Mein Rose' ('My Love, My Rose')[74] – unaware that Steed and the police were moving in on him before he could escape to Rio. It was a bitter and infatuated Prendergast who was seized by the authorities and imprisoned [JOKE].

By autumn 1966, Emma had moved to a new flat in the shadow of a monstrous office block [MISS]. Although no address was specified[75], it was 'in town' [NEVE], north of some country roads [SEET] but south of Whittlesham Heath and Fitzroy Lane [EPIC]. Beside the front door was a large silver door buzzer with 'Emma Peel' written over the top of it; close friends such as Steed knew that there was a secret button at the top left of the door jam which would unlock the door from the outside [FEAR, TIME] thus meaning that Steed could gain access before Emma arrived home and help himself to her drinks [VENU]. On the inside of this door, a rough human dummy could be hung for Emma's fencing practice [VENU] and the door itself could be secured from unwanted visitors by a chain [SEET] and a bolt [FEAR].

This door gave access into the large 'L' shaped living area of the wood-floored flat. To the left of the door were some chairs, a standard lamp and a large painting on the wall, while to the right was a red piano standing in a deep alcove which was painted a strong scarlet with white flowers forming a music score on staves [eg FEAR]; the piano could also be moved out from the alcove when it was to be played [VENU]. Sometimes a black metal plinth supporting a wrought iron bird sculpture was placed on this corner [TIME, VENU], adjacent to a pine cabinet which stood beneath a large bronze wall plaque [BIRD] and two small pairs of wall lights. At the back of the apartment was a pot plant or a lamp on a low table [BIRD], standing beside a tall, narrow set of French windows [FEAR] with a balcony [STAT]. A light rug covered the wooden floor [WING]. Although she originally had a white telephone [BIRD], Emma soon swapped this for a red model [WING, TIGE]. Emma also had a tape recorder system hooked up to her phone which allowed her to leave pre-recorded

---

[74] Deutsche Phon, R 236, 78rpm. The summary report gives the translated title as 'My Love, My Tender Beautiful Rose'.

[75] An unconfirmed source suggests it was 'on the highest point of Hampstead.' *The Laugh Was On Lazarus*, p39. A similar source refers to it as being in 'Primrose Hill'. *The Passing of Gloria Munday*, p126. A third mentions 'Emma's Hampstead penthouse'. *The Afrit Affair*, p8.

messages for Steed when he phoned her [BIRD]; this unit was housed beside the phone on a table [VENU]. Her phone number appears to have been 389 2223 [BIRD].

The main furniture in the sparse living area was a very ornate three-piece suite consisting of two chairs and a recliner, all upholstered in deep red on white frames [eg FEAR]; these were frequently moved into new positions around the flat as it seemed that Emma often rearranged the furniture [MISS]. There were two sets of spherical hanging lights; one by the front door and one by the French windows [FEAR]. A second standard lamp stood against the wall furthest from the door [FEAR]. An abstract painting also appeared on this wall [TIME] and there were silver candlesticks dotted around [TIGE]. The door to the left of the French windows led to Emma's bedroom [VENU][76], while further along this wall was a second doorway covered by a beaded curtain [VENU] which was possibly the alternate exit from the apartment [STAT]. There must also have been a storage area for Emma's champagne [WING].

The large open-plan space of this studio allowed Emma lots of room for her various hobbies. It was large enough to house a block of concrete in autumn 1966 [FEAR, TIME, BIRD] while she also had a movable workbench for her scientific work [BIRD, SEET]. She also made reference to having a 'fireside' [STAT] – but none was in evidence in the films.

Impressed with her Lotus Elan S2, Emma upgraded to the new model of the Lotus Elan E3[77] soon after it was launched in June 1966, purchasing a powder-blue version of the sports car complete with lights which could automatically fold down into the bonnet [FEAR, TIME, BIRD, VENU, SEET, WING, LIVI, TIGE, NEVE, EPIC, SUP7, NURS, JOKE, WHO?, DOOR, RETU, JUST, POSI, MDVL, MISS]. She kept this parked round the corner in the street by some garages adjoining her new flat [EPIC] or alternatively left it out in the street itself [POSI]. As with her last car, Emma had a dashboard radio [VENU], but this time had a two way radio handset installed into the glove box which meant that she could contact Steed by phone [VENU, JUST].[78] Emma was prepared to loan her car to others when necessary, such as Paul Croft [MDVL] or the strange Ola Monsey Chamberlain [JOKE]. However, otherwise she was very protective of it and was less than pleased to find the threatening villager Mickle at the wheel in Little Storping, only shortly after the Lotus had been used in a fake road crash where it was claimed that Emma had collided with a fence near the village green [MDVL].

By autumn 1966, the Business Efficiency Bureau instruments recorded a true response when she claimed that she and Steed were in 'the same business' [FEAR], and she was soon reporting to the government [SEET]. When investigating the BEB she claimed to be a rival of Steed's in the travel business [FEAR], while she posed as a embezzler to gain access to the fake escape route in time supposedly offered by Thyssen [TIME].

After helping Steed discover how security was being penetrated at the Muswells Back missile installation [BIRD], Emma found her chemical knowledge disproving the invisibility theories of Ernest Quilby, and helping to ruin an enemy plan cooked up by Major Vazin [SEET]. When investigating a series of murders of ruthless businessmen, Emma again posed as a writer from a magazine, this time one owned by Simon Roberts and Son, when

---

[76] Where, one unconfirmed report suggests, Emma had a collection of teddy bears. *Diana*, Issue 213, 17 March 1967.

[77] Registration SJH 499D.

[78] It has also been suggested that one of the lights on the padded leather dash was a homing device which tracked a button on one of Emma's jackets. *The Afrit Affair*, p91.

she went to interview mountaineer Sir Lexius Cray. Later she went to the offices of Winged Avenger Enterprises claiming to be the representative of a company dealing with novelty items which had a 'London Office' [WING]. After being kidnapped by 'ghosts' near the Benedict Mine and held in an underground city in late 1966 [LIVI], Emma started to redecorate her studio apartment, stripping away the existing wallpaper and painting some of the walls green. This work was delayed slightly by another series of murders associated with big cats, which required Emma to approach the PURRR organisation of cat lovers claiming that she had lost her pet feline 'little John' [TIGE].

As 1967 dawned, Emma seemed to have been taken fully on board by the Department, and people now referred to her as being 'from the authorities'[79] [VENU]. This meant that she was now helping to write official reports [NURS]. Her security rating with the Department was high; Emma had access to every file and every secret document [WHO?], was issued with a pass while working for the Treasury which allowed her full access to paperwork [MISS], could walk into a conference room which was barred to everyone except 'top brass' [DOOR] and was involved in checking security on important assignments [DOOR]. She was also aware of the existence of Mother, although there is little evidence to suggest they met [KNOT]. This standing in the Department meant that she was becoming increasingly well known to the 'other side'; Comrade Nutski's file annotations about her read 'Very dangerous. Do not handle at all' [CORR].

It is possible that Emma now had specific Department training. She had previously been able to pick a lock with a pencil [CAST] but was now able to open handcuffs [WHO?] using a toothpick [BREA], crack a safe with ease [CORR], pick office locks [MISS] and had skeleton keys to open vehicles [BREA]. With this new status, Emma's first case of the new year was an investigation into the British Venusian Society, where she again claimed to be from a newspaper, following up on anonymous photos and tape recordings hinting of an invasion by Venusians [VENU]. The next assignment saw her working in co-operation with the enemy, notably Ivan Peppitoperoff, when both sides of the Iron Curtain saw their agents attacked by a third party. Emma managed to infiltrate SNOB, the charm school where the third party was based, and donned fencing gear to pose as Hilda, one of the instructors, and so defeat the killers in combat alongside Comrade Olga Volowoski [CORR].

By spring, Emma's apartment had been redecorated – and for that matter restructured. There was now a far more ornate silver bell pull, although the front door had been shifted into a different part of the external corridor wall. The secret entry button remained [EPIC] but the lock on the front door was later burnt out by the touch of the highly-charged Peter Haworth [POSI]. The main studio was now a more staggered L-shape, with the French windows in the same place; there was more furniture and less of the sparse feeling than before. Entering via the door, the piano alcove – or where the alcove had been – was now directly to the left and had been filled in, leading to a small seating area alongside which there was a sideboard with a set of scales, an urn and a ceramic statue – as well as Emma's glasses and drinks [eg EPIC]. The ornate furniture had been disposed of in favour of two leather armchairs, and also by the front door was a large clock [NEVE]. Emma now had a colour television set with a remote control [NEVE] (although BBC 2 was not to start operating

---

[79] It is also worth noting that while her cover at BEB was the travel industry, 'Informant's Occupation' even at this stage in autumn 1966 was 'INVESTIGATOR' and 'Informant's Industry' was given as 'DETECTION' [FEAR].

a colour service until that summer) and even appeared to have some system which allowed her to review surveillance films of previous missions [NEVE]. There was also a radio tuner [NEVE] and china ornaments clustered around a lamp in the corner [EPIC]. By the new couch and leather seats was a low table [EPIC] and also a black and orange rug [EPIC]. There was a large clock over the bedroom door [WHO?] and a full length mirror in the corner near a bureau [WHO?].

Emma now had two telephones, one red and one green [WHO?] and her telephone number was 629 6291 [MISS]; her calls could be recorded on a reel-to-reel tape recorder [EPIC]. Although her kitchen is not seen in the existing surveillance films, she owned a faulty toaster which Steed attempted to mend [RETU]. It would seem that a certain amount of rewiring needed to be done after Peter Haworth's electrifying visit in summer 1967 [POSI].

In the three years that she had been operating with Steed, Emma's reputation for under-cover work alongside her business skills had become well known. Her beauty, poise and 'animal vitality' made her a perfect star for a down-beat art house movie to be made by old-fashioned director ZZ von Schnerk. Von Schnerk had Emma kidnapped in a taxi by one-time matinee idol Stewart Kirby and then imprisoned at his soundstages where she was made to act out a series of bizarre situations that would climax in her agonising death. Emma retained her wits and was saved from becoming a posthumous star by the arrival of Steed who brought shooting on *The Destruction of Mrs Emma Peel* to a swift conclusion [EPIC].

Emma had little involvement with Steed's next escapade and simply had to follow him by plane to a desolate island where an enemy agent was testing new combat methods – methods which Emma quickly proved were not invincible [SUP7]. She was then instru-mental in averting an attempt to kill the Prime Minister on a train journey, having posed as a writer for women readers when checking up on Admiral Cartney whose office had been implicated [STAT]. An information leak regarding defence bases via the Guild of Noble Nannies was stemmed with Emma's help [NURS], after which Emma suffered a strange ordeal – having her mind placed in the body of an enemy agent called Lola, while Lola took over her identity for several hours until the process could be reversed [WHO?].

Like Steed, Emma now became a target for revenge. An art dealer called 'Paul Beresford' went to great lengths to get to know her, and indeed there was an attraction between the pair which made Steed rather jealous. It turned out that 'Beresford' was the brother of the late Dr Clement Armstrong whom Emma had seen die at the hands of his creations, the Cybernauts, two years before. Tricked into wearing a watch which took control of her nervous system, Emma fell under temporary control of 'Beresford' until Steed managed to release her [RETU].

Around now, Emma's article *Better Bridge With Applied Mathematics* appeared in the June issue of *Bridge Players' International Guide* [JOKE]. Assuming that the next surveil-lance film was a true assignment and not another training exercise in which she was re-enacting the role of Cathy Gale, Emma found herself using a trio of identities to investi-gate the affairs of the Litoff Organisation. First she claimed to have been a school friend of one Miss Judy Chanarin, then to have been a friend of financier Alex Litoff, and finally infiltrating the Litoff offices as a lady from Pedigree Kennels [BREA]. In the wake of a deadly car rally treasure hunt [TREA], Emma donned her journalist mantle again to visit the wealthy Lord Rathbone regarding a series of articles on 'How to become a millionaire' and discovering that Rathbone's life was being threatened [JUST].

Surviving kidnap and use as bait in a trap for Steed [POSI], Emma was delighted to be reunited with her childhood friend Major Paul Croft who had been delayed in his return from Karachi – an event which Emma had eagerly been talking about all week. Having resigned his commission, Paul wanted to settle down and grow things as well as breeding horses; after being in remote corners of the British Empire for years, the former Major hoped that Emma would help him readjust to being with people. Paul had purchased an old house on a hill in Little Storping in-the-Swuff, sight unseen, after spotting an advert in *The Times*, but hours after Emma went to help him and his batman, Private Forbes, move in, Paul was killed. Emma discovered that Little Storping was actually a boomtown where murders were committed for money and the silence of the entire community bought. When she discovered Paul's body in the office of Dr Haynes, Emma was deeply upset – and later lost no time in extracting a physical revenge on Haynes. In the meantime, her subterfuge in alerting Steed to her plight involved a phone call to her husband 'John' – or 'Johnsie-wonsie' – during which she referred to herself as 'Emma' and mentioned their children little Julian, Gordon, Albert and Baby Brian [MDVL].[80]

Emma was unaware that around mid-September, Max Prendergast broke out of jail in Germany. Prendergast had always had a macabre sense of humour, and his time in prison had fuelled a lethal obsession with Emma, whose photographs he had seen in magazines such as *Bridge Player's International Guide*. Believing that not only was he still in love with her, but that she should now die, he used her interest in bridge to lure her to the remote home of Sir Cavalier Rousicana on Exmoor where he planned to first petrify her and then take his final revenge. On arrival, Emma was led to believe that Sir Cavalier had had to attend a London meeting of the IBPC[81] and was then stalked around the empty building. If anything, Emma was more shaken by this chilling experience than when trapped in Keller's automated house. Although she generally retained her calm during these events, she was still relieved by the arrival of Steed and his dispatch of Prendergast [JOKE].

Emma's security training came in useful for the protection of her acquaintance Lord Melford in October 1967 [DOOR] and she was then subjected to both miniaturisation [MISS] and amnesia [KNOT], both thankfully of a temporary nature. One of her final adventures alongside Steed – the man who had become so close and important to her over the last three years – was an investigation into a supposed walking corpse in November 1967, which concluded with her discovering her own synthetic double [NEVE].

Around November came the news that Emma never thought she would hear. Her husband Peter was found alive in the Manaus region of the Amazonian jungle by a Brazilian medical mission [KNOT]. An unsubstantiated record of events suggests that Peter had been found and cared for by the Leopard People, a lost Inca tribe whose leader, Picchu, believed he had fallen from the sun. Suffering from partial amnesia, Peter lived among the Leopard People until the children of the tribe started to die. Picchu then restored his memory so that he would return to the world and stop the disease, spread by the men cutting through the Amazonian jungles.[82] With her husband arriving back in London, Emma made one last visit to see Steed in her official capacity. Kissing him gently on the

---

[80] It is believed that Emma was referring to Julian Wintle, Gordon L T Scott and Albert Fennell – three of the members of the Department surveillance team – and also Brian Clemens, an agent who documented many of her assignments.

[81] International Bridge Players' Convention.

[82] 'Deadly Rainbow', *Steed and Mrs Peel*, Book Two, p4-8.

cheek, she softly whispered, 'Always keep your bowler on in times of stress, and watch out for diabolical masterminds.' The moment of intimacy passed and as Emma departed, Steed thanked her for the three years of danger and friendship – actually addressing her by her Christian name. He then watched thoughtfully as Peter – who clearly had similar sartorial elegance to himself – whisked his wife away in his Rolls-Royce convertible [KNOT].

Having departed from Stable Mews, the reunited couple apparently returned to Pringle on Sea to repeat their brief honeymoon of a few years earlier – although as one unconfirmed report indicated, this was merely the start of another dangerous adventure in which she would encounter the Leopard People... and be reunited immediately with Steed.[83]

There are two other rather strange and bizarre surveillance films which seem to show Emma – or a woman very much like her – from somewhere around 1966-67. The first incident – which is in monochrome and has no dialogue – seems to concern the recovery of a jewel which was stolen from her while she was swimming with dolphins. The second – in colour – has the lady in question in what appears to be Spain, averting an assassination attempt launched using a lethal gas-squirting doll. Although it seems to be Emma in these items, there is no confirmatory material on this point.

Another unconfirmed assignment for Steed around late 1968 saw him reunited with Emma when Tara King went missing. Emma had apparently just returned from six months in the Amazon with the Leopard People; Peter had stayed on for a particularly gruesome ceremony to be performed by the tribe and aimed to be back in England for Christmas.[84] A further such document suggests that some time around 1969, Peter had died – and Steed had not attended the funeral. Alone again, Emma was once more involved in the running of Knight Industries – and again highly sceptical of the prospect of automation as proposed by the graduate Edwin Carruthers.[85]

Paperwork on Emma – notably what appears to be a transcript of her exploits in Little Storping in-the-Swuff – was kept in a 'Top Secret' file by the Department in 1969 [PAND]. By 1977, her exploits still filled three 22423 MA type files in the record office (including files 347 and DM) [DEAD]. A colour photograph of her remained on display in Steed's drawing room [CARD] and he still knew where to contact her. Certainly by August 1977, Emma was no longer known as 'Mrs Peel' – as she told Steed when he telephoned her about an unsolved case from 12 years earlier. Thinking back to their three years of amazing adventures together, Steed fondly commented that Emma hadn't changed and that she was 'Still Mrs Peel to me' [KIL1].[86]

---

[83] 'Deadly Rainbow', *Steed and Mrs Peel*, Books Two-Three. See Appendix B.

[84] 'The Golden Game', *Steed and Mrs Peel*, Book One, p14.

[85] *Too Many Targets*, p57-68.

[86] Emma was of course featured in the Warner Bros biographical picture of Steed's life which incorrectly depicted her as 'Dr Emma Peel, Former Chief of the Prospero Program' – in effect a Government meteorologist. This version of Emma lived in a spacious two-level flat with minimalist furniture, Andy Warhol-style prints on the walls and an automated piano; it was actually the home of architect Richard Rogers in Chelsea and overlooked the Royal Hospital. She drove a silver E-type Jaguar rather than a Lotus. This Emma had had an evil clone of her created by fellow meteorologist Sir August de Wynter, and the 'Ministry' file on her rather ruthlessly described her as a 'psychopathic personality with schizophrenic delusions, suffering from recurring amnesia based on traumatic repression leading to outbursts of anti-social and violent behaviour.' The reaction of the true Emma to this cinematic representation of her is not known.

MISS TARA KING

'Jolly girl... awfully decent sort' was the verdict of Department operative Basil Creighton-Latimer with regards to Miss Tara King [WISH], one of the youngest and highest profile agents working for the organisation by the end of the 1960s. Known for her beauty, style and being a 'Dab hand with a caviar canapé' [GETA], Tara's resourcefulness during an amnesia incident afflicting the Department meant that she had gone from being a fledgling operative undergoing training at Mother's HQ in 1967 to almost immediately becoming the new junior operative assigned to the legendary John Steed [KNOT], and therefore a very young lady involved in some of the more serious counter-espionage cases over the next two years. 'I considered her to be vulnerable, very young and very taken with Steed,'[1] recalled actress Linda Thorson – a colleague of Patrick Macnee's – who knew Tara during the period when she was working with the Department, having been a contemporary of hers at RADA.

Very little is known about Tara's formative years. She seems to have been born around 1947, and having been christened Tara (a name apparently inspired by Scarlett O'Hara's North Georgian plantation in the 1939 film *Gone With The Wind*[2]) she found that in her formative years when she introduced herself most people then responded 'Ra-Boom-Der-Ay'[3] [KNOT]. When she was two years old (around 1949), she spent some time in North Alaska [LOOK]. According to her dossier, her father was an airline pilot and she travelled extensively in Canada where he worked.[4] However, newspaper reports in October 1967 about Tara landing a major role in a television series indicated that she was the 'daughter of a wealthy farmer.'[5] Of her family, she had an uncle called Charles Merrydale[6] who was of Irish descent and who ran his own company [WISH], and an aged aunt in Cheltenham whom she would go and spend the weekends with [TAKE]. There was also another uncle

---

[1] 'Linda Thorson', *Look Who's Talking The Avengers*, p19.

[2] According to Tara's associate, Linda Thorson. 'Linda Thorson', *Look Who's Talking: The Avengers*, p17.

[3] Because of the song 'Tar-ra-ra-boom-der-ay!', originally sung by the celebrated Mama Lou in a St Louis brothel and published by Henry J Sayers in 1891. The piece was popularised in England by musical hall artiste Lottie Collins.

[4] *Featuring The New Avengers*, p22.

[5] *Daily Mail*, 30 October 1967, p3. See also *Daily Mirror*, 30 October 1967, p7.

[6] Erroneously referred to as 'Charles Merryvale' in the summary report.

who once had a double-barrelled shotgun made specially for him but never used it... since the young man married Tara's cousin of his own free will [OVER].

It was apparently through hunting trips with her father that she acquired her ability to handle firearms and to ski.[7] She soon held a pilot's licence[8] – and flew a helicopter during her time with the Department [NOON]. Unconfirmed reports suggest that by 1968, Tara had been in the Congo where she was tied to a stake by cannibals[9] and faced a charging rhino with a jammed gun[10]; stickers from Capetown to Delhi covered her suitcase.[11] It seems that prior to coming to the UK, Tara lived in Toronto where she trained as a secretary after leaving school[12]; this is where she learned her skills in typing and shorthand [CYPH]. Her original career – which she never referred to in the surveillance films – was to be an actress, travelling to London to enrol with RADA, the Royal Academy of Dramatic Art.[13] An unconfirmed report in which Tara once thought about the girls from the office where she had once worked possibly suggests that she had undertaken temp work to supplement her income at this time.[14]

There is little known about Tara's friends and acquaintances. She had a friend called Georgie in the medical profession, and another associate called Gregory [WILD]. There was also another friend whom she persuaded to take part in a little exercise demonstrating how easy it was to frame somebody [THAT]. She had a basic knowledge of chemistry; certainly she knew that ether was inflammable, that potassium chlorate explodes under impact and that she could use pyrochloric acid to burn through metal restrains [CATC].[15] Unconfirmed reports suggest that Tara knew French and German[16]; the surveillance films show that she did not understand Greek [GAME].

It seems that after a couple of years at RADA, Tara opted for a career change. Although during October 1967 it was announced that the newly graduated actress had landed a starring role in a British adventure television film series, Tara instead opted for real-life espionage. The young actress instead joined the Department as Agent 69 [KNOT]. By late autumn 1967 she was undergoing training from instructors such as George Burton at the country estate being used by Mother as his HQ [KNOT]. Two of those training alongside her were a naval officer called Paul Mullard [INTR] and fellow operative Damian Harrison[17], while she also knew another operative called Penman [FALS] early in her career.

Tara was incredibly fit. One enemy agent was impressed that this Spartan of a girl was

---

[7] *Featuring The New Avengers*, p22.

[8] *Featuring The New Avengers*, p22. Confirmed on one unfilmed assignment. *TV Comic*, Issue 991, 12 December 1970.

[9] *The Drowned Queen*, p124.

[10] *The Drowned Queen*, p124.

[11] *The Magnetic Man*, p112.

[12] *Featuring The New Avengers*, p22.

[13] *Featuring The New Avengers*, p22. It is worth noting that this celebrated school for aspiring thespians has had many famous graduates over the years including Dame Diana Rigg CBE, Linda Thorson and Patrick Newell although the celebrated actress Joanna Lumley, famous for her appearances in series such as *Sapphire & Steel* and *Ab Fab*, failed her audition there.

[14] *The Magnetic Man*, p24.

[15] Tara apparently knew about the effects of radioactivity. *TV Comic*, Issue 898, 1 March 1969.

[16] 'Come On In – The Water's Deadly'. *The Avengers Annual*, 1969, p54.

[17] *Too Many Targets*, p23.

not out of breath after ascending the 365 steps of a lighthouse [DONE] and she could turn cartwheels in a most athletic manner [CLUE]. When a large wheel was bowled at her she evaded it skilfully [FOG], effortlessly leapfrogged over the backs of other agents [INTR] and executed an excellent forward roll on a tarmac street when left behind by a milk float she was pursuing [FALS].

Her dossier noted that she was skilled in both judo and karate, and was an excellent shot.[18] Tara practised her judo on cushions at her flat and received further tuition from Steed; she was a quick learner and could soon get her elder off balance [INVA]. Within months, she was able to trounce two of the very best martial arts experts, Cavell and Captain Tim – the latter, who sustained a broken leg, pleaded with her not to tell anyone of her victory [TAKE]. The throw manoeuvres which she used included O-Goshi from ju-jitsu [TAKE] and the judo move Sumi Gaeshi [STAY].

Kicking was a key element of Tara's usual form of combat [eg INVA, GUNS, LOOK] along with well-aimed punches [eg LOOK, WILD, ROTT]; a blow from her hand was powerful enough to lay out female opponents [WILD, STAY]. When in full combat she very energetic, flinging herself about [INVA], leaping at her attackers [INTR] and propelling herself into her adversaries by springing off the wall with her feet [CATC]. On other occasions she tended to evade rather than attack, but nevertheless had the strength to throw a colossus through the wall of a hut [DONE]. The throw was one of Tara's most common moves [CYPH, WILD, FALS, TAKE]. She was very confident with this technique – as she demonstrated on the Honourable Teddy Chilcott [WILD].

Even when restrained, Tara was a formidable opponent. Tied up, she could grab a man around the neck with her legs [THAT] and fight with bound hands [OVER]. She co-ordinated very well with Steed when they found themselves in fisticuffs together [GAME], and in more exotic fights demonstrated her talents at knife throwing [NOON] and even the skill of a matador [KEEP].

However, in addition to conventional unarmed combat, Tara would frequently make use of any potential weapon which came to hand. She fenced with an umbrella [CLUE] and a swordstick sheath [STAY], lashed out with in-trays and out-trays [CLUE, GETA, CLUE], hand-bags [KNOT, GUNS], a mallet [LACE], a telescope [DONE], glass shards [GAME], a spade [NOON], a paddle [FALS], a rolling pin [WISH], a bucket [INVA], butter pats [WISH], frying pans [WISH], a wine bottle [ROTT] and a spanner [TAKE], while the missiles she flung included a bowler hat [CLUE], crates [GUNS], a vase [LEGA] and a bottle of red wine [ROTT]. Vases [INTR, FOG] and china ornaments [FOG] were items which she favoured for knocking somebody out. She would also bite when necessary [CLUE].

One attacker was blinded by water squirted from Tara's hot water bottle [CLUE] while his colleague tripped on apples which she scattered on the floor, allowing her to knock him out with her painting palette [CLUE]. She lowered a ladder on one man to apprehend him [CYPH] and used a windlass on a well to smash a revolver from the hand of another [NOON], while a ladder and bridle were deployed on an assassin [NOON]. When attacked by Sergeant Blackie at Mr Puffin's balloon stall, she gained the upper hand by bursting a balloon in the face of her assailant, momentarily blinding him [INTR]; her use of sand from a fire bucket had a similar effect [INVA]. One woman received a piano lid in her jaw when she took on Tara [TAKE], who also brought a hat stand down on one attacker [INTR] and pushed grapes

---

[18] *Featuring The New Avengers*, p22.

into the face of another [REQU]. An angle-poise lamp came in handy to slam into the face of Sir Geoffrey Armstrong when he caught her searching his office [FOG].

In a tight spot, Tara was an extremely resourceful lady, using her clothes to wipe clear a tunnel ahead of her [INVA], hurling her shoe to attract Steed's attention [WILD], mixing chemicals to manufacture an explosive [CATC], sliding a plank from a timber pile to concuss an enemy courier [TAKE], triggering an explosive case to blow her way out of the sealed Cunningham Family crypt at St Bartholomew's Church [TAKE] or using a shard of pottery to dig at the bottom of Steed's grave in Paradise Plot [BIZA]. A few months into her new career, she was also planning well – such as when she took over the kitchen of the Elizabethan Hotel, reasoning it was the nerve centre of the establishment [WISH], or transferring from the lift to the ventilation system during an attack on the War Room [THAT].

Tara tended not to rely very heavily on firearms and, while still training, the main weapon which she carried was a brick secreted in her handbag [KNOT]. On one of her early assignments she had a case containing a rifle [INVA], and seemed familiar with the FF70/9 rifles which she and Steed attempted to track down [GUNS]. On another occasion, she found herself firing a sub-machine gun taken from a member of Intercrime [LACE]. When she was acting as Lord Dessington's bodyguard, Steed issued her with his Smith and Wesson Model 19 Combat Magnum .357 revolver which she tended to play with in a rather amateurish manner [LOOK]. Tara herself was later armed with a silver Webley revolver on a couple of missions [XR40, GAME] and also used a Smith and Wesson like Steed's [KEEP]. At her flat, she kept a Beretta 6.35mm automatic hidden in a silver box on a tabletop [THAT].

Like all agents, Tara was trained to withstand interrogation [LACE], although she did later succumb to the Chinese water torture [LEGA]. However, she also devised tortures of her own, applying a feather duster to the bare feet of Mr Sidney Street to elicit necessary information [LEGA]. Tara knew techniques to withstand the forcible use of drugs – principally to refrain from going to sleep – which enabled her to resist a hallucinogenic charade at a critical moment [PAND]. She was also able to withstand an assault on her mind using a sound projector [INTR] but could not master the art of hypnotism [CYPH].

Tara claimed that her powers of survival were instinctive [INVA]. Despite her fear of heights [LOVE][19], Tara was a strong climber who overcame her fears to quickly slide down ladders [CYPH], leap off tall walls [NOON] or scramble down wells [NOON]. She was an excellent swimmer and diver [DONE, KEEP].[20] Apart from heights, her only other fear seemed to be rats [INVA].[21]

After training, Tara was adept at picking locks [XR40] using items such as a hair grip [ROTT] or a metal strip [STAY]. However, it was not a skill she used very often, leading her to comment that her 'breaking and entry' was a bit rusty by November 1968 [FOG]. She was also trained to move quietly when trying to surprise intruders [FALS].

Tara was quite stunning at safe-cracking and under test conditions could perform this task in less than 59.15 seconds [LACE]. Mother particularly prized having Tara on his team because he rated her as having a good analytical mind [WISH]. Tara's mental powers proved

---

[19] It is reported that Tara got butterflies in the stomach at the thought of sky-diving. *TV Comic*, Issue 921, 9 August 1969.

[20] See also 'Come on In – The Water's Deadly', *The Avengers Annual*, 1969, p48.

[21] An unconfirmed and unlikely report suggests that Tara once fainted when a boa constrictor slithered over her foot. *The Drowned Queen*, p124.

useful on many occasions, reasoning out a vital key for a courier case from the phrase 'Love laughs at locksmiths' [TAKE], suggesting the use of the psychiatric trick of 'association of ideas' to recall details from her subconscious [REQU] or deducing that it was love which was making Sir Rodney Kellogg act so strangely [LOVE].

Tara was quickly able to set Steed up to look as guilty as she did when framed, which helped to prove her innocence. Furthermore, Tara was trained to work undercover and knew that the Department would not be fooled by her decoy double being clearly spotted at London Airport [THAT]. She cleverly tricked a man into revealing the details of his contacts to her [TAKE] and similarly conned a captor into dropping her guard by claiming that she had worked her bonds free, when she had not [STAY]. Her lateral thinking saved her life in a duel when she opted not to run for her own weapon, but rather to stop her opponent from reaching his [GUNS].

In terms of personal attributes, Tara had excellent hearing [XR40]. She was very observant, spotting a cigarette on a lighthouse staircase (revealing a hidden room) [DONE], a logo on a vehicle [INVA] and recalling that the type of cigarette smoked by Captain Soo matched a butt left at the home of Lt Roy Casper [INTR]. When visiting the home of Steed's friend Bill Bassett, a glimpse of Steed's bowler and umbrella in the hallway was enough to tell her that Steed had not left; unfortunately, her reaction to this was not subtle enough to escape being noticed [OVER].

By the end of training, Tara was fully conversant with the Department, including the drill for visiting the medical establishment Department S [NOON]. However, initially there were some matters of procedure with which she was not entirely familiar, such as the regulation method of hiding documents in the bottom of a bag [INVA].

Tara was at first very impulsive and acted without thinking [INVA], yet her habit of picking things up which looked of interest sometimes paid dividends [SPLI]. Although Mother found her frivolous at times [LOVE], Tara took great pride in her work [LEGA]. She liked to have solid proof rather than accept a series of coincidences [WISH]. Even after working with Steed for several months, she could still be upset by a death [KEEP].

While she was training, Tara already lived at an open-plan flat at 9 Primrose Crescent, London, W1 [KNOT, THIN], although – despite the printed card she carried with this address [THIN] – it was probably Flat 9 of house 19A judging by the surveillance film [THAT]. The apartment was on an upper floor at a bend in the street [CLUE].[22]

'Goodness gracious me!' exclaimed Mother on seeing Tara's apartment – without fog – for the first time [PAND]. The interior of Tara's flat was incredibly bohemian, full of lots of Victoriana and knick-knacks placed against the background of bright, vibrant colours in a very pop-art fashion, typical of the 'Swinging' London of that era. This potpourri of items which might have been thrown out as junk was referred to as 'objet retrouvé' at the time and had a Parisian flavour. The front door to the flat was in a corridor of the apartment building which had a lift [CLUE, TAKE]. Visitors could use a buzzer to announce their arrival [CLUE] and the door was secured with a chain, Yale latch and bolt [CLUE], while a small silver high-heeled boot mounted on the inside of the door could swing aside, revealing a peep-hole through which Tara could first check on who her visitor was before admitting

---

[22] The architecture is almost identical to a building found on Chalcot Crescent, NW1. It was suggested that Tara had a garage beneath her flat – *The Magnetic Man*, p108 – but in the films she parked her car in the street outside [GUNS].

them [INVA, CLUE, STAY]. However, Tara did not keep this door locked as often as she should, which sometimes allowed unwanted guests [WILD, LEGA].

The front door brought the visitor onto an upper landing of the open living area, beside which there was both a real circular window to the outside world [CLUE] and a false window painted on the wall in an alcove [LOVE] close to a wall-mounted phone [CLUE, LOVE]. There were then two ways to descend to the living area. The conventional way was down the stairs, the banisters of which were prone to being smashed in a fight [CLUE, LOVE]. The other way down was via a fireman's pole [eg KNOT], descending to an area under the landing where there was some shelving [OVER]. The walls were painted in pink, peacock blue, snug grey and Imperial Chinese yellow with lilac woodwork. Giant golden letters and numerals were adhered to the walls. The number '22' appeared by the back door, with '21' on the stairs by the front window [CLUE], 'TK' and 'NO' either side of the back door (with a crown over the 'TK') [eg KNOT] and 'OP' on the wall by the stairs [eg GUNS].

The decor was eclectic to say the least. A pair of stuffed stag heads, one of which was an early 19th century Austrian, were mounted on the wall by the stairs while a large stuffed fish hung over a lacquered cabinet on the left of the bedroom door [eg TAKE]. There were a couple of primitive African paintings and various old-fashioned shop signs which Tara had acquired, including spectacles from an opticians, a giant boot from a boot maker, a huge padlock from a locksmiths, a wooden horse's head from a French meat shop, and a bearded bust of a Turk from a snuff and tobacco shop which stood on a sideboard by the back door. A model vintage car stood on a table by the stairs and there was a small treasure chest on a Victorian post box to the right of the bedroom door. A penny-farthing bicycle hung on the wall above a shelf of china heads on which Tara kept her wigs (one of which, her favourite, Steed accidentally broke [FOG]). Beneath the stairs was a spinning wheel, and a bellows formed part of the decor along with vases of dried flowers [eg KNOT, GUNS, THIN]. One wall held a display of rather lethal blades [WILD] of which Tara proudly said, 'What a collection.' [LEGA] Tara was always picking up antiques and curios at establishments such as Ho Lung's curio shop [FALS] or Xavier Smith's [PAND]. In 1969, she was particularly interested in acquiring a 17th century French bracket clock which had eluded her for some time [PAND].

Tara had a shocking pink carpet (later red), a red rug (under which she hid photographs [THAT]), and numerous cushions scattered about. Two white Chinese pendant lanterns hung from the ceiling and seating was provided by tan leather armchairs, while a bright couch in green, orange and yellow formed a window seat with matching curtains. On one table was a silver lighter [LOVE] while a silver box secreted her Beretta [THAT].

The Yale-locked ornate panelled back door with its stained glass bird (which looked as if it had come from a pub) [eg KNOT] led to a corridor with frosted glass windows [THAT] and in turn led down into a concrete yard at the rear of the building [LEGA]. Somehow – and it is by no means clear how – it was actually possible for Mother's Mini Moke to be driven through the living area of Tara's apartment [FOG].

The blind-covered windows behind the couch area overlooked the street outside [CLUE] and trains could be seen crossing a viaduct in the distance [GUNS, WILD]. Tara smashed one of her own windows playing 'invisible golf' [OVER]. The apartment was air-conditioned – but on one occasion the system went into reverse on a foggy day in November 1968 and filled the living area with a dense pea-souper [FOG]. With sand and sun lamps in position, the flat could make do for a summer holiday [KEEP].

The aforementioned Victorian post box originally served as Tara's drinks cabinet [GUNS] although later she kept glasses and decanters on top of it [THAT, OVER]. Wine was stored carefully in a wine rack in the back corner of the room beneath an abstract painting [THIN], while spirits, including whisky, were kept in decanters on the sideboard by the back door [THAT].

Tara had lots of different phones around the flat [eg KNOT, CLUE] but after working with Steed for only a short while, she soon realised that many of the calls she would receive would be for him [CLUE]. As noted, one of the old phones was mounted on the landing wall by the front door [CLUE, LOVE]. It seems that the different receivers may have been connected to different lines, since her flat was called by two different numbers, one starting 324 [CLUE] and another beginning 46 [WILD]. Certainly her number was known to Nurse Janet Owen who tried to contact Steed at Tara's apartment [WILD].

Tara had a record player of the latest and trendiest design [CLUE, THIN]. In terms of other household appliances, Tara had a Dictaphone on which she could leave messages and reports for Steed [STAY], an upright electric Hoover [THIN] and an electric fan [THIN]. In her drinks sideboard, Tara kept a photographic developing kit [THAT]. The fuses were under the stairs, near a desk which Tara would write at [THIN].

A cupboard and pot plant stood beside Tara's bedroom door, and beyond these was another door adjacent to a dresser containing her crockery, and then another window [LEGA]. Tara's bedroom was never seen, but it seems that she kept her pink teddy bear hot water bottle in there [CLUE] and various blue screens [THAT]. The second door was presumably her bathroom, in which she had a shower [INVA].

In late 1967, Tara was driving an outstandingly rare vehicle – a hand-built maroon AC 428 Spider Cabriolet[23] [KNOT] made by AC Cars of Thames Ditton in Surrey. The vehicle had been in production since October 1965, originally as the AC427 and then revised to the AC428 in January 1967. However, only 19 AC 428s were ever built, with a coachbuilt body manufactured in Italy by Fura and a 7014cc V8 engine. Tara used this automatic vehicle through to early 1968 [SPLI, GETA, LOOK, WILD, XR40, CYPH, CATC] and on one assignment she allowed Steed to take the wheel [INVA]. Unlike all the other AC 428s manufactured, Tara's came complete with air-conditioning – enhanced by Steed accidentally ripping its canvas roof with a magician's sword [LOOK].

Tara was a daring driver [SPLI] and was able to manoeuvre a car superbly on the road, using it to block and cut in front of vehicles which had opponents at the wheel [GUNS]. She could easily throw off a tail [LEGA] and her lightning reactions allowed her to brake quickly but safely when the road was blocked by an obstruction [ROTT]. Tara kept control of the car when a conditioned Steed suddenly grabbed hold of the wheel as she drove through the countryside [STAY]. Steed was certainly impressed enough with her driving skills to trust her with his Rolls-Royce Silver Ghost early on in their partnership [WILD]. When driving for pleasure, she particularly enjoyed being out in the countryside [CATC].

Very keen on fashion[24], according to some reports Tara enjoyed shopping at places such

---

[23] Registration LPH 600D.

[24] Allegedly during one assignment in 1969, Tara found some old military uniforms and commented, 'They'd make Fab Gear for the Younger Generation!' *TV Comic*, Issue 912, 7 June 1969. Two years later while shopping in London she told Steed, 'The Gear in this Boutique is Sensational!' *TV Comic*, Issue 1015, 29 May 1971.

as Boutique Madeleine on Carnaby Street[25] and also on Bond Street.[26] Vibrant colours were highly attractive to her, and unlike Emma she liked to contrast the shades rather than using them to complement. Brightly coloured jacket and skirt – or often miniskirt – combinations for Tara included items in forest green [WILD], gold [SPLI], navy blue with pink trim [GETA], maroon jersey [XR40], bright yellow with navy [CATC], pink [KEEP] and lime green [STAY]. She also wore similarly bright trouser suits in blue [LOVE], red [CATC], pale mustard Levi cord [DONE], a green and lime check [INTR] and a stylish grey Spanish cut with matching top hat and gloves [LEGA]. She had a distinctive leather zipped motorcycle jacket [WILD, KEEP] and a taste for tartan [GUNS, DONE, STAY]. One new outfit she bought specially for Steed comprised purple trousers with a maroon blouse and boa [FALS] while other notable items included a long purple dress [PAND] and a zipped Indian-style top [PAND].

Tara favoured wearing culottes which she had in green [LACE], brown [GETA, GUNS, WILD], light blue [LOOK], orange [GUNS] and black [GAME]. Sometimes these would be part of a set with a waistcoat like a brown gabardine [GETA, GUNS]. Again, Tara had numerous bright waistcoats in shades of pale blue [WILD], lilac [KEEP], dark blue (fastened by a chain) [CYPH, GAME] and purple [FALS] amongst others. Her blouses were just as bright, including pinks [GAME, KILL], greens [FALS, LOVE] and reds [REQU]. When not wearing jackets, Tara would sometimes wear long cardigans [eg INTR, WISH, THAT]. She had an array of polo necks in various colours, but often wore black [eg LOOK], beige [eg LOOK] or brown [eg STAY]. Occasionally, she wore tee-shirts [XR40, GAME]. Like Emma and Cathy, Tara also had an army of formal dresses including a white silken item with a hood [SPLI, GETA], a pale blue number [CYPH, GAME?] and a short white silk design with lace cuffs for attending the opera [LOOK].

Tara had a few fur coats [KNOT, GUNS, CATC, LACE][27] as well as overcoats in various vivid shades [eg GUNS, LACE], a red Hussar maxi-coat [SPLI], a white double-breasted coat [LACE, BIZA] and a Cossack-style red coat with black fur hood and cuffs [FOG]. She would wear scarves on occasion [eg SPLI, DONE], some of which matched her outfits [WILD, CYPH]; she also wore ties and neckerchiefs of various designs [eg SPLI, PAND]. Tara usually favoured black gloves [eg GUNS, FOG] but had various sets to match her wardrobe [GUNS, LEGA, SPLI]. Her range of hats included berets in tartan [GUNS] and white [DONE] and some broad-brimmed hats [XR40, CATC]. Tara particularly enjoyed the fashionable image of knee-length boots which she generally wore in black [eg GETA, PAND] although she also had pairs in brown [GETA, STAY] and red [NOON].

At home, Tara wore a peacock blue silk Kimono-style robe with coloured dragons [INVA, WILD, XR40, LEGA], a purple slipper satin gown with pale blue ostrich feather trim [WILD] and some bath robes [KNOT, INVA]. When sailing, she had yellow oilskins [OVER] and for camouflage work she had appropriate fatigues [THAT]. For a fancy dress party, she donned a cat-style outfit with mask, black body and green boa [XR40].[28]

Tara wore large earrings [WILD, XR40], various rings on her left hand [eg ROTT, PAND], and an anti-magnetic, shock-proof, waterproof, chronometer type watch (which ran fast)

---

[25] *The Drowned Queen*, p8.
[26] *The Magnetic Man*, p22.
[27] It has been suggested that Tara wanted a chinchilla fur. *The Magnetic Man*, p24.
[28] Tara apparently wore Western gear for a party at the 'Lazy J' Western Style Dude Ranch and Holiday Camp. *TV Comic*, Issue 987, 14 November 1970.

[GAME] and which Steed recognised [PAND] on her left wrist [eg LACE], along with the occasional metal bracelet [eg REQU, CLUE]. Steed gave her a pearl necklace for her birthday [KEEP], the sort of item that she would often wear [eg XR40, LOVE]. She also sported beads [eg GAME] and a silver necklace [FALS]. Most of all, she liked diamonds [GUNS].

Tara at first wore her brunette hair in a bob [eg KNOT, XR40] – which is how she appeared on her photo ID card [NOON] – but in spring 1968 had it cut shorter [eg CYPH, NOON]. A couple of times in early 1968 she wore her hair down [LOOK, WILD, MORN] and would wear it up on dressy occasions [BIZA]. She used hair grips [ROTT, PAND] and had an assortment of wigs as disguises [GUNS, INVA, LACE].[29] Sometimes Tara sported large circular spectacles [GAME] and wore sunglasses when necessary [WILD, KEEP]. She occasionally carried a handbag [eg LOOK, LACE, STAY]. Tara painted her fingernails [eg CLUE, REQU] (also doodling on the back of her hand [CLUE]) and could recognise exclusive French perfumes like Reckless Abandon [LOVE]. She ordered a case of Lilly of the Valley from Bellchamber Brothers [LOVE].

On her missions, Tara carried her current ID card [NOON, INTR], both her own address card [FOG] and Steed's [LOOK], a lock pick [XR40] and a box of matches [FOG]. She would occasionally use a miniature camera [LACE, THAT] or a wristwatch camera [THAT].

Like so many of Steed's associates, Tara was partial to a glass of champagne – often with Steed or at his apartment [GETA, XR40, NOON, LEGA, KILL, THAT, BIZA] and would bring him a bottle, knowing how much he loved it [LEGA]. She smuggled an extra special vintage with 'every grape hand-trod' in for him when he was incarcerated at Department S [NOON], no doubt in return for the 1957 bottle he had brought her when she was at home with her injured ankle some months earlier [CLUE]. She also took the opportunity to quaff the exotic grapes at the Peace Conference where Steed was in charge of security in 1968 [KEEP].

While at the Elizabethan Hotel, she ordered a very dry sherry [WISH], and also appeared to enjoy this drink on other occasions [KEEP, PAND]. When inducted at Centre 53, she ordered a brandy at the establishment's bar [INTR], and kept a good brandy at her flat [INTR, FOG] along with whisky [THAT]. Red wine was another favourite which she had at home [INTR]; she also enjoyed this at the Elizabethan [WISH] and indulged in the most expensive glass of red wine ever which had the Black Pearl dissolved in it [LEGA]. This was also an area where she had a knowledge of vintage, commenting of the wine she was served at Wainwright Timber Industries that the '53 was not a good year [ROTT]. She was not above helping herself to a drink at Steed's flat [CATC] while at her own flat she had numerous bottles of Meudon and Heim which she swigged from when in triumphant mood [THIN]. However, her favourite tipple was apparently a tall crystal glass of crushed ice permeated with grenadine laced with a mixture of Cantonese saki and crème du violette, topped with a measure of calvados, a tablespoon of Devonshire Cream and a fresh, unripe strawberry [SPLI]. While on assignment, she would decline drinks from the likes of Lord Dessington [LOOK] or Professor Palmer [ROTT]. Tara's preferred beverage was coffee which she drank at Steed's [GETA, GAME, REQU] and offered to him when he visited [CLUE].

One of Tara's favourite meals was a great big juicy rare fillet steak [DONE], and by April 1968 she and Steed had their own favourite restaurant to dine at, where she would offer to pay [CYPH].[30] She was quite adept at cookery herself and was happy to cook at Steed's to

---

[29] Also see *Moon Express*, p54.

[30] It is possible that Tara periodically dieted. *TV Comic*, Issue 897, 22 February 1969.

his recipes [ROTT]. She was able to whip together a crown roast with the help of Basil Creighton-Latimer [WISH] and also had her own secret recipe for soup which included a tablespoon full of yoghurt [INTR]. While not allergic to caviar (which she apparently liked[31]), champagne, oysters or quail, she was allergic to ragweed [CATC].

Even though Steed stated that Tara did not smoke [THAT], she did carry a cigarette lighter when working undercover at Cypher HQ in April 1968 [CYPH] and also had a silver lighter on her table back at the flat [LOVE]. Tara declined snuff when it was offered to her [THIN].

Tara did not particularly care for parties and attempted to get as many as possible (eg 14) over and done with in one evening [LEGA]. On another occasion in spring 1968 she went to a fancy dress party dressed as a cat [XR40] and apparently attended another party in Hastings on one occasion.[32] She did however have a great love of all types of music and went to a lot of different concerts [LOOK] as well as the opera [LOOK] and – apparently – the ballet [WILD]. At home she listened to LPs of jazz [CLUE] and dance music [THIN] and her collection included Stan Kenton's 1958 Capitol LP *The Stage Door Swings*. Tara read fashion magazines [GUNS, FALS] and, apparently, *The Times*[33] as well as books like *Code Cracking for Beginners* [GETA] and *Hypnosis – It's* [sic] *Theory and Practice* [CYPH]. When it came to finances, Tara preferred to have her assets in cash rather then invested on the stock market [LOOK]. For her vacation, her favoured venues appeared to be somewhere she could ski [CLUE] or sunning herself on the beach in Bermuda [STAY].[34] There was also one unconfirmed report that she joined Steed on holiday in Western Scotland on a grouse shoot.[35]

Tara continued to ski [CLUE, LOOK][36], went sailing [OVER] and said that she enjoyed motor racing (although whether as a spectator or participant is unclear) [LOOK].[37] While staying at the Elizabethan Hotel, the excuses given for her being unable to come to the phone – that she was riding[38], playing tennis or swimming – all seemed quite plausible to Steed [WISH].[39] Tara also seemed quite adept on the trampoline [GUNS]. She and Steed would often discuss a case over an indoor pastime. Steed was able to beat her at table tennis [LOOK] and it seems that she was not terribly good with bar billiards either [WISH]. At Steed's flat, they would also play chess [CYPH][40] and cribbage [FALS] together, but when

---

[31] *The Magnetic Man*, p29.

[32] 'Mary, Mary...', *The Avengers Annual*, 1968, p68.

[33] *The Magnetic Man*, p62.

[34] Apparently, Tara liked to go to the coast and get a really good tan. *TV Comic*, Issue 977, 5 September 1970.

[35] 'Are You A Clansman, Mr Steed...?', *The Avengers Annual*, 1968, p34.

[36] An unconfirmed report suggests that Tara had to cancel a skiing holiday in Switzerland during 1968. *The Gold Bomb*, p5.

[37] Other unconfirmed reports indicate that Tara also cycled. *The Gold Bomb*, p87; *TV Comic*, Issue 962, 23 May 1970; 'The Golden Game', *Steed and Mrs Peel*, Book Three, p91-92.

[38] Images of Tara riding exist in unconfirmed reports such as 'Thou'rt An Interfering Varlet, Mr Steed...', *The Avengers Annual*, 1969, p77; *TV Comic*, Issue 983, 17 October 1970; Issue 1036, 23 October 1971. She also apparently rode a giant cat. *TV Comic*, Issue 1020, 3 July 1971.

[39] It is possible that Tara also played croquet. *TV Comic*, Issue 1070, 17 June 1972.

[40] Tara apparently found watching a chess tournament boring. *TV Comic*, Issue 1030, 11 September 1971.

she attempted to do a card trick with Steed her colleague spoilt it [LOOK].

When not on assignment, Tara enjoyed sketching and painting [CLUE] and shopping [GETA]. Judging by her successful 'brim graft' on one of Steed's bowlers, she was adept at needlework [CLUE]. She enjoyed baking, making and icing a three-tier wedding cake [THIN], and could dextrously assemble a house of cards [WISH]. She was not terribly punctual [INVA, LOOK]. She liked dogs, but was not able to give such a pet the exercise it needed [TAKE].

Musically, Tara could also play the piano [SPLI] and the organ – on which she could perform a repetitive easy-listening number which became associated with her [THIN] – and discovered to her astonishment that she could play a cool jazz riff on a trumpet [TAKE]. Emitting a sharp whistle by placing her fingers in her mouth [FALS], Tara had a habit of singing to herself when she was on her own [GUNS].

By 1967, Steed was already a legend in the Department, and even before her first meeting with him – when she accidentally attacked him in the grounds of Mother's HQ – Tara had already studied Steed's file when she was still classed as a 'new recruit' [KNOT]. At this point, Tara's training was incomplete; for example, she had been taught how to administer the single-handed death grip but was not yet familiar with the counter-move. Assuming that Steed would want her address and phone number, Tara furnished these in her ornate handwriting – and thus it was her that Steed contacted her when he suffered a bout of amnesia. With a strong belief in Steed, Tara disobeyed the orders of her superiors and helped Steed to expose her own trainer, George Burton, as a traitor [KNOT].

A short time later, towards the end of 1967, Tara graduated from training – the same day that Basil Creighton-Latimer started his probationary agent's course [WISH]. She was soon to renew acquaintances with her hero, John Steed. This came about when she was assigned to Steed who had requested a new colleague from Mother [KNOT]. She described her new assignments as being to 'investigate developments' [DONE] as a 'secret agent' [NOON]. Steed quickly took her under his wing and although she was still very much learning her new trade, within a year he knew that she was sharper, brighter and more intelligent than many other security operatives, such as those at Centre 53 [INTR].

Tara's attitude towards Steed was often that of a little puppy dog that would always be around, looking up adoringly at her master. There was an element of hero worship from their first encounter [KNOT], but as time went on the two became close friends on a more equal footing, albeit with Steed always retaining the upper hand. On their early assignments, Tara would hug Steed with relief, knowing that he had never let her down [INVA], and when incarcerated at the Elizabethan Hotel she was sure that Steed would come and rescue her, and was delighted to hear that he worried about her [WISH]. When separated from him, she missed him dreadfully [WISH, KILL], writing him a postcard every hour on the hour [KILL]. She started to speak in idioms which she had most likely adopted from him [WISH]. The Honourable Teddy Chilcott – who had his eye on Tara – became very jealous of Steed, and while Steed was showing no particular attention towards Tara (apart from his usual gentlemanly charms), Tara's conversation had a habit of revolving around her hero [WILD]. On another occasion, she admitted that to relate everything she knew about Steed could take quite some time [INTR]. Soon she knew his tastes in champagne [NOON] and where he kept his revolver [FOG].

Tara knew about Steed's previous involvement with Janice Flanders [CLUE], but his cheery behaviour on another occasion led her to fear that he had met another girl [STAY].

She was less than keen on the idea of Steed alone protecting young Miss Miranda Loxton at a hideout [REQU] or remaining underground with some scantily clad 'angels' [BIZA]. She was delighted to pose as his wife [INVA] and on another unfilmed mission allegedly suggested that he pose as her fiancé.[41] The very sight of him was even powerful enough to help her resist a hypnotically-implanted order [LOVE]. Although attracted to Tara, Baron Von Curt was quick to realise that Steed meant a very great deal to her [KEEP]. Even when she attended a party in summer 1968, although she danced with three princes, eight lords, 14 baronets and 21 viscounts, all of these encounters were superficial as in her mind she only wanted to dance with Steed [LEGA].[42] While there is no direct evidence for a sexual relationship between them from the surveillance films, Linda Thorson recalled that Macnee's circle of friends had a different attitude at the time. 'We took the sex relationship for granted,' she said, 'and Tara, like Emma before her, did sometimes stay overnight – but it was all very civilised.'[43]

Another trait which revealed her great devotion to Steed was that Tara claimed to be able to recognise the sound of Steed's approaching Rolls-Royce Silver Ghost [WISH]. 'She had a great deal of love for Steed and would have died for him, without question,'[44] commented Thorson, adding, 'I think Tara was a very grown-up girl who was going to go on to great things and was in there to learn the job and do her best.' Tara worried about Steed [FALS] and wanted to defend him [GAME] to the extent of shielding him with her own body [INTR]. She became furious with those who would not help her in this respect [NOON] and once hit Steed over the head with a bottle of champagne in order to protect him [NOON].

Not believing that Steed could suffer delusions or breakdowns [STAY], Tara trusted him implicitly [FALS] and was upset when she had to lie to him [STAY]. However, she did not inform him that she had leave coming up for fear that he might have it cancelled [KILL], and anticipated that he would try to foist an itinerant Fang the Wonder Dog on her [TAKE].

Like Steed, by 1968 Tara seemed to have a Red Card pass which she used at the Ministry of TSI [SPLI]. As such, no doors were locked to her; she could go anywhere and check on anyone [GUNS]. On what seems to be her first proper assignment with Steed, Tara made use of her blonde wig to check on tests regarding a stolen consignment of FF70 rifles. She was then captured and forced to fight a duel as a demonstration of the rifles during an auction [GUNS]. While visiting the Ballistic Research Centre, Tara drove a different car from her usual AC. Presumably a Department pool car which she used when necessary, this vehicle was a bright red Lotus Elan +2[45] with sleek bodywork and folding lights [GUNS, LACE]. The car, which had a 1588cc engine, had been introduced by Lotus in June 1967 as a sports car for a young family.

Presumably in December 1967, Tara was taken off the active service list after she bruised and badly dislocated her left ankle when she collided with a handsome Italian who was also skiing on the upper slopes. Confined to Primrose Crescent, Tara was able to undertake research work by phone into Steed's investigation of a series of murders, but also

---

41 *The Gold Bomb*, p9.

42 One report suggests that Tara did not know the difference between a gavotte and a waltz. *TV Comic*, Issue 934, 8 November 1969.

43 *The Complete Avengers*, p160.

44 'Linda Thorson', *Look Who's Talking The Avengers*, p19.

45 Registration NPW 999F .

became a sitting target for the two killers – whom she successfully dealt with, despite her incapacity [CLUE].

Tara had to apparently spend several weeks off her feet over Christmas 1967, but was ready for action again in the New Year. As 1968 arrived, Tara was delighted to find herself posing as a blonde 'Mrs Steed' when she visited the Alpha Academy on the trail of a missing colleague. Breaking into the academy grounds one evening, Tara found herself the quarry in a lethal hunt for a group of the highly-trained Alpha students, and undertook the endurance test of the Tunnel. However, her fighting skills were not yet as finely honed as they would later become and she was easily overpowered by the students [INVA].

While investigating the death of an agent inside the headquarters of the Ministry of TSI, Tara was captured by enemy agents at a faked road accident and taken to Nullington Private Hospital where Dr Constantine saw her as a suitable subject to have her psyche fused with that of Boris Kartovski, one of Steed's old adversaries who was now kept alive only on life support. Steed was able to rescue Tara from the process in the nick of time [SPLI].

By now, Tara was starting to socialise with Steed more and more, and met many of his friends. When she met Paul Ryder and George Neville, two of Steed's oldest colleagues, for the first time, they were both highly impressed with her. When three enemy agents escaped from the Monastery prison, Tara helped with checking on Lubin at 'the Ministry' [GETA].

In March, when the board members of the Caritol Land and Development Corporation were picked off by killer clowns, Tara was put in charge of protecting Lord Dessington. Tara was ill at ease, at first following him much too closely and then being easily distracted, allowing Dessington to plummet to his death through an open window when a carpet was whisked from under his feet. Giving pursuit, she was captured by the clowns and taken to Vauda Villa where she was handed to a magician called Fiery Frederick who wanted to perfect his act of burning a woman in half. Climbing into the rear end of a pantomime horse costume behind Steed, Tara infiltrated a meeting of vaudevillians and helped overpower them and their controller [LOOK].

By now, the Honourable Teddy Chilcott, a rather pushy upper-class young gentleman, had got a crush on Tara and started forcing his attentions on her. While Tara was as charming as possible in return without forthrightly rejecting his advances, Teddy became obsessed with her 'cloak and dagger' work with Steed, and became immensely jealous of Tara's senior colleague – making him an ideal pawn to dispose of Steed who had been used as a witness to a series of hypnotically-induced murders. Again, Tara was still rather new to the nasty side of the security game and was shocked when one man fell to his death from a fire escape [WILD].

A sabotage attempt on the computer George/XR40 saw a rare chance for Tara to go undercover, dropping her English rose tones in favour of her North American accent, posing as Prunella, the niece of computer expert Sir Wilfred Pelley who was being held prisoner in his own home [XR40].

From around March 1968, the assignments for Steed and Tara were issued directly to them by Mother, and Tara also had her brunette bob cut shorter. The leaking of information from HQ Cypher Division at Lessington meant an undercover mission for her as a secretary, something which Mother saw as an 'opportunity' for her – indicating that the young agent was still cutting her teeth with the Department [CYPH].

With Steed under house arrest, Tara really had her chance to shine when taking over his investigation into a security leak at the Carmadoc Research Establishment on the coast where she drove a green Mini Moke provided by the base. The young agent was also now able to prove herself more experienced in the field than another operative, a Ministry man called Watney, and – having survived being forced off a cliff-edge into the sea – Tara was able to wrap up the case where Steed had failed, showing how beams of light were allowing a group of enemy agents based at the lighthouse of Colonel Withers to eavesdrop on conversations at the solar test laboratory [DONE].

Posing as a jewel thief with Steed, a blonde-wigged Tara was able to attract the attentions of Intercrime, and her ability to crack a safe within seconds ensured that she was able to join the organisation. However, when she was held hostage against Steed's compliance to Intercrime's Great, Great Britain Crime, she managed to escape by donning a lab coat and posing as a computer technician at Intercrime HQ. Temporarily, Tara was driving the Lotus Elan +2 again which had a tyre blown out by Intercrime gunfire in a multi-storey car park [LACE].

When Steed waited to overpower double agent Jimmy Merlin, Tara fell victim to one of the sleeping gas bombs which Merlin – who found her very pretty – had just stolen from the Ministry of TSI, and thus slept through a major evacuation in May 1968 [MORN]. She was then kidnapped and used as the incentive for Steed to enter into a macabre game of Super Secret Agent against a man called Daniel Edmund [GAME]. Investigating the deaths of a series of Ear, Nose and Throat specialists in June led to Tara being captured and subjected to freezing temperatures at the Cold Cure Clinic by Dr Frank Glover – resulting inevitably in a cold [CATC].

By late spring 1968, Tara had acquired a new car. Presumably impressed with the Lotus Elan, she now switched from the AC 428 to a red Lotus Europa Mark I[46] [FALS, LEGA, WISH, ROTT, LOVE, STAY, THAT, THIN, REQU, PAND]. Originally launched in October 1966, this two-seater closed coupé was the result of a collaboration with Renault and had a 1470cc engine beneath its low-slung fibreglass body. The car was sabotaged on one occasion [WISH] while on another it was stolen by a timber man called Sandford who drove it for eight miles, abandoned it and let all the air out of the tyres [ROTT].

By now, Tara was herself becoming quite a highly-regarded name in the Department alongside her famous partner, and was recognised by Sykes and his fellow miscreants at Dreemykreem Dairies. Having identified that Dreemykreem were implicated in an outbreak of untruths which prevented the blackmailing Lord Edgefield from being brought to justice, Tara was ducked in a vat of drugged milk which caused her only to tell lies – and was then imprisoned in a giant salted butter machine until rescued by Steed [FALS].

When Steed was injured and sent to Department S, Tara was the first to visit her hero with armfuls of presents on 19 June. As usual, Tara's youthful spirits and good looks attracted male attention, with Sir Rodney Woodham Baines – another Department S patient – attempting unsuccessfully to flirt with her. This was also the day that an attempt was made on Steed's life at the remote, isolated unit. Standing virtually alone, Tara successfully defended the invalid Steed against two killers called Grant[47] and Farrington[48] who had been hired by Gerard Kafka [NOON].

---

[46] Registration PPW 999F.

[47] Referred to as 'Norman Grant' in summary report.

[48] Referred to as 'Kyle-Farrington' in summary report.

Tara continued to have a busy social life with the upper echelons in summer 1968. Taking a falcon dagger left to the recovered Steed for identification, Tara inadvertently alerted more interesting parties to the whereabouts of the highly-valued item, and cracked under the Chinese water torture inflicted firstly by the Baron von Orlak and then Sidney Street [LEGA].

While Steed and Tara were assigned the leisurely task of liaising as official observers at a peace conference, Tara acquired a 'husband' again briefly when she encountered the dashing blonde nobleman Baron Von Curt who was hiding in her wardrobe at Ye Olde Sun Hotel[49] to evade the attentions of two girls called Helga and Miranda with whom he had arranged the same rendezvous. When Tara agreed to pose as his wife to extricate him from his embarrassment, the Baron found himself enchanted by her and – possibly in a move to evade a third girl – drove Tara to Mother's HQ in his sports car. Von Curt subsequently invited Tara to his country house which, by an astounding coincidence, he had loaned to the authorities to stage the peace conference. In the following hours, the Baron revealed his expertise with a rapier as he and Tara attempted to determine the real Steed from a number of impostors [KEEP].

With some leave due and nothing special on, Tara decided to check up on her Uncle Charles Merrydale who had been taking an extended holiday at the Elizabethan Hotel for over a month. On arrival at the hotel, Tara discovered that her uncle was in fact being held prisoner on behalf of his company secretary, Kendrick, who aimed to take over the business in his absence. When Tara's own attempts to leave the hotel were hampered, she hatched a plan to blow the cover of the organisation in charge – and also exposed Maxwell, one of the guests, as the mastermind behind the scheme [WISH].

Equipped with a pink and purple pass to give her a week's leave, Tara enjoyed some sun, sand and sea and purchased Steed an inflatable dinghy as a present [KILL]. She then rejoined Steed to investigate a series of deaths connected with the timber industry, during which she was captured by the cohorts of the insane Wainwright [ROTT]. A fake message from Mother then tricked Tara into accompanying Colonel Mannering and Captain Soo to Centre 53, supposedly on a TOHE course but in fact a cunning ruse used by enemy agents to get security operatives to divulge confidential information when their guard was down [INTR].

A security leak at Missile Redeployment led Tara – posing as a journalist writing the article *Perfumes of the Aristocracy* – to visit the perfumiers Bellchamber Brothers on the track of a rare scent which she recognised. Later she fell under the spell of subliminal messages of passion and became so obedient to the words of Casanova Ink's Nigel Bromfield that she nearly threw herself out of a window with remorse over their hopeless romance. Steed saved her yet again [LOVE].

Cured of the romantic conditioning, Tara was part of the team following a talking attaché case as it passed along a chain to a traitor. One of the men she confronted was Cavell, who admired her style and on whom she used her wiles to make him believe that she was his contact. Taking Cavell's place, Tara then posed as 'Tara Cavell', a martial arts expert, when she encountered the next link in the chain, Captain Tim, whom she beat in combat. Later in the assignment, Tara was forced to commandeer a green mini belonging to the vicar of St Bartholomew's Church [TAKE].

---

[49] Judging by the surveillance film, this pub is the one on the village green in Northaw, Hertfordshire.

Tara was sympathetic and helpful to Steed when it seemed that he had lost all memory of his three week holiday on the continent at the start of November. Captured by a man called Proctor, she was forced to make Steed believe that he had killed a fellow agent – but managed to escape the enemy's clutches [STAY]. Shortly afterwards, Tara found herself helping track down 'the Gaslight Ghoul' who was attacking foreign delegates at a Disarmament Conference... and ended up with her right foot caught in a man trap at the Gaslight Ghoul Club's Black Museum when stalked by the killer, Mark Travers, prior to another rescue by Steed [FOG].

For Christmas, Tara gave Steed a gold propelling pencil with a crown on the top [REQU]. Tara had learned a great deal during 1968 and Steed commented that she was now 'very experienced'. Now a highly-capable agent in her own right, she was given a two week solo assignment to break the security of the underground War Room which had been devised by Steed. Tara found a weakness in the defences, but was unknowingly being set up to look like she was handing over secrets to a foreign agent called Gregor Zaroff who was in the pay of a man called Dangerfield. Because of the increasing concerns about Tara's reliability from within the Department, Mother had to take the step of reducing her Security Rating first to Zero Minus and then to Zero Minus One when it seemed she could have gone over to the 'other side'. Under house arrest for the first time, Tara was then captured by Dangerfield while his assistant, Kate, flew from London Airport to the East in her clothes. Again, Steed was on hand to rescue Tara and restore her security rating [THAT].

While doing some research on a strange metal box at home for Steed, Tara came under attack from the object which flung bolts of electrical power around the flat. Her quick thinking allowed her to drain its power with her household appliances, after which she used her favourite Meudon and Heim to short it [THIN]. Tara was then caught in an explosion at Steed's flat and awoke in hospital with two broken legs to be informed by Major Firth that Mother had been killed and that Steed was unknowingly carrying a booby-trapped pen. It was therefore necessary to locate the hideout where Steed was protecting Miranda Loxton, a vital witness against Murder International. Tara soon realised that she was being tricked; her legs were not broken, Mother was alive and the hospital was a fake. She escaped her captors and managed to locate Steed's real hideaway [REQU].

The resemblance between Tara and Pandora, a woman who was to have married former Department operative Gregory Lasindall on 18 November 1915, allowed Henry Lasindall, the controller of the Archives, to hatch a plan with his brother Rupert to trick their Uncle Gregory into revealing the location of a vast dowry originally intended for Pandora. Henry set up Tara – who was not on a mission at the time – to be kidnapped at the premises of Xavier Smith, and when she awoke at Seven Pines, Barsworth, she was kept in a drugged state and treated as if she were Pandora back in November 1915. It was now that Tara's red Lotus was destroyed by Henry Lasindall in an attempt to make Steed and the Department believe that Tara was dead. Running it off the road and placing a skeleton dressed in Tara's clothes at the wheel, Lasindall doused the Lotus in petrol and set it alight. At the last minute, Tara managed to overcome the medicated illusion and was rescued by Steed – whom she thanked with the gift of a clock with a very loud chime [PAND].

Tara went sailing in the channel in February, but returned fairly quickly to join Steed at the home of his friend Bill Bassett, where she discovered the household being held prisoner by one Fenton Grenville [OVER]. She was then stunned and deeply upset by the apparent death of Steed – something which she steadfastly refused to believe could be true until she could see his body. In fact, Steed was investigating the escape route used by embezzlers via the Happy Meadows cemetery, in the last of his and Tara's assignments to be subject to surveillance filming [BIZZ].

It is possible that Tara was working with Steed as late as 1972 – and there is allegedly French surveillance footage from as late as 1975 showing them sipping champagne together. Alongside Cathy and Emma, a framed colour photograph of Tara adorned Steed's lounge at his country home in 1976 [CARD], while paperwork about her filled four 22423 MA files (332, 347, 401 and OMC) in the Department archives in 1977 [DEAD]. However, there is little or no evidence of anybody like Tara operating in the espionage field since – aside from one incident in Los Angeles in October 1986 when a woman answering her description posed as 'Agent Gregory', a fake FBI agent, in a plot to shoot the Russian boxer Illya Ivanovich Gabinov and so cause a major international incident.

MIKE GAMBIT

Born around 1943, it seems that Michael Gambit – or Mike as he was generally known – joined the Department in either the late 1960s or the early 1970s after a rather adventurous life. Of his family, very little is known. He claimed to be 'as British as the Union Jack' [GLAD] and indeed had Irish blood in him from his granny's side [ANGE]. The only other relative mentioned in the surveillance films is an aunt who thought that he should wear pyjamas in bed (which he did not) and who, in the 1970s, sent him a pair for his birthday each year... which he simply stored in his spare bedroom [SLEE].

Gambit's upbringing was not a privileged one and his recollections suggest a basic working-class background. He grew up in a house without a garden of any sort, and learnt to bowl a mean cricket ball in his back yard [DEAD]. He claimed to have had a 'knockabout education' [RAT] and certainly never went to prep school [NEST] or learnt subjects such as Latin [DEAD]. Nevertheless, despite the difference in social origins, Steed never looked down on him. In Steed's mind, nobody could help their background [FACE].

Gambit's formal education came to a halt in the late 1950s when, at the age of 14, he joined the Navy and was soon climbing up mizen masts [DEAD]. In 1960, he was busy discovering sex [RAT]. Between leaving the Navy and joining the Department, Gambit's career is unclear.[1] Certainly he was a motor driver, apparently at Formula One standard[2], and raced at Le Mans in France, Monza in Italy and Daytona in the USA... crashing at all of them[3] [MIDA]. One dossier – unconfirmed by the surveillance films – indicates that Gambit was a major in the Parachute Regiment, after which he used his 'comprehensive knowledge of warfare'[4] as a mercenary. The same dossier indicates that he wrestled crocodiles. Other sources indicate that after serving with 'the Paras' he was 'seconded to the SAS (Special Air Services)'[5] and that his time as a mercenary saw him active in Africa[6] ('in the Congo'[7]) and the Middle East[8] and where he gained experience of 'guerrilla

---

[1] In one unconfirmed report, Gambit told Purdey that after leaving school he had 'just knocked about a bit... I hitch-hiked across Europe.' 'The Sleeping Dragon', *Daily Mirror*, 11 October 1976, p17.

[2] *Featuring The New Avengers*, p37.

[3] An alternate transcript also refers to Spa in Belgium. *The Eagle's Nest*, p185.

[4] *Featuring The New Avengers*, p37.

[5] *The Avengers* (Rogers), p173.

[6] *The New Avengers Annual*, 1977, p5.

[7] *The Avengers Anew*, p12.

warfare'.[9] It is also possible that he had spent time in Canada, since he was knowledgeable about the country prior to an assignment there in 1977 [COMP]. Certainly, Gambit did not join the Department any earlier than 1967, as he was not around during Steed's first two encounters with the Cybernauts [LAST].

As with Purdey, Steed was to comment that he taught Gambit all that he knew [KIL2]. Amongst the many skills which Mike displayed was an ability to fly a helicopter [CARD][10] – although he had no prior experience of flying light aircraft [TRAP] – and a talent for breaking in without even bruising a lock which led him to describe himself as 'a pro' [ANGE]. He was able to use the computer system run by the Department to select data records [ANGE] and was familiar with the Department's *modus operandi* from the 1950s [RAT].

Despite his 'knockabout education', Gambit had a wide range of knowledge and interests. He knew about the myths of King Midas [MIDA] and Daedalus [RAT] from a girlfriend who majored in Greek [RAT], and was also aware of Professor Waterlow, a leading authority on bird migration [CAT]. Like Purdey, Gambit was also a bit of a movie buff and seemed to know his subject better than she did; for example, Gambit was quite right that Walter Huston and not John Huston was the lead in the 1948 Humphrey Bogart movie *The Treasure of Sierra Madre* [MIDA].

Gambit had sharp reactions, enabling him to quickly extinguish a timed incendiary device [MIDA]. Generally he could read body language well enough to identify a gunman [LION], but at other times was too impulsive to distinguish between friends and enemies [TRAP]. He could also be vengeful – relishing the chance to avenge the death of CIA agent Marty Brine by taking a swing at Soo Choy [TRAP].

Swimming underwater proved no problem for Gambit [NEST]. He could also quickly determine the locking point of a door and open it with a kick [SLEE], as well as deducing a course from the stars [TRAP]. He was very observant, realising that certain archive files from 1960-65 lacked a layer of dust [RAT], smelling alcohol from a nearby illicit still [EMIL], or recognising that the absence of a church bell's toll pin-pointed the location of a hit-man [KIL2]. Gambit was also blessed with an excellent memory for a face, be it that of killer Tom O'Hara [GLAD] or Tarka, another assassin whom he had seen in official files [BASE]. Having observed the clues, Gambit's approach to a problem was basic. Sometimes he was right [TALE, 3HAN] but at other times his deductions were wrong – notably when his suspected armour-plated lightweight alloy sewer buggy turned out to be a vast rat [GNAW].

A man of deeds rather than words, Gambit disliked bureaucracy which stood in the way of doing his job, and would be curt with needlessly officious people [NEST]. He saw himself as sceptical, but nevertheless rational [RARE].

Gambit was an extremely fit man in the 1970s, able to scale high gates with ease [MIDA] and not averse to crashing through a glass door or window [TARG, DEAD, ANGE, COMP]. He claimed to have a lot of practice at smashing in doors [3HAN] and had no hesitation about leaping onto the back of a hit-man's departing car [DEAD]. He had a good head for heights

---

[8] *The Avengers* (Rogers), p173.

[9] *The Avengers* (Rogers), p173.

[10] It is possible that Gambit also piloted a helicopter on another unfilmed assignment. 'The Sleeping Dragon'. *Daily Mirror*, 12 October 1976, p21. An alternate transcript suggests he flew a helicopter in the hunt for Irwin Gunner. *To Catch a Rat*, p97.

and was happy either scaling a Victorian folly [DEAD] or leaping some way down to the ground in hot pursuit [LION]. While in France in August 1977, he was able to run, leap and kick a tree holding a Russian sniper before the gunman had chance to open fire on him – a testament to the training of concentration instilled in him by his karate master [KIL1].

Judging by the celluloid evidence, Gambit was quite an expert of martial arts such as judo. His approach to combat – especially one-on-one – was often very silent and detached, allowing his opponent to make the first move and, when they were off their guard, to move in quickly and overpower them with a series of quick and powerful judo-like blows that first winded and then disabled [eg NEST, 3HAN, HOST, TRAP]. Much of Gambit's expertise in unarmed combat was thanks to 'Spence'[11], one of the Department trainers [CARD]. Part of this training dealt with how to beat a bullet, and to anticipate and deflect it – a trick he had seen done only once prior to his own successful attempt in Paris in August 1977 [KIL2]. All this official training was apparently augmented by instructions from a karate master who taught him that anything was possible, as long as he could focus his mind and concentrate on the feat at hand [KIL1].

By 1976 Gambit's theory had been supplemented by practice. Indeed, when he was forced into a life or death fight with Spence, it was the pupil who triumphed over the master [CARD]. Gambit was a match for many trained assailants – and even dispensed black eyes to four Metropolitan police at the Lakeshore Boulevard West Motel in Toronto, claiming that it was a reflex action [BASE]. The size of his opponents was not necessarily an obstacle. He easily threw Choy, an oriental physical education attaché who had been rated a Top Class Bodyguard Grade A – or 'Grade B' according to Gambit [MIDA].

Gambit's methods of fighting could be very ruthless, such as forcing a man's hand against a furnace inspection window so that the intense heat would make him drop his gun [CARD]. He also had an excellent knowledge of the vulnerable pressure points of the human body, and was able to render an opponent unconscious with a hand deftly placed at the right spot on the neck [SLEE]. When Gambit used his pole-axing blows on his target, they could be out for hours [CARD]. A quick punch was all that was needed to render the unwary unconscious [FACE, 3HAN, DIRT] – that or a single chop to the neck [SLEE, GLAD] or a blow to the side of the head [ANGE].

Alongside Purdey, Gambit formed an excellent fighting duo; one of their 'party tricks' was for Gambit to bend down behind an assailant while Purdey kicked their opponent over his back [LAST]. The pair would practice together in the Department gym [DEAD] where Gambit would also spar with Spelman [HOST]. Both Purdey and Gambit could also co-ordinate superbly with Steed to overcome enemy agents, such as when Purdey and Steed pinioned Nada, allowing Gambit to beat the Russian killer into submission [GLAD]. Steed commented that Gambit was a very tough man to come up against – and as such on the occasion when the two men did face each other, it was only by fighting dirty and applying a swift knee to the groin area that Steed was able to triumph [HOST]. While very much admiring his young colleague's martial arts skills, he felt that Gambit tended to watch his opponent's hands for their next move, rather than anticipating them by watching their eyes [HOST].

Taking a leaf from Purdey's book, by 1977 Gambit was starting to adopt more kicks in his fighting style which he successfully employed against the soldiers of Soo Choy [TRAP] as well as rapidly removing guns from the hands of opponents [ANGE, COMP, BASE] or deliv-

---

[11] According to an alternate transcript, 'Spence' was apparently Bill Spencer. *House of Cards*, p37.

ering the final overpowering blow [GLAD]. He could also restrain with an arm lock [FACE]. Gambit was a resourceful fighter. He would use half a playing card flicked in the face to distract an assailant [CARD] or divert the attention of an armed lady with his verbal charms until he could take her weapon from her [ANGE]. Opponents might be shut in sarcophagi [MIDA] or have their blow-darts blown back at them [TARG].

Across his assignments, there were only a few opponents who gave Gambit any trouble – such as Spelman's hired heavy Marvin [HOST] and The Unicorn who rated Gambit as a complete professional [LION]. In the fight with The Unicorn, and also an encounter with a large Canadian hooch brewer on the Woodbridge-Toronto road, it was Purdey who would come to his rescue [LION, EMIL]. Nevertheless, Gambit would not concede defeat in the Canadian incident [EMIL]; a proud man, his partners knew that he never admitted that he needed help [GNAW].

Leaping onto a bi-plane wing during take-off [TALE] and standing in the middle of a road to play 'chicken' with an oncoming lorry [OBSE], Gambit demonstrated that he was immensely brave. He was also tenacious, running some surveillance film over and over again until he found a clue in it [DIRT].

While he was extremely proficient in unarmed combat, Gambit was also seen as one of the Department's 'Armoury Experts' [TRAP] and had a vast knowledge of firearms and other weapons. His favoured weapon was a .357 Smith and Wesson Model 19 Combat Magnum revolver [NEST, LAST, TALE, CAT, 3HAN, GNAW, HOST, TRAP, DEAD, RARE, LION, KIL2, COMP, BASE] which he referred to as a Magnum .38 [NEST]; he also had a chromed version of this revolver which he seldom used [OBSE]. Generally Gambit carried his Magnum in a holster worn under his left shoulder [eg HOST, TRAP, DEAD] and sometimes Purdey would borrow this handgun while in the field [BASE]. For particularly tricky customers such as The Unicorn, Gambit took no chances; he would carry up to four guns, including .32 Beretta Model 70 Automatics strapped to his ankle and in his sock [LION].

Like the other Department agents, Gambit had been trained to shoot to kill in circumstances when another agent's life was directly threatened [OBSE], although for bringing in a target alive he would instead go for a leg shot to disable [HOST]. So skilled was he in the use of firearms that Gambit could comfortably fire a gun in each hand when the occasion demanded [TARG], drive and discharge a handgun at the same time [KIL2], and could outdraw other members of the Department [GNAW].

For recreation, Gambit favoured a pump-action shotgun for clay pigeon shooting [FACE]. In addition to the familiar firearms at his disposal, Gambit was always keen to try new weapons on the HQ shooting range [HOST]. On the occasion of hunting a possibly mechanised enemy in the London sewers, Gambit accessed a shell gun from the Department armoury, knowing that it could stop a tank at 30 paces [GNAW]. Recognition of different sorts of bullets was second nature to him [KIL2].

In addition to firearms, Gambit was proficient at improvising other weapons when the situation demanded them. Purdey's bra became a slingshot [DIRT] and his tie and shoes became a bolas [TRAP]. He was adept with a bow and arrow [TRAP].[12] Gambit was also very well-versed in other weaponry, from a wartime X5 pin grenade [KIL1] through to what

---

[12] Gambit apparently practised on an archery range. 'The Gambit Gambit', *The New Avengers Annual*, 1978, p5. An unfilmed report suggests he could also defend himself with a Japanese samurai sword. 'The Gambit Gambit', *The New Avengers Annual*, 1978, p2.

sound a mortar made [EMIL].

Gambit usually carried an ID card [NEST, CAT, DEAD, COMP, GLAD] and a cigarette lighter [SLEE]; however, he did not tend to be encumbered with lots of exotic spying gadgetry of the sort that would be associated with James Bond [COMP]. The ID card which he carried by 1977 indicated that he was a British agent [COMP, GLAD]. The card number for 'GAMBIT' was 70530 with an expiry date of '2/4/78' and applied to 'ALL COUNTRIES WESTERN NATO – INTERNATIONAL' [GLAD].

Emerging from his apparently lower-class background, Gambit clearly became a self-made man in the 1960s, and by the 1970s had attained not only a rich lifestyle, but also integrated with the higher strata of society with ease. According to Purdey, Gambit was mean with money [LAST]. He liked to sleep in late on a Sunday [SLEE] and his idea of heaven was a mixed sauna and a licensed bar [TALE].

From 1973 [DEAD], Gambit lived 'round the corner' from Purdey [NEST] in the Shoreditch area of Central London [SLEE], not far from a branch of the Consolidated Bank Ltd [SLEE] and within 20 minutes drive of an airport (presumably Heathrow) [TRAP]. The apartment block[13] housed a total of 50 people [SLEE], and Gambit's abode was a state-of-the-art affair, its open-plan living area fitted out with numerous modern devices and decorated with graphic art [NEST]. The spacious main area incorporated a breakfast bar and kitchenette built on a black and turquoise brick surface [eg SLEE], a seating area, dining table and a sofa which – set into a low wall – could slide out to form a bed at the touch of a control [LAST, SLEE]. Behind this was a curtain of fine chains which led to a raised area where the wall was adorned with various rifles, handguns [eg LAST] and crossbows [eg TALE]. This area also housed a high chair and drawing board [DIRT]. Hi-fi featured prominently in the living area, with large speakers strategically positioned [LAST]. A radio was built into one of the low wall surfaces [LAST] and Gambit also owned both a white television [TALE] and a home movie projector, the screen for which could be erected in the kitchen area [DIRT]. The overall décor was red and white with black trim, with three spotlights mounted over the door [SLEE]. Other furniture included black canvas and tubular steel chairs [eg LAST], a glass-topped dining table by the window overlooking the road [TALE] a fur-covered recliner [eg FACE], a Buddha head [DIRT], rubber plants and white marble statuettes [LAST]. One wall held a number of mirrors on its deep turquoise brickwork [FACE]. Among the gadgets Gambit kept in the lounge were a trimphone complete with a speaker facility [NEST, FACE, TALE], although he also had a slender green stalk phone [DIRT]. All in all, Steed agreed that the flat had style – although he had to admit that it was not his style [SLEE].

Gambit's apartment also had a spare room for visitors – a modern but Spartan affair decorated in bright green with wall-mounted television, cupboards (in which Gambit stored all the unopened packets of pyjamas), book shelf and trimphone [SLEE]. It was possible for people such as Purdey to let themselves into the apartment if Gambit was out or asleep [LAST], although there was also a chain on the front door [DEAD]. One regular visitor in 1976 was Charlie, a sparrow who had adopted Gambit and who would sing to him at dawn... often to Gambit's chagrin [SLEE].

Gambit's main form of transport was a red Jaguar XJS[14] [NEST, MIDA, LAST, CAT, TARG, 3HAN, HOST, TRAP, RARE, LION]. This was an automatic vehicle, fitted with a radio telephone

---

[13] These apartments were very similar indeed to those in Carlton House Terrace, SW1.
[14] Registration NRW 875P.

handset [HOST]; the vehicle had its tyres shot out by enemy agent Ivan outside an embassy [3HAN]. His other vehicle for off-road or countryside assignments was a white Range Rover[15] [LAST, RAT, CAT, TALE, TRAP, OBSE]. This too was fitted with a radio telephone [RAT, TALE] which could connect to Steed's home telephone [TALE].

Ever impulsive, Gambit was also happy to commandeer any other vehicles which he needed in the pursuit of his duty, including a white Citroen from a conference centre car park when his own XJS was parked in [NEST], a three-wheel van to pursue the criminal Grima through the streets of Paris (which he likened to driving at Le Mans) [LION], the car of a woman driver to give chase to a hit-man who was escaping in a Toronto Star van [COMP], and even Metropolitan Police Car 6418 while on assignment in Ontario – on which he enjoyed using the siren [GLAD]. Unfortunately, these vehicles were seldom returned to their owners intact; Gambit used the three-wheel van to ram a lorry [LION] and performed the same trick with the lady's car to halt the Toronto Star vehicle [COMP].

Gambit was a consummate driver after his time in the motor-racing world. His reactions were fantastically sharp, and his additional Departmental training had shown him how to safely punch out a windscreen shattered by gunfire [NEST], or shoot a gun with one hand and driving a vehicle with another [KIL2]. He handled vehicles well when driving off-road [RAT], while in built-up areas he managed to weave in and out of traffic and other obstacles with great skill [MIDA]. It was his ability controlling a vehicle which allowed him to save a man called Frank Turner from two enemy agents, and a short while later to pursue a bi-plane in which Turner was making his escape [TALE]. However, while driving overseas, he could be easily distracted and forgot which side of the road to drive on [GLAD]. Gambit also knew that in the absence of petrol, he could run a car off 'hooch' [EMIL].

While on duty, Gambit attempted to emulate Steed's sartorial elegance with a range of well-cut, trendy suits, including a three-piece dark brown with a double hip pocket [eg NEST, FACE], a brown checked three-piece with gold silk lining [eg NEST, TRAP], a sharp two-piece pinstripe [eg, MIDA, EMIL] and a light grey three-piece [eg MIDA, ANGE]. He tended to wear plain-coloured shirts with his suits [eg NEST, KIL2], sometimes choosing an item with white collar and cuffs to contrast with a colour [eg FACE, TRAP]. He also sported stripes [eg CAT, DEAD] and checks [eg DEAD, BASE], with cufflinks [eg 3HAN]. A tie normally accompanied a suit, his favourites being a brown patterned item [eg NEST, TARG], a navy blue with a white polka dot [eg MIDA, FACE] and a plain brown [eg LAST, GNAW]. He also had a black tie for more sombre occasions [eg GNAW]. More casually – such as when riding – he would sport a cravat [TARG, GNAW, HOST]. For formal occasions, parties and nights out, he had his familiar dinner jacket which often appeared with a frilly shirt [LAST, 3HAN, LION, KIL2], as well as a formal tie and tails [HOST].

In addition to the suits, Gambit had a wide range of less formal attire which reflected more the styles of the times. There was a brown suede leather casual jacket [eg RAT, GNAW], a light brown double-breasted blazer [eg CAT, SLEE], some knitted jackets [RARE, OBSE, BASE] and – during 1977 – various velour zip tops in blue [eg ANGE], green [eg LION] and brown [eg GLAD]. Several of these he wore with light polo neck sweaters [eg GNAW, 3HAN]. His trousers were often fashionably flared [eg TRAP] and his shoes were elastic-sided [eg CAT].

As noted, at home Gambit was not into pyjamas [SLEE] and slept wearing nothing more than a gold chain around his neck [LAST]. He owned a white judo suit for work-outs at the

---

[15] Registration LOK 537P.

gym [HOST, DEAD] and cricketing whites with a flat cap [DEAD]. Gambit tended to wear a small ring on the little finger of his right hand [eg CAT, TARG], a silver watch (usually on his left wrist) [eg, GNAW, EMIL] and followed the contemporary fad for medallions [3HAN, DEAD].

When it came to food, Gambit was equally at home dining out in style in London [SLEE] or grabbing a quick snack at a roadside stand such as The Chef's Hat [TALE]. He tended to prefer a cup of coffee over tea [NEST, SLEE, DIRT], while in the alcoholic stakes he was partial to Scotch (which he would carry a bottle of during particularly cold, dismal missions) [LAST, GNAW], Napoleon's Cognac [KIL1], champagne [LAST, LION, KIL2], and ice-cold beer which he liked to drink straight from the bottle [SLEE]. He did not like Schnapps [NEST] and had problems digesting rather strong illicit hooch [EMIL]. It also seems that he could mix a Martini 'well enough' [DEAD] and was known to carry a hip-flask for a quick swig when working late [DEAD]. As usual, there was always a supply of wine and champagne at Steed's home during most visits [3HAN, HOST, KIL1].

In terms of participating sports, Gambit enjoyed a game of squash although claimed that he was 'not that good' [CARD]. He also played tennis, sometimes against Purdey [TRAP], and enjoyed a few overs of cricket against Steed – who felt that Gambit's delivery was a little weird and more akin to a baseball player's pitch [DEAD]. Gambit also liked a canter on horseback, and took full advantage of the facilities at Steed's Stud – even feeling confident enough about his abilities to wager the odd fiver with Steed as to who could out-race who. As it turned out, Steed and Gambit were evenly matched [TARG]. He and Steed also enjoyed a spot of clay pigeon shooting [FACE].

For indoor sports, Gambit was also no stranger to games such as bar billiards [FACE] or snooker [3HAN], and would have enjoyed a game of Scrabble with Purdey if it was not for the fact that she cheated [LAST]. As a spectator, Gambit preferred watching the pacey baseball rather than the more sedate cricket [DEAD], and agreed with the Bishop of Lichfield that golf was a somewhat absurd game [ANGE]. His history of betting on horses was not good and he lost a lot of money – usually on tips from Purdey [LAST]. He also did the football pools, which gave him an understanding of the mathematics of permutations and combinations [ANGE].

Gambit shared a similar sense of humour with Steed in many respects [CAT], although at other times his more obvious quips fell flat with his colleagues [LION]. Many of his jokes were quite excruciating, such as his comment about enemy agent Ivan Halfhide having his pyjamas on when he was found in Lake Ontario because he was 'diving to the bed of the lake' [BASE]. He also had a joke about a plastic fig leaf which he seems rather proud of [ANGE]. Gambit retained his humour and flippancy even in the most perilous situations such as being held at gun-point [ANGE] or threatened with decapitation [TRAP]. Like Purdey and Steed, he was soon able to laugh off the dosage of curare which threatened both their lives [TARG]. His humour was coupled with a sense of fun, seen in the way that he decided to give Controller Bradshaw a taste of his own medicine at the Target Range, not realising that he was condemning the easy-going technician to death [TARG].

Musically, Gambit played the piano (very badly according to Purdey) [LAST], did not play the bassoon [CAT][16] and could whistle 'Colonel Bogey' [NEST]. Despite some of the abstract graphic pieces in his flat, he did not understand modern sculpture [3HAN]. He could

---

[16] An unconfirmed pictorial report suggests that Gambit may have played the guitar. 'Hypno-Twist', *The New Avengers Annual*, 1977, p47.

perform some basic sleight-of-hand card tricks [CARD] and other unconfirmed reports suggest that he used to like *Popeye* cartoon films[17] and could do the crossword in *The Times* in 15 minutes.[18]

By the mid-1970s, Gambit was well known for his attentions towards attractive women, and joked that he would get on well with an ornithologist as they were both experts on 'birds' [CAT] while also quipping to a maths teacher that he was 'good with figures' [DEAD]. Indeed, as with many macho men of the time, he claimed to have a little black book packed with girls' telephone numbers [FACE], while another of his favourite tomes was supposedly *Hints for a Growing Boy* [SLEE]. By 1976, it was common knowledge in the Department that he had 'been around quite a bit' [RAT]. Events cited in this murky past were an affair connected to a typing pool, an incident with an under-secretary's under-secretary (which apparently was nothing more than jealous rumours) and an undercover job with a so-called 'Russian Countess' where Gambit had taken the term 'undercover' quite literally [RAT]. He once had a girlfriend who majored in Greek [RAT].

However, despite his apparent appetite for women, Gambit was a gentleman, as could be seen when he carefully covered the legs of a woman in a taxi cab who was thrown into an enforced sleep by the release of S-95 over London [SLEE]. He also strongly believed that a man would never leave a woman – an opinion which Purdey opposed [BASE].

In 1975, Gambit took three bullets scrambling over 'the Wall', and was given a blood transfusion in Germany [NEST]. Some time prior to 1977, he had managed to survive an attempt on his life by Irish hit-man Tom O'Hara [GLAD]. By late 1975, Gambit was working alongside Purdey [GNAW], over whom he was still claiming seniority through to 1977 [BASE]. Gambit was a very close friend of Purdey whom he considered to be very beautiful [CARD]. At times, he could find her irritating, which she would tease him about [EMIL]. The pair mastered the sounds of certain bird calls to signal to each other [DIRT].

Despite all the flirting with Purdey and his very deep attraction and friendship with her, it seems that there was never anything more sexual between Gambit and his subordinate. The teasing and joking was all part of a relationship which also had aspects of Gambit looking after Purdey, almost like a big brother. When it seemed that Purdey was to die from curare poisoning, a frantic Gambit determinedly announced that he would break the rules and hunt down those responsible for her death [TARG]. Similarly, when fearing the deaths of both Purdey and Steed at the Briantern Health Farm, Gambit aimed a gun directly at the head of Coldstream and announced that he would kill him in warm blood if his friends perished [ANGE].

Gambit had immense admiration and respect for Purdey, declared that she was a 'great girl' [SLEE] and knew that she was a real lady [FACE]. They would socialise together, getting a little tipsy on a boat trip (on which nothing happened between them) [FACE], playing tennis [TRAP], going out to dinner [TALE] or down to the disco [TRAP]. She was prepared to come and join him in his flat when he felt lonely [DIRT]. However, at times Gambit would take unfair advantage – on one occasion unnecessarily allowing her to get undressed before revealing his presence in her flat (and paying the price) [CARD], and offering dinner with her as a valuable prize in a wager on another [CARD]. When he did flirt with her, she never felt threatened [NEST, CARD, LAST, DIRT], and he was able to identify himself to her with

---

[17] *House of Cards*, p111.
[18] *The Eagle's Nest*, p131.

some intimate, and probably saucy, comment [CAT]. However, unlike some of Purdey's other men friends, by spring 1977 Gambit had never been invited to dinner to meet Purdey's mother – although he did know her mother's telephone number [HOST].

Nevertheless, there was a very protective streak in Gambit with regards to his partner, and on one occasion he suspected that Steed was using his concern for Purdey against him [HOST]. Purdey very much believed that he was jealous of the attentions paid to her by a fellow agent called Larry, although Gambit declared that this was because the extrovert Larry was a 'first class fool' [3HAN]. There were similar reactions from him when Purdey seemed to be forming a friendship with CIA agent Marty Brine [TRAP], and when Larry Doomer – Purdey's former fiancé – entered her life again, Gambit delivered a threatening message to Doomer that he was a 'close friend' of Purdey. However, Purdey did not want to discuss her past liaison with Gambit – and indeed Gambit had to kill Larry to save Purdey's life shortly afterwards [OBSE].

In late 1975, Gambit also worked with Edward Harlow, feeling close enough to him to visit his grave on the first anniversary of his death [GNAW]. It is also possible that he was working on the screening of other agents with an official called Torrance [FACE] and – with Purdey – had encountered opposition agent Ivan Halfhide [BASE]. By the start of 1976, it seems that Gambit and Purdey had both been assigned to become members of Steed's inner circle. Gambit was now a well-established agent in the Department and there were even had facsimiles of him on the Target Range [TARG]. He was also high on the list of 'incorruptibles' held by the Department computer [ANGE] and found that on his first assignment for the Department in Canada in 1977, he was already known to security chief Paul Baker who had cleared him for 'Z' Security [COMP].

Being a very up-to-date gentleman, Gambit felt that Steed was somewhat old-fashioned [NEST]. Nevertheless, he admired Steed and was also capable of liking and admiring the activities of other agents active on both sides, such as Juventor [3HAN]. Gambit soon had tremendous faith in his new superior – obeying Steed's order to tackle an armed man in the sure knowledge that Steed must have already disabled the man's gun [TALE]. He soon admitted that he had learnt not to distrust Steed's instincts and experience [SLEE]. Off duty, Gambit would address Steed socially as 'John' [SLEE].

After exposing Felix Kane as a Department traitor and apparently seeing him perish [LAST], Gambit was involved in the investigation into the hiring of an assassin called 'Midas' [MIDA]. As 'Mike', a teen idol, he was part of a distraction exercise to deliver Professor Vasil from the clutches of Perov at an airfield, and later saved Purdey from a Russian sleeper called 'Dr Tulliver' [CARD]. Having taken over the security at the von Claus lecture a little too late to prevent a kidnap, Gambit then did research with the German authorities and arranged a date with a German archivist called Helga for 24 April 1976 before joining Steed and Purdey on the island of St Dorca [NEST]. He was also too late to protect W Richard Foster from a lethal attack by a bird, but his purchase of a basket of cats saved Purdey's life at the Sanctuary of Wings [CAT].

When Purdey and Steed were incapacitated by lethal doses of curare, Gambit fought on alone through the Target Range and defeated Draker, the man behind the scheme, to recover the vital antidote for his friends [TARG]. Exposing the replacement of key security people with look-alikes, Gambit executed a plan he hatched with Steed. Using his ancestry to adopt an authentic Irish accent, Gambit went undercover to the Mission for the Distressed and Needy as Terry Walton from Dublin, a smelly, unshaven lush – a role which

Gambit thought was great fun. As 'Walton', Gambit claimed to have killed himself, and helped in identifying 'Craig' – another *doppelgänger* – as the traitor in Home Security [FACE].

Gambit did a lot of legwork on the tracking of Burt Brandon's legendary evidence against a government official, and bravely stopped Frank Turner escaping with it by leaping onto the wing of his bi-plane [TALE]. When the Three Handed Game was threatened, Gambit was assigned to protect Helen McKay. Having found Helen attractive when studying her file photo, Gambit was pleased when she seemed to reciprocate these feelings... only because she needed a nude model for her modern art sculpture. He was unfortunately unsuccessful in protecting her from having her mind drained by Juventor [3HAN].

In August, Steed stayed over at Gambit's flat in the spare room – and next morning both men discovered that everyone else in the area had been put to sleep by S-95 gas. Making his way across London with Steed, Gambit adopted one of his simplest disguises – the camouflage clothes worn by one of the robbers in Brady's gang [SLEE]. As an armoury expert, it was the firepower which Gambit took down into the sewers of London which ultimately dealt with the colossal rodent on the loose beneath the city [GNAW]. It was also possibly around now that Gambit thoroughly enjoyed an assignment in New York, specially offered to him by Steed [OBSE].

When his friend Travis[19] was fatally knifed attempting to deliver some vital film showing the 19th Division Special Commandos acting as mercenaries overseas[20], the investigation into the rogue army unit became a personal one for Gambit. His versatility at accents again came in useful when he posed as the dishonourable Major Gambit, a Scot transferred as a new adjutant to the Commandos with a fabricated history involving misappropriated regimental funds, womanising and misuse of company property [DIRT]. In early 1977, Gambit attempted to track down rogue agent Irwin Gunner alongside Purdey [RAT], and shortly afterwards found himself tangling with the Cybernauts – and injuring his right hand when engaging in a fight with one of the metal men. He then sustained further injuries when a Range Rover was pushed into him [LAST].

By 1977, Gambit was rated as one of the top professionals in his field, even by his opponents [LION]. Around spring that year, Gambit had a major redecoration of his flat. The walls and doors were repainted with warmer colours such as orange, lime green and brown, and there were more shelves dotted around the place [TRAP, DEAD]. The cold, modern look was out as the automatic bed was replaced by steps leading up to the raised section of the main area [DEAD]. The fur-covered recliners were removed and a patterned floral sofa took their place [TRAP]. The stark graphic art was gone and softer pencil sketches were now displayed on the walls, alongside various mobiles [TRAP]. The early 1970s trimphone had also vanished, replaced with a white receiver of conventional design [TRAP, DEAD]. Nevertheless, there was still an open quality to the living space – largely because after four years, Gambit had still not unpacked [DEAD].

When it seemed that Steed was handing over the Allied attack plans to enemy agents, the terrible situation arose where it was Gambit who was reluctantly detailed by Tommy McKay to bring Steed in. In a direct confrontation, the master triumphed over the pupil – but Gambit's belief in Steed was soon restored and together they collaborated in releasing

---

[19] An alternate transcript referred to him as 'Peter Travis'. *Fighting Men*, p5.

[20] The same report names this as Umbezi. *Fighting Men*, p6.

Purdey from the clutches of a traitor in the Department [HOST]. After being in on a drugs intercept in Windsor, Gambit enjoyed a cuddle (complete with brandy and mints to hand) on his sofa with a girl who – judging by the fact that she was allowed to handle his revolver – was also attached to the Department or an associated security body. In the middle of one such tryst, Gambit and his colleagues were lured onto a plane and delivered into the estate of Soo Choy in East Anglia. Ranked against a private army, Gambit's skills in mercenary combat came flooding back as he improvised an arsenal of weapons for the ensuing game of cat and mouse [TRAP].

Digging back into Steed's past brought Gambit into contact with maths teacher Miss Penny Redfern at his colleague's old school. He quickly invited Penny out for a drink on their first meeting – despite the fact that earlier he claimed to have a date that night with a woman who had done a round-the-world cruise with five men for company. Indeed, such was the attraction returned by Penny that the teacher told her headmaster that she would happily choose Mike over and above the school. However, work always came first and – as with her predecessor – a telephone call to Gambit's apartment saw the beau having to make his apologies and head out into action, helping Steed in another rescue of Purdey, this time from the supposedly dead defector, Mark Crayford [DEAD].

Gambit was highly sceptical about the supernatural powers claimed by medium Victoria Stanton when she warned the team about a threat on Steed's life [RARE]. After research into a possible link between a series of deaths, Gambit was the member of the team who finally exposed Department official Coldstream as an enemy sleeper behind the deadly subliminal images being implanted at Briantern Health Farm. Turning the charm on in a tight situation, Gambit invited Jane, Coldstream's secretary, out to dinner and kissed her while she held him at gun-point. Shortly afterwards, Gambit received a minor gunshot wound in the right arm from Coldstream [ANGE].

In June, the appearance of Larry Doomer brought out the protective side of Gambit's nature. In a life-or-death stand-off alongside a Bloodhound missile, Gambit saw that Purdey's life was directly in danger and had no choice other then to loose off a fatal shot at Doomer – an act which it took Purdey some time to get over [OBSE].

When a series of assignments took him to France in summer 1977, Gambit was delighted at the prospect of talking to French girls in the Surete [LION] and also attending the Moulin Rouge [LION] and the Follies [KIL1, KIL2]. Having enthusiastically taken part in the apprehension of The Unicorn, Gambit was also involved in a car chase through the French capital in pursuit of one of the late assassin's men [LION]. Shortly afterwards, he returned to France with his colleagues to find himself fighting cryogenically preserved Russian soldiers from the 1940s [KIL1, KIL2]. On this assignment, he used the vehicle assigned to Steed [KIL2].

On 16 August, Gambit encountered Dr Jeanine Lepage at a post-mortem and there was an immediate attraction between English agent and French medico. A date was quickly arranged at her home, Apartment B, 24 Rue de Fleur. Jeanine claimed to be an excellent cook and felt that Gambit had 'the look of an imaginative man'. Although the date was set for 8.30 pm that night, other events prevented the rendezvous [KIL1, KIL2]. Again, he was injured in action; Gambit's right hand required another period in bandages after he bravely deflected a bullet with the butt of his revolver, while a few days later he had his left hand injured from a gunshot fired by Colonel Stanislav. For his valour in this affair, he was awarded the Mongolian Medal by the Soviet Comrade Kerov [KIL2].

Visiting Canada in the late summer to help identify the enemy agent Scapina, Gambit was involved in another car chase, this time through the suburbs of Toronto, and was arrested several times by the Metropolitan police who did not believe his claims of being an English secret agent. The first time, Staff Sergeant Talbot of Station D took him in for ramming a *Toronto Star* van, and he was later jailed for trespassing on the private property of architect Berisford Holt [COMP]. While on assignment in Toronto, Gambit was given a Triumph TR7[21] which was red with a white speed stripe and a black vinyl roof [COMP, GLAD]. This too was equipped with a radio telephone [GLAD].

The subsequent holiday in Ontario was cut short when Gambit was needed to help track down a top Russian operative who was training a new breed of local killers [GLAD]. After this, he returned briefly to England – but was soon summoned back across the Atlantic by Steed to help with the location of a Russian base within the vicinity of Lake Ontario. When needing to scare enemy agent Ivan Halfhide with a telephone call in Toronto, Gambit used a bizarre French accent akin to Peter Sellers' masterful comic creation Inspector Clouseau [BASE]. His last firmly accounted mission was then to expose a double agent in Canadian intelligence known as The Fox [EMIL].

The incident with The Fox was the last confirmed mission for Gambit alongside Steed and Purdey, although it seems that they may still have been active as a unit into early 1978.[22] While it has been suggested that in 1979 he was a still a prominent agent using the alias 'Charles Bind' and encountered a *doppelgänger* of himself, the evidence available is distinctly inconclusive.

---

21 Registration MHF 292
22 *The New Avengers Annual*, 1978.

PURDEY

Whatever Purdey's Christian name is, it has remained a closely guarded secret. In the same way that she eschewed all issues to do with titles or forms of address (when asked if she was 'Miss or Mrs' she replied, 'Just Purdey' [MIDA]), Purdey was only known by her surname during both her time with Steed and – prior to that – in her former career as a ballet dancer [OBSE]. The family name of Purdey, though, suggests connections with James Purdey, the world famous gun manufacturer who established himself as the proprietor of the most famous gun-making business in London as early as the 1820s.

According to one unconfirmed report, Purdey had an American grandmother who was 'Quite a gal out West in her youth'.[1] Another incident not covered in the surveillance films revealed some details about one of her relatives, Harold Purdey, her great uncle who wrote the book *Empires At Any Cost*. Great Uncle Harold was the black sheep of the family who made three fortunes operating criminal rings in the Colonies, had a talent for mayhem, and stole from his own South African diamond mines. Although he received a knighthood, Harold was ultimately thrown out of Africa, although it was rumoured he died having hidden £1,000,000 in diamonds on his estate. He was buried in the church where Purdey's stepfather later tried out his sermons, and which had a series of secret passages leading to the Purdey home.[2]

Purdey seems to have been born around 1946. According to one of the Department dossiers, she was born in India where her father was a brigadier in the British Army.[3] Her mother was a 'marvellous woman' and described by those who met her as 'beautiful' [HOST]. Purdey emphatically inherited her good looks.

Of the rest of her family, Purdey seemed close to her Uncle Elly – Elroyd Foster – a colonel in the British Army. Although elderly by 1976, he enjoyed his niece's visits at his home of stuffed animals and trappings from the days of the Empire [DIRT]. It would seem that it was from her father and her uncle that Purdey gained her knowledge about the Army. She was able to recognise the crest of the 'Glorious 19th' Commandos, and knew that their nickname of the 'Mad 19th' derived from the exploits of Colonel 'Mad Jack' Miller [DIRT].

Always slim and slender, Purdey may have been nicknamed 'Skinny' while at school [ANGE]. She seemed to have had a very happy childhood, with memories of days out with

---

[1] *To Catch a Rat*, p151.

[2] 'Go And Grin Somewhere Else!', *The New Avengers Annual*, 1977, p55-56.

[3] *Featuring The New Avengers*, p30.

her parents (notably a trip out boating one Wednesday afternoon around 1960 [RAT]). Her talents for co-ordination and agility meant that she always enjoyed dancing in various forms, and she once quipped that she could tap dance before she could walk [3HAN]. Her education was described in her dossier as 'international' since she travelled with her father to trouble spots such as Cyprus and Aden.[4] The same document noted that while studying the arts in Peking, she apparently learned Chinese martial arts, enhanced by her learning the little-known French martial art panache[5] when she concluded her schooling at the famous university of La Sorbonne in Paris. In addition to gaining a knowledge of France and the French language [KIL1], it was here that Purdey learnt to play the French game of boule, becoming so proficient that she became a member of the ladies' team at the university [LION]. Although it is unclear what her primary subjects of education were, she was certainly knowledgeable on subjects such as the Civil War [RAT] and the Greek myths of Daedalus [RAT]. She also had an extensive vocabulary and an impressive ability to express herself (superior to that of Mike Gambit) [DIRT].

However, it seems to have been towards the end of Purdey's time at the Sorbonne that tragedy struck. Some years earlier, her father had been seconded to the Secret Service – a line of work which unfortunately eventually placed him in a position to be shot on espionage charges in 1966 (although Purdey herself never specifies that he was a spy in the available films) [CARD]. Her mother was to remarry over the next few years – this time to a bishop who had a passion for roses [CARD].[6] It is worth noting that since Purdey's father was shot as a spy and the bishop was an acquaintance of Roland – a Department agent – there may well have been an espionage or security connection with the Purdey family prior to their daughter joining the Department in the early 1970s. Purdey continued to try to visit her mother regularly [HOST].[7]

When Steed described her as 'Graceful [and] very nubile' [CARD] he was outlining two of the reasons why Purdey's original career as a ballet dancer was a very apt one. By 1970, she was performing with the Royal Ballet, already using only her surname to stamp her presence on the company lists. In her mid-20s, Purdey was still in the chorus line alongside the likes of Anton Unguer, John Hemmings, Natasha Osato, Ann Roy, Linda Jones, Vivian Thompson and June Anders [OBSE].

Also by 1970, Purdey was in a loving relationship with Larry Doomer, a young and dedicated RAF officer. Doomer loved planes; his father had taught him to fly since, as a trouble-shooter with an oil company, Doomer senior[8] had his own plane to commute to business sites in Texas, Alaska and the Middle East. Coming from an affluent family, Doomer had a flat at 2A Hamil Court, London W1 which Purdey effectively moved into, although she still maintained her own flat as well. Her very feminine touch was evident around the home, with a dressmaker's dummy and various cuddly lions hidden amongst the wicker furniture which was the vogue of the day [OBSE].

Purdey and Doomer were very much in love and discussed their plans for marriage at

---

[4] *Featuring The New Avengers*, p30.

[5] *Featuring The New Avengers*, p30.

[6] Apparently the Bishop had worked out in Africa. *House of Cards*, p59.

[7] See 'What a lousy way to run a business!', *The New Avengers Annual*, 1977, p31; 'Go And Grin Somewhere Else!', *The New Avengers Annual*, 1977, p59.

[8] Referred to as 'Edgar Doomer' in the transcript.

length. A plot of land near Milton Keynes in Buckinghamshire had already been purchased for their 'dream house', complete with kitchen, garden, drawing room, dining room and a love seat which Purdey romantically dwelt upon. Children were also a possibility in their future, although Purdey was keen that the couple should have a dog – a 'great, big woofly thing' [OBSE].

The Purdey who danced with the Royal Ballet and fell in love with Larry Doomer was a very different lady to the Purdey who later worked with the Department. Doomer had described his fiancée as having 'just a touch of fairy princess,' and indeed Purdey was a very feminine, light-hearted, fluffy and 'girlie' young lady [OBSE].

However, the dream was shattered by an incident reminiscent of the tragedy which Purdey had suffered herself four years earlier. Even as Mr Doomer was planning to fly back from the Middle East especially for his son's wedding, he was charged with spying by the authorities. His car was stopped in a desert territory by three soldiers and forced over a shallow precipice so that he could be captured. One Thursday in May 1970, Doomer senior was taken out before a firing squad and shot dead [OBSE].

Larry Doomer was informed of his father's death in a telegram from the Foreign Office the following morning – the same day that his copy of the *Daily Telegraph* carried the headline 'Middle Eastern Emissary Flies Out Today'. Doomer found himself staring at a photograph of the Arabian diplomat whom he believed was responsible for his father's execution. With only hours before the emissary left the United Kingdom, Doomer took his career in his hands and set out for the airfield to gun down the VIP. However, Purdey – having found both telegram and headline at the Hamil Court flat – managed to arrive at the airfield just in time to prevent Doomer from pulling the trigger. As his quarry flew safely out of the country, the enraged Doomer slapped his fiancée and walked away. The romance was over [OBSE].

With Doomer behind her, Purdey threw herself into her work; at the time the relationship broke up she was already due to appear in *Le Lac Des Cygnes* (*Swan Lake*), a July 1970 production featuring lead dancers such as Phyllis Mann, Anita Ladre, Olga Bokosi, Maria Finda, Lynn Dane, Edward Joy and Michael Soams [OBSE]. Within a few years though, she was looking at a new profession which would still put her fitness and co-ordination to good use. Purdey claims that her career with the Royal Ballet came an end when she was thrown out for being 'too tall' [NEST][9], and by 1976 the fact that she was an ex-ballet dancer was known to quite a few people in the Department – such as Felix Kane [LAST].

It would seem that Purdey joined the Department – or one of the official security organisations – soon after the split from Doomer. Certainly when Doomer tried to contact her shortly after their separation, he was unable to find her. Also, given the fact that by 1976 she was working directly as part of Steed's close-knit trio, Purdey must have proved herself as a top operative by late 1975, suggesting that her extensive training and induction was around 1971-72. When meeting Doomer again in 1977, Purdey explained to him that she did not dance any more, but now did 'Something quite different' [OBSE].

Purdey's senses were finely honed. Her ears could detect the low drone of a helicopter at some distance [CARD]. She was blessed with excellent powers of observation and memory to recall a scar on a man's leg [RAT], find an overlooked bird ring [CAT], detect a

[9] In summer 1977, Purdey's height was 1.732m and her weight was 58.967 kg [COMP].

trail of carrion [GLAD], puzzle over wet grass [BASE] or spot droplets of blood in undergrowth [BASE]. She could also quickly spot a gunman in a crowd from his body language [LION]. However, she was not always aware of a sniper behind her [TARG].

Purdey believed that she had an incisive mind [TARG] and disliked being interrupted as it disturbed her concentration [BASE]. She put great faith in her deductive reasoning – swallowing a poison capsule to show it contained only water, and thus guessing the next move by Perov [CARD]. With an eye for detail, she could deduce information from a photograph with ease [CARD, COMP]. She seemed to know a little about architecture, being able to identify a church with a flintstone Saxon tower [CARD] and could spot signs of radioactivity [GNAW].[10]

Purdey's diction was quick and clear and she tackled tongue-twisters with ease [3HAN]. She could adopt American [FACE, BASE] and Canadian [BASE] accents, and also do what Gambit thought was a poor impersonation of one of their cinema heroes, Humphrey Bogart [CAT]. Having a piano in her flat [eg LAST, OBSE], she played the instrument well and with a sense of humour [RARE]. Alongside Steed and Gambit, she could whistle a confident 'Colonel Bogey' [NEST], and she and Gambit mastered distinctive bird calls to signal to each other [DIRT].

It seems that Steed himself was instrumental in the training of agents in the early 1970s, commenting once that he taught Purdey all she knew [KIL2]. In terms of language training, in addition to her French skills, Purdey was soon able to read Russian [KIL1] and various Arabic languages [RARE].

Computer training meant that Purdey could successfully interrogate official Department files held in the main database[11] [ANGE] and was able to operate similar equipment such as the Canadian 'Control Data' card selector [COMP]. More practical technical training meant that she could undertake electrical and mechanical work [LION]. Purdey could swim underwater [NEST] and could move around stealthily [eg NEST]. Other skills presumably acquired during training were the ability to pick locks with a piece of wire [RAT], gain entry to buildings [ANGE] and pilot a helicopter [SLEE]. She was also able to perform first aid, dressing Gambit's injured fist [LAST] and constructing a make-shift sling from Gambit's shoulder holster and a few sticks to brace Steed's broken arm [TRAP].

Purdey was an immensely trustworthy operative who would not betray the work of the Department even to other offices like D16 [RAT]. She would, however, playfully question the identity of her fellow agents during a security alert [CAT]. Purdey was a very keen agent and wanted to be in on the action [EMIL]; when she was left out of the plan, she would usually determine her own avenue of investigation [CAT]. She had immense pride in her work and that of her colleagues [BASE]. At times, Purdey could be threatening – such as when she dropped a boule on the foot of Henri Duval [LION]. She could also be very brave, acting as a diversion to let Gambit escape from the 19th Division Commandos [DIRT], and having to be dragged back from a burning car by her colleagues when she attempted to recover vital evidence [EMIL].

Ever the ballerina, Purdey liked to remain fit and supple by exercising at home [LAST,

---

[10] An unconfirmed report also revealed her tangential knowledge that the average cloud weighs 30,000 pounds. 'A Fluid Situation', *The New Avengers Annual*, 1978, p53.

[11] Apparently a Mark-7B computer. 'Go And Grin Somewhere Else!', *The New Avengers Annual*, 1977, p58.

FACE]. Breaking Department regulations, she would at times take her phone off the hook when she wanted peace and quiet [NEST]. She could perform on an Army assault course as well as a lieutenant[12] and his men [MIDA]. She could scale high walls [SLEE, ANGE], drainpipes [TARG] and gates [MIDA] with ease, had no problem with heights [TARG, LION] and could leap down from a roof confidently [TARG]. She also knew how to fall, and so was not injured when thrown from her motorcycle when its tyre was shot out [TALE].

Purdey's method of unarmed combat relied heavily upon her acquired skills in panache.[13] A combination of Canne and the 19th century method of kick-boxing known as savate, la panache had been created in 1955 by Parisian instructor Roger Lafond and incorporated some Japanese hand-to-hand combat elements. Purdey blended this with kung-fu [DEAD] and karate-style kicks – and the moves she had learnt as a ballerina [NEST] plus a degree of tap [3HAN].

Trained by 'Spence' at the Department's gym at HQ from her first days as an agent[14], Purdey was told by her tutor that she fought with too much compassion – although she could throw him through the gym doors [CARD]. Defeated opponents, such as the Russian agent Chislenko, felt that she fought well – for a woman [GNAW]. She would also spar in practice with Gambit at HQ [DEAD] and claimed that she could break a man's back in three places if he lied to her [RAT].

Purdey's most notable form of self-defence or attack was high ballet-style kicks, with her flashing foot dealing out pain on impact [NEST, FACE, CAT, SLEE, HOST, TRAP, KIL1], disarming [CAT, TALE, GNAW, 3HAN], or merely keeping an assailant at bay [MIDA, CARD, LAST]. She could kick a pencil from a man's hand and catch it in the heel of her boot [TARG] or propel a bomb into the vehicle of the bomber [LION]. Sometimes a kick meant her opponent falling [SLEE, 3HAN] possibly to their doom if one of her colleagues was threatened [MIDA]. Like Emma, Purdey's legs were strong enough to lock around a man's neck and throw him [CARD] and she could kick doors open [SLEE, DIRT, EMIL]. Her flying assault was strong enough to rip a man's trousers [RAT] and she could hurl a man onto a roof [DIRT]. Assailants would also be subdued by having their head slammed against walls [GNAW].

When Purdey was truly furious, a single punch would put a man out cold [CARD, GLAD, EMIL] while at other times she administered a chop to the neck [KIL2]. With women she tended to punch, slap and twist arms [ANGE]. Fighting with Gambit, the pair had various 'party tricks' which they could employ [LAST] and both co-ordinated well with Steed [GLAD]. Although proficient with an arm-lock [FACE], she could be overconfident with this manoeuvre [RAT]. Purdey was also resourceful with the items around her, using a wooden table to keep killer birds at bay [CAT] and wielding a clothes rail to fend off an attacker at a clothes store [SLEE].

Seldom resorting to firearms, from 1976 Purdey used a chrome Beretta Model 70 .32 ACP Automatic[15] [CARD, RAT, LAST] which she carried in her purse [RAT]. This was finally crushed by the cybernetic hand of Kane in early 1977 [LAST]. After this Purdey used a small

---

12 Referred to as 'Henry' in an alternate transcript. *The Eagle's Nest*, p169.

13 *Featuring The New Avengers*, p30.

14 An unconfirmed report notes that Purdey's instructor told her when facing an opponent, 'Their eyes... always watch their eyes.' 'The Sleeping Dragon', *Daily Mirror*, 12 October 1976, p21.

15 An alternate transcript of the Gunner affair erroneously referred to this as a pearl-handled Derringer which Steed believed belonged to Purdey's American grandmother. *To Catch a Rat*, p151.

black automatic, believed to be another Beretta Model 70 .32 ACP [TRAP, OBSE] and a chrome small-calibre Browning automatic [LION]. She could quickly dismantle and reassemble a 9mm Browning Automatic at the Target Range which she enjoyed using a great deal – being able to throw a can in the air and shoot it at close range [TARG]. Her shooting skills were excellent and she attained 99 per cent on the Department range [TARG].[16]

Only occasionally did Purdey show fear, such as when confronted by Zarcardi and his lethal falcon [CAT], suddenly being attacked by an archer [FACE], realising that she was in a minefield [DIRT] or when assaulted by the cyborg Kane [LAST].[17]

During an assignment, Purdey could think with lighting speed to cover incidents like Gambit crashing, gun in hand, into a church in Meacham (by acting like an outraged bride – to his embarrassment) [RAT], using a tongue-twister to prove the identity of Perov [3HAN], posing as a shop window dummy to avoid pursuers [SLEE], throwing objects such as milk bottles to create distractions [SLEE], taking the hand brake off Colonel Stanislav's car so that it would hit him [KIL2], leaping over a lethal incinerator chute [COMP], or using her own body to protect a vital hand-print on a car roof from being washed away at Roy's Carwash in Woodbridge [EMIL]. She was also methodical, taking Burt Brandon's shoes for analysis [TALE] and realising the connecting factor in the attacks on the Three Handed Game triumvirate [3HAN].

In her active service in the early 1970s, it seems that Purdey worked overseas on some assignments. On one occasion she went missing for a month in the jungles of Brazil. Bitten by a tarantula (in a sensitive place), her life was saved by a tribe of Indians with whom she was living, whose treatment combated the spider's poison in her system. Unfortunately, Purdey was never debriefed on this episode to the full satisfaction of the Department and, as such, her computer records continued to hold a month's unaccountable gap, meaning that in times of internal investigation she could not be considered to be above suspicion [ANGE].

Purdey's idea of a perfect assignment was normally dinner at the Palace, lunch at the Houses of Parliament and four or five fashion shows [OBSE]. She loved clothes and shoes, and adored a chance to study the Parisian fashions [KIL1]. Even in 1970 she had been stylish [OBSE] and by 1976 had acquired a style which was distinctive but also – in notable contrast to Cathy and Emma – decidedly feminine. Her vast and ever-changing wardrobe included items like a yellow batik-patterned silk dress in pleated chiffon [NEST] and numerous sleeveless [eg LAST, RAT, TALE, DEAD, LION, KIL2] and pinafore dresses [FACE]. Some of Purdey's outfits were diaphanous lurex and velvet items worn over a leotard which could be removed for combat [NEST, MIDA, FACE]. One distinctive item was a white hooded dress covered in red lipstick-mark motifs which was ideal for Paris [ANGE, KIL2] but the skirt was sucked away by a ventilator in Toronto to reveal shorts underneath [COMP].

Occasionally, Purdey adopted a tomboyish look. One notable outfit was a maroon velvet two-piece suit which she wore with a white shirt bearing a lavender and mauve stripe, and a wide white tie [RAT]. She also had a pink and white striped knitted trouser suit [HOST], a

---

[16] There are also references to Purdey using a gold-plated revolver. 'A Funny Thing Happened On The Way To The Palace', *The New Avengers Annual*, 1977, p15.

[17] It has also been suggested that Purdey hated rats. 'The Sleeping Dragon' *Daily Mirror*, 13 October 1976, p21.

sleeveless knitted jacket [RARE, GLAD], a beige jacket, waistcoat and trousers ensemble (ideal for Steed's stables) [RARE] and a rather loud white, red, green and blue bomber jacket with matching trousers [BASE]. For formal occasions, she had a sharp black three-piece suit [OBSE]. She wore various blouses, often white [eg CARD, COMP] but increasingly patterned as 1977 wore on [eg RARE, EMIL]. Along with the tomboy look, Purdey had a number of neck ties [eg 3HAN, ANGE] including a distinctive checked item [RARE, GLAD]. She was also known to wear a cravat [GNAW] and frequently sported a choker [3HAN, GNAW, RARE].

Other notable fashion items were a variety of long cardigans [eg RAT, 3HAN] – one of which adorned her facsimile on the Target Range [TARG] – a blue and green oriental top and trousers [CARD], a beige plastic cape and skirt [LAST], a fleece jacket [RAT][18], a pink blouse with the word 'SPORT' on the back [TARG], a brown corduroy waistcoat and jeans [KIL1] and a green and white tabard bearing the word 'KANSAI' [LION]. She often wore polo necks with these [eg LAST, RAT]. Purdey had a fur coat [NEST] and a light trench coat [GNAW, DIRT]. She seldom wore hats, and those she owned included a woollen affair [MIDA] and a broad-brimmed hat with a leopard skin band [DIRT]; rarely, she sported a head scarf [GNAW]. When on her motorcycle she wore black gloves [TALE, OBSE] and also had some blue mittens [TRAP]. Purdey often wore scarves [eg MIDA, EMIL] many matching her outfits [eg CARD, CAT].

Purdey tended to wear fashionable high boots of various colours such as red [eg NEST], black [eg CARD], fawn [eg DIRT], white [eg TRAP], grey [eg EMIL] and brown [eg EMIL]. She also wore high-heeled shoes [eg CARD, COMP], black stockings and suspenders [RAT, TARG]. Purdey's nightwear was either a cream or white night dress [TARG, GNAW] or loose-fitting blue silk pyjamas with lilies on them [SLEE]; she also had a white silk dressing gown [CARD].

When training, Purdey had a gold silk combat suit [CARD, DEAD] as well as pink and black leotards for her exercises at home [LAST, FACE]. For dirty work she had a blue and white striped rugby shirt and denim jeans [GNAW] or denim dungarees [RARE]. It is also notable that Purdey seemed to have designed her own patriotic 'logo', a rampant lion picked out as a fluttering Union Jack which adorned one of her blue tee-shirts [BASE] and also a black cotton jump-suit with red and white trim and the name 'PURDEY' which she wore when on her motorbike [TALE]. The name 'PURDEY' also decorated her white crash helmet [CAT], a blue wetsuit [BASE] and a tee-shirt [TRAP].

Purdey usually wore a ring on the small finger of her right hand [eg NEST, LACE, HOST, TRAP], although she later switched to wearing this on the small finger of her left hand [eg RARE, BASE] as she had done in the early 1970s [OBSE]. As 1977 wore on, she started wearing two rings on her right hand [eg BASE], some with larger stones [eg ANGE, EMIL].

Usually Purdey could be seen wearing small pearl keepers in her ears [eg CARD, DIRT, LION], but would pick something more ornate for a special occasion [SLEE] while looking longingly at some diamond pairs in the looted window of Montague Jewellers [SLEE]. Purdey nearly always wore a fine gold chain about her neck [eg CAT, DIRT, HOST, KIL1, EMIL] and occasionally sported a pearl necklace [FACE]. She would wear a watch on either right [KIL2] or left [GLAD] wrists, along with a wristband [3HAN]. Sometimes she would also wear a metal bracelet [eg ANGE, BASE] or even a charm bracelet [TARG] – and was known to hang

---

[18] This jacket seems to be the one which Purdey wore for her file photograph and was used for identification by people such as Dr Prator [FACE] and Draker [TARG].

a 'stupid little pen-knife thing' on a cord from her neck [TRAP]. Sometimes, Purdey would carry a handbag or purse [LAST] in which she would keep her revolver [RAT] or a radio transmitter [LION]. She would occasionally wear a purse about her neck on a cord [COMP] or carry a smaller shoulder bag [eg COMP, OBSE].

For most of 1976 and early 1977, Purdey's blonde hair was fashioned into a distinctive mushroom bob cut [eg NEST] – a contrast the long tousled look she had adopted in 1970 [OBSE]. She was proud of her hair and liked to check it in a mirror [KIL2]. From summer 1977, she had a more layered variation of the design [eg LION, BASE] which she would occasionally wear in a short pony tail for an evening out [COMP]. She used a bright pink lipstick called Sins of Youth [NEST].

Like Emma Peel before her, Purdey was extremely aware of her femininity – most strongly indicated when she undressed in a sexy manner while standing before a mirror in her flat [FACE]. She was able to play upon a guard's desire to 'touch' her as a distraction [MIDA], was able to get close enough to Cromwell of D16 to get him in an arm-lock [RAT], played on Terry and the other soldiers of the 19th Division Special Commandos to impress her with tales of bravery at the local pub [DIRT] and could fool a captor into undoing the bonds at her ankles, unleashing her dangerous kick [TALE]. Purdey said she needed her beauty sleep [NEST] and would enjoy a shampoo and blow dry even inside a car wash [EMIL]. In general though, she objected to women being used as things of amusement – like the dancing girls of Paris [KIL2].

When it came to men, Purdey's friend, actress Joanna Lumley, recalled that, 'She didn't care about being pretty or trying to attract men, because that seemed to happen all the time anyway.'[19] Purdey herself believed that men were more restless and changeable than women [BASE], while also observing that, 'Inside every woman there's a degree of pure cat' [DEAD]. She had dinner with colleague George Stannard (a couple of times) [NEST] and Cromwell [CARD], while George Myers bet her £100 against an intimate meal on their shooting performance [TARG]. She did not object strongly when offered as the prize in a competition between suitors [CARD]. Zarcardi felt that she had 'beautiful eyes' [CAT], Colonel Miller found her 'attractive' [DIRT] and Roger Masgard believed she was 'charming' [3HAN]. In return, Purdey felt that a fellow agent called Larry was handsome, rugged, charming and sexy [3HAN] and also found visiting CIA agent Marty Brine rather handsome, accepting his dinner date. When Brine observed that Purdey was so perfect that somebody must have made her, Steed replied, 'Some have tried, many have floundered.' [TRAP] She was put out when Colonel Martin kissed Steed and Gambit on the cheeks in admiration – but not her [KIL2]. Nevertheless, she was angry when a man called her his 'sweetheart' [HOST].

There was a mischievous side to Purdey's character that enjoyed teasing people, such as Mr Lewington who was scared of flying [CAT]. Sometimes this perkiness could backfire and look tactless, notably when she attempted to cheer up Steed, not realising that he had just heard about Mark Clifford's death [FACE]. Purdey displayed good humour even when being hunted after a plane crash [TRAP] or shaking off a fatal dose of curare [TARG]. However, she did not enjoy Gambit's more obvious puns [LION].

Living alone, Purdey was domesticated. She could wash, sew and iron [RAT]. She was very proud of her omelettes [RAT, LION], notably one cooked French-style [MIDA, 3HAN]; she

---

[19] *Joanna Lumley – The Biography*, p143.

could also whip up beef, a steak or a lasagne [3HAN], and made a tomato salad using a vast, chemically-enhanced tomato grown by scientist Charles Thornton [GNAW]. Purdey liked to eat steak *au poivre* at the George Cinq in Paris [NEST]. When going out for dinner with Gambit she relished Italian, such as Milanese... and was less then impressed by the roadside cuisine of The Chef's Hat [TALE]. She also liked to eat while being driven by Gambit, consuming oranges [MIDA] or marshmallows [RAT]. Feeling that the marshmallow was 'a neglected little beast' she would cook a marshmallow pie when it was 'in season' [3HAN].

As for drink, Purdey very much enjoyed wine when dining out or with friends [RAT, 3HAN], although her favourite tipple – as known by her uncle – was a gin with a measure of orange, a dash of bitters, and ginger ale with ice (although her uncle disapproved strongly of the ice, saying it was only fit for peasants and polar bears) [DIRT]. She was partial to a bloody Mary when in the pub with the boys [DIRT][20] and also mixed her own concoctions, such as a cocktail she whipped up for a friendly cricket match in 1977 which Steed christened a 'purdka' (vodka, lemonade and gin – with bitter to cheer up the gin) [DEAD]. She was also familiar enough with Russian drinking customs to call 'Nostrovia' and smash the glass when the occasion called for her to down some vodka in Soviet company [GNAW]. She savoured everything from a Napoleon cognac at the Chateau War Museum in France [KIL1] to illicit hooch brewed in Ontario [EMIL]. And – as with almost any associate of Steed's – she soon developed a taste for champagne [eg LAST, LION, KIL2, COMP] which he would even deliver to her as she hung beneath a helicopter [DIRT].

Purdey played tennis [TRAP] and boule [LION], and it is possible that she had javelin experience [TRAP]. She cheated at Scrabble [LAST] and also played cards [HOST] and – judging by the set in her flat – chess [CARD]. Purdey picked horses to back at random [RAT] and passed these onto Gambit as bad tips [LAST]. She watched her male colleagues play snooker [3HAN] and cricket [DEAD].

By 1976, Purdey had taken a gutted basement in London and refurbished it in feminine art decor and art nouveau styles using shades of lilac and pink to make what she described as 'the biggest bed-sitter in the world.'[21] Her flat, Number 5 [LAST], was in a quiet London road [LAST][22] around the corner from Gambit's [NEST] in the Shoreditch area of London, near a branch of the Consolidated Bank Ltd [SLEE]. Purdey could rendezvous with her colleagues at an airport – presumably Heathrow – within 20 minutes of a Red Alert [TRAP].

Coming 21 steps down from the road [RAT], the front door opened into the main open-plan living area. This contained a pink three-piece suite, wicker chairs, a rug, a chess set, various painted screens, a sundial, ornate lamps and shades, 1930s art nouveau posters, numerous pot plants, a white TV set, a hi-fi, a trim phone, a lilac and white piano, and ornaments on pedestals [eg CARD, TARG, SLEE, LAST]. Along one wall was a large mirror and, flanked by lilac curtains, a pair of exercise barres which enabled Purdey to maintain her dancer's training [FACE, LAST]. There was also a mirrored make-up area [LAST]. At the rear of the room was a kitchen surface with pine units, white chairs and a table [LAST]. There was a second phone mounted on the wall by the front door [RAT]. During 1976, Purdey moved the kitchen chairs and table to the front of the flat adjacent to the alcove with barred

---

[20] An unfilmed report suggests Purdey also liked to drink a tomato juice with a dash of Worcestershire, or a grapefruit juice. 'What a lousy way to run a business!', *The New Avengers Annual*, 1977, p32.

[21] 'Room at the Top'. *The New Avengers Annual*, 1978, p49.

[22] The road itself, although unidentified, bears a strong resemblance to St Peter's Square, London W6.

windows by the front door [SLEE, HOST]. Lighting was on a dimmer switch [LAST].

The bedroom, decorated in gentle colours and lots of white, was separated from the living area by a curtain of beads [eg NEST] adjacent to a display case of ornaments and drinks [SLEE, HOST] in which she kept Larry Doomer's letters and photograph [OBSE]. There was also a long mirror [LAST]. Beside her bed she kept a white telephone, and in the bed itself was a white teddy bear [NEST]. The phone was later replaced by a trimphone with a long cord [SLEE, TRAP]. Likewise, an alarm clock featuring characters from the children's television series *The Magic Roundabout* [SLEE] was replaced by another model with a luminous dial within months [GNAW]. The light was controlled by a cord beside the bed [GNAW]. Another alcove off the bedroom apparently led to the bathroom [SLEE]. Patrick Macnee was less impressed with the decor, describing it as being 'Like a tart's boudoir.'[23]

The flat was not terribly secure with its Yale lock [SLEE], chain on the door and a wire cage behind the letter box [LAST]. A Russian sleeper called 'Dr Tulliver' was able to break in [CARD] as was a kidnapping party [HOST] and the door was smashed in by Steed and Gambit on occasion [TARG, SLEE].

In 1976, Purdey enjoyed driving a mustard yellow MGB drophead sports model[24] – a flighty little sports car which reflected her fun nature [MIDA, CARD, LAST, TARG, FACE, 3HAN, SLEE, GNAW]. Purdey was an excellent driver in reverse as well as forward [TARG], could punch out a shattered windscreen and avoid gunfire [SLEE][25]; she could however be distracted by Gambit's flattery [CARD]. Purdey also owned a motorbike – a yellow Yamaha DT250 Enduro[26] which she controlled with utmost precision [CAT]. Purdey's aptitude on two wheels meant that she would often borrow similar transport when the situation arose, such as a gendarme's motorcycle when in the French countryside [KIL1].

In terms of her artistic tastes, by the mid-1970s Purdey found that her sense of humour was very much in tune with the plays of the contemporary English wit Noel Coward or the 17th century French writer Jean-Baptiste Poquelin, better known as Moliere [LAST]. For music, she enjoyed the compositions of Ludwig van Beethoven [TARG]. She clearly had little or no empathy with modern or abstract art, as shown by her lack of understanding for the symbolism of the sculptural work of Helen McKay [3HAN]. She apparently read *The Times* and could do its crossword in ten minutes.[27]

To relax, Purdey would sometimes go out to the disco with Gambit [TRAP] and also relished sunbathing *au naturel* [OBSE]. She enjoyed watching films a great deal and found that – like Gambit – she was a bit of a film buff and they would debate items of trivia such as whether Walter Huston or John Huston directed the 1948 Humphrey Bogart movie *The Treasure of Sierra Madre* (indeed, Gambit seemed slightly more knowledgeable than her in this arena) [MIDA]. Her two viewings of the 1954 Howard Keel musical *Rose Marie* gave

---

[23] *Stare Back and Smile*, p132. One transcript described the flat thus: 'A hookah... A chess board laid out with a half-finished game on it. A collection of fob watches. A typewriter. A miniature wine rack containing quarter bottles of champagne... Another chess board laid out for a game to commence.' [NEST].

[24] Registration MOC 232P.

[25] An unconfirmed report suggests that Purdey could keep control of a vehicle when its tyres were shot out. 'Fangs for the Memory!', *The New Avengers Annual*, 1977, p9.

[26] Registration LLC 950P.

[27] *The Eagle's Nest*, p131,171.

her all the background she had of Canada [COMP] and she was very aware of clichéd lines from Westerns [BASE], assorted battle tactics and standard quotes like 'Let's get the hell out of here' [TRAP].

By late 1975, Purdey was working for Mike Gambit on incidents such as the break-in at the Ministry where fellow agent Edward Harlow was killed [GNAW]. It may also be around now that they tangled with Soviet agent Ivan Halfhide for the first time, although he evaded them and later appeared working in Toronto in 1977 [BASE]. It is also possible that she had worked in partnership with another agent called Merton whose approach she was familiar with [CAT]. Purdey's rise through the Department was rapid. By 1976, she was one of the top agents, famous enough to have mannequins of herself included at the automated Target Range [TARG].

Purdey felt that Gambit had style [FACE] and – although she would not admit it to him – cared about him a great deal [FACE]. She did not feel threatened or bothered by his flirting [NEST, CARD, DIRT, DEAD] and liked him to fuss over her [TARG], even deliberately playing on his jealousy [3HAN]. She was however furious when he deliberately took advantage of a situation to see her in a state of undress [CARD], although she was happy for Gambit to reveal her leg in the course of duty to distract members of the 19th Division Special Commandos [DIRT]. There was clearly an intimacy between them – evident when he whispered something in her ear which uniquely identified him [CAT] – although on another occasion when they got tipsy on a boat trip on a river, nothing happened [FACE]. They did have dinner together on occasion [TALE] or go to the disco – where she could read his mind after he had consumed a few drinks [TRAP]. Although she wept when she believed he had been killed by 'Walton', his *doppelgänger* [FACE], Purdey was not sufficiently close to Gambit that she would discuss her past with Larry Doomer with him [OBSE]. By spring 1977, Gambit had still not been invited for dinner with Purdey's mother – unlike his colleague, Spelman [HOST].

Around the very start of 1976, Purdey was reassigned to work with Steed alongside Gambit; when neither Steed nor Gambit were available she reported to Craig, the Executive in Charge of Home Security [FACE]. Steed was a senior Department figure, a hero and a legend to her – but in a very different manner to how Tara King had doted on her colleague almost a decade earlier... although, as Gambit noted, Purdey never mentioned Mrs Peel [LAST]. When Gambit commented that Steed was old-fashioned, Purdey immediately leapt to his defence saying that the same could be said of St Paul's, yet both had 'survived a very long time' [NEST]. In Purdey's eyes, this charming and avuncular figure was 'the best' [SLEE], 'beautiful' [CARD], 'gallant' [LAST], a 'wonderful man' [SLEE] whom she felt was a true gentleman [KIL2]. Comparing him to teak, Purdey believed that Steed was inflexible and dependable [HOST], finding the act of putting her head on his shoulder to be comforting [DEAD]. She tried to be sensitive to his feelings and memories [LAST] and could tell when he was worried [LAST]. She also knew his tastes in things such as the ballet [RARE] but not as obsessively as Tara. Purdey would fiercely defend her new superior in the face of others [RARE] and maintained that even if he had murdered a colleague, his reason for doing so would have been justified [RARE]. She appeared to have a major confession to tell him once when it seemed they were on the point of death, saying, 'Steed, I want to tell you something...' as automated walls moved in on them [ANGE], and on a later occasion hugged him with joy on discovering that he had not been killed by a gunshot [KIL2].

Having witnessed the apparent demise of Felix Kane [LAST], one of Purdey's first missions with Steed in March 1976 ultimately involved the protection of a visiting princess from the lethal touch of Midas. Purdey[28] was captured during this investigation and at one point it seemed that she would be given over to Midas as his 'plaything' – presumably meaning a gruesome, disease-ridden death as the result of rape. Nevertheless, it was her expert fighting footwork which saw Midas eventually captured [MIDA].

As part of the diversion to help Steed execute the defection of Professor Vasil, Purdey posed as a cheerleader with a gang of girls screaming for their trendy teen idol 'Mike' (ie Gambit). When the Russian 'House of Cards' scheme was activated after the apparent death of Ivan Perov, it was Purdey who had to break the news to Steed that Joanna, his latest lady friend, was in fact a Russian sleeper ordered to kill him. Once more, Purdey was instrumental in the final overpowering of Perov [CARD].

When the remote Scottish island of St Dorca needed investigating to locate the kidnapped Dr von Claus, Purdey came ashore by covert means in a wetsuit to give cover for Steed, and briefly found herself imprisoned by the Third Reich followers using the local monastery as their cover [NEST]. Her role in the investigation into the death of Hugh Rydercroft led to her being captured by the bizarre Zarcardi at his Sanctuary of Wings, and coming under a brutal attack from the birds under his control. Purdey was saved only by her quick thinking, and two basketfuls of cats purchased by Steed and Gambit [CAT].

Always hoping to match Steed's perfect score on the Target Range, Purdey's expertise with a handgun was shown to be only 99 per cent perfect. Unfortunately, the one sniper's pellet which had marked her right shoulder was infected with curare and soon she was in a coma. Luckily Gambit and Steed – who was also infected – managed to brave the shooting course and acquire the antidote which saved her life [TARG].

When it became clear that a Mission for the Distressed and Needy was somehow involved in the replacement of key security people with *doppelgängers*, Purdey investigated alone, first donning the guise of a bespectacled middle-aged Salvation Army lady with a home counties accent. Convinced that the charitable organisation was implicated, Purdey then went undercover as 'Lolita', a working class, frizzy-haired, gum-chewing, bejewelled girl who had some stolen money from a bank job pulled by her boyfriend. As such, this allowed her to be 'trained' by Dr Prator to become a perfect double for herself, and was duly dispatched to kill the 'real' Purdey – unaware that the fake 'Gambit' that she had been training with at the Mission was in fact the real one, and that Craig, the one person she felt she could trust, was the original *doppelgänger* who controlled the whole scheme [FACE].

During the summer of 1976, Purdey seemed to exchange the Yamaha for a red Honda motorcycle[29] which she was still riding in 1977 [TALE, OBSE]. This was a model which allowed her a great deal of manoeuvrability denied to her by a car, such as being able to squeeze through the narrow gap between a wall and a removal lorry [TALE] and navigating the rough terrain of woodlands in Buckinghamshire [OBSE]. The vehicle did sustain damage on one occasion when a tyre was shot out by two enemy agents called Poole and Roach [TALE].

During the long search to acquire the sensitive material secreted years earlier by Burt Brandon, Purdey was both shot from her motorbike and then kidnapped by Poole and Roach,

---

[28] The transcript for this incident – and others – refers to Purdey under the alias 'Charly' [MIDA, CARD, NEST, DIRT].

[29] Registration OLR 471P.

two operatives hired by the enemy. She was released when Steed pulled off an excellent bluff – and took her revenge quite adequately with her hands tied behind her back [TALE].

Purdey's charge in the protection of the triumvirate who comprised the 'Three Handed Game' was Roger Masgard who performed professionally on stage as 'Masgard, the Memory Man'. Unfortunately during one of Masgard's performances at a theatre in Wimbledon, Purdey was too distracted in his dressing room trying out a clown make-up and wig to prevent him from being snatched and having his memory plundered by the mercenary agent Juventor. Purdey later more than made up for her failure, employing her tap-dancing skills against Juventor, whose mind inhabited the body of tap dancer 'Tap' Ranson. A swift kick sent Juventor flying from the stage down into the orchestra pit at the theatre [3HAN].

When a quantity of S-95 was used to put the population of Central London to sleep one Sunday in August, Purdey fought a lone battle for survival to get out of the affected area, having been locked out of her flat in nothing more than her silken pyjamas, forcing her to borrow a red Mini from a sleeping driver at the end of her road. Evading the raiding parties co-ordinated by Brady, Purdey attempted to hide from her pursuers by posing as a shop window display mannequin ('Today's Biggest Offer') at a store called Marian's. She then took on the guise of a mercenary helicopter pilot, supposedly ready to fly Brady, his accomplice Tina and their loot to safety from Westland Heliport [SLEE].

It transpired that Purdey's role in the investigation of possible covert surveillance in the sewers of London tied in to the death of Harlow a year earlier. The growth serum research completed privately by Charles Thornton had accidentally created a giant rat down in the tunnels, and Purdey found herself menaced by both the vast rodent and Thornton when she made her own investigations – saved by Steed's quick thinking and a plastic bag filled with a noxious concoction [GNAW].

Purdey decided to call on Uncle Elroyd for help when it seemed that the 19th Division Special Commandos were acting as mercenaries overseas. Deciding to chat up some of the commandos in the local pub was a mistake, since Purdey was soon placed in confinement by the ruthless Colonel 'Mad Jack' Miller. Escaping with the help of Gambit, she strayed into a minefield – to be rescued by Steed in a champagne-equipped helicopter [DIRT].

By 1977, Purdey was a very prominent figure in the Department; The Unicorn rated her as one of the best professionals [LION], while Paul Baker of Canadian security was well aware of her skills [COMP] and the Soviet Captain Malachev had seen her face in his country's files on many occasions [BASE].

Early in 1977, Purdey worked with Gambit to try to locate Irwin Gunner, an agent who had suddenly become active again after 17 years. Checking up on Gunner's old colleague, John Cledge, Purdey became engaged in a brief struggle with an 'assailant' who turned out to be Cromwell, the head of D16. Cromwell charmed Purdey with the invitation for a dinner date, which she accepted – although she realised in the nick of time that Cromwell was the traitor Gunner was trying to expose [RAT].

It was Steed's care and admiration for Purdey which made her a target for the vengeful Felix Kane, who had survived the inferno which engulfed him a year earlier. Aided by the legs and an arm cannibalised from a Cybernaut, Kane launched a horrific attack on Purdey in her basement flat so that her mutilation and death would cause Steed grief. Although Purdey fought bravely against the cyborg assailant, it was Steed's use of plastic skin on the metal limbs which finally saved her life [LAST].

Kane's terrifying assault on Purdey meant a lot of redecoration to her flat after the damage that had been inflicted; her piano was wrecked along with a number of her ornaments [LAST] but it was soon replaced [HOST, OBSE]. Also in early 1977, Purdey swapped her MGB for a bright yellow Triumph TR7[30] [HOST, TRAP, RARE, ANGE]; it was this vehicle that was left by the kidnapper Vernon at Steed's home in spring 1977 to prove that Purdey was being held hostage [HOST].

Purdey was targeted by double agent Spelman (whose real name was Spelenovitch) as part of a scheme to discredit Steed and so undermine confidence in the entire Department. In fact, she had got to know Spelman quite well, even to the extent of taking him to dinner with her mother. Three heavies called Vernon, Packer and Marvin were hired to kidnap Purdey from her flat, placing her chloroformed body in a coffin, and holding her captive in a disused Haunted House attraction at an obsolete funfair in North London. Valuing Purdey above any secret documents, Steed was prepared to hand over the ransom demanded of him – but with Gambit's help, Spelman was overpowered [HOST].

During a drugs interception in Windsor, Purdey rather enjoyed working with handsome Marty Brine, and accepted a dinner date with the CIA agent just before he was gunned down by a courier. The fact that the hand-over had been thwarted made Purdey a target of revenge for drugs baron Soo Choy, and with Gambit and Steed she was lured onto an aircraft and flown to the villain's estate in East Anglia, successfully engaging in jungle warfare against Soo Choy's private army [TRAP].

Purdey now started to redecorate her flat, replacing the pinks and lilacs with shades of beige and cream [RARE]. When Steed's old rival Mark Crayford returned to England after being declared dead by the Russians, Purdey again became a kidnap victim and bait in a trap for Steed – held captive at an old Victorian folly where Crayford had once triumphed over his school friend. A dual rescue by Steed and Gambit saved Purdey's life again [DEAD]. Purdey then tried to clear Steed's name when he was implicated in the murder of his colleagues by Graham Wallace, an embezzler inside the Department who was about to be exposed [RARE].

By now, the basement flat had been redecorated in a far lighter colour scheme, and a green telephone installed. More pine furniture was in evidence now as well [ANGE, OBSE]. The next assignment took Purdey and Steed first to Paris (where she dressed as a nun when wishing to leave the George V hotel in Paris unobserved by Russian agents) and then to the border between East and West. Purdey undertook her own investigation of Briantern Health Farm, survived stretching in a traction machine, and was saved by Gambit from what she believed was certain death – being crushed by moving walls in a maze alongside Steed [ANGE].

During the Queen's jubilee celebrations that June, two images from Purdey's past returned to haunt her. Firstly, she was offered a plum security assignment by Steed which involved her protecting a visiting VIP – none other than the man whom Larry Doomer had been sure had had his father killed. Secondly, the day after she turned the assignment down, Purdey was helping Steed investigate a fire at an RAF base when she came face to face again with Squadron Leader Doomer.[31] The meeting was upsetting for her – and later

---

[30] Registration OGW 562R. An unconfirmed report suggests that this vehicle had an anti-theft alarm. 'What a lousy way to run a business!', *The New Avengers Annual*, 1977, p31.

[31] It is interesting to note that Doomer's home betrayed the same taste in graphic art as Gambit's.

compounded when it became clear that Doomer himself had hired two mercenaries called Kilner and Morgan to start the fire, allowing him a distraction so that he could tamper with a missile due for a demonstration the next day [OBSE].

In the exercise, 'Red Leader' Doomer claimed that his final Bloodhound missile had gone haywire and blown up in mid-air; in fact, he had ditched it into a sand bank near Milton Keynes. He then planned to launch the missile at the Houses of Parliament during the VIP visit, killing the man he held responsible for his father's death. The rocket was hidden in a pit on the patch of land where he and Purdey had planned their 'dream house' seven years earlier. Having extracted his revenge, Doomer planned to go to Africa and operate as a pilot [OBSE].

Doomer attended a party given by Steed where he told Purdey that he still wanted her – and received a slap in the face from a furious ex-ballerina who was still not ready to discuss what had happened with her colleagues. Realising that the missile would be detectable in photographs taken by the Eye of God satellite, Doomer kidnapped General Canvey, the officer in charge, and intercepted the shots of the area. By now, it was evident what Doomer was planning – and Doomer himself was *en route* to launch the Bloodhound. Claiming that Doomer was not mad, just badly hurt and obsessive, Purdey asked for a five minute start on Steed and his colleagues in order to talk to her former fiancé. When Steed refused, Purdey shot out the tyres on his Range Rover and took off on her motorbike with tears in her eyes. While Gambit dealt with Kilner and Morgan, Purdey found herself engaged in a stand-off with Doomer at the missile site. Ultimately, Gambit had no option other than to shoot Doomer – who was directly threatening Purdey's life. Purdey was upset by Doomer's death, not least because she doubted that she would have opened fire if Gambit had been similarly threatened [OBSE].

Having helped tracking Steed's old adversary The Unicorn in England, Purdey was delighted to return to Paris and enthusiastically joined in with the hit-man's capture – shortly before The Unicorn was shot by one of his own men and an elaborate charade had to be staged to make it appear that the dead killer was still alive [LION]. Purdey soon returned to France in August when Steed was finally able to close a case that had been open since 1965. Indeed, for her role in subsequently preventing the outbreak of World War III, Purdey was awarded the Little Mother of the Earth and Tractor Drivers and Heavy Industry Award from Comrade Kerov [KIL1, KIL2].

When on assignment overseas, Purdey drove a red Mini while in Paris [LION] and in Canada was allocated a yellow Toyota Corolla hatchback[32] [BASE, EMIL] which was equipped with a radio telephone [EMIL].

While waiting at an airfield in Kent for a courier bearing a vital clue to the identity of the agent Scapina, Purdey received flesh wounds to her left arm from the machine gun fire of a hidden assassin. She quickly recovered for her first trip to Canada where she found herself incarcerated in the automated Canadian Security Building in Toronto, which turned out to be SCAPINA itself. Avoiding all the computerised traps, Purdey triggered the building's sprinkler system and short-circuited the control computer [COMP]. Before she returned to England, Purdey was also involved in preventing Karl Sminksy and his men from carrying out an attack on the relocated Canadian Security Building with their bare hands [GLAD].

---

[32] Registration LRM 022.

Summoned back to Toronto shortly afterwards, it was Purdey who first firmly located the position of 'Forward Base', the Russian HQ which had been hidden on the shoreline of Lake Ontario since 17 April 1969 [BASE]. She then went undercover in an attempt to infiltrate the organisation which was paying The Fox, a double agent in Canadian Intelligence. Captured by two men called Mirschtia and Kalenkov, she managed to escape imprisonment at Puck's Circus, and then posed as a cleaning lady to follow another enemy agent called Arkoff who was involved in The Fox's final payoff in the lake at Humber Bay Park [EMIL].

As with her colleagues, Purdey's current whereabouts are unknown. It seems likely that she was still active alongside Gambit and Steed into early 1978. Since then there have been unsubstantiated reports that she has been undertaking charity work, became involved with an antiques dealer in Suffolk while commuting back and forth between South America, and even spent some time cast away on a desert island.

24

THE DEPARTMENT

'They walk in twilight,' was how one Oriental adversary of Steed and his colleagues described their mode of operation [TRAP]. Trying to pin down details on the people Steed works for is like trying to snare a shadow. Even during the surveillance films, there is little consistency of terminology and procedure which leans towards the theory that the group was a team of trained experts in various fields, applying themselves wherever needed. Some described their work as 'cloak and dagger' [NUTS] and Steed himself remarked that he was employed in 'an odd business' [MAND]. However, it was probably Purdey who summed up the remit of her colleagues best, declaring, 'Trouble is our business' [GLAD].

First and foremost, it is difficult to come up with a *name* for the body. One of the most commonly used terms is the one adopted by Don Macpherson for the 1998 movie: 'The Ministry'.[1] It is easy to see where this terminology comes from. In a number of the surveillance films, Steed is said to be from 'the Ministry' [VENU, XR40, POSI, ROTT, PAND] and carries a 'Ministry security pass' [NOON, KEEP]. Tara checks files at 'the Ministry' [GETA] and one of the medical security inmates offers to pull strings for her at 'the Ministry' [NOON]. A highly unreliable source suggested that Steed and Tara worked for 'a department known only as the Ministry'[2] which 'Major' Steed described – with tongue firmly in cheek – as the 'Ministry of Exceptionally Important Affairs'.[3]

The only problem with this was that Steed's people worked for many different Ministries including the Ministry of Ecology [CAT], Ministry of Agriculture [ROME, GNAW] and Fisheries [LOBS], Ministry of Defence [SEET, MISS, CYPH], Ministry of Technology [NEVE, XR40], Ministry of TSI [SPLI, MORN], Ministry of Science [DWAR], Ministry of Works [HAND][4], Ministry for Promotion [MIND], Ministry of Eastern Affairs [PRIN], War Ministry [VENU][5] as well as working with the Ministry of Health [WILD] and Ministry of Information [FACE] plus members of various unspecified Ministries [eg SELL, CYBE, DUST, TIME, NURS, RETU, GUNS, LOVE, TALE]. It was not one single 'Ministry'.

In the early 1960s, the body was usually referred to as 'the Organisation' by Steed [SELL], while hit-man Olaf Pomeroy referred to 'your Organisation' [BEAR] and One-Six

---

[1] The film gave the Ministry motto as 'In Unity We Stand Strong For Our Country'.

[2] *Moon Express*, p3. See also *The Magnetic Man*, p35.

[3] *Moon Express*, p79.

[4] See also 'Epidemic of Terror'. *Look Westward/The Viewer*, 5 October 1963.

[5] Also possibly the Ministry of Transport. *TV Comic*, Issue 1,000, 13 February 1971.

spoke of a 'large Organisation' [MIRR]. Tara too referred to it as 'the Organisation' [KNOT]. The diving group of smugglers known as 'the Frogs' believed that Steed and his colleagues were representing 'British Intelligence' [FROG] and when addressing Steed, an adversary called Merridon referred to 'your intelligence service' [KILL]. Steed was known to call 'Security' [TWOS] and describe himself as from 'Security' [TAKE] as well as referring to 'my security people' [FOG]. 'The Section' was another term applied to the group [WRIN].

However, the name which has been adopted for this work is 'the Department', which is how it is referred to on a number of occasions [FEED, TWOS, FALS, KILL, STAY, THAT, REQU, MIDA, RAT, HOST, ANGE]; for example, Steed commenting, 'I'd better alert the Department,' [STAY] and Tara being referred to as 'with the Department' [THAT].

The Department has apparently been going since World War I [PAND] and one of the best descriptions of its function came from Patrick Macnee, writing with novelist Peter Leslie in 1965: 'a small and select band of men and women more off-beat than [MI5, MI6 or SOE]. They are available for any kind of work, anywhere. They can overlap or circumvent all or any of the others.'[6]

The protection of visiting VIPs [NEED, KING, DECA, SELL, CART, CONC, BRIM, PRIN, OUTS, OBSE] – or indeed their horses [TROJ] – was a prime role for the Department, which would also investigate kidnappings or incidents concerning overseas allies [MOON, KEEP]. Potential sabotage [SLIP, COUR, MOUS] and threats to the country's early warning system [DRES, GRAV] came within their remit, along with general matters of national security which could lead to world panic [DWAR] including nuclear threats [NOV5, BARG, MORN]. Associated with this was investigation into blackmail [SCHO, DUST, FALS, TALE], defection [GIRL, MIRR, HOLE, CARD], apprehending of assassins [BEAR, REMO, LION] and monitoring enemy agents [MIRR, TWOS, QUIC, TOWN, MIDA, GLAD] or, ideally, exposing them [COMP, BASE, EMIL].

In the early 1960s, the Department was also heavily involved in investigating home-grown crime such as murder [DANC], arson [ROSE], paid beatings [FRIG], theft of diamonds [DOUB], paintings [MIRR] and bullion [CAGE], insurance scams [BAIT], protection rackets [BOOK], missing official papers [MIRR], counterfeiting [ROOT, MEDI] and the recovery of stolen money [DOWN] or diamonds [MIRR]. Smuggling also fell into its arena, tracking down illegal importers of drugs [SNOW, CONS, LOBS, TRAP], guns [BULL], diamonds [DIAM, DANE, ROCK, BREA], gold [FLEE, MIDA], ambergris [WHAL] and ivory [ELEP]. The team combated organised crime [INTE, WOND, NOON, LACE], took an interest in anti-terrorism techniques [SLEE] and aided in witness protection [REQU].

The murder of officials [HIST, VENU, CAT, ROTT], businessmen [CYBE, MARK, DIAL, SUCC, WING, FEAR] or American doctors [CATC] attracted the Department's attention – as did other bizarre deaths [SURF, HUNT, TIGE, POSI, KIL1] and missing people [TOY, SURR, DIRT] or fish [CAST]. They also looked into 'escape routes' for miscreants [SPRI, TIME, BIZA]. Steed and Emma described their territory once as things which 'Appear without warning...' – 'And disappear without trace...' [TIGE].

Scientific espionage relating to British developments was a prime concern [NIGH, CLAY, WARL, EGGS, UNDE, BROK, ROOM, HOLE] as was, to a lesser extent, industrial espionage [HAND]. The group also undertook military investigations [ESPR, DIRT] and national security issues such as the Allied attack plans [HOST] and US war policy documents [3HAN]. Its

---

[6] *...deadline*, p18.

couriers transported fuel samples [PROP], medical formulas [MORT] and sensitive papers [DISP, TREA].

The Department became involved when there were security breaches at establishments or groups such as the Carmadoc Research Establishment [DONE], the Deepdale Atomic Energy Commission [SHAD], Winterwell Atomic Research Station [MOUS], the CFEE [BUTL], the Department of Forestry Research [ROTT], Project CUPID [LOOK], Cypher HQ [CYPH] (and other cipher issues [FEED, MIRR]), the DEWLine System [MONT], the Muswells Back missile installation [BIRD], United Europe [DOOR], the War Room [THAT], the World Disarmament Committee [FOG] as well as defence meetings [NURS], embassies [GNAW], research laboratories [RADI, AIR, DRAG], naval bases [ZEBR], RAF bases [OBSE], state ordnance depots [GUNS], Government strong rooms [MIND], peace conferences [KEEP] and scientific conferences [NEST]. Other cases arose because of strange reports [TOWN, LIVI, INVA, NEVE] or there simply being 'Odd people involved' [SECO].

The Department also had a procedure which was referred to as 'Red Alert'; the exact nature of this alarm is unclear, but given the political climate of the day it would seem possible that this related to a potential nuclear strike from one of the superpowers such as Russia or America [TRAP].

Controlled from HM Government [SECO] at Whitehall [BROK], the Department liaised with the aforementioned Ministries and UNESCO [ELEP], the War Office [HUNT, DANG], the War Department [DRES], the Army Training Centre [DIRT], the Foreign Office [TROJ], the Treasury [COUR, WHAL, MISS], the MOTC [CYPH], NATO [BOX], the NUTSHELL [NUTS], the CIA [TRAP], D16 [RAT], the Supply Commission [BULL], C5 [OBSE], the Home Office [TALE], Interpol [INTE] and other security bodies such as PANSAC [OUTS] and MI12 [CYPH].

By the 1970s there was a formal HQ [HOST] known as 'the Ministry building' [ANGE] and apparently in London [GLAD]. This had a gymnasium [CARD, DEAD, HOST], a firing range [HOST] and a bar [RARE]. The Department also had agents across the world in Europe [PAND] including Paris [ANGE], the Eastern Sector [ANGE], behind the iron curtain [DEAD], the Far East [MIDA], Montreal [MONT], Tangiers [BULL], Rome [MAUR] and Austria [WRIN].

There were also specific initiatives such as the Floral Network [WHO?] or the Special Service [REQU]. Different sections of the organisation were responsible for the disposal of corpses [STAT], intercepting post and phone calls [FEED, BAIT, HOST, RARE], issuing espionage equipment [THAT], a forensic team [BROK, INTR, STAY, CAT, TALE], a medical division [TAKE, TARG], a scientific team known as 'The Lab' [BEAR, TAKE], a file archive [PAND, RAT, TARG, DEAD, RARE, TRAP], overseas security [DEAD], a monitoring room at Whitehall [RAT] and a pathological lab [BIRD]. Specialist establishments included a security prison called 'the Monastery'[7] [GETA], a nursing home called Department S [NOON], an interrogation holding centre called 'the Unit' [WRIN], an automated Target Range [TARG] plus safe houses for interrogation [QUIC, CARD] and meeting places like B Complex [RARE].

Steed reported to a number of superiors in the available surveillance films. The following pages provide a brief run-down on each of them.

---

[7] Now apparently used as Ashridge College near Little Gaddeston, Hertfordshire.

'5'

'5' was the superior of Steed and an agent called Tobert in 1961. Based in an office at Whitehall – phone number Whitehall 0011 – where he recorded phone conversations, he suffered from a poor liver [ROOT].

ONE-SIX

A balding, no-nonsense individual with close-cropped hair and a hearing aid in his left ear, One-Six was one of the last superiors under the 'One' identification system to act as Steed's superior in early 1963. He tended to be well-dressed in a dinner jacket or dark suit [MIRR], with a tie or a dapper Panama hat when in the Mediterranean [FROG]. One-Six ran a team of about ten men in London, briefed in the back room of a seedy bar, outside which stood a woman called Iris. It seems that One-Six, in a reluctantly benevolent manner, helped Iris out with 'young David'. One-Six had a low opinion of Steed, feeling it would be best to make him do office paperwork and telling him, 'There are no lone wolves on my team.' 'Just old foxes,' replied Steed [MIRR].

ONE-SEVEN

Another balding senior officer in rather Victorian attire, who in early 1963 was monitoring the information leak from Professor Aubyn's research department at St Luke's College, where he was staying with his old friend, the Vice-Chancellor. Enjoying a beer at The Volunteer, he disapproved of Steed's use of Venus Smith. It seems he had worked with Steed before, commenting, 'Your cover usually has a large element of wishful thinking.' He smoked cigarettes in a holder and quoted Samuel Johnson [SCHO].

ONE-TEN

'He contracts the 'undercover' work, but he will always keep the arrangements on a PERSONAL basis,'[8] noted an internal memo on One-Ten in February 1961. The balding, One-Ten was a very incisive man [DISP] and was usual found wearing a dark suit [BEAR, CLAY] in his office in London [BEAR], although later on he would arrange meetings elsewhere such as a pub [WARL], a sauna bath [CLAY] or a ceramics museum [CLAY] – a trait later picked up by Mother, one of his successors.

Steed worked with One-Ten frequently during 1961 and 1962, and was not afraid to argue against his orders [BEAR]. They had apparently been in the Department around the same length of time, since One-Ten commented about a hit-man who had been in the business 'as long as you and me' [BEAR]. When Steed began to feel too personally involved on an assignment, One-Ten would take him out of the game [BEAR]. One-Ten could be quite

---

[8] *The Complete Avengers*, p15. Their emphasis.

ruthless, instructing Caroline Evans not to rescue Steed after he had been caught trying to break into a girls' finishing school as this might compromise the operation [SPRI]. Steed grudgingly commented that his boss 'Can be amazingly efficient' on one occasion [INTE].

In 1962, Steed was concerned when One-Ten was not available at the time of M Roland's visit to London [SELL], but was soon reporting to him in Jamaica – finding his boss dressed in a dapper suit with Panama hat and dark glasses [DISP]. It was on this occasion that One-Ten arranged for Cathy Gale to be Steed's cover on a journey from Jamaica to Santiago [DISP]. One-Ten's attitude to Cathy was to change sharply, and in the coming months he would disapprove of Steed's use of 'amateurs' [CLAY].

One-Ten smoked [DISP] and enjoyed a pint at a pub in Covent Garden where he would meet Steed [WARL]. He also drank Scotch [REMO]. He knew his Sunderland China [CLAY] and was bothered about his tan – asking Steed to oil his back [REMO]. While in the province of Aluda, One-Ten enjoyed applying sun-tan lotion to actress Nicole Cauvin, suggesting that they could go to Antibes and stay at the four star Bonne Auberge [REMO].

ONE-TWELVE

'One of my elders and betters,' was how Steed described the pudgy faced man who directed Steed when One-Ten was not available in 1962 during the visit to London of M Etienne Roland. Steed seemed ill at ease with his new boss, and although One-Twelve knew that he was 'very good', he still had Steed tailed by another agent called Fraser. One-Twelve was a hard taskmaster, remarking, 'There is never an explanation for a failure to carry out an assignment,' and – in more reflective mood – asking, 'Who's to guard the guards themselves?' He was an art lover who admired a bust of Canadian Marc-Aurele de Foy Suzor-Cote, and liked to meet people at the British Museum. Steed felt he was 'quite a connoisseur' [SELL].

ONE-FIFTEEN

In 1961, One-Fifteen sent Steed to investigate sabotage and security at a research centre trying to solve the problem of a radiation resistant material suitable for space travel [DRAG].

CHARLES

A fair-haired, portly figure wearing an old school tie [SHAD, WRIN], a trilby [WRIN] and carrying a cane [SHAD] or battered briefcase [SHAD], Charles was the man whom Steed reported to in late 1963. He had an office a mile away from Steed's [WRIN], did the crossword [WRIN], hated smoking [WRIN], ate ice cream [SHAD], spoke Latin [SHAD] and clearly admired good food and wine [WRIN]. Charles saw it as the privilege to break the rules [WRIN]. An unconfirmed report suggests that Charles had held British Intelligence together for 15 years prior to his retirement in 1964, and was briefly involved with the Department again in 1969-70.[9]

---

[9] *Too Many Targets*, p4,5,10,11,16 etc.

COLONEL ROBERTSON

Most likely a senior member of the Department in 1966 whom Steed reported to [PRIN] and made requests from [JACK] on various occasions by phone; this was probably also the 'Colonel' whom Steed reported to around the same time on another case [SUCC]. The Colonel had a loud voice and was apparently argumentative with Steed [PRIN].[10]

MOTHER

'Mother knows best' [KNOT] was a suitable motto for members of the Department when this highly experienced operative was in charge of personnel and disappearances, a few months prior to becoming top man in the Department.

His date of birth obscure, Mother was apparently a fat, wrinkled baby.[11] He had brothers and sisters[12] and was a chubby lad who played on the beach with a bucket and spade.[13] Schooled at St Gargoyles[14], he made a point of returning to the school in his adult life to present the prizes on sports day as an 'old boy'[15] where even the headmaster simply introduced him as 'Mother'.[16] Mother also seemed to mix in high society, commenting on one occasion that he had known Lady Vanessa Cholmondley Davenport since she came out in 1938 [LOVE]; he was also friends with Lord and Lady Wallingstone.[17]

Of Mother's family, he had a nephew called Basil Creighton-Latimer[18] who apparently joined the Department in late 1967. Basil and Mother had little in common, and the rather awkward nephew was only sent on assignments when absolutely necessary [WISH]. Mother greatly preferred the company of his two maternal aunts, Harriet and Georgina. Living in a mews flat[19], both were keen readers of espionage and murder novels by Agatha Christie and Earl Stanley Gardener. As such, they were delighted when their nephew could tell them tales involving guns and violence, and harboured hopes that he would be able to allow them visits to a morgue or to Scotland Yard's famous Black Museum. While Georgina was always delighted by Mother's stories, Harriet was far more picky about detail [LACE]. It seems that Mother also had a tall, thin, haughty Aunt Gertrude.[20]

---

[10] It is possible that this was the Colonel who handed assignments to Steed and Emma around 1965-66, sometimes by radio. *TV Comic*, Issue 731, 18 December 1965. He was a gaunt-faced man with an office in London. *TV Comic*, Issue 736, 22 January 1966. See also *TV Comic*, Issue 751, 7 May 1966; Issue 761, 16 July 1966.

[11] 'The Spirit of Christmas', *TV Comic Annual*, 1970, p52.

[12] 'The Spirit of Christmas', *TV Comic Annual*, 1970, p53.

[13] 'The Spirit of Christmas', *TV Comic Annual*, 1970, p52.

[14] *TV Comic*, Issue 1072, 1 July 1972.

[15] *TV Comic*, Issues 1070-1078, 17 June – 12 August 1972.

[16] *TV Comic*, Issue 1073, 8 July 1972.

[17] *TV Comic Holiday Special*, June 1972.

[18] It is possible that Basil was the nephew who brought Mother Christmas presents. 'The Spirit of Christmas', *TV Comic Annual*, 1970, p49.

[19] Which appears to be Weymouth Mews, London, W1.

[20] *TV Comic*, Issues 1070-1078, 17 June – 12 August 1972.

From some of Mother's comments, it seems that he was once very active in the field. Disabled in the 1960s, he instead applied his mind to problems and the acquisition of knowledge, commenting on one occasion: 'I've nothing else to do but think. It's my job to know these things' [CATC]. One unconfirmed report suggests that Mother had been a field operative during the War in France. In a senior position, the officer fussed over his charges like a mother tending his flock, which led to his operatives calling him 'Mother'. On hearing the name he apparently liked it and adopted it, later using it as his code-name[21] and creating other 'family' code-names in the Department [eg STAY].

Mother was apparently wounded in France[22] and this confined his 5' 11" frame to a wheelchair for the rest of his career; he weighed in at about 20 stone. It is not entirely clear when Mother joined the Department. Certainly he had an excellent working knowledge of code-names used during World War I [PAND] and was *au fait* with various cases undertaken by Steed and Emma over the period 1966 to 1967, enabling him to relate specific incidents to his aunts for amusement [LACE].[23]

By 1967, Mother was in charge of personnel and missing agents at a remote country estate which also functioned as a training ground. Located in an office full of ladders, filing cabinets and the uniforms of the three armed services, Mother could move about using a frame of hanging straps suspended from the ceiling; 'the only exercise I get,' he explained. He had an aide called Filson and was in contact with Washington [KNOT].[24]

Steed and Mother already seemed to know each other prior to the amnesia incident, and Mother was one of the few people to call him 'John' [KNOT] – in comparison to the more formal 'Steed' which he adopted from the time when Steed became his direct subordinate. Steed felt that Mother was 'vulnerable at the best of times' [KNOT].

By spring 1968, Mother was a department head, on the same footing as Colonel Stonehouse [TAKE]. It was a cardinal error to even admit to the existence of Mother outside the immediate Department [INTR]. In this new position, Mother reported directly to a minister [CYPH]. He would also take on special assignments, such as spending three months assembling a detailed dossier on the blackmailer Lord Edgefield for Sir Joseph Tarlton [FALS]. Also, when it suited him, he was happy to test new equipment for the armed forces [KEEP]. He was so proud of his Department's success record that when some puzzle appeared insoluble, he would consider passing it to another section [BIZA].

Mother made it a point to acquaint himself with all rumours – no matter how malicious these might be to him personally [TAKE]. As such, he developed an excellent instinct and a twitch of his nose meant something was amiss [CYPH]. When the situation arose, Mother could still enter the fray against an opponent, making good use of the weapons available [REQU]. Although he seemed to have a collection [LACE] and expert knowledge of firearms [LOVE], he himself did not carry a gun [LACE].

Mother had quite a reputation for being ill-tempered, although this was an aspect which

---

21 *Too Many Targets*, p15.

22 This would seem to dispel one theory that Mother was Defence Committee-member Sir George Collins of Park Mansions, who was known to be able-bodied in early 1967 [NURS].

23 Strangely enough, the surveillance footage of these events has been spliced into the film concerning the Great Great Britain Crime.

24 It is possible that Mother later returned to this office. 'May I Have This Trance?...', *The Avengers Annual*, 1969, p33.

he generally only displayed to those whom he believed to be incompetent in the execution of their duty [FALS, THAT] or when circumstance was against him [LOVE]. However, he did not like hearing his word questioned [LACE], having the obvious pointed out to him [KNOT], listening to people quote regulations he himself had compiled [KNOT] and was furious when told what to do by his subordinates – on one occasion bawling, 'I was making life and death decisions when the only choice in life you had to make was to eat your baby cereal or to spit it out!' [THAT]. Another source of irritation was that although he had fantastically acute hearing (rated A1+) [KEEP], he had a deep hatred of noise [NOON, PAND] and would generally attempt to find peaceful surroundings for his base of operations, which included tranquil spells underwater [KEEP]. Despite his often irritable nature, Mother was also capable of playing small jokes on colleagues [LACE] and did not even mind having fun poked at his portly appearance [STAY].

In his position, Mother was a target for assassination attempts [STAY].[25] When away on leave, Mother passed control of the Department over to Father [STAY]. Mother had various powers which included the ability to order an exhumation [BIZA] and to make arrangements for agents visiting Department S [NOON].

No doubt recalling his own experience in the field, Mother frequently dispensed advice on attitude and approach. When Tara went missing, he was very concerned that Steed should not worry about her as this would make him think below par [CATC]. Similarly, he did not want Steed to be aware of his burden when an assignment was effectively an exercise to clear Mother himself of bring a traitor [TAKE].

Mother voiced the opinion that there was no room for sentimentality in Department work [DONE], and he could be very tough on his operatives. He brutally told Lt Roy Casper to check the corpse of his former contact, Izzy Pound, for a pulse to shock Casper into the realisation that he had been duped [INTR]. 'Sorrow is a negative after-the-event emotion,' Mother declared, favouring instead positive action to remedy any unfortunate or tragic situation [INTR]. He valued dedication to duty very highly [BIZA]. It also seems that Mother had a mean streak towards his employees, only allowing Steed and Tara a single day's holiday [KEEP]. An unconfirmed report suggests that he had a Scrooge-like attitude to Christmas.[26]

That is not to say that Mother was entirely without sentiment himself. When it seemed that Tara had been killed in a car incident he was very deeply upset, taking the unprecedented step of leaving his office to personally visit Steed with the news and offer his old colleague a leave of absence [PAND].

From early 1968, Mother allocated many of the most taxing cases to Steed, to whom he had assigned promising new recruit Tara King in late 1967. As such, Steed and Tara were frequently given work which had defeated Mother's other agents, or matters associated with internal security where there was no question as to their loyalty. However, it is not clear how exclusive use of Department agents was. When Tara went missing once, Mother was not sure if she was currently engaged on a case or not [PAND].

Mother's trust in Steed was virtually unshakeable [FALS, STAY, THAT] – aside from a nagging suspicion that Steed might be buying his personal drinks on expenses [NOON]. Mother would bend the rules in situations where he trusted Steed's instinct [THAT] and

---

[25] Also *TV Comic*, Issues 935-941, 15 November – 27 December 1969; Issues 1070-1078, 17 June – 12 August 1972.

[26] 'The Spirit of Christmas', *TV Comic Annual*, 1970, p50.

confidential matters of internal investigation would be handed over to Steed [INTR]. In return, Steed never had any doubts about Mother's loyalty – commenting that he was above suspicion, despite his 'foibles' – and was one of his few confidantes when a trap was sprung to reveal a traitor whom both men suspected was Major Glasgow [TAKE]. Steed and Mother were also obviously good friends outside work, and Mother always enjoyed visiting his top agent... largely so that he could sample Steed's cellar [REQU].

It is possible that Mother had been instrumental in Tara's training and grooming her as one of his key agents. When it seemed that Tara might have 'gone over' to the other side, Mother wanted to see her name cleared above all else... although he had a nagging doubt that Tara could possibly have turned traitor [THAT]. Mother still found her young outlook on life to be a rather frivolous one at times [LOVE], and he was taken aback when Tara kissed him in relief [REQU]. And, although he trusted both Steed and Tara implicitly, Mother was rather concerned about the pair being together unchaperoned when Steed's home-made rocket shot skywards with his two key agents alone on board [BIZA].

Mother's usual mode of dress was a three-piece pinstripe suit [eg CATC, DONE] although at other times he favoured a plain black jacket and waistcoat with grey striped trousers [KEEP, BIZA]. An old-fashioned pocket watch on a chain was slung across his rounded stomach [eg KNOT, LOVE], a white handkerchief sprouted from his breast pocket [eg CATC, STAY], and a patterned bow tie [eg KNOT, STAY] was his favoured neckwear, sometimes wrapped around a high-winged shirt collar [KEEP, THAT, LACE]. On occasion, Mother's sense of the theatrical led him to adopt other garb, such as the checked cape reminiscent of the popular image of Sherlock Holmes as he was driven around the foggy neighbourhood of Gunthorpe Street during November 1968 [FOG]. Off duty, Mother remained immaculately turned out, sporting a rich green velvet smoking jacket and black cape with black bow tie [LACE]. His one concession to jewellery was a small ring on the little finger of his left hand [eg INTR, REQU]. Although confined to his chair – in which he very much enjoyed being trundled when in a creative mood [TAKE] – he was also often seen carrying a dark walking cane [eg KNOT, BIZA].

Whether it was because of his eternal quest for a peaceful base of operations, or as a security measure to avoid assassination attempts, Mother's HQ tended to move from place to place. Since he did refer to his own chambers being redecorated on one occasion, it is tempting to speculate that maybe this process took the best part of a year and was the reason for all Mother's shifts of venue [NOON]. Between spring 1968 and spring 1969, Mother could be found atop a lifeguard's chair in the middle of an outdoor swimming pool in a secluded, walled garden [DONE]; on the top deck of a red Leyland double-decker bus in London Transport livery[27] apparently running the 707 route to Piccadilly Circus, and bearing a 'Remember Mother's Day' advertisement down the side [FALS]; in a bare lilac room with ladders and large scale models of fuel tankers and a Bentley convertible [CYPH]; still in the Bentley convertible in the middle of a field [CYPH]; in a concrete roof-top area with an empty swimming pool and various step-ladders as well as décor including candles and a throne [CATC]; at Steed's apartment, 3 Stable Mews [NOON]; in an underwater office with an airlock being tested for the Navy in a river located downstream from the Old London Road

---

[27] Registration OLD 666. It is possible that Mother used this on two other unfilmed occasions. 'The Museum Mystery!', *TV Comic*, Issue 896, 15 February 1969; 'What's A Ghoul Like You Doing In A Place Like This?', *The Avengers Annual*, 1969, p58. This 'Mobile Headquarters' was incorporated by Don Macpherson into his screenplay for the 1998 movie about Steed.

and left at the salmon nets [KEEP]; in a room of black and white photographic blow-ups of Department agents where Mother was perched on a mobile, counterweighted set of scales [WISH]; in a conference room at a brewery with vats of vodka, cognac and sherry [KILL]; in a verdant indoor garden with statues, columns and garden furniture accessed via a fake telephone box standing beside a wall on a street [INTR][28]; at an underground site with a frieze of the Oval cricket ground as it was in 1880, accessed by agents dropping in through a hole in the road alongside a 'Danger – Men at Work' sign [LOVE]; in a room full of lacquered and painted screens and partitions [TAKE]; at Father's office [STAY]; in a castle tower, possibly at 'the Monastery' [THAT]; in a balloon, enjoying uninterrupted bliss [THAT]; in a spacious artistic room with statues and abstract art [LACE], and in a luxurious library room in what appeared to be a large house, complete with a snooker table [BIZA]. Other unconfirmed venues for Mother's base of operations included a mine in the Rhondda Valley in Wales[29], a roundabout in a seaside fairground one cold January[30], Lord Nelson's famous flagship *HMS Victory* in Portsmouth[31], sampling the waters at an old Roman Baths in a spa town[32] and at the rear of a pub.[33] Apparently Mother hated to be more than 20 minutes from Westminster[34] and one report suggests that he briefed Steed and Tara from his London HQ over a close-circuit television system linked to a seaside Punch and Judy show.[35]

.ccording to Steed, Mother leaving his HQ was 'like a cuckoo leaving its nest' [PAND]. On several rare occasions, Mother did venture out from HQ, visiting Tara King's apartment when she disappeared and then visiting Steed at Stable Mews to tell his colleague that she had supposedly been killed [PAND], seeing Helen Pritchard in Ward 10 at Humpington Hospital [BIZA] or paying a visit to see Steed's home-made rocket [BIZA]. On one occasion, Mother apparently even came to the scene of the investigation, meeting Steed and Tara at the offices of the *Daily Chronicle* in Fleet Street.[36]

Mother's main aide was a six foot tall, silent blonde lady in her early 20s known only as Rhonda [CATC, DONE, CYPH, FALS, NOON, WISH, KILL, INTR, LOVE, TAKE, STAY, FOG, THAT, PAND, LACE, REQU, BIZA]. It was the fact that Rhonda never seemed to speak (or was not the 'chatty type') that most appealed to Mother [NOON, LACE] and she was his most constant companion from around April 1968 onwards. On one occasion around spring 1968, Mother explained that Rhonda had lost her voice – although it is not clear if this was a temporary malady or a permanent handicap [LACE] – and he once observed that if Rhonda ever made a squeak there was skulduggery afoot... [LACE].

Rhonda was clearly a very athletic woman, easily capable of handling herself in a fight against any man [REQU] as well as being a strong swimmer [DONE, KEEP]. As a bodyguard, she was armed and always ready to defend her superior [LACE]. However, these attributes were seldom required in her supervision of Mother, and it was more usual that she would be

[28] Which appears to be Cavendish Place, London, NW8.
[29] 'Don't Go Down the Mine, Dad... (Mother's Already There)'. *The Avengers Annual*, 1969, p22-23.
[30] 'Come On In – The Water's Deadly', *The Avengers Annual*, 1969, p47.
[31] *TV Comic*, Issues 949-950, 21-28 February 1970.
[32] *TV Comic*, Issue 956, 11 April 1970.
[33] *Too Many Targets*, p22-23.
[34] *Too Many Targets*, p96.
[35] *TV Comic*, Issue 1023, 24 July 1971.
[36] *TV Comic*, Issue 1044, 18 December 1971.

making the drinks [FALS], acting as a chauffeur [CYPH, FOG, LACE] or simply pushing her boss around in his wheelchair [TAKE, THAT, PAND, LACE]. From the available surveillance footage, it is also known that she painted [LACE] and was an accomplished bowler at cricket [LOVE]. During spring 1968, Mother did also have two other female assistants alongside Rhonda during the time of Steed's house arrest [DONE] and it also seems that Gould, who posed as the mobile HQ bus conductor around the same time, was another direct aide [FALS].

Almost invariably, Mother's office would contain his six beloved telephones which housed lines M1 to M6 and were transported around by his aides in a suitcase [NOON]. These were his primary means of contact with the Ministry and agents all over the globe, and indeed he was known to use up to four of these lines at any one time [NOON]. The phones were coloured red, white, green (later replaced by grey), black, blue and yellow [eg DONE, REQU]. The red phone was most often used by Mother to contact people including a Swahili speaker [CATC], MI12 [CYPH], internal security [NOON] and also Steed via his car phone [KILL]. The black phone was line M3 [BIZA], the yellow phone (M4) also took external calls [INTR], the white phone seemed to take news from organisations such as the police [WISH] and the green (later grey) phone (M6) linked to Department S security [NOON] and took external calls from agents [INTR, BIZA]. Steed was permitted to use the blue phone by Mother on occasions [CATC] and Mother regularly seemed to be in contact with Grandma [BIZA, CATC].[37] Delighting in peace and tranquillity, Mother ensured that the telephones all had silencers on them to reduce their bells to a gentle, muffled buzz [NOON]. Agents calling into Mother needed to dial only a special two digit code to be immediately connected, and all conversations on these lines were recorded [STAY]. On occasion, Mother was also equipped with a mobile phone unit complete with speaker, a portable radio set [BIZA], and a radio with a handset and a Union Jack attached to the aerial [TAKE].

Mother was quite a connoisseur of alcohol and this would usually be present in whichever location he had placed his office [CYPH, INTR]; his favourites seemed to be Scotch [CATC, FALS, WISH], brandy [KEEP, ROTT, THAT], and a little red wine [TAKE] although he was also known to have champagne on hand [DONE]. He was very fond of port [NOON] and felt that it was very important to take soda in whisky [TAKE]. As noted, he relished having a colleague such as Steed who shared his fine taste, and spared no time in drinking his way through Steed's versatile cellar [NOON]. However, Mother seemed reluctant to let his relatives know how much he enjoyed his drink, claiming to his aunts that he only drank whisky for 'medicinal purposes' [LACE] when they generally offered him 'five fingers of old red-eye' [LACE]. He could also wield a mean ice shaker [REQU].

In terms of food, Mother was rather partial to oysters (although too many of them gave him trouble in the abdomen) [FALS] and was quite fond of cheese and crackers [KILL]. He was also known to enjoy the odd ice cream [CATC].

Another of Mother's favourite treats was a good cigar which he would lovingly draw and bite on as the mood took him [eg CATC, BIZA]. Indeed, he seemed a connoisseur of smoking, remarking that a man who smoked custom-made, hand-rolled cigarettes containing Virginia and Turkish tobacco with a preponderance of Oriental herbs must be 'evil incarnate' [INTR].

When out and about on the roads, Mother would be chauffeured in a variety of vehicles, ranging from a 1965 silver Bentley S3 Continental Drophead Limousine Coupe[38] with

---

[37] Mother also dictated reports to Grandma [TAKE].
[38] Registration 257 HYT.

coachwork by HJ Mulliner[39] [CYPH] right the way through to cruising the streets of London in a white Mini Moke[40] decorated with flags, blue and orange stripes and a radar dish for navigating in the fog [FOG].

Mother could speak at least one Oriental language [FALS], and while he abhorred hyperbole [TAKE] was himself inclined to get carried away with the sound of his own voice [FOG].[41]

Although not explicitly seen in the surveillance films, other evidence shows that Mother apparently lived in a rather grand country house with a croquet lawn[42] and was attended by a butler.[43] It is possible that this was the headquarters which doubled as a training ground in 1967 [KNOT]. Of his London accommodation, one report suggests that in December 1969 Mother lived alone in a dingy place to economise on his rent[44] but by late 1971 had moved to a large house in a London crescent (with five steps up to the door).[45]

For pastimes, Mother very much enjoyed a game of cards, which he would play with Steed [LACE] as well as sharing rubbers of bridge with Colonel Berman [NOON] – something which Colonel Mannering also claimed he and his wife indulged in [INTR]. Mother still enjoyed a game of cricket [LOVE] and was at the right level for snooker [BIZA]. Other hobbies included ventriloquism [LACE], gardening [INTR] and taking snapshots with an old-fashioned box camera [BIZA].

Two other unfilmed and undated reports from around late 1967 and late 1968 seem to indicate that Mother, although still wheelchair bound, was a far more portly, clean-shaven, balding man accompanied by a leggy blonde female aide. It is most likely that this was the Mother that Steed worked with from 1967 and that his features have been changed in the illustrations for security purposes, but his headquarters in the first instance were on board an ornate pink pleasure boat in a lake[46], while those in late 1968 were in a sewer-like chamber accessed from a gentlemen's public lavatory.[47]

It is possible that by 1970, the remit of Mother's role had expanded. He was one of the official observers at the demonstration of the Delta Five-Zero vertical take-off bomber[48] and the following year found himself on board the flight of an experimental high altitude bomber when a strange force hit the country and prevented him from landing for some time.[49] An unsubstantiated report suggests that Mother was still Steed's superior during 1976.[50] He too was depicted in the 1998 Warner Bros movie about Steed.[51]

---

[39] 'The Avengers Change Gear'. *The Avengers Annual*, 1969, p32.

[40] Registration THX 77F.

[41] In one unfilmed case, Steed feared that Mother would 'ramble on for hours'. *TV Comic*, Issue 1073, 8 July 1972.

[42] *TV Comic*, Issue 922, 16 August 1969; Issue 1070, 17 June 1972.

[43] *TV Comic*, Issue 936, 22 November 1969.

[44] 'The Spirit of Christmas', *TV Comic Annual*, 1970, p51.

[45] *TV Comic*, Issue 1050, 29 January 1972.

[46] 'Deadly Rainbow', *Steed and Mrs Peel*, Book Two, 1991, p14.

[47] 'The Golden Game', *Steed and Mrs Peel*, Book One, 1990, p6-7.

[48] *TV Comic*, Issue 970, 18 July 1970.

[49] *TV Comic*, Issues 1038-1043, 6 November – 11 December 1972.

[50] *The Eagle's Nest*, p5-7,107.

[51] In *The Avengers*, Mother was 'Head of The Ministry, Elite Intelligence', a dandruff-ridden, moustached figure in a wheelchair who liked macaroons, smoked cigarettes and reported to the Prime

FATHER

A blind lady, Father took over when Mother was away on leave. She wore dark glasses and a grey suit. Apparently an expert in cranial sculpture, she had fantastic senses of hearing and touch; all the items in her office had a textural quality or made distinctive sounds. She also knew a Chinese way of releasing tensions by stroking stones [STAY]. Father was also depicted in the 1998 movie about Steed.[52]

Minister. His office was a library beneath the Thames near Tower Bridge (actually a manipulation of the Royal Naval College near Greenwich). He wore a pinstriped suit, drank tea and had a (speaking) female aide called Brenda.

[52] The film showed Father in a negative light as a scientist who had worked on a cloning experiment and fallen in love with Sir August de Wynter. A traitor to the Ministry and a rival of Mother, Father was apparently killed when a balloon she was riding beneath collided with the signs atop the offices of Wonderland Weather.

APPENDIX A

This is the list of the files and surveillance films available from the Department. The codes used throughout this book are listed alphabetically, after which are given the rather fanciful titles accorded to the assignments (with alternate titles footnoted where available), the code number[1], the name of the Department operative(s) who documented the incident (along with aliases where appropriate[2]), the date of compilation, and then the dates on which the material was issued to both UK[3] and US[4] intelligence services.

Some very early files were issued on the day of completion. Note that some material from 1967 to 1969 was made available in the US prior to gaining full clearances in the UK, while no items prior to 1964 were made available in the US until 1991.

Those responsible for overseeing transcriptions were Patrick Brawn (December 1960 – August 1961), Reed de Rouen (August – October 1961), John Bryce (May – November 1962), Richard Bates (December 1962 – March 1964), Brian Clemens (November 1964 – March 1966), Philip Levene (October 1967 – June 1968) and Terry Nation (July 1968 – March 1969).

The dates are as given on the files and have not been corrected (eg NEVE where the file date is 14 February 1967, yet the film was clearly shot in November 1967).

---

[1] Code numbers are only available for 1960s reports. Items marked * are unconfirmed.

[2] It has been suggested that Philip Levene's codename alias in the Department was Daffodil and that he was one of Major B's Floral Network in 1967. However, since Daffodil was killed in 1967 and Levene's name still appears on documented cases into 1968 this seems unlikely. Similarly, Jeremy Burnham has been believed to be a former enemy agent who posed as the Reverend Jonathan Anesbury at Little Bazeley in 1965, but who subsequently defected.

[3] ie The Midlands office up to 1967 and the London office after the location move in 1968; other regional offices sometimes took the material on earlier dates.

[4] Generally the New York office.

3HAN: *Three Handed Game*. Compiled by Dennis Spooner and Brian Clemens,
August 1976. Issued: 19 January 1977 (UK), 12 January 1979 (US)

AIR: *The Deadly Air*. Code 3420.* Compiled by Lester Powell, 7 September 1961.*
Issued: 16 December 1961 (UK)

ANGE: *Angels of Death*. Compiled by Terence Feely and Brian Clemens, April 1977.
Issued: 15 September 1977 (UK), 29 September 1978 (US)

AUNT: *The Girl From Auntie*.[5] Code E.64.10.18. Compiled by Roger Marshall,
c.23 October 1965. Issued: 22 January 1966 (UK), 6 June 1966 (US)

BAIT: *A Change of Bait*. Code 3421. Compiled by Lewis Davidson, 20 September 1961.
Issued: 23 December 1961 (UK)

BARG: *Death at Bargain Prices*. Code E.64.10.5. Compiled by Brian Clemens,
17 February 1965. Issued: 23 October 1965 (UK), 11 April 1966 (US)

BASE: *Forward Base*. Compiled by Dennis Spooner, August 1977.
Issued: 24 November 1977 (UK), 3 November 1978 (US)

BATM: *Death of a Batman*. Code 3609. Compiled by Roger Marshall, 14 August 1963.
Issued: 26 October 1963 (UK), 1991 (US)

BEAR: *Mr Teddy Bear*. Code 3506. Compiled by Martin Woodhouse, 4 August 1962.
Issued: 29 September 1962 (UK), 1991 (US)

BEHI: *Don't Look Behind You*.[6] Code 3606. Compiled by Brian Clemens, 5 July 1963.
Issued: 14 December 1963 (UK), 1991 (US)

BIGT: *The Big Thinker*. Code 3514. Compiled by Martin Woodhouse,
13 December 1962. Issued: 15 December 1962 (UK), 1991 (US)

BIRD: *The Bird Who Knew Too Much*.[7] Code E66.6.3. Compiled by Brian Clemens,
from initial work by Alan Pattillo, October 1966. Issued: 11 February 1967 (UK),
10 March 1967 (US)

BIZA: *Bizarre*. Code E.67.9.31. Compiled by Brian Clemens, 3 March 1969.
Issued: 21 April 1969 (US), 21 May 1969 (UK)

BOOK: *Brought to Book*. Code 3366. Compiled by Brian Clemens, 12 January 1961.
Issued: 14 January 1961 (UK)

BOX: *Box of Tricks*. Code 3517. Compiled by Peter Ling and Edward Rhodes,
17 January 1963. Issued: 19 January 1963 (UK), 1991 (US)

BREA: *The £50,000 Breakfast*. Code E66.6.20. Compiled by Roger Marshall,
from initial work by Roger Marshall and Jeremy Scott, 20 July 1967.
Issued: 14 October 1967 (UK), 28 February 1968 (US)

BRIE: *Brief for Murder*. Code 3600. Compiled by Brian Clemens, c.12 April 1963.
Issued: 28 September 1963 (UK), 1991 (US)

BRIM: *A Touch of Brimstone*.[8] Code E.64.10.21. Compiled by Brian Clemens,
December 1965. Issued: 19 February 1966 (UK), n/k (US)[9]

---

[5] The title refers to the MGM espionage TV spy series *The Man from UNCLE* inspired by cases of the United Network Command for Law and Enforcement which began in 22 September 1964 on NBC and was shown on BBC1 from 24 June 1965.

[6] Referred to on early paperwork as *The Old Dark House*.

[7] The title is inspired by *The Man Who Knew Too Much* an Alfred Hitchcock thriller filmed in 1934 and 1956.

[8] Referred to on early paperwork as *The Hellfire Club*.

BROK: *The Secrets Broker*. Code 3613. Compiled by Ludovic Peters, 19 October 1963.
Issued: 1 February 1964 (UK), 1991 (US)

BULL: *Bullseye.*[10] Code 3508.* Compiled by Eric Paice, 20 September 1962.
Issued: 20 October 1962 (UK), 1991 (US)

BUTL: *What the Butler Saw*. Code E.64.10.22. Compiled by Brian Clemens, January 1966.
Issued: 26 February 1966 (UK), 28 July 1966 (US)

CAGE: *The Gilded Cage*. Code 3614. Compiled by Roger Marshall, 25 October 1963.
Issued: 9 November 1963 (UK), 1991 (US)

CARD: *House of Cards*. Compiled by Brian Clemens, May 1976.
Issued: 26 October 1976 (UK), 20 October 1978 (US)

CART: *Death a la Carte.*[11] Code 3604. Compiled by John Lucarotti, 7 June 1963.
Issued: 21 December 1963 (UK), 1991 (US)

CAST: *Castle De'ath*. Code E.64.10.15. Compiled by John Lucarotti, 20 August 1965.
Issued: 30 October 1965 (UK), 2 May 1966 (US)

CAT: *Cat Amongst the Pigeons*. Compiled by Dennis Spooner, June 1976.
Issued: 16 November 1976 (UK), 17 November 1978 (US)

CATC: *You'll Catch Your Death.*[12] Code E.67.9.9. Compiled by Jeremy Burnham,
24 May 1968. Issued: 7 October 1968 (US), 16 October 1968 (UK)

CHAR: *The Charmers*. Code 3623. Compiled by Brian Clemens, 27 February 1964.
Issued: 29 February 1964 (UK), 1991 (US)

CLAY: *Immortal Clay*. Code 3516. Compiled by James Mitchell, 10 January 1963.
Issued: 12 January 1963 (UK), 1991 (US)

CLUE: *The Curious Case of the Countless Clues.*[13] Code E66.6.27.
Compiled by Philip Levene, 19 January 1968. Issued: 3 April 1968 (US),
5 February 1969 (UK)

COMP: *Complex*. Compiled by Dennis Spooner, July 1977.
Issued: 10 November 1977 (UK), 5 January 1979 (US)

CONC: *Concerto*. Code 3601. Compiled by Terrance Dicks and Malcolm Hulke,
26 April 1963. Issued: 7 March 1964 (UK), 1991 (US)

CONS: *Conspiracy of Silence*. Code 3522.[14] Compiled by Roger Marshall, 1 March 1963.
Issued: 2 March 1963 (UK), 1991 (US)

CORR: *The Correct Way to Kill*. Code E66.6.9. Compiled by Brian Clemens,
early February 1967. Issued: 11 March 1967 (UK), 24 March 1967 (US)

COUR: *Dead on Course.*[15] Code 3501. Compiled by Eric Paice, 26 May 1962.
Issued: 29 December 1962 (UK), 1991 (US)

CYBE: *The Cybernauts*. Code E.64.10.7. Compiled by Philip Levene, March 1965.
Issued: 16 October 1965 (UK), 28 March 1966 (US)

---

[9] This surveillance film was originally subjected to restricted availability.

[10] Referred to on early paperwork as *Dead on Target*.

[11] Referred to on early paperwork as *Fricassee of Death*.

[12] Referred to on early paperwork as *Atishoo, Atishoo, All Fall Down*.

[13] Referred to on early paperwork as *The Murderous Connection*.

[14] Erroneously referred to as 3255 on some documents.

[15] Referred to on early paperwork as *The Plane Wreckers*.

CYPH: *Super Secret Cypher Snatch.*[16] Code E.67.9.10. Compiled by Tony Williamson, 14 June 1968. Issued: 30 September 1968 (US), 9 October 1968 (UK)

DANC: *Dance with Death.* Code 3376.* Compiled by Peter Ling and Sheilagh Ward, 13 April 1961. Issued: 15 April 1961 (UK)

DANE: *Death of a Great Dane.* Code 3511. Compiled by Roger Marshall and Jeremy Scott, 1 November 1962. Issued: 17 November 1962 (UK), 1991 (US)

DANG: *The Danger Makers.* Code E.64.10.20. Compiled by Roger Marshall, c.13 December 1965. Issued: 12 February 1966 (UK), 4 July 1966 (US)

DEAD: *Dead Men are Dangerous.* Compiled by Brian Clemens, March 1977. Issued: 8 September 1977 (UK), 24 November 1978 (US)

DECA: *The Decapod.* Code 3507. Compiled by Eric Paice, 13 September 1962. Issued: 13 October 1962 (UK), 1991 (US)

DIAL: *Dial a Deadly Number.* Code E.64.10.4. Compiled by Roger Marshall, c.22 January 1965. Issued: 4 December 1965 (UK), 21 July 1966 (US)

DIAM: *Diamond Cut Diamond.* Code 3371.* Compiled by Max Marquis, 18 February 1961. Issued: 18 February 1961 (UK)

DIRT: *Dirtier by the Dozen.*[17] Compiled by Brian Clemens, October 1976. Issued: 5 January 1977 (UK), 22 December 1978 (US)

DISP: *Death Dispatch.* Code 3503. Compiled by Leonard Fincham, 23 June 1962. Issued: 22 December 1962 (UK), 1991 (US)

DIST: *The Far Distant Dead.* Code 3418.* Compiled by John Lucarotti, 14 August 1961. Issued: 19 August 1961 (UK)

DONE: *All Done With Mirrors.* Code E.67.9.8. Compiled by Leigh Vance, 13 June 1968. Issued: 13 November 1968 (UK), 2 December 1968 (US)

DOOR: *Death's Door.* Code E66.6.17. Compiled by Philip Levene, 7 June 1967. Issued: 7 October 1967 (UK), 31 January 1968 (US)

DOUB: *Double Danger.*[18] Code 3415.* Compiled by Gerald Verner, 6 July 1961. Issued: 8 July 1961 (UK)

DOWN: *Hunt the Man Down.* Code 3374.* Compiled by Richard Harris, 12 March 1961. Issued: 18 March 1961 (UK)

DRAG: *Dragonsfield.*[19] Code 3422.* Compiled by Terence Feely, 27 September 1961.* Issued: 30 December 1961 (UK)

DRES: *Dressed to Kill.* Code 3617. Compiled by Brian Clemens, 6 December 1963. Issued: 28 December 1963 (UK), 1991 (US)

DUST: *Silent Dust.*[20] Code E.64.10.13. Compiled by Roger Marshall, 2 July 1965. Issued: 1 January 1966 (UK), n/k (US)

DWAR: *The White Dwarf.* Code 3520. Compiled by Malcolm Hulke, 14 February 1963. Issued: 16 February 1963 (UK), 1991 (US)

---

[16] Also referred to as *Sepet Sucpre Cncehc Sypare*. Referred to on early paperwork as *Whatever Happened to Yesterday?*

[17] The title is inspired by the 1967 war movie *The Dirty Dozen.*

[18] Referred to on early paperwork as *Confession from a Dead Man.*

[19] Referred to on early paperwork as *The Un-Dead.*

[20] Referred to on early paperwork as *Strictly for the Worms.*

EGGS: *The Golden Eggs*. Code 3518. Compiled by Martin Woodhouse, 31 January 1963.
  Issued: 2 February 1963 (UK),1991 (US)

ELEP: *The White Elephant*. Code 3616. Compiled by John Lucarotti, 22 November 1963.
  Issued: 4 January 1964 (UK), 1991 (US)

EMIL: *Emily*. Compiled by Dennis Spooner, August 1977.
  Issued: 1 December 1977 (UK), 9 February 1979 (US)

EPIC: *Epic*. Code E66.6.11. Compiled by Brian Clemens, 27 February 1967.
  Issued: 1 April 1967 (UK), 14 April 1967 (US)

ESPR: *Esprit De Corps*. Code 3624. Compiled by Eric Paice, 11 March 1964.
  Issued: 14 March 1964 (UK), 1991 (US)

FACE: *Faces*. Compiled by Brian Clemens and Dennis Spooner, July 1976.
  Issued: 14 December 1976 (UK), 13 October 1978 (US)

FALS: *False Witness*.[21] Code E.67.9.12. Compiled by Jeremy Burnham, 11 July 1968.
  Issued: 6 November 1968 (UK), 25 November 1968 (US)

FEAR: *The Fear Merchants*. Code E66.6.1. Compiled by Philip Levene,
  early September 1966. Issued: 21 January 1967 (UK), 27 January 1967 (US)

FEED: *Please Don't Feed the Animals*. Code 3375. Compiled by Dennis Spooner,
  30 March 1961. Issued: 1 April 1961 (UK)

FLEE: *The Golden Fleece*. Code 3603. Compiled by Roger Marshall and Phyllis Norman,
  24 May 1963. Issued: 7 December 1963 (UK)

FOG: *Fog*.[22] Code E.67.9.24. Compiled by Jeremy Burnham, 31 December 1968.
  Issued: 17 February 1969 (US), 12 March 1969 (UK)

FRIG: *The Frighteners*. Code 3412.* Compiled by Lt.-Col. Jasper Davies
  (alias 'Berkely Mather'), 25 May 1961. Issued: 27 May 1961 (UK)

FROG: *A Chorus of Frogs*. Code 3523. Compiled by Martin Woodhouse, 8 March 1963.
  Issued: 9 March 1963 (UK), 1991 (US)

GAME: *Game*. Code E.67.9.11. Compiled by Richard Harris, 25 June 1968.
  Issued: 23 September 1968 (US), 2 October 1968 (UK)

GETA: *Get-A-Way!* Code E66.6.29. Compiled by Philip Levene, 15 February 1968.
  Issued: 24 April 1968 (US), 14 May 1969 (UK)

GIRL: *Girl on the Trapeze*.[23] Code 3370.* Compiled by Dennis Spooner,
  11 February 1961. Issued: 11 February 1961 (UK)

GLAD: *The Gladiators*. Compiled by Brian Clemens, July 1977.
  Issued: 6 September 1978 (UK), 19 January 1979 (US)

GNAW: *Gnaws*.[24] Compiled by Dennis Spooner, October 1976.
  Issued: 21 December 1976 (UK), 29 December 1978 (US)

GRAV: *The Gravediggers*.[25] Code E.64.10.8. Compiled by Malcolm Hulke,
  c.14 April 1965. Issued: 9 October 1965 (UK), 4 August 1966 (US)

GUNS: *Have Guns – Will Haggle*.[26] Code E.67.9.4. Compiled by Donald James,
  November 1967/29 February 1968. Issued: 1 May 1968 (US), 11 December 1968 (UK)

---

[21] Referred to on early paperwork as *Lies*.

[22] Referred to on early paperwork as *The Gaslight Ghoul*.

[23] Referred to – rather strangely – on early paperwork as *The Man on the Trapeze*.

[24] The title is a play on the popular 1975 movie *Jaws* which concerned a killer shark.

[25] A variant surveillance film exists entitled *The Grave-Diggers*.

HAND: *Six Hands Across a Table*. Code 3524. Compiled by Reed R. de Rouen,
15 March 1963. Issued: 16 March 1963 (UK), 1991 (US)

HIST: *A Sense of History*. Code E.64.10.24. Compiled by Martin Woodhouse,
February 1966. Issued: 12 March 1966 (UK), 20 June 1966 (US)

HOLE: *The Thirteenth Hole*. Code E.64.10.16. Compiled by Tony Williamson,
c.15 September 1965. Issued: 29 January 1966 (UK), 18 August 1966 (US)

HOST: *Hostage*. Compiled by Brian Clemens, February 1977.
Issued: 17 November 1977 (UK), 8 December 1978 (US)

HOUR: *The Hour that Never Was.*[27] Code E.64.10.14. Compiled by Roger Marshall,
20 July 1965. Issued: 27 November 1965 (UK), 25 April 1966 (US)

HUNT: *Small Game For Big Hunters*. Code E.64.10.17. Compiled by Philip Levene,
c.1 October 1965. Issued: 15 January 1966 (UK), 4 April 1966 (US)

INTE: *Intercrime*. Code 3515. Compiled by Terrance Dicks and Malcolm Hulke,
29 December 1962. Issued: 5 January 1963 (UK), 1991 (US)

INTR: *The Interrogators*. Code E.67.9.19. Compiled by Richard Harris and
Brian Clemens, 22 October 1968. Issued: 1 January 1969 (UK), 20 January 1969 (US)

INVA: *Invasion of the Earthmen*. Code E66.6.26. Compiled by Terry Nation,
21 November 1967. Issued: 27 March 1968 (US), 15 January 1969 (UK)

JACK: *The House That Jack Built*. Code E.64.10.23. Compiled by Brian Clemens,
January 1966. Issued: 5 March 1966 (UK), 16 May 1966 (US)

JOKE: *The Joker*. Code E66.6.15. Compiled by Brian Clemens, 11 April 1967.
Issued: 29 April 1967. (UK), 12 May 1967 (US)

JUST: *You Have Just Been Murdered*. Code E66.6.21. Compiled by Philip Levene,
2 August 1967. Issued: 28 October 1967 (UK), 24 January 1968 (US)

KEEP: *They Keep Killing Steed*. Code E.67.9.15. Compiled by Brian Clemens,
29 August 1968. Issued: 11 November 1968 (US), 18 December 1968 (UK)

KIL1: *K is for Kill: Part One – The Tiger Awakes.*[28] Compiled by Brian Clemens,
June 1977. Issued: 27 October 1977 (UK), 23 March 1979 (US)[29]

KIL2: *K is for Kill: Part Two – Tiger by the Tail.*[30] Compiled by Brian Clemens, June 1977.
Issued: 3 November 1977 (UK), 23 March 1979 (US)[31]

KILL: *Killer*. Code E.67.9.17. Compiled by Tony Williamson, 27 September 1968.
Issued: 30 December 1968 (US), 22 January 1969 (UK)

KING: *Kill the King*. Code 3419.* Compiled by James Mitchell, 30 August 1961.
Issued: 2 September 1961 (UK)

KNOT: *The Forget-Me-Knot*. Code E66.6.25. Compiled by Brian Clemens,
19 January 1968. Issued: 20 March 1968 (US), 25 September 1968 (UK)

---

[26] The title comes from a western adventure, *Have Gun – Will Travel* which ran on CBS TV from 1957 to 1963 and on CBS radio from 1958 to 1960. It seems that some of the surveillance film was initially completed in advance and referred to as *Invitation to a Killing*. Code E66.6.30.

[27] The title is inspired by the 1956 war espionage film *The Man Who Never Was*. Referred to on early paperwork as *An Hour to Spare* and *Roger and Out*.

[28] Referred to on transcript as *The Long Sleep – Part One*.

[29] Forms a single item in US registry with Part Two.

[30] Referred to on transcript as *The Long Sleep – Part Two*.

[31] Forms a single item in US registry with Part One.

LACE: *Homicide and Old Lace.*[32] Code E.67.9.27. Compiled by Malcolm Hulke and
Terrance Dicks[33], November 1968/23 January 1969. Issued: 17 March 1969 (US),
26 March 1969 (UK)

LAST: *The Last of the Cybernauts...??* Compiled by Brian Clemens, May 1976.
Issued: 2 November 1976 (UK), 9 March 1979 (US)

LEGA: *Legacy of Death.*[34] Code E.67.9.14. Compiled by Terry Nation, 9 August 1968.
Issued: 4 November 1968 (US), 20 November 1968 (UK)

LION: *The Lion and the Unicorn.*[35] Compiled by John Goldsmith, May 1977.
Issued: 29 September 1977 (UK), 15 December 1978 (US)

LIVI: *The Living Dead.* Code E66.6.7. Compiled by Brian Clemens,
from initial work by Anthony Marriott, early January 1967.
Issued: 25 February 1967 (UK), 3 March 1967 (US)

LOBS: *Lobster Quadrille.* Code 3625. Compiled by Richard Bates and Brian Clemens
(collective alias 'Richard Lucas'), 20 March 1964. Issued: 21 March 1964 (UK),
1991 (US)

LOOK: *Look – (stop me if you've heard this one) But There Were These Two Fellers...*
Code E.67.9.5. Compiled by Dennis Spooner, 19 March 1968.
Issued: 8 May 1968 (US), 4 December 1968 (UK)

LOVE: *Love All.* Code E.67.9.21. Compiled by Jeremy Burnham, 18 November 1968.
Issued: 3 February 1969 (US), 19 February 1969 (UK)

MAND: *Mandrake.* Code 3620. Compiled by Roger Marshall, 16 January 1964.
Issued: 25 January 1964 (UK), 1991 (US)

MARK: *The Murder Market.* Code E.64.10.2. Compiled by Tony Williamson,
18 December 1964. Issued: 13 November 1965 (UK), 30 May 1966 (US)

MAUR: *The Mauritius Penny.* Code 3510. Compiled by Malcolm Hulke and
Terrance Dicks, 18 October 1962. Issued: 10 November 1962 (UK), 1991 (US)

MDVL: *Murdersville.* Code E66.6.23. Compiled by Brian Clemens, 25 August 1967.
Issued: 11 November 1967 (UK), 7 February 1968 (US)

MEDI: *The Medicine Men.* Code 3615. Compiled by Malcolm Hulke, 8 November 1963.
Issued: 23 November 1963 (UK), 1991 (US)

MIDA: *The Midas Touch.* Compiled by Brian Clemens, April 1976.
Issued: 9 November 1976 (UK), 1 December 1978 (US)

MIND: *The Master Minds.* Code E.64.10.3. Compiled by Robert Banks Stewart,
8 January 1965. Issued: 6 November 1965 (UK), 11 July 1966 (US)

MIRR: *Man in the Mirror.* Code 3521. Compiled by Geoffrey Orme and
Anthony Terpiloff, 22 February 1963. Issued: 23 February 1963 (UK), 1991 (US)

---

[32] This title is inspired by the 1944 thriller *Arsenic and Old Lace*. It seems that the main narrative was
a result of early surveillance originally referred to as *The Great Great Britain Crime* or *The Great
Great Britain Case* (Code E66.6.32), while the material with Mother visiting his aunts is also noted as
Tall Story on early reports.

[33] Brian Clemens apparently helped to compile some material on this mission concerning Mother and
his aunts.

[34] Referred to on early paperwork as *Falcon*.

[35] Referred to on transcript as *Lion and Unicorn*.

MISS: *Mission... Highly Improbable.*[36] Code E66.6.24. Compiled by Philip Levene,
22 September 1967. Issued: 18 November 1967 (UK), 10 January 1968 (US)

MONT: *Mission to Montreal.*[37] Code 3500. Compiled by Lester Powell, 12 May 1962.
Issued: 27 October 1962 (UK), 1991 (US)

MOON: *Crescent Moon.*[38] Code 3369.* Compiled by Geoffrey Bellman and
John Whitney, 4 February 1961. Issued: 4 February 1961 (UK)

MORN: *The Morning After.* Code E.67.9.20. Compiled by Brian Clemens,
5 November 1968. Issued: 29 January 1969 (UK), Aug/Sep 1969 (US)[39]

MORT: *One for the Mortuary.* Code 3377.* Compiled by Brian Clemens, 26 April 1961.
Issued: 29 April 1961 (UK)

MOUS: *Build a Better Mousetrap.* Code 3610. Compiled by Brian Clemens,
28 August 1963. Issued: 15 February 1964 (UK), 1991 (US)

NEED: *The Yellow Needle.*[40] Code 3413.* Compiled by Patrick Campbell, 8 June 1961.
Issued: 10 June 1961 (UK)

NEST: *The Eagle's Nest.* Compiled by Brian Clemens, April 1976.
Issued: 19 October 1976 (UK). 5 September 1978 (US)

NEVE: *Never, Never Say Die.* Code E66.6.10. Compiled by Philip Levene,
14 February 1967. Issued: 18 March 1967 (UK), 31 March 1967 (US)

NIGH: *Nightmare.* Code 3368.* Compiled by Terence Feely, 28 January 1961.
Issued: 28 January 1961 (UK)

NOON: *Noon Doomsday.* Code E.67.9.13. Compiled by Terry Nation, 30 July 1968.
Issued: 28 October 1968 (US), 27 November 1968 (UK)

NOV5: *November Five.* Code 3611. Compiled by Eric Paice, 27 September 1963.
Issued: 2 November 1963 (UK), 1991 (US)

NURS: *Something Nasty in the Nursery.* Code E66.6.14. Compiled by Philip Levene,
2 April 1967. Issued: 22 April 1967 (UK), 5 May 1967 (US)

NUTS: *The Nutshell.* Code 3602. Compiled by Philip Chambers, 10 May 1963.
Issued: 19 October 1963 (UK), 1991 (US)

OBSE: *Obsession.*[41] Compiled by Brian Clemens, May 1977.
Issued: 6 October 1977 (UK), 10 November 1978 (US)

OUTS: *The Outside-In Man.*[42] Code 3622. Compiled by Philip Chambers,
12 February 1964. Issued: 22 February 1964 (UK), 1991 (US)

OVER: *Take-Over.* Code E.67.9.30. Compiled by Terry Nation, 21 February 1969.
Issued: 14 April 1969 (US), 23 April 1969 (UK)

PAND: *Pandora.* Code E.67.9.26. Compiled by Brian Clemens, 17 January 1969.
Issued: 10 March 1969 (US), 30 April 1969 (UK)

---

[36] This title is derived from the TV espionage/crime adventure series *Mission: Impossible* which originally ran on CBS from 17 September 1966 and began on Associated-Rediffusion on 5 January 1968. Strangely referred to on early paperwork as *The Disappearance of Admiral Nelson.*

[37] Referred to on early paperwork as *Gale Force.*

[38] Referred to on early paperwork as *Kidnapping by Consent.*

[39] Originally to have been issued in US on 27 January 1969.

[40] Referred to on early paperwork as *Plague.*

[41] Referred to on early paperwork as *Missile.*

[42] Referred to on early paperwork as *The Twice-Elected.*

POSI: *The Positive Negative Man*. Code E66.6.22. Compiled by Tony Williamson,
    31 August 1967. Issued: 4 November 1967 (UK), 17 January 1968 (US)

PRIN: *Honey For the Prince*. Code E.64.10.26. Compiled by Brian Clemens,
    4 March 1966. Issued: 26 March 1966 (UK), n/k (US)

PROP: *Propellant 23*. Code 3505. Compiled by Jon Manchip White, 21 July 1962.
    Issued: 6 October 1962 (UK), 1991 (US)

QUIC: *Quick-Quick Slow Death*.[43] Code E.64.10.19. Compiled by Robert Banks Stewart,
    c.12 November 1965. Issued: 5 February 1966 (UK), n/k (US)

RADI: *The Radioactive Man*.[44] Code 3372.* Compiled by Fred Edge, 25 February 1961.
    Issued: 25 February 1961 (UK)

RARE: *Medium Rare*. Compiled by Dennis Spooner, April 1977.
    Issued: 22 September 1977 (UK), 26 January 1979 (US)

RAT: *To Catch a Rat*. Compiled by Terence Feely, June 1976.
    Issued: 30 November 1976 (UK), 16 February 1979 (US)

REMO: *The Removal Men*.[45] Code 3509. Compiled by Roger Marshall and Jeremy Scott,
    4 October 1962. Issued: 3 November 1962 (UK), 1991 (US)

REQU: *Requiem*. Code E.67.9.29. Compiled by Brian Clemens, 13 February 1969.
    Issued: 31 March 1969 (US), 16 April 1969 (UK)

RETU: *Return of the Cybernauts*. Code E66.6.18. Compiled by Philip Levene,
    15 June 1967. Issued: 30 September 1967 (UK), 21 February 1968 (US)

ROCK: *Death on the Rocks*.[46] Code 3512. Compiled by Eric Paice, 15 November 1962.
    Issued: 1 December 1962 (UK), 1991 (US)

ROME: *The Grandeur That Was Rome*.[47] Code 3607. Compiled by Rex Edwards,
    19 July 1963. Issued: 30 November 1963 (UK), 1991 (US)

ROOM: *Room Without a View*. Code E.64.10.9. Compiled by Roger Marshall,
    29 April 1965. Issued: 8 January 1966 (UK), 27 June 1966 (US)

ROOT: *Square Root of Evil*. Code 3367. Compiled by Richard Harris, 21 January 1961.
    Issued: 21 January 1961 (UK)

ROSE: *Ashes of Roses*. Code 3373.* Compiled by Peter Ling and Sheilagh Ward,
    4 March 1961. Issued: 4 March 1961 (UK)

ROTT: *The Rotters*. Code E.67.9.18. Compiled by Dave Freeman, 8 October 1968.
    Issued: 16 December 1968 (US), 8 January 1969 (UK)

SCHO: *School for Traitors*. Code 3519. Compiled by James Mitchell, 9 February 1963.
    Issued: 9 February 1963 (UK), 1991 (US)

SECO: *Second Sight*. Code 3612. Compiled by Martin Woodhouse, 11 October 1963.
    Issued: 16 November 1963 (UK), 1991 (US)

SEET: *The See-Through Man*. Code E66.6.5. Compiled by Philip Levene,
    late November 1966. Issued: 3 February 1967 (US), 4 February 1967 (UK)

---

[43] Referred to on early paperwork as *The Quick-Quick-Slow Death*.

[44] Curiously enough, Fred Edge documented a similar incident for the Canadian Intelligence Service in 1959.

[45] Referred to on early paperwork as *The Most Expensive Commodity*.

[46] Referred to on early paperwork as *Pillar of Salt*.

[47] Referred to on early paperwork as *The Glory That Was Rome*.

SELL: *The Sell-Out.*[48] Code 3502. Compiled by Anthony Terpiloff and Brandon Brady,
9 June 1962. Issued: 24 November 1962 (UK), 1991 (US)

SHAD: *Man with Two Shadows.* Code 3605. Compiled by James Mitchell, 21 June 1963.
Issued: 12 October 1963 (UK), 1991 (US)

SLEE: *Sleeper.* Compiled by Brian Clemens, September 1976.
Issued: 12 January 1977 (UK), 6 October 1978 (US)

SLIP: *Death on the Slipway.* Code 3414.* Compiled by James Mitchell, 22 June 1961.
Issued: 24 June 1961 (UK)

SNOW: *Hot Snow.* Code 3365. Compiled by Ray Rigby, from initial work by
Patrick Brawn, 30 December 1960. Issued: 7 January 1961 (UK)

SPLI: *Split!* Code E66.6.28. Compiled by Brian Clemens[49], 1 February 1968.
Issued: 10 April 1968 (US), 23 October 1969 (UK)

SPRI: *The Springers.* Code 3411.* Compiled by John Whitney and Geoffrey Bellman,
11 May 1961. Issued: 13 May 1961 (UK)

STAT: *A Funny Thing Happened on the Way to the Station.* Code E66.6.13.
Compiled by Brian Clemens from initial work by Roger Marshall (collective alias:
'Brian Sheriff'), 22 March 1967. Issued: 15 April 1967 (UK), 28 April 1967 (US)

STAY: *Stay Tuned.* Code E.67.9.23. Compiled by Tony Williamson, 13 December 1968.
Issued: 24 February 1969 (US), 26 February 1969 (UK)

SUCC: *How to Succeed... at Murder.*[50] Code E.64.10.25. Compiled by Brian Clemens,
February 1966. Issued: 19 March 1966 (UK), 13 June 1966 (US)

SUP7: *The Superlative Seven.* Code E66.6.12. Compiled by Brian Clemens,
13 March 1967. Issued: 8 April 1967 (UK), 21 April 1967 (US)

SURF: *A Surfeit of H_2O.* Code E.64.10.10. Compiled by Colin Finbow, c.11 May 1965.
Issued: 20 November 1965 (UK), n/k (US)

SURR: *Man-Eater of Surrey Green.*[51] Code E.64.10.12. Compiled by Philip Levene,
c.11 June 1965. Issued: 11 December 1965 (UK), 25 August 1966 (US)

TALE: *The Tale of the Big Why.* Compiled by Brian Clemens[52], August 1976.
Issued: 7 December 1976 (UK), 2 February 1979 (US)

TAKE: *Take Me To Your Leader.* Code E.67.9.22. Compiled by Terry Nation,
29 November 1968. Issued: 10 February 1969 (US), 5 March 1969 (UK)

TARG: *Target!* Compiled by Dennis Spooner, July 1976.
Issued: 23 November 1976 (UK), 12 September 1978 (US)

THAT: *Who Was That Man I Saw You With?* Code E.67.9.25.
Compiled by Jeremy Burnham, 10 January 1969. Issued: 3 March 1969 (US),
19 March 1969 (UK)

THIN: *Thingumajig.*[53] Code E.67.9.28. Compiled by Terry Nation, 21 January 1969.
Issued: 24 March 1969 (US), 2 April 1969 (UK)

---

[48] Referred to on early paperwork as *Traitor.*

[49] With assistance possibly from Dennis Spooner.

[50] Referred to on early paperwork as *How To Succeed at Murder... Without Really Trying.*

[51] Referred to on early paperwork – probably incorrectly – as *Man Eater of Ferry Green.*

[52] The transcript was prepared by Philip Broadley and Brian Clemens.

[53] Referred to on early paperwork as *It.*

TIGE: *The Hidden Tiger*. Code E66.6.8. Compiled by Philip Levene, mid-January 1967.
Issued: 4 March 1967 (UK), 17 March 1967 (US)

TIME: *Escape in Time*. Code E66.6.2. Compiled by Philip Levene, early October 1966.
Issued: 28 January 1967 (UK), 10 February 1967 (US)

TOWN: *The Town of No Return*.[54] Code E.64.10.1. Compiled by Brian Clemens,
13 November 1964/ c.30 July 1965. Issued: 2 October 1965 (UK),
1 September 1966 (US)

TOY: *Toy Trap*. Code 3416.* Compiled by Bill Strutton, 20 July 1961.
Issued: 22 July 1961 (UK)

TRAP: *Trap*. Compiled by Brian Clemens, March 1977. Issued: 13 October 1977 (UK),
2 March 1979 (US)

TREA: *Dead Man's Treasure*. Code E66.6.19. Compiled by Michael Winder, 5 July 1967.
Issued: 21 October 1967 (UK), 13 March 1968 (US)

TROJ: *Trojan Horse*. Code 3621. Compiled by Malcolm Hulke, 30 January 1964.
Issued: 8 February 1964 (UK), 1991 (US)

TUNN: *The Tunnel of Fear*. Code 3417.* Compiled by John Kruse, 3 August 1961.
Issued: 5 August 1961 (UK)

TWOS: *Two's a Crowd*. Code E.64.10.11. Compiled by Philip Levene, c.28 May 1965.
Issued: 18 December 1965 (UK), 9 May 1966 (US)

UNDE: *The Undertakers*. Code 3608. Compiled by Malcolm Hulke, 2 August 1963.
Issued: 5 October 1963 (UK), 1991 (US)

VENU: *From Venus With Love*.[55] Code E66.6.4. Compiled by Philip Levene,
early November 1966. Issued: 14 January 1967 (UK), 20 January 1967 (US)

WARL: *Warlock*.[56] Code 3504. Compiled by Doreen Montgomery, 7 July 1962/Dec 1962.
Issued: 26 January 1963 (UK), 1991 (US)

WHAL: *Killer Whale*. Code 3525. Compiled by John Lucarotti, 22 March 1963.
Issued: 23 March 1963 (UK), 1991 (US)

WHO?: *Who's Who???* Code E66.6.16. Compiled by Philip Levene, 18 April 1967.
Issued: 6 May 1967 (UK), 19 May 1967 (US)

WILD: *My Wildest Dream*. Code E.67.9.6. Compiled by Philip Levene, 1 April 1968.
Issued: 6 January 1969 (US), 7 April 1969 (UK)

WING: *The Winged Avenger*. Code E66.6.6. Compiled by Richard Harris,
early December 1966. Issued: 17 February 1967 (US), 18 February 1967 (UK)

WINT: *Dead of Winter*.[57] Code 3423.* Compiled by Eric Paice, 18 October 1961.*
Issued: 9 December 1961 (UK)

WISH: *Wish You Were Here*.[58] Code E.67.9.16. Compiled by Tony Williamson,
12 September 1968. Issued: 18 November 1968 (US), 12 February 1969 (UK)

---

[54] The title is possibly inspired by the 1954 movie *Point of No Return*.

[55] The title is inspired by the 1957 biography *From Russia, With Love*, one of Ian Fleming's accounts of the espionage career of James Bond, briefly Steed's bully at Eton. Referred to on early paperwork as *The Light Fantastic*.

[56] Referred to on early paperwork as *Zodiac*.

[57] Referred to on early paperwork as *The Case of the Happy Camper*.

[58] Referred to on early paperwork as *The Prisoner*.

WOND: *The Little Wonders*. Code 3619. Compiled by Eric Paice, 3 January 1964.
Issued: 11 January 1964 (UK), 1991 (US)

WRIN: *The Wringer.* Code 3618. Compiled by Martin Woodhouse, 20 December 1963.
Issued: 18 January 1964 (UK), 1991 (US)

XMAS: *Too Many Christmas Trees*. Code E.64.10.6. Compiled by Tony Williamson,
c.1 March 1965. Issued: 25 December 1965 (UK), 11 August 1966 (US)

XR40: *Whoever Shot Poor George Oblique Stroke XR40?* Code E.67.9.7.
Compiled by Tony Williamson, 17 April 1968. Issued: 30 October 1968 (UK),
9 December 1968 (US)

ZEBR: *Traitor in Zebra*. Code 3513. Compiled by John Gilbert, 29 November 1962.
Issued: 8 December 1962 (UK), 1991 (US)

APPENDIX B

In addition to the surveillance films, associated transcripts and summary reports, the Department archives hold a number of other 'mission reports' catalogued in a different manner, disguised as books and children's comics for discreet transportation. These incidents, often involving recurrent themes and locations, lack a feeling of authenticity with regards the behaviour of the key protagonists, and indeed conflict with facts established elsewhere; for example, Steed and his colleagues are frequently depicted as working closely with – or even directly for – the police. As such, these items have largely been kept separate from the main text.

One of the most dubious aspects of these reports is that – given the time span covered in total – in some years such as 1966 and 1968 it seems that Steed, Emma and Tara would simply not have had enough days to cram in all these incidents around the surveillance films which we knew definitely took place. Also, considering some of these incidents concern legendary monsters, ghosts, giant beanstalks and aliens, one suspects that many of these 'missions' had no basis in reality whatsoever, but were designed as mis-information. They are included in this appendix for completeness and curiosity value alone.

The earliest such incident seems to come from 1961 when Steed was working with Dr David Keel. How Ming, a dying Chinese undercover colleague of Steed's, arrived on Keel's doorstep having inadvertently being given a drug consignment by a gang.[1]

Looking into the convenient death of George Gracechurch Minton in a motor accident near Naples around 1963, Steed involved Cathy Gale, a friend of Minton's daughter. Flying to Naples, Cathy and Steed encountered dubious German and Italian characters, and in London exposed an international blackmail gang.[2] A dying colleague of Steed's called Tony attempted to pass on to him samples of a killer germ which had struck the village of Warbury. Reporting to the Chief, Cathy and Steed were detailed to stop the germ warfare threat made by a group called Terror Ltd who wanted £6,000,000 in gold to deter them from infecting Britain's reservoirs.[3] Steed and Cathy protected Queen Olivia of Richenstein when the royal travelled to Scotland and was kidnapped during a train crash

---

[1] 'The Drug Peddler'. *TV Crimebusters*, 1962.

[2] *The Avengers*. Compiled by Douglas Enefer. Issued: 1963 (UK).

[3] 'Epidemic of Terror'. *Look Westward/The Viewer*, 14 September – 19 October 1963; *TV Post*, 5 December 1963 – 9 January 1964; *Saturday Manchester Evening News and Chronicle*, 14 June – 1 August 1964.

by Count Sergovan.[4] In the Middle East, Steed and 'Miss Catherine G_.' worked undercover as air stewards to guard Sheikh Abal against his military executive Colonel Hassam, and then saved the Sheikh's life in North Africa.[5] Steed investigated freak lightning strikes on major buildings claiming to be from the Ancient Monument Preservation Society. These were found to be connected to an electronic super computer constructed at a Darwell research centre which planned to control humanity by mental conditioning during a television broadcast. Steed now claimed to be an observer from SMUT[6] to halt the transmission.[7]

Around 1965, Steed set out for a drive in the country with his new colleague Emma Peel, only to discover a stolen briefcase thrown into the back of his Bentley. This contained secret plans of a nuclear reactor. When Emma was kidnapped by foreign spy, Yanto Colmo, Steed rescued her and the plans by infiltrating a fun fair as a clown and a dummy dragon.[8] When government scientist James Harmon vanished in a flash of light, Steed and Emma fought two laser-wielding foreign spies, Franz and Helmut.[9] Strange glowing objects appearing over London were investigated on orders from the Colonel. These 'fireballs' were created by Count Voro, the 'Firemaster of the World', who planned to ignite London into an inferno; Emma and Steed pretended to be two of his robot servants.[10] A colleague code-named 'British Agent Alpha 1' apparently vanished from a small plane in mid-air as he returned from Europe. Steed and Emma – again reporting to the Colonel – followed his trail and rescued him from the clutches of a scientist called Grenfell.[11]

In January (presumably 1966)[12], the death of former Home Secretary Sir Arthur Smeck-Hudson involved Steed in another investigation for a superior known as 'His Nibs'[13] who suspected Hudson of passing information via a defecting Russian doctor, Tamara Petrova. Steed stood for parliament at the Brawhill by-election while Emma enrolled at L'Ecole des Croupiers in Monte Carlo to expose a Mafia scheme to undermine British confidence and security.[14] *En route* to a country house party, Steed and Emma found themselves held up

---

[4] 'Quest for a Queen'. Compiled by John Malcolm. *Look Westward/The Viewer*, 2 November – 7 December 1963; 'A Queen in Pawn', *TV Post*, 16 January – 20 February 1964; 'Quest for a Queen'. *Saturday Manchester Evening News and Chronicle*, 8 August – 26 September 1964.

[5] 'Operation Harem'. *Look Westward/The Viewer*, 21 December 1963 – 22 February 1964; *Saturday Manchester Evening News and Chronicle*, 1 February – 28 March 1964; *TV Post*, 27 February – 23 April, 1964.

[6] Society for Multilateral Use of TV.

[7] 'The Runaway Brain'. *Look Westward/The Viewer*, 7 March – 9 May 1964; *Saturday Manchester Evening News and Chronicle*, 4 April – 7 June 1964.

[8] Artist's impressions by Pat Williams. *TV Comic*, Issues 720-725, 2 October – 6 November 1965.

[9] Artist's impressions by Pat Williams. *TV Comic*, Issues 726-730, 13 November – 11 December 1965.

[10] Artist's impressions by Pat Williams. *TV Comic*, Issues 731-735, 18 December 1965 – 15 January 1966.

[11] Artist's impressions by Pat Williams. *TV Comic*, Issues 736-740, 22 January – 19 February 1966.

[12] Hussey noted – incorrectly – that Steed was living at Westminster Mews; by this time he was living at Queen Anne's Court. *The Floating Game*, p44.

[13] 'His Nibs' is an obscure figure whom Patrick Macnee also referred to in some of his works (eg *...deadline, Dead Duck*). It is possible that he was in fact many people that Steed reported to (eg the Colonel, Mother), all combined into an unidentifiable amalgam. Similarly, a minion of 'His Nibs' was Benson, who frequently drove a London taxi cab and would collect Steed for meetings with his boss. 'His Nibs' also seemed to have cases referred to him by Fletcher of MI5.

by a trio of highwaymen, who seemed to believe that the pair were carrying a roll of secret microfilm sought by enemy agents Pedro and Alonso.[15] On the south coast, Steed and Emma then tested a new listening device on board a motor yacht at the orders of the Colonel, protecting it from international spies, Kroger and Hendrik.[16] The Colonel next gave Steed and Emma the task of delivering two pet cheetahs to their owner, the visiting Sheik Abdul of Samara, whose life was threatened by his half-brother Yussuf.[17] Spending Hogmanay in Scotland with Sir Jocelyn, Steed and Emma encountered a false alarm over the theft of top secret atomic documents.[18]

In early April 1966[19], 'His Nibs' asked Steed and Emma to investigate the appearance of dead people walking around London. The duo were aided by another security operative, Oxford law graduate George Washington from Jamaica, and uncovered a plan to attack the Pentagon with a hydrogen bomb by 'Message' Morrison, a vicar whom Steed had known in the war.[20] Driving up to Blackpool in his Bentley as part of a rally over the May 1966 bank holiday, Steed encountered young pop singer Gloria Munday who was subsequently killed in a teenage riot. Investigating with approval from 'His Nibs', Steed escaped from HM Prison, Kirkham and – with the help of Emma and George – exposed a plan to control the youth of Britain via radio broadcasts.[21]

A country picnic for Steed and Emma was disrupted by the appearance of two battling Roman soldiers – one of whom was a spy called Helmut, one of a number of enemy agents working on a film. Steed became a Roman gladiator extra, and was saved from the enemy by Emma in her guise as Britannia.[22] Even on holiday, Steed and Emma found a gang led by Stroheim, one of their sworn enemies, on board their cruise liner, the *Orontes*.[23] The Colonel then assigned Steed and Emma to protect Professor Johnson and his mirage maker from foreign spies Hans and Franz.[24]

A series of British scientists were kidnapped via a vanishing cabinet used in the stage act of Wander the Wizard. Steed posed as Jacko, Wander's assistant, after his friend Professor Brand went missing, while Emma posed as electronics scientist Professor Peel to get kidnapped herself.[25] Steed and Emma also outwitted an attempt by Russian master spy

---

[14] *The Floating Game*. Compiled by Anthony Hussey (alias 'John Garforth'). Issued: January 1967 (UK), April 1967 (US).

[15] Artist's impressions by Pat Williams. *TV Comic*, Issues 741-745, 26 February – 26 March 1966.

[16] Artist's impressions by Pat Williams. *TV Comic*, Issues 746-750, 2 April – 30 April 1966.

[17] Artist's impressions by Pat Williams. *TV Comic*, Issues 751-755, 7 May – 4 June 1966.

[18] Artist's impressions by Pat Williams. *TV Comic Annual*, September 1966.

[19] Hussey still noted – incorrectly – that Steed was living at Westminster Mews. *The Laugh was on Lazarus*, p32.

[20] *The Laugh Was On Lazarus*. Compiled by Anthony Hussey (alias 'John Garforth'). Issued: January 1967 (UK), May 1967 (US).

[21] *The Passing of Gloria Munday*. Compiled by Anthony Hussey (alias 'John Garforth'). Issued: March 1967 (UK), July 1967 (US).

[22] Artist's impressions by Pat Williams. *TV Comic*, Issues 756-760, 11 June – 9 July 1966; 'The Roman Invasion'. *John Steed – Emma Peel*, Issue 1, November 1968.

[23] Artist's impressions by Pat Williams. *TV Comic Holiday Special*, June 1966.

[24] Artist's impressions by Pat Williams. *TV Comic*, Issues 761-766, 16 July – 20 August 1966; 'The Mirage Maker'. *John Steed – Emma Peel*, Issue 1, November 1968.

[25] Artist's impressions by Pat Williams. *TV Comic*, Issues 767-771, 27 August – 24 September 1966.

Lev Petrovoski to infiltrate the General Staff.[26] When Steed visited his friend Sir William at the West Country market town of Dunminster, he discovered that the hamlet was prey to a band of ruffians who called themselves the Mohocks whom he defeated with Emma's help.[27] A man called Ralph Haig was killed by karate blows linked to a mysterious 'K' club which Steed infiltrated as a kung-fu expert and again put out of action with Emma's help.[28] Steed and Emma investigated the deaths of a number of men who had been acquitted of crimes but then killed and had a card with the word 'Spies' placed on their corpses. Posing as a journalist for *The Globe*, Steed exposed former police and magistrates acting as vigilantes called SPIES – The Society for Punishment of Immune Enemies of Society.[29] Assigned by his superior to investigate the theft of a Zambian order from the IPAC offices, Steed visited the plant as an efficiency expert (occasionally under the alias 'Drake') with Emma as his secretary and set a trap for employee Bill Kerry.[30]

Steed and Emma helped Special Branch track a master of disguise in London to Madame Tussaud's.[31] They then traveled to Scotland to act as bodyguards for the young Prince Abdul Bey of Arania and saved him from kidnap by 'the Brotherhood'.[32] When a figure called the Miser claimed that he would rob all the banks in London at midnight, Steed and Emma cornered the puny villain at a wax museum.[33] The disappearance of General Frobisher, Admiral Caine and the Foreign Minister was linked by Emma to their wives ordering a new golden wire and silk dress from top fashion designer Madame Zingara. Posing as the wife of Air Vice-Marshal Clinton, Emma found the dresses exerted a hypnotic influence and arranged for her 'husband' – Steed – to be kidnapped.[34]

Enjoying a weekend fishing in the Norfolk Broads, Steed and Emma encountered a group of Vikings led by Venka who stole an atom bomb to demand autonomous rule for their village, and who were infiltrated by Steed disguised as a blonde Norseman.[35] Attempting to solve a string of jewel robberies, Steed and Emma tangled with Black Heart and her Seven Dwarves who operated from a toy shop base and planned to steal some French royal jewels from Beauville Castle.[36]

Steed was distracted from writing his war memoirs (suggested by 'His Nibs') by the death of an army motorcycle courier, which in turn led to an investigation into a Nazi movement of

---

[26] 'A Funny Thing Happened On The Way To The Palace', *The New Avengers Annual*, September 1977.

[27] 'The Mohocks'. Artist's impressions by Mick Anglo. *The Avengers*, 1966.

[28] 'The K Stands for Killers'. Artist's impressions by Mick Anglo. *The Avengers*, 1966.

[29] 'No Jury... No Justice!'. Artist's impressions by Mick Anglo. *The Avengers*, 1966.

[30] 'Deadly Efficient'. Artist's impressions by Mick Anglo. *The Avengers*, 1966.

[31] Artist's impressions by Pat Williams. *TV Comic Annual*, September 1966.

[32] 'Baby, it's cold outside'. Artist's impressions by Emilio Frejo with Juan Gonzalez Alacrejo, *Diana*. Issues 199-201, 10 – 24 December 1966.

[33] 'The Miser Strikes at Midnight'. Artist's impressions by Emilio Frejo with Juan Gonzalez Alacrejo, *Diana*. Issues 202-204, 31 December 1966 – 14 January 1967.

[34] 'The Mystery of the Golden Dress'. Artist's impressions by Emilio Frejo with Juan Gonzalez Alacrejo, *Diana*. Issues 205-208, 21 January – 11 February 1967.

[35] 'Vengeance of the Vikings!'. Artist's impressions by Emilio Frejo with Juan Gonzalez Alacrejo. *Diana*. Issues 209-211, 18 February – 4 March 1967.

[36] Artist's impressions by Emilio Frejo with Juan Gonzalez Alacrejo, *Diana*. Issues 212-215, 10 – 31 March 1967.

'Werewolves' led by Ludwig Harris, a Swindon farmer who claimed to be Adolf Hitler. After investigations in Bavaria as an English journalist, Steed rejoined Emma and saw that Harris's plans were foiled.[37] Steed and Emma then found that Steed's friend, TV reporter Tom Partridge, had been attacked by his own dogs. This was part of a revenge hatched by Professor Klein whose 'Antagoniser' light beam could make animals violent.[38] Steed and Emma were also witnesses to the attempted kidnap of Princess Helga of Varania, and the trail led to an international assassin called the Mad Hatter who sold Steed a bowler containing a snake.[39]

When attending a fancy dress ball at Lord Tweezle's, Steed and Emma were attacked by Chang Tu and his group of assassins known as the Secret Six.[40] When Steed took Emma to the races, he was followed and subsequently captured by a number of men interested in his winnings – only to be rescued by Emma and the police.[41] Attending a conference, Emma and Steed realised that Mr Semyonov, the Russian trade advisor, had been replaced by a double and Steed's cricketing skills defeated the impostor.[42]

Investigating strange markings made in the countryside, Steed and Emma uncovered a plot at a local airfield hatched by an agent of the Bazavia Air Force posing as the game-keeper of Sir John Hanley.[43] Steed took Emma up the M4 to the Chiltern village Western Montgomery for a meeting of the Thoroughbreds of the Past vintage and veteran cars, so that she could drive a Frazer-Nash in a hill-climb, standing in for famous driver Prince Chundraganath Chalongse to decoy assassins.[44] Steed and Emma travelled on the *Arcadia*, a pleasure cruiser transporting £5,000,000 in gold bullion and two dozen missiles along the Suez Canal, and defeated hijackers Franklyn Chisholm and 'Professor' Al Hartley.[45] Steed's fishing holiday in a remote part of Scotland bizarrely made the newspapers, and he found local villagers threatened by a group of men who had concealed a nuclear missile base inside an old castle.[46] Steed and Emma parachuted into enemy European territory to rescue captured agent Hamish Donnell from secret police interrogation – and identified the 'Hamish' they rescued as Colonel Hrade of Intelligence.[47] While spending a weekend in Cornwall, Steed found a hidden passage used by smugglers and was nearly thrown into the sea to drown.[48] Handling security at a multi-national peace conference at the New Empire Hotel for 'His Nibs', 'Major' Steed called in Emma to help thwart the strange machinations

---

[37] *Heil Harris!*. Compiled by Anthony Hussey (alias 'John Garforth'). Issued: March 1967 (UK), September 1967 (US).

[38] Artist's impressions by Emilio Frejo with Juan Gonzalez Alacrejo, *Diana*. Issues 216-218, 7 – 21 April 1967.

[39] 'The Mad Hatter's Party!'. Artist's impressions by Emilio Frejo with Juan Gonzalez Alacrejo. *Diana*. Issues 219-220, 28 April – 5 May 1967.

[40] 'The Fatal Fancy Dress Ball'. Artist's impressions by Emilio Frejo with Juan Gonzalez Alacrejo. *Diana*. Issues 221-224, 12 May – 2 June 1967.

[41] 'Odds against Steed'. Artist's impressions by John Stokes. *The Avengers Annual*, September 1967.

[42] 'Double Trouble'. Compiled by Peter Leslie. *The Avengers Annual*, September 1967.

[43] 'Flying Eagles'. Artist's impressions by John Stokes. *The Avengers Annual*, September 1967.

[44] 'A Race Against Time!'. Compiled by Peter Leslie. *The Avengers Annual*, September 1967.

[45] 'Sunset in the East'. Compiled by Peter Leslie. *The Avengers Annual*, September 1967.

[46] 'Steed's 'Holiday''. Artist's impressions by John Stokes. *The Avengers Annual*, September 1967.

[47] 'A Question of Intelligence'. Compiled by Peter Leslie. *The Avengers Annual*, September 1967.

[48] 'A Brush With Disaster'. Artist's impressions by John Stokes. *The Avengers Annual*, September 1967.

of 'The Afrit' – one Professor Hamid, whose plan to trigger World War III using the Project Fastslap bombers was averted.[49]

Immediately after rejoining her husband Peter around November 1967[50], Emma was whisked away for a second honeymoon at Pringle-on-Sea – where Mother asked Steed to investigate the disappearance of some motorway surveyors. Emma exposed a scheme hatched by two Americans to alienate the world towards the Incan Leopard People from South America, and the Peels returned to Bolivia to help the tribe.[51]

Now working with Tara King, 'His Nibs' assigned 'Major' Steed and the young agent to the security detail of the *African Queen*, the world's first luxury submarine liner, on its maiden voyage from Southampton to New York. Posing as a ballroom dancing instructor and a physiotherapist, the pair prevented Captain Wimperton from turning his own vessel to piracy.[52] Around June 1968[53], Tara went missing while investigating a security leak of computer codes controlling nuclear missiles. Assigned by Mother, Steed called upon Emma to help locate his new colleague, held captive by Steed's old Eton school chum, Hilary 'Four Eyes' Fox, whose macabre games were an attempt to acquire the codes to the Hangman Defence System.[54] Called to Scotland Yard by 'His Nibs' (who was now referred to as a General), 'Major' Steed (who was about to have a two week holiday in Cannes) and Tara (who was about to go skiing in Switzerland) were asked to trace the source of radioactive gold which was coming into the country. The gold was shielding consignments of Uranium-235 destined for a nuclear bomb, and collected by a man disguised as a Newfoundland dog.[55] Invited to the tailors' establishment of Morrison and Wagpenny, Steed was overpowered and his clearance papers given to his double – 'Number One' – whose plans to take Steed's place at the secret trials of a new missile tank were foiled.[56] At a fairground, Tara and Steed intercepted information being passed on by microdots in a shooting gallery between the fair's owner, Signor Monticelli and spy Yano Yakimoto.[57] On holiday in West Scotland, Steed and Tara were looking for Druid Caves and uncovered a plan by the Laird of MacIrmahill, who believed he was heir to the throne of Scotland, to destroy a nearby dam with an old Wellington Bomber.[58] Mother assigned Steed to find out

---

[49] *The Afrit Affair*. Compiled by [John] Keith Laumer. Issued: April 1968 (US). Steed was apparently 45 at the time, thus making the year 1967. p9.

[50] Oddly enough, Steed refers to a total eclipse not happening until after 'the Seventh'; there were total eclipses on 2 November 1967 in the South Atlantic, 22 September 1968 in Russia and China and 7 March 1970 in Mexico – none of which seem to coincide with Emma's reunion with Peter. 'Deadly Rainbow'. p43.

[51] 'Deadly Rainbow'. Compiled by Anne Caulfield, Artist's impressions by Ian Gibson. *Steed and Mrs Peel*, Books Two and Three, 1991-92.

[52] *The Drowned Queen*. Compiled by [John] Keith Laumer. Issued: June 1968 (US).

[53] Emma commented that she had just spent six months with the Leopard People. 'The Golden Game'. p14.

[54] 'The Golden Game'. Compiled by Grant Morrison, Artist's impressions by Ian Gibson. *Steed and Mrs Peel*, Books One to Three, 1991-92.

[55] *The Gold Bomb*. Compiled by [John] Keith Laumer. Issued: September 1968 (US).

[56] 'Clothes Make the Man...'. Artist's impressions by John Stokes. *The Avengers Annual*, September 1968.

[57] 'All the Fun of the Fair Mr Steed...?'. *The Avengers Annual*, September 1968.

[58] 'Are You a Clansman, Mr Steed...?'. Artist's impressions by John Stokes. *The Avengers Annual*, September 1968.

how secrets were being leaked via the Sunnylands Health Clinic. Enrolling as a patient, Steed found Doctor Koestl was using a machine to read brain patterns during hypnotism.[59]

Collecting a case supposedly containing valuable papers in Hong Kong to take back to 'His Nibs' in London, Steed was amazed when the contents mysteriously changed into millions of dollars in banknotes. Back in London, Steed was menaced by metal objects under the control of stage magician CT Fung.[60] Fletcher of MI5 referred Mrs Violet Pingree to 'Major' Steed when she was concerned about the behaviour of her husband, Wellesley. Posing as her Uncle Alec Cameron and niece Maud Cameron, Steed and Tara discovered that Wellesley was being tricked into purchasing plots of land on the moon by a man called Cregmore Tebbet.[61]

Off the Cornish coast, Steed and Tara investigated a gold smuggling operation for Mother under the cover of entering a cross Channel race; the gold smuggled by Captain Whittaker-Walker had been made into a yacht's mast.[62] Driving back to London from the South Coast, a puncture led Tara to see a huge Venus fly trap, created by Botanist Alpha and Colonel Smythe via hormonic conversion.[63] Steed and Tara were rushed to a Ministry of Defence Research Centre at Glen Leven where Bobby, the son of one Professor Braithwaite, had been kidnapped and held at Castle Tannockburn by Said Ghabul, an international spy.[64] When Steed and Tara found a 'Guy' in a pram outside Steed's flat on 30 October (presumably 1968), it exploded 15 minutes later. Steed then identified his attacker 'Fawkes' as being the Commando Colonel.[65] When Brigadier Trudshaw, Admiral Hornbeam and Air Marshal Golightly, three high-ranking Ministry of Defence officers, went missing just before Christmas, Steed and Tara found that they had been shrunk by a device created by the elderly Mr Spooner, the manager of the toy department at Durrbridge's department store.[66]

When the naturalist Sir Edmund Whittington's prehistoric African seeds grew into lethal, fast-growing ivy Steed and Tara were called in by Gilbert Carter of the Ministry of Agriculture and rescued Whittington from the insane bio-chemist Dr Jason A Grimstone.[67] When channel swimmer Commander Swainson vanished in the sea in January while searching for an enemy submarine, Mother summoned Steed and Tara to a sea-side fairground. Tara was captured by the sub commander, Piotr, and lured him into a trap at a military base.[68] Mother assigned Steed and Tara to look after GRID[69], a machine that could determine the age of

---

[59] 'Mens Sana, and all that...', *The Avengers Annual*, September 1968.

[60] *The Magnetic Man*. Compiled by Norman Daniels. Issued: December 1968 (US).

[61] *Moon Express*. Compiled by Norman Daniels. Issued: February 1969 (US). This incident seems to date from 1968 since reference was made to the Americans not being ready to land on the moon for another year. p98.

[62] 'Avast There, Mr Steed...', *The Avengers Annual*, September 1968.

[63] 'Mary, Mary...'. Artist's impressions by John Stokes. *The Avengers Annual*, September 1968.

[64] Artist's impressions by Tom Kerr. *TV Comic*, Issues 877-883, 5 October – 16 November 1968.

[65] 'Good Guys and Bad Guys'. *The Avengers Annual*, September 1969.

[66] Artist's impressions by Tom Kerr and unknown. *TV Comic*, Issues 884-889, 23 November – 28 December 1968.

[67] Artist's impressions by John Canning. 'Seeds of Destruction!', *TV Comic*, Issues 890-895, 4 January – 8 February 1969.

[68] 'Come on In – The Water's Deadly', *The Avengers Annual*, September 1969.

[69] Gamma Ray Indication Device.

artefacts but it was stolen by Professor Theodore Wyckham of the British Museum.[70]

Steed and Tara were part of the reception committee to greet President Frederick Diaff of Gunthstat, but found themselves dealing with a sudden hypnosis-created riot, induced by ice lollies sold at a local cinema. Tara fell under the influence of the strange refreshment, but the projectionist was exposed as Diaff's rival.[71] Tara and Steed were also detailed by Mother to protect Sheikh Sayid Mahmoud of Saluzan when he came to Britain to sign an oil deal. The Sheikh was also dealing with criminal arms dealer Jasper Groat but Steed managed to swap consignments, and received the finest racing camel in Saluzan as a gift.[72] A call from his former boss Charles alerted Steed to a strange situation in which the Department was being destroyed. Dr Keel and Cathy Gale were kidnapped, and Steed joined forced with the widowed Emma to face a new breed of Cybernauts developed by Dr Bennett Cowles and a cybernetic clone of Dr Armstrong.[73]

Mother assigned Steed and Tara to locate Professor Blomhammer's stolen Mark IV Mole, a robot laser-boring device stolen by a gang of criminals planning to steal the Crown Jewels – the successful mission leading Steed and Tara to receive a royal 'thank you' at Buckingham Palace.[74] Cancelling a holiday, Steed and Tara were summoned to Scapa Flow in the Orkney Islands by Mother who asked them to investigate a company called Marine Electronics. Attending a board meeting on a luxury yacht as ship's cook and stewardess, the pair exposed the King Neptune-like Managing Director as Ludovick Croza, an old adversary of Steed, and foiled his attempt to kidnap two scientists.[75] Assigned to investigate by Mother, Steed and Tara checked out UFO sightings at the United Kingdom Atomic Energy Authority and confirmed that the aliens were two heavies hired by Professor Plantagenet Hogarth whose lighthouse rocket was aimed at the United Nations fleet at Spithead.[76] An unlikely incident concerned Steed and Tara visiting a country estate called Fable Land where the pair encountered fictional characters – part of an attack on the retired Sir Percy from the Ministry of Records by the Chief Librarian, Silas Bookworm, who had invented a 'Three Dimensional Books' machine.[77] Attending a demonstration of the air defence system DAMOCLES, Steed and Tara witnessed the test missile glow red and become rubbery – a phenomenon controlled by Professor Niarchos and Hercules who then attacked Mother in his HQ down a Welsh mine.[78] Steed's recurrent nightmare about leaping from London's newest skyscraper made Mother send both Steed and Tara for a holiday in Paris. Here, Steed fell under the hypnotic suggestion of a man called Hypnos and was implanted with instructions to kill the Benwatu Ambassador at the Grand Reception back in London – a scheme averted by Tara.[79] Mother then asked Steed and Tara

---

[70] 'The Museum Mystery!'. Artist's impressions by John Canning. *TV Comic*, Issues 896-901, 15 February – 22 March 1969.

[71] Artist's impressions by John Canning. *TV Comic*, Issues 902-907, 29 March – 3 May 1969.

[72] 'Tiger of the Desert!'. Artist's impressions by John Canning. *TV Comic*, Issues 908-913, 10 May – 14 June 1969.

[73] *Too Many Targets*. Compiled by John Peel & Dave Rogers. Issued: November 1990 (US).

[74] Artist's impressions by John Canning. *TV Comic*, Issues 914-920, 21 June – 2 August 1969.

[75] Artist's impressions by John Canning. *TV Comic Holiday Special*, June 1969.

[76] Artist's impressions by John Canning. *TV Comic*, Issues 921-927, 9 August – 20 September 1969.

[77] 'Fable Land', *TV Comic Annual*, September 1969.

[78] 'Don't Go Down the Mine, Dad... (Mother's already there)', *The Avengers Annual*, September 1969.

[79] 'May I have this Trance?...', *The Avengers Annual*, September 1969.

to attend a Grand Party and Ball at Batley Abbey given by Sir Hubert Corringham who was a kidnap target. Sir Hubert had already been replaced by a double by the enemy agent Miroff, but the plan was foiled with help from the ghost of the Sixth Baronet.[80]

Out driving with Tara, Steed found his car tyres punctured by metal spikes, after which they were attacked by a knight in armour – the work of Professor Conwell a man who believed that he was living in an age of chivalry, and whose ultrasonic machine was used by a farmer called Jurgens in a plan to kill all livestock in Britain.[81] The kidnap of President Umboko of Mosambia by African warriors led Steed and Tara into a plan to depose Umboko by General Nawabie. Steed and Tara managed to infiltrate a fancy dress ball at the Mosambian Embassy as a 'Laughing Cavalier' and a lady ice cream vendor to foil the scheme.[82] Receiving free tickets for a charity performance, Tara helped stage magician Professor Mesmo in his act but remained under his control with orders to kill Mother. Steed and a safely restored Tara then encountered a strange convention of criminals posing as warlocks at a country house.[83]

When Steed received a model soldier from a military toy shop called The Hussar, he and Tara visited the establishment to be overcome by gas and captured by Captain Kettle, an officer cashiered from the army for cowardice, who projected them into a strange fantasy world using a bizarre machine.[84] Shortly before Christmas (presumably 1969), Tara and Steed were keen to leave Headquarters early – but found that Mother was in a particularly Scrooge-like frame of mind. On the advice of medical officer Dr Pythagoras Plum, Steed and Tara took a leaf from Charles Dickens's *A Christmas Carol* and used films and tape recordings to cure Mother of his meanness and depression.[85]

After an attempt on the life of Admiral Horatio Broadside before a NATO fleet exercise, Mother assigned Tara and Steed to protect him on a treasure hunt at sea from an attack by former U-Boat commander Von Cramer.[86] When work on a new motorway was held up by the appearance of Roman ghosts, Mother assigned Steed and Tara who found the culprit was Squire Fabian Witherspoon, a 'Guy Fawkes'-type character who was planning to dynamite the road.[87] Mother had Steed and Tara find out what fate befell agent David Rothwell, found on the Yorkshire moors. Rothwell had tangled with a Zeppelin commanded by Wilhelm Sigwald, the Kaiser of Crime, who was planning to hold the Government to ransom with a fake germ bomb.[88] When the vertical take-off bomber Delta Five-Zero aircraft went missing in a huge rainstorm, Steed, Tara and Mother connected this with the disappearance of meteorologist Dr Weatherby from a weather control centre and found that on the Scottish island of Morag Skerry the enemy planned to paralyse Britain with a renewed Ice Age.[89]

The theft of a payroll by cowboys in the New Forest was linked by Steed to his latest

---

[80] 'What's a Ghoul like you doing in a place like this?', *The Avengers Annual*, September 1969.

[81] 'Thou'rt an interfering varlet, Mr Steed...', *The Avengers Annual*, September 1969.

[82] Artist's impressions by John Canning. *TV Comic*, Issues 928-934, 27 September – 8 November 1969.

[83] Artist's impressions by John Canning. *TV Comic*, Issues 935-941, 15 November – 27 December 1969.

[84] Artist's impressions by John Canning. *TV Comic*, Issues 942-948, 3 January – 14 February 1970.

[85] 'The Spirits of Christmas'. *TV Comic Annual*, September 1970.

[86] Artist's impressions by John Canning. *TV Comic*, Issues 949-955, 21 February – 4 April 1970.

[87] Artist's impressions by John Canning. *TV Comic*, Issues 956-962, 11 April – 23 May 1970.

[88] Artist's impressions by John Canning. *TV Comic*, Issues 963-969, 30 May – 11 July 1970.

[89] Artist's impressions by John Canning. *TV Comic*, Issues 970-977, 18 July – 5 September 1970.

assignment from Mother – the recovery of top secret missile plans stolen from Davenly in Hampshire. The trail led to the 'Lazy J' Western Style Dude Ranch and Holiday Camp in the New Forest and Eastern agent Boris Patervitch.[90] When a low-flying aircraft sprayed fertiliser over an RAF base, Steed and Tara found that plants and insects were growing to giant proportions – the fertiliser dust being developed by a farmer called Johnson for his own garden.[91] Returning from a weekend away, Steed found Tara at his flat with news that Sir Geoffrey Master, the millionaire builder, had fallen from one of his buildings after receiving a model of 'Humpty Dumpty' – the first of several victims of bankrupt builder Rufus Green who was bidding for a government hydro-electric scheme.[92] At the Ministry of Transport, Mother informed Steed and Tara of an attempt to wreck an express train carrying gold bullion – and the pair exposed stationmaster Septimus Crump who planned to steal the next consignment of gold in revenge for his station being closed.[93] Proving that a prehistoric monster was roaming the Cambrian Mountains of Wales was the next assignment given to Steed and Tara by Mother. Near the village of Pandy Mynydd, the dinosaurs were finally revealed as the robotic creations of Professor Merlin Jones who used a high frequency invention to roll time back.[94] In one of the least credible assignments, Steed and Tara were called to the toy department of a London department store by Mother in connection with a Junior Scientist's set from which a giant beanstalk had grown at a South Down government research establishment. At the top of the plant was Kang the Terrible, a giant warrior of Gengis Khan, imprisoned for 700 years.[95]

A holiday for Steed and Tara at Little Frampton-on-Sea, was cut short by orders from Mother. The pair protected Colonel Flubbergast, the retiring Chief of the Secret Service, from his arch-enemy Cedric the Terrible.[96] Steed and Tara were then detailed to protect electronics expert Professor Muddle-fuddle from Baron Guy Lopez of Rook Castle at an international chess championship at the Royal Albion Hall.[97] Strange signals beamed from a disused satellite in space made the population dance uncontrollably – meaning that Mother, aboard an experimental aircraft, could not land because of staff dancing on Northfield Aerodrome's runway. Having been underground at HQ, Steed and Tara located the pirate radio ship from which the signal was being beamed by Discord Danny the Delinquent DJ.[98]

Mother summoned Steed and Tara to the Fleet Street offices of the *Daily Chronicle* and informed them that a huge meteor was apparently to collide with Earth – the prelude to a bizarre experience where the pair were confronted by gnome-like time travelling aliens.[99] Steed and Tara were sent to Scotland by Mother to investigate sightings of a monster which had stopped work on a new power station beside a Loch; the creature was a harmless baby,

---

[90] Artist's impressions by John Canning. *TV Comic*, Issues 978-988, 12 September – 21 November 1970.

[91] Artist's impressions by John Canning. *TV Comic*, Issues 989-995, 28 November 1970 – 9 January 1971. 'A strange adventure, Steed' commented Tara at its conclusion.

[92] Artist's impressions by John Canning. *TV Comic*, Issues 996-999, 16 January – 6 February 1971.

[93] Artist's impressions by John Canning. *TV Comic*, Issues 1000-1006, 13 February – 27 March 1971.

[94] Artist's impressions by John Canning. *TV Comic*, Issues 1007-1014, 3 April – 22 May 1971.

[95] Artist's impressions by John Canning. *TV Comic*, Issues 1015-1022, 29 May – 17 July 1971.

[96] Artist's impressions by John Canning. *TV Comic*, Issues 1023-1029, 25 July – 4 September 1971.

[97] Artist's impressions by John Canning. *TV Comic*, Issues 1030-1037, 11 September – 30 October 1971.

[98] Artist's impressions by John Canning. *TV Comic*, Issues 1038-1043, 6 November – 11 December 1971.

[99] Artist's impressions by John Canning. *TV Comic*, Issues 1044-1051, 18 December 1971 – 5 February 1972.

cut off from its mother by a new wall.[100] Mother then had Tara and Steed track £5,000,000 hijacked from an armoured van by Sir Cedric Cramp of Carver Hall and his Civil War Society, who were producing counterfeit notes.[101] Invited to tea at Mother's country house, Steed and Tara were to accompany Mother and his Aunt Gertrude to present the prizes at his old school, St Gargoyle's, where two rather incompetent assassins, Waldo and Gremlin, aimed to dispose of Mother.[102] Taking a summer holiday, Steed and Tara found Jasper Groat at work in the village of Wallingstone-on-Mole, using drugged milk in a plan to steal Wallingstone Diamonds.[103] Steed and Tara travelled to Nottingham to protect Sir Reginald Blower, the mastermind of a new town at Sherwood Forest, and were confronted by a group of Merrie Men...[104]

One very odd unfilmed report strangely prefigures the incident with the Russian K-agents in 1977 which formed the double-length surveillance film – in the same manner as the dual incidents at the Litoff Organisation in 1962 and 1967. A postman called Sam Hurley was killed in the Suffolk village of Wentwick by a Chinese soldier in obsolete uniform. Steed, Purdey and Gambit worked alongside Major Francis and captured the young soldier, whose ID revealed him to be Private Foo Semoi, born in 1925. All his targets had been obsolete, and Professor Chambers detected that the soldier had a radio receiver in his skull – part of a sleeping army secreted in England in 1946. As the Chinese Ambassador explained to Steed, the soldiers had been woken by a faulty satellite. One agent, Captain Hi Ling, had orders to provoke World War III by assassinating the Prime Minister at the House of Commons. Steed used his steel-lined bowler to slam Hi Ling into Big Ben's massive bell at the vital moment.[105]

When a colleague called Peter Peters was found with poison injected vampire-style into his neck, Purdey, Gambit and Steed came up against Martin Count, a former optics agent who had been fired and was taking revenge from a film studio.[106] When Steed went to receive his third decoration from the Queen, his former adversary Lev Petrovoski kidnapped him on the Mall, but he was rescued from a country mansion by Purdey and Gambit.[107] On her way to visit her mother, Purdey went missing in the village of Amblecombe after having a drugged drink at a pub, allowing Steed and Gambit to discover that the hamlet was now inhabited completely by enemy agents.[108] When Sir James died at his own retirement party, Steed's trio exposed hypnotist Ranji Bangee as a fake employed by Yuri Grenkov and Lord Lacey, Sir James's business rival.[109] While visiting Purdey's family, Steed had arranged to meet with agent George Hinchcliffe who was due

---

[100] Artist's impressions by John Canning. *TV Comic*, Issues 1052-1059, 12 February – 1 April 1972.

[101] Artist's impressions by John Canning. *TV Comic*, Issues 1060-1069, 8 April – 10 June 1972.

[102] Artist's impressions by John Canning. *TV Comic*, Issues 1070-1078, 17 June – 12 August 1972.

[103] *TV Comic Holiday Special*, June 1972.

[104] 'The Woodland Folk', *TV Comic Annual*, September 1972.

[105] 'The Sleeping Dragon'. Compiled by Brian Clemens. *Daily Mirror*, 11 October 1976, p16-17; 12 October 1976, p21; 13 October 1976, p21; 14 October 1976, p21.

[106] 'Fangs for the Memory!' Artist's impressions by John Bolton. *The New Avengers Annual*, September 1977.

[107] 'A Funny Thing Happened On The Way To The Palace', *The New Avengers Annual*, September 1977.

[108] 'What a lousy way to run a business!', *The New Avengers Annual*, September 1977.

[109] 'Hypno-Twist'. Artist's impressions by John Bolton. *The New Avengers Annual*, September 1977.

to tell him about a traitor in the Department. Beneath the local church of Purdey's stepfather, the trio located a computer duplicating the information from their headquarters, operated by Scots patriot Charles Wyatt-Bell, one of Hitler's Death's Head legion.[110]

After 15 years of cat and mouse games with Steed, Comrade Gorsky sanctioned an agent called Sagarin to deploy a hypnotic scheme to kill Mike Gambit, implanting orders in three of Gambit's colleagues.[111] The last of these unconfirmed reports comes from around 1978. Investigating the strange behaviour of Special Service Unit 5 in the Welsh mountains for Captain Bohn, Steed, Gambit and Purdey found a sleeper agent at work, using a drug to induce hydrophobia at the unit.[112]

---

[110] 'Go And Grin Somewhere Else!', *The New Avengers Annual*, September 1977.

[111] 'The Gambit Gambit', *The New Avengers Annual*, September 1978.

[112] 'A Fluid Situation', *The New Avengers Annual*, September 1978.

BIBLIOGRAPHY

BOOKS

Barlow, Geoff, *The Saga of Happy Valley* (Albion Press, 1980)

Carraze, Alain and Jean-Luc Putheaud with Alex J Geairns (ed.), trans: Paul Buck,
 The Avengers Companion (Titan Books, September 1997[1])

Carter, John, *The New Avengers – 2: The Eagle's Nest* (Futura Books, December 1976)

Cartwright, Julian, *The New Avengers – 4: Fighting Men* (Futura Books, March 1977)

Cave, Peter, *The New Avengers – 1: House of Cards* (Futura Books, November 1976)

Cave, Peter, *The New Avengers – 5: The Cybernauts* (Futura Books, September 1977)

Cave, Peter, *The New Avengers – 6: Hostage* (Futura Books, December 1977)

Chapman, James, *Saints and Avengers: British Adventure Series of the 1960s*
 (IB Taurus, April 2002)

Cornell, Paul, Martin Day and Keith Topping, *The Avengers Programme Guide*
 (Virgin Publishing Ltd, March 1994)

Cornell, Paul, Martin Day and Keith Topping, *The Avengers Dossier*
 (Virgin Books, February 1998)

Daniels, Norman, *The Avengers – #8: The Magnetic Man*
 (Berkley Medallion Books, December 1968)

Daniels, Norman, *The Avengers – #9: Moon Express*
 (Berkley Medallion Books, February 1969)

Enefer, Douglas, *The Avengers* (Consul Books, 1963)

Ewbank, Tim and Stafford Hildred, *Joanna Lumley – The Biography*
 (André Deutsch, October 1999)

Harris, Walter, *The New Avengers – 3: To Catch a Rat* (Futura Books, February 1977)

Heald, Tim, *John Steed: An Authorised Autobiography – Volume One:*
 Jealous in Honour (Weidenfeld and Nicolson, October 1977)

Hussey, Anthony (as 'John Garforth'), *The Avengers: The Floating Game*
 (Panther Books, January 1967)

Hussey, Anthony (as 'John Garforth'), *The Avengers: The Laugh was on Lazarus*
 (Panther Books, January 1967)

---

[1] An English translation of Carraze, Alain and Jean-Luc Putheaud, *Chapeau melon et bottes de cuir*
(Hutieme Art Editions, 1990)

Hussey, Anthony (as 'John Garforth'), *The Avengers: The Passing of Gloria Munday*
  (Panther Books, March 1967)
Hussey, Anthony (as 'John Garforth'), *The Avengers: Heil Harris!*
  (Panther Books, March 1967)
Kaewert, Julie, *The Avengers* (Titan Books, August 1998)
Laumer, [John] Keith, *The Avengers – #5: The Afrit Affair*
  (Berkley Medallion Books, April 1968)
Laumer, [John] Keith, *The Avengers – #6: The Drowned Queen*
  (Berkley Medallion Books, June 1968)
Laumer, [John] Keith, *The Avengers – #7: The Gold Bomb*
  (Berkley Medallion Books, September 1968)
Lumley, Joanna, *Stare Back and Smile* (Viking, October 1989)
Macnee, Patrick and Marie Cameron, *Blind in One Ear* (Harrap, September 1988)
Macnee, Patrick with Peter Leslie, *...deadline* (Hodder and Stoughton, November 1965)
Macnee, Patrick with Peter Leslie, *Dead Duck* (Hodder and Stoughton, May 1966)
Macnee, Patrick with Dave Rogers, *The Avengers and Me* (Titan Books, May 1997)
Macpherson, Don, *The Avengers Original Movie Screenplay* (Titan Books, August 1998)
Miller, Toby, *The Avengers*, (BFI Publishing, September 1997)
Peel, John and Dave Rogers, *Too Many Targets* (St Martin's Press, November 1990)
Rogers, Dave, *The Avengers* (Independent Television Books Ltd, March 1983)
Rogers, Dave, *The Avengers Anew* (Michael Joseph Ltd, July 1985)
Rogers, Dave, *The Avengers: The Making of the Movie* (Titan Books, August 1998)
Rogers, Dave, *The Complete Avengers* (Boxtree, March 1989)
Rogers, Dave, *The Ultimate Avengers* (Boxtree, August 1995)
Rogers, Dave and SJ Gillis, *The Rogers and Gillis Guide to The Avengers*
  (SJG Communications Services, November 1998)
The Avengers Annual (Souvenir Press Ltd/Atlas Publishing and Distribution Co Ltd,
  September 1967)
The Avengers Annual (Atlas Publishing Company Ltd, September 1968)
The Avengers Annual (Atlas Publishing Company Ltd, September 1969)
The New Avengers Annual (Brown Watson, September 1977)
The New Avengers Annual (Brown Watson, September 1978)
TV Comic Annual (TV Publications Ltd, September 1966)
TV Comic Annual (Polystyle Publications Ltd, September 1969)
TV Comic Annual (Polystyle Publications Ltd, September 1970)
TV Comic Annual (Polystyle Publications Ltd, September 1972)
TV Crimebusters (TV Publications Ltd, 1962)

PERIODICALS AND MAGAZINES

Anglo, Mick, *The Avengers*, Thorpe and Porter, 1966
Bentley, Chris (ed.), *Bizarre*, Issues 1-3/Extra
  (The Avengers Mark One Appreciation Club, Jul 1990-1991)
Hearn, Marcus (ed.), *The Avengers: The Official Souvenir Magazine*
  (Titan Magazines, August 1998)

McKay, Anthony with Annette Hill and Chris Bentley, *A Guide to Avengerland*
  (Dead Man's Treasure/Fanderson, June 1999)
Morrison, Grant and Anne Caulfield, *Steed and Mrs Peel*, Books One to Three
  (Acme Comics, March 1991(dated 1990) – June 1992)
Rogers, Dave (ed.), *Look Who's Talking The Avengers* (OTTA, April 1986)
Rogers, Dave (ed.), *Stay Tuned*, Vol 1 No 1 to Vol 3 No 9
  (Dave Rogers/Bowler Enterprises, Spring 1987 – February 1999)
Rogers, Dave (ed.), *On Target*, Issue 1 to Vol 3 No 2 (Dave Rogers, 1982-1986)
Diana (DC Thompson and Co Ltd, Issues 199 – 224, 10 December 1966 – 3 June 1967)
Featuring The New Avengers (Independent Television Books Ltd, September 1976)
John Steed – Emma Peel (aka *The Avengers*, Issue 1) (Gold Key, November 1968)
June and School Friend (Fleetway Publications Ltd,
  Issues 52 – 63, 29 January – 16 April 1966)
TV Comic (TV Publications Ltd, Issues 720 – 771, 2 October 1965 – 24 September 1966)
TV Comic (Polystyle Publications, Issues 877 – 1078, 5 October 1968 – 12 August 1972)

RECOMMENDED WEBSITES

Devotees of Steed and his compatriots can be found all over the world, and many are conducting their own incredible research into the agents' careers. David K Smith runs the excellent *The Avengers Forever* (http://theavengers.tv/forever/), Mike Noon established both *Dead Duck – The Avengers Merchandise Archive* (http://deadduck.theavengers.tv/) and *...deadline – The Avengers Press and PR Archive* (http://deadline.theavengers.tv/), Alan and Alys Hayes celebrate the radio dramatisations of Steed's adventures at *Avengers on the Radio* (http://aor.theavengers.tv/), Alan Hayes and Mike Noon collaborate on the unfilmed adventures in *The Avengers Illustrated* (http://wingedavenger.theavengers.tv/), Anthony McKay co-ordinates research into the places visited by Steed and his colleagues in *A Guide to Avengerland* (http://avengerland.theavengers.tv/) and Piers Johnson's *Mrs Peel – We're Needed* (http://www.dissolute.com.au/avweb/) is simply staggering in detail. An excellent place to discuss the exploits of Steed and his colleagues is *The Avengers.TV International Forum* (http://forum.theavengers.tv/).

ACKNOWLEDGMENTS

Neil and Sue Alsop, David Auger, Chris Bentley, Lee Binding of Contender, Canal+ Image UK, Anthony Brown of *TV Zone*, Andrew Cartmel, Julie Cartwright and Chris Gabb, Brian Clemens, Simon Coward, Kevin and Elaine Davies, The Department, Michael Dunford, Eton College, Dick Fiddy of the BFI, Dennis Hall, Alys and Alan Hayes, Trish Hayes of the BBC Written Archive Centre, Marcus Hearn, John Herron, Annette Hill, Chris Johnson, Laurie Johnson, Mark One Productions, Andrew Martin, Anthony McKay, Stephen McKay and Janet Fishwick, Hilary McPhail, Ralph Montagu, Mother, Mike Noon, Chris Perry, Richard Reynolds, Michael Richardson of *Action TV*, Dave Rogers, David Schleicher, Frank Shailes, David K Smith, Studio Canal, Simon Vivian, Martin Wiggins and various contributors to *The Avengers TV International Forum*.